at Global Knowledge Certification Press

Don't let the <u>real</u> test be your first test!

Included on CD-ROM

i-Net+™ CERTIFICATION TEST YOURSELF PERSONAL TESTING CENTER

Master the skills you need to pass the i-Net+ exam using the TEST YOURSELF Personal Testing Center on CD-ROM—the most effective i-Net+ exam simulator and knowledge-building tool available. Choose the Live Exam mode for a timed exam or choose the Practice Exam mode, which lets you set the pace, displaying in-depth answers as needed. This CD-ROM features more than 250 interactive, exam-based i-Net+ questions, detailed score reports by exam topic, and a unique benchmarking tool that charts your progress. It's the closest you can get to having your own personal i-Net+ exam trainer!

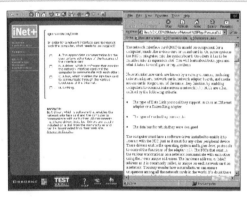

TEST YOURSELF
IN PRACTICE EXAM OR LIVE EXAM MODE

Experience realistic exams on your own computer with the interactive TEST YOURSELF software. Use the Practice Exam mode so you can pause the exam and link back to the text for more information, or use the Live Exam mode—a timed exam that simulates the actual i-Net+ exam.

OTHER UNIQUE TESTING FEATURES

- All exam questions randomly generated from a pool of 250 questions for a different test experience each time

- Hyperlinks to expert-written text for further explanations

- Written and prepared by professionals who have taken and passed the exams

- All CompTIA i-Net+ test objectives covered in detail

- Includes Internet Explorer 5 on CD-ROM

ASSESS YOURSELF

Detailed score reports show which exam topics need further study and how your score compares to the required passing score.

BENCHMARK YOURSELF

Chart your progress with the Bench-marking Tool—the scoring feature that records and graphs your exam scores over time.

SYSTEM REQUIREMENTS:

A PC running Internet Explorer version 5 or higher.

i-Net+™ Certification
Study Guide

i-Net+™ Certification Study Guide

Syngress Media, Inc.

Osborne/McGraw-Hill

Berkeley New York St. Louis San Francisco Auckland Bogotá Hamburg London Madrid Mexico City
Milan Montreal New Delhi Panama City Paris São Paulo Singapore Sydney Tokyo Toronto

Osborne/McGraw-Hill
2600 Tenth Street
Berkeley, California 94710
U.S.A.

For information on translations or book distributors outside the U.S.A., or to arrange bulk purchase discounts for sales promotions, premiums, or fund-raisers, please contact Osborne/**McGraw-Hill** at the above address.

i-Net+™ Certification Study Guide

1234567890 DOC DOC 019876543210

Book p/n 0-07-212230-7   and   CD p/n 0-07-212231-5
parts of
ISBN 0-07-212232-3

Publisher Brandon A. Nordin	**Acquisitions Coordinator** Tara Davis	**Computer Designers** Gary Corrigan Dick Schwartz
Associate Publisher and Editor-in-Chief Scott Rogers	**Series Editor** Maxwell Miller, Ph.D.	Roberta Steele
Acquisitions Editor Gareth Hancock	**Technical Editor** Patrick Santry	**Illustrators** Robert Hansen Brian Wells
Associate Acquisitions Editor Timothy Green	**Copy Editor** Adaya Henis	Beth Young
Editorial Management Syngress Media, Inc.	**Proofreader** Linda Medoff	**Series Design** Roberta Steele
Project Editors Eva Banaszek Janet Walden	**Indexer** David Heiret	

FOREWORD

From Global Knowledge

At Global Knowledge we strive to support the multiplicity of learning styles required by our students to achieve success as technical professionals. In this series of books, it is our intention to offer the reader a valuable tool for successful completion of the i-Net+ certification exams.

As the world's largest IT training company, Global Knowledge is uniquely positioned to offer these books. The expertise gained each year from providing instructor-led training to hundreds of thousands of students worldwide has been captured in book form to enhance your learning experience. We hope that the quality of these books demonstrates our commitment to your lifelong learning success. Whether you choose to learn through the written word, computer-based training, Web delivery, or instructor-led training, Global Knowledge is committed to providing you the very best in each of those categories. For those of you who know Global Knowledge, or those of you who have just found us for the first time, our goal is to be your lifelong competency partner.

Thank you for the opportunity to serve you. We look forward to serving your needs again in the future.

Warmest regards,

Duncan Anderson
President and Chief Executive Officer, Global Knowledge

The Global Knowledge Advantage

Global Knowledge has a global delivery system for its products and services. The company has 28 subsidiaries, and offers its programs through a total of 60+ locations. No other vendor can provide consistent services across a geographic area this large. Global Knowledge is the largest independent information technology education provider, offering programs on a variety of platforms. This enables our multi-platform and multi-national customers to obtain all of their programs from a single vendor. The company has developed the unique Competus™ Framework software tool and methodology which can quickly reconfigure courseware to the proficiency level of a student on an interactive basis. Combined with self-paced and on-line programs, this technology can reduce the time required for training by prescribing content in only the deficient skills areas. The company has fully automated every aspect of the education process, from registration and follow-up, to "just-in-time" production of courseware. Global Knowledge Network through its Enterprise Services Consultancy, can customize programs and products to suit the needs of an individual customer.

Global Knowledge Classroom Education Programs

The backbone of our delivery options is classroom-based education. Our modern, well-equipped facilities staffed with the finest instructors offer programs in a wide variety of information technology topics, many of which lead to professional certifications.

Custom Learning Solutions

This delivery option has been created for companies and governments that value customized learning solutions. For them, our consultancy-based approach of developing targeted education solutions is most effective at helping them meet specific objectives.

Self-Paced and Multimedia Products

This delivery option offers self-paced program titles in interactive CD-ROM, videotape and audio tape programs. In addition, we offer custom development of interactive multimedia courseware to customers and partners. Call us at 1-888-427-4228.

Electronic Delivery of Training

Our network-based training service delivers efficient competency-based, interactive training via the World Wide Web and organizational intranets. This leading-edge delivery option provides a custom learning path and "just-in-time" training for maximum convenience to students.

ARG

American Research Group (ARG), a wholly-owned subsidiary of Global Knowledge, one of the largest worldwide training partners of Cisco Systems, offers a wide range of internetworking, LAN/WAN, Bay Networks, FORE Systems, IBM, and UNIX courses. ARG offers hands on network training in both instructor-led classes and self-paced PC-based training.

Global Knowledge Courses Available

Network Fundamentals
- Understanding Computer Networks
- Telecommunications Fundamentals I
- Telecommunications Fundamentals II
- Understanding Networking Fundamentals
- Implementing Computer Telephony Integration
- Introduction to Voice Over IP
- Introduction to Wide Area Networking
- Cabling Voice and Data Networks
- Introduction to LAN/WAN protocols
- Virtual Private Networks
- ATM Essentials

Network Security & Management
- Troubleshooting TCP/IP Networks
- Network Management
- Network Troubleshooting
- IP Address Management
- Network Security Administration
- Web Security
- Implementing UNIX Security
- Managing Cisco Network Security
- Windows NT 4.0 Security

IT Professional Skills
- Project Management for IT Professionals
- Advanced Project Management for IT Professionals
- Survival Skills for the New IT Manager
- Making IT Teams Work

LAN/WAN Internetworking
- Frame Relay Internetworking
- Implementing T1/T3 Services
- Understanding Digital Subscriber Line (xDSL)
- Internetworking with Routers and Switches
- Advanced Routing and Switching
- Multi-Layer Switching and Wire-Speed Routing
- Internetworking with TCP/IP
- ATM Internetworking
- OSPF Design and Configuration
- Border Gateway Protocol (BGP) Configuration

Authorized Vendor Training

Cisco Systems
- Introduction to Cisco Router Configuration
- Advanced Cisco Router Configuration
- Installation and Maintenance of Cisco Routers
- Cisco Internetwork Troubleshooting
- Cisco Internetwork Design
- Cisco Routers and LAN Switches
- Catalyst 5000 Series Configuration
- Cisco LAN Switch Configuration
- Managing Cisco Switched Internetworks
- Configuring, Monitoring, and Troubleshooting Dial-Up Services
- Cisco AS5200 Installation and Configuration
- Cisco Campus ATM Solutions

Bay Networks
- Bay Networks Accelerated Router Configuration
- Bay Networks Advanced IP Routing
- Bay Networks Hub Connectivity
- Bay Networks Accelar 1xxx Installation and Basic Configuration
- Bay Networks Centillion Switching

FORE Systems
- FORE ATM Enterprise Core Products
- FORE ATM Enterprise Edge Products
- FORE ATM Theory
- FORE LAN Certification

Operating Systems & Programming

Microsoft
- Introduction to Windows NT
- Microsoft Networking Essentials
- Windows NT 4.0 Workstation
- Windows NT 4.0 Server
- Advanced Windows NT 4.0 Server
- Windows NT Networking with TCP/IP
- Introduction to Microsoft Web Tools
- Windows NT Troubleshooting
- Windows Registry Configuration

UNIX
- UNIX Level I
- UNIX Level II
- Essentials of UNIX and NT Integration

Programming
- Introduction to JavaScript
- Java Programming
- PERL Programming
- Advanced PERL with CGI for the Web

Web Site Management & Development
- Building a Web Site
- Web Site Management and Performance
- Web Development Fundamentals

High Speed Networking
- Essentials of Wide Area Networking
- Integrating ISDN
- Fiber Optic Network Design
- Fiber Optic Network Installation
- Migrating to High Performance Ethernet

DIGITAL UNIX
- UNIX Utilities and Commands
- DIGITAL UNIX v4.0 System Administration
- DIGITAL UNIX v4.0 (TCP/IP) Network Management
- AdvFS, LSM, and RAID Configuration and Management
- DIGITAL UNIX TruCluster Software Configuration and Management
- UNIX Shell Programming Featuring Kornshell
- DIGITAL UNIX v4.0 Security Management
- DIGITAL UNIX v4.0 Performance Management
- DIGITAL UNIX v4.0 Intervals Overview

DIGITAL OpenVMS
- OpenVMS Skills for Users
- OpenVMS System and Network Node Management I
- OpenVMS System and Network Node Management II
- OpenVMS System and Network Node Management III
- OpenVMS System and Network Node Operations
- OpenVMS for Programmers
- OpenVMS System Troubleshooting for Systems Managers
- Configuring and Managing Complex VMScluster Systems
- Utilizing OpenVMS Features from C
- OpenVMS Performance Management
- Managing DEC TCP/IP Services for OpenVMS
- Programming in C

Hardware Courses
- AlphaServer 1000/1000A Installation, Configuration and Maintenance
- AlphaServer 2100 Server Maintenance
- AlphaServer 4100, Troubleshooting Techniques and Problem Solving

About Syngress Media

Syngress Media creates books and software for Information Technology professionals seeking skill enhancement and career advancement. Its products are designed to comply with vendor- and industry-standard course curricula, and are optimized for certification exam preparation. Visit the Syngress Web site at http://www.syngress.com.

Contributors

James Stanger (Ph.D., MCSE, MCT, CIW) is a writer and network consultant currently living in Southern California. He is a Microsoft Certified Systems Engineer, Microsoft Certified Trainer, and a Certified Internet Webmaster Security Professional. He consults for Axent, IBM, DigitalThink, Evinci, and ProsoftTraining.com. He has also done consulting work on various projects for the i-Net+ certification. His areas of expertise include TCP/IP, firewalls, proxy servers, general network security, and UNIX and Windows NT administration.

André Paree-Huff (CCNA, MCSE+I, ASE, A+, Network+, i-Net+) has been working in the computer field for over seven years. He is currently working for Compaq Computer Corporation as a Network Support Specialist, level III, for the North America Customer Support Center in Colorado Springs, CO. André handles troubleshooting network hardware, specializing in Layers 2 and 3 of the OSI model. André has co-authored two network-related technical manuals and has been a technical editor on many others. He is currently working toward his CCIE.

Amy Thomson (A+, MOUS Master) is a software and A+ instructor in Halifax, Nova Scotia, and she has over ten years of experience in dealing with computer hardware and applications. Amy has taught computer classes from one end of Canada to the other and back again. She holds an Honours B.Sc. in Psychology and is currently preparing for certification as an MCSE.

Paul Burrer (MSCE, MCT, MCNI, MCNE, A+) is an independent consultant and technical trainer with over five years of experience in the networking field. He is the sole owner of PRB Consulting, a company that provides IT consulting services for small- to mid-size businesses, as well as training services for education centers across the nation. Paul lives in the Dallas area with his wife and daughter and spends way too much time on the computer for his wife's liking. Paul can be reached at pburrer@yahoo.com.

Michael Cross (MCSE, MCPS, MCP+I, CNA) is a Microsoft Certified Systems Engineer, Microsoft Certified Product Specialist, Microsoft Certified Professional + Internet, and a Certified Novell Administrator. He has diplomas in computer programming and network support and is currently finishing two university degrees.

Michael is the Network Administrator, Internet Specialist, and a Programmer for the Niagara Regional Police Service. In addition to administering their network, programming, and providing support to a user base of over 800 civilian and uniform users, he is Webmaster of their Web site at http://www.nrps.com and also develops and maintains their local intranet.

Michael also owns KnightWare, a company that provides consulting, programming, networking, Web page design, computer training, and various other services. He has served as an instructor for private colleges and technical schools in London, Ontario, Canada. He has been a freelance writer for several years and has been published over two dozen times in numerous books and anthologies. He currently resides in St. Catharines, Ontario, Canada.

Technical Editor

Patrick Santry (MCT, MCSD, MCP+SB, i-Net+) has been involved in Web development and management for over five years. He specializes in systems integration for business-to-business e-commerce applications. Patrick currently works for a large chemical and mechanical products manufacturer in Erie, PA, as a Senior Information Systems Specialist. His responsibilities include Web server management, Web development, and integration. In his spare time he runs a Web site devoted to Web professionals located at http://www.santry.com. Patrick dedicates his writing efforts to his family: his wife Karyn, his daughters Katie and Karleigh, and his son Patrick Jr. (aka PJ).

Series Editor

Maxwell Miller (Ph.D., CIW, CIT, i-Net+) is a consultant specializing in e-business and IT training and certification. Max provides consulting services in the areas of instructional systems design, competency management, distance learning, curriculum architecture, and psychometrics. Formerly, Max was the Chief Content Architect of ProsoftTraining.com and co-led the development of the IBM-Certified Internet Webmaster (CIW) Internet certification program. He has managed the development of numerous commercial IT training products, including software and courseware; CBT; WBT; and distributed learning solutions for customers, including the Gartner Group, Netscape Communications, IBM, Citibank, and GE. Max began his career as a Telecommunications Systems Engineer at AT&T Bell Labs in Holmdel, NJ; and has served as a Senior Scientist consultant to the Federal government in the areas of IT systems architecture, imagery analysis, and sonar classification for automatic target recognition. Max completed his doctorate in Applied/Cognitive Science and Acoustics at the Catholic University of America in Washington, DC, and holds a masters degree in Human Factors Engineering. He can be contacted at mail24558@pop.net.

Acknowledgments

We would like to thank the following people:

- Richard Kristof of Global Knowledge for championing the series and providing access to some great people and information.
- All the incredibly hard-working folks at Osborne/McGraw-Hill: Brandon Nordin, Scott Rogers, and Gareth Hancock for their help in launching a great series and being solid team players. In addition, Timothy Green, Tara Davis, and Janet Walden for their help in fine-tuning the book.

CONTENTS AT A GLANCE

CONTENTS

PREFACE

This book's primary objective is to help you prepare for and pass the required i-Net+ certification exam so you can begin to reap the career benefits of certification. We believe that the only way to do this is to help you increase your knowledge and build your skills. After completing this book, you should feel confident that you have thoroughly reviewed all of the objectives that CompTIA has established for the exam.

In This Book

This book is organized around the actual structure of the i-Net+ exam administered at CompTIA Testing Centers. CompTIA has let us know all the topics we need to cover for the exam. We've followed their list carefully, so you can be assured you're not missing anything.

In Every Chapter

We've created a set of chapter components that call your attention to important items, reinforce important points, and provide helpful exam-taking hints. Take a look at what you'll find in every chapter:

- ■ Every chapter begins with the **Certification Objectives**—what you need to know in order to pass the section on the exam dealing with the chapter topic. The Certification Objectives headings identify the objectives within the chapter, so you'll always know an objective when you see it!

- ■ **Exam Watch** notes call attention to information about, and potential pitfalls in, the exam. These helpful hints are written by MCSDs who have taken the exams and received their certification—who better to tell you what to worry about? They know what you're about to experience!

- **On the Job** notes point out procedures and techniques important for coding actual applications for employers or contract jobs.

- **Certification Exercises** are interspersed throughout the chapters. These are step-by-step exercises that mirror vendor-recommended labs. They help you master skills that are likely to be areas of focus on the exam. Don't just read through the exercises—they are hands-on practice that you should be comfortable completing. Learning by doing is an effective way to increase your competency with a product.

EXERCISE

- **From the Classroom** sidebars describe the issues that come up most often in the training classroom setting. These sidebars give you a valuable perspective into certification- and product-related topics. They point out common mistakes and address questions from actual classroom discussions.

- **Q&A** sections present problems and solutions in a quick-read format. For example

QUESTIONS AND ANSWERS

What if a user wishes to save a file to a pre-existing filename?	Inform the user that a file by that name already exists and prompt him or her about whether to overwrite the file.
What if a CFile object throws an exception during construction?	Ensure that the program cannot go on to attempt to use that object.

- The **Certification Summary** is a succinct review of the chapter and a restatement of salient points regarding the exam.

- The **Two-Minute Drill** at the end of every chapter is a checklist of the main points of the chapter. It can be used for last-minute review.

- The **Self Test** offers questions similar to those found on the certification exams, including multiple choice and fill-in-the-blank. The answers to these questions, as well as explanations of the answers, can be found at the end of each chapter. By taking the Self Test after completing each chapter, you'll reinforce what you've learned from that chapter, while becoming familiar with the structure of the exam questions.

Some Pointers

Once you've finished reading this book, set aside some time to do a thorough review. You might want to return to the book several times and make use of all the methods it offers for reviewing the material:

1. *Re-read all the Two-Minute Drills*, or have someone quiz you. You also can use the drills as a way to do a quick cram before the exam.

2. *Re-read all the Exam Watch notes.* Remember that these are written by people who have taken the exam and passed. They know what you should expect—and what you should be careful about.

3. *Review all the Q & A scenarios* for quick problem solving.

4. *Re-take the Self Tests.* Taking the tests right after you've read the chapter is a good idea, because it helps reinforce what you've just learned. However, it's an even better idea to go back later and do all the questions in the book in one sitting. Pretend you're taking the exam. (For this reason, you should mark your answers on a separate piece of paper when you answer the questions the first time.)

5. *Complete the exercises.* Did you do the exercises when you read through each chapter? If not, do them! These exercises are designed to cover exam topics, and there's no better way to get to know this material than by practicing.

6. *Check out the Web site.* Global Knowledge Network invites you to become an active member of the Access Global Web site. This site is an online mall and information repository that you'll find invaluable. You can access many types of products to assist you in your preparation for the exams, and you'll be able to participate in forums, online discussions, and threaded discussions. No other book brings you unlimited access to such a resource. You'll find more information about this site in Appendix B.

The CD-ROM Resource

This book comes with a CD-ROM that contains test preparation software, providing you with another method for studying for the exam. You will find more information on the testing software in Appendix A.

How to Take an i-Net+ Certification Examination

By André Paree-Huff, ASE, A+, CCNA, i-Net+, MCSE+I, Network+

Excel Professionally with the i-Net+ Certification

CompTIA has again created a certification to help you stand out professionally. The new i-Net+ certification follows in the footsteps of its predecessors, and it is quickly proving to be a highly accepted, great benchmark for Internet knowledge.

CompTIA has developed the i-Net+ certification to give IT professionals a chance to prove their knowledge to their employers and customers in the area of Internet, extranet, and intranet technologies. Similarly to the Network+ and A+, i-Net+ certification is vendor neutral: it was developed with help from people representing various companies to make sure that it remains a neutral certification.

Over 6,000 people in over 20 countries signed up to take the beta version of the test, proving that this certification may quickly become a standard for knowledge and experience baseline assessment. Presently, the test is being offered in English in 22 countries.

Why Choose the CompTIA i-Net+ Certification?

There are several reasons why you should choose the CompTIA i-Net+ certification. Some of them are

- **Recognition** You will be recognized for your knowledge and experience.

- **Customer satisfaction** Customers are more satisfied with the service received from a certified professional.

- **Confidence**   You will feel more confident with your knowledge when you are with your customers, having passed the certification exam.

- **Career Advancement**   Many companies reward or promote employees who have proved their knowledge with certification.

Computerized Testing

Considering the popularity of CompTIA's certifications, and the fact that certification candidates are spread around the world, the only practical way to administer tests for the certification program is through Sylvan Prometric testing centers. Sylvan Prometric provides proctored testing services for Microsoft, Oracle, Novell, Lotus, and CompTIA's other certifications; the A+ computer technician certification; Network+; and the CDIA certifications. In fact, most companies that need secure test delivery over a wide geographic area use the services of Sylvan Prometric. In addition to delivery, Sylvan Prometric also scores the tests and provides statistical feedback on the performance on each test question to the companies and organizations that use their services.

Typically, several hundred questions are developed for each new certification examination. The questions are first reviewed by a number of subject matter experts for technical accuracy and then are presented in a beta test. The beta test usually lasts two to three hours due to the large number of questions. After a few weeks, CompTIA uses the statistical feedback from Sylvan to check the performance on the beta questions.

Questions are discarded as too easy if the majority of the test takers gets them right, or as too difficult if the majority gets them wrong. A number of other statistical measures are taken for each question. Although the scope of our discussion precludes a rigorous treatment of question analysis, you should be aware that CompTIA and other vendors spend a great deal of time and effort making sure their examination questions are valid. In addition to the obvious desire for quality, the fairness of a vendor's certification program must be legally defensible.

The questions that survive statistical analysis form the pool of questions for the final certification examination. This pool is what the questions for the actual test are drawn from. Each time you take the exam you will receive a new set of questions; you might see some of the same questions, but don't count on remembering the exact question for a retake.

Exam Information

The i-Net+ certification exam is a Sylvan Prometric delivered exam. The test is comprised of a question pool with each tester receiving 72 questions. Each test question weighs exactly the same, no matter if the question is a true/false, single-answer, or multiple choice. In order to receive a passing grade, you must answer 53 questions correctly. This will give you the required 73% needed to achieve the certification.

You will be given 90 minutes to complete 72 questions; you will have, therefore, 1.25 minutes for each question. If you do not know the answer within 30 seconds of looking at the test, you are advised to make an educated guess, mark the question, and move on quickly. Once you have finished the last question, return to the questions you marked for a more in-depth look. Use your time wisely and remember that an unanswered question is always wrong; thus, if you have no idea of the correct answer, take your best guess.

The test is in a non-adaptive form, which means that you can move forward and backward to rethink your answers. Many times a test question will be answered later in the test in the form of a question.

Example:

Question 10. Which of the following is considered a fruit?
A. Apple
B. Potato
C. Cow
D. Garlic

Question 23. An apple is a _____?
A. Animal
B. Mineral
C. Building supply
D. Fruit

CompTIA might soon start following the testing practice of Cisco, Microsoft, and Novell and change its tests to an adaptive form, in which each question is based on the previous question. Thus, if you get two questions in a row correct, you will not be asked any additional questions in that category; but if you miss two out of three, you will automatically be asked an additional three questions in that category. Adaptive tests are better for both Sylvan and the vendor because you can get more test subjects in the same period, as most adaptive test takers rarely take over 30 minutes to either pass or fail a test. For the vendor, it assures greater security, as the test taker receives fewer questions to remember when leaving.

Questions on a Computerized Certification Exam

Computerized test questions can be presented in a number of ways. Some of the possible formats are used in CompTIA certification examinations, and some are not.

True/False

Think back to school and the test you forgot to study for. What was the one type of question you hoped for? True/False! CompTIA does not use this type of question, because you always have a 50 percent chance of guessing the correct answer.

Multiple Choice

The majority of the i-Net+ certification questions are in the multiple-choice format, with either one correct answer or more than one correct answer. In the case of multiple-choice questions with more than one correct answer, the candidate may or may not be told how many answers are correct.

Example:

Which networking protocols are routable? (Choose two.)

or

Which networking protocols exist in the Network Layer of the OSI model? (Choose all that apply.)

You may see both variations on CompTIA certification examinations, but the trend seems to be toward the first type, in which candidates are told explicitly how many answers are correct. Questions of the "Choose all that apply" variety are more difficult and can be confusing, so you will not see as many of this type, as CompTIA does not intend to trick you.

Graphical Questions

Graphics are sometimes used as exhibits to help present or clarify an exam question. These may be network diagrams or pictures of networking components. It is often easier to present the concepts required for a complex performance-based scenario with a graphic than it is with words. Expect only a couple of graphical questions on your i-Net+ exam.

Test questions known as "hotspots" actually incorporate graphics as part of the answer. These questions ask the certification candidate to click a location or graphical element to answer the question. For example, you might be shown the diagram of a network and be asked to click an appropriate location for a bridge. Your answer would be correct if you clicked within the hotspot that marked the correct location. The i-Net+ exam may have a few of these graphical hotspot questions. Expect only a couple of hotspot questions on your exam.

Free Response Questions

The free response question requires a free response, type-in answer. This type of question might present a TCP/IP network scenario and ask you to calculate and enter the correct subnet mask in dotted decimal notation. This type of question is not often used; the beta i-Net+ exam I took recently does not contain any free response questions.

Testing Job Performance

CompTIA certification focuses on timeliness and the ability to perform job tasks. Even performance-based multiple-choice questions do not really measure performance. Another strategy is needed to test job skills.

With unlimited resources, it would not be difficult to test job skills. In an ideal world, CompTIA would fly i-Net+ candidates to a test facility (much as Cisco does for the CCIE), place them in a controlled environment with a team of experts, and ask them to plan, install, maintain, and troubleshoot an Internet, intranet, and extranet and to design and implement a Web server and pages. In a few days at most, the experts could decide whether each candidate should or should not be granted i-Net+ certification status. Needless to say, this is not likely to happen. The cost would be prohibitive, and it would be impossible to test more than one person on a set of equipment at a time.

Another more practical way to test performance is to use the actual software and create a testing program to present tasks and automatically grade a candidate's performance when the tasks are completed. This cooperative approach would be practical in some testing situations, but the same test that is presented to i-Net+ candidates in Boston must also be available in Bahrain and Botswana. Many Sylvan Prometric testing locations around the world cannot run 32-bit applications, much less provide the complex networked solutions required by cooperative testing applications.

The most workable method of measuring performance in today's testing environment is a simulation program. When the program is launched during a test, the candidate sees a simulation of the actual software that looks and behaves just like the real thing. When the testing software presents a task, the simulation program is launched and the candidate performs the required task. The testing software then grades the candidate's performance on the required task and moves to the next question. In this way, a 16-bit simulation program can mimic the look and feel of 32-bit operating systems, a complicated network, or even the entire Internet.

Simulation questions provide many advantages over other testing methodologies, and simulations are expected to become increasingly important in computer certification programs. Studies have shown that there is a very high correlation between the ability to perform simulated tasks on a computer-based test and the ability to perform the actual job tasks. Thus, simulations enhance the validity of the certification process.

Another benefit of simulations is in the area of test security. It is just not possible to cheat on a simulation question. In fact, you will be told exactly what tasks you are expected to perform on the test. How can a certification candidate cheat? By learning to perform the tasks? What a concept!

Knowledge-Based and Performance-Based Questions

CompTIA Certification develops a blueprint for each certification examination with input from subject-matter experts. This blueprint defines the content areas and objectives for each test, and each test question is created to test a specific objective. The basic information from the examination blueprint can be found on CompTIA's Web site at http://www.comptia.org.

Psychometricians categorize test questions as knowledge-based or performance-based. As these terms imply, knowledge-based questions are designed to test knowledge, and performance-based questions are designed to test performance.

Some objectives demand a knowledge-based question. For example, objectives that use verbs such as "list" and "identify" tend to test only what you know, not what you can do.

Example:

Objective: Types of URLs to access a given type of server.

Which two transport protocols can be used to display an HTML document on a Web browser? (Choose two.)
A. FTP
B. HTTPS
C. mailto
D. HTTP
Correct answers: B and D

The i-Net+ exam consists primarily of straightforward, knowledge-based, multiple-choice questions that can be answered fairly quickly if you know your stuff. These questions do not present complex scenarios to confuse you.

Other objectives use action verbs such as "install," "configure," and "troubleshoot" to define job tasks. These objectives can often be tested with either a knowledge-based question or a performance-based question.

Example:

Objective: Cookies

Knowledge-based question:
Where do you configure an Internet Explorer 5.*x* Web browser to accept cookies?
A. File | Properties Cookies
B. Tools | Internet Options | Security tab
C. Options | Cookies
D. View | Options | Security | Cookies
Correct answer: B

Performance-based question:
You want to ensure that you have a reliable tape backup scheme that is not susceptible to fire and water hazards. You are backing up three Windows NT servers and would like to completely back up the entire system. Which of the following is the most reliable backup method?
A. Configure the backup program to back up the user files and operating system files: complete a test restore of the backup; and store the backup tapes offsite in a fireproof vault.
B. Configure the backup program to back up the entire hard drive of each server, and store the backup tapes offsite in a fireproof vault.
C. Copy the user files to another server; configure the backup program to back up the operating system files; and store the backup tapes offsite in a fireproof vault.
D. Configure the backup program to back up the user files and operating system files, and store the backup tapes offsite in a fireproof vault.
Correct answer: A

Even in this simple example, the superiority of the performance-based question is obvious. The knowledge-based question asks for a single fact, but the performance-based question presents a real-life situation and requires that you make a realistic decision. Thus, performance-based questions give more bang (validity) for the test author's buck (individual question).

Study Strategies

There are appropriate ways to study for the different types of questions you will see on a CompTIA Network+ certification examination.

Knowledge-Based Questions

Knowledge-based questions require that you memorize facts. There are hundreds of facts inherent in every content area of every Network+ certification examination. There are several tricks to memorizing facts:

- *Repetition* The more times your brain is exposed to a fact, the more likely you are to remember it. Flash cards are a wonderful tool for repetition. Either make your own flash cards on paper or download a flash card program and develop your own questions.

- *Association* When facts are connected within a logical framework, they are easier to remember. Try using mnemonics, such as "All People Seem To Need Data Processing" to remember the seven layers of the OSI model in order.

- *Motor Association* It is often easier to remember something if you write it down or perform some other physical act, such as clicking a practice test answer. You will find that hands-on experience with the product or concept being tested is a great way to develop motor association.

The emphasis of CompTIA certification is job performance, so there are very few knowledge-based questions on CompTIA certification exams. There are important reasons that you should spend time learning file names, IP address formulas, and other minutiae.

Performance-Based Questions

Most of the questions you will face on a CompTIA certification exam are performance-based scenario questions. These questions are superior to simple knowledge-based questions, but the job task orientation of CompTIA certification extends the knowledge you need to pass the exams; it does not replace this knowledge. Therefore, the first step in preparing for scenario questions is to absorb as many facts relating to the exam content areas as you can. In other words, go back to the previous section and follow the steps to prepare for an exam composed of knowledge-based questions.

The second step is to familiarize yourself with the format of the questions you are likely to see on the exam. You can do this by answering the questions in this study guide, or by using practice tests. The day of your test is not the time to be surprised by the complicated construction of some exam questions.

For example, one of CompTIA Certification's favorite formats of late takes the following form found on Microsoft exams:

- *Scenario:* You have a network with . . .
- *Primary Objective:* You want to . . .
- *Secondary Objective:* You also want to . . .
- *Proposed Solution:* Do this . . .

What does the proposed solution accomplish?

A. It achieves the primary and secondary objectives.
B. It achieves the primary but not the secondary objective.
C. It achieves the secondary but not the primary objective.
D. It achieves neither the primary nor the secondary objective.

This kind of question, with some variation, is seen on many Microsoft Certification examinations and will be present on your i-Net+ certification exam.

At best, these performance-based scenario questions really do test certification candidates at a higher cognitive level than knowledge-based questions do. At worst, these questions can test your reading comprehension and test-taking ability rather than your ability to administer networks. Be sure to get in the habit of reading each question carefully to determine what is being asked.

The third step in preparing for CompTIA scenario questions is to adopt this attitude: Multiple-choice questions aren't really performance based. These scenario questions are just knowledge-based questions with little stories wrapped around them.

To answer a scenario question, you have to sift through the story to determine the underlying facts of the situation and apply your knowledge to determine the correct answer. This may sound silly at first, but the process we go through in solving real-life problems is quite similar. The key concept is that every scenario question (and every real-life problem) has a fact at its center, and if we can identify that fact, we can answer the question.

Exam Blueprint

The i-Net+ exam is divided into six major areas. These areas are broken down here to show you the areas that will be covered. Each area is further broken down into objectives on the test. You will be tested extensively in each of these areas, so prepare as well as you can for each section.

Testing Area	% of Examination (Approximately)
i-Net Basics	10%
i-Net Clients	20%
Development	20%
Networking	25%
i-Net Security	15%
Business Concepts	10%

The objectives for the test, as well as other information about the CompTIA certification exams, can be found on CompTIA's Web site at http://www.comptia.org.

Scheduling the Test

To take the i-Net+ certification test, you will need to contact Sylvan at 1-877-803-6867, in the United States. Not all testing centers offer all tests, so you may not be able to take the test at the center closest to you. You can also schedule a test by using Sylvan's online registration system at http://www.2test.com.

If for some reason you are unable to keep your test appointment, you must cancel your appointment by 7:00 P.M. Central Time on the day before your scheduled exam date. You can reschedule your exam at that time or wait until later to do so. Your test must be rescheduled within one year of the original test date or all monies paid are forfeited.

A fee of $185.00 (price at the time this book went to press) is required for each attempt at the test. Payment must be made prior to scheduling the test, in the form of voucher, credit card, bank transfer, or check. If you pay by personal check, Sylvan will bill you or your company by invoice for the cost and must receive the check before you schedule your testing time.

When you have scheduled your test, you will be given some important information. You should make note of this information so that, in case of any problems on your test day, you will have all information ready to give the proctor. This information will be

- Test number
- Date of test
- Location
- Seat number
- Confirmation number

Taking the Test

On the day of the test, try to arrive at the testing center about 10 to 15 minutes early to sign in and get your paper and pencil. Make sure you take with you two forms of ID: one must include a photograph, and both must include a signature.

The picture ID may be any of the following:

- Driver's license
- State ID
- Work ID
- Military ID
- Passport

Please remember not to bring any cell phones, pagers, or study material into the testing center, as they are not allowed in the testing area.

The Stress Is Over

After you end the test you will immediately receive on your monitor a report of your score, as well as notification whether you passed or failed the exam. You will need to stop by the proctor's desk to pick up a hard copy of your test results for your records. If you passed the exam, you will receive a packet in the mail in approximately four to six weeks with your certification certificate and a letter of congratulations from CompTIA.

Good luck!

i-Net+

COMPUTING TECHNOLOGY INDUSTRY ASSOCIATION®

I

i-Net Basics

CERTIFICATION OBJECTIVES

This chapter provides you with an introduction and overview of the Internet. You will learn about the origins and evolution of the Internet and the emergence of internal private networks called *intranets*. You will be familiarized with underlying Internet technologies including the World Wide Web, Web browsers, Web servers, and Uniform Resource Locators (URLs).

You are also going to become aware of the issues that affect Internet/intranet/extranet site functionality and performance, including bandwidth constraints, customer and user connectivity, and connection access points and speed. You will see how e-business leverages these technologies by linking organizations to their supply chain, including business partners, suppliers, distributors, customers, and end users using extranets and the Internet.

CERTIFICATION OBJECTIVE 1.01

Introduction to the Internet

The Internet is perhaps best described as the world's largest *Inter*connected *Net*work of networks. There is no centralized control of the Internet; instead, many millions of individual networks and computers are interconnected throughout the world to communicate with each other. The Internet is not only technology, it's a global community of people, including corporations, nonprofit organizations, educational institutions, and individuals.

The early roots of the Internet can be traced back to the Advanced Research Projects Agency (ARPA). ARPA is an agency within the United States Federal Government formed by the Eisenhower administration in 1957 with the purpose of conducting scientific research and developing advanced technologies for the U.S. military.

One of ARPA's research areas was developing a large-scale computer network that could survive a serious nuclear attack. This network came to be known as *ARPAnet*. ARPAnet was designed to ensure reliable communications between individual computers (nodes), even in the event of failures between connecting computer networks. The architecture of ARPAnet provided the foundation for the Internet as we know it today.

The Internet was originally comprised almost exclusively of government research centers and universities within the United States. Today, the Internet continues to expand internationally as it is commercialized. The major obstacle to further growth in underdeveloped countries is the lack of a reliable telecommunications infrastructure. In third-world nations and parts of Eastern Europe, modern telephone systems are typically not available.

History and Evolution of the Internet

Different organizations have been involved in the development of the Internet, including the United States Federal Government, academic organizations, and industry. The Internet has gone through many stages of technology development. This timeline highlights the major events that led to its development.

- **1962**   The report *On Distributed Communications Networks* is published by the Rand Corporation. It proposes a computer network model in which there is no central command or control structure, and all nodes are able to reestablish contact in the event of an attack on any single node.

- **1969**   The Department of Defense (DoD) commissions ARPA for research into computer networks. The first node on this network is at the University of California at Los Angeles (UCLA). Other computers on the network are at the Stanford Research Institute, the University of California at Santa Barbara, and the University of Utah.

- **1982**   TCP/IP is established as the data transfer protocol for ARPAnet. This is one of the first times the term "Internet" is used. The DoD declares TCP/IP to be the standard for the U.S. military.

- **1986**   The National Science Foundation (NSF) creates NSFnet, which eventually replaces ARPAnet, and substantially increases the speed of communication over the Internet.

- **1989** Tim Berners-Lee at CERN drafts a proposal for the World Wide Web.

- **1990** ARPAnet is superseded by NSFnet.

- **1991** Gopher is introduced by the University of Minnesota.

- **1992** The World Wide Web (WWW) is born at CERN in Geneva, Switzerland.

- **1993** The Mosaic World Wide Web browser is developed by the National Center for Supercomputing Applications (NCSA). Mosaic was the first Web browser with a graphical user interface. It was released initially for the UNIX computer platform, and later in 1993 for Macintosh and Windows computers.

- **1994** The Netscape Navigator Web browser is introduced. The Web experiences phenomenal growth.

- **1995** Sun introduces the Java programming language. Netscape Navigator 2.0 ships with support for Java applets. Navigator becomes the dominant Web browser.

- **1996** Users in almost 150 countries around the world are now connected to the Internet. The number of computer hosts approaches 10 million. The number of commercial applications of the Internet increases dramatically.

- **1997** *Intra*connected *Net*works, or *intranets*, are deployed based on Internet technologies.

- **1998** Commercial applications of the Internet expand, including business-to-consumer e-commerce, e-auctions, and e-portals.

- **1999** America Online (AOL) acquires Netscape and partners with Sun Microsystems. E-business applications expand to extend e-commerce to business-to-business extranets linking the supply chain, including customers, suppliers, business partners, and distributors together.

Management and Control of the Internet

One of the most frequently asked questions is, "Who controls the Internet?," or "Who runs the Internet?" The best answer is *no one* and *everyone*. The roots of the Internet grew out of research sponsored by ARPA. As the technology evolved, the NSF became involved in the expansion and management of the Internet in 1984. Both NSF and ARPA were organizations funded entirely, or in part, by the U.S. Government working closely with academic institutions. The control and management of domain names was passed from NSF to Network Solutions, Inc. Network Solutions had a monopoly on the distribution of domain names until 1999 when the process was opened up to other companies.

Today, no single organization, government, or nation controls the technology, content, or standards of the Internet. Because the Internet fosters international cooperation, it is often referred to as the *global community*. International standards bodies, including the Internet Engineering Task Force (IETF), the Internet Society (ISOC), and the World Wide Web Consortium (W3C), are leading the process to develop international standards.

Commercialization of the Internet has contributed to its rapid expansion and constant evolution. Most large corporations have an Internet presence in the form of a Web site or e-commerce site. The use of intranets today is as common as the use of LANs was in the 1980s. The rapid deployment of e-business will increasingly link business and technology in the new millennium.

Evolution of the World Wide Web

The idea for the Web is attributed to Tim Berners-Lee of CERN, the European Laboratory for Particle Physics in Geneva, Switzerland. In 1989, Berners-Lee conceived the architecture for the Web as a *multimedia hypertext information system* based on a client/server architecture. The major events in the evolution of the World Wide Web is also covered in the timeline presented previously in "History and Evolution of the Internet" (see 1989 and 1992–1999).

Like the Internet, the Web is a network composed of many smaller computer networks. Specialized servers—referred to as *Web servers*—store and disseminate information, and Web clients—referred to as *Web browsers*—download and display the information for end users.

Web Browser Evolution

The first-generation Web browser developed at CERN was character based. It was very primitive by today's standards and only capable of displaying text (e.g., Lynx browser). It wasn't until the Mosaic browser became available in 1993 that the potential of the Web began to be realized.

Mosaic was developed at the National Center for Supercomputing Applications (NCSA) by a team of software engineers led by Marc Andreesson. Mosaic was the first graphical browser to take advantage of the multimedia capabilities of the Web. Equally important, Mosaic was cross-platform, allowing users to view the same Web pages on Windows, Macintosh, and UNIX computer platforms.

In 1994, Andreesson left NCSA and co-founded Netscape Communications Corporation in Mountain View, California. In 1995, the Netscape Navigator Web browser quickly became the most widely used cross-platform Web browser on the market. Netscape integrated all of the features of Mosaic, and added many new features and capabilities as well.

The second-generation Netscape Navigator browser, version 2.0, was released for general availability in February 1996. Many new capabilities were incorporated into Netscape 2.0, including support for Java applets, Acrobat files, Shockwave files, and built-in HTML authoring.

Components of the Internet

The Internet is based on these fundamental technology components:

- Internet clients
- Internet servers
- Communications protocols

Internet Clients and Web Browsers

Internet clients represent computer nodes or client software such as Web browsers, e-mail, FTP, and newsgroup clients. When a client requests data from a server, information is *downloaded.* Alternately, when a client transfers data to a server, it is *uploaded,* as shown here:

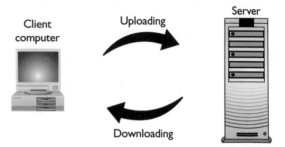

The computer and network infrastructure underlying the WWW is the same as that of the Internet. What differentiates the Web from the Internet is the multimedia capability offered by Web browsers and servers. A Web browser is a client application that displays multimedia hypertext documents (Web pages). Examples of Web browsers include Microsoft Internet Explorer and Netscape Navigator.

exam
ⓦatch

The CompTIA i-Net+ exam is based on vendor-neutral standards; however, you should be familiar with actual vendor implementations and products based on these standards to do well on the exam. For example, when discussing browser concepts, you should be familiar with the most recent versions of both the Netscape and Microsoft Web browsers.

Internet Servers

A server (also called a *host*) is a computer or software application that makes available (or *serves* the client) data and files. Internet servers are available for the Web, Mail, News, and other Internet services.

The purpose of a Web server is to store and disseminate Web pages, interact with the client browser, and process user transactions and requests such as database queries. Web servers are available for all popular computer platforms and operating systems, including Windows, Macintosh, and UNIX. Essentially, a Web server is sitting and listening for a request from a browser to download a document (Web page) residing on the server. The purpose of the server is to "serve" documents to a client and interact with backend systems such as databases and other servers.

Web documents are written using the *HyperText Markup Language* (HTML). HTML is a Web-based *standard* that describes how Web documents are displayed in a Web browser or *thin client*. A thin client may be a Web browser, network computer, personal digital assistant, or any device capable of displaying HTML. Since HTML is a cross-platform language, the same Web pages can be viewed in various browsers on Windows, Macintosh, and UNIX computer platforms. As newer types of thin clients emerge, the Web will become a pervasive part of our lives.

A common misconception about the WWW is that a thin client maintains a continuous connection with the Web server. In fact, once the information is downloaded from the server to the browser, the transaction is completed, and the connection is terminated. The information in the browser is viewed without remaining connected to the server. In order to download new information, a new transaction is required.

Figure 1-1 shows the relationship between a Web browser and a Web server. A Web browser requests a document by entering the address of the document, which is its *Uniform Resource Locator*—otherwise known as a URL or Web address. A connection is attempted between the client and the

---

FIGURE I-I   Interaction between a Web browser and a Web server

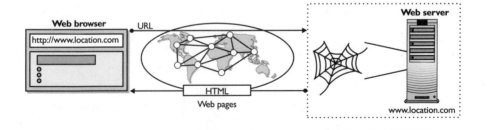

server, and, if successful, a document is downloaded from the server and viewed in the browser.

For example, consider connecting to the CompTIA Web site. To do this, the URL for CompTIA—http://www.comptia.org—is entered in the browser location text field. The browser attempts to make a connection to the CompTIA Web server. If the connection is successful, a Web page (HTML file) is downloaded to the client browser that made the request, as shown in Figure 1-1, and the connection is closed.

INTRANETS AND EXTRANETS   Both intranet and extranet technologies are based on the same open standards that make up the Internet. Intranets are *intra*connected *net*works that are usually restricted to *internal* access only by a company's employees and workers. Oftentimes, an intranet is located behind a firewall to prevent unauthorized access from a public network.

The term *extranets* is derived from the external networks that connect an Internet site, or connects an Internet site to another Internet site using the Internet. In a sense, it's an extension of an Internet/intranet site to another site on the Internet where information and resources may be shared. Common examples of extranets are links between business partners that need to share information such as sales data or inventories.

E-COMMERCE AND E-BUSINESS   The terms *e-commerce* and *e-business* have become almost as pervasive as the use of Internet. The "e" stands for *electronic* and is used to separate the traditional use of terms like commerce, business, and mail from the corresponding computer or Internet-based usage of these terms.

What exactly do e-commerce and e-business mean? E-commerce is about selling products and services over the Internet in a secure environment and is a subset of e-business. E-business is about using Internet technologies to transform key business processes to capitalize on new business opportunities; strengthen relationships in the supply chain with customers, suppliers, business partners, and distributors; and become more efficient and, in the process, more profitable. The Internet, intranets, and extranets serve as the enabling e-business and e-commerce technologies. You will learn about this in later chapters.

Internet Protocols

The Internet is inherently a multivendor computing environment composed of computers from many manufacturers using various network devices, operating systems, languages, platforms, and software programs. In order for this diverse array of hardware and software components to interoperate (or connect and work) with each other, there must be a standard method or language of communication. This language is referred to as a *protocol.*

The Internet is based on scores of protocols that support each of the types of services and technologies deployed on the Internet. The basic suite of protocols that allows this mix of hardware and software devices to work together is called *TCP/IP.*

TCP/IP   Transmission Control Protocol/Internet Protocol. TCP/IP became the Internet's standard data transfer protocol in 1982 and is the common protocol (or *language*) that allows communication between different hardware platforms, operating systems, and software applications. TCP/IP is a packet-switching system that encapsulates data transferred over the Internet into digital "packets."

It is important to understand that clients, servers, and network devices on the Internet must be running the TCP/IP protocol. This is true for Windows, Macintosh, and UNIX computer platforms.

On a Windows-based client, the TCP/IP protocol is implemented through a software *device driver,* sometimes referred to as the TCP/IP "stack." In Windows 95/98 and Windows NT, the TCP/IP stack is built into the operating system.

HTTP   HyperText Transfer Protocol. The HTTP protocol operates together with the TCP/IP protocol to facilitate the transfer of data in the form of text, images, audio, video, and animation.

Internet Services

The Internet is a combination of many types of services, and each has its own associated protocol. It has evolved from a time when only text-based files and e-mail could be transferred from one computer to another. The most common Internet services are

- **E-mail**   Based on Post Office Protocol (POP) and Simple Mail Transfer Protocol (SMTP).
- **File Transfer**   Based on the File Transfer Protocol (FTP) and it is used to transfer ASCII and binary files across a TCP/IP network.
- **Newsgroups**   Network News Transfer Protocol (NNTP) is used for newsgroups.
- **World Wide Web**   HyperText Transfer Protocol (HTTP) is used for the Web.

Other Internet services include Telnet, IRC Chat, Archie, and Gopher. Most of these services are available using the Web and e-mail.

While each of these services is layered on top of the TCP/IP protocol, they are entirely separate. Originally, these services were isolated from each other. To download a file, you needed a dedicated FTP application. To send or receive e-mail, you needed a dedicated e-mail application. As the Internet and the Web have evolved, these capabilities have been integrated into Web browsers. This eliminates the need for dedicated client applications. Figure 1-2 illustrates the types of services that are currently supported by Web browsers.

FIGURE 1-2   Multiple Internet services available via the Web

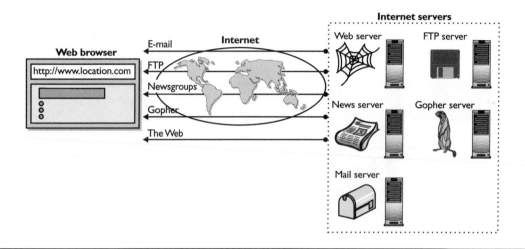

CERTIFICATION OBJECTIVE 1.02

URL Components and Functions

A URL is a unique address on the Internet, similar to an e-mail address. A URL specifies the address of a server, or a specific Web page residing on a server on the Internet. A URL also specifies the transfer protocol.

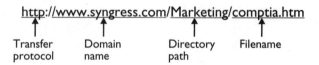

Transfer   Domain   Directory   Filename
protocol   name   path

- The *transfer protocol* is the method of transferring or downloading information into a browser such as HTTP (for Web pages), FTP (for files), or NNTP (for USENET news).

- The *domain name* specifies the address of a specific Web server to which the browser is connecting. Similar to a telephone number, it must be unique.

- The *directory path* is the name and directory path of the file on the server being requested by the browser (optional).

- The *filename* is the name of the Web page being requested by the browser.

CERTIFICATION OBJECTIVE 1.03

Types of URLs

As explained in the preceding section, URLs vary with respect to the selected *transfer protocol*. The transfer protocol is the method by which information is transferred across the Internet. The transfer protocol determines the type of server being connected to, be it a Web, FTP, Gopher, mail, or news server. Table 1-1 lists the major transfer protocols.

The Domain Name

The domain name is the Web server address. The domain uniquely defines a company, nonprofit organization, government, individual, or any other group seeking a Web address. The traditional way of specifying the server domain name is http://www.*location*.com. However, server names do not have to be specified this way. For example, sometimes the "www" is omitted

TABLE 1-1	Transfer Protocol	Server Type	URL Syntax
Major Transfer Protocols Supported by Web Clients	http	Web	http://www.*location*.com
	ftp	FTP	ftp://ftp.*location*.com
	gopher	Gopher	gopher://gopher.*location*.com
	news	Newsgroup	news://news.*location*.com
	mail	e-mail	mailto://*person*@*location*.com
	file	Local drive	file:///c:/directory/*filename*.htm

and the server name is specified as *location*.com (or *location*.net, *location*.edu, etc.).

The first part of the domain name is usually the name of the company, person, or organization. The second part, called the *extension*, comes largely from a set of conventions adopted by the Internet community.

Domain Name Extensions

URLs also vary with respect to the domain name extensions. Domain names must be qualified by using one of the following six extensions for sites within the United States. For sites outside of the United States, country codes are used in place of the domain extension. Table 1-2 lists the primary domain extensions in use.

Directory Path and Filename

The directory path is the location of the directory in which the file is located on the Web server. The directory path is sometimes called the *path statement*. The filename is the name of the document being requested by the Web browser. The filename is part of the directory path. The default filename when entering only the server name is usually index.htm or index.html.

TABLE 1-2	Domain Extension	Description
Primary Domain Extensions for U.S.-Based Web Site.	.com	Commercial business
	.net	Network or Internet Service Provider (ISP)
	.edu	Educational institution
	.gov	United States Government
	.mil	Military
	.org	Any other organization (often nonprofit)
	us, uk, de, etc.	International country codes

Internet Port Number

An Internet port number (also referred to as a *socket number*) distinguishes between running applications. In some cases, a port number may be required and is appended to the server name, such as http://www.*location*.com:80 (80 is the default port for Web services). The port number can usually be omitted and the server's default port will be used.

The most commonly used port numbers are

FTP	Port 21
Telnet	Port 23
SMTP	Port 25
HTTP	Port 80

Assigning Domain Names

The group in charge of managing the Domain Name System (DNS) is the Internet Corporation for Assigned Names & Numbers (ICANN). ICANN is a nonprofit organization, the purpose of which is to verify that no duplicate domain names are assigned. As of June 1999, ICANN accredited 42 companies from 10 countries to offer domain name assignment services. Updated information on ICANN can be obtained from

http://www.icann.org/registers/accredited-list.html

The Internet Assigned Numbers Authority (IANA) is a voluntary organization that has suggested some new qualifiers that further differentiate hosts on the Internet, as shown in Table 1-3.

IP Addresses

Each domain name has a corresponding number assigned to it referred to as an *Internet Protocol* address, or IP. "IP" is the second part of the "TCP/IP" protocol.

TABLE 1-3	Qualifiers	Description
IANA Suggestions for New Qualifiers	.firm	Business or firms
	.shop	Business offering goods and services to purchase
	.arts	Entities offering cultural and entertainment activities
	.web	Entities offering activities based on the WWW
	.nom	Individual or personal nomenclature
	.info	Entities providing information services

Just as a domain name is unique, so is the IP address. IP addresses are what Internet routers use to direct requests and route traffic across the Internet. IP addresses are also managed by ICANN.

Domain Name System

The system designed to assign and organize addresses is called the Domain Name System (DNS). The DNS, devised in the early 1970s, is still in use today. The DNS was designed to be user friendlier than IP numbers. Often, an IP address has an equivalent domain name. In these cases, a server on the Internet can be specified using its IP number or domain name. Domain names are much easier to remember than IP addresses.

Domain names were created so that URLs could be user friendly and people would not have to enter the difficult-to-remember IP address. An example of an IP address is 209.0.85.150. This is the IP address that maps to www.comptia.org.

When you enter a domain name, a special *domain name server* (a dedicated computer at your ISP) looks up the domain name from a special file (called a *routing table*) and directs the message to the appropriate IP address on the Internet.

EXERCISE 1-1

Converting Domain Names and IP Addresses

In this exercise, you will access a Web site using both its domain name and its IP address. Given one of the addresses, you will use a reverse lookup system to convert back and forth between the two representations.

1. Go to http://network-tools.com/ and click one of the Mirror link sites labeled 1 through 6. Scroll down the page until you see the input area, shown here:

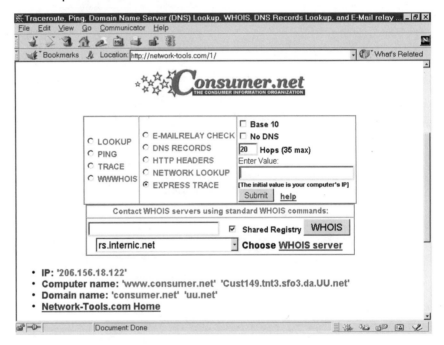

2. Type the URL www.comptia.org in the Enter Value field, click the Lookup radio button, and press SUBMIT. This is called a *reverse domain lookup*.

3. Notice the IP address is returned in the text field in place of the domain name, as shown here:

```
┌────────────────────────────────────────────────────┐
│  ○ LOOKUP    ○ E-MAILRELAY CHECK  ☐ Base 10        │
│  ○ PING      ○ DNS RECORDS        ☐ No DNS          │
│  ○ TRACE     ○ HTTP HEADERS       20  Hops (35 max) │
│  ○ WWWWHOIS  ○ NETWORK LOOKUP     Enter Value:      │
│              ◉ EXPRESS TRACE      209.0.85.150      │
│                                   Submit    help    │
├────────────────────────────────────────────────────┤
│  Contact WHOIS servers using standard WHOIS commands: │
│  www.comptia.org          ☑ Shared Registry  WHOIS │
│  rs.internic.net      ▾  Choose WHOIS server       │
└────────────────────────────────────────────────────┘
```

4. Go to your Web browser and in the location window type the IP address as **http://209.0.85.150/**, then press ENTER. This will take you to the CompTIA Web site. Try typing **http://www.comptia.org** to verify that this takes you to the identical location.

5. Go to your Web browser and type the IP address as **http://209.0.85.150/** in the location window, and press ENTER. This will take you to the CompTIA Web site.

You can also do a lookup on an IP address and it will return the domain name. Feel free to experiment with some of the other services available using http://network-tools.com/.

Internet Site Performance and Reliability

The performance and reliability of an Internet or intranet site is critical in order to attract and retain users. If Web pages take too long to load, the site does not work reliably, or users are frustrated because they need a superfast connection in order to view the site, both the users and sponsors of the site will be disappointed. This next section describes the critical success factors for creating a high-performance and reliable Web or intranet site.

Internet Connectivity

Connecting to the Internet may seem like a transparent process to the user, but in order to understand how users connect to the Internet, each of the various communication and interface points must be understood. Data travels from the user's computer to a remote server, and vice versa. Understanding the path it takes is important to being able to troubleshoot system performance and reliability problems.

Gateways

A gateway is a device used for connecting networks using different protocols so that information can be passed from one system to another, or one network to another. Gateways provide an "onramp" for connecting to the Internet. A gateway is often a server node with a high-speed connection to the Internet. Most individuals and smaller organizations use an Internet Service Provider (ISP) as their gateway to the Internet.

There are two primary methods of connecting to the Internet: dial-up connections using a modem, and direct connections. In both cases, you need an ISP. An ISP is analogous to a cable television company that provides access to various cable television systems.

Internet Service Provider (ISP)

Until 1987, access to the Internet was limited to universities, government agencies, and companies with servers on the Internet. In 1987, the first commercial ISP went online in the United States, providing access to organizations and companies that did not own and maintain the equipment necessary to be a host on the Internet.

An ISP is your gateway to the Internet. An ISP maintains a dedicated high-speed connection to the Internet 24 hours a day. In order to connect to the Internet, you must first be connected to your ISP. You can obtain a dedicated line that provides a continuous connection to your ISP (for an additional fee), or connect to the Internet only when necessary using a modem. Figure 1-3 illustrates a typical dial-up connection for an end user using an ISP as a gateway to the Internet.

FIGURE 1-3   Dial-up connection using an ISP as a gateway to the Internet

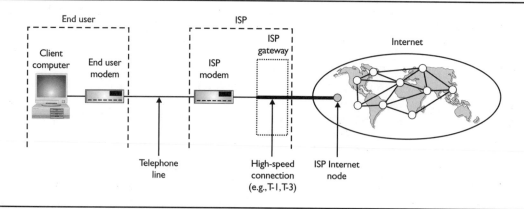

Internet Backbone

The high-speed infrastructure that connects the individual networks on the Internet is referred to as the *backbone*. A backbone is a high-speed conduit for data to which hundreds and even thousands of other smaller networks are connected.

Each backbone is operated and maintained by the organization that owns it. These organizations, usually long distance carriers, regional phone companies, or ISPs, lease access to their high-speed backbones to other organizations. The most prominent groups are ISPs and Telecommunications Companies (TelCos).

Types of Internet Access and Bandwidth

There are two primary methods of connecting to the Internet. A *dial-up* connection using a modem, or a *direct* connection directly to an ISP or the Internet backbone. Dial-up connections include analog modems that can operate at a maximum speed of 56K, and Integrated Services Digital Network (ISDN) connections with a maximum throughput of 128K a second. Both operate using standard telephone lines to the Central Office of the Telco.

Direct connections are carried over high-speed data lines. There is a wide range of direct connection speeds available. Direct connections can be established at speeds as slow as 56 Kbps and as fast as 45 Mbps. The higher-speed direct connections are called T1 and T3 connections. T1 connections operate at 1.5 Mbps. A T3 connection can range in throughput from 3 Mbps to 45 Mbps. T1 connections are very common for business, and T3 connections are used by ISPs and Telcos. The main difference between these two connection methods is speed and cost.

Connection speeds are measured in either kilobits per second (Kbps) or megabits per second (Mbps). A mega*bit* (Mb) is a million bits, and a kilo*bit* (Kb) is a thousand bits. A mega*byte* (MB) is a million bytes, and a kilo*byte* (KB) is a thousand bytes. Don't confuse bits and bytes. One byte = eight bits. Note that bits are represented by a lowercase "b," and bytes are shown as an uppercase "B." A typical dial-up modem connection operates at speeds of either 28.8 or 56.6 Kbps. Direct connections are usually measured in Mbps and are many times faster than dial-up connections.

An advantage of a dial-up connection is it only requires a standard phone line and a modem, and is relatively inexpensive. As an alternative to a T1 connection for home and small business users, others methods such as cable modems and Digital Subscriber Line direct access are becoming available in most major markets. These options tend to cost much less than leasing T1 or fractional T1 lines. With a fractional T1, you are sharing the "pipe" with other users or organizations, which can have a significant impact on performance.

Internet Site Functionality

There are many factors that can influence the functionality of the Internet or a Web site. Some of these factors are related to the Internet backbone, including network traffic and congestion; some relate to the quality, reliability, and security of the hosting site; and still others are related to the design and usability of a Web site. All of these factors contribute to the overall user experience when accessing the site.

Performance Issues

In order to understand performance issues, the entire end-to-end communications infrastructure must be considered. For example, if users are becoming frustrated because the access to your company Web site is sluggish, there may be a variety of reasons for the poor performance.

First, it might be that their connection speed to the Internet is too slow. Perhaps they are using an older-generation modem that is slower than 56.6 K. Alternatively, their ISP may have a slow connection to the Internet that is where the bottleneck is. Extending out the infrastructure, the problem may be that the Internet is congested, and response time to your site is slow. This may be the case during the peak hours during a normal work week.

Finally, the problem might be on the host or server end of the connection. Issues on this end could be poor performance related to the bandwidth of an ISP, the speed of the Internet servers, or the amount of traffic on their site. If a lot of users are accessing their servers and engaging in a high level of transactions, performance will be slow for all other users. Sometimes security services can be the culprit when running Secure Socket Layer (SSL). In order to troubleshoot performance, network engineers use a variety of tools such as Ping, Traceroute, and other proprietary network management tools to isolate performance problems.

Usability and Audience Access

Another performance issue that affects overall site functionality is the design and architecture of your Internet site. It is important to keep in mind that your site needs to be designed taking into account the access and connection speeds of your *users*. You may have a direct T3 connection to the Internet, and the fastest Web servers available, but if your users are connecting through a slow dial-up connection, performance can be significantly degraded.

Always design to the lowest common denominator if that is your target audience. Alternately, if you are building an intranet site and all of your users are connecting over a LAN, you may not be so concerned about performance issues.

on the **Job**

Before designing a Web site, you should conduct a user survey and analysis to determine the range of connection speeds used by customers and end users to connect to your network. By current standards, the lowest common denominator is considered to be a 28.8 K or 56.6 K modem connection.

Issues with Embedded Graphics

One of the greatest impacts on user performance is the size, format, and techniques used for embedded graphics. Always strive for fast-loading graphics, whether they be photographic images, line art, or other graphics.

Performance issues are often tied to graphics files being too large and taking too long to download over an ordinary modem connection. This design pitfall can be addressed by using compression algorithms on the graphic files, scaling the graphic down in size, selecting the optimal graphic file format, or reducing the number of colors in an image.

Nothing looks uglier than a Web page that is supposed to have an embedded graphic file and instead has a generic file icon showing a question mark. This is usually caused by a mistake in the HTML document. Either the image file is not where the HTML document is trying to access it from, or, in some cases, the file may be corrupted and fails to load, or hangs up while downloading the page. Users sometimes disable image loading within their browsers if this is impacting their performance.

One workaround is to present users with two types of sites: one that is optimized for high-speed connections and another that is optimized for slower modem connections. The downside of this approach is that it takes the additional resources to maintain and update both sites. A clever design architecture can minimize the impact of maintaining two sites instead of one.

FROM THE CLASSROOM

Creating Fast-Loading Image Files

If your Web pages don't download quickly, you are likely to lose users. They will become impatient and move on to another site. Adding graphics poses a performance tradeoff. Does the value of the graphic file justify the increased performance hit when downloading the page? Here are some tips for creating high-performance images:

- Reduce the screen size of the image file whenever possible. Every bit you trim from an image means better performance. Users with laptops and small screens will benefit as well.

- Use the appropriate image format. For line art, text images, and illustrations, use a GIF file format that is smaller than JPEG. For photographs and high-resolution images, use JPEG with comression.

- Reduce the number of colors in your images by using black and white whenever possible and downsampling the number of colors from 256 to fewer. Experiment to see what works.

- Use image compression tools that can decrease the file size of GIF and JPEG images even after you have scaled them down and reduced the number of colors.

- Reuse the same graphics whenever possible so they are retrieved from the disk cache instead of having to download new images.

- Add WIDTH and HEIGHT tags to your images (specified in pixels). This tells the browser to allocate the space on the screen for images and begin downloading the text content before the images have finished loading.

—*Maxwell Miller, Ph.D.,*
CIW, CWT, i-Net+

CERTIFICATION SUMMARY

This chapter provided you with an introduction and overview of the Internet. You became familiar with the origins and evolution of the Internet and the emergence of internal private networks called *intranets*. You were also familiarized with underlying Internet technologies including the World Wide Web, Web browsers, Web servers, and Uniform Resource Locators (URLs).

You also learned about factors that affect Internet/intranet/extranet site functionality and performance, including bandwidth constraints, customer and user connectivity, connection access points, and throughput. Last, you learned how e-business leverages these technologies by linking organizations to their supply chain, including business partners, suppliers, distributors, customers, and end users using extranets and the Internet.

TWO-MINUTE DRILL

- ❑ The Internet is perhaps best described as the world's largest *inter*connected *net*work of networks.

- ❑ ARPA is an agency within the United States Federal Government formed by the Eisenhower administration in 1957 with the purpose of conducting scientific research and developing advanced technologies for the U.S. military.

- ❑ International standards bodies, including the Internet Engineering Task Force (IETF), the Internet Society (ISOC), and the World Wide Web Consortium (W3C), are leading the process to develop international standards.

- ❑ The idea for the Web is attributed to Tim Berners-Lee of CERN, the European Laboratory for Particle Physics in Geneva, Switzerland.

- ❑ HTML is a Web-based *standard* that describes how Web documents are displayed in a Web browser or *thin client*.

- ❑ The basic suite of protocols that allows the mix of hardware and software devices to work together is called *TCP/IP*.

- ❑ On a Windows-based client, the TCP/IP protocol is implemented through a software *device driver*, sometimes referred to as the TCP/IP "stack."

- ❑ A URL specifies the address of a server, or a specific Web page residing on a server on the Internet.

- ❑ The first part of the domain name is usually the name of the company, person, or organization. The second part, called the *extension*, comes largely from a set of conventions adopted by the Internet community.

❑   The group in charge of managing the Domain Name System (DNS) is the Internet Corporation for Assigned Names & Numbers (ICANN).

❑   A gateway is a device used for connecting networks using different protocols so that information can be passed from one system to another, or one network to another.

❑   The high-speed infrastructure that connects the individual networks on the Internet is referred to as the *backbone*.

SELF TEST

The following Self Test questions will help you measure your understanding of the material presented in this chapter. Read all the choices carefully, as there may be more than one correct answer. Choose all correct answers for each question.

1. You are teaching a course to the new hires in the IT department describing the difference between a LAN and the Internet. The best description for the Internet is

   A. The largest local-area network in the world

   ✓ B. The world's largest interconnected network of networks

   C. A network used for internal corporate use

   D. A global community of Internet Service Providers (ISPs)

2. The early roots of the Internet can be traced to

   A. Network Solutions, Inc.

   B. Gopher and the World Wide Web

   ✓ C. The United States Government and the ARPAnet

   D. Tim Berners-Lee

3. Organizations responsible for the management of the Internet include

   ✓ A. Internet Engineering Task Force (IETF)

   B. Internet Society (ISOC)

   C. World Wide Web Consortium

   D. All of the above

4. The idea for the World Wide Web is attributed to

   A. Netscape

   ✓ B. Tim Berners-Lee of CERN

   C. Mark Andreesson

   D. The U.S. Government

5. You are in the process of designing an internal corporate intranet, and one of the Web developers asks you if you are standardizing on a client. He is referring to

   ✓ A. A computer node or software such as a Web browser

   B. A communications protocol

   C. Software that serves applications across networks

   D. Security device such as a firewall

6. The purpose of a Web server is to

   ✓ A. Store and disseminate hypertext documents

   B. Request documents from a Web browser

   C. View hypertext documents

   ✓ D. Interact and process requests from a Web browser

7. Intranets and extranets are based on the following Internet technologies

   A. Web clients and servers

B. Hypertext documents and HTML

C. TCP/IP and HTTP protocols

✓ D. All of the above

8. Your CEO gives you a big promotion and says you are now the e-business guru. Which of the following statements would you include in a speech to your IT department describing e-business?

✓ A. Capitalizes on Internet technologies to transform key business processes and strengthen relationships with business partners, suppliers, and customers

✓ B. A means to become more efficient and more profitable

C. Was developed jointly by Netscape and Microsoft

✓ D. Selling products and services over the World Wide Web with e-commerce

9. Select from the following the correct explanations for the listed Internet protocols and their corresponding Internet services

✓ A. TCP/IP—Enables communications over the Internet

B. POP and SMTP—Enables e-commerce transactions

✓ C. HTTP—Enables communications on the World Wide Web

✓ D. FTP—Used for transferring ASCII and binary files

10. Which answer best describes the elements of a Uniform Resource Locator (URL)?

A. Domain name, Port Number, File Path, XML

B. HTML, Domain name, File Path, Port name

✓ C. Transfer Protocol, Domain name, File Path, Port Number

D. XML, Domain name, Client Address, File Path

11. Which of the following groups is in charge of managing the Domain Name System?

A. Internet Society (IS)

✓ B. Internet Corporation for Assigned Names & Numbers   ICANN

C. World Wide Web Consortium (W3C)

D. Internet Engineering Task Force (IETF)

12. An Internet Service Provider (ISP) is responsible for providing users

A. A gateway to the Internet

B. Dedicated or dial-up connections to the Internet

C. Internet backbone connectivity

✓ D. All of the above

13. Home users are likely to connect to the Internet using the following type of access:

→ A. Dial-up modem connections

B. Direct T1 or T3 connections

→ C. ISDN or cable modems

✓ D. A and C

14. Customers and users are sending e-mail messages to the Webmaster complaining about the performance and functionality of a newly launched Web site. There are

many factors that might be responsible, including

A. Internet backbone traffic and congestion

B. Quality, reliability, and security of the hosting site

C. Design and usability of a Web site

✓ D. All of the above

15. Users are frustrated because the access to your company Web site is sluggish. There may be a variety of reasons for the poor performance. Your job is to troubleshoot the problem. Select which two problems might account for the poor performance.

A. Their connection speed to the Internet may be very slow and is the problem.

B. You are using TCP/IP instead of HTTP as the communications protocol.

C. The hosting site servers may not be able to keep up with user requests.

D. Users need to upgrade their operating system to improve network performance.

16. You are asked to design a commercial e-commerce site that will be accessed primarily by end users, students, and housewives. It would be good practice to design your site to be

A. Optimized for users with fast direct connections to the Internet

B. Designed for business users who connect from their place of work

C. Designed for users who connect using slower dial-up connections with modems

D. None of the above

17. You are asked by the MIS Director to speed up the performance of the Web site. One of the biggest problems you have noticed is how slowly Web graphics load. What are some possible fixes to this problem?

A. Reduce the size of graphics files.

B. Transform all graphics into GIF files.

C. Use fewer colors if possible without degrading graphic resolution.

D. Convert all files to JPEG format.

18. You are the Webmaster and notice that the company logo on the homepage does not load and there is an ugly generic file icon in its place. The problem could be

A. The image file has become corrupted.

B. The image file is too large and takes too long to download.

C. The image file is no longer in the location that the HTML document is pointing to.

D. The number of colors in the image file is too few.

19. The Internet Backbone is best described as

A. The service provided by ICANN and W3C

B. A high-speed infrastructure that connects the individual networks on the Internet

C. Extranet connectivity points

D. The suite of Internet protocols

SELF TEST ANSWERS

1. **B.** The Internet is perhaps best described as the "world's largest *inter*connected *net*work of networks." There is no centralized control of the Internet; instead, many millions of individual networks and individual computers are interconnected throughout the world to communicate with each other. The Internet is not only technology, it's a global community of people, including corporations, nonprofit organizations, educational institutions, and individuals.
   A is incorrect because the Internet is a global internetwork, not a local network. **C** describes an intranet. **D** is wrong because the Internet consists of more than just ISPs.

2. **C.** The early roots of the Internet can be traced back to the *Advanced Research Projects Agency* (ARPA). ARPA is an agency within the United States Federal Government formed by the Eisenhower administration in 1957 with the purpose of conducting scientific research and developing advanced technologies for the U.S. military.
   A is incorrect because Network Solutions is an organization responsible for registering domain names. **B** is incorrect because Gopher and the World Wide Web came later after the Internet was conceived. **D** is incorrect because Tim Berners-Lee is the father of the World Wide Web.

3. **D.** Today, no single organization, government, or nation controls the technology, content, or standards of the Internet. Because the Internet fosters international cooperation, it is often referred to as the *global community*. International standards bodies, including the Internet Engineering Task Force (IETF), the Internet Society (ISOC), and the World Wide Web Consortium (W3C), are leading the process to develop international standards.

4. **B.** The idea for the Web is attributed to Tim Berners-Lee of CERN, the European Laboratory for Particle Physics in Geneva, Switzerland. In 1989, Berners-Lee conceived the architecture for the Web as a *multimedia hypertext information system* based on a client/server architecture.
   A is incorrect because Netscape is responsible for creating the first commercial Web browser, and **C** is incorrect because Marc Andreesson is a cofounder of Netscape. **D** is incorrect because the U.S. government did not invent the Web.

5. **A.** Internet clients represent computer nodes or client software such as Web browsers, e-mail, FTP, and newsgroup clients. When a client requests data from a server,

information is *downloaded.* Alternately, when a client transfers data to a server, it is *uploaded.*

B is incorrect because communications protocols are the language for communicating across networks. **C** is incorrect because application software runs on servers or clients. **D** is incorrect because a firewall is a network device that is related to the server side, not the client.

6. **A** and **D.** The purpose of a Web server is to store and disseminate Web pages, interact with the client browser, and interact with backend systems such as databases and other servers.

   B and **C** are incorrect because Web browsers are used to request and view Web pages.

7. **D.** Both intranet and extranet technologies are based on the same open standards that make up the Internet, including client/server technology, HTML, TCP/IP, and HTTP. Intranets are *intra*connected *net*works that are usually restricted to internal access only by a company's employees and workers. Often, an intranet is located behind a firewall to prevent unauthorized access from a public network. The term *extranet* is derived from the external networks that connect an Internet site or an Internet site to another Internet site using the Internet.

8. **A, B,** and **D.** *E-commerce* is about selling products and services over the Internet in a secure environment and is a subset of e-business. *E-business* is about using Internet technologies to transform key business processes to capitalize on new business opportunities; strengthen relationships with customers, suppliers, business partners, and distributors; and become more efficient and, in the process, more profitable. The Internet, intranets, and extranets serve as the enabling e-business and e-commerce technologies.

   C is incorrect because Netscape and Microsoft both have e-business strategies but did not develop a joint strategy, as they are fierce competitors.

9. **A, C,** and **D.** The Internet is a combination of many types of services, and each has its own associated protocol. TCP/IP enables communications over the Internet; Post Office Protocol (POP) and Simple Mail Transfer Protocol (SMTP) are used for e-mail; HyperText Transfer Protocol (HTTP) is used for the Web; FTP is for transferring ASCII and binary files across a network.

   B is incorrect because POP and SMTP protocols enable e-mail and Internet messaging rather than e-commerce.

10. **C.** A Uniform Resource Locator (URL) is a unique address on the Internet, similar to an e-mail address that specifies a Transfer Protocol, Domain name, File Path. A directory name and port number are optional.
A, B, and **D** are incorrect because HTML and XML are languages for creating Web pages and are not part of a URL.

11. **B.** The group in charge of managing the Domain Name System is the Internet Corporation for Assigned Names & Numbers (ICANN). ICANN is a nonprofit organization, the purpose of which is to verify that no duplicate domain names are assigned. The IS, W3C, and IETF are concerned with other standards-based matters.
A, C, and **D** are incorrect because the IS, W3C, and IETF are responsible for developing other Internet standards.

12. **D.** An ISP is your gateway to the Internet. An ISP maintains a dedicated high-speed connection to the Internet 24 hours a day. In order to connect to the Internet, you must first be connected to your ISP. You can obtain a dedicated line that provides a continuous connection to your ISP, or connect to the Internet only when necessary using a dial-up connection.

13. **D.** Home users are likely to connect to the Internet using a dial-up connection using a modem, Integrated Services Digital Network (ISDN), or a cable modem.
B is incorrect because business users and ISPs are likely to connect using direct T1 and T3 connections.

14. **D.** Many factors can influence the functionality of the Internet or a Web site. Some of these are related to the Internet backbone, including network traffic and congestion; some relate to the quality, reliability, and security of the hosting site; and still others are related to the design and usability of a Web site. All of these factors contribute to the overall user experience when accessing the site.

15. **A and C.** It may be that the users' connection speed to the Internet is too slow. Perhaps they are using an older-generation modem that is slower than 56.6 K. Alternatively, their ISP may have a slow connection to the Internet where the bottleneck resides. Extending out the infrastructure, the problem may be that the Internet is congested and response time to your site is slow. This may be the case during the peak hours during a normal work week. Finally, the problem might be on the host or server end of the connection. Issues on this end could be poor performance

related to the bandwidth of their ISP, the speed of the Internet servers, or the amount of traffic on their site. If a lot of users are accessing their servers and engaging in a high level of transactions, performance will be slow for all other users.
B is incorrect because TCP/IP is the standard Internet communications protocol and HTTP is layered on TCP/IP. **D** is incorrect because a user's O/S does not affect the performance of the network.

16. **C.** Another performance issue that affects overall site functionality is the design and architecture of your Internet site.
A is incorrect because it is important to keep in mind that your site needs to be designed taking into account the access and connection speeds of your users. **B** is incorrect because you may have a direct T3 connection to the Internet, and the fastest Web servers available; but, if your users are connecting through a slow dial-up connection, performance can be significantly degraded. Always design to the lowest common denominator if that is your target audience.

17. **A and C.** Performance issues are often tied to graphics files being too large and taking too long to download over an ordinary modem connection. This design pitfall can be addressed by using compression algorithms on the graphic files, scaling the graphic down in size, selecting the optimal graphic file format for a particular image type, or reducing the number of colors in an image.
B and D are incorrect because GIF or JPEG files have specific applications and usage.

18. **A and C.** A Web page with a generic file icon showing a question mark is usually caused by a mistake in the HTML document. Either the filename of the image does not exist where the HTML document is trying to access it from, or, in some cases, the file may be corrupted itself and fails to load, or hangs up while downloading the page.
B is incorrect because a generic file icon only appears if the graphic file cannot be located. **D** is incorrect because it takes longer to download image files as their number of colors increases.

19. **B.** The high-speed infrastructure that connects the individual networks on the Internet is referred to as the *backbone*. A backbone is a high-speed conduit for data to which hundreds and even thousands of other smaller networks are connected. Each backbone is operated and maintained by the organization that owns it. These organizations, usually long distance carriers, regional phone companies, or Internet Service Providers (ISPs),

lease access to their high-speed backbones to other organizations. The most prominent group are ISPs and Telecommunications Companies (TelCos).

A is incorrect because ICANN and W3C are concerned with Internet standards, not the backbone. C and D are wrong because extranets are external networks and Internet protocols are a common communications language.

i-Net+

COMPUTING TECHNOLOGY INDUSTRY ASSOCIATION®

2

Indexing and Caching

CERTIFICATION OBJECTIVES

I n this chapter we are going to look at two important concepts that help make the Internet the highly functional communication device we know it to be. The first part of the chapter will cover the concepts and implementations of caching. We will also cover the end-to-end process of caching, going from the client to the Web server. In the second half of the chapter, we will examine the various types of search indexes and methods of utilizing them effectively. In addition to utilizing other search engines, we will cover topics related to indexing and searching our own Web site. Finally, we will look at META tags and how they can help you configure your Web site for better searching.

CERTIFICATION OBJECTIVE 2.01

Web Caching

Caching is the process of storing requested objects at a network point closer to the client, at a location that will provide these objects for reuse as they are requested by additional clients. By doing so, we can reduce network utilization and client access times. When we talk about Web objects or objects in general, we are simply referring to a page, graphic, or some other form of data that we access over the Internet, usually through our Web browser. This storage point, which we refer to as a *cache*, can be implemented in several different ways, with stand-alone proxy caching servers being popular for businesses, and industrial-duty transparent caching solutions becoming a mainstay for Internet Service Providers (ISPs). Within this section, we will focus on different aspects and implementation issues of Web caching, as well as the methods for determining a proper solution on the basis of the situation requirements.

Web Caching Client Benefits

A request for a Web object requires crossing several network links until the server housing the object is reached. These network crossings are referred to as hops, which generally consist of wide area network (WAN) serial links and routers. A typical end-to-end connection may span 15 hops, all of which add latency or delay to the user's session as objects are directed through routers and over WAN links. If a closer storage point for recently accessed objects is maintained, the number of hops is greatly reduced between the client and the original server. In addition to the reduced latency, larger amounts of bandwidth are available closer to the client; typically, cache servers are installed on switched fast Ethernet networks, which can provide up to 200 megabits per second data-transfer rates. With these speeds, the limiting factor becomes the link speed between the client and the provider's network where the caching server is located. Even though caching servers can benefit users of smaller networks, the solution tends to be more effective when implemented with a larger user base. This is due in part to the expiration period of cached items and the fact that larger user bases exhibit higher degrees of content overlap, and more users can share a single cached item within a shorter period of time.

Web Caching Increases Network Performance

Because of the rising demand for bandwidth and the associated costs, we must find alternatives to adding additional circuits. A look at the traffic statistics available at http://www.wcom.com/tools-resources/mae_statistics/ gives us an idea of how peak times affect network utilization. Web caching allows us as network administrators and system engineers to reduce bandwidth peaks during periods of high network traffic. These peaks are usually caused by a large number of users utilizing the network at the same time. With a caching solution in place, there is a high likelihood that users' requests will be returned from the cache without the need to travel over a WAN link to the destination Web server.

Determining Cache Performance

It is apparent that caching can provide increases in network performance, reduce latency, and maximize bandwidth. The question that a network administrator usually faces in evaluating a current or proposed caching solution is not how, but how much. Most cache performance analyses are done on the basis of a cache hit ratio:

Requests Returned from Cache / Total Requests = Cache Hit Ratio

This is the number of requests that are to be retrieved from the server's cache divided by the total number of requests. The cache hit ratio is usually expressed as a percentage, with the higher number representing a better-performing cache.

Caching Server Placement

Because object cache is time dependent, caching becomes more effective as the number of users increases. The likelihood of 10 users sharing Internet objects is fairly small compared to duplicated object access for 20,000 users. Because of this trend, it becomes necessary to implement caching servers in strategic locations across the network. These locations are determined by weighing such factors as available upstream bandwidth, protocol usage, supported client base, client connection speeds, client traffic patterns, staffing, and server considerations.

EXERCISE 2-1

Hands-On Latency and Bandwidth Comparison

Increased distance between client computers and the origin servers adds latency and increases the risks of bottlenecks. Most connections will pass over 10 to 20 routers before an end to connectivity is established. These routers along the network path are referred to as *hops*. The TCP/IP Trace route utility can determine the number of hops between your current location and another point on the Internet. Local caching servers typically are located within two or three hops of client computers. To use the Trace route utility, you must have a computer running the TCP/IP protocol suite, connected to the Internet (or Local Area Network), and know the IP address or fully qualified domain name (FQDN) of the host you wish to trace to. The syntax on a Windows computer is as follows:

Tracert 192.233.80.9

Compare this to your corporate Web server, your ISP's Web site, or another machine on the LAN.

Once you have seen a comparison of the hops and the Time To Live (TTL) counts for both Trace route commands, you can now relate the difference by bringing the two sites up in your browser. Depending on the overall file size of the viewed pages, you should see a considerable performance difference between the two visited Web sites. This exercise helps to demonstrate the two main client benefits for utilizing proxy servers: reduced latency and increased speed (throughput).

Passive Caching

Passive caching represents the most basic form of object caching. Passive caching servers require less configuration and maintenance, but at the price of reduced performance. Passive caching, as the name implies, makes no attempt to "prefetch" Internet objects.

Passive caching starts when a caching server receives an object request. The caching server will check for the presence of the requested object in its local cache. If the object is not available locally, the caching server will request the object from the location originally specified by the requesting client, this is referred to as the origin server. If the object is available locally, but the content is determined stale by examining the Time To Live property (TTL), then it will also request the object from the origin server. Finally, if the object is available within the caching server's local cache, and the content is considered fresh, then the server will provide the content to the requesting client directly. After the caching server fulfills the user's request, the object is inserted into the server's local cache. If the disk space allocated for caching is too full to hold the requested objects, previously cached objects will be removed on the basis of a formula that evaluates how old the content is, how often an object has been requested, and the size of the object.

Unlike active caching, passive caching is performed strictly on a reactive basis. Passive caching would be a good choice for locations with limited support personnel, and where the performance gains would not merit the added configuration and tuning required by active caching.

In addition to the most popular configuration as stand-alone servers, passive caching servers can be configured as members of clusters for fault tolerance, and as array members for performance gains. This is not typically done, because the expense of additional caching servers is usually justified only when qualified personnel are available to configure, maintain, and tune complex caching setups.

Active Caching

Active caching servers use a proactive approach referred to as *prefetching* to maximize the performance of the server's cache by increasing the amount of objects that are available locally on the basis of several configurations and a statistical analysis. If the likelihood that a requested object will be retrieved from a local cache is increased, performance gains are seen in the overall cache server process. Active caching takes passive caching as a foundation and builds upon it with increased performance and enhanced configuration options.

With most passive caching servers, an object that is retrieved from an origin server is placed in the cache, and a Time To Live (TTL) property is set. As long as the TTL has not expired, the caching server can service client requests locally without the need to recontact the origin server. After the TTL property for the object has expired, additional client requests will reinitialize the caching process.

Active caching builds up to this process by initiating proactive requests for specified objects. Active caching servers can use several factors to determine what objects to retrieve before any actual client requests are received. These factors can include network traffic, server load, objects' TTL properties, and previous request statistics.

Active caching helps maintain higher levels of client performance. When clients can access pages that are stored in a caching server, the transfer speed is increased, and overall session latency is reduced. With active caching, clients have a higher cache hit rate, allowing more objects to be returned from a point closer to the client and returned at a higher speed. Active caching will also check the objects that are cached locally, and will refresh the objects during off-peak periods before they expire. This helps to maximize unused network time and increase the likelihood of returning fresh data.

Caching Related Protocols

The use of caching requires the use of a protocol. There are three protocols used in caching. These protocols are the Internet Cache Protocol, the Caching Array Routing Protocol, and the Web Cache Communication Protocol. Each protocol has a very defined usage, as well as pros and cons.

Internet Cache Protocol

Internet Cache Protocol (ICP) allows several joined cache servers to communicate and share information that is cached locally among the servers. ICP is based upon the transport layer of the TCP/IP stack, utilizing a UDP or connectionless-based communication between the configured servers. With ICP, adjoining caching servers are configured as ICP Neighbors. When a caching server that is acting as an ICP Neighbor receives a request and does not have the object available locally, it will send an ICP query to its ICP Neighbors. The ICP Neighbors will in turn send replies that will indicate whether the object is available: "ICP Hit," or the object is not available: "ICP Miss." While ICP can improve performance in a group of caching servers, it introduces other performance-related issues. Because ICP is required to send requests to each participating ICP Neighbor for a nonlocally available object, the amount of network traffic will increase proportionally as the number of joined caching servers increases. The other downside of utilizing ICP is that additional requests add to the latency of the users' session due to the wait period for ICP replies. ICP servers also tend to duplicate information across the servers after a period of time. This may seem like a benefit initially; the duplication of content across cache servers in an array will lower the overall effectiveness, which will be evident in our cache hit ratio.

Caching Array Protocol

The Caching Array Routing Protocol (CARP) provides an alternative method to ICP to coordinate multiple caching servers. Instead of querying neighbor caches, participating CARP servers use an algorithm to label each server. This algorithm, or *hash*, provides a way to determine the location of a requested object. This means that each participating server knows which array member to check with for the requested object if it is not present on the server that received the request.

In contrast to ICP-based arrays, CARP-based arrays become more efficient as additional servers are added. CARP was originally developed by Microsoft, but has since been adopted by several commercial and freeware caching solutions.

Web Cache Communication Protocol

The Web Cache Communication Protocol was developed by Cisco in order to provide routers with the ability to redirect specified traffic to caching servers. With WCCP version 2, the previous limitations of single routers have been replaced with support for multiple routers. This is important in environments in which the router introduced a single point of failure. WCCP reads into the TCP/IP packet structure and determines the type of traffic according to which port is present in the header. The most common TCP/IP port is port 80, which is HTTP traffic. This allows the router to forward Web requests to a caching server transparently while maintaining direct access for other protocols such as POP3 or FTP.

Transparent Caching

Transparent caching servers require additional complexity and configuration at the gateway point where the client requests are redirected to the cache servers. Since most Web protocols are TCP based, redirection happens at the transport layer (layer 4) of the OSI model. Transparent cache clients are unaware of the middleman, and are limited in their ability to control if the request is returned from the origin server or the cache.

Single-Server Caching

Single-server caching is the idea that you have one server acting as the caching server. This is generally seen primarily on a small LAN; more than 10 or 12 users will easily overrun a single-cache server.

Clusters

Clusters are groups of systems linked or chained together that are used in the caching of information for a company or ISP. By having a cluster of cache servers you can reduce bandwidth while increasing production time for users, as they do not have to wait for the page to be retrieved from the Internet.

Hierarchies

Hierarchical caching occurs when you place a cache server at each layer of your network in a hierarchical fashion just as you do with routers. Your highest cache server would be just inside your firewall, which would be the only server responsible for retrieving information from the Internet. This server or cluster of servers would then feed downstream to other cache servers such as department, building, or location cache servers.

Parent-Sibling

The parent-sibling caching works much like the hierarchies' caching except that the sibling caches are all working together. Each sibling cache is aware of what the other caches are storing and can quickly request from the correct cache server. If a new request comes in, the siblings will send the request to the parent cache server, which will either return the requested information or retrieve it.

Distributed Caching

Distributed caching is much like proxy clusters. The idea is that you have several proxy servers working together to reduce the load of retrieving the information from the Internet. This also acts as a fault tolerance, so that if one of the proxy server goes offline, the others will automatically be able to respond to the requests.

CERTIFICATION OBJECTIVE 2.02

File Caching

In addition to causing HTTP traffic, file transfers that take place across the Internet consume large amounts of network bandwidth as well. The file transfer protocol represents a means for a connection-oriented exchange of information between two systems. In the early days of the Internet, FTP was a mainstay among mostly UNIX-type systems. FTP's cross-platform communication capability has led it to become one of the most popular standards for data transfer. Because FTP sessions tend to involve larger amounts of data than a typical HTTP session, benefits from caching FTP objects can be substantial.

Using caching for FTP requests in a large company can reduce request time and bandwidth dramatically. If 50 employees downloaded a 1MB file each morning, and each request were made directly to the server housing the file that is maintained in the corporate office, it would require 50MB of data to be downloaded across the network, probably via a WAN connection. If a cache server were implemented, only the first request for the data would be directed to the housing server; each additional request for the same data would be served by the cache server.

Proxy Caching

Proxy caching works through a cooperative connection between the browser and the caching server, rather than between the browser and the remote origin server. When a client is configured to use a particular caching proxy server (or any proxy server, for that matter), it directs all of its requests for a particular protocol (HTTP, FTP, Gopher, and so on) to the port on the proxy server specified in the browser configuration. Because several different protocols can be proxied and cached, most browsers allow for different configurations for each protocol. For example, we can specify that HTTP (port 80) requests be sent to our Web-caching server, which could be located at 192.168.0.2 at port 8080. At the same time, we can configure our clients' Web browsers to send FTP (port 21) requests to our file-caching server located at 192.168.0.3 at port 2121. This allows for dedicated servers to provide caching for different protocols. This also allows for better management of network resources; if one server is responsible for caching all data, it will have to time out more quickly, due to space requirements.

HTTP requests to a target Web server, and the browser directs them to the cache. The cache then either satisfies the request itself or passes on the request to the server as a proxy for the browser (hence the name).

Proxy caches are particularly useful on enterprise intranets, where they serve as a firewall that protects intranet servers against attacks from the

Internet. Linking an intranet to the Internet offers a company's users direct access to everything out there, but it also causes internal systems to be exposed to attack from the Internet. With a proxy server, only the proxy server system need be literally on the Internet, and all the internal systems are on a relatively isolated and protected intranet. The proxy server can then enforce specific policies for external access to the intranet.

The most obvious disadvantage of the proxy configuration is that each browser must be explicitly configured to use it. Earlier browsers required manual user setup changes when a proxy server was installed or changed, which was a support headache at best for ISPs supporting thousands of users. Today, a user can configure the current version of either Navigator or Internet Explorer to locate a proxy without further user involvement.

(Note that, eventually, browser setup and support will be completely automated. A typical browser will automatically find whatever resources it needs, including caches, each time it begins operation. At that time, proxy caches will be completely transparent to the browser user. Today, however, transparency issues are a key inhibitor to the use of proxy caches.)

Another disadvantage of the proxy configuration is that the cache itself becomes another point of system failure. The cache server can crash and interrupt Internet access to all intranet systems configured to use the proxy for access. The cache server can become overloaded and become an incremental performance limitation. To help ensure that the server is not overloaded, it should be running only proxy software and should have large amounts of storage and memory installed. A high-end processor such as a Pentium III or RISC chip would also help ensure that the proxy/cache servers do not cause a network bottleneck.

CERTIFICATION OBJECTIVE 2.04

Cleaning Out Client-Side Cache

Up to this point, we have focused on server-side caching. If we focused entirely on server-side caching, we would be ignoring the fact that the most prevalent form of caching takes place on the client itself. This client cache is designed to reduce the load times for objects that are static in nature, or dynamic objects that haven't changed since the client's last visit. The client cache stores these objects locally on the client computer, within memory, and in an allocated section of hard disk space. Both Microsoft's Internet Explorer and Netscape's Navigator browsers have settings that allow the user to control caching functions and behaviors. The different settings include the location of the cache, the size of the cache, and the time when the browser compares the cached objects to the ones on the remote Web server.

The most important aspect of client-side caching is that is requires storage space on the hard disk to work effectively. Once the disk space allocated for caching has become full, it can no longer work properly. It is for this reason that it must be emptied periodically to maintain maximum performance.

It is generally a good idea to periodically clean this cache out or have it set for a lower number of days so that it will automatically be flushed. By setting the history to a high number, beyond 14 days, you run the risk of retrieving stale information from cache, and of not being able to store additional information in cache if the allotted space is full.

By controlling the amount of cache being used and the TTL of the cache, you can increase your performance and decrease the network bandwidth usage drastically, as your browser will always check the local cache before sending a request out either to a proxy server or to the orginating server.

EXERCISE 2-2

Changing the Amount of Cache Disk Space
Internet Explorer 5.x

1. Start Internet Explorer.

2. In the Tools menu, click Internet Options.

3. In the General tab, in the Temporary Internet Files section, click Settings (Figure 2-1).

4. Change the "Amount of disk space to use" setting by dragging the slider (Figure 2-2).

5. Click OK, and then click OK again.

Internet Explorer 5.x:
Internet settings

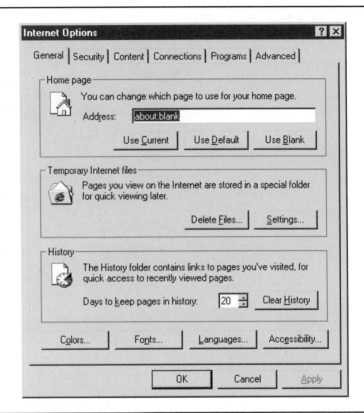

Internet Explorer 4.0, 4.01

1. Start Internet Explorer.

2. In the View menu, click Internet Options.

3. In the General tab, in the Temporary Internet Files section, click Settings.

4. Change the "Amount of disk space to use" setting by dragging the slider.

5. Click OK, and then click OK again.

Internet Explorer 3.x

1. Start Internet Explorer.

FIGURE 2-2

Internet Explorer 5.*x*:
Temporary Internet File
properties

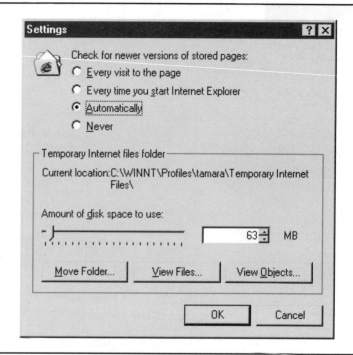

2. In the View menu, click Options.

3. Click the Advanced tab.

4. In the Temporary Internet Files section, click Settings.

5. Change the setting by dragging the slider.

6. Click OK, and then click OK again.

Netscape Navigator 4.*x*

1. Open the Edit menu and choose Preferences.

2. Click the Advanced category and select Cache.

3. Click the Clear Disk Cache button and the Clear Memory Cache button (Figure 2-3).

4. Click OK.

Preference screen shot for
Netscape 4.x Cache
settings

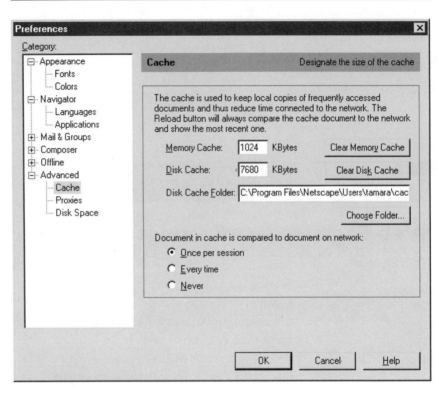

CERTIFICATION OBJECTIVE 2.05

Server May Cache Information As Well

Web servers are designed to handle multiple simultaneous requests from
Internet clients in the most efficient matter. Because the pages and objects
that a Web server provides are stored on a hard disk or a disk array, there
can be latency experienced while the information is retrieved. Commonly
used information can be stored in the Web server's memory, and it can

be returned more efficiently without the added processor utilization and latency from disk I/O. The amount of data that can be cached on a Web server depends on the amount of physically available memory. Most Web servers face a performance bottleneck in the area of memory, which will limit the amount of data the Web server can cache. This is one of the many reasons that it is prudent to load test and monitor server performance on a regular basis.

CERTIFICATION OBJECTIVE 2.06

Web Page Update Settings in Browsers

In the dilemma caused by the necessity to choose between a transparent caching server and a proxy-caching server, a significant area of consideration is that of client configuration. While some large ISPs use proprietary clients, most customers demand the use of a client of their choice. A proxy client needs to be configured to direct its Internet requests to a specific proxy server. Early proxy clients required that the settings be manually entered into each client. Even with today's technologies, this would make proxy caching difficult to implement on a large basis, especially for ISPs. There has been a tremendous amount of effort expended on developing solutions that provide for the performance, fault tolerance, and security of proxy caching servers while reducing the effort to configure clients. This has led to such technologies as Proxy Automatic Configuration files and the Web Proxy Automatic Discovery protocol.

Proxy Automatic Configuration

Proxy Auto Configuration (PAC) files allow the browser to reconfigure its proxy settings based on information stored within this file. During the initial client installation, a URL is supplied to direct the browser to check for updates on a periodic basis. The code is usually written in JavaScript and stored at a location within the local area network, or at the remote access point. Both Netscape and Internet Explorer browsers support this function, making it feasible to deploy in mixed environments.

The following is a JavaScript function that determines how the current protocol being used redirects the browser to the appropriate proxy server. If no appropriate protocol or proxy server is determined, the client will attempt to establish a direct Internet connection. This can be extremely useful in a setting in which only certain protocols should be retrieved from proxy servers.

```
function DetermineProxy(url, host)
}
if (url.substring(0, 5) == "http:") {
return "PROXY myWebProxy:80";
}
else if (url.substring(0, 4) == "ftp:") {
return "PROXY myFTPProxy:80";
}
else if (url.substring(0, 6) == "https:") {
return "PROXY mySSLProxy:8080";
}
else {
return "DIRECT";
}
```

Web Proxy Automatic Discovery Protocol

This protocol allows a browser to automatically detect proxy settings. Web Proxy Automatic Discovery (WPAD) is supported through the use of the dynamic host control protocol (DHCP) and the Domain Name Server (DNS) system. Once the proper settings are configured, DHCP and DNS servers can automatically find the appropriate proxy server and configure the browser's settings accordingly. To supply the client with the necessary configuration through DHCP, the DHCP server must support the DHCPINFORM message. If this is not available you will need to use DNS. WPAD is currently supported only in Internet Explorer 5, making it a viable solution only in strictly defined networks.

Static Index/Site Map

A static index allows visitors to your Web site to choose from a list of hyperlinks that will direct them to the appropriate content. This is very similar to a book's table of contents. As Webmasters, we must ensure that we structure our information in a manner that is easily understood and navigated. Static indexes allow us to explicitly define where content is located and to assist visitors by placing these links in a readily accessible area such as the homepage. By defining these areas of content and placing static indexes, we allow the users to spend their time more efficiently and encourage them to visit our site again.

Static indexes need to be layered out in an easy-to-understand manner so that the user will be able to locate the item or area of choice quickly and easily. A static index does not change unless a Web designer or Webmaster updates the page. This does not allow users to search the site for the content they wish to locate. A good example of this can be found at http:\\www.snap.com; the tabs across the top center of the page are a static index that allows you to go quickly to the section you choose by clicking.

EXERCISE 2-3

Site Information Comparison
Pick two Internet sites that you are familiar with, preferably two with similar content. Analyze how information is being presented—do you have to search? What happens if you don't know what you are looking for and are just doing general browsing?

Keyword Index

The amount of information contained on a Web site can be overwhelming. Users wish to locate what they are looking for quickly. The idea of keywords has become a very important part of searching a Web page for content. A user can enter a keyword such as "1957" on a car parts page and be given all the content that has been marked with "1957." The following is an example of how keywords are coded into a page:

```
<META NAME="keywords" CONTENT="keywords for your site here">
```

Depending on the operating system you are using and the Web server software you have installed, there are some keywords that are reserved. These are words that are used by the software for other purposes. The words "and," "or," "add," "Join," and "next" are all reserved and are used by the OS or other software. They cannot be used as part of your keyword list. It is recommend that you make your keywords as specialized for your page as possible. If you were creating the car parts Web page used in the preceding example, you would not want to use the word "car" as a keyword, as all your pages would be returned as a good result to the user.

CERTIFICATION OBJECTIVE 2.09

Full-Text Index

A full-text index stores all the full-text words and their locations for a given table, and a full-text catalog stores the full-text index of a given database. The full-text service performs the full-text querying. This allows Index Server to make use of the structure of the document, rather than just using the raw content. It indexes full text in formatted data such as Microsoft Excel or Word documents. Index Server also has the ability to look inside private data formats via the open standard IFilter interface. Unlike some other systems that are limited to text files, Index Server can read a variety of document formats.

Index Server is a great idea for sites containing large amounts of data in documents that a user might use in research. The program will take each document and record every word, with the exception of words contained in the noise words list. Noise words lists are used for words that will appear too many times to be of use for a search; examples are a company's name, or words such as "the," "and," and "I." Researchers do not want to be returned 10,000 results with their search; they would rather be returned 10.

Searching Your Site

When designing your Web site, you need to keep in mind who will be accessing the site for information. Languages are written with various characters. Character sets for the majority of the world are listed in Table 2-1. These character sets include the normal letters and numbers of the language, as well as special characters (for example, Greek letters ΔΦΩ would fall under character set 1253).

Searching Content

When you search the Internet, the content of your search or the way you enter your request will determine your results. If you need to search for information on a specific topic or subtopic, you should know how to word your request so that you get answers only to what you are asking. If you performed a search on "computer modems" on http://www.altavista.com, you would receive 1,499,930 pages in response to your request, but if you searched for "computer modems," you would reduce that number to 4,449 pages returned—still a large number, but much smaller than the response to your orginial request.

Boolean Operators

Boolean searches are simply based upon evaluating a statement or expression to determine whether it is true or false. Boolean statements are composed of Boolean operators such as AND, OR, and NOT. With these operators, you can articulate your search to whatever degree is necessary by including and excluding relative subjects. Boolean queries tend to be used in simple queries to eliminate a certain property or information from a result set. Boolean-based searches reflect logic that is typically used in programming languages, which is great for programmers, but can be too complicated for normal users.

| TABLE 2-1 | Character Sets Used in Web Coding | |

Base Charset	Display Name	Aliases (Charset IDs)
1252	Western	us-ascii, iso8859-1, ascii, iso_8859-1, iso-8859-1, ANSI_X3.4-1968, iso-ir-6, ANSI_X3.4-1986, ISO_646.irv:1991, ISO646-US, us, IBM367, cp367, csASCII, latin1, iso_8859-1:1987, iso-ir-100, ibm819, cp819, Windows-1252
28592	Central European (ISO)	iso8859-2, iso-8859-2, iso_8859-2, latin2, iso_8859-2:1987, iso-ir-101, l2, csISOLatin2
1250	Central European (Windows)	Windows-1250, x-cp1250
1251	Cyrillic (Windows)	Windows-1251, x-cp1251
1253	Greek (Windows)	Windows-1253
1254	Turkish (Windows)	Windows-1254
932	Shift-JIS	shift_jis, x-sjis, ms_Kanji, csShiftJIS
EUC-JP	EUC	Extended_UNIX_Code_Packed_Format_for_Japanese, csEUCPkdFmtJapanese, x-euc-jp
JIS	JIS	csISO2022JP, iso-2022-jp
1257		Windows-1257
950	Traditional Chinese (BIG5)	big5, csbig5, x-x-big5
936	Simplified Chinese	GB_2312-80, iso-ir-58, chinese, csISO58GB231280, csGB2312, gb2312
20866	Cyrillic (KOI8-R)	csKOI8R, koi8-r
949	Korean	ks_c_5601, ks_c_5601-1987, Korean, csKSC56011987

Boolean searches tend to retrieve more accurate results than other searches, but add the complication and effort of writing proper queries. Boolean searches also require at least a little amount of pertinent knowledge to complete effective searches. Since Boolean searches are based upon True/False conditions, improperly executed queries may return no relevant matches.

Wildcard Searches

Wildcard searches allow searches to match a certain pattern instead of being restricted to a fixed word or phrase. The accepted character for wildcard searches is the asterisk. The asterisk can be placed at the beginning or the end of a search word or phrase. For example, instead of searching for computers OR computing OR computation, it would be more efficient to search for compu*.

Wildcard searches are some of the easiest to perform, as you are not required to have a great deal of knowledge or information to perform these searches. Be aware, though, that a wildcard search will return many more results then you are likely to want to search through. If you do decide to use a wildcard search, utilize the "search these results" feature of many search engines to narrow your search results down to a manageable number.

Natural Language Queries

Natural language queries represent increased technology that allows users to search on the basis of naturally formed phrases, sentences, or questions. The effectiveness of searches based upon natural language becomes more reliant on the search engine technology rather than depending on the wording of the query.

At the present time natural language queries are still in the developmental stage. Very few search engines are powerful enough to handle the additional overhead of performing this type of search. As development continues in speeds of processor and memory, this type of search will become a norm.

Compound Queries

Individual queries can be combined to form a compound query. This allows for separate operators to be combined, retrieving the most accurate result set. An example would be "+computer AND +databases OR +relational AND +databases." Table 2-2 lists several compound queries and their meanings. To

TABLE 2-2		Types of Search Operators

Operator	Character Used	Definition of Operator
OR Operator	OR	The OR operator between two words or other values means you are searching for items that contain one of the words. Example: "job or career."
NOT Operator	NOT	The NOT operator between two words or other values means you are searching for documents that contain the first word before the NOT operator, but not the second word that follows it. Example: "job not contract."
AND Operator	AND	The AND operator between two words or other values means you are searching for documents that match both the search items, not just one of them. Example: "career and technology."
Minus operator	–	When the minus operator is present before a search item, the results will exclude all items containing that search term. For example, "Technology Careers –biotech" will help you search for high-tech jobs outside the biotech industry. This is another representation of the AND operator.
Plus operator	+	The plus operator works inversely to the minus operator. When the plus symbol is present before a word or search phrase, this indicates that the term must be present to match the search request. Example: "+careers +benefits." This is another representation of the AND operator.
Wildcard character	*	The asterisk wildcard will allow you to search for all items or phrases that match a particular pattern. For example, searching for com* will allow you to search for all items that begin with the letters "com."
Quotation marks	" "	Quotation marks define exact phrases that must be present in search results. For example, "eCommerce Careers" will return results that will help filter nonpertinent information about standard commerce-related jobs.

obtain a complete listing of the compound queries that are allowed for a particular search engine, you can check the Help feature on the engine.

Indexing Your Site for a Search

Search engine placement is becoming more and more important. With the numbers of Web sites growing and growing, users are relying more upon search engines to sort between content they are looking for and nonpertinent information. Some of the smaller search engines will index sites without requiring that a request be submitted for a certain URL or domain. With most of the larger high-profile commercial engines, it is necessary to register your site for a search. Once you have registered your site, or even a few key pages, you will be in line to have your site "crawled" by a visiting spider. A spider is simply an application running on a remote server that views raw HTML information and META tags and records information within the search engines' database. The process of crawling is the spider visiting your site, going through every page that is accessible via a hyperlink, and recording that information back to a database.

Excluding Directories from Search

There might be some information that is not appropriate to index with search engines; adding a robots.txt file in the base of your Web directory can prevent this. A robots.txt file is merely an ASCII-based file that indicates what directories are acceptable for searching, and those that should be excluded. This is an example of a robots.txt file:

```
User-agent: *
Disallow: /private
Disallow: /users
```

These three lines in a robots.txt file will tell the user-agent "* = all" that they are not allowed to search any directory starting with /private or /users. If you wish, you can enter a specific user-agent such as yahoo, lycos, or any other search utility. Additional examples or a complete explanation of the Robots standards can be found at http://info.webcrawler.com/mak/ projects/robots/robots.html.

Search Optimization with META Tags

Adding META tags to the HTML code of your Web pages allows developers to emphasize specific content within their pages. The standard tags that search engines support are AUTHOR, DESCRIPTION, and KEYWORDS. The syntax for implementing each of these tags is listed here.

```
<META NAME="author" CONTENT="content's author goes here">
<META NAME="description" CONTENT="description goes here">
<META NAME="keywords" CONTENT="keywords go here">
```

There are additional META tags, but you should maintain a level of compatibility within your tags across the range of search engines you wish to be indexed with. By using these three tags, you maintain this compatibility across the top commercial search engines.

CERTIFICATION SUMMARY

In this chapter, we have focused on the different technology, protocols, and implementations of caching and indexing. While working with caching protocols, we have seen how and when they are used. We have seen file caching, transparent caching, and proxy caching. We have learned how to clean out the cache on client software to increase response time. We have examined different types of ways to index your site so that users or visitors are able to maneuver quickly and easily throughout your site. We have shown how to use static maps to take a user to a defined area of the site such as customer service, news, or weather. Finally, we have learned how to best index your site for a search so that you can return high-quality results.

✓ TWO-MINUTE DRILL

- ❏ Caching is the process of storing requested objects at a network point closer to the client, at a location that will provide these objects for reuse as they are requested by additional clients.

- ❏ A request for a Web object requires crossing several network links until the server housing the object is reached. These network crossings are referred to as *hops*, which generally consist of wide area network (WAN) serial links and routers.

- ❏ Passive caching represents the most basic form of object caching.

- ❏ Active caching servers use a proactive approach referred to as *prefetching* to maximize the performance of the server's cache by increasing the amount of objects that are available locally on the basis of several configurations and a statistical analysis.

- ❏ The use of caching requires the use of a protocol. There are three protocols used in caching. These protocols are the Internet Cache Protocol, the Caching Array Routing Protocol, and the Web Cache Communication Protocol.

- ❏ Transparent caching servers require additional complexity and configuration at the gateway point where the client requests are redirected to the cache servers.

- ❏ Clusters are groups of systems linked or chained together that are used in the caching of information for a company or ISP.

- ❏ Hierarchical caching occurs when you place a cache server at each layer of your network in a hierarchical fashion just as you do with routers.

- ❏ The parent-sibling caching works much like the hierarchies' caching except that the sibling caches are all working together.

- ❏ Distributed caching is much like proxy clusters. The idea is that you have several proxy servers working together to reduce the load of retrieving the information from the Internet. This also acts as a fault tolerance, so that if one of the proxy server goes offline, the others will automatically be able to respond to the requests.

- ❏ The file transfer protocol represents a means for a connection-oriented exchange of information between two systems.

❑ Proxy caching works through a cooperative connection between the browser and the caching server, rather than between the browser and the remote origin server.

❑ The most prevalent form of caching takes place on the client itself. This client cache is designed to reduce the load times for objects that are static in nature, or dynamic objects that haven't changed since the client's last visit. The client cache stores these objects locally on the client computer, within memory, and in an allocated section of hard disk space.

❑ Most Web servers face a performance bottleneck in the area of memory, which will limit the amount of data the Web server can cache. This is one of the many reasons that it is prudent to load test and monitor server performance on a regular basis.

❑ Proxy Auto Configuration (PAC) files allow the browser to reconfigure its proxy settings based on information stored within this file.

❑ A static index allows visitors to your Web site to choose from a list of hyperlinks that will direct them to the appropriate content.

❑ The amount of information contained on a Web site can be overwhelming. Users wish to locate what they are looking for quickly; therefore, the idea of keywords has become a very important part of searching a Web page for content.

❑ A full-text index stores all the full-text words and their locations for a given table, and a full-text catalog stores the full-text index of a given database. The full-text service performs the full-text querying.

SELF TEST

The following Self Test questions will help you measure your understanding of the material presented in this chapter. Read all choices carefully, as there may be more than one correct answer. Choose all correct answers for each question.

1. When determining cache performance, _____ divided by number of requests = hit ratio.

   A. Number of requests returned from the Internet

   B. Total number of requests to Internet for company

   C. Number of requests returned from cache server

   D. Number of requests denied

2. Browsers can be configured to reconfigure the proxy settings without users' interaction. What type of file is maintained on the local host that configures the browser?

   A. HTML script

   B. C++ file

   C. .exe file

   D. JavaScript

3. If you were coding a Web page that would include Japanese characters, what would you need to include in the coding of the page?

   A. The correct keyboard type

   B. This cannot be done on an American keyboard.

   C. The correct base character set

   D. A META name for the characters

4. The benefits of Web caching are (choose all that are correct)

   A. Decreased need to access the Internet for same data

   B. Increase in network bandwidth

   C. Decreased cost of Internet service

   D. Increase in the number of users that can access the Internet

5. Prefetching is done in what type of cache?

   A. Passive Cache

   B. Internet Cache

   C. Active Cache

   D. Caching Array

6. To allow for quick maneuvering of your Web page to predetermined areas, it is recommend that you code _____ into your pages.

   A. Static index

   B. Full-text search engines

   C. META tags

   D. Web caching

7. Information stored on the local system, the user's system, is called

   A. Web server cache

   B. Proxy server cache

C. Client cache

D. Memory

8. The process of storing information for future request is called

A. Proxy

B. RAM

C. Caching

D. Indexing

9. If you wanted to search a site for all words beginning with "comp," what search request would you use?

A. Comp-

B. Comp*

C. Comp+

D. Comp and

10. If you wished to search the Internet for the sentence "It was the best of times," how would need to enter your query?

A. It+was+the+best+of+times

B. Best+times

C. Best and Times

D. "It was the best of times"

11. Cache is also present on the local system in your WWW explorer, be it Internet Explorer or Netscape. What properties of this cache can you manage? (Choose all that are correct.)

A. Amount of disk space allotted to cache

B. Time to Live

C. Location of cache

D. Type of pages stored in cache

12. Search engines have advanced in their ease and ability to aid researchers in finding exactly what they are looking for. What is the newest type of search engine?

A. Keyword

B. Character set

C. Boolean

D. Full-text

13. How does CARP retrieve a requested page?

A. Uses passive caching

B. Uses ICP hits and ICP misses with neighboring cache servers

C. Uses an algorithm to label each server on the basis of what it contains

D. Uses hierarchies in which each cache server asks the next higher server for the data until it is retrieved from cache or the originating server

14. File caching can be a great benefit in what application?

A. HTTP

B. Telnet

C. FTP

D. Printing

15. What protocol is used for detecting a proxy server on a network?

A. DHCP

B. PAC

C. ICP

D. WPAD

16. What can be done to ensure security and exclude directories from searches on a Web server?

    A. Add the directory name you do not wish to have searched to the exclude_search.dat file.

    B. Add exclude.txt to the top of the directory you do not wish to have searched.

    C. Add nosearch.txt to the bottom of the directory that you do not wish to have searched.

    D. Add robots.txt to the end of a directory that you do not wish to have searched.

17. You have been requested to install a proxy server on your company's network. What must be done to provide proxy services to the users on the LAN?

    A. The server must be configured with each user's IP address.

    B. The router must be configured to direct all Internet request to the proxy server.

    C. Each user station must be configured to use the proxy server.

    D. Nothing; once the proxy server is online it will automatically proxy Internet requests.

18. +computer AND +database or +relational AND +databases would be an example of

    A. Natural language queries

    B. Wildcard queries

    C. Compound queries

    D. Boolean queries

19. To allow better searches of your site, a Web designer can add _____ to your site.

    A. Keyword indexes

    B. Wildcard

    C. Boolean

    D. Static indexes

20. What does it mean to have your Web site crawled?

    A. Visitors navigate through your Web site, clicking links to go further and further down on your site.

    B. When your Internet connection is very poor, your Web site is said to be crawled, meaning that users move VERY slowly on your site.

    C. When you register with a search engine, it will crawl your site to record information into the search database.

    D. None of the above.

21. Proxy can be used for what applications?

    A. Telnet

    B. FTP

    C. WWW

    D. E-mail

22. Web servers that receive many requests for a set page, usually the main or homepage, can do what to decrease the response time?

    A. Move the data to the center of the disk for quicker I/O response time.

    B. Store the page in memory for quicker response time.

C. Store the page on a proxy server other than the originating server and allow it to service the requests.

D. Have a pointer to the main page from a blank page and send that blank page upon request so that it will cut down on response time.

23. What is the most important item to consider when configuring client-side cache?

A. Amount of physical memory

B. Amount of virtual memory

C. Amount of hard disk storage space

D. Speed of your network adapter

24. To utilize single-server caching, what is the greatest number of users recommended to be on the LAN to ensure that the server is not overrun?

A. 5

B. 10

C. 25

D. 50

25. What type of caching are you running when the end user has no awareness of the caching?

A. Cluster cache

B. Hierarchies

C. Transparent

D. Single-server caching

SELF TEST ANSWERS

1. **C** is correct. Requests returned from cache / total request = cache hit ratio.
   A, B, and **D** are all incorrect; these numbers have no bearing on the cache hit ratio.

2. **D** is correct. A PAC file writing Java is maintained on the local system and configures the browser each time it is activated. It can be configured to check for a new JavaScript at predefined times and a predefined location. This allows for updates to the browser's proxy settings without the need for human invention.
   A is incorrect; HTML is used for generating Web pages. **B** is incorrect; C++ is a programming language. **C** is incorrect; .exe files are executable—for example, IE.exe, which is run to create an IE window.

3. **C** is correct. Each language has its own character set that includes the letters and numbers used in that language. For the characters to be displayed correctly, you must have the correct character set encoded in the page.
   A is incorrect, because the keyboard has no bearing on what characters are displayed. You could copy them from a file and never use the keyboard. **B** is incorrect, because with the correct charset, any type of character can be created. **D** is incorrect, because META tags are not used for this type of function.

4. **A, B,** and **C** are all correct. Caching decreases the need to access the Internet; as data is stored in the cache server, it increases network bandwidth when cache servers are placed through the network and decreases the cost of Internet service. Some ISPs charge on the basis of the amount of data that is transmitted. If a page is requested only one out of the 15 times it is needed, this reduces the cost by a factor of 15.
   D is incorrect, because caching has no bearing on the number of users that can access the Internet.

5. **C** is correct. Prefetching is done in active cache systems, when a system retrieves a page before it is requested on the basis of data on past requests.
   A is incorrect, because in passive cache a page is retrieved only when it is requested. It is then put into cache in case the request is made again before the Time To Live timer runs out on the request. **B** is incorrect, because Internet Cache is a protocol, not a type of cache. **D** is incorrect, because Caching Array is also a protocol, not a type of cache.

6. **A** is correct. Static indexes allow a visitor to quickly move through your Web page.
   B is incorrect, because search engines are great for sites with large amounts of data or large number of pages, but they do not help in the quick maneuvering of a site. **C** is

incorrect, because META tags have no bearing on the maneuvering of a site. **D** is incorrect, because caching is used to store a page in memory for quick retrieval, not for moving throughout a Web site.

7. **C** is correct. This is the cache on the local system that houses currently accessed Web pages for quick retrieval upon a request for the same page again. This can be easily configured via IE or Netscape for length and amount of data to be cached.
A is incorrect, because a Web server cache is a dedicated server, not the client server.
B is incorrect, because a proxy server cache is used in conjunction with the Web server to retrieve and retain data from the Internet. **D** is incorrect, because memory is a physical part of the hardware of a system.

8. **C** is correct. Caching is the process of storing information so that subsequent requests do not require that the information be pulled from the originating server.
A is incorrect, because proxy is the process of retrieving the information on behalf of a system or user. **B** is incorrect, because RAM is memory in the system. **D** is incorrect, because it refers to how information is organized on a server for easy retrieval.

9. **B** is correct. You would enter **comp*** to retrieve all words beginning with "comp."
A, **C**, and **D** are other forms of switches for searching but not for a wildcard search switch.

10. **D** is correct. To retrieve an exact parsing, you need to enter the query in quotes.
A is incorrect, because it would return any page that had the words "it," "was," "the," "best," "of," and "times" located anyplace, not just in the exact order and placement. A page with "it was found to be the best time to get out of the house" would be returned. **B** is incorrect, since many search engines do not use the words "it" and "the." This would be a good option, but again it would search the page for the word "best" and then the word "times" anyplace on the page.

11. **A**, **B**, and **C** are all correct. You can control all of these properties of a local cache.
D is incorrect; you have no control over what pages are stored in cache. You can, however, mark a page for static cache and give it a per-fetch time frame in some explorers such as IE.

12. **D** is correct. Full-text search is on the horizon. This allows a user to enter a question or sentence and retrieve data pertaining to it. The search engine analyzes the question and retrieves the material pertaining to it.
A is incorrect, because keywords are used in marking data on a Web site for quick retrieval based on a given word. This has been used for a long time in Web page

encoding. **B** is incorrect, because character sets have nothing to do with the search engine. **C** is incorrect, because Boolean was one of the first search engine search criteria developed. It is very cumbersome.

13. **C** is correct; CARP uses an algorithm to label the cache servers on the basis of the data provided that they contain in their cache. The more servers in the array, the better CARP operates.
    A is incorrect, because in passive caching, a page is retrieved and stored only after it has been requested. This can be used in conjunction with the CARP protocol. **B** is incorrect, because ICP hits and misses are used in the Internet Cache Protocol. **D** is incorrect, because it is yet another form of caching and has no bearing on the protocol being used.

14. **C** is correct. File caching can allow for FTP files that are retrieved by several people or the same person several times to be stored in cache and retrieved from said cache instead of the originating server. This can greatly reduce the network overhead and bandwidth.
    A is incorrect, because HTTP uses cache but not file cache. **B** is incorrect, because Telnet has no use for cache as data transferred to and from the client system is not stored or reused. **D** is incorrect, because printing does not use cache.

15. **D** is correct: Web Proxy Automatic Discovery Protocol is used to discover proxy servers on a network. It can be used along with DHCP to learn the proxy server's IP address.
    A is incorrect, because DHCP is used for autoconfiguration of IP addresses and some other TCP/IP settings. **B** is incorrect, because PAC is used for autoconfiguration of Web browsers; it is a JavaScript stored on the station. **C** is incorrect, because ICP is a protocol used between cache servers to communicate and share information.

16. **D** is correct. By adding robots.txt you will keep a directory from being searched while a search on a site is being performed.
    A, **B**, and **C** are all incorrect, because doing any of these will not keep a directory from being searched.

17. **C** is correct. Each end user station must be configured to use the proxy server. Without this configuration, the stations will try unsuccessfully to acquire their data directly.
    A is incorrect, because the proxy server has no knowledge of end stations' IP addresses. **B** is incorrect, because the router has no knowledge of the proxying being done. **D** is incorrect, because there must be some sort of configuration done on the end user system to allow users to utilize the proxy server.

18. **C** is correct. This is an example of compound queries, which use multiple search properties to help ensure that the requested results are returned.
A, B, and **D** are all incorrect. Natural language queries would include something like "What are computer databases or relational databases?" Wildcard queries would include something like data* and would return anything beginning with "data." Boolean queries are true-or-false queries.

19. **A** is correct: Keyword indexes can help visitors better search for information on your Web page. An example of a keyword index is <META NAME="keywords" CONTENT="Keywords for your site here">.
B and **C** are incorrect, because they are types of searches. **D** is incorrect, because it is used to navigate a Web site more easily, but keywords are used to search a Web site.

20. **C** is correct; once you register your site with a search engine, it will crawl your site to record all information available about your site to add to the search database. Then, when a user searches on a subject, the database will have all the needed information about your site to compare that search against.
A, B, and **D** are all incorrect.

21. **B** and **C** are correct. You can use proxy for FTP and WWW connections. Using proxy allows for only a set number of PCs to be physically tied to the Internet, and the rest are secured from the Internet, as those looking at your site see only the proxy server(s).
A and **D** are incorrect, because you cannot use proxy for a Telnet or e-mail connection.

22. **B** is correct. If the page or pages are stored in memory, the response time can be reduced drastically. If the server does not have to go to a storage device to retrieve the requested information, the response in returning the page to the requester is much lower.
A is incorrect. This choice would not reduce the response time for a request. If the page were stored anyplace on a hard disk, this would increase the response time. **C** and **D** are incorrect, because this would increase the response time, as it would be necessary to perform either an additional request from another proxy server or to find the page in either cache or disk storage after the orginal blank screen was returned.

23. **C** is correct. You must be concerned most with the amount of free space on your hard drive. If your drive fills up or there is too little room for the cache to operate, it can and will become a bottleneck in your operations.
A is incorrect, because memory plays a part in everything on a system, but physical storage space is the biggest concern for cache. **B** is incorrect, because virtual memory only plays a part in how a program runs; again, it requires physical hard drive space in

order to swap the memory in and out. **D** is incorrect, because the speed of your NIC has no bearing on the cache.

24. **B is correct.** It is not recommend to have more than 10 or 12 users at most on a single-cache server network. With more users than this, you will easily overrun the server, and the response time will be longer than the time needed to request the pages directly from the originating server.

    A is incorrect, because a single-cache server can handle 10 to 12 at most. **C** and **D** are incorrect, because 50 users would easily overrun the cache server.

25. **C is correct.** Transparent caching is exactly that: transparent to the users, who are completely unaware of its existence. Transpartent caching does not require modifications to the client machine.

    A, B, and **D** are all incorrect. For these to work the user must be aware of them or at least have software configured to use them. This may be via a technican manually setting up the caching on the end user system, or via a script run at the time the user logs into the network.

3

i-Net Clients

W hen a person first attempts to use the Internet, the experience can go one of two ways. It can seem almost magical, with lots of things to do that are fun and exciting, or it can be the most frustrating event one has ever experienced. Often, how a person responds can be translated to his or her experience with the Internet client. An Internet client is the user's window to the Internet, allowing him or her to view this global village and the information it offers. It is software that interacts with servers on the Internet, providing ways to access information, pictures, programs, and other content of a Web site.

In this chapter, we'll discuss the importance of the Internet client, and topics that need to be addressed for the client to function properly. We'll look at software and hardware supporting an Internet client and see what configurations need to be made for a client to function properly. We'll also discuss various types of client applications, and tell you when and where different client applications would be used. This information will enhance your own experiences with the Web and enable you to provide greater support to other users and make their experiences positive ones.

CERTIFICATION OBJECTIVE 3.01

Infrastructure Supporting an Internet Client

Each city has an infrastructure, and the global village of the Internet is no different. An infrastructure is the underlying features or framework of a system. In the case of a city, these features would include telephone lines for communication, roadways for transportation, and other elements that allow the city to function. For the Internet and intranets, the infrastructure consists of such things as protocols for transport of data, network connections to enable proper communication, and so on. The infrastructure is the basic systems that allow it to function.

As we'll see in the sections that follow, a number of basic systems support the Internet client. For most of the systems we'll discuss, if one were to fail, users would be unable to access the Internet. At the very least, they would miss out on some of the features they'd come to expect from the Internet.

Each system making up the infrastructure works with other systems to enable users to access the Internet as a whole, or the diverse elements making up the Internet.

TCP/IP Stack

TCP/IP is an acronym for Transmission Control Protocol/Internet Protocol. A *protocol* is a set of rules as to how data is packaged, transmitted, and received. It controls how data is sent over a network. The TCP/IP protocol suite is a set of protocols incorporated into software. Once installed on a computer, it can be used to communicate with other computers that also use TCP/IP. To communicate with another computer, such as a server, both the client and server need to be using the same protocol. TCP/IP is a standard, routable protocol that most large networks (especially the Internet) use. It provides the ability to connect dissimilar systems so they can communicate with one another. This means that UNIX, Microsoft platforms, and Macintosh can all communicate on the same network.

The U.S. Department of Defense Advanced Research Projects Agency (DARPA) originally developed TCP/IP in the 1960s and 1970s as part of an experiment in transmitting data between computers. DARPA wanted computers to be able to send and receive data, without having to physically connect them with network cabling. While initial experiments succeeded in sending data over the telephone lines between a computer in Massachusetts and a computer in California, the transmission speeds were incredibly slow.

To understand their problem, put yourself in the place of these researchers. You're attempting to download a large file that's being sent as a steady stream of data. Since the entire file is being sent this way, it will tie up the transmission wire for the time of the transfer. The wire can't be used for anything else—communication, transfer of other files, and so forth. If the file becomes corrupted while being sent, the entire file will need to be sent again. This will increase the transmission time, possibly requiring you to keep trying to download the file over and over again.

The problem led to the development of TCP/IP and packet switching. TCP/IP provided a common protocol that dictated how the data was to be sent and received. Packet switching provided the ability to break data into smaller chunks that are, at most, a few kilobytes in size. Each packet is transmitted separately, providing a more efficient use of the media (i.e., telephone lines or network cable). If one of these packets becomes corrupted, the entire file doesn't need to be resent, just that particular packet.

The way that TCP/IP performs packet switching is that a sending computer breaks the file into smaller parts and then adds a code to the beginning and end of each packet. The code added to the beginning of the packet is called a *header.* The header provides information on where the packet originated, the destination, and what relationship it bears to other packets being sent. This allows the receiving computer to reorganize the packets so they become a duplicate of the original file. Additional code is added to the packet, which allows the receiving computer to check whether the packet was corrupted during transmission.

Once the packet is broken up, and the wrapper code is added, it is sent over the network. During its travel over the transmission wire, specialized hardware or computers, called *routers,* will intercept the packets and view the information contained in the header code. These routers use tables that provide a listing of other routers and computers on the network. Based on the destination contained in the packet's header, the router will either retransmit the packet to the destination computer or—if that computer isn't part of the router's local network—retransmit the packet to another router. The router determines the best possible path for the packet to take on its way to the destination of the receiving computer.

At the final destination, the receiving computer analyzes the wrapper code on the packet and determines whether it is corrupted or not. If corrupted, it sends a message back to the sending computer asking to resend the packet. If it is not corrupted, it reassembles the packets into their original state. Because the wrapper code contains information that shows its relationship to other packets being sent, the packets don't need to be sent or received in order. Different packets may travel along different routes on the network, and retransmitted data may be sent out of their original order.

To help understand how TCP/IP performs these actions, we'll look at how TCP/IP maps to a conceptual four-layer model. As seen in Figure 3-1, these layers consist of Application, Transport, Internet, and Network. The Application layer is the layer of TCP/IP where applications gain access to a

FIGURE 3-1

Four-layer conceptual
model of TCP/IP

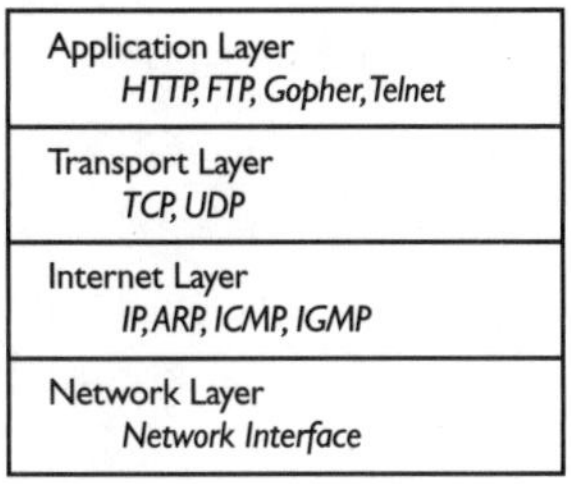

| Application Layer |
| *HTTP, FTP, Gopher, Telnet* |
| Transport Layer |
| *TCP, UDP* |
| Internet Layer |
| *IP, ARP, ICMP, IGMP* |
| Network Layer |
| *Network Interface* |

network. This is the layer in which your Internet client or an Internet server accesses the services and utilities provided by TCP/IP. The next layer is the Transport layer, which provides communication sessions between computers. Next is the Internet layer, which encapsulates packets in code to provide addressing and routing information. This gives the packet the information necessary to route packets between computers and networks. Finally, the Network layer, or Network Interface layer, is responsible for putting frames of data on the transmission wire and pulling frames off the wire. In the paragraphs that follow, we'll discuss each of these layers in detail.

The Application layer is the topmost layer of the TCP/IP conceptual model, and provides the means for applications to access a network. When you enter the address of a Web site into your browser, it is the Application layer that your browser accesses so that the Web page is displayed. On the Internet server's end, the Application layer provides an access point to send the requested data over the network.

It is at the Application layer that you specify the protocol, service, or utility that will be used to access data over the Internet or local area network. These include

- **HTTP**   HyperText Transfer Protocol. HTTP is the client/server protocol used by the World Wide Web. It is used by Internet browsers to retrieve HTML (HyperText Markup Language) documents from Web servers, and by Web servers to send Web pages.

- **FTP**   File Transfer Protocol. FTP was developed to transfer files between computers on a TCP/IP network. For example, if you wanted to download a program from an Internet site, FTP could be used to send the file to your computer.

■ **Gopher**   Client/server software and a simple protocol that enables users to search and retrieve files from Gopher servers on the Internet. Using the Gopher service, Internet providers can create links to other servers, annotate files and directories, and create custom menus for use by Gopher clients.

■ **Telnet**   Client/server software and a simple protocol that enables users to log in to remote computers to run programs and access files. Like Gopher, Telnet goes back to the early days of the Internet and is less frequently used.

Although TCP/IP is often referred to as if it were a single protocol, it is in fact a suite of protocols. As such, to install FTP, HTTP, and the other protocols discussed in this section, you need to install TCP/IP and the supporting clients (e.g., Web browser or FTP client) on your computer. You don't need to install every individual protocol, as they are all part of the TCP/IP protocol suite.

The Transport layer of the four-layer conceptual model is where transport protocols are used to provide communication sessions between computers. One of two protocols may be used to deliver the data.

■ **TCP**   The Transmission Control Protocol used to provide connection-oriented, reliable sessions between computers. TCP is commonly used when large amounts of data are being sent, or acknowledgment of data being received is required.

■ **UDP**   The User Datagram Protocol that provides connectionless communication between computers. It doesn't guarantee that packets will be delivered, and is generally used to send small amounts of data or data that isn't crucial for delivery. Any reliability of data being sent is the responsibility of the application, not this protocol.

Which of these two protocols is used to transport data depends on the protocol used at the Application layer. The method of delivery determined at the Application layer dictates whether UDP or TCP is used. For example, FTP uses TCP for transporting data. If you were to use FTP to download a file, TCP would automatically be used as the transport protocol.

The Internet layer of the conceptual model is where data is wrapped in the code that contains addressing and routing information. This layer is made up of four protocols that provide routing information.

- **IP** Internet Protocol. IP has the primary responsibility for routing packets between networks and hosts on a TCP/IP network. It also specifies the format that the packet will take.

- **ICMP** Internet Control Message Protocol. ICMP is used to send messages and report errors on the delivery of packets. These control messages and error reports are sent between the server and the gateway to the Internet or another section of a large network.

- **IGMP** Internet Group Management Protocol. IGMP is used to report the memberships of computers (hosts) in a particular multicast group. *Multicasting* is the ability to send messages to a select group of computers. For example, if you were to send e-mail to a mailing list, each member on that list would receive a copy of that message. Multicasting is different from broadcasting, because with broadcasting a message is sent to everyone on the network. The IGMP protocol is used to inform the local router that it wants to receive memberships addressed to a multicast group.

- **ARP** Address Resolution Protocol. ARP is used to obtain the hardware addresses of hosts located on the same physical network.

The final layer of the conceptual model is the Network layer, which is also called the Network Interface layer. This is where the packet of data is passed from the network card or modem onto the transmission wire. It is at this point that the data has passed from the Internet server or client and is on its way to the receiving computer.

exam
ⓦatch

Remember that all of the protocols in the TCP/IP protocol suite are installed with TCP/IP on your computer. TCP, IP, HTTP, FTP, and the other protocols mentioned in this section are all part of the TCP/IP suite. As such, to install all of these protocols, you only need to install TCP/IP on your computer.

Hardware Platform

Hardware is a vital part of the infrastructure supporting an Internet client. *Hardware* is a blanket term for physical components on which applications run, use to connect to software available on servers, or use to perform some specific purpose. For example, a browser will run on the computer, use a monitor to display information, and use a modem to connect to the Internet. As we'll see in the sections that follow, a considerable amount of hardware can be used to access services on the Internet. These include your computer, handheld devices, WebTV, and Internet phone.

Personal Computers (PCs)

Personal computers, also referred to as *desktop computers*, are designed for individual users. These computers can be placed on a desktop, and are made up of components that gather input from a user (such as through a keyboard or mouse), process data, store data on a hard disk, and output information (such as through a monitor). Other components, such as a modem or network card, enable the user to connect to other computers, like over the Internet.

Personal computers are used to run a variety of applications. These applications have minimal requirements that must be met if the application is to install and run properly. For example, the application needs a certain amount of RAM, processor power, and storage space to install and run. If the requirements aren't met, the application won't function. For this reason, it is important to check the minimal requirements of an application against the hardware making up your PC.

Handheld Devices

Handheld devices are computers and other pieces of equipment that are small enough to fit and operate in your hand. An example of this is a handheld computer, also called a *palm-top* because it fits in the palm of your hand. These handheld devices can even run a version of Windows called Windows CE, which has a GUI interface similar to that found in Windows 95 or NT. Using such a device, you can access such Web services as e-mail.

One drawback to handheld PCs is that they have an extremely small keyboard or electronic pen for input and navigation, which makes using the device difficult. Another problem is that they have small screens to view output from the computer. It is for this reason that handheld PCs still haven't replaced notebook computers as a small, portable way of computing.

A notebook computer is a larger handheld device that can be used to access the Internet, but is still small enough to carry around easily. They are roughly the size of a hard cover book, and have computing power comparable to desktop PCs. They can run the same applications, including operating systems and Internet client programs.

A new handheld device used to access Internet services is the cellular phone, some of which have the ability to retrieve e-mail from the Internet. The e-mail can be viewed on a screen on the phone. Some cell phones also provide the ability to connect with a cable to the modem of your computer. This is particularly advantageous for notebook computer users who may want to dial in to the Internet when not near a telephone.

WebTV

WebTV is a Microsoft product that allows those without computers to access the Web through a television and a box that's similar in appearance to those used for cable TV. With these two requirements, you then sign up with a WebTV access service.

WebTV connects to the Internet with a modem and a telephone line. The speed of connection depends on the WebTV box being used. Two versions are available: Classic and Plus. If the Classic model of WebTV is used, users connect at 33,600 bps. If the Plus version of WebTV is used, users can connect at 56K.

Users browse Web pages and can access Internet services using WebTV's browser and a handheld remote control. If users wish, they can purchase a keyboard separately for use with WebTV, but this isn't required. WebTV uses the television as an output device, the same way that a computer uses a monitor.

WebTV is also available as part of Microsoft Windows 98. Once this is installed on your system, you can view TV listings for your area. If you have a TV tuner card, you can also view TV shows on your computer. To install WebTV on a Windows 98 machine, 30.6MB of free disk space is required.

Installing WebTV on Windows 98

1. From the Windows Start menu, select Settings | Control Panel.

2. Double-click on the Add/Remove Programs icon.

3. Select the Windows Setup tab. When Windows has finished searching your system for installed components, click the check box for WebTV for Windows, and then click OK.

4. Windows will begin copying the files necessary for installing WebTV. When it has finished, you will be asked to reboot your computer. Click Yes to reboot your computer, so that your system settings can be changed.

5. From the Windows Start menu, select Programs | Accessories | Entertainment. Click WebTV for Windows. When WebTV loads, click Next.

6. Click the link to get TV listings from the Gemstar G-Guide. A browser window will open, and you will then be required to enter your postal or ZIP code. After entering this, select the cable provider nearest you from the listing that appears. Once this is done, click Get Listings to download TV listings. This option is only available for users in Canada and the United States.

7. As the listings download, click the screen for WebTV for Windows. Click Next to continue. A tour of the TV Program Guide will begin. Watch the tour, and then click Next to continue.

8. Click Finish to end the installation.

Internet Phone

Internet phone is a recent innovation to the Internet, allowing users
to talk verbally with one another as if they were using a normal telephone.
Communication takes place over the Internet, allowing one user with an
Internet phone to talk with other users with Internet phones without having
to pay for long distance charges.

Operating System

Of all the components that make up the infrastructure of an Internet client,
the most basic element is the operating system. It provides the ability to
perform basic tasks, such as recognizing input from a mouse or keyboard,
sending output to a monitor or printer, and allowing you to store and keep
track of files and directories. Without an operating system, you wouldn't be
able to run an Internet client because no computer can run without it.

Operating systems provide a number of ways in which you or applications
can interact with it. Applications interact with the operating system by working
with programming code that enables the application request services and access
functionality provided by the system. This code is called Application Program
Interfaces (API). As a user of the operating system, you may use a set of
commands to work with the system. For example, to view a listing of files in
a DOS operating system directory, you would use the dir command. Other
operating systems, such as Macintosh's System 8 operating system or the
Windows 9x or NT operating system, enable you to view these same files
through a Graphical User Interface (GUI). Rather than typing in commands,
you can interact with the operating system by clicking menus and objects
in the GUI interface.

Operating systems provide a platform on which other software can run
and provide a layer between applications and the underlying hardware. This
layer is important to software developers, as it frees them from having to
provide proprietary drivers for each piece of hardware. Users familiar with
older applications, such as DOS applications, will remember needing to
install different drivers to work with each program installed on a computer.
With newer operating systems, developers use drivers provided by the

operating system, enabling them to focus on the functionality of their application rather than on what hardware different users will use. Such applications run on top of the operating system, and are written specifically for the operating system being used. Because there are a number of different operating systems available, it is important that you check what operating system an Internet client or other software is written for. Some software may not run as expected on certain platforms. For example, a Windows 98 Internet client can't run on a machine running a DOS operating system, and one written for Windows NT can't run on a Macintosh.

Network Connection

To access an intranet or Internet Web site, you and other users will require some sort of network connection. As you will see in this discussion, a network connection consists of hardware and software working together, so that you can access network resources. In terms of hardware, your computer will need a modem or network interface card (NIC), which is used to pass data onto and pull data off of the transmission wire. The transmission wire itself may be network cabling connected to your LAN, or an active telephone line. In addition to this, you will need software installed to connect to the network, and an active account that will enable you to access network resources. Regardless of whether you're connecting to an intranet on your LAN, connecting to the Internet through a LAN, or connecting to the Internet from a stand-alone computer, these are the basic components comprising a network connection.

If your computer is located on a network, you should already have the ability to connect to your corporate intranet. Intranets use the same technologies as the Internet on TCP/IP networks. This means that if your computer is part of a TCP/IP network that has an intranet, all you will need is a Web browser and other software to access the intranet site. As we'll see later in this chapter when we discuss configuration issues, only a few modifications need to be made to access an intranet site over an existing TCP/IP network.

on the
Job

Don't assume that just because a network is running TCP/IP that it also has an intranet. Not all TCP/IP networks use Web pages or Internet applications, but many do take advantage of this, and many more existing networks will incorporate such functionality in the future. Intranets enable users to access commonly used information from a central location. They are especially useful for distributing computer training and help-desk information, mission statements, general orders on how to perform common tasks, and so on. Despite the growing popularity of intranets, don't assume that every TCP/IP network has one—many don't.

If you have a computer located on a LAN with a permanent connection to the Internet, you won't need any additional hardware to connect to the Internet. Computers on a network already have NICs installed, so that they can access resources on a LAN. To connect to the Internet via the LAN, you would, however, need to contact your network administrator for instructions on how to connect. This is because many organizations with permanent connections use a *proxy server*. A proxy server is a computer that stands between the LAN and the Internet. The proxy server software on this network server allows computers on the LAN to access the Internet through the proxy server's IP address. The address consists of four sets of numbers that are three digits or less, which identify the computer on the TCP/IP network. As we'll see when we discuss configuration issues, to access the Internet through the proxy server, you need to know the IP address of the proxy server.

While connections to an intranet are generally done through a NIC, connections via a modem are by far the most common method of connecting to the Internet. Most users connecting from home or small offices don't have permanent connections to the Internet; instead, they use temporary dial-up connections through an Internet Service Provider (ISP). In such cases, the ISP provides installation disks that configure the dial-up connection for you, and may supply Web browsers or other clients to access the Internet service. Windows 95 and 98 also have a Connection Wizard that walks you through the process of setting up your Internet connection.

We'll discuss the steps necessary to set up a dial-up connection, and the information required for such configuration, later in this chapter.

While the most popular method of connecting to the Internet is with a dial-up connection that uses the telephone line, there are a number of other technologies available. The choice of technology used in a business or home is determined by a combination of factors, usually revolving around price and connection speed. Prices are changing, and in many cases dropping, so our discussion will revolve around issues of technology rather than financial benefits or drawbacks.

As mentioned, dial-up connections that use telephone lines are a conventional method of accessing the Internet. This is often referred to as POTS (Plain Old Telephone Service), in which the media used for data transmission is also used for voice communication. Using a modem, you can connect at speeds up to 56 Kbps (kilobits per second). This means that if you have a 56K modem, you can transmit or receive 56,000 bits of data each second.

Integrated Services Digital Network, or ISDN, is another common method of connectivity. It is a set of standards for transmitting data over copper wires and other media. This media allows you to transmit and receive data at speeds up to 128 Kbps. Instead of a modem, you use an ISDN adapter. The ISP also uses an ISDN adapter at their end to allow ISDN connectivity. In addition to data, ISDN allows you to communicate by voice, as you would with POTS.

Two levels of service are available with ISDN: Basic Rate Interface (BRI) and Primary Rate Interface (PRI). BRI is designed for home and small business users, and PRI is designed for larger user bases such as large enterprises. BRI consists of two 64 Kbps bearer channels (or B channels) and one 16 Kbps delta channel (or D channel). The B channel is used for transmitting and receiving data and voice, and the D channel is used to send and receive information used for control and signaling. In North America, PRI is made up of 23 B channels and one 64 Kbps D channel, while in Europe PRI consists of 30 B channels and one D channel.

Digital Subscriber Line, or DSL, allows users to connect at speeds ranging from 512 Kbps to 8 Mbps. Theoretically, the technology provides speeds up to 8.448 Mbps (megabits per second), but typical connections are considerably lower than this. While POTS uses analog signals to transmit data, DSL uses high-bandwidth digital copper telephone lines for the transmission of data and voice. This allows homes and businesses to benefit from high-speed transmission, while enjoying the DSL's ability to carry both data and voice simultaneously. In other words, users can talk on the telephone while surfing the Web.

Like DSL, cable modems are becoming a popular method of accessing the Internet. As with DSL, there is a continuous connection. Cable modems connect through copper cabling, such as that used for cable TV. In fact, many cable TV providers are doubling as ISPs because of this technology. A special adapter is installed in your computer, which is usually an Ethernet adapter. Once the adapter, necessary drivers, and client are installed, you are able to connect through cable TV lines to the Internet at speeds ranging from 512 Kbps to 52 Mbps.

Web Browsers

Web browsers are applications that are primarily used to display text and images on the World Wide Web. Web browsers provide the ability to interpret and display HTML documents, which are documents that are written in the Hypertext Markup Language and contain indicators (called *tags*) that dictate how text and graphics are to be formatted. Web browsers read the formatting information of the tags, and then display the text or image accordingly. A more common term for such documents is "Web pages."

As we saw earlier in this chapter, Web browsers use HTTP to transfer Web pages from a server to a Web browser. Whenever you enter the address of a Web site, such as www.comptia.com, the browser automatically uses HTTP to transfer the HTML document from the server to your computer. While the browser may use other protocols discussed in this chapter to access sites and files on the Internet, HTTP is the one primarily used by Web browser applications.

The first GUI Web browser, Mosaic, was developed in 1992. By providing an easy-to-use interface, users were able to easily access Web pages. Mosaic was developed at the National Center for Supercomputing Applications at the University of Illinois in Urbana, Illinois. The person primarily responsible for Mosaic was a young man in his early 20s named Marc Andreesson, who led the project. Andreessen left the project to become part of Mosaic Communications, which evolved into a company called Netscape Communications that produces the Netscape Navigator browser. Mosaic, in updated versions, is still available as a commercial product.

While Mosaic was the first graphical browser, and Netscape became the first browser to be widely used by the public, these are not the only browsers on the market. Microsoft Internet Explorer followed, becoming primary competition for Netscape. A number of smaller companies and ISPs (such as America Online) also came out with their own browsers. However, at present, Netscape and Microsoft produce most of the browsers used on the Internet.

Each of the browsers discussed so far allows you to view graphics on the Web; however, some don't. The most popular text-only browser on the market is Lynx, developed at the University of Kansas for students to access UNIX servers. It has become a popular browser for accessing the Internet when only text needs to be viewed or when graphics aren't required. It is commonly used among blind and visually impaired users who "view" Web pages by listening to a voice synthesizer that reads textual information displayed through the browser.

Most Web browsers provide the same features and abilities of viewing Web pages. This is because they adhere to standards that are set by the World Wide Web Consortium (W3C). This organization sets the standards that are to be followed in developing Web pages and the browsers that view them. Despite this, many browsers also include proprietary features. This means that in order to view a Web page that exploits these features, you must use that particular browser. These innovations occasionally become accepted standards by W3C, and are then implemented in other browser types.

E-mail

E-mail is electronic mail, and another of the primary services of the Internet. These are messages that can be sent and stored from one computer to another. Using a mail client, you can create messages, attach files to them, and transmit them over the Net. The message first goes to a mail server, and is then sent to the mail server on which the receiving user's e-mail account is located. When the user connects to the mail server with

FROM THE CLASSROOM

A common question that students ask about Web browsers is, "which is the best one to use?" Unfortunately, there is no answer to this, except to say that the best browser to use is the one you're most comfortable with. While the manufacturer of each browser will say theirs is the best, you should use one that suits all of your needs and that you find easiest to use.

If you're creating an intranet and have to choose the browser that everyone in your organization will use, it is important that you choose one, and only one, browser. Don't let

users run several different browsers, as you'll have a difficult time supporting them when problems arise. The same applies to e-mail applications and other client applications that will be used to access the site and its services. By setting one browser as your organization's browser, you and the rest of your IT staff can become experts in the use of that browser. When users have problems, you'll be able to answer their questions quickly and effectively.

—*Michael Cross,*
CNA, MCSE, MCPS, MCP+I

his or her mail client, these messages are downloaded and can then be displayed through the mail client. E-mail was one of the first services provided by the Internet, and continues to be one of the most popular uses of the Internet.

E-mail is directed to people on the Internet through e-mail addresses. These identify the user who the message is for, and the location on the Internet that the user has an e-mail account through. For example, let's say you had the e-mail account mcross65@hotmail.com. When the message is sent over the Internet, it is directed to hotmail.com. It then goes to Hotmail's DNS table, which decides where the message is to travel to from there. Generally, the message would go to a mail server at Hotmail. The server then attempts to deliver the message to a mailbox belonging to someone with the username mcross65. The @ symbol separating the username and domain signifies that the user is "at" that location on the Internet. If the user exists, the message is delivered. If the user does not exist, the message is usually discarded, and a new message is created to inform the sender that the message was undeliverable.

E-mail can be sent to individuals or groups of people. This is done through distribution lists and software called an *e-mail reflector*. This software contains a listing of users who are to receive e-mail. An e-mail message that is to be sent to those on the list is then sent to the e-mail reflector. By sending a message to an e-mail address that is assigned to the software itself, the e-mail reflector forwards a copy of the message to each person on the distribution list. This allows large groups of people to receive regular newsletters, information, and so forth. People interested in receiving such information can add themselves to distribution lists when visiting sites that offer information on topics or products. Such mailing lists are the source of SPAM, which is unsolicited e-mail.

Simple Message Transfer Protocol, or SMTP, is a common protocol used for sending e-mail messages. SMTP is installed on machines as part of the TCP/IP protocol suite. Because SMTP has a limited ability to queue messages on the receiving end, Post Office Protocol 3, or POP3, is the protocol often used on the receiving end of e-mail messages. POP3 is often used by Internet servers to receive and store mail. While both SMTP and POP3 have the ability to both send and receive mail, most Internet servers use both of these protocols for e-mail.

TCP/IP Ports

Any client software that uses TCP/IP uses an identifier called a *port*. When FTP, Telnet, SMTP, or other software and protocols are running, they monitor this port constantly. In other words, the server listens to this port for requests for service, and the client application uses this port number to request services like Web pages, mail, and so forth. Server applications or processes using TCP/IP have at least one assigned port number, which is called a *Well Known Port Number*. A listing of commonly used Well Known Port Numbers is shown in Table 3-1.

| | | TABLE 3-1 |
| | | |

TABLE 3-1

Well-Known Port
Numbers

Name	Port Number	Description
DNS	53	Domain Name Server
FTP	20	FTP (File Transfer Protocol) Data
FTP	21	FTP (File Transfer Protocol) Control
Gopher	70	Gopher
HTTP	80	Hypertext Transfer Protocol
POP3	110	Post Office Protocol 3
SMTP	25	Simple Mail Transfer Protocol
Telnet	23	Telnet
TFTP	69	Trivial File Transfer Protocol

CERTIFICATION OBJECTIVE 3.02

Use of Web Browsers and Various Clients

Internet clients are designed with specific purposes and uses in mind.
One may be designed to display Web pages, another to access files from an
FTP site, to send and receive e-mail, or access some other service available
on the Internet or corporate intranet. In recent years, however, this has
changed in that universal clients have been developed to access a number
of different services. This enables users to access multiple services through
a single client.

In this section, we will discuss the use of a number of popular and traditional clients. We'll discuss a number of clients that are designed to access individual services, and see when one client should be used over another. We'll also discuss universal or all-in-one clients that access more than one Internet service, and see that some universal clients may not be the all-in-one Internet clients you'd expect.

FTP Clients

FTP clients are applications that make the File Transfer Protocol, or FTP, easy to use. FTP is designed for the transmission of files across the Internet or networks using TCP/IP. When you install TCP/IP on your computer, FTP is also installed. From a command prompt, you can enter commands specific to FTP that will enable you to transfer files. To make using FTP easier, FTP clients use menus and toolbars to invoke these commands and display information through a GUI.

When you access an FTP site using an FTP client, it appears similar to viewing files and directories on your hard disk. You can tunnel down into directories and subdirectories, and move up from subdirectories to parent directories. You can choose the files you want and download them to your disk. This provides a fast, efficient way of getting the information you want quickly without having to navigate through various Web pages.

Because FTP sites don't use Web pages, there is usually a file called a *directory map*. This is a listing of directories and files on the FTP server, and usually provides a description of each file. This is an important resource on FTP sites, as it can be difficult—or impossible—to find the program, document, or other file you want without a directory map.

Telnet Clients

Telnet clients are terminal emulation programs that run on TCP/IP networks. Terminal emulation means that the software allows your computer to run like an older dumb terminal, and connect to mainframes, Bulletin Board Systems (BBSs), and other servers. The Telnet software on your computer connects your PC to a Telnet server. Commands entered through the Telnet client are executed on the server as if they were being entered directly on the server console.

Telnet clients allow you to access information in a text-based manner. Universities, government institutions, and other organizations provide Telnet services to enable users to access information, download files, send e-mail to one another, and so on. They are a great way to access data, without having to wait for graphics to download and display in your browser.

While Telnet services are still available on the Internet, they aren't as popular as they were some years ago. When connecting to a Telnet server, you are greeted with menus similar to those found in DOS programs. There are no graphics, and commands are entered via the keyboard. The only commands that can be executed with a mouse are those found on the menus of the Telnet client itself. Figure 3-2 shows what it looks like when a Telnet client is connected to a Telnet server. The commands available from a Telnet server appear in the main window of the application, while other Telnet commands are available through the menu appearing at the top of the application.

FIGURE 3-2

Telnet client connected to a Telnet server

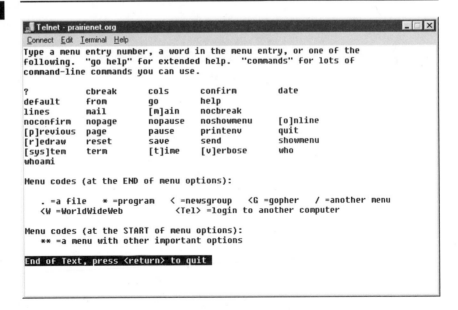

EXERCISE 3-2	**Using Telnet**

Using Telnet

1. Connect to your ISP.
2. From the Windows Start menu, click Run, and then type **telnet**.
3. When the Telnet window appears, select Remote System from the Connect menu. This will display the Connect dialog box.
4. Type **prairienet.org** in the Host Name field, and then click Connect.
5. Once connected, type **visitor** as your login name, and **guest** as your password.
6. Browse through the site. When you're ready to end your session, select Disconnect from the Telnet Connect menu.

E-mail Clients

E-mail clients are applications that enable you to send electronic messages to other users on your intranet or Internet. A number of e-mail clients are available on the market, including Eudora Pro, Outlook Express, and many others. These clients have the ability to create new messages, check mail on an Internet mail server, and read mail. You can also attach files to a message, enabling you to send documents, graphics, programs, and other files over the Internet.

Users on a Novell NetWare 5 network may also find GroupWise advantageous. This is an application and service that provides e-mail on a corporate intranet. One of the benefits of GroupWise is that users are able to access e-mail messages using a browser. By accessing a Web page that verifies their username and password, GroupWise users can view e-mail over an intranet Web page.

All-in-One Clients/Universal Clients

As the Internet becomes increasingly popular, all-in-one, or Universal, clients have become commonplace. This type of client software enables users to access Web pages, FTP sites, Telnet sites, e-mail, and more through a single application. Rather than having several applications running at once, you can access diverse Internet services through a single program or suite of programs.

As more features are added to applications, a program can become monolithic in size. For this reason, programmers have taken to modular programming. This involves breaking a large program into a number of modules or smaller executables. In terms of Internet clients, this can be seen in suites such as Internet Explorer or Netscape Communicator. While the Web browser can access Web pages, Telnet, FTP sites, and so forth, a separate e-mail application is available for transmitting and receiving messages. Even with this, some e-mail applications also provide access to other services such as newsgroups.

Newsgroups are directories of messages and files available on a news server. They are similar to message groups that appear on dial-in Bulletin Board Services, where messages are posted publicly and can be viewed by everyone. Files, such as graphics or programs, are also available in newsgroups. To access newsgroups, you can use specialized client software, such as Forte's Free Agent, that enables you to view and post messages or download files.

Microsoft Outlook Express is an example of software that combines the abilities of two diverse Internet clients. Using this software, which is part of the Internet Explorer suite, you can send and receive e-mail, attach files, and connect to newsgroups. Once connected, you can then browse through the public messages in various groups, post new messages, read other people's public messages, and download files to your local hard drive.

Web browsers, such as Internet Explorer and Netscape Navigator, also combine the abilities of different Internet clients. Web browsers' primary purpose is to display Web pages. However, these browsers have the ability to list files available on an FTP site. For example, by typing **ftp.microsoft.com** in the address bar of your browser, you will be able to navigate directories and view files available on the Microsoft FTP site.

Many browsers also have the ability to launch other programs if the Web browser itself is unable to access a particular kind of site. For example, let's say you were using Internet Explorer and wanted to access a Telnet site. Specify the protocol being used, and the name of the site would open the associated program. In the case of accessing the Telnet site we visited in Exercise 3-2, you would type **telnet:// prairienet.org** in the address bar of the browser. Since Telnet sites can't be supported directly through Internet Explorer, the browser would automatically open the Telnet application.

Earlier in this chapter, we mentioned that e-mail is sent and received through e-mail programs such as Eudora Pro, Outlook Express, and other e-mail applications. However, there are sites that provide e-mail services that are accessible through a Web browser. A popular example of this on the Internet is Hotmail, which is found at www.hotmail.com. Another popular example for intranets is Novell's GroupWise. When accessing e-mail with a Web browser, a Web page is displayed asking for your username and password. Once this is entered and submitted, a new page is displayed showing e-mail messages that have been received by that server. You can select a received message and read it through your browser, reply to messages, or send new ones. There is also the capability of attaching files to messages. One of the obvious benefits to having e-mail accounts set up in this fashion is that you can view your e-mail from any computer. You don't need to configure an e-mail application to retrieve your e-mail, or worry about being unable to access e-mail that resides on another computer.

EXERCISE 3-3

Using Microsoft Internet Explorer or Netscape Navigator to Access FTP Sites

1. Connect to the Internet, and open your Web browser.

2. In the address bar of your browser, type **ftp://ftp.microsoft.com**.

3. A listing of directories and files will appear in the browser window. Find the file dirmap.txt and double-click it. A new window will open showing the contents of this file.

4. Browse through the various directories on the FTP site.

When to Use Each Browser

While Universal or all-in-one clients enable you to access multiple services, it's important to remember that certain features may not be available if that's all you use. For example, while a Web browser can access FTP sites, and send and receive e-mail, its primary purpose is to display HTML documents. The features included in the browser are focused on the display of Web pages, so the ability to do such things as spell-check your e-mail isn't present.

The same holds true for other clients. E-mail clients such as Outlook Express and Eudora Pro are designed to send and receive e-mail. Newsreaders, such as Forte Free Agent, are specifically created to access newsgroups. Telnet clients are designed for accessing Telnet sites, and FTP clients are designed for accessing FTP sites. If you are going to be browsing such sites frequently, you may find that an application created for that purpose is easier to use, and has greater functionality.

Basic Commands to Use with Each Client

As with any application, there are a number of commands and controls that you should be familiar with when using Internet clients. Some of these are text commands that can be typed in, while others can be executed by clicking objects or menu items in Windows-based programs. In the paragraphs that follow, we'll discuss a number of the common commands and controls with which you should have some familiarity.

Web browsers are the most-used type of client on the Internet. While there are numerous Web browsers available for you to use, many of the elements found in each browser interface are consistent. For example, as seen in Figure 3-3, browsers have a menu bar, toolbar, and address bar. The menu bar appears at the top of the browser. Each menu contains a number of items that invoke commands when you click them.

The File menu contains commands that deal with files. These include the HTML documents viewed through the browser, and those you wish to open. The Open command under this menu is used to open Web pages stored on your hard disk or to display Web pages found on specific Web sites. The New command enables you to open a second instance of the browser. The Print command is also found under this menu, enabling you

---

FIGURE 3-3

Menus and toolbars found in Microsoft Internet Explorer 5

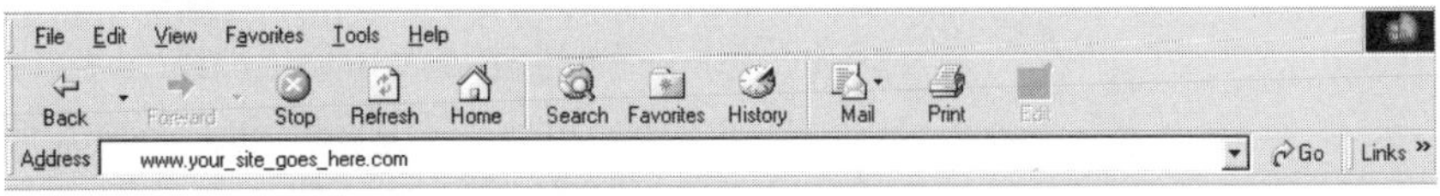

to print the Web page currently being viewed, while the Save or Save As commands allow you to save the HTML document to disk. Finally, the Exit or Close command allows you to exit the browser.

The Edit menu provides commands that deal with editing the Web page. While you can't directly edit a Web page residing on a Web site, this menu has commands that allow you to cut, copy, and paste elements of the Web page or the Web page in its entirety. Some browsers, like Internet Explorer, also have a Select All command that will select the entire Web page. Once selected, you can then cut or copy it. If this isn't done, you will have to manually select an item to cut or copy by dragging your mouse over an area of the Web page. Depressing your left mouse button and moving the mouse over an area of the page will make such a selection. Finally, a particularly useful command on the Edit menu is the Find or "Find on this page" command. This will enable you to search the page for a word or phrase of text. You will especially find this command useful if you are looking for a particular word, topic, or phrase in a lengthy Web page.

The View menu contains commands that deal with what will be displayed in the browser, or how the browser itself will appear on your screen. Commands that may appear under this menu will toggle the display of various toolbars. This will enable you to view extra toolbars in your browser, or hide them if they aren't being used. Other commands appearing here may include a Stop command to cease the loading of a Web page. This is useful if there is an error in the page, or if it is taking a long time to load in the browser. The Refresh or Reload command can then be used to download the Web page again, so that it can be fully displayed.

If you are creating or learning how to create Web pages, the Source or View Source menu item may be useful to you. This will enable you to view the HTML or programming code used to create a Web page. This command will display the code in the browser window, or launch another application such as Notepad or an HTML editor. If you've ever wondered what went into writing HTML documents, or how someone created a particularly interesting Web page, this command will allow you to see the code.

At times, you may find a Web site you'll want to visit over and over again. In such a case, you'll want to use a menu called Favorites, Bookmarks, or something similar. This menu contains commands to add the names of favorite

Web sites to a list. Once a favorite Web page has been bookmarked, its name will appear under the menu. When you click on the menu, the browser will display that Web page.

The Tools menu includes commands dealing with configuring your browser, or possibly launching other applications. For example, in Internet Explorer, items under this menu will launch e-mail applications or newsreaders. Other menu items allow you to modify preferred settings for your browser.

The Help menu is an important menu in any application. This menu will allow you to search and view topics with which you have questions or problems. Other items appearing under this menu will show information about the browser, such as the name and version number.

Beneath the menu bar, you will find toolbars that have buttons to invoke various commands. These buttons are usually visual representations of frequently used commands found under menus. For example, such buttons may enable you to print the Web page, display a list of favorite Web sites, and so forth. Other toolbars may provide additional features. For example, in Microsoft Internet Explorer 5, a radio toolbar is available. This allows you to listen to radio stations over the Net, and even save links to the stations you prefer listening to.

The address bar appears by default at the bottom of the menus and other toolbars, and is used to enter the Uniform Resource Locators (URLs) of Web sites you wish to visit. It is here that you type the Web site address, and after pressing ENTER on your keyboard or clicking Go to the right of the address bar, that Web site's default page will appear in the main browser window. For example, you could type **www.comptia.com** in the address bar to visit that site. If the browser has the ability to browse FTP sites, as is the case with most current browsers, you could also enter the URL of those sites.

If your Web browser doesn't have the ability to browse FTP sites, or if you prefer using textual commands to browse a site, you could enter FTP commands from the DOS prompt. A number of commands are available through FTP, and these commands are available once TCP/IP has been installed on your system. To use these commands, you begin by typing **FTP** at the command prompt, followed by the name of the site you wish to visit. Once connected, you may be required to enter a username and/or password, and you will then be able to use the commands shown in Table 3-2.

TABLE 3-2

Common FTP Commands That Can Be Entered from a Command Prompt

FTP Command	Description
!	Escape to the shell. This will enable you to escape from FTP to the DOS command prompt.
?	Prints help information.
append	Appends information to a file.
ascii	Sets the ASCII transfer type.
bell	Has your computer beep when a command has been completed.
binary	Sets the binary transfer type.
bye	Logs off the FTP site. Causes the session to terminate, and exits back to the DOS prompt.
cd	Changes the remote working directory. This allows you to navigate through directories on the remote computer, the same way you'd navigate through directories on your local hard drive in DOS.
close	Terminates the FTP session. Similar to the bye command, but doesn't exit to DOS.
delete	Deletes a file on a remote computer. To delete the file, the filename would appear after the delete command.
dir	Lists the contents of the directory you're browsing on the remote computer.
disconnect	Terminates the FTP session. Identical to the close command, and similar to the bye command except that doesn't exit to DOS.
get	Used to receive or download a file from a remote computer.
help	Provides help information specific to the FTP utility being used.
lcd	Used to change the local working directory. This is the directory on your local hard disk.
ls	Lists the contents of the directory you're browsing on the remote computer. This is identical to the dir command.
mdelete	Used to delete multiple files located on the remote computer.

TABLE 3-2	FTP Command	Description
Common FTP Commands That Can Be Entered from a Command Prompt *(continued)*	mdir	Used to list the contents of multiple directories on a remote computer.
	mget	Receive or download multiple files from a remote computer.
	mkdir	Creates a directory on the remote computer.
	mls	Lists the contents of multiple directories located on the remote computer.
	mput	Used to send multiple files to a remote computer.
	open	Used to establish a connection with a remote computer. From the FTP prompt, you can enter the open command followed by the URL of the FTP site you wish to visit.
	prompt	Used to force interactive prompting between commands.
	put	Used to send a file to a remote computer.
	pwd	Forces the working directory on a remote computer.
	quit	Used to terminate an FTP session and exit to the DOS prompt. Identical to the bye command.
	recv	Used to receive a file from a remote computer.
	remotehelp	Displays help information that is specific to the FTP server to which you're currently connected.
	rename	Renames a file on the remote computer.
	rmdir	Removes or deletes a directory on the remote computer.
	send	Sends a single file to the remote computer.
	status	Shows your current status. Using this command displays connection information and details of how elements of the session will be handled.
	trace	Used to toggle the tracing of packets used in the FTP session.
	type	Used to set the file transfer type used in the session.
	user	Sends new user information. This enables you to log in to the server as a different user.

on the **job**

It can be difficult remembering all the FTP commands, and you'll generally only remember the ones you use most in your job. That's why the help and remotehelp commands are particularly important. The help command provides you with a listing of commands available in FTP. To view a description of a particular command, type HELP followed by the command you want information on. The remotehelp command is used to view a listing of commands that are used by the FTP server to which you're currently connected.

CERTIFICATION OBJECTIVE 3.03

Configuring the Desktop

Much of using the Internet or a corporate intranet is software related, and like any programs, some configuration is necessary if the software is to function properly. This not only includes configuring the Web browser itself, but elements of your operating system, so that your computer can connect to various servers. Once configured, you will then be able to connect to the Internet or your intranet, and use the benefits and features offered.

For the remainder of this chapter, we'll discuss how and why such configurations are made to your system. We'll see how TCP/IP, including the default gateway, subnet mask, IP addresses, and so on, is configured. We'll discuss HOSTS files, and why they are important, especially on corporate Intranets. Finally, we'll compare DHCP and static IP addresses, and talk about other configurations you may want to set on your browser.

TCP/IP Configuration

From the networking point of view, TCP/IP is the language of the Internet. It is used to identify a computer on the Internet or your local TCP/IP network, and provides rules on how computers will communicate and transfer data. As such, configuring TCP/IP is of vital importance to the functionality of browsers and other applications on the Internet and local intranets.

Once TCP/IP has been installed on your computer, there are two places that it can be configured on a Windows NT or 9*x* computer:

- Dial-up Networking, where you configure settings used to connect to an ISP or a remote TCP/IP network
- Network, which is an applet found in the Control Panel

It may seem redundant to have two places in which to configure TCP/IP; however, there is a good reason. The Network applet is used to configure a computer to connect to a network. For example, let's say your computer is a workstation on a LAN. The Network applet would be used to configure TCP/IP so that you can access network resources. Dial-up Networking is used to connect to remote computers. If you were connecting to the Internet or dialing in from a remote location to another TCP/IP network, you would make configurations here. This would allow you to keep one set of configuration information for your LAN, and still connect to the Internet or another remote network.

It is important to keep such configuration information separated, and geared toward the network you're connecting to, because TCP/IP identifies your computer on a network, and uses information that determines how other servers on a different network can be contacted. It does this through several important pieces of information:

- IP address
- Subnet mask
- Default gateway address

Computers on a TCP/IP network, like the Internet, are identified by IP addresses. The IP address shows which network your computer is a part of, and where on the network your computer (also called a *host*) resides. This is similar to the address of your house, where part of the address shows the street you live on, and the other part shows where on the street you're located. The address itself is comprised of four sets of digits, separated by periods. Each set of numbers can be comprised of one to three digits, ranging from 0 to 255. An example of an IP address would be 201.131.3.3. Valid IP addresses for the network you're connecting to can be acquired through your network administrator or the ISP you're using to connect to the Internet.

Some IP addresses cannot be used on a network. IP addresses cannot start with the numbers 127, as these are used for loopback functions; for example, 127.0.01 would loop any packets back to your computer. This could be used to check whether TCP/IP is working on your machine, but cannot be used as a valid IP address. IP addresses also can't be made up of all 255's or 0's. 255 is a broadcast address and is used for sending messages to all computers on a network. IP addresses comprised of all zeros are interpreted as "this network only," and can't be used by a machine as an IP address.

At the beginning of this section, we mentioned that part of an IP address shows what network you're on, while the remainder identifies your computer on that network. Part of the IP address is the network ID, stating that your computer is part of a particular network. The remainder of the IP address identifies the computer or host itself. For example, if your IP address were 201.131.3.3, the network ID might be 201.131 (the beginning of the address), while the 3.3 (the end of the address) would be the host ID. The *subnet mask* allows the computer to distinguish what parts of the IP address are the network ID and host ID.

Subnet masks are used to block parts of the IP address to distinguish the network ID from the host ID. Like an IP address, the subnet mask is made up of four sets of 1–3 digit numbers. If a set of numbers is 255, the corresponding set in the IP address is identified as part of the network ID. If the set of numbers in the subnet mask is a zero, the corresponding set in the IP address is part of the host ID. For example, let's say your IP address is 201.141.30.5 and your subnet mask is 255.0.0.0. Since the first set of numbers in the subnet mask is 255, this would mean that the first set of numbers in the IP address (201) is your network ID. The remaining three sets of numbers in the subnet mask are all zeros, indicating that the last three sets in the IP address are your host ID. To illustrate this further, compare the subnet mask to the IP addresses in Table 3-3 to see how the subnet mask blocks out (i.e., masks) the network ID.

TABLE 3-3	How Subnet Masks Distinguish the Network ID from the Host ID		
IP address	201.131.3.3	201.131.3.3	201.131.3.3
Subnet mask	255.0.0.0	255.255.0.0	255.255.255.0
Network ID	201	201.131	201.131.3
Host ID	131.3.3	3.3	3.3

Using the IP address and subnet mask, the computer can see if you're attempting to connect to a computer on your local network or to a remote computer. If it is to be sent to a computer on your network, it is sent directly. If on another network, it needs to use a *default gateway*.

A default gateway is a computer or other hardware that will forward messages and data to another network. If data is meant for a computer on a remote network, it is sent to the default gateway and forwarded from there. The way that your computer knows what computer is the gateway is by configuring it with the IP address of the default gateway.

As mentioned earlier, you can set up the IP address, subnet mask, and default gateway for your computer through the Network applet in the Control Panel or through Dial-up Networking. Although the appearance may differ, essentially the same type of information can be added through each.

In Windows NT 4.0 Workstation, you can double-click the Network applet in the Control Panel to open the network properties. When the Network Properties dialog box appears, clicking the Protocols tab will allow you to view a number of protocols currently installed on your system. If TCP/IP does not appear in the listing, clicking New on this tab will allow you to install it. If TCP/IP already appears in the listing, double-clicking this entry or clicking Properties on this tab will open the TCP/IP properties. By default, the tab that appears is the IP Addresses tab. It will display fields in which you can enter an IP address, subnet mask, and default gateway. You'll notice that the option selected by default states that you can have an IP address automatically assigned to you. This is only used if your network uses a DHCP server, which is usually the case for Internet connections. We will discuss DHCP in greater detail in the section that follows. To enter an IP address specifically assigned to you, click the option that states "Specify an IP address," and then type the IP address assigned to you by your network administrator.

Press TAB once to move to the next field, and either accept the default subnet mask of 255.255.255.0 or enter the subnet mask issued to you by your network administrator. Finally, tab down to the next field, and enter your default gateway address. Again, you would get the address of the default gateway from your network administrator.

To set up an IP address in Dial-up Networking, go to the Windows Start menu. Here, select Programs | Accessories, and then click Dial-up Networking. This will open a new window showing your current dial-up connections. Right-clicking one of these connections will display a menu, enabling you to select Properties to bring up the Dial-up Networking properties for that connection. When the Properties dialog box appears, click the Server Types tab, and then click TCP/IP Settings. This will make the TCP/IP Settings dialog box appear, as shown in Figure 3-4.

In this screen, you'll notice that there are additional fields for DNS and WINS. These are naming systems that map the names of computers to IP addresses, and vice versa. DNS is the Domain Name System, and was developed as a distributed database for identifying domains and hosts on

FIGURE 3-4

TCP/IP Settings dialog box

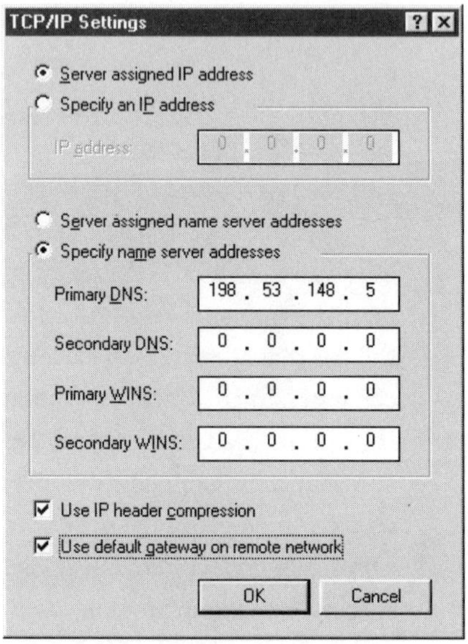

the Internet. You can imagine how difficult it would be to remember IP addresses for each site you wanted to visit on the Internet. What DNS does is, when a URL is entered into your browser, the domain name is sent to a DNS server. It searches a database and returns the IP address for that particular server, so you can then access it. If you were to type in the IP address for a server, a DNS server could compare the IP address and send you the domain name, so that it appears in the address bar of your browser.

WINS is the Windows Internet Name Service, and gives Windows NT Servers the ability to resolve NetBIOS computer names on a TCP/IP network. You'll remember that when you first installed Windows NT or 9*x* on a computer, you were asked to name the computer. This is the NetBIOS name, and is a friendly name used to identify a computer. WINS keeps a database that is dynamically updated on the NT network, adding NetBIOS and IP addresses to it as new computers are found. When WINS is used on a network, client computers register their names with the WINS server as they connect to the network. The WINS server then maps the names of these computers to their IP addresses. When a WINS client requests a resource from one of these clients, the WINS server resolves the name and returns the IP address to the requesting computer.

exam
Watch

WINS is a Microsoft technology that runs on Windows NT Servers. DNS servers can be used on NT networks, but are available for other platforms as well. DNS is used on the Internet for name resolution; therefore, while WINS may not be required to connect to an Internet server, DNS is.

DHCP vs. Static IP

So far, we've discussed configuring computers with static IP addresses. Static IP addresses are IP addresses that are assigned to one—and only one—user. The IP address is manually entered into the TCP/IP configuration, and no other computer on the network is able to use that address. Static IP addresses are commonly used on networks and corporate intranets, allowing administrators to track what users are doing, control their access, and access the user's computer by connecting to the IP address of that user's computer. The drawback to this method is an added burden to administration in that you must keep records of what IP addresses have been assigned to which users. If two computers were to use the same address on the network, each user would receive error messages and experience problems when accessing network resources. Another problem with static IP addresses is that even if a user isn't connected to the network, that particular IP address cannot be used. The IP address is assigned to the user whose machine you've configured it with. If you were to run low on available IP addresses, other users who are currently on the network couldn't share the IP address.

Although you can configure each computer on a network to use its own, individual IP address, it may be easier to have IP addresses automatically assigned to users as they log in to the network. This is where the Dynamic Host Configuration Protocol (DHCP) comes into play. DHCP allows you to dynamically assign and configure a user's network settings as he or she logs in to your network. DHCP manages the allocation of IP addresses and eliminates many of the problems associated with manually configuring a client computer. When a client has been configured to use DHCP, it requests the following information from a DHCP server when connecting to the network:

- IP address
- Subnet mask
- Default gateway address

Upon receiving the request, the DHCP server then selects an IP address from a pool of available addresses stored in a database on the DHCP server. It offers one of these addresses to the client, and if it accepts the address, the IP address is "leased" for a specific period of time.

IP addresses are issued to the client for only a certain period of time, which means that the client doesn't monopolize the address. Each time the client connects to the network, or to an ISP's Internet server, he or she can be issued a new IP address for the length of the connection. The length of time the IP address is leased is configured on the DHCP server. Because this allows a limited pool of addresses to be used by a large group of client computers, DHCP is commonly used on the Internet. It allows ISPs to provide Internet access to more users than they have IP addresses for.

DHCP and static IP addresses can be set through the TCP/IP properties on your computer. This is available through the Network applet found in the Control Panel on Windows 9x and NT computers. It is also available through the properties of a Dial-up Connection found in Dial-up Networking in Windows 9x and NT computers. Configuring settings through the Network applet is generally done when you are making TCP/IP configurations for a local network. When connecting to Internet sites, you should make changes through the properties of a specific dial-up connection. This will enable you to make configurations for each dial-up connection without affecting TCP/IP settings for your network.

HOSTS File Configuration

While DNS servers offer an effective way of mapping host and domain names to IP addresses, they are overkill when used on smaller networks. After all, if users only need to access a single or small handful of computers, having a DNS server is probably more than you need. For example, you wouldn't want to have a DNS server set up on your network so users could find a single intranet server. When this is the case, *HOSTS files* are a useful alternative.

HOSTS files are static files that map hostnames to IP addresses. In other words, when new hosts are added to a network, the HOSTS file isn't automatically updated. You need to open the HOSTS file manually, and then add the new host or domain name to the file. An example of a HOSTS file is shown in Figure 3-5.

You add an entry to a HOSTS file by opening and editing the file. The HOSTS file can be edited with any text editor, and is found in the *systemroot*\SYSTEM32\DRIVERS\ETC directory of a Windows NT computer, or in the Windows directory of your Windows 9x computer. You then type a new entry at the bottom of the file. The IP address is typed first; then, after pressing TAB, you enter the host or domain name that your computer will use to find the computer at that IP address. Each entry can be up to 255 characters in length, and entries are not case sensitive.

The drawback to using HOSTS files is that a HOSTS file must reside on each computer on your network. In other words, if you have an intranet site

FIGURE 3-5

HOSTS file

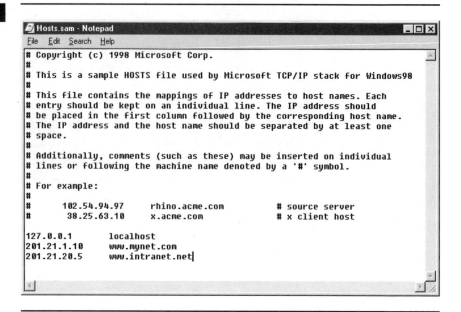

```
Hosts.sam - Notepad                                                    _ □ ✕
File  Edit  Search  Help
# Copyright (c) 1998 Microsoft Corp.
#
# This is a sample HOSTS file used by Microsoft TCP/IP stack for Windows98
#
# This file contains the mappings of IP addresses to host names. Each
# entry should be kept on an individual line. The IP address should
# be placed in the first column followed by the corresponding host name.
# The IP address and the host name should be separated by at least one
# space.
#
# Additionally, comments (such as these) may be inserted on individual
# lines or following the machine name denoted by a '#' symbol.
#
# For example:
#
#      102.54.94.97      rhino.acme.com          # source server
#      38.25.63.10       x.acme.com              # x client host

127.0.0.1       localhost
201.21.1.10     www.mynet.com
201.21.20.5     www.intranet.net
```

that you want users to access, you have to update the HOSTS file on each
network workstation. When the host or domain name is entered into a
browser, or used by another application on that computer, it then checks the
local HOSTS file for the proper IP address. Because the HOSTS file is read in
a linear fashion, the most commonly accessed domain names and hostnames
should appear at the top of the file. This will allow the application to find the
host or domain name more quickly.

Configuring Your Browser

Configuring settings that determine how your browser will function and
connect to the Internet is an important part of a user's Internet or intranet
experience. If users can't connect, or the browser behaves in a manner that
is confusing or difficult, users will become frustrated with the Internet,
intranet, and the person who set it up for them (i.e., you). While browser
settings vary from manufacturer to manufacturer and version to version,
some are consistent among all.

Many of the settings for an Internet Explorer Web browser are contained in the Internet Options applet, found in the Control Panel. Similar settings to this may be found in the Options for a browser developed by other manufacturers. Upon opening it, you will see a dialog box with several tabs, which we'll discuss in this section. The first tab is the General tab, shown in Figure 3-6. This is where you set basic elements of your browser. The first field on this tab is where you can enter the homepage the browser will use. You can type in the URL of the page that will open when your browser opens or when Home in your Web browser is clicked. If your browser is currently open, you can click Use Current to have the Web page displayed in it as your homepage. Use Default will set the homepage to the manufacturer's default setting, and Use Blank will have no Web page appear when the browser is open.

The section below the Home page is where you can configure Temporary Internet File settings. When you are browsing Web pages, the

FIGURE 3-6

The General tab of Internet Options

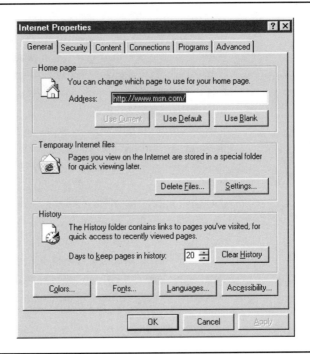

HTML documents, images, Java classes, and other files are downloaded from the server to a Temporary Internet File directory on your local hard drive. The browser then reads these files from your hard disk. The Temporary Internet File section of the General tab enables you to delete these files from your hard disk by clicking Delete Files. You can also click Settings to bring up another dialog box, in which you can set how much hard disk space will be used for these files and when your browser should check for newer versions of pages currently in the directory. You can also change the directory used for these temporary files.

The History section is where you configure how long your browser will keep links to previously visited pages. These previously visited pages can be viewed by clicking the arrow on the address bar of your browser. You can set the number of days these links will be kept, or delete the history by clicking Clear History. If the number of days is set to 0, no history will be kept.

The Security tab of Internet Options, shown in Figure 3-7, allows you to specify security settings for your browser. Here, moving a slide bar allows you to set one of several levels of security and limit what the browser will do on the Internet. Clicking Custom Level enables you to select specific options of how the browser will interact with sites. For example, you can control whether the browser can download files, use Java applets, and so forth. You can also specify restricted sites that shouldn't be visited, and others that are trusted.

The Content tab is used to control what users can view through the browser, and has additional security features. The first section of this tab, shown in Figure 3-8, is the Content Advisor. A number of Web pages on the Internet have their Web pages rated through RSACi. RSACi is the Recreational Software Advisory Council for the Internet services, and it allows Web page authors to have their pages rated in much the same way that movies are rated. By clicking Enable, you can control whether browser users can view different levels of sex, violence, language, and nudity. Once setting the levels of content that can be viewed, you can then enter a password to keep other users from changing these settings.

FIGURE 3-7

The Security tab of Internet
Options

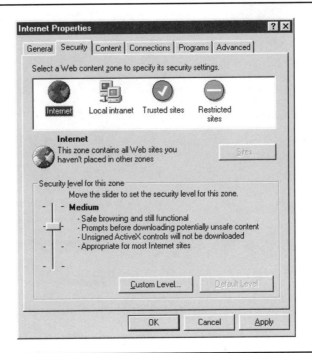

The Certificates tab is used to ensure that Web sites send verification
of who they are, before personal information is sent. It is also used to
positively identify you to secure Web sites. Clicking Certificates will allow
you to view certificates currently used by your computer, while clicking
Publishers will view a listing of various sites that you trust.

Personal Information is the final section of the Content tab. AutoComplete
allows you to set whether Internet Explorer can complete fields on Internet
forms automatically. This will have the browser enter common information
(your name, address, etc.) on forms you're completing on the Internet. You
can also set it to remember usernames and passwords used on sites you've
previously visited. Internet Wallet allows you to specify credit card information
used when shopping on the Net. This saves you from having to enter your

FIGURE 3-8

The Content tab of
Internet Options

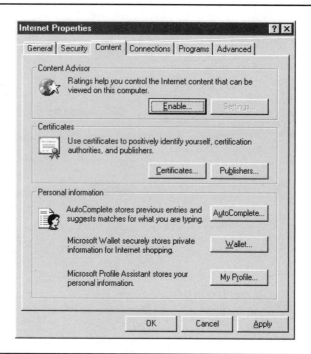

credit card number or address information repeatedly. Finally, My Profile
allows you to specify personal information about yourself.

The Connections tab allows you to configure how you will connect to
the Internet via a modem or LAN. The first section of this tab allows you
to invoke the Internet Connection Wizard, which takes you through the
process of configuring your computer to connect to the Internet. Once you
click this button, a Wizard opens, asking you to enter information related
to your Internet account. Before using the Internet Connection Wizard,
however, you will need the following information from your ISP:

■ The dial-up number of your ISP, which is the telephone number
that your computer will dial to connect to the ISP's server.

■ Your username and password.

- Whether you have a SLIP or PPP account, which is the type of connection to your ISP. While PPP is faster and newer than SLIP, some providers still use the SLIP protocol.

- Whether an IP address is automatically assigned to you, or whether you have an assigned IP address. In most cases, the IP address will be assigned to you automatically through DHCP.

- IP addresses of the primary and secondary DNS servers.

- The name of the mail server, and the protocol the mail server uses for incoming and outgoing mail. In many cases, POP3 will be used for incoming mail, and SMTP will be used for outgoing mail.

- The name of the news server.

Once you have this information, you can then invoke the Internet Connection Wizard and input the information into the fields as requested. If you don't have an existing Internet account, you can use the Internet Connection Wizard to find one. The Wizard will dial a toll-free number, and download a listing of ISPs in your area.

When you've set up an account, it will appear in a listing below the button that invokes the Internet Connection Wizard. Here you are allowed to Add, Remove, and modify Settings of connection accounts. Double-clicking on a connection account in the listing will also display additional properties of that account.

Finally, the section below this allows you to configure LAN settings. Earlier in this chapter, we discussed some of the various ways to connect to the Internet. One of these was through a network that—if you're in a large company—may use a proxy server. You'll remember that a proxy server is software residing on a server that acts as a barrier between your local network and the Internet. It allows computers on the network to access the Internet through a single IP address, and provides a measure of security against hackers. The proxy server will include various features for tracking what users are doing on the Internet, and generally includes methods for blocking users from accessing certain sites or limiting them to certain sites on the Net.

Configuring a computer to use a proxy server is done through Internet Options in Microsoft Windows. The Connections tab provides fields to set the IP address of the proxy server on your network. Depending on the browser version or Windows operating system you're using, the fields will either appear on the Connection tab itself, or by clicking LAN Settings on the Connections tab. If you click this button, the screen shown in Figure 3-9 will appear. Clicking the "Use a proxy server" check box will activate the fields below, where you then enter the IP address of your proxy server.

You'll also notice a check box to "Bypass proxy server for local addresses." If this isn't checked, a proxy server will be used for all local IP addresses. This may require extra permissions by your network administrator, and will often slow connections to other hosts on your TCP/IP network. Often, it is best to have this check box checked, if performance is an issue.

Advanced opens another dialog box that enables you to set IP addresses for different proxy servers. This is useful when you want to have different

FIGURE 3-9

Configuring LAN settings through Internet Options

Local Area Network (LAN) Settings

Automatic configuration

Automatic configuration may override manual settings. To ensure the use of manual settings, disable automatic configuration.

☑ Automatically detect settings

☐ Use automatic configuration script

Address [ ]

Proxy server

☑ Use a proxy server

Address: 198.200.80.2   Port: 80   [Advanced...]

☐ Bypass proxy server for local addresses

[OK]   [Cancel]

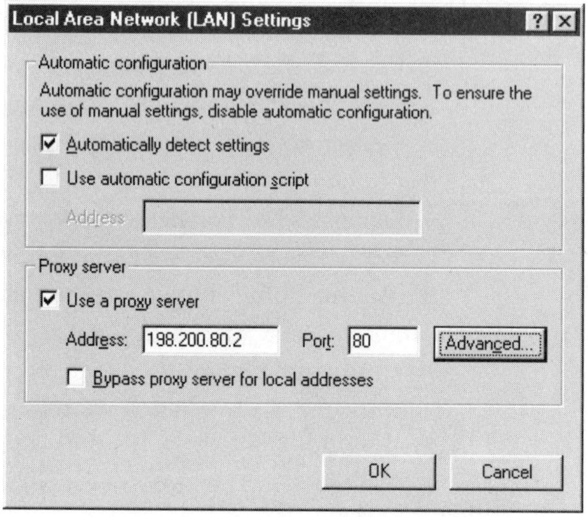

proxy servers controlling access to HTTP, FTP, Gopher, Secure, and other sites on a network or the Internet. If only one proxy server is used on your network, you don't need to configure settings in the Advanced dialog box.

Configuring Your Browser to Connect to the Internet Through a LAN

1. From the Windows Start menu, select Settings | Control Panel.
2. Double-click the Internet Options icon.
3. Click the Connections tab.
4. Click the "Connect to the Internet using a local area network" option, and then click the "Connect to the Internet using a local area network" check box. If this doesn't appear on the tab, click LAN Settings, and when the dialog box appears, click the "Use a proxy server" check box.
5. Type the IP address of your proxy server.
6. Click OK to accept your changes.

The next tab in Internet Options is Programs (Figure 3-10). Here you can specify the default programs that Windows will use for different Internet services, including the default HTML editor, e-mail program, newsreader, Internet call, calendar program, and contact list. To change the current program used for a service, simply click the drop-down list for that program. Different programs on your system will appear in the listing.

The final tab in Internet Options is the Advanced tab. This contains a listing of various configurations, including printing and browsing options, how Internet Explorer will handle multimedia, and a number of security issues. This tab should not be played with unless you understand each of the dozens of options offered.

Now that we've discussed so many topics dealing with Internet clients, let's look at some common questions you may encounter in learning and working with the Internet.

FIGURE 3-10

The Programs tab of
Internet Options

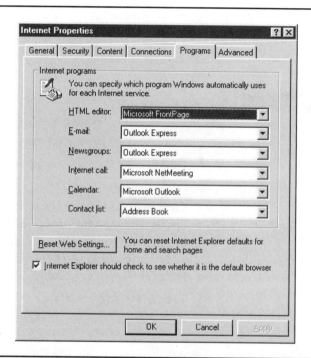

QUESTIONS AND ANSWERS

Users on the corporate intranet I'm creating use the Internet at home. Some like Lynx, others like Internet Explorer, and still others like Netscape Navigator. Should I let them run whatever they like at work to access the intranet?	No. Choose one browser as the corporate standard for all users to use. The more Internet client applications in use, the more difficult it will be to provide user support. Choose the Internet clients that best suit your intranet, and that you and the other staff in your Information Systems (IS) team are expert enough to support.
I've installed WebTV for Windows on my Windows 98 computer, but I can't view any television shows. Why?	You probably don't have a TV tuner card installed on your computer. This will enable you to view television shows on your PC. WebTV for Windows will still run on your computer, but will be limited to displaying TV listings.
We have just added a permanent Internet connection on our network. However, users are unable to connect to the Internet. What is most likely the problem?	If you are using a proxy server to connect network users to the Internet, it is possible that the proxy server settings haven't been configured on the workstation. Ensure this has been set, or users won't be able to connect to the Internet.

CERTIFICATION SUMMARY

In this chapter, we discussed the importance of the Internet client, and topics that need to be addressed for the client to function properly. Considerable hardware and software supports an Internet client, and configurations need to be made for a client to function properly. First, we saw that the infrastructure supporting an Internet client is made up of such things as the TCP/IP protocol suite, which is a group of protocols dictating how data is transferred from computer to computer. In addition to TCP/IP, the Internet client also depends on hardware, the operating system, and other elements that make a network connection possible.

We also saw that an Internet client isn't merely a Web browser like Internet Explorer or Netscape Navigator, and that a number of different applications may be used to access Internet services. These include e-mail programs, FTP clients, Telnet clients, or all-in-one browsers that provide access to multiple services. As we saw, while applications made by various manufacturers may have slightly different interfaces, there are common commands that can be used with each of the different clients.

For Internet clients to run properly, some configuration needs to be made to your computer. Primary to this is TCP/IP. For TCP/IP to run, you need to configure such things as an IP address, subnet mask, and default gateway. You may also need to configure DHCP, a DNS server address, WINS, HOSTS files, or other elements that enable TCP/IP to function properly on your network or the Internet. After ensuring that this functions properly, and that a connection to the Internet is made successfully, you can then configure settings that will allow the user to enjoy the Internet or your corporate intranet to the fullest.

TWO-MINUTE DRILL

- ❑ TCP/IP is an acronym for Transmission Control Protocol/Internet Protocol.
- ❑ A protocol is a set of rules as to how data is packaged, transmitted, and received. It controls how data is sent over a network.

❑   The Transport layer of the four-layer conceptual model is where transport protocols are used to provide communication sessions between computers.

❑   WebTV enables you to access the World Wide Web through your television and a box that's similar in appearance to those used for cable TV. With these two requirements, you then sign up with a WebTV access service.

❑   Internet phone is a recent innovation to the Internet, allowing users to talk verbally with one another as if they were using a normal telephone.

❑   There are two levels of service available with ISDN: Basic Rate Interface (BRI) and Primary Rate Interface (PRI).

❑   Simple Message Transfer Protocol (SMTP) is a common protocol used for sending e-mail messages. SMTP is installed on machines as part of the TCP/IP protocol suite.

❑   FTP clients are applications that make using the File Transfer Protocol (FTP) easy to use. FTP is designed for the transmission of files across the Internet or networks using TCP/IP.

❑   Telnet clients are terminal emulation programs that run on TCP/IP networks. Terminal emulation means that the software allows your computer to run like an older dumb terminal, and connect to mainframes, Bulletin Board Systems (BBSs), and other servers.

❑   E-mail clients are applications that enable you to send electronic messages to other users on your intranet or Internet. A number of clients are available on the market, including Eudora Pro, Outlook Express, and many others.

❑   Computers on a TCP/IP network, like the Internet, are identified by IP addresses. The IP address shows which network your computer is a part of, and where on the network your computer (also called a *host*) resides.

SELF TEST

1. You are setting up a computer to connect to the Internet. Which of the following protocols will you need to install to connect to the Internet?

   A. TCP/IP

   B. TCP

   C. IP

   D. HTTP

2. You enter the URL of a Web site into the address bar of your Internet browser. Which protocol will be used to retrieve the HTML document (Web page) from this site?

   A. HTML

   B. HTTP

   C. FTP

   D. Gopher

3. You have accessed a site that is specifically designed for the transfer of files. From this site, you can click a program's name and have that software downloaded to your computer. Which of the following protocols would be used to download these files?

   A. ICMP

   B. FTP

   C. ARP

   D. HTML

4. You are transmitting data to another computer over the Internet. Which layer of the TCP/IP conceptual model is responsible for putting frames of data onto the transmission wire?

   A. Application

   B. Transport

   C. Internet

   D. Network

5. You are configuring your e-mail client. Which of the following protocols are generally used for outgoing mail?

   A. POP3

   B. SMTP

   C. HTTP

   D. FTP

6. You are configuring your e-mail client. Which of the following protocols are generally used for incoming mail?

   A. POP3

   B. SMTP

   C. STMP

   D. HTTP

7. A person wants to access the Internet and browse Web pages without incurring the expense of purchasing a computer. Which of the following can she purchase and use to access the World Wide Web?

   A. WebTV

   B. WebTV for Windows

   C. Internet phone

   D. Cellular phone

8. A user who is new to the Internet needs to access the certification information on the Web page of a particular Web site. Into which of the following would you instruct him to type the URL of the site he wishes to visit?

    A. The DOS prompt

    B. The address bar

    C. The address prompt

    D. The Favorites or Bookmark menu

9. You have accessed an FTP site through the command prompt of your computer. Once finished browsing the site, you now want to terminate your session with the FTP server. However, in doing so, you do not want to exit back to the DOS prompt. Which of the following commands could you use? (Choose all that apply.)

    A. bye

    B. close

    C. disconnect

    D. lcd

10. You access an FTP site from the command prompt of your computer. Which of the following commands would you use to view the contents of files and directories on the remote computer? (Choose all that apply.)

    A. dir

    B. lcd

    C. ls

    D. cd

11. You are browsing an FTP site, and have found files you wish to download to your computer. Which of the following commands could be used to receive a file or files from this FTP server? (Choose all that apply.)

    A. get

    B. mget

    C. put

    D. mput

12. A user complains that he can't connect to the network and access your corporate intranet. As such, he can't access the Web pages on the intranet site containing information required for his work. You check the TCP/IP properties for the user and see the window shown next. Assuming the computer is set to use static IP addresses and this default subnet mask, why can't this user connect to the network to access your intranet?

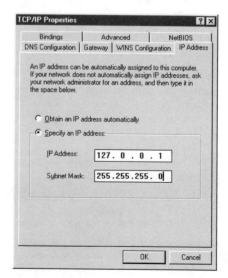

A. The IP address is incorrect.

B. The subnet mask is incorrect.

C. DHCP isn't set.

D. DNS needs to be configured.

13. A user has an IP address of 201.200.50.6 and a subnet mask of 255.255.255.0. This user attempts to access an intranet Web server with the IP address 201.200.79.4. What will happen?

   A. The request for the Web page will be routed through the default gateway.

   B. The request for the Web page won't be routed through the default gateway, as it is on the same network as this computer.

   C. The user won't be able to access the Web site, because he has an invalid IP address.

   D. The user won't be able to access the Web site, because he has an invalid subnet mask.

14. You are configuring a user's computer to access your corporate intranet on a TCP/IP network. Which of the following can be used to resolve the Web site's name of www.myweb.net to an IP address? (Choose all that apply.)

   A. DNS

   B. WINS

   C. Default gateway

   D. HOSTS file

15. Your company has 300 users who work over three shifts. You have a limited number of IP addresses that won't cover the number of computers used on the busiest shift. Fortunately, not all of the users access the intranet at the same time. Which of the following will you use so that users will be able to access the intranet?

   A. DNS

   B. DHCP

   C. WINS

   D. Static IP addresses

16. You have just added an intranet Web server to your local area network. You want users on the network to be able to enter a domain name in the address bar of their browser to access the site. However, as it is a small network, you don't want to add additional server applications to process the domain name and provide the proper IP address. Which of the following will you use to resolve the domain name to an IP address?

   A. DNS

   B. DHCP

   C. WINS

   D. HOSTS files

17. A user is complaining that it is taking a long time to access a regularly used server. The server the user is accessing is your intranet Web server that everyone on the network uses. You think the problem might be the HOSTS file. Which of the

following should you check when reading the HOSTS file?

A. The most commonly used domain names appear as the bottommost entries in the file.

B. The most commonly used domain names appear as the topmost entries in the file.

C. The HOSTS file is updated with the domain name on the intranet server, and not on each computer in the network.

D. The distributed database making up the HOSTS file has been replicated across the network.

18. You are setting up an Internet station at a local library. This particular Internet computer is meant for children, and the library wants to keep small children from viewing sexual material over the Net. What can you do to prevent objectionable material from being viewed through Internet Explorer on this computer?

A. Set the level of Security on the Security tab of Internet options to High.

B. Configure the Content Advisor settings on the Content tab of Internet Options.

C. Configure Connection settings on the Connection tab of Internet Options not to connect to such sites.

D. Nothing. There are no settings to control this.

SELF TEST ANSWERS

1. **A.** TCP/IP is the protocol used on the Internet, and commonly used as the protocol on large area networks. TCP/IP is a suite of protocols, so you only need to install TCP/IP for all of the protocols to be installed.
   B, C, and **D** are incorrect. Because TCP/IP is a suite of protocols, each of these will be installed when TCP/IP is installed. You don't need to install each individual protocol, just TCP/IP.

2. **B.** HTTP, or the Hypertext Transfer Protocol. This is the client/server protocol used by the World Wide Web. This protocol is used by Internet browsers to retrieve HTML (Hypertext Markup Language) documents from Web servers, and by Web servers to send Web pages.
   A is incorrect. HTML is the Hypertext Markup Language used to create Web pages; it is not a protocol. **C** is incorrect. FTP is a protocol designed for the download of files from Internet sites. **D** is also incorrect. Gopher is similar to FTP, and is used to search and retrieve files from an Internet site. Using the Gopher service, ISPs can create links to other servers, annotate files and directories, and create custom menus for use by Gopher clients.

3. **B.** FTP, or the File Transfer Protocol. FTP was developed to transfer files between computers on a TCP/IP network. For example, if you wanted to download a program from an Internet site, FTP could be used to send the file to your computer. Although it is an older protocol, it is still commonly used on the Internet.
   A is incorrect. The Internet Control Message Protocol, or ICMP, is used to send messages and report errors on the delivery of packets. **C** is also incorrect. ARP (Address Resolution Protocol) is used to obtain the hardware addresses of hosts located on the same physical network. **D** is incorrect because HTML isn't a protocol; it is the Hypertext Markup Language, which is used to create Web pages.

4. **D.** The Network layer is where the packet of data is passed from the network card or modem onto the transmission wire. It is at this point that the data has passed from the Internet server or client and is on its way to the receiving computer.
   A is incorrect. The Application layer is where applications gain access to a network. This is the layer in which your Internet client or an Internet server accesses the services and utilities provided by TCP/IP. **B** is incorrect. The Transport layer provides communication sessions between computers. **C** is also incorrect. The

Internet layer encapsulates packets in code to provide addressing and routing information. This gives the packet the information necessary to route packets between computers and networks.

5. **B.** The Simple Message Transfer Protocol, or SMTP, is most often used as the protocol for outgoing mail. In other words, when you send e-mail, SMTP is the protocol generally used.
   A is incorrect. POP3 is the protocol often used on the receiving end of e-mail messages. POP3 is an acronym for Post Office Protocol 3, and is often used to receive and store mail. **C** is incorrect. HTTP is the Hypertext Transfer Protocol, which is used by browsers and servers for requesting and transferring Web pages. **D** is also incorrect. FTP is the File Transfer Protocol, and is primarily used for transferring files—such as during the download of programs—between a server and an Internet client.

6. **A.** The Post Office Protocol 3, or POP3, is often used to receive and store mail. While both SMTP and POP3 have the ability to both send and receive mail, POP3 is most often used for incoming mail, as it has improved abilities for queuing messages.
   B is incorrect. The Simple Message Transfer Protocol, or SMTP, is a common protocol used for sending e-mail messages. SMTP has a limited ability to queue messages; as such, it is generally used for outgoing e-mail. **C** is incorrect because there is no protocol called STMP. **D** is also incorrect. HTTP is the Hypertext Transfer Protocol, and is used by browsers and servers for requesting and transferring Web pages.

7. **A.** WebTV allows users to browse the World Wide Web without the use of a computer. WebTV consists of a box that's similar to a cable TV box, and a remote control. The user's television set is used as a display device. The control allows users to browse the Web through the box, which provides the means of connecting to the Internet.
   B is incorrect because WebTV for Windows is software that's available with Windows 98. This requires you to have a computer, and a connection to the Internet. **C** is incorrect. Internet phone is a way of talking with other people who have an Internet phone over the Internet. It doesn't have the ability to browse Web pages. **D** is also incorrect because—although some cell phones provide e-mail services, or a way of connecting to a computer's modem—cellular phones don't have the ability in themselves to browse Web pages.

8. **B.** The address bar is used to enter the URL or address of the Web site you wish to visit. In this bar, you type in the Web site address, and after pressing ENTER on your

keyboard or clicking Go to the right of the address bar, that Web site's default page will appear in the main browser window.

A is incorrect because Web pages are graphical and cannot be accessed by entering URLs from the DOS prompt. If you attempt to enter a Web site address from the command prompt, you will receive a bad command or filename error. **C** is incorrect because there is no such thing as the "address prompt." **D** is also incorrect. The Favorites or Bookmark menu of a browser is used to store links to visited sites; it is not used to navigate to sites you haven't yet visited.

9. **B, C.** The close and disconnect commands can both be used to terminate a session with an FTP server. In using these commands, the session is terminated, but the user isn't returned to the DOS prompt. This enables him or her to continue working from the FTP prompt.

    A is incorrect because the bye command terminates the session and exits the user back to the DOS prompt. This question states that this was not to happen when the session was terminated. **D** is incorrect because lcd is used to change the local working directory, which is the directory on your local hard disk.

10. **A, C.** The dir and ls commands provide identical functionality when viewing the contents of a directory on a remote computer. The dir command works the same as if you were browsing directories on your local hard disk from a command prompt. The ls command is unique to FTP, but also enables you to list files and directories on the remote computer.

    B is incorrect because lcd is used to change the local working directory. This is the directory on your local hard disk, not the directory on the remote computer. **D** is also incorrect. The cd command is used to change directories on the remote computer. It allows you to navigate the FTP site, but doesn't display the contents of a directory.

11. **A, B.** The get and mget commands are both used to receive or download files from a remote computer. The get command is used to get a file from the server. If you wish to receive multiple files from the remote computer, you could use the mget command.

    C is incorrect because put is used to send or upload a file to a remote computer; in other words, it puts the file on the FTP server. If you wish to send multiple files to the remote computer, you could use the mput command. **D** is also incorrect.

12. **A.** The IP address is incorrect. Some IP addresses cannot be used on a network. IP addresses cannot start with the numbers 127, as these are used for loopback functions.

In this case, 127.0.01 is being used, so TCP/IP would loop any packets back to your computer.
B is incorrect because the question asks you to assume that the subnet mask is correct. **C** is incorrect because the question states that static IP addresses are used. As such, DHCP wouldn't be implemented. **D** is incorrect because this wouldn't keep the user from connecting to the network. If DNS isn't set, the user would be unable to resolve names to IP addresses.

13. **A.** The request will be routed through the default gateway. The default gateway is a computer that handles forwarding data to other segments of a network. In this case, the user has an IP address of 201.200.50.6 and a subnet mask of 255.255.255.0. This means the network ID is 201.200.50 and the host ID is 6. The network the user is trying to connect to has a network ID of 201.200.79, meaning that it will need to be passed through the default gateway.
    B is incorrect because the Web server is located on a remote network. **C** is also incorrect because the user does have a valid IP address. IP addresses can't begin with 127, or consist of all 0's or 255's. This isn't the case with this user's IP. **D** is incorrect because the user does have a valid subnet mask. Subnet masks block part of the IP address to define the network ID and host ID. The 255's of this address designate the network ID, and the final 0 designates the host ID.

14. **A, B, D.** DNS, WINS, and the HOSTS file can all be used for name resolution on a TCP/IP network, allowing the intranet's Web server domain name to be resolved to an IP address. DNS is the Domain Name System, and was developed as a distributed database for identifying domains and hosts on the Internet. WINS is the Windows Internet Name Service, and gives Windows NT Servers the ability to resolve NetBIOS computer names on a TCP/IP network. The HOSTS file allows you to configure each computer that will access the intranet site so that it can resolve the domain name to an IP address.
    C is incorrect. The default gateway address specifies which server will forward data to remote networks; it isn't used for name resolution.

15. **B.** DHCP is the Dynamic Host Configuration Protocol. With this, computers are leased IP addresses when they connect to the network. This will enable the users on the network to have IP addresses. Computers not connected to the network that have IP addresses that are needed by others will lose their lease to an IP address.
    A and **C** are incorrect because WINS and DNS are used for name resolution. They

don't control who has which IP address. **D** is incorrect because there aren't enough IP addresses for all computers on the network. As such, not everyone will be able to access the network from every machine.

16. **D.** HOSTS files are static files that map hostnames to IP addresses, and are an ideal choice for small networks when you don't want to use server applications to resolve domain names to IP addresses. With HOSTS files, a file on each workstation is updated with the IP address and domain or hostname that will be accessed. When new hosts are added to a network, the HOSTS file isn't automatically updated. You need to open the HOSTS file manually and then add the new host or domain name to the file.
    A is incorrect because Domain Name System (DNS) servers must be added to the network to resolve domain names to IP addresses—not a desired result. **B** is incorrect because DHCP (Dynamic Host Configuration Protocol) isn't used to resolve domain names to IP addresses. **C** is also incorrect. WINS (Windows Internet Name Service) must be added to the network to resolve domain names to IP addresses—not a desired result.

17. **B.** The most commonly used domain names appear as the topmost entries in the file. When the host or domain name is entered into a browser, or used by another application on that computer, it checks the local HOSTS file for the proper IP address. Because the HOSTS file is read in a linear fashion, the most commonly accessed domain and hostnames should appear at the top of the file. This will allow the application to find the host or domain name more quickly.
    A is incorrect because the HOSTS file is read in a linear fashion. Therefore, the most commonly used entries should appear toward the top of the file, not at the bottom. **C** is incorrect because the HOSTS file needs to be located with updated entries on each of the workstations on the network. Each computer that will access sites in the HOSTS file will need a HOSTS file. **D** is incorrect because the HOSTS file is a static file appearing on each computer on the network; it is not a distributed database.

18. **B.** The Content Advisor settings available through the Content tab of Internet Options is used to control what users can view through the browser. RSACi (Recreational Software Advisory Council for the Internet services) allows Web page authors to have their pages rated in much the same way that movies are rated. By clicking Enable, you can control whether browser users can view different levels of

sex, violence, language, and nudity. After setting the levels of content that can be viewed, you can enter a password to keep other users from changing these settings. **A** is incorrect because the security settings on the Security tab of Internet Options controls security issues in the browser. This controls what the browser can do, not what the browser can view. **C** is also incorrect because the Connection tab is used to configure Internet connections, not content that can be viewed. **D** is incorrect because recent versions of Internet Explorer provide the ability to control viewable content.

i-Net+™

COMPUTING TECHNOLOGY INDUSTRY ASSOCIATION®

4

i-Net Client Security, Troubleshooting, and MIME

CERTIFICATION OBJECTIVES

4.01	MIME Types and Their Components
4.02	Issues Related to Legacy Clients
4.03	Value of Patches and Updates to Client Software, and Associated Problems
4.04	Advantages and Disadvantages of Using a Cookie, and How to Set Cookies

This chapter discusses various TCP/IP clients, including those you use to collect e-mail, browse the Web, and generally conduct business over the Internet. You will learn more about each, as well as about how Multipurpose Internet Mail Extensions (MIME) form the backbone of the client/server relationship when it comes to e-mail and Web transactions with a browser. In this chapter, you will learn about how MIME originated and how it works today. You will learn how to customize the way your Web browser handles MIME extensions, as well as how to handle problems presented by older Web browsers and e-mail clients. You will learn more about the various types of clients that use TCP/IP, as well as issues regarding legacy clients, updating clients, and security. Finally, you will learn about the nature and purpose of cookies, and how they can help a Web server maintain state, track users, and make a Web session more interactive.

MIME Types and Their Components

MIME establishes standard ways a Web server can deliver files to a client for easy, automatic reading. Back in 1982, RFC822 defined the standard format for text-based e-mail sent via SMTP. This standard was sufficient then, but with the advent of HTML-based e-mail and increasingly sophisticated users of e-mail, the IETF had to either build a new standard, or extend the new one. It decided to extend the existing standard by issuing RFCs 1521 and 1522. These extensions allow more freedom concerning what can be transferred via e-mail. RFC 1521 shows how users can create e-mail messages that use more sophisticated ASCII text but are still compatible with older systems. Because RFC 1521 extends e-mail, yet makes sure these e-mail extensions are backward compatible, the new standard is called the Multipurpose Mail Extensions. RFC 1522 brought even more flexibility to e-mail by allowing users to send non-ASCII text.

Many MIME types exist. The most common are

■ Audio, such as RealAudio

- Video, including RealPlayer, Windows Media Player, QuickTime, and so forth
- Images, including GIF and JPEG
- Virtual Reality Modeling Languages (VRML)
- ASCII Text Readers
- Applications, including Telnet, FTP, IRC Chat, ICQ and Instance Messenger, and NNTP (Network News)

Note that the original purpose of MIME was to extend the capability of e-mail clients and servers. Over the years, however, Web clients and servers have adopted MIME, as well, because it allows them to handle various document types efficiently. All a Webmaster has to do is define a new MIME type, and the Web server will process the MIME type automatically. Once a Webmaster defines a MIME type, the server automatically inserts a special header in the first packets sent during a Web session. Any client that recognizes this MIME type as found in the header sent by the server will automatically choose the correct application to handle that file. If the MIME type is correctly defined in the Web browser, the browser will open the proper application on the fly. However, you will have to define the MIME type in the browser if it has not already been defined for you.

You should consider MIME to be one of the ultimate examples of the client/server model: the server handles some of the processing task, then sends that information to the client so that it can finish the job.

Can a Client Understand Various E-mail Types?

A client will only understand those e-mail or MIME types that are clearly defined. This is why Web browsers such as Netscape Navigator and Microsoft Internet Explorer either use separate e-mail applications or bundle in their own e-mail clients. Most applications, however, use MIME to ensure compatibility. Although a Web server uses MIME to help browsers launch applications by sending information in an HTTP header, e-mail clients do not receive such help from e-mail servers. Rather, the sending and the receiving e-mail clients must be able to exchange formats that are compatible with each other. The Post Office Protocol 3 (POP3) server that stores and forwards e-mail does not use MIME to format messages to the client. Therefore, if you have a client that is not capable of reading the e-mail message sent by your friend, you will not be able to read the message automatically and will have to find an alternative way to read it. In some cases, you won't be able to read the message at all.

Like all modern e-mail clients, Microsoft Outlook has ways to configure itself to receive MIME extensions. First, go to Tools | Options, and you will see the dialog box shown in Figure 4-1.

Click the Mail Format tab; then click the Settings dialog box. Doing so will then present the Plain Text Settings dialog box, shown in Figure 4-2.

FIGURE 4-1

Selecting Plain Text Options in Microsoft Outlook 98

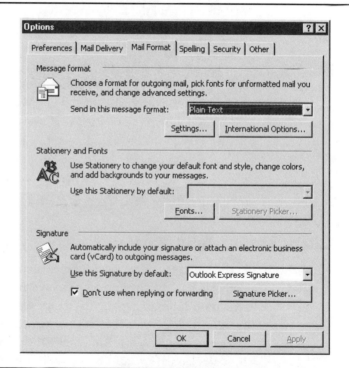

FIGURE 4-2

FIGURE 4-2

The Plain Text Settings dialog box in Microsoft Outlook 97

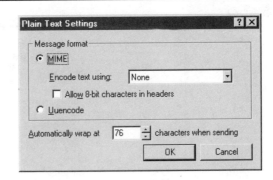

You then have the choice of using standard MIME, or using older 8-bit characters in the headers.

It is possible that a test question will focus on what will happen when a Web browser or e-mail client can't understand a MIME type. For example, older e-mail clients will not be able to process HTML messages, because they do not have a MIME extension to automatically process e-mail. One possible result will be that the e-mail message will get bounced back by an older e-mail server. Another is that the e-mail message will come through, but only as an attachment that you will have to read with a browser.

Defining MIME File Types for Special Download Procedures

For a Web browser, you define MIME types by creating name/value pairs. Figure 4-3 shows the MIME definition for the GIF file type.

The name/value pair for the GIF MIME type is image/gif. It is standard behavior for a Web server to send the image/gif pair in the header, where the browser automatically renders any GIF image with its own internal reader. A Web browser will do the same thing with a document, as well.

FIGURE 4-3

The MIME Type for GIF
Images in Netscape
Communicator 4.5

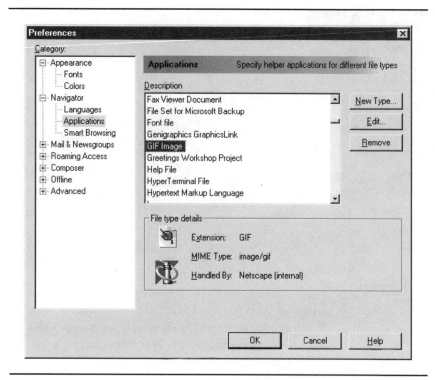

Figure 4-4 shows how Netscape Navigator can automatically process
a Word file by having Microsoft Word launch.

You can also define your own MIME types if you have the proper
information. In Netscape Navigator, for example, you can go into the
Preferences | Applications section and then create your own MIME type.
Now that you understand some of these concepts, let's take a look at
a popular browser and see how it deploys the MIME standard.

EXERCISE 4-1

MIME Types and Their Components

1. Open up Netscape Navigator.

2. Go to Edit | Preferences.

FIGURE 4-4

The Defined MIME Types
for Word Files in Netscape
Communicator 4.5

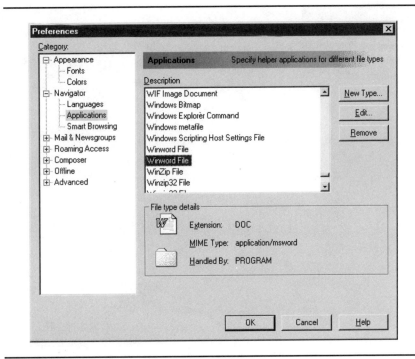

3. Your screen should resemble Figure 4-5.

4. Click in the Applications area, which lies immediately beneath the Navigator section.

5. You should see a long list of applications that Navigator is preconfigured to recognize.

6. Scroll down the Applications window to view the entries, which are arranged alphabetically.

7. Find the GIF Image entry. Notice that it is registered to Netscape as a reader. Note that if you go to the TIF entry, you should find another program, perhaps Paint Shop, Photo Shop, or a Microsoft program that is registered to read this file. This is because the only Web-ready image formats are JPEG, GIF, and PNG.

8. Highlight the GIF Image entry.

FIGURE 4-5

The Netscape Preferences dialog box for Communicator 4.5

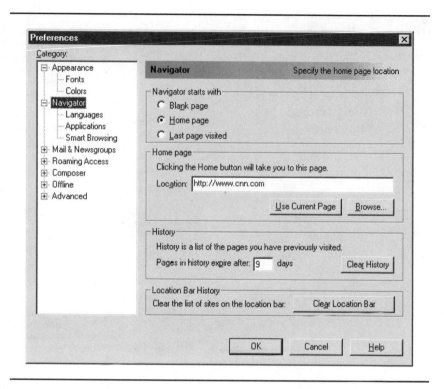

9. After you have highlighted the GIF Image entry, select the Edit button.

10. You now have the option of editing this entry for the Netscape browser.

11. Notice that this image is handled by Navigator. If you wished to, you could change the Handled By entry so that all GIF images downloaded to Navigator could be handled by another application. This would be a mistake, however, because this would render Navigator incapable of handling GIF images internally. So leave these settings at their default by clicking Cancel.

12. Find the Text Document entry. Notice that it has no MIME type enabled. This is because Netscape assigns its own reader for all ASCII text files.

FROM THE CLASSROOM

One of the more confusing elements in regards to MIME is that students think that MIME applies only to e-mail servers and clients. It does not. In fact, you will find that Web servers and Web browsers implement sophisticated MIME implementations.

Arguably, the most sophisticated e-mail use of MIME is the Secure MIME (S/MIME) implementation, which allows users to encrypt e-mail messages to recipients.

—*James Stanger, MCSE, MCT, CIW*

on the **job** *You will find that many end users will try to customize these entries and cause problems with their browsers. Should you run into such problems, you can now fix them quickly.*

CERTIFICATION OBJECTIVE 4.02

Issues Related to Legacy Clients

Two types of legacy clients exist. The first type of legacy client is an application that was widely used before the Internet became popular. The second type of legacy client is an older application, such as the original version of Navigator, or an older e-mail program. Although such applications are clearly Internet-oriented, they nevertheless represent older technology. Thus far you have learned about e-mail and HTML clients. However, many different types of legacy clients use TCP/IP. These include

- The Winsock 1.0 TCP/IP stack, including Windows 95 Dialup Networking (DUN)
- Telnet (VT100 terminal emulator)
- IBM's Systems Network Architecture (SNA) connections (3270 terminal emulator)

Winsock TCP/IP Stack

Older TCP/IP stacks, such as the Windows 95 Dialup Networking (DUN) 1.0, have a variety of issues that make connecting to servers more difficult. These include

- **Slower dial-up access speeds**   The packet size in the original DUN is the same for both PPP and LAN connections. This is no problem if you plan on connecting via an Ethernet connection, or even through a high-speed connection (128 Kbps or higher). However, if you connect using a modem using the original DUN version, your speed will be slower, because packet sizes will always be about 1,500 bits, the same size as if you were making a LAN connection.

- **Compression issues**   Older networking does not support dial-up compression as well, which means slower connection speeds. Also, if the server is using an older stack, it is possible that it will not be compatible with hosts using newer stacks.

- **Encryption**   Older clients use weaker encryption. Older stacks, for example, have a tendency to use simplistic encryption schemes, such as reusing keys. Once you reuse a key, you make it possible for a hacker to crack your encryption scheme and obtain access to your information.

- **Logging**   Older IP stacks do not support logging at the PPP level.

Telnet

It is possible to use Telnet to connect to many older sites. Telnet applications allow you to access a particular machine using a character-based interface. You can use Telnet, for example, to edit files on a UNIX server. For example, many libraries and organizations allow you to connect to sites via Telnet. Whenever you access a system via Telnet, you are said to open a virtual terminal. Many older UNIX servers provide what are called shell accounts. A shell account is the predecessor to modern Point-to-Point Protocol (PPP) accounts. Normally, you would have to use Telnet or a terminal program to access this type of account. Although such accounts are older, they still provide e-mail, Telnet, FTP, and Gopher services. You should note, however, that you can use Telnet for many different very current applications, as well. For example, if you wish to log in to a modern UNIX server remotely, Telnet is a common way to do so.

IBM SNA

You have another way to access legacy sites. Using IBM's Host On Demand program, you can gain access to Systems Network Architecture (SNA) hosts from your Web browser. SNA is an old IBM mainframe network structure that is still quite common, because many companies invested in it in the 1970s and 1980s. Host On Demand can run from either Netscape Navigator or Microsoft Internet Explorer. All you have to do is install it. Once you click a hyperlink that takes you to a SNA host, you see a login screen. Once there, you can then log in and start a 3270 session. Just as with Telnet, once you establish this session, you can access company assets as if you were directly accessing them. Host On Demand keeps the session alive even if you use your browser to go to additional Web pages.

Checking Revision Date

You have to ensure that your software tools suit your needs. It is important that you understand exactly what version you and your clients are using. Checking revision dates will help you do this. For example, many software applications ship with bugs, which are defects in the software. A system bug can merely be annoying, such as when a program contains a spelling error, or a broken part of a user interface. System bugs can also be quite dangerous, because they can either cause system crashes, resulting in loss of productivity, or they can lead to security problems. When a vendor discovers or decides to act upon a bug release, many times it will issue a bug report.

Such bug reports generally cover only certain versions of the service, application, or file. Unless you understand exactly which version you have, you will waste a lot of time trying to update systems that do not require it. For example, when Microsoft issued its "Second Version" of Windows 98, it no longer needed any remedial Year 2000 updates. This surprised many IT professionals who did not keep track of version levels.

Most operating systems and their components get upgraded regularly. UNIX sendmail and bind (DNS) packages have a long history of upgrades and fixes. As of this writing, Windows NT Server 4.0 has been through six service packs, as well as innumerable hot fixes intended to provide the best services. It is your responsibility to discover and document the revision dates of your software.

Manufacturer/Vendor

As you obtain new software meant to enhance your client or server, make sure that you receive it from a reputable vendor. Likewise, make sure that you purchase manufacturer software from a reputable dealer. Many times companies have purchased what they thought was legitimate software, when in fact it was pirated and illegally sold by a third party. Such practices lead not only to licensing issues, but also to support and security problems. If you require support for your products, you will get little or none unless you are careful to purchase software from a reputable place that will stand by warranty guarantees.

Security problems that can arise include the possibility that pirated software can contain viruses, as well as other problems that can compromise your network.

Troubleshooting and Performance Issues

Older clients generally have the following problems:

- Lack of work-saving features
- Incompatible protocols and procedures
- Slower performance

Although some newer clients add unnecessary bells and whistles that end users sometimes have to wade through in order to get to the important items, newer clients are generally the result of detailed research that makes them better. Older clients often use older protocol versions, as well as older compression and encryption techniques that can lead to problems. You should consider that older clients tend to work more slowly than their newer counterparts. The chief issues concerning older clients include

- Lack of vendor support in case of an issue
- Problems with operating system interoperability, including Y2K issues

As you troubleshoot client problems, you will have to make sure that you understand the vendor and version exactly. Otherwise, your diagnosis may be wildly inaccurate. For example, as you approach an end user, make sure that you find out what version of the program she is running. In applications running in Windows, you can usually do this by checking the Help menu in the dialog box. You should also ask whether the application has ever worked before. Try to determine what the end user or another employee did to cause the problem.

Make sure that you do not rush in and change settings and install new programs before you are sure you understand the problem at hand.

Compatibility Issues

It is likely that people who hold on to older clients tend to cause interoperability problems. For example, when Microsoft Word 97 came out, the default files it created were incompatible with Microsoft Word 95 documents. Similarly, e-mail clients that cannot handle HTML attachments can cause problems, because it is possible that some employees will not get all of the information they need via e-mail.

Consider what may happen if you upgrade your servers so that they no longer work with older clients. Consider further that some of your remote sales force will keep using an older TCP/IP stack, or other connectivity software. Even though most server-side software is in fact backward compatible, this is not always the case. Unless you consider backward compatibility and the need to communicate upgrades carefully, you may end up costing your business valuable productivity time.

For example, when you think about using MIME extensions on your Web server, you should take note of the fact that older clients may not be able to handle them. Although it is possible for users to modify their clients by creating new MIME types, it is not likely that the average end user can do this. Even if a particular person can, remember that few people will want to go through that type of inconvenience. Nevertheless, you should always consider legacy Web and e-mail client issues. The Internet solves many of these compatibility issues by using open standards like HTTP and HTML, so that any Web browser can access information across heterogeneous networks.

Value of Patches and Updates to Client Software, and Associated Problems

You have already read about the importance of keeping up to date with the revision dates of your software and with product updates. Vendors release updates and patches for four major reasons:

- The product originally shipped with a flaw that could not be fixed in time.
- A previously overlooked problem was discovered.
- The vendor invented or adopted a new, popular technology, and wishes to update the operating system, service, or application.
- New hacker techniques make existing practices untenable.

Older Windows TCP/IP stacks had problems that allowed hackers to guess how TCP connections were made, allowing hackers to defeat security. Microsoft has been able to issue some patches to solve this problem. Before hacking techniques became so sophisticated, it was acceptable for Microsoft to allow machines to downgrade network encryption so that they could communicate with older LAN Manager servers by sending authentication information in cleartext. However, Microsoft has issued fixes for this problem.

Desktop Security

When it comes to desktop security, you can do more than you think to make sure your information stays as private as possible. This includes the use of screen savers, password protection, security policies, and anti-virus programs. For example, you can have a screen saver activate a number of minutes after your computer senses it is idle. The computer senses whether it is idle by counting the number of minutes that no input has been received from the keyboard or the mouse. Depending upon the system, you can set a password-protected screen saver to activate any number of minutes after the computer senses inactivity.

Most end users are accustomed to security policies that require minimum password length, as well as the additional requirement to change passwords every so often. Sometimes companies require a third element, which is that you can't reuse a password. In some cases, company servers keep a password history that does not allow you to reuse the last three passwords you have chosen. In other words, if you used "howd7d**dy" as a password three months ago, and $c00bidoo for the password last month, you could not use these again. This is referred to as password aging.

Security policies are meant to decrease the likelihood of a hacker's guessing passwords, or being able to crack the passwords of files and packets he or she may have captured. However, when it comes to desktop security, such practices can be disastrous, because end users often write down passwords and keep them in or near their desks. Some will try to hide passwords on the bottom of computer keyboards, or place them on the inside of the computer desk. Still others just give up and write them down on sticky notes and paste them directly to their monitor. Clearly, this type of desktop security is a problem. As an IT professional, you do not want your users to employ such means. One way to keep users practicing safe computing is to create a reasonable security policy. Don't make your security policy too strict. Otherwise, you will end up frustrating users, who will then take the shortcuts listed here.

Another way to ensure that the desktop area is secure is to use password-protected screen savers. This is especially important in well-traveled areas, such as where the receptionist keeps her computer and where it is easy for others to have access to this computer while the receptionist is on break or at lunch. Other ways to ensure desktop security include

- Password-protecting the computer at boot time using CMOS passwords
- Physically securing the CPU so that it can't just "walk away"
- Enforcing username and password-based logins on computers with multiple users

If you take these precautions, you will be able to increase the security of your business.

Virus Protection

Another aspect of desktop security is making sure that computers are protected from computer viruses. A virus is a miniprogram specially designed to interrupt the normal workings of your computer. Some viruses are merely annoying, whereas others are truly destructive. You will learn more about viruses in Chapter 12. The i-Net+ exam, however, will cover ways that you can protect your clients, and one of these is to install anti-virus software. Of course, the best way to protect yourself against a virus is to install a virus program directly on the computer. Here is a partial list of several popular anti-virus vendors:

- Norton AntiVirus (http://www.norton.com)
- PCcillin (http://www.pccillin.com)
- McAfee VirusScan (http://www.mcafee.com)

Regardless of vendor, anti-virus programs require constant updates because hackers are always developing new viruses. Make sure that you update the clients as often as possible. Otherwise, the machines on your network will not be protected. Anti-virus programs can protect only against viruses that they know about; therefore, if you don't update your anti-virus program, it won't be able to protect you.

Other Client-Side Security Threats

ActiveX, Java, and JavaScript applications can present serious security problems. This is especially the case if the end user is not properly educated, or if you or the end user have left e-mail and browser security settings at a low level. ActiveX and Java programs are not dangerous in and of themselves. However, it is possible to develop malicious programs. ActiveX programs have the ability to run with full permissions on your server. This means that someone can create an ActiveX control that, for example, deletes files or crashes your computer. Because ActiveX controls have no built-in security measures, the control can easily cause damage. Such was the case with an old ActiveX control named Internet Exploder. This program crashed the computer upon which it was activated.

Java applets, however, have somewhat more rigorous security measures. Whenever they are run within a Web browser, Java applets are sandboxed, which means they run in their own memory space. Furthermore, sandboxed Java applets can't write directly to the hard drive, nor can they make direct system calls. However, just because Java applets are sandboxed when they are run within a browser, this does not mean that all Java applets and applications are safe. Furthermore, you should understand that the Java language itself is not sandboxed. It is possible to execute Java programs and applets outside the sandboxed Java Virtual Machine in a browser. As a result, Java can become dangerous.

Some anti-virus programs will check Java and ActiveX applications to see whether they have been granted too much access. Nevertheless, you should consider such threats when securing your desktop.

Encryption Levels

All well-known e-mail and World Wide Web clients allow for encryption. Each, however, uses different levels and types of encryption. You should make sure that your clients constantly update their ability to use strong encryption for two reasons:

■ Stronger encryption provides more data confidentiality.

■ If end users fail to upgrade their clients, they may not be able to communicate securely with the rest of the world. Encryption upgrades tend to have problems with backward compatibility. Therefore, updates are essential.

In regard to encryption levels, most agencies, organizations, and vendors use one of four simple types:

■ **None**   This setting does not encrypt data at all.

■ **Trivial**   Although this encryption level does encrypt data, the means of encryption is so weak that almost any application, such as a network sniffer, can decrypt it on the fly.

■ **Moderate**   Packets are encrypted, but with an algorithm that can be broken by a standard computer (for example, a Pentium II 450MHz box) within a period of days. The key length for this type of encryption might be 40 bits. At one time, the United States required all for-export software to allow only 4-bit encryption.

■ **Strong**   Transmissions are encrypted using a key length of at least 128 bits. A key at least this long helps ensure that the only way to break the encryption in a reasonable period of time (say, in less than several months or even years) would be to use a supercomputer. This would cost millions of dollars. Another way to break such code would be to engage in a sophisticated parallel processing scheme, whereby lower-powered computers would work together to crack the keys. At one time, various governments, including that of the United States, had rules against exporting software capable of over 40-bit encryption.

You can use different types of encryption algorithms. These include

- **Rot13** An easily broken encryption scheme. This symmetric key algorithm uses a substitution scheme whereby each letter in the text is replaced by a letter that is 13 characters down the alphabet. For example, the word "romanticism" would become "ebznagvqvfz." Rot13 is short for "rotate alphabet 13 places."

- **DES** A popular symmetric key algorithm adopted by the U.S. government and widely used by many applications.

- **Triple DES** A more secure variant of DES that is also quite popular.

- **RSA** An asymmetric key algorithm that ensures data secrecy across public networks. SSL, for example, uses this algorithm.

- **MD5** A one-way algorithm that you can use to sign documents or create hash code. This algorithm is quite popular.

- **SHA** Another one-way algorithm that you can use to sign documents or create hash code. This is also quite popular.

It is also possible to use these encryption types to encrypt transmissions at different layers of the Open Systems Interconnection model (OSI). The OSI model is a seven-layer model meant to describe how network hosts communicate with each other:

- **Application layer** You can use Secure MIME (S/MIME) or Pretty Good Privacy (PGP) to encrypt e-mail applications.

- **Session layer** You can use Secure Sockets Layer to encrypt Web-based transmissions.

- **Transport layer** Secure Shell (SSH) is an application meant to replace Telnet and the UNIX "rlogin" programs. SSH uses public key cryptography to ensure data remains encrypted.

- **Network layer** A virtual private network (VPN) allows you to encrypt all network communications.

Web Browsers

A Web browser is one of the killer apps in use today. It is arguably only slightly less critical than an e-mail client. Because of its popularity, most vendors, including Microsoft and Netscape, have experienced tremendous pressure to produce the latest and greatest versions. You will learn about e-mail clients in the next section. A Web browser is a key tool because it is possible to use it as a thin client in an Internet, intranet, and extranet setting. A thin client is a client that you can install and use on multiple platforms to access complex applications, services, and servers that reside on the back end (that is, on the server side). Thin clients are less expensive and require less maintenance than PCs.

Before the advent of the Web browser, you had to install a specific client for a specific server. In other words, if you wished to access a database at one time, you generally had to use a dedicated database client. This meant that companies had to develop new software for each application. However, using a Web browser you can access sophisticated back-end solutions such as Web servers and application servers. An application server is a server-side service that runs as middleware between the Web server and a database. Therefore, a Web browser forms a part, or tier, of a rather sophisticated networking solution. In two-tier computing, a back-end server processes all data and allows the client (that is, the Web browser) to format the information on a screen. In three-tier networking, the processing is divided among a client that renders information on the screen; a server that processes information, called business logic; and a database server. Business logic refers to the ability to format data and process it for delivery to a client, such as a Web browser. The practice called *n-tier computing* involves using a client, several servers that distribute the business logic function, and a database. The use of middleware allows a Web browser to access many services, including

- Legacy systems, including CICS servers and mainframes
- Intranet solutions
- SNA networks

Figure 4-6 shows what happens in a typical n-tier transaction. First, a Web client makes a request. It is received by the Web server, which then distributes part of that load to an application server—which, for the purposes of the exam, can be said to help process the business logic. The process is then passed on to the database server that contains the data stores.

Once the data is received, the n-tier architecture then sends the data back to be rendered in the browser.

Therefore, a Web browser is something more than a simple application you use to access Yahoo! or Amazon.com. It has become a key business tool. In order to take advantage of the latest connectivity options a browser

FIGURE 4-6

A typical n-tier transaction

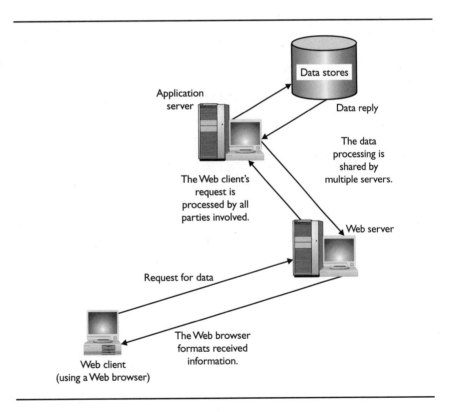

has to offer, you generally need to upgrade your browser. Browser upgrades generally bring these benefits:

- More support for advanced and legacy applications and servers

- Support for more MIME types, including the ability to render XML and PNG graphics, and automatically load advanced audio and video formats

- More sophisticated browsing, including the ability for the browser to remember previously entered URLs, and its ability to supply "http" and even "www" in front of common names

- Better encryption to use in SSL sessions

At one time, upgrading your browser to the latest version was a no-brainer; few people wished to limit their browsing experience by staying with an older browser version. However, patching and updating Web browsers has become rather tricky in the last year or so. This is because most vendors, including Microsoft and Netscape, have experienced tremendous pressure to deliver upgrades at a rapid pace. This has generally resulted in browsers that introduce system bugs.

on the
Job

If you use Microsoft Internet Explorer to upgrade the desktop in Windows NT Server 4.0, you run the risk of confusing the permissions for the login shell (called "explorer.exe"). Confusing the login shell permissions generally results in a login shell that gives you nothing more than a cursor, rather than the icons you would normally expect (for example, the Start button, Network Neighborhood, My Computer, and so forth). Other bugs have introduced rather serious security issues.

Hackers have been able to exploit fourth-generation browsers to

- View the contents of your hard drive.

- Spoof the contents of the address bar, which could lead unsuspecting users to think that they are visiting one site, such as Yahoo!, when they are in fact visiting another.

- Execute programs without the knowledge of the user.

Therefore, you should upgrade your browser only to a version that is known to be stable. One way to ensure this is to wait for consensus about the latest stable version. Consult networking peers and magazines for more information about the latest news concerning browser upgrades.

Although the Y2K bug has largely become a thing of the past, it is a perfect example of the need to upgrade your browser. This is especially the case with Windows 95/98/NT/2000 and Microsoft Internet Explorer. Microsoft uses Internet Explorer as a means to patch its operating system. Although Microsoft does issue service packs, many of these service packs–as well as other applications and services such as Windows NT Option Pack– require you to first install certain versions of Internet Explorer. Therefore, you will likely have to remain aware of the patch levels of your browsers for at least these two reasons.

E-mail Clients

E-mail is arguably the ultimate killer app, because it allows users to communicate quickly and efficiently. In addition to speed, e-mail allows users to keep an archive of documents for future reference. Most e-mail clients provide ways to store information that a user can tailor to his or her own liking. A good e-mail application also provides these features and options:

- **Advanced search capabilities**   These include the ability to search message headers and the entire body text.

- **Attachment storage options**   An e-mail client should allow you to specify where you wish to store attachments.

- **Message format options**   You should be able to send in standard ASCII text, as well as in Rich Text Format and HTML. Older clients that do not have the MIME HTML entry will often process these messages as separate attachments.

- **Address Book**   Most users store e-mail addresses of contacts. You can use a local address book, as well as a remote one. Many e-mail clients allow the use of the Lightweight Directory Access Protocol (LDAP) to view remote, centralized lists of employees and contacts. Centralized lists are effective because you need to maintain only one

list, as opposed to dealing with explaining how to update each
contacts list on the client.

- **Multiple account definitions**   Most e-mail clients allow you to
  check e-mail from e-mail servers.

- **Kerberos support**   Kerberos is a client/server method for
  controlling access to specific network resources. Advanced e-mail
  clients, such as Eudora, allow you to make sure they can work with
  a Kerberos server.

- **Dial-up networking options**   You can configure an e-mail client
  to automatically connect to your ISP, if you are not connected
  to a LAN.

- **S/MIME (including certificates and encryption settings)**
  In order to encrypt communications via S/MIME, you need to
  install your key pair, as well as using the public keys of those with
  whom you wish to communicate. Make sure your e-mail client
  allows this option.

- **Spell checking**   Some e-mail clients contain extensive spelling
  checkers, with the ability to upgrade them.

- **Archiving**   Because of their sheer number, your e-mail client
  should contain the option to compress and store seldom-used
  messages.

- **Autoconfiguration**   Some e-mail clients allow you to specify
  servers that contain scripts to automatically configure all e-mail
  settings.

You may need to upgrade your e-mail client to improve any one of
these options. As with a Web browser, you will want to upgrade in case
of system bugs.

Regardless of these options, you must provide the following:

- **POP3 server address**   This can be either an IP address or resolved
  host name (usually via DNS or WINS). POP3 servers receive and
  store e-mail. They will forward e-mail to an authenticated user who
  is using a properly configured e-mail client.

- ■ **SMTP server address** As with POP3, this can be either an IP address or resolved host name. SMTP servers do not store mail. Their only purpose is to transfer mail from one server to another.

- ■ **Username and password** These are specific to individual users. You may have to enter multiple profiles if you have multiple users using the same application.

Client Standardization

Many companies mandate the use of specific e-mail clients and Web browsers. For example, many companies require a specific Web browser for intranets that offer advanced database search features, connection to proprietary servers, and so forth. One reason for this was that the Webmasters used client-side VBScript. Another reason was that they were using the IIS Web server, which allowed them to use a specific form of encryption with a third-party encryption service that worked best with Internet Explorer. As a result, the company didn't want users working at the help desk using any other browser, because Navigator doesn't work with client-side VBScript.

The reverse is also possible: One company required the use of Netscape Navigator 4.05 because it had a Java Virtual Machine that was most compatible to the version of Java it was using for applets especially designed to make users more productive in their jobs. Another reason was that, at the time, this version seemed to have the fewest serious bugs.

In the same regard, e-mail client standardization is important, especially because it helps save time. Imagine how much time it would take for an IT professional to have to research the system bugs introduced by several different e-mail clients. Also, wouldn't it be easier to standardize to one client? This way, whenever a problem arises, the IT professional has to worry about researching only one application. If she is at all organized, she will be able to keep track of the most common installation and configuration issues so that she can get end users up and running as quickly as possible. Because these applications are mission-critical, it is important that you standardize and streamline all variables as much as possible.

EXERCISE 4-2

Checking Security Levels in Netscape Navigator

1. Start Netscape Navigator.

2. Go to Edit | Preferences. You should see a dialog box. The right side should contain a Category window with the following categories: Appearance, Navigator, Mail & Newsgroups, Roaming Access, Composer, Offline, and Advanced.

3. Click the Advanced icon in the Category window.

4. Expand the window, and then select the Proxies window.

5. From this window, you can enable proxy support in your browser. By default, your browser will be set at the Direct connection to the Internet setting. You have two other options. You can configure the settings manually, or you can choose automatic proxy configuration (see Figure 4-7).

FIGURE 4-7

Netscape Preferences, showing proxy settings

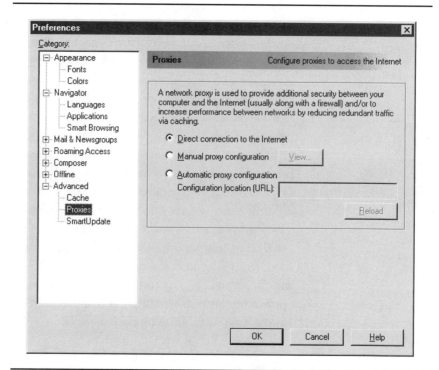

6. Click on the Manual proxy configuration window.

7. Select the View button. Once you have selected the View button, you should be able to see how you can make Navigator work with various proxy servers.

8. Select Cancel and return to your browser.

Advantages and Disadvantages of Using a Cookie, and How to Set Cookies

A cookie is a simple piece of information sent in the HTTP header during a Web transaction between a Web server and a browser. You can transmit (that is, set) cookies using a scripting language, such as JavaScript or VBScript. Using JavaScript, for example, you can have the code that creates cookies reside on the server side, or it can reside on the client side. Netscape Corporation first originated the idea of using cookies with HTTP. When first set, cookies remain in memory. When you close your browser, the cookies are stored on your hard drive in the form of simple text files. Once stored on the hard drive, information in the cookies allows Web servers to extend the functionality of the Web browser.

The primary use of cookies is to maintain state. HTTP sessions generally time out quickly. In other words, the Web server normally drops the TCP connection shortly after a Web page has finished loading. Without cookies, any information entered by a user would be lost as soon as he goes to another site. If the server sets a cookie, however, this cookie stores information created during the session.

Now that you understand the idea of maintaining state with cookies, you have a basic understanding of how cookies help an e-commerce site personalize sites for users. Cookies also help save time during the authentication process. It is possible to set a cookie after an initial successful authentication. Upon subsequent visits, the user will not have to enter username and password information.

Setting a Cookie Without the Knowledge of the User

All Web browsers ship with fairly wide-open security settings. For example, all Web browsers allow sites to set cookies by default. Therefore, it is possible for a Web server to set a cookie without your knowing about it. Although this has caused alarm in some people, this is not necessarily a bad thing; usually, cookies simply help Web sites deliver information to you. They also help personalize your browsing experience. If you give the site your name, for example, via a Web form, the site can deposit a cookie containing your name. That site can then access that cookie when you return and can offer you a welcome message.

In computing, many processes work without the user's explicit knowledge. However, you can customize your browser to control how it processes cookies.

Automatically Accepting Cookies vs. Query

Most browsers have their own versions of the following settings:

- **Allow all**   Usually the default.

- **Prompt before accepting a cookie**   Allows you to select which cookies you will allow and discard others.

- **Deny all**   Forbids your browser to accept any cookies at all.

Older Web browsers, such as Microsoft Internet Explorer 3.0, do not allow you to automatically deny cookies; you have to first be warned about the cookie, and then make the decision to delete it every time.

on the
Job

In an intranet setting, disabling cookies may have a detrimental effect on the browser's ability to function. If an end user is having problems with passwords, for example, check whether the browser is accepting cookies. The reason for this is that the Web server may be trying to set a cookie containing that user's password, but the user's browser won't accept that cookie.

Remembering Everything the User Has Done

One of the more effective—and notorious—uses of cookies is the ability to track users. If you visit a site that uses cookies, it will first set a cookie. When you come back to the site some days later, it is possible for this same site to read the cookie it originally set, and then determine where you have been on the Web, the time you spent at other sites, and so forth.

This occurs if you supply information to a site, and if this site then stores that information in a cookie. Depending upon the information you enter, some sites can use this information to build profiles about you.

Security and Privacy Implications

The activity of using cookies to track user activity has prompted some to argue that cookie use can constitute an invasion of privacy. Although this notion is a bit extreme, Web sites do, in fact, track users all the time. Tracking helps the site's owners tailor the site to customer interests, plan advertising campaigns, and even generate revenue through selling user profiles.

One of the attractions of the Web is the feeling of anonymity it gives people. Many users assume aliases when using the Internet. Because cookies help track user identification, many people feel threatened. The key to ensuring privacy in regard to cookies is to be very careful about what kind of information you will share with a Web site. Chances are, if you give information to a site, it will end up back on your hard drive as a cookie.

One of the cardinal rules Netscape implemented in regard to cookies is that a server has to set its own cookies. In other words, a client must first establish a connection with a server, and that server, or another server in the client's DNS domain, must then set a cookie on the client's computer. However, a company called DoubleClick pioneered a way to get around this rule. DoubleClick has been able to deposit cookies on the computers of end users who have never even visited its site (and therefore have not even contacted DoubleClick's DNS domain). DoubleClick does this by taking advantage of the very popular banner advertisement service it offers. A banner advertisement is a simple animated image or banner that appears on a Web page. It is nothing more than a commercial that exists on a Web page. For example, if you have ever gone to AltaVista (http://www.altavista.com) to conduct a search, a banner ad—usually somewhat related to your search results—will appear along with your results. This banner ad often originates from the DoubleClick organization. However, the ad is embedded within a page that comes from AltaVista. Because this banner ad from DoubleClick seems to originate from the same DNS domain as AltaVista, the cookie is technically legal, even though it really comes from DoubleClick. Once this cookie is deposited, it is possible for companies to track user activity. This is especially the case if an end user enters any personal information, which is then saved in a cookie.

Cookie Storage

Each browser stores its cookie text files differently. Microsoft Internet Explorer 5.0 stores cookies in separate text files. You can view these files according to your user profile. For example, if your name is James and you have installed Windows NT 4.0 Server on your C:\ drive, these files will be in the C:\winnt\profiles*username*\temporary Internet files. In Windows 98, IE 5.0 stores files in the C:\Windows\Cookies directory, as long as you have user profiles enabled. Additional operating systems such as Windows 95 and Windows NT 2000 Professional and Server store cookies differently.

All current versions of Netscape Navigator (4.0 and later) store all cookies in one file in a single directory. If your name is James, and you have installed Windows NT, 2000, or 98 on your C:\ drive, then it will be in the C:\Program Files\Netscape\Users\James\cookies.txt file. An example of this file is shown in Figure 4-8. If multiple users have created user profiles, each user will have his or her own cookie file.

Navigator, for example, limits cookies to 300, whereas IE by default allows cookies to consume as much as 2 percent of your hard drive. Once these limits are reached, your browser will delete the oldest cookie. For more information about cookies, go to Cookie Central (http://www. cookiecentral.com/).

FIGURE 4-8   A cookie file generated by Netscape Communicator 4.5

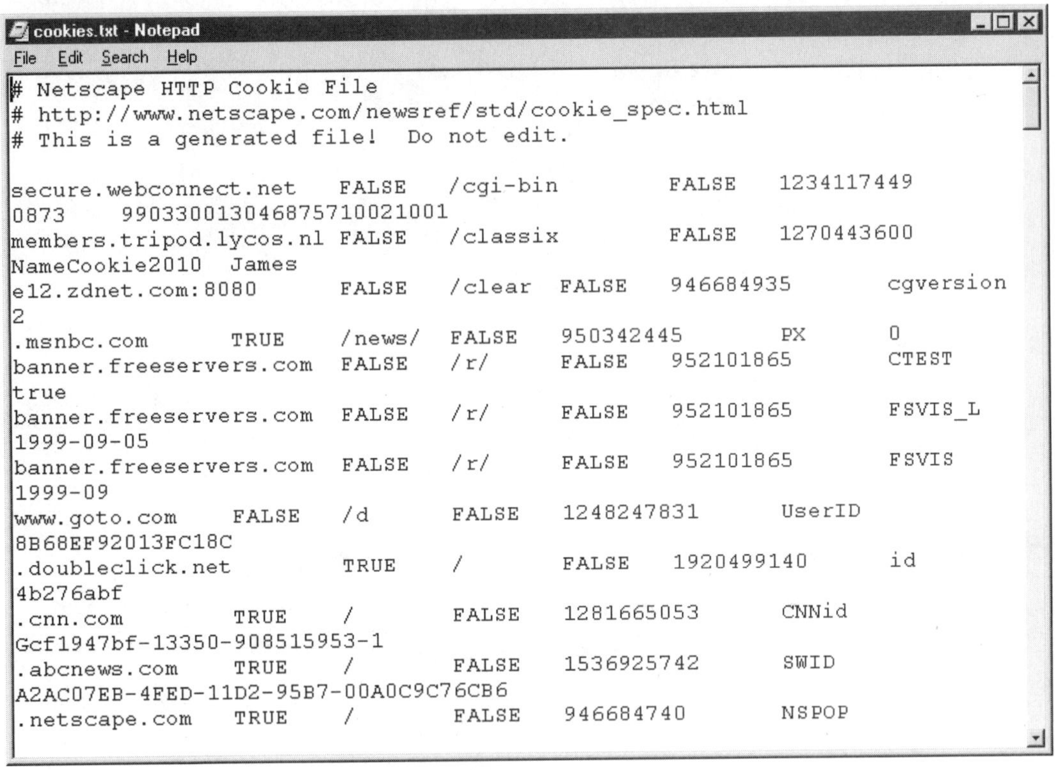

```
cookies.txt - Notepad                                               _ □ X
File  Edit  Search  Help
# Netscape HTTP Cookie File
# http://www.netscape.com/newsref/std/cookie_spec.html
# This is a generated file!  Do not edit.

secure.webconnect.net    FALSE   /cgi-bin       FALSE    1234117449
0873    99033001304687571 0021001
members.tripod.lycos.nl  FALSE   /classix       FALSE    1270443600
NameCookie2010   James
e12.zdnet.com:8080       FALSE   /clear  FALSE   946684935      cgversion
2
.msnbc.com       TRUE    /news/  FALSE   950342445      PX       0
banner.freeservers.com   FALSE   /r/     FALSE   952101865      CTEST
true
banner.freeservers.com   FALSE   /r/     FALSE   952101865      FSVIS_L
1999-09-05
banner.freeservers.com   FALSE   /r/     FALSE   952101865      FSVIS
1999-09
www.goto.com     FALSE   /d      FALSE   1248247831     UserID
8B68EF92013FC18C
.doubleclick.net         TRUE    /       FALSE   1920499140     id
4b276abf
.cnn.com         TRUE    /       FALSE   1281665053     CNNid
Gcf1947bf-13350-908515953-1
.abcnews.com     TRUE    /       FALSE   1536925742     SWID
A2AC07EB-4FED-11D2-95B7-00A0C9C76CB6
.netscape.com    TRUE    /       FALSE   946684740      NSPOP
```

Viewing Cookies Generated by a Web Transaction

1. In Windows 95, 98, or NT, open Windows Explorer.

2. Determine which browser you use, and then use Windows Explorer to navigate to the appropriate directory as indicated in the Cookie storage section.

3. If you are viewing the cookies generated by Navigator, you will have to open the cookies.txt file. If you are viewing the separate cookie files generated by IE, you will have to open individual text files.

4. Although you can view these files, it is generally not a good idea to delete them. Some may contain valuable information. For example, if you have accessed a site that stores your password in a cookie, deleting it will make you have to enter this password again. If you have forgotten the password, you will have to contact someone to get it back.

If an end user somehow deletes or modifies a cookie, the information can be damaged so that the Web server that originally set the cookie will no longer be able to use it. If you ever delete a cookie or tamper with a directory that contains cookies, do so very carefully. Nevertheless, if you delete cookies from your hard drive, you will not damage your browser. You will, however, notice that many of the Web sites you visit will no longer offer the customized browsing experience to which you have probably grown accustomed. As you continue browsing the Web, you will have to repeat the process of allowing sites to deposit cookies on your drive.

<table>
<tr><td>EXERCISE 4-4</td></tr>
</table>

Controlling Cookies in Internet Explorer 5.0

1. Open Internet Explorer 5.0.

2. Go to Tools | Internet Options.

3. Once the Internet Options dialog box presents itself, select the Security tab. Note that IE defaults to Medium security. This setting allows all cookies without warning.

4. Select the Custom Level icon. You should now be looking at the Security Settings section.

5. Scroll down to the Cookies section. You should see that you can enable cookies, disable them, or require a prompt.

6. Write down your current settings.

7. In the "Allow cookies that are stored on your computer" section, select Prompt.

8. Click OK twice to return to the browser.

9. Visit the following sites:
   http://www.msnbc.com
   http://www.microsoft.com (click on any link to register for an item)
   http://www.disney.com
   http://www.ford.com

10. Your browser should warn you that it is asking for permission to set a cookie. You have the option of accepting or rejecting this. It is your choice.

11. Go back to the Cookies section in the Security Settings dialog box and return the cookie settings to their original places.

12. If you wish, experiment with additional settings, including the ability to disable memory-resident cookies, as well as ones stored on your hard drive.

EXERCISE 4-5

Controlling Cookies in Netscape Navigator (or Communicator) 4.x

1. Start Netscape Navigator.

2. Go to Edit | Preferences.

3. Select the Advanced icon.

4. Notice that from this dialog box you can control several items, including the browser that processes cookies.

5. Write down your original settings.

6. Select the "Accept all cookies" dialog box.

7. Select the "Warn me before accepting a cookie" dialog box.

8. Browse several large, commercial Web sites, including the following:
   http://www.msnbc.com
   http://www.microsoft.com (click on any link to register for an item)
   http://www.disney.com
   http://www.ford.com

9. Your browser should warn you that it is asking permission to set a cookie. You have the option of accepting or rejecting this. It is your choice.

10. Go back to the Preferences dialog box and click Advanced.
11. Return your cookie settings to where they were before you started this exercise.

If you wish, experiment with other settings, including accepting no cookies, and the option that attempts to thwart the DoubleClick cookie strategy (Accept only cookies that get sent back to the originating server.)

You now have a better idea of how MIME works. You also know how to work with newer and legacy TCP/IP clients, how to address security and upgrade issues, and how cookies work. You also know how to control cookies. Here are some possible scenario questions and their answers.

QUESTIONS AND ANSWERS

An end user has called you, complaining that he can't access a Web site. You go over to the end user and confirm this. When you ask him to enter the password, he says that he doesn't have to because his browser will remember it for him. He then says that for some reason, the browser no longer remembers the password. What is causing this problem?	Two answers could apply here, both of which require an understanding of how cookies work. First of all, you should ask whether he uses this browser all the time. If he has two browsers on his computer, the problem may be that only one browser has a cookie set that allows him to remember the password. If he uses another browser that has not set this password cookie, then this will explain why the browser no longer remembers. The second answer would be that the user has somehow deleted or modified this cookie, making it impossible for the browser to read the cookie.
You have discovered a problem with an application. It consistently crashes under the same situation. You can duplicate the problem on several systems. The only cause must be some sort of bug in the program. What could you do to solve this problem?	The first step to take would be to check the vendor to see if the company has issued a patch for this particular bug. You can do this by calling the vendor or visiting its Web site. Then, obtain the appropriate patch for the application and install it.

QUESTIONS AND ANSWERS

You notice that e-mail messages sent from a client arrive in text format, but also have an HTML attachment of the exact same message in HTML format. Why is this happening?	The duplicate message has been sent by another e-mail client that sends messages in standard ASCII text and also in HTML format. The messages are identical. Your client can't handle the HTML format, because it doesn't have the proper MIME entry. Therefore, it processes this information as a separate attachment. If you upgrade your client to a more modern version, you will be able to read the message in HTML.

CERTIFICATION SUMMARY

In this chapter, you have learned about various MIME types. You have learned about how MIME first began as a way to extend the format in which e-mail messages were created. You then learned how Web servers have adopted this format. You also learned about S/MIME, and how legacy clients operate on the Web.

This chapter also discusses security and maintenance issues, including the necessity of upgrading clients. Upgrading clients is important, not only for security reasons, but because upgrades allow you to consistently communicate with others using the latest, usually most efficient tools. You also learned about desktop security issues, including ways to implement virus protection, and the fact that applications can apply different levels of encryption. Finally, you learned about cookies. You learned about their basic uses, as well as how to control how a Web server sets them in a browser.

On the exam, you will be tested concerning your ability to discuss what MIME is, and how it relates to newer and older clients. You will be asked to show that you know how MIME allows Web servers and clients to work well together. You will also be asked a question concerning the importance of product updates and patch levels. The chief issues concerning security discussed in this chapter include ways to make sure your desktop is secure. This includes using screen savers, as well as making sure that you keep your anti-virus definitions as current as possible. Finally, you will be tested on your knowledge of how cookies can help a Web site operate more efficiently and track users.

TWO-MINUTE DRILL

❑ MIME establishes standard ways a Web server can deliver files to a client for easy, automatic reading.

❑ The original purpose of MIME was to extend the ability for e-mail clients and servers. Over the years, however, Web clients and servers have adopted MIME, as well, because it allows them to handle various document types efficiently.

❑ In regard to a Web browser, you define MIME types by creating name/value pairs.

❑ You should consider MIME to be one of the ultimate examples of the client/server model: The server handles some of the processing task, and then sends that information to the client so that it can finish the job.

❑ Two types of legacy clients exist. The first type of legacy client is an application that was widely used before the Internet became popular. The second type of legacy client is an older application, such as the original version of Navigator, or an older e-mail program. Although such applications are clearly Internet oriented, they nevertheless represent older technology.

❑ Older TCP/IP stacks, such as the Windows 95 Dialup Networking (DUN) 1.0, have a variety of issues that make connecting to servers more difficult.

❑ It is possible to use Telnet to connect to many older sites. For example, many libraries and other organizations allow you to connect to sites via Telnet. Many older UNIX boxes provide what are called *shell accounts*.

❑ You should note, however, that you can use Telnet for many different current applications, as well. For example, if you wish to log in to a modern UNIX server remotely, Telnet is a common way to do so.

❑ You have to ensure that your software tools suit your needs. It is important that you understand exactly what version you and your clients are using. Checking revision dates will help you do this.

❑ As you obtain new software meant to enhance your client or server, make sure that you receive it from a reputable manufacturer. Likewise, make sure that you purchase manufacturer software from a reputable dealer.

❑ Older clients generally have the following problems:

    ❑ Lack of work-saving features

    ❑ Incompatible protocols and procedures

    ❑ Slower performance

❑ Legacy clients often impede the ability of a company to share information consistently between all workers in a company. It is likely that people who hold on to older clients tend to cause interoperability problems.

❑ It is important to keep up to date with the revision dates of your software and with product updates. There are four major reasons that vendors release updates and patches:

    ❑ The product originally shipped with a flaw that could not be fixed in time.

    ❑ A previously overlooked problem was discovered.

    ❑ The vendor invented or adopted a new, popular technology, and wishes to update the operating system, service, or application.

    ❑ New hacker techniques make existing practices untenable.

❑ When it comes to desktop security, you can do more than you think to make sure your information stays as private as possible. This includes the use of screen savers, security policies, and anti-virus programs.

❑ A virus is a miniprogram specially designed to interrupt the normal workings of your computer. Some viruses are merely annoying; others are truly destructive.

❏ All well-known e-mail and World Wide Web clients allow for encryption. Each, however, uses different levels and types of encryption.

❏ A Web browser is a key tool because you can use it as a thin client in an Internet, intranet, and extranet setting. A thin client is a client that you can install and use on multiple platforms to access complex applications, services, and servers that reside on the back end (that is, on the server side).

❏ E-mail is arguably the ultimate killer app because it allows users to communicate quickly and efficiently. E-mail also allows users to keep an archive of documents for future reference.

❏ Many companies mandate the use of specific e-mail clients and Web browsers. For example, many companies require a specific Web browser for intranets that offer advanced database search features, connection to proprietary servers, and so forth.

❏ A cookie is a simple piece of information sent in the HTTP header during a Web transaction between a Web server and a browser. You can transmit (that is, set) cookies using a scripting language, such as JavaScript or VBScript.

❏ All Web browsers ship with fairly wide-open security settings. For example, all Web browsers allow sites to set cookies by default. Therefore, it is possible for a Web server to set a cookie without your knowing about it.

❏ One of the more effective—and notorious—uses of cookies is the ability to track users.

❏ One of the cardinal rules Netscape implemented in regard to cookies is that a server has to set its own cookies. In other words, a client must first establish a connection with a server, and that server, or another server in the client's DNS domain, must then set a cookie on the client's computer.

❏ Each browser stores its cookie text files differently.

SELF TEST

1. Bill calls you and asks you why he can't read any of the e-mail messages he receives. He is, in fact, able to receive e-mails, but they are illegible. You check the situation and realize he is using an older client. You upgrade the client, and all works well. Which of the following answers best explains why Bill had a problem?

   A. He does not have an e-mail server defined.

   B. His client does not support the e-mail server.

   C. The e-mail server has not authenticated him.

   D. His client does not support the proper MIME type.

2. You wish to view a Tagged Image File Format (TIF) file in your Web browser. After several tries, you find that you can only save the file to disk, or open it in a separate application (Adobe Photoshop). Why is this the case?

   A. You have a legacy Web browser.

   B. Your browser does not have a MIME type defined for this file.

   C. Web browsers support only the GIF, JPEG, and PNG formats.

   D. You need to upgrade your browser.

3. You have just been able to view the latest Mars landing using streaming video. You have Netscape Navigator and RealPlayer already loaded on your system. As soon as you clicked a hyperlink, your browser launched RealPlayer automatically and began to download the information to your browser. How does a Web server facilitate this transaction?

   A. By embedding MIME headers in the HTTP connection

   B. By using MIME

   C. By downloading a special application to your browser

   D. By using IETF standards defined in RFCs

4. You have launched many applications from Microsoft Internet Explorer, including Word. Which of the following applications can MIME deploy? (Choose all that apply.)

   A. TCP

   B. Windows notepad

   C. External applications you define

   D. Internal applications developed especially for the browser

5. You have just encrypted an e-mail message so that no one but the recipient can read

it. Your intended recipient can read the message automatically. Which of the following best describes this activity?

A. You have just used MIME.

B. You have just used S/MIME.

C. You have just used encryption.

D. You have just applied MIME.

6. Your organization has just decided to standardize its e-mail clients so that everyone must use Internet Explorer. Which of the following best explains the reason for standardizing a Web browser?

A. The company wishes to ensure consistent e-mail communication.

B. Legacy Web browsers do not support MIME.

C. Legacy Web browsers are less prone to security issues.

D. Web browsers are legacy clients.

7. Your company mandates the use of version 5.0 of Internet Explorer for its Intranet. Rosa calls and complains that she can't view an important part of the Intranet. She can view other parts, but not the one she needs to fill out a report. You go over to her computer and begin troubleshooting the problem. What could you do to begin solving this issue? (Choose all that apply.)

A. Ask her whether she has installed any new applications.

B. Determine the version number of the Web browser.

C. Reinstall Navigator.

D. Install an older version of Internet Explorer.

8. You have accurately determined that a client needs an upgrade for a particular application. You can't find the one used by the company, but you have your own identical product. Why should you not use your own upgrade? (Choose all that apply.)

A. If something goes wrong later, the end user will not be able to receive technical support.

B. Licensing issues can arise, causing problems for your company.

C. The warranty may be void.

D. The upgrade is the wrong one for your particular company.

9. You notice that your version of Netscape Navigator has a bug. You are using Netscape version 3, which is an old one. Your company does not have a rule concerning which Web browser you can use. What can you do to solve this problem?

A. Go to the Netscape Web site and upgrade to the latest browser.

B. Go to the Netscape Web site and read up on the latest bugs.

C. Send an e-mail to the company concerning the bug.

D. Go to the Netscape Web site, read up on the latest bugs, and upgrade your operating system.

10. The salespeople at your company use Windows dial-up networking. You wish to always ensure they have the latest dial-up networking software, including an updated TCP/IP stack. What are the benefits of using current dial-up networking software? (Choose all that apply.)

    A. Faster dialup speeds

    B. Better compression

    C. Better encryption

    D. Ability to dial up servers at 1.544 Mbps

11. You need to connect to a UNIX server running Red Hat 6.1. You need to access the system as if you were directly sitting in front of it. Specifically, you need to edit a text file on this UNIX system. Which of the following applications allow you to do this?

    A. Internet Explorer

    B. Any Web browser

    C. A virtual terminal

    D. Telnet

12. You wish to activate password protection for your Windows 98 system 15 minutes after it detects that there is no activity via the keyboard or the mouse. What can you do?

    A. Use a screen saver password.

    B. Make sure you have not written down passwords anywhere near your desk.

    C. Employ CMOS passwords.

    D. Create user accounts that require password protection.

13. You need to encrypt a file before sending it on the Web. You have an application available to you that can encrypt a file using 40-bit encryption. Of the categories given below, how would you categorize 40-bit encryption?

    A. It is Rot13 encryption.

    B. It is trivial encryption.

    C. It is moderate encryption.

    D. It is strongly encrypted.

14. Your company wishes to use a Web browser to access legacy mainframes via the World Wide Web. The company has mandated that you must use Netscape Navigator 4.07. What is the name for this type of use for a Web browser?

    A. Thin client

    B. Legacy client

    C. Intranet service

    D. Extranet service

15. Sarah calls and complains that although she has installed the latest approved e-mail client, she can't get her e-mail. You check her e-mail settings and notice that both entries for SMTP and POP3 servers are empty. What is the minimum you have to do in order to let Sarah obtain her e-mail?

    A. Enter the SMTP IP address.

    B. Enter the POP3 server name.

    C. Enter the SMTP and POP3 server name.

    D. Enter the SMTP server name.

16. You wish to allow end users to give their usernames and passwords when they first come to your site. You then wish to allow them to return and enter your site without the password. What specific element of HTTP allows you to do this?

    A. Authentication

    B. Cookies

    C. Stateful connections

    D. User tracking

17. Ryan has noticed that everyone else on his intranet has been able to enter a password-protected site without entering a password. Each person remembers having had to enter a password once, but never again. He, however, has to enter a password all the time. He is using the same browser and version as everyone else. What should he do to solve this problem?

    A. Obtain the latest service patch, and then go to the Web site and reenter his password information.

    B. Check the proxy settings on the browser, and then go to the Web site and reenter his password information.

    C. Enable cookies on his browser.

    D. Enable cookies on his browser, and then go to the Web site and reenter his password information.

18. Carol uses Microsoft Internet Explorer 5.0. She has deleted all of her cookies from her hard drive. What will be the result?

    A. Internet Explorer will no longer load, and she will have to reinstall it.

    B. She will have to reinstall Internet Explorer to obtain full use of cookies.

    C. She will lose many custom settings she is used to, but can regain them.

    D. She will have to reinstall Internet Explorer before she can regain the use of cookies.

SELF TEST ANSWERS

1. **D.** His client does not support the proper MIME type. Older e-mail clients do not have the proper MIME definitions to read e-mail sent in HTML, RTF, and other formats. By upgrading the client, you are giving Bill a newer application that can handle the format your company uses.

   A is incorrect, because Bill was still able to receive e-mail; he just couldn't read it. **B** is incorrect, because the MIME issue is not with the e-mail server, but with the e-mail client sending the message. Authentication is the ability to determine the identity of a person or host, and has nothing to do with the MIME issue being discussed, so **C** is incorrect.

2. **C.** Web browsers support only the GIF, JPEG, and PNG image formats.

   A and **D** are incorrect, because no Web browser supports the TIF image format. **B** is incorrect, because it shows a misunderstanding of MIME: Just because a Web browser doesn't support a particular application or format, this doesn't mean that you can't do anything with the file. If you define a MIME type for the TIF file and then associate that MIME type with another application, such as Paint Shop Pro or Adobe Photoshop, it is possible to have the imaging application launch automatically from the browser.

3. **A.** It describes exactly how a Web server uses MIME. A Web server does in fact embed MIME headings in the TCP headers, which your browser then reads and uses to launch the appropriate application. Remember: the use of MIME is a good example of the client/server relationship, because both the server and the client cooperate in performing a task—this time, the viewing of streaming audio.

   B is incorrect, because even though it does correctly identify the use of MIME, it doesn't describe how the protocol works. **C** is incorrect, because generally this is not what happens in a RealPlayer scenario, especially because the question makes clear that you already have RealPlayer on your system.

4. **B, C,** and **D.** You can use MIME to launch a program such as Notepad, as well as any other external application. You also use MIME to launch applications that may be especially developed for a browser.

   A, TCP, is incorrect, because it is the Transmission Control Protocol, which is not an application. TCP is the means by which HTTP (used by Web servers and browsers) communicate.

5. **B.** You can use S/MIME to encrypt e-mail. Although you can use other means to encrypt e-mail, this is a popular method employed by Microsoft, Netscape, Eudora, and others.
   A is incorrect, because it does not describe the use of encryption. **C** is incorrect, because it does not describe how S/MIME works. **D** is incorrect, because you have in fact just used S/MIME.

6. **A.** Legacy clients can cause serious compatibility issues that can result in inconsistent communication.
   B, C, and **D** are incorrect, because all Web browsers support MIME, legacy clients are not necessarily immune to security problems, and not all Web browsers are legacy clients.

7. **A** and **B.** Before you do anything, make sure you gather as much information as possible. Determine whether the end user (or anyone else) has installed anything new, and then determine whether Rosa is using the correct version of Navigator. Chances are, she is not; using a different version may not affect her ability to view the entire Intranet, but it may cause problems in some areas of the Intranet that use proprietary scripting solutions, applications, Java applets, and other methods that only work with specific browsers.
   C is incorrect, because the company wishes to have all users use Internet Explorer.
   D is incorrect, because you have not found out what version of IE Rosa is running. Never rush to install an application until you take preliminary steps.

8. **A, B,** and **C.** Using your own upgrade will cause problems with technical support, licensing, and the warranty. Consider what would happen if the end user contacted the vendor and gave the license number.
   D is incorrect, because you do, in fact, have the correct version. However, you should take the time to upgrade the application with the one that belongs to your company.

9. **A.** It is likely that your browser has a bug that has been fixed by an application patch or upgrade.
   B is incorrect, because simply reading up on the latest bugs will not solve the problem. **C** is incorrect, because sending an e-mail will not solve the issue in a timely manner. **D** is incorrect, because upgrading the operating system does not address issues with either Netscape or the application.

10. **A, B,** and **C.** Using a more current TCP/IP stack will give you many benefits, including the ones listed here.

D is incorrect, because currently there is no way to use dial-up networking to connect at this speed. You would require something like an Ethernet LAN connection and a connection type called a T-1 line.

11. **D.** A Telnet application allows you to access and control a system as if you were standing in front of it.
    A is incorrect, because even though you can use a browser to access files, you cannot edit them in a browser, unless you have specialized software. A virtual terminal is what a server presents to a Telnet client when the server establishes a session. **B** is incorrect, because no Web browser currently allows you to edit text. Therefore, **C** is incorrect, because a virtual terminal is not an application.

12. **A.** You can use a screen saver to automatically activate any number of minutes after the computer detects a lack of activity.
    B is incorrect, because this desktop security precaution does not activate after any number of minutes. Similarly, CMOS and user passwords do not activate after a number of minutes of inactivity. They activate during the boot process or after a user has logged out.

13. **C.** Whenever you use 40-bit encryption, you are using moderate encryption.
    A is incorrect, because it gives the name of a trivial type of encryption. **B** is incorrect, because trivial encryption can be broken in much less than a day. **D** is incorrect, because strong encryption would require a bit length of at least 128 bits.

14. **A.** Web browser used in this way has become a thin client. Before the Web, it was necessary to create customized, dedicated clients to access a mainframe.
    B is incorrect, because even though an older Web browser can be a legacy client, most of the time legacy clients are old, dedicated clients that run only on certain platforms, given certain situations. **C** and **D** are incorrect, because a browser is an application and not a service; although you can use a Web browser to browse an intranet or an extranet, a Web browser is an application you use to access services.

15. **B.** The minimum amount of information that will allow Sarah to receive e-mail is a valid POP3 server name or IP address.
    A is incorrect, because entering the proper IP address for an SMTP server will allow her to send e-mail, not receive it. **C** is incorrect, because even though you should enter both server names, the minimum amount of information necessary is the POP3

server name, and none other. **D** is incorrect, because entering the SMTP server name will allow you to send e-mail messages only.

16. **B.** Cookies allow you to customize the user experience, which includes giving the ability to store username and password information in a cookie. Once a cookie is set, with a username and password, the user will not have to reenter this information. **A** is incorrect, because authentication is a general communication principle, as opposed to a specific HTTP application. **C** is incorrect, because all Web transactions are stateful; however, Web transactions do not remain live for long. **D** is incorrect, because even though cookies can help enable user tracking, user tracking is not an element of HTTP.

17. **D.** Ryan has to enter his password all the time because his browser does not allow any servers to set cookies. Every time he visits this site, the server tries to set a cookie, but is forbidden access. Once he allows cookies to be set, only half the problem is solved, however, because he then needs to revisit the Web site and enter the information once again. Then the server will store his information on his hard drive. Only on his subsequent visit will the information in the cookies apply and allow him to enter without giving any more information.
    A is incorrect, because he already has the latest browser and patch version. **B** is incorrect, because proxy settings on a Web browser have nothing to do with cookies. **C** is incorrect, because it only solves half the problem; he must then go visit the Web site.

18. **C.** Although it will lead to inconveniences, deleting cookies from Carol's hard drive will not ruin the actual browser. It will, however, ruin custom settings such as passwords, username information, and other features she may already be used to. She will have to browse all of her favorite Web sites again in order to get back the cookies she deleted.
    Therefore, **A**, **B**, and **D** are incorrect, be-cause they all stipulate that she must reinstall Internet Explorer, which is not the case.

COMPUTING TECHNOLOGY INDUSTRY ASSOCIATION®

5

HTML

The Internet may be global in nature, but it does have its own universal language. This doesn't mean English or French, or any of the other tongues that we humans use to communicate with one another. Although the Internet uses programming and scripting languages, which allow you to bring the functionality and advantages of a program to the Net, such languages aren't used on every Web page on the Internet. The language most commonly used on the World Wide Web is HTML. HTML is an acronym for the HyperText Markup Language, and it's used to format the information that's transmitted over the Internet to the Web browser running on your computer.

In this chapter we'll introduce you to HTML, how it works, and variations on HTML—such as Dynamic HTML and Extended HTML. We'll also discuss methods of creating Web pages and of controlling page display, depending on the Web browser being used. By the end of this chapter, you'll not only be prepared for the certification exam, but you'll be able to create Web pages to be proud of.

CERTIFICATION OBJECTIVE 5.01

Understanding HTML

The HyperText Markup Language (or HTML, for short) is what makes the Internet graphical. In the early days of the Internet, people viewed information, sent messages, and played text-based games as if they were using a computer running DOS. Commands would be typed in, and an answer would be returned in the form of a string of characters, or by some other action being performed. As graphical user interfaces (GUI, pronounced "goo-ee") became more popular in the late 1980s, people grew used to interacting with information through graphic interfaces. They didn't want to run DOS-based programs, but wanted to use the computer with programs that ran in Microsoft Windows, Macintosh, or UNIX. It was during this time that Tim Berners-Lee at the University of Illinois's National Center for Supercomputing Applications developed a way for the Internet to become graphical. He developed the HyperText Transfer

Protocol (HTTP), which could transfer what we now call Web pages and other files, and the HyperText Markup Language, which could format the transmitted data into a graphical interface.

HTTP and HTML transformed the Internet into a World Wide Web of interconnected computers, which people could access through GUI or character-based interfaces. Lynx, the first Web browser, was character-based. As the Internet grew, other Web browsers—most of which provided GUI interfaces—followed.

HTTP is a protocol, which is a set of rules that determine how computers communicate with one another. When you sit at your computer and enter the address for a specific Web site or Web page, HTTP is used to get the data making up that Web page. When you enter a Web address or URL (Uniform Resource Locator) like www.comptia.com in your Web browser's address bar, it has http:// already entered at the beginning. This signifies that you're using the HTTP protocol to get the Web page you want displayed. This is also signified by starting the Web address with www, which tells the browser that you'll be accessing a site or page on the World Wide Web through HTTP.

While HTTP transports the Web page from a server to your browser, HTML is used to create Web page documents and dictate how those documents are displayed in your browser. When you developWeb pages using HTML, you type instructions into the HTML document that instructs a Web browser how text is to be displayed, what graphics are to appear, how they are to appear, and what will happen when the end user clicks on them. The Web server that stores the Web page and transmits it to your browser has nothing to do with this. It is all done through the HTML document itself.

exam
ⓦatch

Don't confuse HTTP and HTML. You can think of HTTP as a method of transport, like a truck that carries cargo to a destination. The cargo that HTTP carries is HTML documents (Web pages) and other files used in the display of Web pages.

HTML allows you, as a Web page author, to control the browser content and how it is formatted. HTML also controls some GUI elements, such as buttons, list controls, and so on. Through HTML, you control what the user will see and how a Web site is displayed. In fact, it is the only significant way you have to control a user's Internet experience. Even when scripting languages like JavaScript or VBScript are added to provide greater control over the GUI—including user interaction and window control—HTML remains a constant fixture of the Web page. While the user can configure his or her computer and Web browser to the settings he or she wants, you control the interface used to access data on a Web site.

How HTML Works

There is very little difference between an HTML document and a normal text document created using a program like Notepad.exe.

In fact, as you'll see later in this chapter, you can create HTML documents using Notepad.exe. The person creating the Web page—generally referred to as the *author*—enters textual information into the document. What makes the document different from mere plain text is that HTML is a markup language.

Markup languages use symbols, characters, and statements to format a document. These are placed in the document to indicate how that area of the document should appear when it is viewed or printed. In HTML, the indicators that the author uses are called tags.

Tags are elements that tell a Web browser that the document uses HTML, and how information is to be formatted and displayed. A tag is a letter or statement between the < and > symbols. For example, let's say we wanted to have the following appear in a Web browser:

This is italicized!

To make the words appear italicized when they're displayed, you would enter this in your HTML document:

```
<I>This is italicized!</I>
```

When a Web browser reads this line, the browser interprets the <I> tag as an order to italicize any text that follows. This means that any text following this starting tag will be italicized until the browser reads the closing tag (also called an end tag). A closing tag is identical to the opening (or start tag), except that it uses the / symbol, and specifies that this particular formatting is to end at this point.

The concept of opening and closing tags is an important part of HTML. Remember that the opening tag indicates the start of a particular formatting or HTML element, while the closing tag indicates where that formatting style or element ends.

When a user requests a Web page from a Web server, the page is downloaded to the Web browser that reads the document and interprets these tags. By interpreting the tags and formatting the information between the opening and closing tags, the Web browser displays the HTML document in the manner in which you want it formatted. As we'll see later in this chapter, there are many tags that provide instructions as to what the Web browser displays, and how.

DHTML

DHTML is an acronym for Dynamic HyperText Markup Language, or Dynamic HTML. As its name suggests, it allows a Web page to be dynamically altered once it has been loaded. While HTML allows you to format and display elements of a Web page in a static or unchanging manner, DHTML allows you to change dynamically, display, and move various elements. For example, you might create a DHTML Web page that looks like a Windows desktop, allowing users to drag and drop an image to a different location on the Web page. Another example of DHTML would have the color of text change when the mouse moved over it.

This description of Dynamic HTML makes it sound like a different language from HTML, but it isn't. DHTML is an evolution of HTML, and is a blanket term for new HTML tags and options that have been incorporated into some of the newer browsers, as well as style sheets and programming that, when included together in a Web page, make your HTML document dynamic. Because it combines these technologies and methods, the browser used to view such Web pages must support DHTML. Netscape and Microsoft both implemented support for DHTML in version 4.0 of their browsers, and to a large degree, all of these browsers share common DHTML functionality. Earlier versions of Netscape Navigator and Microsoft Internet Explorer do not offer DHTML support and will not recognize some elements of DHTML pages. This means that if your site used DHTML, you would need to create one version with DHTML and another for users with older browsers, or implement coding in your Web page that will check the type of browser being used and then display the Web page accordingly. Later in this chapter, we'll discuss cross-browser coding in greater detail.

Style Sheets and Cascading Style Sheets

To understand DHTML better, we should take a look at some of its components. Style sheets, cascading style sheets, and layering are common features of a DHTML document. Style sheets are embedded in HTML documents, or linked to an external file, which defines the default styles and characteristics of the Web pages used in a document or Web site. It can define how a page is laid out through the use of the <STYLE>...</STYLE> tag set. By using style sheets, you are ensuring that each page used in your Web site has a consistent look or style. Using style sheets, you can address such issues as what the default background color or graphic will be for your pages, the size and color of text and hypertext links, fonts used, and so on.

In addition to style sheets, there are also cascading style sheets. A cascading style sheet sets the style of a Web page by using multiple style sheets and/or files, and displaying them in a specific order. Later in this chapter, we'll show you how <STYLE>...</STYLE> tags are used to format a Web page.

Document Object Model

Dynamic HTML uses the Document Object Model, which gives Web page authors the ability to treat various elements of a Web page as objects. By treating these elements in an object-based manner, you can name and give attributes (such as color or text style). You can use these named objects in various scripts included on your page, causing headers or status bar information to change when a mouse passes over certain text or graphics, or allowing a user of your Web page to use a mouse to drag and drop images.

This extended scripting ability becomes apparent when you use JavaScript, VBScript, ActiveX, or Java applets in your pages. Because the Web page has been downloaded from the Web server, these changes are implemented independently and immediately on each user's machine. Such changes aren't taking place on the original copy located on the Web server, and don't affect how others will view the page when they visit your Web site.

CERTIFICATION OBJECTIVE 5.02

Creating HTML Pages

You can create HTML pages with a simple text editor, like the Notepad program in Microsoft Windows or the Edit program in DOS. Using such programs, you can enter the information and HTML tags necessary to create your Web page. Once you've written these HTML documents for your Web site, you can then save the document to your hard disk with the extension .htm or .html. By saving an HTML document with one of these extensions, you can then open it with a Web browser like Internet Explorer or Netscape Navigator. In order for others to view the Web page on the Internet, the file has to be saved to a Web server. This action is called "publishing" a Web page.

The file extension of .htm or .html tells the Web browser that this is a Web page, and not a simple text file. As we'll see later in this chapter, the HTML header string is the primary means of identifying the content type of the document. However, it's important that you save your Web page with such an extension. If you saved it with the default .txt extension, an application could save the file as a text file, showing all of the HTML tags, but not showing any of the formatting. The difference between viewing an HTML document as intended and viewing the raw HTML is shown in Figure 5-1.

Before you can save your Web page, you'll need to know how to create one, and that's the point of this section. First we'll discuss the document structure of an HTML document, and then we'll add information and tags to the structure to create a Web page.

FIGURE 5-1

Comparison of HTML
and how it appears
in a browser

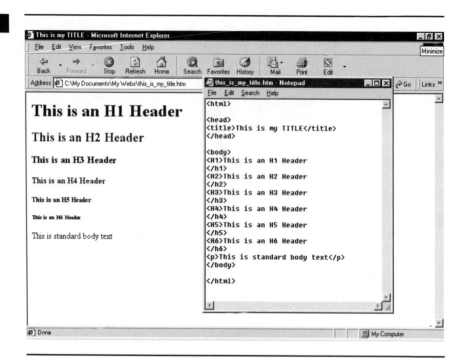

HTML Document Structure

Learning how to author a Web page is a bit like learning how to write. As
you learned in English class, any story or paragraph has a specific structure.
There is a *beginning*, which includes your title and information that sets up
what follows. The *body* of your paragraph or story contains the bulk of the
information you are trying to convey to your reader. Finally, there is a
closing. Web pages are constructed in the same way.

The first step in authoring a Web page is to set up your page, which you
must do using the <HTML>...</HTML> tags. Between these tags, you'll
place other tags that will contain information that will be displayed to the
end user. This would be analogous to writing on a piece of paper. Anything
outside the paper is invisible to the reader, just as anything outside these
tags is ignored by the browser. In a text editor, you type

```
<HTML>
</HTML>
```

The <HTML> tag indicates the start of the HTML document, while the </HTML> tag indicates where it ends.

Between these tags you then enter the <HEAD>…</HEAD> tags, which contain such elements as the title of your Web page and other elements that aren't shown directly to the person viewing the page. Of the tags you can add to the <HEAD>…</HEAD> section of your document, the only required element is the title. The title appears in the titlebar of your Web browser, and is set by using the <TITLE>…</TITLE> tags. For example, in the following example, we see an HTML document set up to use the title "This is my Title":

```
<HTML>
<HEAD>
<TITLE>This is my Title</TITLE>
</HEAD>
</HTML>
```

As is the case with most HTML tags, the text entered between the <TITLE>…</TITLE> tags is displayed to the user.

After the <HEAD>…</HEAD> tags, you place the <BODY>…</BODY> tags, which are used to define the bulk of your Web page's content. Like the body of a paragraph, text written between the <BODY> and </BODY> tags contains most of the information you want to relay to your page's reader and is displayed in the main window of a Web browser. These tags are placed between the </HEAD> tag and the </HTML> tag, so that the entire Web page's structure appears as follows:

```
<HTML>
<HEAD>
</HEAD>
<BODY>
</BODY>
</HTML>
```

In examining the basic structure of HTML documents, you may notice that some tags are written in lowercase, while others appear in uppercase. Either case works, because HTML isn't case sensitive when it comes to tags. While text you place in the body or between tags like the <TITLE>…</TITLE> will appear as it is typed, a Web browser will interpret <BODY>, <body>, <Body>, or any other variation exactly the same. To avoid confusion in reading your HTML document, it is best to choose either upper- or lowercase. The proper style of HTML should have the closing tags matching the case of the opening tag. A mixture of both can make the document more difficult to read, if you later need to troubleshoot or modify the Web page. In addition, such inconsistencies can cause problems when future browsers attempt to view your Web pages.

Another important factor to consider is how HTML processes *whitespace,* which is the space between characters, where nothing has been entered. For example, when you use a text editor, you may press the ENTER key several times, so that there are several spaces between lines. When the browser reads these lines, it ignores these spaces. This means that this text

```
<HTML><HEAD></HEAD><BODY>This is my body</BODY></HTML>
```

would be read by the browser in the exact same way as this:

```
<HTML>
<HEAD>
</HEAD>
<BODY>
This
is my body
</BODY>
</HTML>
```

It is better to separate the document structure on different lines, because it is easier to read. To the browser, however, it makes no difference. You can separate the lines of your document with as many or as few blank lines as you like.

Whitespace applies not only to the number of lines separating each tag, but also to the lines of text that you want to appear in the Web browser. In the preceding example, the line "This is my body" is broken across several lines. However, when the browser reads the line, it will appear as an unbroken sentence, because HTML uses the <BR> and <P> tags to indicate a break in a sentence. The <P> tag breaks your text as if you had pressed the ENTER key in a word processor, so that it becomes double-spaced. The <BR> tag does the same thing, but causes the text to be single-spaced. Table 5-1 demonstrates how to type certain text, and shows how it would appear in a browser.

TABLE 5-1	Text Typed into HTML Document	Text Viewed in a Browser
How HTML is Displayed in a Browser	This is my text	This is my text
	This is \<BR\>my text	This is my text
	This is \<P\>my text	This is my text

When you use the \<BR\> and \<P\> tags, you use no end tag. The \<BR\> causes a break, and only does this once, so it doesn't need a closing tag to show where the formatting ends. The \<P\> tag also does this once and doesn't need a closing tag to show where the formatting ends, but you can use \</P\> to show where your paragraph ends. The \</P\> tag is ignored by the browser but allows it for conformity to other HTML tags. In other words, if you start your paragraph with the \<P\> tag, there will be a double space between the previous paragraph and your new one. To show where the paragraph ends, you may use \</P\>, but you don't have to. It may just make your document easier to read when you modify or troubleshoot it, which may be helpful in future versions of browsers that adhere to such standards.

Comments are a fundamental and vital part of good HTML coding. Comments enable you to make notes on what a section of HTML or scripting does. The comments are ignored by the browser, and are not displayed in the browser. They are only viewed when the HTML source code is viewed through a text editor. The HTML comment begins with \<!-- to mark the beginning of a comment, and uses --\> to mark the end of a comment. An example of this is

```
<!-- This is a comment that will be ignored by Browsers -->
```

By putting this around the script, any browser incapable of executing the script will simply ignore it. If the browser can execute the script, it will ignore the HTML comment and execute the script.

Creating an HTML Document

1. From your Windows Start menu, select Programs and then Accessories. From Accessories, click Notepad.

2. When the Notepad program starts, set up your HTML document's structure, by entering

```
<HTML>
<HEAD>
</HEAD>
<BODY>
</BODY>
</HTML>
```

3. Between the <BODY>...</BODY> tags, type your name, the <BR> tag, and your age.

4. From the File menu, select Save, and then save your document as myfirst.htm.

5. Open your Web browser. From the File menu, select Open, and then type the name and page to the myfirst.htm file you just saved.

6. When the Web page opens, notice that your name and age are shown in the browser's main window, and that the age appears on the line directly below your name.

7. In Notepad, change the <BR> tag to a <P> tag.

8. Between the <HEAD>...</HEAD> tags, type the <TITLE> tag, your name, and then the </TITLE> tag.

9. From the File menu of Notepad, click Save.

10. In your Web browser, click the Refresh or Reload button on your browser's toolbar. Your name and age are now double-spaced, and the titlebar of the browser shows your name.

Formatting Your Text with Tags

Now that you've created a simple Web page, you're ready to make the page more visually appealing. As with creating the document itself, this is done through HTML tags. Using the proper tags with your text in the <BODY>...</BODY> section of an HTML document, you can make your Web page appear however you want it to look.

One of the oldest and most common methods of formatting text in an HTML document is through heading tags. There are six different headings that can be used in a Web page, ranging from a level 1 heading to a level 6 heading. Using these tags, you can quickly change the size of the text. A level 1 heading is the largest size of text, and these progressively decrease in size until they reach the smallest text size, level 6.

The various heading tags are used in the same way as most other tags in HTML. They begin with an opening tag and end with a closing tag. For example, let's say you are creating an HTML document that teaches people how to make a Web page. In such a case, you can use a level 1 heading to state your topic in large text:

```
<H1>How to create a Web page</H1>
```

The <H1> tag tells the browser that the text that follows is to appear in a large size, while the </H1> tag states that any text that follows shouldn't be in this style. This allows you to enter normal text after the heading, so the entire Web page isn't in this format.

If you have subtopics that you want to talk about in such a Web page, you don't want the titles of those topics to appear in quite so large a size. This is a good place to use smaller headings, such as these:

```
<H2>Creating Headings</H2>
```

When such text appears in the browser, it is slightly smaller than the level 1 heading. You can then use <H3>, <H4>, <H5>, and <H6> tags for topics below this. As the number after the H is incremented, the size of the text between the heading tags appears smaller.

In addition to modifying headings, you can also modify the normal body text of your Web page using other tags. If you want to make your text bold, you can use either the <B> or <STRONG> tags. Any text appearing after these tags appears bold. To make the text stop being bold, you use the </B> or </STRONG> tags:

```
<B>This is bold</B>
<STRONG>This is bold too</STRONG>
```

The <B>...</B> tags are used in most current Web pages. The <STRONG>...</STRONG> tags essentially give the same result, but are used for typographical rendering, while <B>...</B> tags explicitly format the text as bold. In most browsers, though, the <STRONG> tag set will have the text appear as bold. Some editors suggest using <STRONG>, while others recommend using the <B> tag set.

Like the tags that make text bold, there are also tags that can be used to make text italic. The tag set you should use to italicize text is <I>...</I>, but using the <EM>...</EM> tags will have the same effect in most browsers. The <EM> tag is used to emphasize text, and like the <I> tag, it results in italicized text in most browsers.

The <U> tag is used to underline text when it appears in a browser. To make text underlined, you use this tag as you use the other tags discussed. Text entered between the <U>...</U> tags will appear underlined when it is viewed in a browser.

on the
Üob

Hyperlinks appear underlined in most browsers, so use the <U>...</U> tags sparingly. If possible, don't use underlined text at all. If you underline text, ensure that the underlined text isn't of the same color as the text of hyperlinks. Otherwise, users may attempt to click the underlined text, thinking that it will make the browser jump to another Web page.

Similar to the <U> tag are the <STRIKE>...</STRIKE> or <S>...</S> tag sets. Instead of underlining text, the <STRIKE> tags cause a line to appear through the text. In other words, the text looks as if it's been crossed or struck out on the screen. The <S> tag is identical to the <STRIKE> tag, but it is a single letter, and so requires less typing on the part of the HTML author.

The <U> and <STRIKE> tag sets have another characteristic in common as well. In HTML 4, both of these tag sets have been deprecated. This means that those particular tags are no longer recommended by the W3C, and shouldn't be used anymore.

on the
Üob

Even though certain tags are deprecated, it's important that you know what commonly used deprecated tags do. This will allow you to modify older Web pages so that they meet the latest recommendations.

While you can still use the tag sets, and browsers will be able to use these indicators for formatting text, future versions of browsers may not support them, so you should stop using them in any future Web pages you create.

The teletype tag, which is sometimes referred to as typewriter text, makes whatever text appears between the <TT>...</TT> tags appear as if it were typed on a typewriter. This allows you to make elements of your Web page take on a typewriter-style typeface, but other tags in HTML will do exactly the same thing. The <CODE>...</CODE>, <SAMP>...</SAMP>, and <KBD>...<KBD> tags also make text appear with the same typeface as the <TT> tag. The difference between these tags is only in where you would use them. The <KBD> tag is for text to be entered by the viewer of the page, the <CODE> tag is for displaying examples of programming or HTML code, while <SAMP> is used for displaying examples of program output. Regardless of this, each is displayed identically.

There are also tags that change the size and position of text entered into an HTML document. By placing text between the <BIG>...</BIG> tags, you can increase the size of text. If you want to decrease the size of text, you can place the text you want to shrink between the <SMALL>...</SMALL> tags. If doing this doesn't respectively increase or shrink the text to a size of your liking, you can stack the tags as shown here:

```
<BIG><BIG><BIG>This increases the size of text</BIG></BIG></BIG>
```

Using multiple instances of <BIG>, however, is generally considered bad form. In such cases, when you want to increment the size of a font, you should use the <FONT>...</FONT> tag set. By entering <FONT+> and the size that you want the font increased in size, you can modify how large your font appears. Similarly, <FONT-> and a number indicating how much a font will be decreased will make your font smaller. The use of <FONT+> is shown in the following example:

```
<FONT+3>This increases the size of text</FONT>
```

The benefit of using <FONT> over <BIG> becomes apparent when you notice how much easier it is to read your HTML code. As Web pages are often modified with new information and styles, it is important to make a Web page's code easy to read and follow.

As you can see by the example of the <BIG> tag set example, you can use more than one HTML tag for a line of text. The same applies to bold, italic, or any of the other modifications mentioned so far. For example, if you wanted to make some text small and bold, you could do the following:

```
<SMALL><B>Your text would go here</B></SMALL>
```

Two other tag sets that modify text will also affect the text's position. These are the superscript and subscript tags. The ^{...} tags will cause text to appear small and raised above the position of other text in a line, while the _{...} tags will cause text to appear small and lower in relation to other body text.

Some text may be more understandable if it is formatted as a list. For example, you may be describing how to do something step by step. In such a case, you may find that it is more understandable to format the instructions in an ordered list. Ordered lists are also known as numbered lists, because when they appear in a Web browser, they look like this:

1. First step

2. Second step

Each step in the list appears with a number before it. Each number increments as more items are added to the list.

Ordered lists are created using the <OL> and </OL> tags. Each item appearing between these tags is formatted so that it appears numbered. For example, if we were going to create the previous numbered listing in an HTML document, we would enter

```
<OL>
        <LI>First step</LI>
        <LI>Second step</LI>
</OL>
```

The items that appear in an ordered list are designated as such, using the <LI> and </LI> tags. The text appearing between these tags appears as list items in the listing. The <OL>...</OL> tags are used to format these list items into an ordered list.

In addition to numbered lists, you can create bulleted or unordered lists. Bullets are generally black dots that appear in front of list items, as shown here:

- First item
- Second item

Unordered lists are used when items in the list don't need to be listed in a set order. For this reason, in HTML, bulleted lists are more commonly referred to as unordered lists. They are created using the <UL> and </UL> tags, as shown here:

```
<UL>
        <LI>First item</LI>
        <LI>Second item</LI>
</UL>
```

As seen in this example, the <UL>...</UL> tags frame the list items. As in ordered lists, each list item is created using the <LI>...</LI> tags, and there is no limit to the number of items between the tags. The <UL>...</UL> tags format the list items, so that they appear bulleted.

exam
ⓦatch

Remember that ordered lists are numbered. They are used for items that need to be in a specific order. Unordered lists are bulleted, and contain list items that don't need to be in any specific order.

There may also be times when you want to center your text, so that it appears in the left, right, or middle of the browser's main window. Justifying text to the left or right of the browser window is done with the

<ALIGN=""> tag, while centering text can be done in two ways. First, you can use the <ALIGN=""> method recommended by the World Wide Web Consortium (W3C). This is done by entering the following into the <BODY>...</BODY> of your Web page:

```
<P ALIGN="CENTER">You would then enter your text here.
```

To have the text aligned to the left or right of the browser window, replace the word "CENTER" with the word "LEFT" or "RIGHT."

You can also enter text between the <CENTER>...</CENTER> tags. These tags aren't recommended by W3C anymore and are considered deprecated, but browsers still support the <CENTER>...</CENTER> tags.

If you want to stress that you're discussing different topics, it may be useful to divide your Web page into different segments. In such a case, you might use the <HR> tag to create a horizontal rule, which is a horizontal line. To create a horizontal rule, you can simply type <HR>, or you can specify attributes that will affect its appearance. For example, you can center the line using the following:

```
<HR ALIGN="CENTER" >
```

You can also specify the width and size (or thickness) of the line by defining attributes of the horizontal rule. For example, if you want to have the line stretch across the entire screen of the browser, and make it thicker than usual, you can do the following:

```
<HR WIDTH="100%" SIZE="5">
```

While this example uses percentages to determine the width, you can also specify it in absolute pixels by replacing the percentage with a set number of pixels. Because its easier to think in terms of percentage, the percentage method is more commonly used.

Such adjustments are made through the parameter attribute. This is made up of settings that enable you to control how text or graphics will appear in the browser. Many tag sets have numerous attributes or parameters that can be used to change the appearance of text or graphics. To view a listing of tags and their attributes, visit the World Wide Web Consortium's Web site at http://www.w3c.org.

FROM THE CLASSROOM

Being able to troubleshoot the HTML documents you create is an important part of creating Web pages. A common problem that students often encounter is that when they bold, itlicize, or do some other formatting to a word or section of text and view the Web page in a browser, they find that the entire document is bold or italicized in that manner, or that a section of text is formatted in an unexpected manner. Often, this is due to the fact that they forgot to use a closing tag. Remember that closing tags tell the browser to stop formatting text in a specific way. For example, let's say that you wanted the word "HTML" bold, and entered the following into the <BODY> of your Web page:

```
The Art of <B>HTML in one easy lesson
```

While the word "HTML" would be bold by this, so would everything else in the HTML document, until the closing tag </B> was read by the browser. If no closing tag were read, then the entire document would be bold.

When text in your Web page is formatted strangely, the first thing you should do is to notice where the improper formatting starts in the text. In the previous example, this would be at the phrase "HTML in one easy lesson." Once you've checked this, open the HTML document in your text editor. You'll then need to read through the document from that point on, and look for tags that require a closing tag. When you find such tags, make sure that a closing tag exists where you want that formatting to end.

—Michael Cross, MCSE, MCPS, MCP+I, CNA

EXERCISE 5-2

Using Headers and Tags in Your Web Page

1. From your Windows Start menu, select Programs and then Accessories. From Accessories, click Notepad.

2. When Notepad starts, type the document structure of the Web page, as follows:

```
<HTML>
<HEAD>
<TITLE>My second Web page</TITLE>
<BODY>
</BODY>
</HTML>
```

3. Between the <BODY>...</BODY> tags, type the names of six of your friends, pets, or others that you may love or like. For each of the six names, use a different heading tag to change its size. For example:

```
<BODY>
<H1>Dad</H1>
<H2>Mom</H2>
<H3>Jennifer</H3>
<H4>Julie</H4>
<H5>Junior the cat</H5>
<H6>Smudge the cat</H6>
</BODY>
```

4. After the line with the level 6 heading, create a horizontal rule that is centered and stretches across half of the browser screen. You can do this by entering the following:

```
<HR ALIGN="CENTER" WIDTH="50%">
```

5. Below the tag you entered in step 4, type the sentence "This line has words that are bold and italicized." Use HTML tags to bold the word "bold" and italicize the word "italicized." You can do this by entering the following:

```
This line has words that are <B>bold</B> and
<I>italicized</I>.
```

6. From the File menu, select Save, and then save your document as mysecond.htm.

7. Open your Web browser. From the File menu, select Open and then type the name and page to the mysecond.htm file you just saved. Notice the way the text appears due to the HTML tags.

Coding Simple Tables and Forms

There comes a point at which you want your Web page to do more than merely display a number of paragraphs, one after the other. When you reach the need to go beyond the most basic level of text formatting, chances are you'll begin to use tables and forms. Tables enable you to split information into columns and rows, and show the information in a more structured and visually appealing manner. Forms allow you to gather information from users.

Using forms, you can get the information you need from users, such as name, address, credit card information, or comments. You can then set up methods that process this information in a specific manner (such as sending it to you through e-mail). In this section, we'll show you how to create both tables and forms for use on your Web page.

Creating Tables

Creating a table starts and ends with the <TABLE>...</TABLE> tags. Between these tags, you then set up rows and cells. Rows are created with the row tags <TR> and </TR>, while cells are defined with the tags <TD>...</TD>. For example, let's say you want to create a table consisting of one column and one row. This means that there is only one cell in the table, so you enter

```
<TABLE>
  <TR>
     <TD>  </TD>
  </TR>
</TABLE>
```

If you want your table to have multiple cells, you in effect create multiple columns. To do this, you insert additional cell tags between the row tags <TR>...</TR>. Any data you want displayed in a particular cell is entered or specified between the cell tags <TD>...</TD>. If you want to add more rows to your table, add more row tags between the <TABLE>...</TABLE> tags.

When you create tables for a Web site, it can get a little confusing when you write HTML to create a table with numerous rows and cells. Because of this, you should get into the habit of indenting your lines of code. In the previous example, each row is indented from where the <TABLE> and </TABLE> tags appear, and the cell tags <TD>...</TD> are also indented from where the row tags appear. This makes it easier to read your HTML code, so that it's less difficult to find problems when they occur in your code. While this may not be an issue with a table that's a single row and cell, it is important when you deal with more complex tables.

Caption Tags

The <CAPTION>...</CAPTION> tags can be used to create a caption for your table. Captions are lines of text that often appear above the table, and tell the reader what information the table contains. This allows a person viewing the table to immediatcly recognize what data the table holds, without having to read surrounding paragraphs. The caption above Table 5-2, for example, tells you that the table contains attributes of the <TABLE> element.

Attributes allow you to control features or characteristics of a table and caption. They enable you to control such things as spacing, the appearance of your table, and the positioning of caption text. By using attributes of the <TABLE> element, you can also specify how wide your table is, whether it has a border, its color, and so forth.

TABLE 5-2   Table Attributes

Attribute	Description
ALIGN	How the table or caption is aligned in relation to other elements in the HTML document. For example, to specify that a caption is to be aligned to the bottom of a table, you would set the align attribute as ALIGN="BOTTOM".
BGCOLOR	Used to set the background color of the table.
BORDER	Used to set the width of lines that outline the table. The border attribute is defined by specifying the number of pixels the border should be. For example, if you didn't want the table to have a border, you would specify BORDER= "0".
CELLSPACING	This sets the space between the border of your cell and the border of the table.
CELLPADDING	This sets the space between the border of your cell and the contents of the cell.
CLASS	Used to specify the class name of a style sheet.
COLS	Used to specify the number of columns in a table.
DIR	Used to specify the direction in which text flows. This is rarely used, but useful in cases of international formatting.
FRAME	Used to specify which sides of the frame surrounding the table are visible. The frame attribute can have any of the following values: VOID, for no frames ABOVE, for the top side of the frame BELOW, for the bottom side of the frame HSIDES, for both the top and bottom sides of the frame (that is, horizontal) VSIDES, for the left and right sides of the frame (that is, vertical) LHS, for the left side RHS, for the right side BOX, for all sides of the frame BORDER, for all four sides of the frame

TABLE 5-2	Table Attributes *(continued)*
Attribute	**Description**
ID	Used to identify an element of the table.
LANG	Used to specify the primary language used for information in the table, such as English.
RULES	Used to set which rules appear between table columns and rows. The values that can be applied to this attribute include NONE, for no rules GROUPS, for rules that appear only between groups ROWS, for rules appearing between rows COLS, for rules appearing between columns ALL, for rules appearing between all elements
STYLE	Used to set a style sheet that will define the appearance of the table.
TITLE	Used to display information as a ToolTip (a colored box displaying the text specified by the title attribute). This is particularly useful when you are creating Web pages for the blind or visually disabled who use audio browsers. Such browsers will speak the title through the PC speaker.
WIDTH	Used to set the width of the table. You can set the width of your table in pixels or by the percent of the screen the table will take up. For example, if you wanted your table to fill the entire width of the screen, you would enter width= "100%".

Using Tables in Web Documents

Tables are commonly used in Web pages, and are valuable in even the simplest Web pages. For example, tables can be used to keep your text properly formatted in a browser window. In surfing the Web, you may have come across paragraphs that are wider than your browser window, forcing you to scroll across to read the text. If you place this text in a table that has a single cell and a width of 100 percent, the contents of the table will fill the width of the browser, even when the window is resized. Should you require further tables in your Web page, you can then nest them. Nesting is putting a table within a table. You can also nest ordered and unordered lists, and so on, within themselves and any tables you create.

In most cases, you'll want to do more than create a simple, single-cell table. You would create multiple cells within the table, and you may want some of these cells to span more than one row or column. This is done with the ROWSPAN or COLSPAN attributes.

ROWSPAN is used to have a single cell span across multiple rows. To illustrate how ROWSPAN works, let's look at the following example of code:

```
<TABLE BORDER="1" WIDTH="100%">
  <TR>
    <TD ROWSPAN="2">This cell spans two rows</TD>
    <TD>This is a single cell</TD>
  </TR>
  <TR>
    <TD>This is a single cell</TD>
  </TR>
</TABLE>
```

The first line shows the border and width attributes of the <TABLE> tag being used. The border is set to a value of 1, so that we can see the table when it is viewed through a browser. The width attribute is set to 100 percent, so that the table fills the width of the browser. Later in the code, we see the ROWSPAN attribute of the <TD> tag being used. In this line, ROWSPAN is set to a value of 2, indicating that the cell is to span two rows. The value of ROWSPAN specifies how many rows the cell will span. The results of this code are shown in Figure 5-2.

FIGURE 5-2

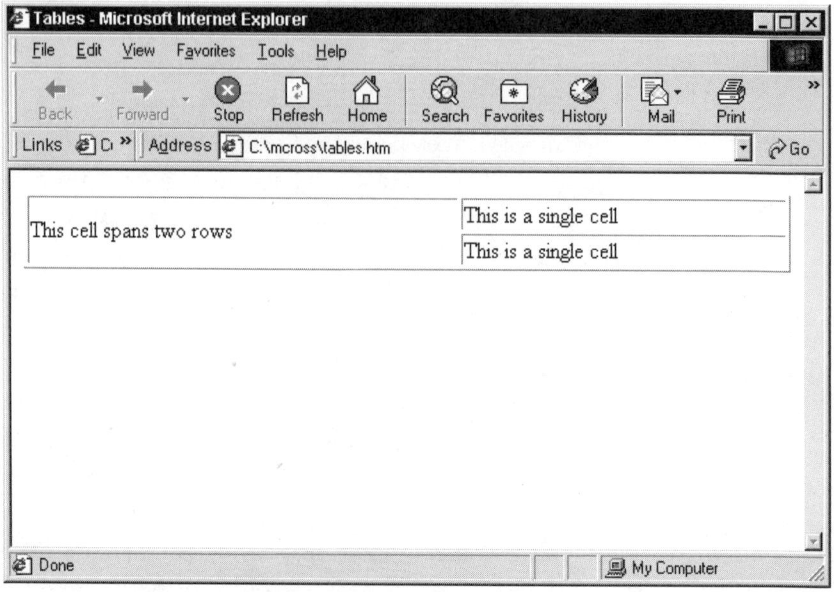

Example of how
ROWSPAN makes a cell
span multiple rows

COLSPAN is similar to ROWSPAN, except that it is used to have a single cell span across multiple columns. The value assigned to COLSPAN specifies the number of columns a particular cell is to span. To illustrate how COLSPAN works, let's look at the following example of code, and then look at the effects of this code when it is viewed through a browser.

```
<TABLE BORDER ="1" WIDTH="100%">
  <TR>
    <TD COLSPAN="2">This cell spans two columns</TD>
  </TR>
  <TR>
    <TD>This is one cell</TD>
    <TD>This is one cell</TD>
  </TR>
</TABLE>
```

As seen in this code, COLSPAN has been set to the number 2, meaning that this particular cell will span two columns. When it is viewed through a browser, it will appear as shown in Figure 5-3.

FIGURE 5-3

Example of how COLSPAN makes a cell span multiple columns

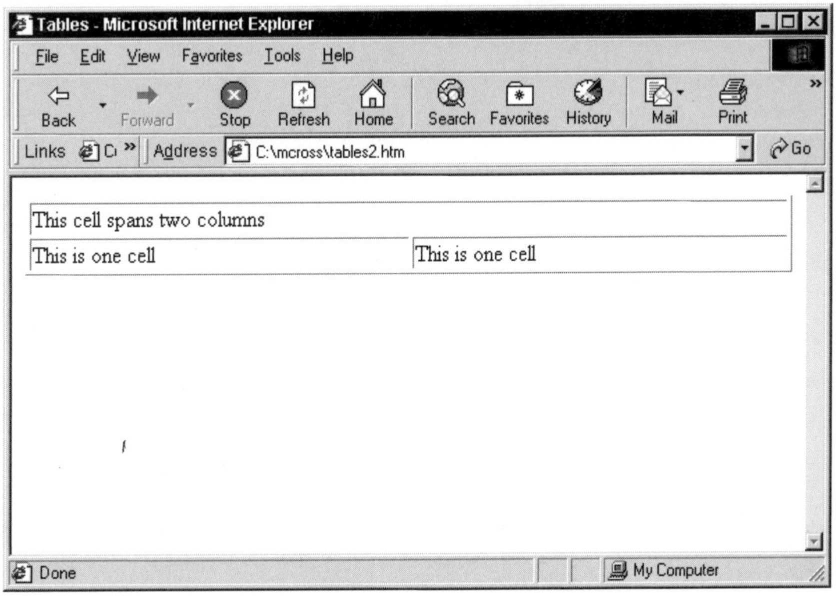

Creating a Simple Table with HTML

1. From your Windows Start menu, select Programs and then Accessories. From Accessories, click Notepad.

2. When Notepad starts, type the document structure of the Web page, as follows:

```
<HTML>
<HEAD>
<TITLE>My third Web page</TITLE>
<BODY>
</BODY>
</HTML>
```

3. Between the <BODY>…</BODY> tags, type the <TABLE>…</TABLE> tags that will specify that you're creating a table.

4. Between the <TABLE>…<TABLE> tags, enter the appropriate tags that will allow you to create two rows and two columns. This can be done by typing the following:

```
<TR>
     <TD></TD>
     <TD></TD>
</TR>
<TR>
     <TD></TD>
     <TD></TD>
</TR>
```

5. In the first cell of the first row, enter your name.

6. Immediately after the <TABLE> tag, enter a caption stating "This is my first table." Specify that the caption is to be aligned at the bottom of the table. This can be done by typing

```
<CAPTION ALIGN =BOTTOM>This is my first
table</CAPTION>
```

7. From the File menu, select Save, and then save your document as mythird.htm.

8. Open your Web browser. From the File menu, select Open, and then type the name and page to the mythird.htm file you just saved. Notice the way the text appears due to the HTML tags.

While tables allow you to display static information, forms can be used to obtain information and feedback from those viewing the page. This data can then be processed in some way through a script or application. For example, if the form asks for a user's name and address, and you click a button on your Web page, this information is sent to you via e-mail.

A form is created using the <FORM> and </FORM> tags. These tags have several optional attributes, which aren't required when creating forms but may be useful in certain situations. These attributes consist of

- **ACTION,** which specifies the URL of the Web server script or application that processes information entered in the form.

- **METHOD,** which specifies how information will be sent. The value of the METHOD attribute can be set to either "GET" or "POST". GET attaches form information to the end of a URL, while POST returns the information by encapsulating it and sending it to a program or script. With CGI, GET truncates after 80 characters, which is why it's best to use POST as the method in which longer messages are sent.

- **NAME,** which is the name of the form

- **TARGET,** which specifies the window location where responses are sent. The target can be set to a particular frame in a window.

Once you've set up the <FORM>...</FORM> tags, and added the optional attributes you decide are useful or necessary to your form's functionality, you can then add elements to your form. These elements provide the ability to enter and retrieve information through the form.

There are a number of different elements that can be added to a form, and each looks different and has a different function. As we'll see in the paragraphs that follow, most of these elements are created using the <INPUT> tag. This tag specifies the method in which data will be entered into the form, or—as in the case of a push button—to indicate that data in the form is to be processed.

A button is one of the most common elements you'll add to a form. When a button element is added to a form, it appears in the Web page as a 3-D Windows push button. The only attributes a button must have are VALUE and NAME. VALUE contains the text that will appear in the button, telling the user what the button is for. The NAME attribute is used to name the element, allowing you to use it in any scripts in your document. To illustrate how you can create a button on your Web page, let's look at the following code:

```
<INPUT TYPE ="BUTTON" VALUE="button text" NAME="ButtonName">
```

When this line of code is entered between the <FORM>...</FORM> tags, you will see a gray button with shaded sides (giving it a 3-D appearance) when you view the document in your browser (see Figure 5-4). The button would also have the words "button text" written across it. If you wrote a script that used the button, you could then refer to it by the name ButtonName.

FIGURE 5-4

Elements that commonly appear on Web pages

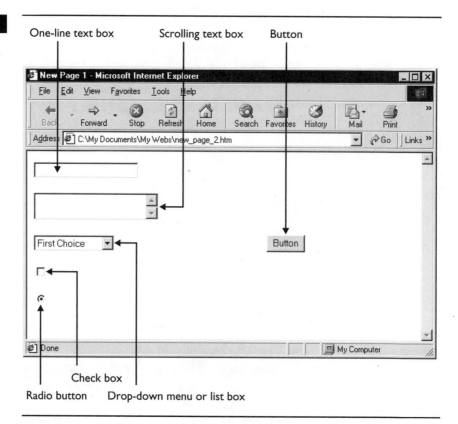

The button element isn't the only button-type object you can place on a form. Two other buttons that often appear on forms are the "submit" and "reset" elements. The Submit button is used to submit the information entered into the form to some processing application or script. The Reset button is used to restore the form to its initial, default values. For example, if your form had a number of areas to enter text, click check boxes, and so forth, the user may decide to reenter all of his or her information. Rather than going through each field and erasing it, or clicking elements to restore them to the way they were before, the user could simply click a Reset button. You can create a Submit and Reset button as follows:

```
<INPUT TYPE ="SUBMIT" VALUE="Submit" NAME="B1">
<INPUT TYPE ="RESET" VALUE="Reset"NAME="B2">
```

As with the button element, the Reset and Submit buttons also have a name attribute. You can use this attribute to name the buttons, and refer to them in any scripting code used in your Web page.

Check boxes are another common element in forms. When viewed through a browser, the check box element appears as a square. When you click it, the check box will appear checked. The text appearing beside a check box is used to indicate choices for the user. When multiple check boxes appear on a form, the user can choose one or more of the check boxes.

Radio buttons are similar to check boxes in that they are used to gather input, by having a user click it to choose an option. Radio buttons are round, and look like an "o" in a browser. When a button is selected, a small dot will appear in it to indicate the selection. Another difference between check boxes and radio buttons is that, while check boxes can be used to accept multiple choices, you can only click a single radio button. In other words, if you had three radio buttons, you could only click one of them. If you clicked another, the first radio button you clicked would be cleared.

Radio buttons and check boxes have the same attributes: VALUE, NAME, and CHECKED. However, some of these attributes have different meanings. For check boxes, the NAME attribute is used to name the element, allowing you to call it in any scripts used in your document. When it is used for check boxes, the name can be different for each check box. You can give each check box the same name, but you don't have to. For radio buttons, the NAME attribute is used to specify what group of radio buttons that particular radio button belongs to. Since only one radio button per group can be checked, the name identifies which group it belongs to. This allows a button to automatically be unselected, when another radio button in the group is selected. The VALUE attribute is generally used only for scripts in your HTML document, or for passing values to the server. It's used to specify the value of a radio button or check box when it's selected. Finally, the CHECKED attribute is used to indicate whether the check box or radio button is initially selected when the Web page is initially loaded. For radio buttons, one must be checked in each group when the Web page is loaded. For check boxes, none or all of them can be checked.

To illustrate the differences between radio buttons and check boxes, let's look at the following code, and then see how it's displayed in a browser:

```
<HTML>
<HEAD>
<TITLE>Check Form</TITLE>
</HEAD>
<BODY>
<FORM>
  <P>Choose your age:</P>
  <P><INPUT TYPE ="RADIO" VALUE="1" NAME="group1">Under 30<BR>
  <INPUT TYPE ="RADIO" VALUE="2" NAME="group1" CHECKED>30-65<BR>
  <INPUT TYPE ="RADIO" VALUE="3" NAME="group1">Over 65</P>
  <P>Enter your favorite color(s): </P>
  <P><INPUT TYPE ="CHECKBOX" NAME="C1" VALUE="1">Blue<BR>
  <INPUT TYPE ="CHECKBOX" NAME="C2" VALUE="1">Red<BR>
  <INPUT TYPE="CHECKBOX" NAME="C3" VALUE="1">Green</P>
</FORM>
</BODY>
</HTML>
```

As you can see in this code, each of the radio buttons has the name "group1." This means that when one of the radio buttons in the group is selected, the others in that group will be deselected. This is because radio buttons are used when you want the user to choose only one option or choice. In this example, users can only be one age, so they are only allowed a single choice. Contrary to this, check boxes are used in situations in which the user may make multiple choices, such as choosing different favorite colors. Each of the check boxes has a different name, since they don't need to belong to a group and can be named individually. You'll also note that—as is required—one of the radio buttons is checked by default. When this code appears in a browser, it looks like what's shown in Figure 5-5.

Entering text is essential to most forms. In many cases, you want to either gather individual input from users, or obtain a way to contact them. After all, if a user orders a product through your form, you'll need to gather the user's name, credit card information, and where you should deliver the product. In other forms, such as one that gets feedback from users, you may ask for the person's e-mail address and a place for people to enter their comments. If you have an area of the Web site that requires security, the users could be asked to enter a password. No matter why you're asking them for this data, the fact remains that you'll need to provide a method for users to input textual information.

FIGURE 5-5

Example of check boxes and radio buttons in a Web page

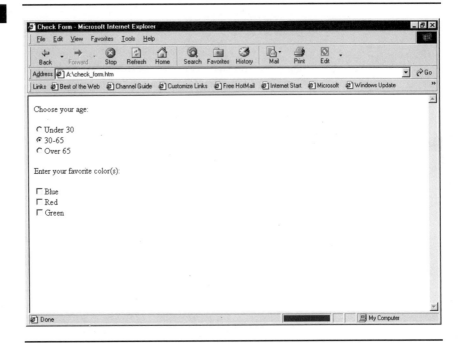

HTML has three commonly used elements for textual input: TEXT, TEXTAREA, and PASSWORD. The TEXT element is used for situations in which the user needs to enter a single line of text, such as name, username, age, and so forth. The PASSWORD element is similar to the TEXT element, except that it hides whatever the user types by displaying asterisks instead of text. The TEXTAREA element is also similar to the TEXT element, except that it can accept multiple lines of text. You often see the TEXTAREA element being used for accepting comments or feedback.

The TEXT element is created using the <TEXT> tag, and has three attributes that are commonly used. The use of this tag and its attributes are shown in the following example of code:

```
<INPUT TYPE ="TEXT" NAME="T1" SIZE="20" VALUE="Enter name here">
```

The first attribute in this line of code is the NAME attribute, which specifies the element's name. The SIZE attribute is used to define the width of the text box on the screen. The size of the TEXT element is measured in characters. The value associated with it defines how many characters can be entered in the text field, before the user needs to use the arrow keys to scroll across to see additional text. Finally, the VALUE attribute is used to set the text that will appear when the Web page first loads. This can tell the user what to enter or—if it is VALUE=""—it can be left blank.

The PASSWORD element appears as a box on a Web page, just like a normal TEXT element. The difference is that when the user types in a word (such as a password), the field displays only asterisks. This protects the user. If someone were looking over the user's shoulder when the password was being entered, that person wouldn't be able to read the user's password. You can create a password field on a form using the following example of code:

```
<INPUT TYPE ="PASSWORD" NAME="T2" SIZE="20">
```

As you can see in the example, the PASSWORD element has a NAME attribute to specify the element's name. The SIZE attribute is also used with this element, specifying the length of the field in characters. Each of these attributes is identical to those used with the TEXT element.

The TEXTAREA element is used to take larger amounts of text than the TEXT or PASSWORD elements. Unlike either of the two previously mentioned elements, the TEXTAREA element is designed for multiple lines of input and has both an opening and closing tag. A TEXTAREA is created using the <TEXTAREA> and </TEXTAREA> tags, as shown here:

```
<TEXTAREA ROWS="2" NAME="S1" COLS="20">Enter Comments here</TEXTAREA>
```

When you create this element, anything you type between the <TEXTAREA>...</TEXTAREA> tags will appear inside the TEXTAREA. This basically sets its initial value, allowing you to enter brief instructions or other information. Like the other elements, the NAME attribute is used to define the element's name. It differs from the other elements in the use of ROWS and COLS, which are used to control the width and height, respectively, of the TEXTAREA. The ROWS attribute sets how many lines of text will be visible, while the COLS attribute sets how many characters wide the TEXTAREA will be. For example, in the code in the example, the TEXTAREA is 2 rows high and 20 characters wide. A user who enters three or more lines of text will need to scroll to see the additional text.

While the TEXT, TEXTAREA, and PASSWORD elements allow independent input on a user-to-user basis, there will be times when users will be entering similar information. For example, if you were asking the gender of a user, there would be one of two answers: male or female. If you were asking for an address, the street addresses of most users would be different, but the states and provinces that many live in would be the same. In such cases, it might be useful to provide a form element to allow users to choose from a selection of possible responses.

HTML provides the means to create a selection list in your form. Selection lists, which are often referred to as selection menus or drop-down lists, are created using the <SELECT> and </SELECT> tags. As shown in the following example, options (choices) are placed between the opening and closing tags to fill the listing.

```
<SELECT NAME ="GenderList" SIZE="1">
    <OPTION VALUE ="Male">Male</OPTION>
    <OPTION VALUE="Female">Female</OPTION>
    <OPTION SELECTED VALUE="Undisclosed">Undisclosed</OPTION>
</SELECT>
```

The <SELECT> tag has several attributes that are used to modify the listing. As we've seen with other HTML tags, the NAME tag is used to provide the element with a name that can be referred to in scripts. The SIZE attribute is used to specify how many of the choices are seen before the user clicks the selection list. If SIZE="1", then only one option is displayed. If this is set to 2, then two options are shown. More options are displayed when the user clicks the selection list itself. While, by default, the user can only choose one of these options at a time, more than one can be selected if the MULTIPLE attribute is used. The <SELECT MULTIPLE> tag allows users to select one or more choices from the list.

Choices are added to the selection list using the <OPTION> tag, which is placed between the <SELECT>…</SELECT> tags. In looking at the preceding example of code, you may have noticed that there is a closing tag (</OPTION>) that can be used. The </OPTION> tag isn't required, and is actually ignored by browsers. The <OPTION> tag acts as a delimiter and thereby doesn't require a closing tag. Like the </P> tag for paragraphs, this closing tag provides consistency with other HTML tags. Despite the fact that a browser will still display the <OPTION> if a closing tag isn't used, you should use an </OPTION> tag to close off any options you provide. This will avoid any trailing spaces that may be needed being stripped by a client or server-side script. Any text appearing after the <OPTION> tag appears as a possible selection in the listing. Using the VALUE attribute, you can assign a value to the option chosen by the user, which can be used in a script in your HTML document or by a script or program on the server. The VALUE attribute allows you to display one value to the user, and pass another value to a client or server-side script. For example, you could have an option of yes with the value of 1 and an option of no with the value of 2. The value could be passed to a script or program that would then process these values accordingly. Finally, the "selected" attribute can be added to specify the option that is chosen by default when the Web page first loads. Unless the MULTIPLE attribute is used in the <SELECT> tag, then only one option can be selected.

```
<HEAD><TITLE></TITLE><BODY></BODY></HTML><BODY></BODY><TR><TD></TD><TD></TD>
</TR><TR><TD></TD><TD></TD></TR>
```

Building Your Page with More Advanced Tags

Although a good portion of any Web page you create will consist of text entered into the <BODY>…</BODY> section of your HTML document, there are times when you'll want to punch up your page by adding tags and text to the <HEAD>...</HEAD> of your Web page. While the <TITLE>...</TITLE> tag set is the only one required in the <HEAD>...</HEAD> section, there are more advanced tags that can be used in your HTML documents. You can add other elements that can be useful to browsers and search engines, and may improve the quality of your Web page. Metadata can be added to the <HEAD>...</HEAD> section to help define visual elements and determine how accessible your HTML document will be on the Web. Metadata isn't a tag in itself, but it is used to describe a group of tags that include

- STYLE
- BASE
- META

In the paragraphs that follow, we'll go through each of these tags and explain how they are useful in Web page design.

Cascading Style Sheets (CSS)

Cascading style sheets are a part of DHTML. Style sheets are embedded directly into the <HEAD>...</HEAD> section of your HTML document using the <STYLE>...</STYLE> tags. Between these tags, you specify defaults for how your page or elements of your page should appear in a browser. To illustrate how this is done, let's look at an example of HTML.

```
<STYLE>
body{background-color: aqua; color: navy; font-family:
 Arial; font-size: 12; font-style: italic; margin: 0.5in}
</STYLE>
```

If this code were placed in the <HEAD>...</HEAD> section of your Web page, it would change the page so that, when viewed in a browser, it has an aqua background, navy blue text, and a ½-inch margin. It would also change the text so it would use an italicized, 12-point, Arial font. Rather than having you modify each line of text entered into your HTML document, the <STYLE>...</STYLE> tags allow you to lay out the style of your document before any text is entered.

Hyperlinks

The base element is used to provide a base URL from which all links in the <BODY>...</BODY> of the page are referenced. To understand the <BASE> element, we must first discuss how to create a hyperlink.

Hyperlinks are associated with images or text (which usually appears underlined) in a Web page. They are entered in the <BODY>...</BODY> section of your Web page. When the user clicks the hyperlinked image or text, the browser takes them to a Web page or performs an action associated with the hyperlink. To create a hyperlink, you use the anchor tags <A>...</A> combined with the hyperlink reference (HREF=) that refers to the URL or action to be performed. For example, in the following code, the first line has a hyperlink that refers to the URL of the Comptia Web site. If this hyperlink were clicked, the default HTML document for that Web site would appear in the browser. The second line shows a hyperlink with the word "mailto:" and an e-mail address. This hyperlink indicates that, when the link is clicked, mail is to be sent to the specified e-mail address. It is this prefix that indicates the action and protocol to be used. This could be mailto://, news://, http://, and so forth. If mailto:// were used, the user's e-mail program would open, with the e-mail address entered in the To: field.

```
<A HREF ="http://www.comptia.com">Comptia Website</A>
<A HREF="mailto:someone@microsoft.com">Webmaster</A>
```

Regardless of the action or URL associated with the hyperlink, the text between the <A>...</A> tags is what will appear on the Web page. This text will appear underlined, indicating that it is a hyperlink to another document or for sending e-mail to someone.

With hyperlinks, you don't need to specify a complete URL to access a particular HTML document.

```
<A HREF="my.htm">Local document</A>
```

With this hyperlink, a document called my.htm is referenced. Because there is no Web site specified as to where the HTML document resides, it would be assumed by the Web server that this document resides on the same Web site, and in the same directory, as the document currently being viewed. For example, if you were viewing a document in the /Webpage directory of www.comptia.com, then the Web server would try to return a document in that directory at that Web site. This would be the same as if you entered **www.comptia.com/Webpage/my.htm** in the address bar of your browser.

Now that we have a better understanding of hyperlinks, let's return to the discussion of the <BASE> element. Earlier, we mentioned that the <BASE> element is used to provide a base URL from which all links in the <BODY>...</BODY> of the page are referenced. For example, let's say you had the following code added to the <HEAD>...</HEAD> of your HTML document:

```
<BASE HREF ="http://www.comptia.com">
```

With this code, any hyperlink on your page would have this Web site appended to the hyperlink reference. For example, let's say you had a hyperlink to a page called my.htm. With the <BASE> element, the URL in the <BASE> tag would be appended to this page. If the <BASE> tag were the same as the one in the previous example, that would mean the reference to my.htm would be appended to become http://www.comptia.com/ my.htm.

META Tag

The META element is primarily used by Web search engines and Spiders. Web search engines are used to search for specific Web pages, based on the keywords you enter into the engine. Spiders search the Internet for new pages to add to the search engine. One method in which data about a Web page is entered into a search engine is through the META element, and its NAME and CONTENT attributes.

```
<META NAME="description" CONTENT="This is my description">
<META NAME ="keywords" CONTENT="Web, HTML, Internet">
```

In the first line of this code, the NAME attribute states that this line contains a description of the Web page. This description is specified by the CONTENT attribute. When the page appears as a result of a search, the description will generally appear below the name of the page. The name is obtained by the search engine through the <TITLE>...</TITLE> tags of your Web page. The next line is another META element, but you'll notice that the name now states that this line contains keywords describing the page. These are the words that someone may enter into a search engine about a certain topic. Because of this, it's important that you enter into the CONTENT attribute as many keywords as possible about your page. This will give your page a better chance of appearing in a search engine.

The <SCRIPT>...</SCRIPT> tags are used to indicate that the code appearing between these tags is a scripting language that is to execute as a program. For example, you might enter JavaScript or VBScript code that performs some action when a user clicks a button on a form. To specify the type of language being used between these tags, you use the LANGUAGE attribute, as shown in the following example:

```
<SCRIPT LANGUAGE ="JavaScript">
      ...Scripting code would go here...
</SCRIPT>
```

When the browser reads these lines, it sees that the scripting language being used is JavaScript. It then executes the code accordingly, performing whatever action the code was created to do.

Difference Between Text Editors and GUI Editors

Until this point, we've discussed writing HTML documents through a text editor, like Notepad.exe. However, this isn't the only way to create Web pages. There are a number of editors on the market that are GUI editors, which allow you to see what the Web page will look like as you create it. Such editors include Microsoft FrontPage, NetScape Composer, HotDog, and many others. These editors work like a desktop publishing program. You don't need to enter tags for most of the contents of your Web page. You type the text you want; format it with buttons on a toolbar or through menus in the editor; and insert images, forms, and tables as you would in a word processing or desktop publishing program. A number of the GUI editors include templates, which have much of the formatting already set up for you.

Just because GUI editors work on a WYSIWYG (What You See Is What You Get) principle, it doesn't mean that you don't need an understanding of HTML. A number of elements—such as metadata, scripting, and so on—need to be manually entered into the document. Some GUI editors, such as Microsoft FrontPage, realize this need and provide a way to edit the HTML coding with the GUI editor. This keeps you from having to save the document in the GUI editor, and then open the same document in a text editor. Additional features in some GUI editors include the ability to preview what the document will look like, and how it will function, without your having to open it in a browser.

Depending on the GUI editor being used, you will also find a number of tools and features that make creating a Web page easier. GUI editors like Microsoft FrontPage include a toolbar that enables you to modify graphics within the editor. For example, after inserting a graphic, you could make parts of the graphic transparent in the Web page. While not all GUI editors provide this ability, newer GUI editors are providing a greater array of options for creating incredible Web pages.

Whether you decide to use a GUI editor or not, you will need a good text editor. Some GUI editors, like Microsoft FrontPage, recognize this need and provide you with a built-in text editor so that you can work directly with the HTML. Some features provided by some of the better text editors include color coding or tags, closing tags that are automatically inserted, and intellisense-type technology that provides you with the attributes of a tag as you type it. With other editors, the distinctions between GUI editors and text editors are blurred, providing toolbars that insert tables, form elements, images, and so forth, directly into your HTML document. While you're not provided with a WYSIWYG interface, tools are provided to make working with HTML even easier.

Compatibility Between Browsers

Tim Berners-Lee created HTML, and his World Wide Web Consortium (W3C) makes recommendations on the latest versions of HTML, but they don't control which tags are actually used in Web pages and browsers. For example, earlier in this chapter, it was mentioned that the <U>...</U> tags can make text appear underlined in a browser. In the latest version of HTML, the W3C no longer recommends using this tag; but most browsers (including the latest versions of Netscape Navigator and Microsoft Internet

Explorer) continue to read these tags and underline text because many Web pages on the Web still use them, and for that reason, Netscape and Microsoft choose to ignore the recommendation. The fact is that if Web page authors use tag sets or technologies in their Web sites, the companies that make the Internet browsers will generally follow suit. After all, as a Web page author, you're the one who helps make the Web what it is.

Just as browser developers tend to ignore recommendations to stop supporting certain HTML tags, one company may see a future in supporting one technology or new tag set, while another may choose to wait and see whether Web page authors start using it before offering browser support. For this reason, one browser may support something used in your Web page, while another may not. To make the issue even more complicated, some browsers on the market are jumping ahead of W3C recommendations, and offering HTML extensions and features that work only with that company's particular browser. This means that a feature that works in Microsoft Internet Explorer may not work as expected—if at all—in Netscape Navigator or other browsers.

exam
Watch

It is important to remember that HTML is a vendor-neutral standard that is owned by the W3C. Tags that are part of this standard, and recommended by the W3C, are meant to be employed and will work with any browser that is compliant with that version of HTML. Browser manufacturers like Netscape and Microsoft occasionally develop proprietary tags that may not work with other browsers. Because such tags aren't part of the HTML standard, browsers created by other manufacturers that don't employ the proprietary tag won't be able to interpret it.

To some degree, you will need to decide which browsers your Web site will be geared to support.

There are hundreds of browsers and browser versions on the market, and some of these won't support what you may consider to be common elements. For example, Lynx is a text-based browser, meaning that it won't display graphics. If you were creating a Web site that was to be accessed by visually impaired users, then Lynx would be a common browser that users of your site would use. In addition, browsers created before a new version of HTML won't be able to interpret the newest additions to the standard. For example, a browser created before HTML 4 won't be able to interpret a tag added to that standard. This would, however, mean that users of other browsers would be limited to a certain degree. What may look perfect in one browser may not look as good in another browser.

Due to the sheer number of browsers available to users on the Web, you can't check how your page looks in every browser on the market. Still, you should see how your Web page looks in the major browsers, Netscape Navigator and Microsoft Internet Explorer.

Over 90 percent of the browsers used on the Internet are manufactured by these two companies. If the page looks okay in these, then a majority of users will be able to view your page the way you want it to be seen. You can provide links from your main page, with recommendations as to which browser is best to view your site. If you don't want to make recommendations, then cross-browser coding is another option for your page.

Creating Cross-Browser Coding in HTML

Cross-browser coding can be used to enable your Web page to be viewed in any browser, and allows you to create HTML documents or parts of HTML documents that will run only in specific browsers.

In other words, a user who is viewing your Web page with Netscape Navigator will see one version of your page. Users viewing with Internet Explorer will see another version, while users with other browsers will see yet another version of your Web page. Such cross-browser coding can be added to your HTML document using any one of a number of scripting languages, such as JavaScript or VBScript.

With such a script, you can determine the type and version of the browser being used to view the page. Once this information has been retrieved by your code, you can then have the HTML created for that browser type and version returned to the browser so it can be properly viewed. To do this, you'll need to know something about crating such scripts in your document.

```
<SCRIPT></SCRIPT></SCRIPT><SCRIPT></SCRIPT>
.
\<BODY><BODY></SCRIPT><SCRIPT>
```

QUESTIONS AND ANSWERS

What does HTML stand for?	HTML is an acronym for Hypertext Markup Language.
Why are there some HTML tags that do the exact same things?	Some older tags have been replaced with newer tags that have the same effect. Examples of this are the <B> and <STRONG> tags that bold text, and the <I> and <EM> tags for italicizing text. The World Wide Web Consortium (W3C) changes their recommendations to using these newer tags, which often require less typing, but generally the older ones will still work in browsers. For some tags, like <TT>, <SAMP>, <CODE>, and <KBD>, the reason for having different tags that do the same things lies in where they are used. Each of these tags provides the reader of the HTML code insight into why the code is there.
I tried to italicize a single word in a sentence appearing in my Web page. Now the entire Web page from that point on is italicized. What could have caused this?	This is probably because you forgot to use a closing or end tag after the word you wanted italicized. You need to put an </I> tag in the place where you want italics to stop being used. Closing tags specify where a particular type of formatting is to stop.
I've written cross-browser compatible code in my HTML document using JavaScript. However, when I try to load the page in an older browser, an error occurs. Why might this be?	If the browser doesn't support scripting, then it may be experiencing an error upon reaching the JavaScript. To fix this error, use the <!-- and --> tags that indicate that text between these tags is a comment that can be ignored. If the browser doesn't support JavaScript, then the script will be ignored. If JavaScript is supported, then the script will execute and provide browser-specific content.

CERTIFICATION SUMMARY

HTML is an acronym for the HyperText Markup Language. Markup languages use formatting commands to format how text is displayed in a Web browser. It is through HTML that you're able to use the Internet in a graphical, point-and-click fashion.

The way HTML works starts with the Web page residing on an Internet server. When a user types a URL (such as www.comptia.com) into a browser's address bar, an HTML document is requested. The Web server uses the HTTP protocol to send the Web page to the browser, which then reads the document and all of the HTML tags contained in it. These tags determine how the Web page will be displayed in the browser.

When writing an HTML document, there are a large number of tags that can be used to format the text and the Web page itself. In addition to this, you can improve the look and functionality of your Web page using tables, forms, and metadata. By adding these elements to a Web page, you not only enhance the end user's experience with your pages, but can also add such abilities as users being able to use form fields to send data, and search engines being able to acquire data about the page.

After creating an HTML document, it is important that you check how the Web page appears in more than one browser. Some elements and features in a Web page may not appear exactly the same—if at all—in certain browsers. While in many cases the inability to display aspects of your page will only be aesthetic, this will give you insight into how a user of the page will see it. If the element or feature is important enough, you can then recommend a certain browser in which to view the page, or provide code that is specific to the browser currently being used.

You can also write code using Javascript or other scripting languages, which allow you to determine the type of browser being used to view the Web page. Using such code, you can retrieve information on the name of the application being used to view the HTML document, and the version of browser being used. This allows you to write HTML and script that is specific to a particular type and version of browser.

TWO-MINUTE DRILL

- ❑ The language most commonly used on the World Wide Web is HTML.
- ❑ While HTTP accesses the World Wide Web and transports the Web page from a server to your browser, HTML is used to create Web page documents and dictate how those documents will display in your browser.
- ❑ *Markup languages* use symbols, characters, and statements to format a document. These are placed in the document to indicate how that area of the document should appear when it is viewed or printed. In HTML, the indicators that the author uses are called tags.

❏ *Tags* are elements that tell a Web browser that the document uses HTML, and how information is to be formatted and displayed. A tag is a letter or statement between the < and > symbols.

❏ DHTML is an acronym for Dynamic HyperText Markup Language, or Dynamic HTML. As its name suggests, it allows a Web page to be dynamically altered once it has been loaded.

❏ Tables enable you to structure information into columns and rows, and present the information in a more interesting and effective manner. Forms allow you to display and gather information from users, and provide an interactive way of doing business on the Web. Using forms, you can get the information you need from a user, such as name, address, credit card information, or comments. You can then set up methods that process this information in a specific manner (such as sending it to you through e-mail).

❏ When you create tables for a Web site, it can get a little confusing when you write HTML to create a table with numerous rows and cells. Because of this, you should get into the habit of indenting your lines of code.

❏ Attributes allow you to control features or characteristics of a table and caption. They enable you to control such things as spacing, the appearance of your table, and the positioning of caption text. By using attributes of the <TABLE> element, you can also specify how wide your table is, whether it has a border, its color, and so forth.

❏ Although a good portion of any Web page you create will consist of text entered into the <BODY>...</BODY> section of your HTML document, there are times when you'll want to punch up your page by adding tags and text to the <HEAD>...</HEAD> of your Web page. While the <TITLE>...</TITLE> tag set is the only one required in the <HEAD>...</HEAD> section, there are more advanced tags that can be used in your HTML documents. You can add other elements that can be useful to browsers. You can add search engines, and you may improve the quality of your Web page. Metadata can be added to the <HEAD>...</HEAD> section to help define visual elements and determine how accessible your HTML document will be on the Web.

❑ Hyperlinks are associated with images or text (which usually appears underlined) in a Web page. They are entered in the <BODY>...</BODY> section of your Web page. When users click on the hyperlinked image or text, the browser takes them to a Web page or performs an action associated with the hyperlink.

❑ Cross-browser coding can be used to create HTML documents or parts of HTML documents that will run only in specific browsers. In other words, a user who is viewing your Web page with Netscape Navigator will see one version of your page. Users viewing with Internet Explorer will see another version, while users with other browsers will see yet another version of your Web page.

SELF TEST

The following Self Test questions will help you measure your understanding of the material presented in this chapter. Read all the choices carefully, as there may be more than one correct answer. Choose all correct answers for each question.

1. You have decided to create a Web page, and you need to control how data will be displayed in the user's Web browser. Which of the following determines how a Web page will be displayed in a Web browser, and can be used by a Web page author to control the display of information?

    A. HTTP

    B. HTML

    C. The Web browser used to access the Web pages

    D. The Web server that sent the Web pages to the Web browser

2. You are creating an HTML document and want to enter a title for your page, which will appear in the browser's titlebar. In which of the following would you enter the <TITLE>…</TITLE> tags containing this title?

    A. <BODY>…</BODY>

    B. <HEAD>…</HEAD>

    C. <FOOT>…</FOOT>

    D. <STYLE>…</STYLE>

3. You are creating a Web page and want to use heading tags to display textual information in different sizes. Which of the following tags would display text in the largest size?

    A. <H1> *the largest*

    B. <H2>

    C. <H6>

    D. <H7>

4. You want to have your text appear bold when your HTML document is displayed in a browser. Which of the following tags would you use to do this? (Choose all that apply.)

    A.

    B. <B>

    C. <EM>

    D. <STRONG>

5. You want to have your text appear italicized when your HTML document is displayed in a browser. Which of the following tags would you use to do this? (Choose all that apply.)

    A. <EM>

    B. <I>

    C. <TT>

    D. <STRONG>

6. You are creating a Web page for a local newspaper, and decide to make some of the text on the page appear as if it were typed on a typewriter. Which of the following could be used to make the text appear this way? (Choose all that apply.)

   ✔ A. <CODE>
   ✔ B. <TT>
   C. <HR>
   ✔ D. <SAMP>

7. You have a Web page that discusses several different issues. You decide to separate these topics with a line that stretches across 90 percent of your Web page. This line should be centered in the middle of the Web page. Which of the following would you use to create this line?

   A. <LINE SIZE ="90%" ALIGN="center">
   B. <LINE ALIGN ="center" WIDTH="90">
   ✔ C. <HR ALIGN ="center" WIDTH="90%" *L/HR>*
   D. <HR SIZE ="90%" CENTER>

8. You are preparing to create a table in your HTML document. Which of the following tags would you use to create a table cell?

   A. <TR>
   B.
   ✔ C. <TD> *table data*
   D. <TC>

9. You have created a form on your Web page, and now want to create a button using the <INPUT> tag. Which of the following is used with the <INPUT> tag to determine what text will appear on the button's face? In this case, the word "button" would appear on the face of the button.

   A. INPUT="button"
   B. NAME="button"
   ✔ C. VALUE="button"
   D. TEXT="button"

10. You have created a form that will survey users of your Web site, and are placing controls on this form that will allow users to enter input. When users answer these questions, you want to control the types of answers they give. Users will be able to answer questions by clicking only choices that you create. For each of the answers, you want users to be able to make multiple selections from a listing of possible choices. Which of the following will you use on this form? (Choose all that apply.)

   A. Radio buttons
   B. Check boxes
   C. Text areas
   D. Selection lists

11. You have written a considerable amount of text in a single paragraph, and now want to create a single, blank line between this paragraph and another. Which of the following tags will you use?

    A. </P>

    B. <P>

    C.

    D. None of the above. When you type in the text editor, press ENTER to create a new paragraph.

12. You have created a selection list on a Web page form. Which of the following tags must be used to create choices that will appear in the listing? (Choose all that apply.)

    A. <SELECT>

    B. <OPTION>

    C. <SCRIPT>

    D. </OPTION>

13. You have the following line of HTML entered into your Web page:

    ```
    <U>Clicking the text that follows will
    take you to the
    <A HREF="http://www.comptia.com"
    >Comptia Website</A>
    ```

    Which of the following is a problem that users will experience when they view this through a browser?

    A. The HTML is split over several lines, so the hyperlink won't work correctly.

    B. There is no closing tag for <U>, so text won't appear underlined.

    C. All text will appear underlined, so the user may click underlined text, thinking that it's a hyperlink that doesn't work.

    D. The <U> tag won't work, because most browsers ignore the <U> tag.

14. You have entered text into your HTML document, and have decided that this text would be easier to follow if it were numbered. You decide to create a list of items, with each item numbered. Which of the following would you use?

    A. <OL>

    B. <UL>

    C. <IL>

    D. <NL>

15. You have entered text into your HTML document, and have decided that this text would be easier to follow if it were bulleted. You decide to create a list of items, with each item bulleted. Which of the following would you use?

    A. <OL>

    B. <UL>

    C. <IL>

    D. <BL>

16. You have entered text into your HTML document, and have decided that this text

would be easier to follow if it were in a list. In this text, some items will appear bulleted, while other text will appear as items in a numbered list. Which of the following tags would you use to specify items in each list?

A. <UL>

B. <OL>

C. <IL>

D. <LI>

17. You have created a Web page that uses a form to gather input from users. Which of the following elements would you use for the user to enter a single line of text, such as a name, username, age, or other short amount of information? The user should be able to view his or her input as it is typed into the field.

A. <TEXT>

B. <TEXTAREA>

C. <PASSWORD>

D. <TXT>

18. You have created a Web page that uses a form to gather input from users. Which of the following elements would you use for the user to enter a password that will enable him or her to enter a secure site? The text entered into this field should not be visible to the user.

A. <TEXT>

B. <PASS>

C. <PASSWORD>

D. <PWORD>

19. You have created a Web page that uses a form to gather input from users. Which of the following elements would you use for the user to enter comments and feedback on your Web site? The user should be able to enter multiple lines of text.

A. <TEXT>

B. <TEXTAREA>

C. <PASSWORD>

D. <TXTAREA>

20. You have created a Web page that uses some proprietary tags developed by Microsoft for Internet Explorer 5. When users view this page with browsers developed by other manufacturers, what will happen?

A. The Web page will be viewed the same in each browser.

B. Text and graphics using the proprietary tags won't display as expected in some or all of the other browsers.

C. There are no proprietary tags. All tags are created by W3C.

D. The browsers will interpret the tags and attempt displaying the formatted elements by "guessing" what the author was attempting to do. This is similar to the way fonts are displayed when a user doesn't have a specific font used in the page.

SELF TEST ANSWERS

1. **B.** HTML is the Hypertext Markup Language, which is used to create Web pages. Tags in the page are used to indicate how text will be displayed, what graphics are to appear in the page, hyperlinks associated with text and graphics, and so forth. As HTML formats the information in the document, it is what determines how the document will be displayed.

   A is wrong, because HTTP is the Hypertext Transfer Protocol, which is used by the user's computer and the Web server to transmit information. The user uses HTTP to request a Web page, while the Web server uses HTTP to transmit the HTML document and other files to the user's Web browser. **C** is wrong, because although the Web browser displays HTML documents, and has settings that can control what data is displayed and how it is displayed, it is out of the control of the Web page author. Except in intranet settings, the user controls the Web browser and a Web page author can't go to each person's computer and configure each set of settings. **D** is wrong, because the Web server stores and sends the HTML documents to the user, but isn't used to dictate how data is displayed to the user.

2. **B.** The title of your Web page is text placed between the <TITLE> and </TITLE> tags. These tags are placed in the <HEAD>...</HEAD> section of your Web page. By entering text between the <TITLE>...</TITLE> tags, and placing them in the <HEAD>...</HEAD> section of the document, the text will appear in the titlebar of the browser.

   A is wrong, because the <BODY>...</BODY> section of your Web page contains information that appears in the main window of the Browser. **C** is wrong, because a Web page doesn't have a <FOOT>...</FOOT> section in its Web page structure. **D** is wrong, because the <STYLE>...<STYLE> tags are placed in the <HEAD>...</HEAD> section of the HTML document to create a style sheet.

3. **A.** Heading tags allow you to display text in different sizes. To display text in the largest size possible using heading tags, you would use the <H1> tag. Text that follows this tag would be larger than normal text, or any of the other level of headings. **B** is wrong, because a level 2 heading (<H2>) is slightly smaller than an <H1> tag. **C** is wrong, because a level 6 heading, created with the <H6> tag, displays text smaller than any other heading level. **D** is wrong, because there are only six levels of headings available with these tags.

4. **B** and **D.** The <B> and <STRONG> tags are used to make text appear bold when an HTML document is viewed through a browser. However, each of these is supported by browsers, and will make text appear bold.

   A is wrong, because the <BR> tag is used to cause a line break, and have the text appear as if the words or paragraphs are single-spaced. **C** is wrong, because the <EM> tag is used to emphasize (that is, italicize) text.

5. **A** and **B.** The <I> tag is used to italicize text. The <EM> tag is used to emphasize text, which in most browsers means that text will appear italicized. Although the <EM> tag is older, it will still work in most browsers.

   C is wrong, because the <TT> tag is the teletype (sometimes called typewriter text) tag. This makes text appear as if it were typed with an old typewriter. **D** is wrong, because in most browsers, the <STRONG> tag will make text appear bold.

6. **A, B,** and **D.** The <CODE>, <TT>, and <SAMP> tags can all be used to make text appear as if it were typed on a typewriter. In addition to those listed here as choices, you could also use the <KBD> tag. The <TT> tag is used in general instances when you want text to appear in a typewriter-style typeface. The <KBD> tag is for text to be entered by the viewer of the page, the <CODE> tag is for displaying examples of programming or HTML code, while <SAMP> is used when displaying examples of program output. Regardless of this, the way each is displayed is identical.

   C is wrong, because the <HR> tag is used to create a horizontal rule. This is a horizontal line that will appear on your Web page, and is generally used to separate sections of your page.

7. **C.** To create a horizontal rule, you would use the <HR> tag. You can set attributes of the horizontal rule to set its width and alignment. Using ALIGN="center" specifies that the horizontal rule is centered on the Web page. Using WIDTH="90%" specifies that the line will stretch across 90 percent of the Web page.

   A and **B** are wrong, because you don't create a horizontal rule using the word LINE. **A** is also wrong, because the SIZE attribute is used to set the thickness of the horizontal rule, and not the width of the line. **B** is also wrong because it specifies the width in pixels rather than percent. It specified it in pixels because the percentage symbol is missing after the size of width. **D** is wrong, because you don't set the width of a horizontal rule with SIZE, but with the WIDTH attribute. It is also wrong, because you would need to use the ALIGN attribute to set the alignment of the horizontal rule.

8. **C.** The tag used to specify a table cell is <TD>. Text written between the <TD> and </TD> tags will appear in that particular cell in the table.

   A is wrong, because the <TR> tag is used to create a table row. **B** is wrong, because the <BR> tag is used to break a sentence to a second line. This makes the text appear as if it were single-spaced. **D** is wrong, because there is no tag in a table called <TC>.

9. **C.** VALUE contains the text that will appear in the button, telling the user what the button is for. When VALUE="button" appears in the <INPUT> tag, the word "button" is displayed on the face of the button.

   A is wrong, because INPUT="button" is used to create the button, but has no effect on what will appear on the button's face. **B** is wrong, because the NAME attribute is used to name the element, allowing you to use it in any scripts used in your document. **D** is wrong, because there is no TEXT= attribute associated with the <INPUT> tag.

10. **B and D.** Check boxes and selection lists can be used in cases in which you want users to be able to choose an answer from a list of possible choices. With check boxes, you can pose your question, followed by a listing of choices that are selected by clicking a check box. Selection lists are drop-down lists of choices. Users can click this control and chose an option from the listing. By using the MULTIPLE attribute, users are able to choose more than one option from the listing.

    A is wrong because you can only select one radio button in a group of such controls. In other words, if you had three radio buttons, you could only click one of them. If you clicked another, the first radio button you clicked would be cleared. **C** is wrong, because text areas allow users to type their answers. The question states that you want to control the users' input, by having them select an answer from a listing of possible choices. This can't be done with a text area control.

11. **B.** The <P> is the PARAGRAPH tag. This tag breaks your text onto separate lines, so that a blank line appears between one line of text and another. In your browser, this will appear as if you had pressed the ENTER key in a word processor, so that it becomes double-spaced.

    A is wrong, because the </P> tag is ignored by a browser. It can be used to denote the end of one paragraph, but aside from this, it has no value in writing HTML. It is only available for consistency with other HTML tags, which use an end or closing tag to show where certain formatting ends. **C** is wrong, because the <BR> tag doesn't create a blank line between one paragraph and another. It will move text after the <BR> tag to the next line. It appears in the browser as if the two lines of text are single-spaced from one another. **D** is wrong, because pressing the ENTER key in a text editor won't separate the text in the browser. The browser will ignore whitespace such as this, and will merge the different lines of text together.

12. **B.** The <OPTION> tag is used to create options or choices that will appear in a selection list. Any text following this tag will appear as an available choice in the listing.
    A is wrong, because the <SELECT>...</SELECT> tags are used to create the selection list itself. The question states that this has already been done. To create options that fill the selection list, the <option> tag must be used. **C** is wrong, because the <SCRIPT>...</SCRIPT> tags are used in the Web page to specify that code for a script appears between these tags. **D** is wrong because the </OPTION> tag isn't a necessary requirement of creating options for a selection list. The </OPTION> tag isn't required, and is actually ignored by browsers. The <OPTION> tag acts as a delimiter and thereby doesn't require a closing tag.

13. **C.** All text in the document will appear underlined in the document, so users may click underlined text thinking that it's a hyperlink that doesn't work. The <U> tag is used to underline text when it appears in a browser, and underlined text is also used to indicate a hyperlink.
    A is wrong, because HTML can be split over several lines in a document, without affecting its functionality. This is because browsers ignore whitespace in HTML, so the multiple lines would be read as if it were on the same line. **B** is wrong, because any text after the <U> tag will appear underlined. If no </U> closing tag is used, then all text in the document after the <U> tag will be underlined. **D** is wrong, because most Browsers do read the <U> tag, and will underline any text following this tag. While the W3C has removed the <U>...</U> tags from the current HTML recommendation, most browsers continue to read this tag as a cue to underline any text that follows (until reaching the closing tag).

14. **A** is correct. Ordered lists are created using the <OL> tag. Each item appearing after this tag is formatted with a number. When the <OL>...</Ol> tags are used, each of the items within these tags will appear with a number before them. For each item in the list, the number before it is incremented. **B** is incorrect, because the <UL> tag is used to create an unordered, or bulleted, list. **C** and **D** are incorrect, because there are no <IL> or <NL> tags used in HTML for creating lists.

15. **B** is correct. An unordered, or bulleted. list is created using the <UL> tag. Each item appearing after this tag is formatted with a bullet, which usually appears as a black dot in front of the text. When the <UL>..</ul> tags are used, each item within these tags will appear with a bullet before it. **A** is incorrect, because the <OL> tag is used for creating ordered lists. An ordered list has items appearing with a number before it. **C** and **D** are incorrect, because there are no <IL> or <NL> tags used in HTML for creating lists.

16. **D** is correct. The <LI> tag is used to specify list items that will appear in an ordered (numbered) or unordered (bulleted) list. Text that appears between the <LI> opening tag, and the </LI> closing tag, will appear as a list item. These tags are used regardless of whether the list item appears in an ordered or unordered list. **A** is incorrect, because the <UL> tag is used to format list items into an unordered (bulleted) list. **B** is incorrect, because the <OL> tag is used to format list items into an ordered (numbered) list. **C** is incorrect, because there is no <IL> tag in HTML for creating list items.

17. **A** is correct. The TEXT element is used for situations in which the user needs to enter a single line of text, such as name, username, age, and so forth. It is created with the <TEXT> tag. When this is used, a single line text box appears on the Web page. **B** is incorrect, because the text area is used for larger amounts of text, such as for accepting comments or feedback. The TEXTAREA element is created with the <TEXTAREA> tag. **C** is also incorrect. The PASSWORD element is similar to the TEXT element, except that it hides whatever the user types by displaying asterisks instead of text. Finally, **D** is incorrect, because there is no <TXT> element in HTML.

18. **C** is correct. The PASSWORD element is used for input that is not meant to be viewed by the user. It is similar to the text element, except that it hides whatever the user types by displaying asterisks instead of text. The PASSWORD element appears as a box on a Web page, just like a normal TEXT element. The difference is that when the user types in a word (such as a password), the field displays only asterisks. This protects the user. If someone were looking over the user's shoulder when the password was being entered, that person wouldn't be able to read the user's password. **A** is incorrect, because the TEXT element allows users to view data that is typed into

this type of field. The TEXT element is used for situations in which the user needs to enter a single line of text, such as name, username, age, and so forth. **B** and **D** are both incorrect, as these aren't tags that are part of HTML.

19. **B** is correct. The TEXTAREA element is used to take larger amounts of text than the TEXT or PASSWORD elements. Unlike either of the two previously mentioned elements, the text tag is designed for multiple lines of input and has both an opening and closing tag. A text area is created using the <TEXTAREA> and </TEXTAREA> tags. **A** is incorrect, because while the <TEXT> element accepts text, this element is used to create a single-line text box. It cannot accept multiple lines of text. **B** is incorrect for the same reason. While <PASSWORD> accepts text, input is hidden from the user, and only a single line of text can be entered. **D** is incorrect, because there is no <TXTAREA> element in HTML.

20. **B** is correct. Text and graphics using the proprietary tags won't display as expected in some or all of the other browsers. Tags that are part of the HTML standard recommended by the W3C, are meant to be used and will work with any browser that is compliant with that version of HTML. Browser manufacturers like Netscape and Microsoft occasionally develop proprietary tags that may not work with other browsers. Because such tags aren't part of the HTML standard, browsers created by other manufacturers that don't employ the proprietary tag won't be able to interpret it. **A** is incorrect, because the proprietary tags won't be recognized by some or all of the other browsers. **C** is incorrect, because some browser manufacturers occasionally develop proprietary tags that may not work with other browsers. Finally, **D** is incorrect, because the browser will be unable to interpret or "guess" how the page elements were to be formatted.

6

Multimedia

I n Chapter 5, you learned how HTML documents can be created. This chapter goes one step further by discussing the use of various graphic, video, and audio files that can help you create a truly dynamic Web page.

This chapter also describes some additional software you may need to access various file types, and it tells you which file types are the most appropriate for achieving the desired effect and accessibility on your Web pages. You'll also learn how to implement these file types into your Web page, and, finally, you'll learn how to test your Web page for possible errors, bottlenecks, and other problems.

CERTIFICATION OBJECTIVE 6.01

Popular Multimedia Extensions or Plug-ins

Web browsers allow you to view the HTML code and basic graphics that make up many Web sites. However, because technology is always improving, there are some types of files that your browser may not support. If your browser cannot read a particular file located on a Web site, you will not be able to access that site. When this is the case, your browser relies on its *plug-in* applications for help.

Plug-ins are small applications that run within your browser to extend its abilities to read nonnative file types. Plug-ins are also sometimes referred to as *extensions* because they extend the normal capabilities of the browser. You can load plug-in applications from CD, or download them from the Internet. Once the plug-in is installed, your browser will use it to access files that it normally couldn't access on its own. This section describes some popular plug-ins and the types of files they support.

on the job

Plug-ins are not the same as "helper programs." Plug-ins work with the browser and are used to run or display files directly within a Web page. Helper programs are a bit older than plug-ins, and they run files within a separate application window.

There are a number of versions in the QuickTime family. They are designed for creating and viewing movie files, typically those with a .mov or .qt extension. More recent versions of QuickTime also include 3-D or Virtual Reality capabilities, and are referred to as QTVR. When used as a plug-in, QTVR can allow you to view movies or still graphics, or listen to audio files.

QTVR uses 3-D rendering, in which an image is captured from many different angles. The different views of the image are then rendered, or combined, to create one object with many different surfaces. This "virtual" reality allows users to see the object as if they were moving around or through it.

QuickTime files are not supported by most operating systems and browsers, so a special QuickTime plug-in is required to view movie or 3-D files on the Internet. You can find the QuickTime plug-in at http://www.apple.com. The QuickTime application can also run WAV, MIDI, Flash, and AVI files, and can be used to display PNG and BMP files, among many others.

Flash

The Flash plug-in allows you to view Macromedia, Inc., Flash animations and audio files. Flash files use *vector* graphics, which display objects as a collection of lines, rather than as a collection of individual dots or pixels, as bitmapped graphics do. This allows the image to retain a high resolution, even after resizing, and vector files use fewer of the computer's resources when they are displayed. Vector and bitmapped graphics are explained in more detail later in the chapter.

Flash files are often embedded in a Web page so that an animation or video runs as long as the Web page is loaded. If you have the Flash plug-in, the Web page will load normally. However, if you do not have the Flash plug-in, or if you have an outdated version, you will be prompted to download it before you can view the Web site.

Shockwave

Shockwave, also developed by Macromedia, Inc., is an improvement over Flash because, as well as supporting animation, video, and audio, it also allows for user interaction. Shockwave is often used to create online games that the user can play by clicking different items within the graphic or animation. Shockwave is also used for online tours that can offer different information, depending on which part of the graphic the user clicks.

Shockwave files typically have the extension .swf, for Shockwave Flash. SWF files are not supported by browsers or operating systems, so a special Shockwave plug-in is required to view these files online. The Shockwave plug-in will also support the same file types that the Flash plug-in supports. Shockwave and Flash plug-ins can be downloaded free from Macromedia at http://www.macromedia.com.

RealPlayer

The RealPlayer plug-in is another application that you can use to run animation, video, and audio files over the Internet. RealPlayer differs from QuickTime, Flash, and Shockwave in that it was designed to run real-time multimedia. Real-time multimedia includes video and audio that comes to you directly from the source, and has not been previously saved on a Web server. For example, if you watch an online broadcast, you are seeing the event as it happens, in "real" time. Only recently has Shockwave been able to support this type of media.

The full RealPlayer application also includes channels for news, sports, entertainment, and other types of up-to-date information. Figure 6-1 shows the RealPlayer application window. Aside from its own native .rm, .ra, and .ram files, the RealPlayer plug-in will also run QuickTime movies, Shockwave files, and sound files.

Windows Media Player

The Windows Media Player, developed by Microsoft, will also allow you to view real-time multimedia. This application is included in Windows 98 and Windows 2000, and can be downloaded from the Internet for use with older operating systems, either as a plug-in or as a full application.

The Windows Media Player will display still graphics, and run many types of video, animated, or audio files, such as .wav, .avi, .gif, and .jpeg. It will support QuickTime movies, but not QTVR files, and it cannot support RealPlayer or Shockwave files.

The RealPlayer application allows you to view news, sports, and other channels for up-to-date information

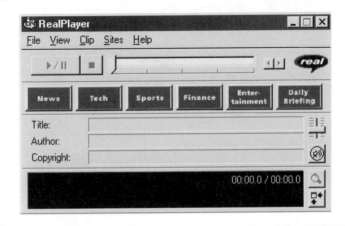

Installing Multimedia Extensions or Plug-ins Using Windows Update

The instructions for this exercise assume that you have Internet Explorer 5 installed on your machine, and that they are using a Windows 9x or NT 4 or later operating system. If you use an older browser or operating system, the results of this exercise will vary.

1. From the Start menu, click Windows Update. Internet Explorer 5 will open, showing the Web page at http://windowsupdate.microsoft.com.

2. On this Web page, click Product Updates. A new window will open, instructing you that your system is being checked to see what components—including plug-ins—have been previously installed.

3. The resulting page will show a listing of components that can be downloaded and installed. An example of this Web page is shown in Figure 6-2. The page will only show what components haven't been installed yet. Scroll down the Web page until you reach the Multimedia section. You will find this under the Internet subsection of Additional Windows Features. Some of the plug-ins seen here may include Flash and Shockwave.

4. Select the plug-in you want to install by clicking the check box beside that plug-in's name. An "x" will appear in the check box, indicating that it has been selected.

FIGURE 6-2   Windows Update allows you to install plug-ins

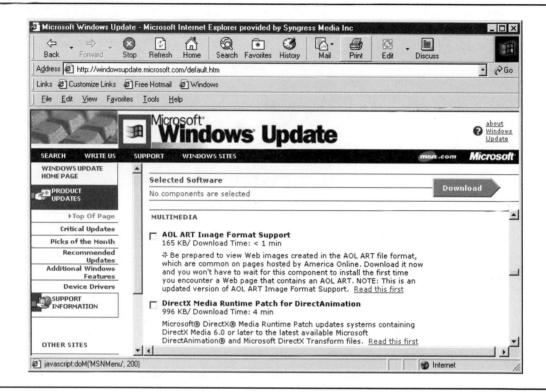

5. Click the Download button on this Web page.

6. The resulting page will show a listing of the plug-ins you selected. Click the Start Download button on this Web page to continue.

7. Depending on the components you choose to install, a dialog box with an end-user licensing agreement may appear. Click the appropriate button to agree to this, and the download and installation will begin. Depending on the components, other steps may be required, and you may need to reboot your computer. Follow any instructions appearing on the screen, and agree to reboot the computer as required.

Uses and Benefits of Various Multimedia File Formats

With or without browser plug-ins, you are likely to run into many file types on the Internet. This section will help you to understand the characteristics of the various file types, as well as the benefits and disadvantages of using them on the Internet.

This section will first introduce you to the types of imaging format, compression, and streaming abilities that are supported by multimedia files. You will then learn the specific characteristics of common file types, and, finally, you will learn how to implement various files into your Web pages.

Raster vs. Object-Oriented Images

One defining characteristic of image files is whether they use raster or object-oriented imaging. The type of imaging used can affect readability by graphics programs, and can also affect the resolution of the image when it is enlarged.

Raster Images

Raster images (also referred to as *bitmaps*) display graphics and animations pixel by pixel. That is, a raster graphic is simply a compilation of individual dots on the screen. The dots of color have no relationship to each other, so if one pixel is changed, the others remain unaffected.

This imaging method is very common because it is easily recognized by most graphics applications. However, raster images are unaffected by improvements in screen resolution because each pixel will maintain its original color. Raster images can also appear grainy when they are enlarged because of this pixel-by-pixel imaging. Figure 6-3 shows how a simple bitmapped circle appears before and after enlarging.

FIGURE 6-3

Bitmapped images can appear grainy when they are enlarged, because each pixel is displayed independently of the others

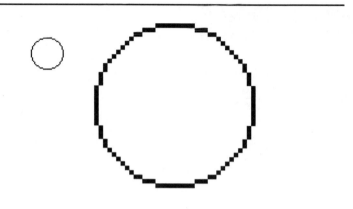

Finally, because raster images recognize only pixels, you may have trouble manipulating or layering shapes in a graphic. For example, you can draw a circle in a bitmapping application and color or resize it. When another object is added, it simply becomes another part of the image. It cannot be colored, removed, or resized independently of the circle that is already in the image (try it in Windows Paint—draw a circle, and then draw a square overlapping it; you cannot work with the two shapes independently).

Object-Oriented Images

Object-oriented images can provide better resolution and resizing ability than raster images because they treat elements as objects, rather than as independent pixels. For example, you saw in Figure 6-3 that when a raster image is enlarged, it can appear grainy. Object-oriented images (vector images) will treat a circle as a circle, regardless of how much it is enlarged. Figure 6-4 is a representation of a vector circle before and after being enlarged. Each element of a vector image is treated as a separate, complete object so that you can color, move, or remove one object at a time. Vector images provide a visual advantage over raster images, but are not supported by all graphics applications.

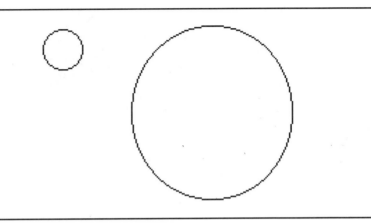

Compression Types

Another differentiating characteristic of file formats is the type of compression they support. As you will see, some file types do not support compression at all. However, many image types support *lossy* compression, which means that redundant parts of the image are removed from the file. This can mean a loss of resolution or clarity of the image, but the benefit is that lossy files provide more compression than other types. The more a lossy image is compressed, the less resolution it will retain. Most graphics programs will allow you to select the desired balance between compression and clarity.

The opposite of lossy compression is called *lossless* compression. This is a method of compressing a file without removing data from it. Although a lossless file cannot be compressed as much as a lossy file, you will not be sacrificing any of the file's data, so the resolution and clarity of the image will not be affected.

Streaming Media

Multimedia files can be accessed in a number of ways from the Internet. When you visit a Web site that runs audio, video, or animation within the browser, the file is said to be *streaming*. Typically, the multimedia file will run as soon as you access the Web site, and will continue as long as the Web page is loaded.

When you access streaming media, the file is sent from the Web site's server to your computer. The plug-in or browser in your computer is responsible for playing the file so that it appears to be coming straight from the Web site.

An advantage of using streaming media on a Web site is that the file doesn't have to be downloaded before the user can play it. The file will play while the user is browsing the site, and this can be a good way to draw attention to your site and keep users' interest.

However, streaming media can cause the Web page to load slowly for those who have older computers or browsers. Depending of the speed of the Internet connection, the media can appear "choppy" if the file is not received quickly enough by the user's computer. Finally, including streaming media can decrease access to your site, since it will be accessible only to those users who have the proper plug-ins.

Nonstreaming Media

The alternative to streaming media is nonstreaming media, which does not run directly from the Web site through the browser. Nonstreaming media must be downloaded by the user before it can be played.

An advantage to including nonstreaming files on your Web site is that once the file is downloaded, users can play it over and over without having to make subsequent Internet connections. The file can be saved on the hard drive, so the user can play it at will, or incorporate it into other applications.

Another advantage of using nonstreaming media is that it does not restrict access to your Web site. When a Web page contains streaming media, users must have the proper media plug-in in order to view the Web page. However, when a Web page uses nonstreaming media, the user can choose to ignore the download, or download the file with the intent of obtaining the proper plug-in at a later time. In either case, the user will be able to view the rest of the Web site without having to first obtain a media plug-in.

Interlacing

Interlacing is a method of image loading. When an image is interlaced, it gradually fades into view until the image is clear. Pixels are loaded throughout the entire image in the first wave. More and more pixels are loaded during each wave until the entire image is loaded. Figure 6-5 illustrates the concept of interlacing.

Noninterlaced images load line by line from the top down, until the entire image is visible. Figure 6-6 illustrates the concept of a noninterlaced image. An advantage to interlacing a graphic is that the user can usually make out the image before it has finished loading. This enables the user to make quick decisions about waiting or moving on, without having to wait for the entire image to become entirely clear.

FIGURE 6-5

Interlaced objects gradually fade into view until they are fully loaded

FIGURE 6-6

Noninterlaced images load from the top down until the entire image is visible

GIF

Graphic Interchange Format (GIF) files are one of the most commonly used file formats on the Internet. The GIF file family includes GIF87a and GIF89a. All GIF files are raster images, so they can be read by almost any Web browser or graphics application. This means they are accessible to a majority of Internet users. Also, GIF files use a method of lossless compression called LZW (Lempel-Ziv Welch) compression, so image quality is not sacrificed for file size. All GIF files can be used for displaying still graphics, and the GIF89a version is also able to support interlacing and animation. GIF89a is described in more detail in the next section. GIF files are supported by almost all browsers, so no additional plug-in or application is required in order to view them.

GIF89a

GIF89a files are newer than their 87a counterparts, and most GIF files that you will come across on the Internet are version 89a. GIF89a files have all the abilities of the 87a version, but are also able to support interlacing and animation.

Graphic animation is accomplished by compiling a number of similar images that have only a few slight differences between them. When these images are played quickly in order, they can give the appearance of motion. For example, assume an animation shows a person tap dancing. To achieve this effect, many images of the person are created, with the feet in a slightly different position on each image. When the images are shown quickly in sequence, the person appears to be dancing. GIF89a files can support animation because a single file can contain multiple images. GIF87a files can contain only a single image, so they cannot support animation.

JPEG

JPEG (Joint Photographic Experts Group) files are also very popular on the Internet. Like GIF files, they are almost universally recognized by Web browsers, so they are accessible without the aid of a plug-in. JPEG images provide 32-bit photolike quality, so they are ideal for photos or other scanned images.

Another feature of JPEG files is their use of lossy compression. Although image quality can be sacrificed when the image is compressed, most graphics applications allow you to select a balance between quality and size.

Although JPEGs do not support animation, they do support a "fading in" effect, similar to that of an interlaced GIF. When this feature is enabled in a JPEG file, it is called a *progressive JPEG*. Unfortunately, while almost all browsers can read a JPEG, only newer ones can read progressive JPEGs.

PNG

Portable Network Graphics (PNG) files use a relatively new technology that improves upon older GIF files. In fact, PNG files are expected to replace GIFs as one of the most commonly used file formats. Like GIF files, PNG files use lossless compression and support interlacing, but they do not support animation.

An advantage of PNG files is that they allow for manipulation of image colors and opacity. You can save a PNG file in gray scale, black and white, or true color. You can also set particular areas of the image to be completely or semitransparent (opaque), which allows you to create a layering effect.

A disadvantage of using PNG files is that they are not accessible to all users. Because this is a relatively new file format, it is not supported by older browsers.

TIFF

Tagged Image File Format (TIFF) files are another very popular file format. TIFF files, which can be identified by the .tif extension, provide excellent color support and resolution, so they are ideal for scanned photographs. TIFF files use raster graphics, and offer the same color manipulation options as PNG files (black and white, gray scale, true color). TIFF files are also able to take advantage of either lossless or lossy compression.

All of these characteristics mean that TIFF files offer great flexibility, so they have become very popular in desktop publishing. However, TIFF files are not supported by most Web browsers, so an additional plug-in or imaging application is required to view a TIFF on the Internet.

BMP

There are many types of bitmapped image formats, including GIF and PNG files. Another type of bitmapped image format is BMP, which is short for the word "bitmap" itself. BMP files are very common, and the technology has been around for a very long time. As with most older technologies, BMP files have the advantage of being easily accessed. Although BMP files are not universally supported by browsers, they are supported by almost all imaging applications, so a majority of people can access them.

However, because BMP technology is older, it does not support high resolution, high color, animation, or interlacing. BMP files are also unable to take advantage of the types of compression discussed in this chapter. Therefore, although BMP files are easily accessible, they do not offer many options; and because they are large, they can take a long time to download.

MOV

There are three basic types of computer video files: MOV, MPEG, and Video for Windows. Files with the .mov extension are QuickTime movie files. They typically contain animation or video, and may be accompanied by audio clips. MOV files can support bitmapped or vector images, and can be streamed or downloaded from the Internet. The biggest advantage of MOV files is their accessibility. Because this is an older file format, MOV files are supported by a variety of applications, including Windows Media Player, RealPlayer, Flash, and Shockwave.

MPEG

MPEG stands for Moving Picture Experts Group, and includes a series of standards for video and audio compression. MPEG files are video and/or audio files that use lossy compression, in which only the changing parts of each frame are saved. There is generally no noticeable quality loss in MPEG files that have been compressed. This type of compression makes it easier to use MPEG files on the Internet, since MPEG files are typically quite large.

There are two current MPEG video standards: MPEG-1 and MPEG-2. Most of the MPEG files you will see are MPEG-1, since the MPEG-2 standard is typically reserved for use by DVD-ROMs. The MPEG family also includes MP3 files, which support audio only. All files in the MPEG family can be either streamed or downloaded from the Internet. MPEG video files usually have the extension .mpg, and MP3 files have a .mp3 extension.

Because the MPEG standard is very popular, it is supported by a number of applications, including RealPlayer and Windows Media Player. MPEG files typically provide better video and audio quality than other video formats.

AVI

AVI stands for Audio Video Interleave. It was developed as part of the Microsoft Video for Windows family. Because of its association with the Windows platform, AVI has become a standard for video and audio files. AVI files use a technology that is easily read by other applications, including Windows Media Player and QuickTime, so these files can be easily accessed without the use of additional plug-ins or applications.

A disadvantage to using AVI files is that they display video at only about 30 frames per second and have a lower resolution than MPEG or MOV files. Therefore, although they are very popular, they do not provide the quality that MPEG and MOV files do. Also, AVI files do not support streaming, so they must be downloaded in order to be viewed.

PDF

In addition to image and video formats, there are a number of translation file formats that allow users to share data across different platforms or incompatible applications. One such format is PDF, which stands for Portable Document Format. The PDF format was designed by Adobe Systems as a method of saving documents so that they can be viewed by others in their original formatting.

When a document is created on a particular computer, it contains the fonts, layout, and graphics supported by that computer. Unfortunately, the document may appear altered when it is viewed on other computers. For example, suppose a document is created using the font Comic Sans. If the document is then viewed on a machine that doesn't have the Comic Sans font, the computer will automatically substitute a different font. The same is true for layout options and image formats. The result is a document that does not look like the original.

Saving a document in the PDF format can solve this problem by capturing an image of the document, rather than saving the document itself. Because the document is now treated as an image, it contains the same look as the original, regardless of the fonts and layouts on the reader's computer.

Unfortunately, since the document is now an image, it cannot be edited by the receiver. Also, a special application or plug-in is required to view the file. The plug-in is called Acrobat Reader, and can be downloaded free from http://www.adobe.com. The plug-in is small enough that it can be sent as an attachment to those who you expect to open the PDF file.

RTF

RTF stands for Rich Text Format, and is used to convert files into ASCII so that they can be opened by other, often incompatible, applications. ASCII is almost universally recognized by word processors, e-mail applications, and graphics applications. The result is that although the file may look different from the original, the reader will be able to open and edit it from within almost any application. This is the conceptual opposite of the PDF file format, which sacrifices the ability to edit a file in order to preserve the original formatting.

The RTF format is ideal for use on the Internet, because it allows you to create files that will be accessible to most users, regardless of the applications they are using. There are no special plug-ins or applications required to save or open an RTF file. Most programs that can read RTF also include a "Save as RTF" option.

PostScript

PostScript is a language used by laser printers to define how printouts should look. When a document is sent to a laser printer, a PostScript command file is created with specifications about how the document is to be printed. The printer's on-board interpreter is responsible for carrying out these commands. PostScript images and fonts are treated as objects, so they can be resized and printed with a high resolution.

The PostScript language, developed by Adobe Systems, is the industry standard for laser printing. PostScript files have the extension .ps, and contain line after line of printer commands. That is, the PostScript file does not contain the actual document to be printed; rather, it contains instructions on *how* the associated document is to be printed.

EPS

Encapsulated PostScript (EPS) files allow you to see the results of the commands in a PostScript file. Recall that the PostScript file itself contains only commands. The EPS file shows you how a document will appear once these PostScript commands are applied to it. The EPS file itself contains a bitmapped "print preview" of the document to be printed.

BinHex

Another type of translation file format is BinHex, which is short for Binary Hexadecimal. "Binary" refers to the computer's native language, consisting of 1's and 0's. Hexadecimal is a 16-base language that uses the numbers 0–9 and the letters A–F. One of the most common implementations of Hexadecimal is the ASCII coding system, which can be read by almost every type of computer, regardless of the application, platform, or operating system being used.

When the BinHex file format is used, data is converted from the originating computer's binary code into ASCII (hex). The receiving computer recognizes the ASCII coding, and converts the data into its own binary code. This allows data to be sent from a PC to a MAC computer, or from a Windows machine to a UNIX machine, for example.

BinHex is supported by most Web browsers and e-mail programs. You can also use separate encoding applications to encode and decode BinHex files, including the very popular WinZip compression application. Files that have been saved in BinHex format have the extension .hqx or .hex.

Adding Multimedia to Web Pages

You should now be familiar with the file types and plug-ins commonly used on the Internet. The focus of this section is the implementation of various file types in your Web pages.

Adding Graphics to a Web Page

In the previous chapter, we talked about how to create Web pages to provide information and entertainment to users. We saw how Web pages are made up of several key parts. <HTML>...</HTML> specifies the beginning and end of the Web page. <HEAD>...</HEAD> contains information that's used by the browser or other elements of the HTML document. <TITLE>...</TITLE> defines the title of the HTML document, which will appear in the titlebar of your browser. Finally, <BODY>...</BODY> is where the bulk of your Web page will be written, and it contains the content that will appear in the main window of the browser. Together, the basic structure of a Web page appears as follows:

```
<HTML>
<HEAD>
   <TITLE>Your title appears here</TITLE>
</HEAD>
<BODY>
</BODY>
</HTML>
```

What wasn't discussed in the previous chapter is how graphics can be added to your Web page. You can use images to punctuate a point you're making through text, provide a visual diversion from large amounts of text, or offer illustrations of what you're talking about. Through such images, you can take a page from being raw information to appearing polished and complete.

Graphics are added in the <BODY>...</BODY> section of an HTML document. You specify what image is to be added using the <img> tag with the src="" attribute. The filename of the GIF, JPEG, or other image file is entered between the quotes. For example, if you had a file named mypicture.gif stored in the same directory as your Web page, you would enter the following into the <BODY>...</BODY> section of your HTML document:

```
<img src="mypicture.gif">
```

If the file were stored in a directory other than where the Web page was saved, you would put the complete path and filename between the quotes. <img src=""> tells the browser that an image is to appear, and the source (that is, filename) equals that specified between the quotation marks.

The file format used with the <img src=""> tag can be any of the image files mentioned in this chapter. This includes animated images like GIFs. It does not, however, include movie files, like MOVs, AVIs, and so forth. For that, you need to use the dynsrc="" attribute. <img dynsrc=""> is used the same as <img src=""> with a few exceptions. It is used for dynamic images—in other words, movie file formats. The filename and, if necessary, the path to the file, is specified between the quotation marks, as seen in the following example:

```
<img dynsrc="mymovie.mov">
```

When added, to an HTML document, the MOV file called mymovie.mov would be set up to play in the browser. To make it play, a special attribute, the start attribute, would be added.

The start attribute is used to specify when the movie file should begin playing. This has two settings: fileopen and mouseover. To illustrate this, let's look at the following piece of HTML code:

```
<img dynsrc="mymovie.mov" start="fileopen">
```

This line would specify that mymovie.mov is to be played through the browser. The start="fileopen" attribute signifies that the movie should begin playing as soon as the file is loaded into the browser. If start="mouseover", then the movie would begin playing when the user moved his or her mouse over the place where the movie resided in the page. Before this, only the first frame in the movie would be visible.

Movies also have a control attribute. When the control attribute is added to the <img dynsrc=""> tag, it specifies that controls for the movie are to appear in the browser. This generally consists of a Play/Stop button and a slide bar. The Play button appears similar to that found on a VCR. When an arrow appears on the button, the movie will begin to play. When a square appears in the button, you can click the button to stop the movie. The slide bar allows you to click it, and to control where in the movie the movie should begin playing.

Whether or not dynamic or static images are used, the <img> tag has a width and height attribute. Using these you can specify the height and width of your image in either pixels or percent. For example, the following line would have the picture mypicture.gif appear with a height of 250 pixels and a width of 400 pixels:

```
<img src="mypicture.gif" width="400" height="250">
```

Another attribute for animated images, such as animated GIFs or movies like AVIs or MOVs, is the loop attribute. This defines how many times an animated GIF or movie is to play before it stops. If loop="1", then the image will run from beginning to end once, and then stop. If loop is applied a value greater than this, then it will play that many times. If "-1" or "infinite" appears, then it will play repeatedly. For example, the following animated gif is specified to play indefinitely and never stop in the following line of HTML:

```
<img src="animated.gif" loop="infinite">
```

Adding Images as Backgrounds

Images can also be added as a background to your Web page. This allows you to have a picture displayed behind other images or text on your HTML document. To add a background image, you would use the <background=""> attribute of the <BODY> tag. This is shown in the following example:

```
<BODY background="mybackground.gif">
</BODY>
```

As you can see, the background attribute appears within the <BODY> tag. The name of the image is specified between quotations marks after the equal symbol (=). This sets what picture will appear behind text and images on the Web page.

In addition, you can also have sound files play when your Web page first opens. This is done with the <bgsound> tag. This tag is placed between the <HEAD>...</HEAD> section of your HTML document. To understand how this is used, let's look at the following line of HTML:

```
<bgsound src="background.wav" loop="1">
```

In this code, the source of the background sound is the file background.wav. This is the file that will be played in the background when the Web page loads. You'll also note that the loop attribute appears here, as it did when we discussed adding images to your HTML document. In this case, the sound file will play once and then stop. If loop="-1", then it would play indefinitely. If another number were set for the loop attribute, then the file would play that many times.

Using Icons for Links

Images are also very popular as links to other Web pages, or to specify where to click to perform some other action. For example, you might have an image of a house to specify where users should click to return to your homepage. You might also have the logo of a software application that users can download when they click the icon. Not only does this make your Web page more attractive, but also it provides clarity as to where users should click to perform some desired action.

As explained in the previous chapter, you create hyperlinks with the <a href=""> tag. The Web page's filename or the URL of the Web site or page this link will take the user to is entered between the quotations. For example:

```
<a href="www.comptia.com">Comptia Web site</a>
```

As we can see in this code, a hyperlink for www.comptia.com has been created. When the user clicks on the words "Comptia Web site," the browser will load the default Web page for that site. When text is used for a hyperlink, it usually appears underlined to let the user know a hyperlink exists there. The </a> closing tag specifies where the text used for the hyperlink ends. Any text appearing after this will be normal text.

Graphics can also be used for hyperlinks. These can be static image files, like GIFs or JPEGs, or movie files appearing in the Web page like MOVs or AVIs. The way a graphic is specified as a hyperlink is by entering the tags for the graphic between the <a href=""> and </a> tags. In other words, you put a graphic in place of where you would normally enter the text you want used for the link. To illustrate this, let's look at the following line of code:

```
<a href="www.comptia.com><img src="comptia.gif"></a>
```

The first part of this line specifies the location to go to when the hyperlinked graphic is clicked. Following this, we see that the graphic comptia.gif is to be used to represent the link. Finally, the hyperlink is closed off with the </a> tag. This tells the browser where the link ends, so that any text or graphics that follow aren't linked to this Web site as well.

It is important to note that if the user weren't using a browser that supported a particular file format, the image wouldn't appear on the page. This would occur if a user were viewing the page with a textual browser, which only viewed text on pages and didn't support any graphics. It would also occur if an older browser were used, one that didn't support a newer type of file format. To show what the image represents, such as a link to another page, you can use the alt="" attribute with the <img> tag. To illustrate this, let's look at the following line:

```
<img src="home.jpg" alt="Return to Home Page">
```

If the browser didn't support the PNG file format, the image wouldn't be displayed. Instead, the words "Return to Home Page" would appear where the image was to be displayed. This is also useful if users know they want to navigate to a certain page, but they don't want all of the graphics to load on the page before navigating. When they see these words, they can click that area and jump to another Web page.

The Process of Pre-Launch Site/Application Functionality Testing

Once you've created your HTML document, and added the multimedia you want to it, you may think you're ready to throw it up on the Web. After all, that's what all the work was for, and you're more than ready to present it to the world. Before you do that, though, it's wise to see your Web pages through the eyes of a user.

All too often, HTML authors and programmers separate themselves from the people who will use their work. They've spent hours writing HTML, added multimedia, and perhaps even programmed in a few surprises. Now they are anxious to throw it up on the Web, hear the compliments of those who hired them, and use the Web site. After all this hard work, however, they fail to use the Web page as a user would. They forget to go through and check what they've written, to see how the page performs and to determine the effects that their work will have on various browsers or the overall site itself.

For the remainder of this chapter, we'll discuss how to test your Web pages, so that you avoid having such problems being discovered by the public. While it may be frustrating for you to find a glitch in your Web page, it's even worse to have a user find it. After all, you'll have problems seen by many, but reported by few. While a hundred users will think bad thoughts of you and click away from your site, you'll be lucky if one person tells you about the problem. It's much easier if you—and, if possible, a colleague or friend—check your work before it's released on the World Wide Web.

Checking Hot Links

One of the most common problems on the Internet is hyperlinks that don't work properly. A user may click a link to another page, and receive an error message saying that the Web page doesn't exist. The reason this is so common is that pages are frequently and unpredictably moved on the Internet. While the Web page may have been there when you started your work, it is no longer at that URL. Perhaps the owner of that Web site moved to a different URL, took the page off the server, or decided to take down the site. Whatever the reason, it's important to check hyperlinks on your Web pages when you first put the page on the Web, and semiregularly after that.

There are a few different methods for checking hot links. *Hot links* are hyperlinks that work. *Cold links* are those that fail when you click them. One method is to use software or services that check the links for you. There are a number of services on the Web that will check links for you, such as LinkExchange or WebGarage, and a few applications on the market that check links on your Web pages. Some HTML editors, like Microsoft FrontPage, include features that will go through a Web page and ensure that when the link is clicked, a Web page will appear. Unfortunately, if you mistyped the URL, but entered the address of another Web site that actually exists, the wrong Web site may appear. This may also occur if the original owner of the site sold the address to another company. Such software will report that the link is still active, unable to realize that the link points to the wrong Web site.

on the !
j o b

Having a hyperlink point to the wrong Web site can be extremely embarrassing. Such was the case for an HTML course at one school. The book being used had an exercise that taught how to create a hyperlink. The URL being used for the link pointed to a Web site that had public domain graphics and multimedia. Unfortunately, after the book was written, the URL was sold to another company. When the students used the URL for their hyperlink, it took them to a site specializing in adult pornography. Since the URL was active, it wouldn't have registered as a problem by software that checked for dead or cold links. The link was hot . . . a little too hot, as the school found out.

Such software also has a problem when it comes to images or text that you meant to be used as a hyperlink, but failed to code as one. If you don't add HTML tags to make text or images into a link, it will appear as standard text or as a normal graphic. Since mistakes happen when you're coding, the only way to find this kind of error is by checking the page manually.

The best way to check for hot links is to use the Web page. Open the page in a browser, and move your mouse over each hyperlinked text or image. The mouse pointer on your screen will change appearance when it is passed over the link. In most cases, it will change from an arrow into a hand. Click each link to ensure that it takes you to a site that's still active, and is the site you expected to go to.

Unfortunately, manually checking links can become impractical if there are hundreds or even thousands of links on your Web site. In such cases, you will need to use automated methods, such as those mentioned in this section. You can also use one of the greatest resources available to your Web site: the people who use it. Provide easily accessible links for users to send you e-mail. Such a link can easily be added to any navigation appearing on Web pages. If you make it possible for users to give you feedback, they can tell you when a particular link is down, or no longer contains the content you mentioned.

Testing Browsers

While the World Wide Web Consortium, W3C, makes recommendations on HTML, they are just that: recommendations. Manufacturers of Web browsers may implement most of these recommendations in their browsers, but they will also ignore some recommendations and add other tags that can only be used by that browser. Because of this, it's important that you don't just use one browser to check your Web page.

At a bare minimum, you should use the most common browsers to view your Web pages before they're on the Web. Most people on the Internet use Microsoft Internet Explorer or Netscape Navigator. While you could use other browsers, you should always use these two to view how your pages look.

Once you've tested your site with the latest version of a particular browser, you should also check how the page displays with previous versions. If your Web page is cutting edge, and uses the latest technologies, your page may not be accessible when it is viewed with an older version. For example, if the page used Shockwave, and this wasn't supported in an older version of a browser, the user may not be able to view anything on the site or navigate to other areas.

Once you've checked a Web page in one resolution, you should consider changing the current resolution, and then view the Web page again. In doing so, you may find that some users may need to scroll horizontally to read paragraphs or view images. You may also find that some applets or graphics may not appear as expected. Testing in this way will enable you to see what the page would look like if a user were viewing the page with a resolution different from the one you used when you created and initially viewed the page.

In testing with various browsers, browser versions, and resolutions, you'll notice that some effects included in your Web pages may work in one browser, while others will fail to function in another. This is because one or the other may not support certain tags or attributes. You may also find that your Web page doesn't look as expected in one of the browsers. This gives you the choice of either altering your page until it looks good in both browsers, or adding recommendations to the homepage of your Web site. For example, you may put a notice on the initial page of your Web site that "This Web site is best viewed with . . . " and then mention the browser it appears best in.

Access to the Site

Accessibility to a site is another important aspect of testing. If users type a URL, or attempt to access an area of your site, you should ensure that they have the accessibility you designed the site to give. In other words, they should be able to get to the areas you want them to access, and be restricted from areas designed for privileged users.

You should test a site with more than one browser. In addition to using various types of browsers, you may also find it beneficial to look at your page using various versions of browsers. Remember that by having a cutting-edge Web site, you may be alienating users who are running earlier versions of a browser. Users who access your site with a browser version that was developed before certain tags used in your Web page may be unable to view the page properly. If the browser version was released before certain scripting or programming languages were out, the users may not be able to view the page or areas of that page. This is a particular problem if you have Java applets, JavaScript, Shockwave, or other effects for your navigation. If the browser can't interpret this, a user may be unable to get into your site or navigate to other pages within the site. Whenever you use Java applets or JavaScript for navigation, you should consider whether it's appropriate to have standard hyperlinks for navigation as well. You may also want to consider offering two versions of your Web site: a high-end version with lots of programming, and a low-end version for older browsers.

Graphics can also be a problem for some users. If a user is using a textual browser that only views text and not images, then multimedia won't be viewable, so you should consider using the ALT="" attribute for any graphics. Text entered in the quotations will be displayed as the graphic is loading, or if the image can't be displayed.

Another aspect of testing is ensuring that when a URL is entered, and a specific Web page isn't specified in the address, a default Web page appears. For example, let's say you entered the URL www.comptia.com. Notice that you didn't specify the HTML document to display in this address. When the browser accesses this address, a default Web page will appear. This is generally a Web page titled Default, Index, or Welcome (often with the file extensions .htm or .html). The default Web page's name is configured in the Web server, so you should check your Web server's documentation or consult your Internet Service Provider (ISP) for information as to what the default Web page should be named.

It is also important to remember that most Web servers on the Internet are UNIX servers. This means that any names you use for Web pages and directories are case sensitive. If you create a Web page called MYPAGE.HTM and provide a link to mypage.htm, your page won't display when the link is clicked. UNIX views this as two different filenames, and will return an error, thinking that the page doesn't exist. The same holds true for directories. You can have two directories with the same name, one that is named in uppercase, and the other in lowercase.

Finally, if you have secure areas for your site, you will want to ensure that common users are not easily allowed access. For example, you may have an area of your site that is accessible only to users with specified usernames and passwords. You can add security to areas of your Web site through scripts, directory permissions, password fields on Web pages, and more. This will allow you to keep out unwanted or unwelcome visitors. After adding whatever level of security you deem fit, you will want to check such pages, to ensure that people who don't enter a username or password can't get in.

E-commerce Site Testing

As you add more to a Web page, more things can go wrong. This is especially true when you're running an e-commerce site, or implementing additional server software. If you have scripting languages, applets, or other programming, it's possible to create conflicts that will corrupt the display of your Web page or cause damage at the server side.

Because you don't want to cripple the important parts of your site, such as those designed to make money, it's wise to use a test server before you implement Web pages on the Internet. A *testing server*, also called a *staging server*, is used to view how a Web site functions, and how Web pages may affect the overall performance and functionality of a site. By setting up e-commerce or other server software on your computer or on a network server, you can test your Web pages and programming without corrupting the actual site used by the public.

Another important testing area for e-commerce sites is checking how your Web page interacts with the server software. Before opening the e-commerce site to the public, enter a number of orders through your Web page for the e-commerce software to process. Check to ensure that these orders were recorded properly.

Once you've determined how the site handles orders that are placed, you should determine whether credit card transactions are properly processed. If credit card transactions are sent to your site, and are processed on a server you control, you can enter mock transactions and view how the e-commerce site handles them. If another server, such as one controlled by a banking or other financial institution, handles credit card numbers, you will need to make arrangements with them. This will let those controlling the processing of these transactions know that a test is being conducted, and that someone isn't attempting to enter fraudulent credit card numbers to make purchases.

You should also test and monitor any databases used on your e-commerce site, and ensure that any data being stored in the database isn't being lost or corrupted. By establishing this early, and preferably before the e-commerce site is active on the Net, you'll save yourself from losing customer information, orders, credit card information, and so forth. You should also ensure that others aren't able to access the database directly. You don't want someone to be able to view any data you don't want him or her to view in the database. Imagine the horror of your customer list, with all their personal and credit card information, being viewed by everyone—or an unscrupulous hacker—on the Internet.

Load Testing

As more visitors come to your Web site, your Web server can be affected to varying degrees. Defects may occur in the way Web pages are displayed, or the Web server may have serious problems in handling the number of requests. Web server software often has a limit to the number of users it can handle, and its hardware may be unable to support the usage the server is experiencing. When this limit is reached, you may need to upgrade to server software and hardware that is better able to handle the load, or split your Web site across several servers.

In performing load testing, most of your work will revolve around hardware issues. The focus will be on the following areas:

- CPU utilization
- Available RAM
- Available bandwidth

If the server's connection to the Internet is too slow, it will be waiting for user input or will be bogged down in trying to transmit data to users. This will mean that you'll need to upgrade your connection, perhaps through a T1 line. If the server has too little memory, it will be slow in processing requests, data may become corrupt, and the server may go down unexpectedly. If virtual memory is used on the server, and disk space is used for additional memory, it can lead to hard disk failure. Data from RAM will be swapped back and forth between the hard disk and RAM, slowing the performance and possibly causing data loss. Adding more memory to the server will solve this problem in most cases. If not, splitting the load between multiple servers may be required. If there isn't enough processing power in the server, the effects will be similar to that of insufficient RAM, and may cause the processor to fail. If CPU utilization is high, you will need to upgrade your server's CPU or split the load across multiple servers.

To perform load testing, you will often need to purchase software that tests your Web site. This will provide information as to probable problems encountered by users, and how fast the Web pages load. Your Web server software may also provide utilities that track the number of users, the days and times they commonly use certain Web pages, or other data. Most of these software packages simulate loads and transactions, and log accordingly. Checking server logs for HTTP errors can also provide insight.

If the Web server's operating system is Windows NT Server, then you may not want additional software to check hard disk performance. NT Server comes with Performance Monitor, or PerfMon, which can monitor and log performance. By using this tool, you can view the utilization of the CPU, available and used RAM, hard disk performance, and other issues that can affect the performance of your NT Web Server.

On the basis of the information you obtain, you can then decide how to approach the problem. If certain areas of your site are being used more frequently than others, such as Web pages that offer downloads of files and programs, you can put those Web pages and associated files on another server. When people visit your site, you can use hyperlinks that detour them to the other server. This balances the load on your site across multiple servers. You can also balance the load on your Web server by running Web site–related software on other computers. For example, if you used a database in your Web site, you could move the database to a separate server. If this still wasn't enough, you could split the database across multiple database servers. There are also clustering and load balancing applications that are specifically geared toward the issues discussed in this section.

Testing with Speed Connections

Life would be easier for HTML authors if everyone had a T1 connection at home. Unfortunately, much as every surfer would like one, this isn't the case. Many areas have faster home Internet access through cable TV lines; there are fast modems on the market, and technologies that improve connection speed. However, it's important to remember that according to some statistics, most people access the Internet with 28.8K or 33.6K connections. What this means is that others may not see your Web pages appear in the browser as fast as you do.

If you have a fast connection to the Internet, it is important to connect at varying speeds to see how fast your Web pages download and display in a browser. You can easily check this by changing your modem settings, and then reconnecting to the Internet. It is most important to check how the Web pages display at slower speeds. In doing so, you will then be able to determine whether users with slower connections will be able to properly view your Web pages.

A common mistake new Web page authors make is to forget how fast a Web page displays when it is loaded from their local hard disk. If you preview your Web page in a browser, and it is opened from the local hard drive, you won't see what the average user will see. This is because there is no download time involved. The pages and multimedia it contains don't need to travel across the Internet to your computer.

If you do want to determine speeds without changing your modem settings, there is software that can check how fast a Web page will download and display at different speeds. A number of applications available on the Internet determine how fast a page will download and load into a browser. Some HTML editors have this ability included in them.

Now that we've discussed plug-ins, multimedia formats, inserting graphics, and testing your site, let's look at some of the common questions people have dealing with these issues.

QUESTIONS AND ANSWERS

If I want to view different file formats, will I need to install every plug-in and application onto my computer?	In most cases, no. Many plug-ins and applications support more than a single type of media. However, not all formats are supported by every plug-in or application. The best way to determine whether an install is needed is to install common plug-ins or applications that support many different media formats. An example of this would be Windows Media Player. As you come across formats not supported by the viewer or plug-in, you can install them as needed.
Which is the best multimedia format to use for Web pages?	Although the developers of each media format will tell you otherwise, the best file format to use really depends on your requirements. JPEGs provide superior compression to GIFs, but progressive JPEGs are a newer format and not supported by all browsers. Therefore, interlaced GIFs might be a better choice over progressive JPEGs in this situation. The best way to decide on a format is to determine what's important for a particular page: wide support of browsers, use of file format, compression vs. image quality, and so forth.
Are there times when I won't need to test my Web pages with various browsers?	Yes. If you are creating Web pages for an intranet site, and all users will be using the same browser type, then don't waste your time testing with other browsers. For example, if everyone using the intranet only has Internet Explorer installed, then don't bother testing with Netscape or Mosaic. However, try to keep track of various versions of the browser being used. If some users are using IE4 and others are using version 5, then test your pages with both versions.

CERTIFICATION SUMMARY

In this chapter, you were introduced to some common browser plug-ins. Plug-ins, or extensions, are used by the browser to read file formats that are not supported by the browser itself or by existing applications on the computer. The QTVR plug-in allows you to view QuickTime Virtual Reality files. The Flash plug-in allows you to view vector graphics and animations. Shockwave is an evolution of Flash, and lets you access online interactive games. Both the RealPlayer and Windows Media Player plug-ins allow you to view real-time broadcasts.

This chapter also described a number of common file formats, as well as their differentiating characteristics and advantages, such as their use of lossy or lossless compression, support for animation, ability to be interlaced or streamed, and their use of bitmapped or vector graphics. In general, older formats provide the advantage of accessibility, while newer formats provide superior quality and better compression methods. Translation formats were also discussed. PDF allows you to retain the original look of a document across incompatible platforms. RTF is an almost universal plain text file format that can be read by almost any computer application. PostScript is an object-oriented laser printer language, and BinHex translates between ASCII and binary to allow the same file to be read by various applications.

Finally, this chapter focused on the importance of testing your Web pages, to ensure that they operate as expected. Testing includes checking hyperlinks, viewing the page within various browsers and at various speeds, checking accessibility to the site, load testing, and ensuring that your site isn't corrupted by changes you make. If you test to see that your site operates properly, it will appear more professional, and it will be easier to use.

TWO-MINUTE DRILL

- ❑ *Plug-ins* are programs that can be installed on your computer and add their functionality to the Web browser. Another term for plug-ins is *extensions*, as these applications extend the capabilities of the browser.

- ❑ Plug-ins are different from so-called helper programs, which are separate applications that launch in their own window.

- ❑ Flash was developed by Macromedia, Inc., as a method of creating graphic-intensive Web pages that have high performance at lower speeds. Flash files can be added to Web pages as a way of displaying animation and audio, and allowing interaction. They are extremely compact and stream from any Web server.

- ❑ Shockwave is another technology developed by Macromedia, Inc., that takes multimedia on the Web one step further. Using Shockwave, you can add multimedia to your Web page as objects. Not only can you view animation and video, and listen to audio, you can actually interact with a Shockwave object.

❑ RealPlayer is an application and plug-in that enables you to view and listen to streaming audio and streaming video over the Internet.

❑ Windows Media Player is similar to RealPlayer in a number of ways. Developed by Microsoft, the Windows Media Player allows you to view and/or listen to streaming video and audio. This allows you to watch broadcasts, listen to the radio, view video files, or listen to audio files on the Web. Like RealPlayer, Windows Media Player also has a Web page where you can browse through various audio and video files to watch and hear.

❑ GIF (Graphic Interchange Format) is an image format that is extremely popular on the Web. Most browsers support this format, allowing a broad range of your audience to be able to view any such images through their browsers.

❑ Along with GIF, JPEG is one of the most common image formats you'll use and come across on the World Wide Web.

❑ One of the benefits of JPEG is its use of compression.

❑ PNG (pronounced "ping") is an acronym for Portable Network Graphics, and is expected to be the license-free answer to GIFs.

❑ TIFFs are one of the most commonly used graphic formats, and they are supported by most imaging applications and major Web browsers.

❑ BMP is an abbreviation of the word *bitmap*, which is another name for *raster graphics*.

❑ PDF (Portable Document Format) can usually be identified by the file extension .pdf. This format is used to capture a document as an image, so that it can be viewed and printed exactly as intended.

❑ RTF (Rich Text Format) is a file format that was developed by Microsoft to allow the exchange of text files among various applications and operating systems.

❑ PostScript is used to define the look of a page when the page is sent to an output device like a printer or plotter.

❑ EPS (Encapsulated PostScript) is the file format used by PostScript to allow users to preview a PostScript font or image.

❑ The QuickTime plug-in and QuickTime Player application is used to view movies. MOV files, identified by the file extension .mov, are QuickTime movie files.

❑ MPEG (Moving Picture Experts Group) is a file format providing digital video and audio.

❑ AVI (Audio Video Interleaved) was developed by Microsoft as a file format for movies. These movies may contain both audio and video, and must be fully downloaded before they can be played.

❑ BinHex is a popular encoding method that is used to convert data from binary to ASCII.

❑ Streaming media is a relatively new and popular method of transferring data to browsers. With this, data is sent in a continuous stream from the Web server to the browser on your computer. As the data is received, it is buffered and displayed.

❑ Before you throw your HTML document up on the Web, don't forget to go through and check what you've written, to see how the page performs and to determine the effects that your work will have on various browsers or the overall site itself.

SELF TEST

1. While surfing the Web, you come across a Web page with a type of multimedia that your browser doesn't support by default. Which of the following will display the multimedia as part of the Web page, so that no other applications need to be started?

   A. Helper program

   B. Plug-in

   C. Browser

   D. None of the above

2. You want to create images for your Web site using vector graphics. Which of the following formats can you use?

   A. GIF87a

   B. GIF89a

   C. Flash

   D. BMP

3. You are preparing graphics for use on your Web site, and have decided to use a file format that uses compression. You want to remove redundant information from the graphic. What type of compression is this?

   A. Lossless

   B. Losser

   C. Lossy

   D. Redundant

4. You have decided to add some movies to your Web site. The method you have decided on for transmitting this data involves data running continuously from within the browser. What type of media is this?

   A. LZW

   B. Nonstreaming

   C. Streaming

   D. Real

5. You have decided to create animated graphics for your Web page. Which of the following image formats can you use?

   A. GIF87a

   B. GIF89a

   C. BMP

   D. PNG

6. You are preparing JPEG files for use on your Web site. You want the JPEG images to gradually fade into view while the Web pages are being loaded. What is the name of this feature?

   A. Interlaced

   B. Progressive

   C. Wavy

   D. Lossy

7. You are preparing graphics for use on your Web site, and have decided to use a file format that uses compression. You are concerned about the image quality suffering when your images are compressed. Which of the following multimedia formats will allow you to

compress files without sacrificing image quality?

A. GIF

B. JPEG

C. BMP

D. MPEG

8. You are creating a Web site, for a local band, that will allow people to download digital music files. Which of the following file formats should you use?

A. MPEG-1

B. MPEG-2

C. MPEG-3

D. MP3

9. You are creating a Web site for a government agency. The agency wants people browsing the site to be able to download various documents in their original formatting, regardless of the type of word processor they are using. Which file format should you use?

A. PDF

B. BinHex

C. RTF

D. Any of the above

10. You are using BinHex to send a document from your Windows computer to a colleague, who uses a UNIX computer. How will BinHex convert the data?

A. Between ANSI and binary

B. Between ASCII and ANSI

C. Between Macintosh and binary

D. Between binary and ASCII

11. You are preparing to insert a graphic into your Web page. The filename of the graphic you will insert is mypicture.gif. Which of the following lines of code will you use to add the graphic to your Web page?

A. <img="mypicture.gif">

B. <img src="mypicture.gif">

C. <img dynsrc="mypicture.gif">

D. <img mypicture.gif>

12. You are preparing to add a graphic to your Web page. Into which section of the HTML document structure would you add the code necessary to insert an image file?

A. <HEAD>...</HEAD>

B. <BODY>...</BODY>

C. <IMG>...</IMG>

D. <GRAPHIC>...</GRAPHIC>

13. You are preparing to insert a movie file into your Web page. The filename of this file is mymovie.avi. Which of the following lines of code will you use to add the graphic to your Web page?

A. <img src="mymovie.avi">

B. <imgdyn src="mymovie.avi">

C. <img dynsrc="mymovie.avi">

D. <img dynscr="mymovie.avi">

14. You have added code to your HTML document that inserts a movie file on your

Web page. The file format of this movie is MOV. Which of the following would you add to this line of code to have the MOV file begin playing as soon as the Web page is loaded in a browser?

A. start

B. start="load"

C. start="fileopen"

D. start="mouseover"

15. You have added an animated GIF to your Web page. You want this GIF to run though its sequence of images continuously, as long as the Web page is loaded in the browser. Which of the following attributes and settings would you add to specify that this animated GIF is to run indefinitely?

A. loop="0"

B. loop="-1"

C. loop=">1"

D. run="indefinite"

16. You have created an HTML document, and you have decided to add an image as the background for your Web page. Which of the following would you use to specify the image that will appear in the background, assuming the image was called backgrnd.jpg?

A. <HEAD background="backgrnd.jpg">

B. <BODY background="backgrnd.jpg">

C. <BODY bgcolor="backgrnd.jpg">

D. <BODY backgrnd.jpg>

17. You have created an HTML document, and you decided to have a sound file play once when your Web page is first opened. Which of the following would you use to specify the sound file to play, assuming the filename is music.wav, and where would you add this line of code?

A. <bgsound src="music.wav" loop="1"> would be added between the <BODY> and </BODY> tags.

B. <bgsound src="music.wav" loop="1"> would appear between the <HEAD> and </HEAD> tags.

C. <sndfile="music.wav"> would appear between the <BODY> and </BODY> tags.

D. <bgsound="music.wav> would appear between the <HEAD> and </HEAD> tags.

18. You want to use an image in your Web page as a hyperlink. When the user clicks a file called icon.gif, the browser will open the CompTia Web site (http://www.comptia.com). Which of the following lines of code would you enter into your HTML document to do this?

A. <a href="icon.gif"><img src="www.comptia.com"></a>

B. <a href="www.comptia.com"><img src="icon.gif"></a>

C. <a href="www.comptia.com>icon.gif</a>

D. <img src="icon.gif"><a href="www.comptia.com></a>

19. You have created an HTML document and are preparing to put it up on your Web site. You want to ensure that all hyperlinked images and text work, and that they point to the Web sites you want them to point to. You want to avoid links not working, pointing to inactive sites, or pointing to incorrect sites or sites that have changed their content. Which of the following will you do to check this? (Choose all that apply.)

    A. Use software that checks hyperlinks for you.

    B. Check each hyperlink manually.

    C. Use different browsers.

    D. Check for text that is underlined in the Web page.

20. You are trying to access your Web site. When you enter the URL, an error message appears saying that the Web page cannot be found. You know that you've uploaded all of the HTML files and multimedia for your site, but you can't access them unless you type in the full URL that includes HTML document names. What is most likely the problem?

    A. The HTML files are corrupt.

    B. The homepage of your Web site doesn't have the proper default page name.

    C. You didn't check with multiple browsers.

    D. You are accessing the site at a slow connection, so the Web page is taking a while to load.

SELF TEST ANSWERS

1. **B** is correct. Plug-ins are small applications that extend the abilities of the Web browser to support file types that the browser normally couldn't access on its own. Plug-ins will run multimedia files within the browser itself, so you may not even be aware that it is running.

   A is incorrect, because these allow you to view multimedia files by playing them in a separate window. **C** is incorrect. Although browsers can support some file types on their own, this scenario states that the browser doesn't support this particular file by itself. **D** is incorrect, because it states that the correct answer is not given.

2. **C** is correct. The Flash application can be used to create object-oriented (vector) graphics. These image types display elements as objects, rather than as independent pixels. This allows you to take advantage of higher resolutions and to enlarge images without losing clarity.

   A and **B** are both incorrect, because all files in the GIF family are bitmapped (raster) graphics that display images pixel by pixel. **D** is also incorrect, because this file format supports raster images only.

3. **C** is correct. Lossy compression removes redundant information from the file when the file is compressed. In this type of compression, image quality can be sacrificed for a smaller file size, but lossy compression provides much greater compression than lossless compression.

   A is incorrect, because this type of compression is the opposite of lossy compression. In lossless compression, no data is omitted from the file, so it cannot be compressed as much, but image quality is not sacrificed. **B** is incorrect, because there is no such term as "losser" compression. **D** is incorrect, because although the redundant information will be removed from the file, the proper term is "lossy," not "redundant."

4. **C** is correct. This type of media runs online while the user is visiting the host Web site. The file is sent to the user's computer, at which point the computer is responsible for playing and looping the multimedia if required.

   A is incorrect. LZW stands for Lempel-Ziv Welch, and is a type of compression used by GIF files. **B** is incorrect, because this is the opposite of streaming data. Nonstreaming data cannot be viewed online within the browser. It must first be downloaded before it can be played. **D** is incorrect, because this is not a valid media type.

5. **B** is correct. This is a bitmapped image format the uses lossless compression, and is able to support animation. A single GIF89a file can contain many images. If the

images are displayed quickly in order, they can give the impression of movement or animation.

A is incorrect. One of the major differences between GIF87a and GIF89a files is that only GIF89a files can support animation and interlacing. **C** and **D** are incorrect, because these file types are only capable of storing one image. Animation relies on the ability of one file to display multiple images.

6. **B** is correct. Progressive JPEGs fade into view, rather than loading line by line from the top down. This gives users the chance to decipher the image, and either wait or move on, before the image is entirely loaded. Progressive JPEGs look very much like interlaced GIFs.

A is incorrect. Interlaced files are capable of fading in, but when this characteristic is applied to a JPEG file, it is called progressive, not interlaced. **C** is incorrect, because this is not a valid multimedia term. **D** is incorrect, because this is a type of file compression, where redundant or unnecessary parts of an image are removed to decrease the size of the file.

7. **A** is correct. GIF files use lossless compression, so image quality is not sacrificed when the image is compressed. However, this type of compression does not reduce the size of the file as much as lossless compression does.

B and **D** are incorrect, because both of these formats use lossy compression. This means that unnecessary parts of the file will be removed. This can cause image quality to suffer. **C** is incorrect, because these files do not use compression.

8. **D** is correct. You should use MP3 files. MP3 is part of the MPEG family, but is used for audio files only. They cannot support video, but provide much better sound than either MPEG-1 or MPEG-2 files.

A and **B** are incorrect, because although these files can include sound, they are designed for video. They are not capable of supporting sound quality as good as that of MP3 files. **C** is incorrect, because this file type doesn't exist. The MPEG family includes MPEG-1, MPEG-2, MPEG-4, and MP3. There is no such thing as MPEG-3.

9. **A** is correct. You should use PDF. This file format is used to capture an image of a document. This means that the document will look the same to anyone viewing it, regardless of the type and capabilities of their word processor. The Acrobat Reader application is required for viewing PDF files.

B is incorrect, because this is a translation format that converts data between binary and ASCII. **C** is also incorrect, because this is an almost universally understood plain text language. In both BinHex and RTF files, the document will appear differently on various computers, depending on each machine's interpretation of the ASCII or RTF code. **D** is incorrect, because PDF is the only valid answer.

10. **D** is correct. Different applications and platforms use different binary coding. However, almost all computers and applications can understand ASCII (hex) coding. BinHex files are coded by the originating computer from binary to ASCII. The receiving computer decodes the ASCII file into its own form of binary code.

    A and **B** are both incorrect, because they refer to ANSI data, which is not supported by BinHex. **C** is incorrect, because it states that BinHex is used to convert data between Macintosh and binary. Although BinHex is often used on Macintosh computers, it is not limited to this platform. BinHex uses binary and ASCII, which can be read by Macintosh or PC computers.

11. **B** is correct. You can add images to your HTML documents using the <img> tag. To specify the filename and, if necessary, the path to the file, you use the src="" attribute of the <img> tag. The path and/or filename is entered between the quotations. Therefore, to add a graphic named mypicture.gif to your Web page, you would use the following line of code:

    <img src="mypicture.gif">

    A is incorrect, because it lacks the src attribute. If this line were used, an error would result. **C** is also incorrect. The dynsrc attribute is used to specify that a dynamic source file, such as a MOV or AVI file, will be inserted into the HTML document. When static graphic files, like JPEGs or GIFs, are used, the src="" attribute is used. Finally, **D** is incorrect, because the filename isn't in quotations and isn't proceeded by src=.

12. **B** is correct. Image files must be inserted between the <BODY> and </BODY> tags in the HTML document structure. This is the section of the HTML document that will actually be displayed by the browser.

    A is incorrect, because the <HEAD>...</HEAD> section of the HTML document is used for information read, but not displayed by the browser. **C** is incorrect, because <IMG> refers to a type of command tag, not a section of the HTML document. Also, the <IMG> command is not accompanied by the closing </IMG> tag. **D** is incorrect, because there is no <GRAPHIC> or </GRAPHIC> tag in the HTML document structure.

13. **C** is correct. Movies, such as those of the AVI or MOV file formats, can be added to a Web page using the <img> tag with the dynsrc="" attribute. This is followed by

the filename of the movie and, if necessary, the path to the file is entered between the quotations.

A is incorrect, because the src="" attribute is used to specify a static file, like a GIF or JPEG, is to be inserted into the Web page. It is not used for movie files. **B** is incorrect, because there is no tag called <imgdyn>. **D** is incorrect, because of a spelling error. The <img> tag has a "dynsrc" attribute, not "dynscr."

14. **C** is correct. When start="fileopen" is added to the line of code specifying which movie file is to be played through the Web page, the movie will begin playing as soon as the Web is loaded into the browser.

    A and **B** are both incorrect. Although the start attribute is used to specify when the movie file should begin playing, it needs to be equated to one of two settings: fileopen or mouseover. **D** is incorrect, because if the command is start="mouseover", then the movie would begin playing when the user moved his or her mouse over the place where the movie resided in the page. In this scenario, the movie begins as soon as the Web page is loaded.

15. **B** is correct. The command loop="-1" will cause the animation to loop indefinitely. The loop attribute is for animated multimedia, such as animated GIFs or movies like AVIs or MOVs. This defines how many times an animated GIF or movie is to play before it stops. If "-1" or "infinite" appears, then it will run as long as the Web page is loaded. **A** is incorrect, because this command indicates that that browser should not run the animated GIF at all. It would appear in the Web page with only the first frame showing. **D** is incorrect, because there is no run attribute or setting called "indefinite."

16. **B** is correct. You can add images as a background to your Web page using the background attribute of the <BODY> tag. This command would cause the JPEG file to appear in the background of the Web page, while displaying graphics or text on top of it.

    A is incorrect, because it suggests using the background= code within the <HEAD> tags. Anything that is to be displayed by the Web browser must be entered within the <BODY> tags. **C** is incorrect, because the bgcolor command is used to display solid colors, not graphics, in the background. **D** is incorrect, because the background attribute isn't being invoked. The background= command must be used to mark this file for use in the background.

17. **B** is correct. The <bgsound> tag is used to play sound files when the Web page first opens. The src="" attribute specifies the filename of the sound file to play, while loop="1" is used to specify the number of times the sound file should play. This tag is placed in the <HEAD>...</HEAD> section of your HTML document. **A** is incorrect, because the <bgsound> tag, and the settings affecting this tag, must be added between the <HEAD> and </HEAD> tags, not the <BODY>...</BODY> tag set. **C** is incorrect, because there is no tag called <sndfile>. **D** is incorrect, because the src="" attribute of the <bgsound> tag is missing from this line of code, as is the loop="1" attribute and setting.

18. **B** is correct. A graphic can be specified as a hyperlink is by entering the tag for the graphic between the <a href=""> and </a> tags. In other words, you put a graphic in place of where you would normally enter the text you want used for the link. **A** is incorrect, because in this case, the link tag references the image, and the image tag references the hyperlink. **C** is incorrect, because this line of code doesn't specify that an image is to be used as a link. The text between the hyperlink reference and the closing </a> tag will appear as underlined text with this code, and act as a textual hyperlink. **D** is incorrect, because in this case, the image tag appears before, not between the hyperlink tags.

19. **B** is correct. The best way to check hyperlinks is to do it manually. Click all hyperlinked text and images to see that they point to the correct URL, and that there is an active and expected Web page at that address. **A** is incorrect, because software that checks hyperlinks won't be able to distinguish whether the hyperlink points to the Web site you wanted. It can only check to see if a Web page exists at that URL. **C** is incorrect, because if a hyperlink works in one browser, it will work in others. The point of testing your site with various browsers is to ensure the page looks the same in each. **D** is incorrect. Some links are displayed as underlined text. However, text can be formatted with an underline, even when it is not being used as a hyperlink. Conversely, not all links display an underline.

20. **B** is correct The homepage of your Web site doesn't have the proper default page name. When the browser accesses a URL without a specific HTML document being specified, a default Web page will appear. This is generally a Web page titled default, index, or welcome (often with the file extensions .htm or .html). The default Web page's name is configured in the Web server, so you should check your Web server's documentation or consult your Internet service provider (ISP) for information as to what the default Web page should be named.

A is incorrect, because this question states that if you enter the URL with the name of an HTML document, a Web page appears. A corrupt HTML file will result in an error, and no Web page will be displayed. **C** is incorrect. Although Web pages may not appear as expected in other browsers, URLs are understood universally by browsers. If a URL works in one browser, it will work in others. **D** is incorrect, because it states that the Web page is just loading slowly. If a URL exists, it will show the same information to a fast computer as it will to a slower computer.

7

i-Net Languages

Developing real-world Web solutions requires a good deal of knowledge about the environments you are presented with. To select the proper tools for the job you will require, at the minimum, a basic understanding of the terms and technologies that drive the client/server development world.

Database knowledge is one of the most-often used Web resources. Knowing this, it's important to note the differences between types of databases and how to connect those databases to your application.

In this chapter, we will discuss some of the current popular technologies and when to use them. Finally, we will discuss what role databases play in these technologies.

CERTIFICATION OBJECTIVE 7.01

Programming-Related Terms and Internet Applications Development

In the next sections we're going to cover some of the primary terms associated with Internet development and their applications.

API

API is an acronym for application program interface. These interfaces are the set of commands that an application uses to request and carry out lower-level services performed by a computer's operating system or access functionality of another program. API provides several advantages to the programmer. These advantages include extending the functionality of your application, standardization of commands, and decreasing hardware requirements. We will discuss each of these advantages in depth.

Extending the functionality of your application is most certainly one of the biggest advantages of using API. The ability to use powerful methods offered by another application or the operating system itself makes API a very notable technology in this chapter.

Visual Basic provides many functions within the language itself. However, Visual Basic cannot access system information, tell you who is currently logged in to the computer, or even provide the installation directory of Windows. These are important functions that you may need to access within your application. Windows API can provide thousands of functions that would otherwise be unavailable to a Visual Basic programmer. But API does not stop at Visual Basic. API can be used by most of today's development environments. In fact, one downside to API is that most API documentation, if it exists at all, is written for C/C++ programmers.

API also standardizes application calls. This is very useful because much of the functionality that you may need has probably already been developed, tested for bugs, and documented for use by programmers of many backgrounds. By using API, you are ensuring that your program will return the desired result.

Finally, API can minimize the use of system resources and, therefore, decrease the demand of massive hardware requirements. By using existing functions, especially those connected with the operating system, you minimize the amount of memory and space your program will use.

Today, computer hardware may seem to be a nonissue. However, you should not always assume that because hardware is so readily available that excessive resources would be available to your program.

CGI

Common Gateway Interface, or CGI, defines the communication link between the Web server and Web applications. What does this mean? Simply put, CGI gives network or Internet access to specific programs of your choice. CGI communicates over the Hypertext Transfer Protocol, known as HTTP. CGI provides access to your server's applications over the HTTP protocol.

CGI acts as a "middleman" in an Internet application. Your Web browser requests a CGI script or application from a Web site. In doing so, the Web server executes the CGI application on the server. The application then returns information to the Web server. The Web server then returns the output to your Web browser. CGI, with the aid of the Web server software, acts as a mediator, passing information back and forth between the server's applications and your Web browser.

SQL

SQL (often pronounced "sequel"), or Structured Query Language, is the common communication method between databases. The history of SQL began in the late 1970s, when IBM began developing it in a lab in San Jose, California. SQL is a nonprocedural language that will let you decide what data you want to select from a database. The term "nonprocedural" describes what data is returned as opposed to how the database performs the action. From database to database, although the interface and management may be different, SQL is the common thread that you can use to define the information that will be returned.

While ANSI (American National Standards Institute) and ISO (Industry Standards Organization) both govern the standards for this language, there will be some slight changes from one database to the next. In addition, many database management systems (DBMs) provide extensions to SQL that are proprietary. This is common, but it is necessary to note the differences between standard SQL and the proprietary extensions.

Databases tend to confuse the average person. Terms like "table," "recordset," "field," "relationship," and "query" tend to scare people away. SQL, however, is easy to understand and is a language with logical syntax. Let's consider a very small database and show how SQL can retrieve data from that table. Let's assume that the database has a table called "Books" and another called "Authors." Table 7-1 shows the fields for these two tables.

TABLE 7-1

Structure of a Database

Books Fields	Authors Fields
ISBN *primary key	AuthorID *primary key
AuthorID *foreign key	FirstName
Title	LastName
Publisher	Country
PublishedDate	Email

These tables are obviously not a good start for a real database; so don't try to start your own bookstore on the basis of this example!

Let's say you wanted to write a SQL statement that showed you a complete list of all the books you have on file. The SQL command would look something like this:

```
SELECT * FROM Books
```

Now say you want to be able to display all books, as well as the author's name next to each individual book. You would have to use the SQL keyword "join" in order to join two related tables from a database. The join statement takes one field from each table and uses the values from these two fields to create a relationship between the two tables. In our example, these fields would be AuthorID, which is the primary key of the Authors table, joining this table on the foreign key of AuthorID in the Books table. We'll cover relational databases more thoroughly later in this chapter.

Table 7-2 shows some basic SQL statements and their definitions.

ISAPI

ISAPI (Internet Server Application Programming Interface) is a set of program calls that allows you to create a Windows Web-based application that will run faster than a CGI application. One of the disadvantages of a CGI application is that each time it is requested, it runs as a completely new and separate process. This takes up system resources as each instance, or request, runs in its own address space. This is inefficient, especially if many users request the application. In an ISAPI application, you create a dynamic link library application file that can run as part of the Hypertext Transfer Protocol application's process and address space. This is known as running in process. The DLL is loaded into the Web server when the HTTP service is started. The DLL remains in memory as long as it is needed; it doesn't have to be located and read into storage each time the application is requested.

It is easy to convert CGI applications into ISAPI applications without having to recode the program's logic. However, the application does need to

TABLE 7-2	SQL Method	Description and Example
Simple SQL Statements and Their Definitions	SELECT	Can be followed by the field name of the data that you want to display in your query's results. You can also specify an asterisk (*) to grab all the fields in a particular table or view. Example: `SELECT MyField FROM MyTable`
	FROM	Used to specify what table(s) or view(s) contains the fields that you want to display. Example: `SELECT MyField FROM MyTable`
	WHERE	Used for passing criteria on your query results. Example: `SELECT * FROM MyTable WHERE MyField = 'MyValue'`
	INSERT	Used for inserting data into your database table. Example: `INSERT INTO MyTable (Field1, Field2) VALUES ('Value1, 'Value2')`
	INTO	Used for inserting values into a table. This word passes the name of the table into which you want to insert data. Example: `INSERT INTO MyTable (Field1, Field2) VALUES ('Value1, 'Value2')`
	VALUES	Specifies the values to pass to the specified fields into which you want to insert data. Example: `INSERT INTO MyTable (Field1, Field2) VALUES ('Value1, 'Value2')`
	DELETE	Deletes a row from a table based on criteria that you pass. Example: `DELETE FROM MyTable Where Field1 = 'MyValue'`

be written to be thread-safe. This allows a single instance of the DLL to serve multiple users.

A special kind of ISAPI DLL is called an ISAPI filter. An ISAPI filter can be instructed to execute for every HTTP request. It can also be instructed to execute only for certain file types. You can create an ISAPI filter for logging, encryption or decryption, authentication, or many other purposes. A common filter is the Active Server Page (ASP) filter. This file-mapped filter executes script code stored in any file with an .asp extension. Many other filters have been created for other file types. Windows NT can now support

PERL by using an ISAPI filter for PERL. This allows a ported version of PERL to execute any files with a .pl file extension.

ISAPI applications can be much more effective than CGI applications, especially in high-use scenarios. ISAPI applications run in the same process as the Web server's HTTP service and, therefore, don't require loading and unloading or their own address space.

DLL: Dynamic Linking and Static Linking

Earlier in this chapter we discussed API. In this section, we will discuss the idea of the API storage unit, the dynamic link library (DLL). We will also discuss the difference between statically linking functions and dynamically linking them.

First, let's start by defining a DLL. It is a collection of functions or a collection of programs that can be called upon by another program. The word "library" suggests that it can store a vast set of functions that can be "checked out" when they are needed. These functions are then stored in a file, usually with a .dll extension.

The advantage of packaging functions together outside your standard programs is that they do not get loaded into memory until they are needed. You can create large programs that perform many functions and communicate with many devices without taking up a large amount of system memory. When a DLL function is needed, it is loaded and run. The system can then release that library from memory when it is no longer needed. For instance, if a user opens up a graphics program, it does not need to load a printer or scanner driver. However, when the user wants to scan in a photo or print out his newest graphics, the program loads the appropriate library and executes the functions as needed. When the user has completed his scan or print job, the DLL releases the resources it used.

Static linking a function means that it is loaded with the main program. The function is loaded into memory whether or not it is in use. While this may sound like a major problem, static linking has its advantages. You would want to static link a function if it were used repeatedly throughout a program. Some functions may take up massive processing power if they are constantly being linked and unlinked. For this reason, static linking is still used, and rightly so.

In summary, static linking is used for functions that are used consistently and constantly throughout your program. Static linking is loaded at runtime and, therefore, uses more system memory (RAM). Dynamic linking is used for program functions that are not used often in your program or are not accessed constantly. Dynamic linked functions can be called upon when they are needed by your main program. DLLs are storage units for functions.

Client- and Server-Side Scripting

Client- and server-side scripting are important elements in Internet development. They allow the interaction of customers with data of all types. On the server side, scripting allows the programmer to access server resources such as SQL Server databases, custom COM objects, MTS components, and more. Server-side scripting allows the programmer to place the business logic on the server. This provides several advantages.

The first advantage of server-side scripting is that your business logic is stored in one place. Business logic comprises the rules to which your applications must conform. For instance, your business logic may state that prices for a product vary by geographic location: Canada and the United States. If your rules change, your code needs updating in one place only. Not only does this make updates easier, it also makes them less time consuming and costly. Updating software on the client side can pose a number of technical problems. If you're using client-side code for your business logic, you must make certain that each user who uses your system has the most current version of your software. We will go into more detail on the different tiers of an application later in this chapter.

FROM THE CLASSROOM

The 8-Second Rule: Optimize Your Code

A general rule of thumb for Web applications is to keep response times to 8 seconds and under. Most users will leave your site if they have to wait more than 8 seconds to receive a reply. When it comes to e-commerce applications, this could mean a loss of potential revenue. In order to avoid this, there a couple things you can do when developing server-side code in order to optimize performance.

- If you open an object, make sure you close it and set it back to nothing.

- Use localized variables.

- Separate HTML from your logic as much as possible. Try to do all your processing first; build a string in your code that contains the HTML, and then do one print or write to output the HTML. Avoid nesting logic in the HTML.

- Keep database connections to a minimum. Try to get all your data in one query instead of multiple queries.

- Avoid too many transfers or transactions over network resources. If possible, keep all servers that will interact with the Web site on a small subnet in order to maximize network throughput.

- Avoid using too many variables that need to be stored on the server. If possible, pass variables through the URL instead of storing them on the server, such as the use of session variables on ASP.

The main thing to understand is in Web development, there are many variables that can affect performance. As a Web developer, you need to understand network issues and know how to code effectively in order to develop a high-performance site that provides your users with a good experience, and in the process creates return customers.

—Patrick J. Santry,
MCSD, MCT, MCP+SB, i-Net+

CERTIFICATION OBJECTIVE 7.02

Popular Client-Side vs. Server-Side Programming Languages

In this section, we will describe the various scripting and application development languages available to you as a Web developer. We also find out when to use various development technologies. There may be technologies, such as VBScript, for example, that run on the client side and that are unique or proprietary to specific browsers. There may also be instances when it makes sense to use one technology based upon the server platform the Web site is running on.

Java

Java is a programming language developed by Sun Microsystems (http://www.sun.com) in 1995. Java was developed specifically for use in distributed applications and, more specifically, for the Internet. A common misconception about Java is that it can create applets only for Web pages. This is completely untrue. Java is capable of compiling completely stand-alone applications that run on a server, as well as full-featured applications for the workstation. While the Web-embedded application is the most known and possibly the most recognizable Java product, applets certainly do not define the full capability of Java.

Java was based on the popular C++ language. Much of the syntax and libraries created for Java were modeled after those items popular with C++. The main difference that separates the two languages is that Java applications do not permit references to data outside their own resources. This means Java cannot create conflicts in another application. More important, the fact that Java cannot contain references to data, memory, or other resources outside itself enforces the security necessary for distributed applications.

Java is also portable. This means that applications developed on one operating system can also be run on another. Applications can be developed on a UNIX platform, and you are assured that it will run on a Windows platform. This is accomplished by two ideas introduced with Java: the Java Virtual Machine and compiling to byte-code. Byte-code is an abstraction of compiled code that serves as an instruction set. The Java Virtual Machine can interpret these instructions. This is done so that the virtual machine can be changed on any operating system to read the byte-code instructions as desired. In this model, the Java virtual machine acts as a mediator between the byte-code instruction set and the processor, all along executing the commands one item at a time. In another model for Java byte-code interpretation, we can use a JIT compiler. JIT stands for "just in time." A JIT compiler usually comes with the Java virtual machine specific to the platform it runs on. A JIT compiler will essentially recompile the byte-code instructions into platform-specific code. This allows the byte-code to be sent immediately to the systems processor and, therefore, usually makes the code faster. This is effective for functions that are called upon repeatedly.

Java has been used in various capacities. When Java first came out, most of what you saw on the Web was small applets used to brighten up a Web site. Java has matured now to offer the developer a way of developing middle-tier objects, which the Web user does not see. These middle-tier objects contain most of a company's business rules in order to interact with a back-end database, legacy system, or any other type of information store.

Java has also been used to port languages like VBScript over to the UNIX/Linux environment. There are several companies that use the Java SDK to port the popular Active Server Pages (ASP) platform over to UNIX environments. This allows a VBScript to be truly multiplatform—and all provided by Java. We'll be discussing ASP later on in this chapter.

Java also provides other services such as database connectivity, server-side processing such as Java Server Pages, and much more. To find out more about Java, you can visit the Sun Microsystems Web site at http://java.sun.com.

JavaScript

JavaScript is different from the compiled language Java. JavaScript carries some of the syntax of Java and even carries some of the same functions. However, JavaScript is different in that it is interpreted rather than compiled. A compiled program is converted into language that the computer can understand. An interpreted program must be fed one command at a time into an interpreter. Because of this, JavaScript is much slower than compiled Java. Since the scripting language is interpreted, it also removes the necessity of using low-level data types and sticks to one basic type: a variant.

In most programming languages, various data types are used to define variables. Those data types restrict the type of information that can be stored in them. This usually includes integers, strings or characters, bytes, and numbers. JavaScript, along with most scripting languages, only has a variant data type. Variant is a generic container that can hold any type of data. While this may sound convenient, it is a disadvantage to the popular scripting language. Containers or variables of type variant use more memory than the primitive data types of other languages.

JavaScript is a very popular language for Web developers. JavaScript allows developers to create scripts to change images when your mouse passes over them, calculate payments, validate data, and change styles of any element on the Web page. JavaScript is the most popular of scripting languages for basic Internet use because it works on most of today's popular browsers and operating systems. It is important to note, however, that while there is a standard for JavaScript, implementation may vary from browser to browser.

PERL

Practical Extraction and Reporting Language (PERL) is an interpreted scripting language. While PERL is generally used on UNIX-platformed Web servers, it has been ported to many other operating systems as well. Since PERL is interpreted, it is compiled just before execution. It can be compiled into either C code or cross-platform byte-code.

PERL has been optimized for scanning text files, extracting information from those files, and reporting the results. PERL is also a good language for many common system tasks. Because of its capabilities, PERL is regarded as an exceptional choice for a CGI application development language.

The language is intended to be easy to use rather than precise and small. Some of the best features of the C—awk, sed, sh, and tr—are combined into PERL. This was not an accident. PERL was intentionally built this way so people familiar with those popular languages would have less difficulty learning and using it. PERL's expression syntax resembles C's expression syntax. PERL is unique among most programming utilities in that it will not limit the size of your data or run into other memory constraints. If your server has the memory and system resources, PERL has the ability to handle the entire file as a single variable.

CGI applications run in their own address space and require loading and unloading for each request. However, plug-ins can be installed for some servers so that PERL is loaded permanently in memory. This reduces compile time and results in faster execution of PERL scripts.

C

In 1972, Dennis Ritchie at Bell Laboratories formed a new computer language. This language as you can probably guess by the section subheading, was named C. The language was modeled after a previous language called B, which was also developed at Bell Labs by Ken Thompson.

Before we get too far, we must understand why these people decided to write these languages. It wasn't for pure enjoyment. It wasn't simply to prove skill. It was to fill a very obvious need. In 1969, Ken Thompson and Dennis Ritchie were developing a new operating system called UNIX for the PDP-7 computer. I'm sure that name is not new to most of you. The language was originally coded in an assembler. Once UNIX was functional, it was evident that a higher-level language would be needed. Doug McIlroy then introduced TMG to the group. Ken Thompson decided to implement Fortran for UNIX and so began coding it in TMG. What resulted was not Fortran at all, but a new language and compiler. Ritchie sensed that a better language would be needed. B didn't do any type checking; that is, it didn't verify the type of data stored in variables. Ritchie then created C, modeling it after the B language. UNIX was soon recoded in C for the PDP-11.

As you can imagine, with all these languages being thrown about and rapidly changing, C got a little mixed up. C was powerful and flexible, and programmers began adopting it as their favorite language. However, several different variations of C started sprouting up all over the place. Slight differences between the variations made it difficult to move from one company to the next and read the code. It was because of this that the American National Standards Institute (ANSI) created a small committee to decide the standard definition of the language. In 1983 those standards were formed to create what we know as ANSI Standard C. Most compilers these days can compile to this standard.

So, if C was written so long ago for UNIX, why should you use it today? That good question deserves a good answer—or a few of them.

C is a very powerful and very flexible programming language. There are no limitations to what can be done with C. Any application can be written in C. Device drivers that communicate directly with hardware can be written in it, as well as desktop applications and games. Operating systems have been developed in C, as well as compilers for other languages. Because of this power and flexibility, C is still very useful today.

Age has only refined the C programming language. Because C has been around for so long, it has been tried and tested repeatedly. It has continually been revised and standardized. Because of its power and ability, numerous programmers have adopted C. Those numerous programmers have coded add-ons and helper functions that have improved the language itself.

C is small. There are not many keywords, or reserved words, in the C language. Keywords are the basic terms that make up the functionality of the language. These terms range from instructions to initiate and end a loop to those used for simply declaring the existence of a variable. A small keywords set ensures an easy-to-understand, uncluttered language. The limit to the number of keywords does not define the limits of the language, however. You will find that the few keywords used are well chosen and effective. Table 7-3 shows the reserved words for ANSI C.

For the most part, these are common English terms. You can pretty well guess what each one of these terms does. That was very much the intent of C: to be simple and powerful.

The last reason to use C is because it is modular. This means that common actions in a program can be combined into a function. A function is simply a group of statements that can be called from the rest of the program. This is common when the program calls the same statements more than once. Modularity allows for clarity in logical programming.

asm	auto	break	case	char
const	continue	default	do	double
else	enum	extern	float	for
goto	if	int	long	register
return	short	signed	sizeof	static
struct	switch	typedef	union	unsigned
void	volatile	while		

Modularity also allows for code reuse. The same functions can be stored and used repeatedly at the programmer's discretion.

C++

C++ is more than just a very strange-looking grade. C++ is yet another language to choose from that also has its good points. So, logically, if C replaced B, wouldn't C++ be the next generation language to replace C? The reason the next version of C is named C++ is that in the C language, in order to increment a value by one, you use the operator ++, hence C++. C++ is the next step past C, but only in that it has added a few things for a new environment. C++ is an object-oriented language that allows programmers to code in the style of everyday life, with interaction of one object to another. Each object has its own characteristics, properties, events, and methods of operation.

Visual Basic

Visual Basic is a programming language from Microsoft. The word "visual" comes from the idea that dragging and dropping objects and controls on the form can create the program's interface. BASIC is the name of the language from which VB was formed. Some developers would argue that Visual Basic is simply an environment and that BASIC is the language you code in. While this may be technically true, the BASIC language has changed drastically and is very dissimilar to the original BASIC.

Visual Basic is easy to learn and fast to code with. Visual Basic is a wonderful tool for Rapid Application Development (RAD). Because of the speed with which you can develop fully functional applications with Visual Basic, it is often used to create an application prototype that will later be written in another language. Because of Visual Basic's ease of use, it has become very popular, pulling in about three million developers, according to Microsoft.

The newest versions of Visual Basic have made it even more popular. Applications coded in Visual Basic can now be compiled to native code—the same code a program written and compiled in C or C++ would create! Not only can Visual Basic use objects coded in other languages, it can compile objects for use in other languages. While Visual Basic is not truly an object-oriented programming language, efforts have been made to allow the creation of COM DLLs and COM EXEs.

Visual Basic can now be used to create everything from server-side objects to simple applications with a graphical user interface. Visual Basic can connect to databases, access sequential files, and even use a large portion of the Windows API. This means that while Visual Basic has no direct hardware access, it can access APIs written in other languages that can perform those functions.

Visual Basic's data abilities range from the simplest of client applications that retrieve data from a local database to multitier applications that combine information from AS/400, Oracle, and nonrelational data sources such as directory servers. Visual Basic can access these data sources via ODBC, OLE DB, or Microsoft's popular ActiveX Data Objects. Since Visual Basic is touted as a Rapid Application Development language, the data development tools are integrated directly with the Visual Basic IDE. These development tools can be used to access any data source that uses ODBC, OLE DB, or ADO. Along with these development tools are included data-aware controls that allow direct data binding.

VBScript

VBScript is yet another interpreted scripting language. VBScript is provided by Microsoft and is a smaller subset of its Visual Basic programming language. VBScript is similar to other Web-based script languages like JavaScript, Tcl, PERL, and REXX. Because VBScript is similar to Visual Basic in syntax, it makes transitioning between the two painless. Someone who codes in Visual Basic should be able to learn VBScript rather quickly.

Like JavaScript, VBScript is easier and faster to code than more complex, more structured, compiled languages such as C, C++, and Visual Basic. This makes VBScript ideal for smaller programs or as a glue to combine and execute larger compiled programs. For instance, VBScript is often used in the ISAPI-based, Microsoft Active Server Pages discussed later in this chapter. VBScript is often used in ASPs to connect to databases, execute compiled programs and return their results, and act upon specialized server-based objects.

VBScript is Microsoft's answer to ever-so-popular JavaScript. Both JavaScript and VBScript function with an interpreter that comes with a Web browser. VBScript was designed for use in Web pages opened in Microsoft's Internet Explorer Web browser. VBScript can communicate with the Web browser itself, as well as with ActiveX controls, automation servers, Java applets, and other client-side applications.

One drawback to VBScript is that Netscape's browser does not support it. Because of this, VBScript is best suited for intranet Web sites that use the Internet Explorer browser only.

JScript

JScript is an interpreted script language from Microsoft that is designed for use within Web pages. It adheres to the ECMAScript standard developed by Microsoft and Netscape. It is basically Microsoft's equivalent to the earlier and more widely used JavaScript.

The main difference between JScript and JavaScript is that JScript is object-oriented in nature. This allows add-ons to the core language.

XML

We now move on to one of the most exciting new developments in Internet development technologies. Extensible Markup Language (XML) is a flexible way to define commonly used information formats. The format and the data itself may then be shared on the World Wide Web, in intranets, and even in desktop applications. Let's look, for instance, at a bookseller who uses a standard or common way to describe information about a book. The format of the data would include standard information for author, title, ISBN, and year published. You could then describe each book's information format with XML. If each bookseller used the same data format, a user could send a search agent or custom program to each bookseller's Web site, gather book data, and then make a valid comparison of price, shipping costs, and so on. Any individual or group of individuals that wants to share information in a consistent manner can use XML.

"That sounds great, but why is it so 'exciting'?," you say. This technology can change the way Web search engines work. It can change the way we browse for Internet information. Currently, Web search engines crawl from Web site to Web site. On each page the engine indexes all the keywords and then files the page in its database. This means that a Web site that has nothing to do with dogs may show up in a search for "dogs" because the Web's author used that word once or twice on his page. With XML, the data on a page can be formatted commonly to allow search engines not only to index pages more quickly, but also to report on searches more accurately. Furthermore, more applications will be developed to use XML to allow you to search many sites with the same data. Can you imagine a program that could go to each car dealer's Web site and make a comparison of vehicles for you? XML is exciting because it allows you to not only provide your data, but also define the container in which the data is held. Essentially, once XML has become more widely adopted by Web developers, the entire Internet will serve as a huge database that can be tapped by any application that needs information.

The World Wide Web Consortium is the organization that defines XML's format and use. XML is similar to the language of today's Web pages, HTML. Both XML and HTML contain markup symbols to describe the contents of a page or file. HTML, however, only defines the graphical layout of data on a page. XML describes the page's content in terms of what data is being described and the data itself. For example, <BOOK> could indicate the information to follow was information about a book. This means that XML files can be processed purely as data, or they can be stored with similar data on another computer similar to a database, or the data can be displayed much like an HTML document. For example, the application in the computer receiving the XML document might provide book reviews from Amazon.com, BarnesandNoble.com, and fatbrain.com all on the same page.

The word "extensible" in Extensible Markup Language means that the tags available to XML are limitless and self-defining. You are not limited to a certain amount of tags as you are with HTML. XML is actually a simpler and easier-to-use subset of the Standard Generalized Markup Language (SGML). SGML is the standard for creating a document structure.

Early XML applications include Microsoft's Channel Definition Format (CDF), which describes a channel. Microsoft's channels are a portion of a Web site that downloads to your hard disk, and are updated periodically as information changes. A specific CDF file contains data that specifies an initial Web page and how frequently it is updated. Many other XML applications are springing up across the Net. Medical applications now allow doctors to define the format in which a patient's medical chart can be stored. Applications related to banking, e-commerce, personal profiles, legal documents, part lists, and more are anticipated.

VRML

Virtual Reality Modeling Language (VRML) is a language used for describing three-dimensional image sequences and user interactions with them. VRML allows you to build a sequence of visual images into Web pages. A visitor to your site can interact by viewing, moving, rotating, or otherwise interacting with your three-dimensional scene. For example, prototypes of new products can be developed to display a rotating view of the products. The user would be allowed to zoom in on the product or turn it to view it from any angle.

To view a VRML file, you need a VRML viewer application that can be plugged into a Web browser. While VRML was once a very cool idea and is still used in a few Web sites, it is quickly being replaced by other media interaction technologies such as Sun's Java or Macromedia's Shockwave.

ASP

Active Server Pages (ASP) have been touched on slightly in earlier portions of this chapter. Here we will learn a little more about what ASP is and how it can be used. An ASP can be an ordinary HTML page that includes one or more scripts that are processed on the Web server before the page is sent to the user. An ASP is somewhat similar to CGI applications in that they both involve programs that run on the server. Typically, the script in the ASP at the server uses input received in the user's request for the page to access data from a database. The ASP then builds or customizes the page on the fly before sending it to the requestor. A good example of this is MSN.com. MSN.com allows you to define how you want your page to be displayed when you visit again. When you return, the ASP looks up your information in the server's database, formats the page as you described, and returns the HTML for the page.

It's important to note that the ASP code itself never appears to the user. All of the programming logic of the site is hidden to the user. Viewing the source of an ASP inside a browser only returns the ASP's resulting HTML output. This is very important, because most ASP source code includes the location of a database and, in many instances, the username and password needed to access that database. If the source of the ASP were revealed, a Web site cracker could use that information to compromise your server.

ASP is a feature of the Microsoft Internet Information Server (IIS). However, new programs are allowing ASPs to be used with other Web servers. ChiliSoft creates an add-on for Apache, Lotus, Netscape, and O'Reilly Web servers that allow you to run ASPs on Solaris, AIX, HP UX, and Linux. Since the server-side script is building a plain HTML page, it can be delivered to almost any browser.

ASP allows you to use any scripting language your server defines as an ISAPI filter. While VBScript and JScript are the native formats usually used in ASPs, other languages are available. ActiveState creates an add-on to IIS that allows you to run PerlScript, a subset of PERL, within ASPs.

As is true of ISAPI filters, IIS maps files with an .asp suffix to the program, which analyzes the script within ASPs. When a file with an .asp extension is requested, IIS retrieves the file, runs it through the ASP program DLL, and returns the resulting HTML code to the user's browser.

Having the knowledge of multiple scripting languages and being able to function on both the UNIX and Microsoft platforms will increase your value on the job market and make your job easier in most heterogeneous corporate environments.

When to Use the Languages

With all these tools available, you might start to wonder which one you should use for your next project. While some of the uses for each were discussed earlier in each language section, I'll try to shed a little more light on which tool is right for which job.

The first thing to consider is where the application is going to run. What environment is the application going to require? Is the application running in an Intranet or Internet site? Can you control what browsers are used for the site? Does the code need to be secured to prevent theft? These are all questions that need to be answered.

As already stated in this chapter, the following are often used on server-side applications: JavaScript, VBScript, Java, Visual Basic, C/C++, ASP, PERL, and even XML. You may say, "Wait as second! Some of those look like client-side technologies!" You are correct is saying that. Many of today's technologies can be used both on the client and on the server. JavaScript and VBScript are often used within Active Server Pages on the server side. Java, while known for its client-side applets, can also create server-side servletts. XML can be used anywhere. It allows data to be uniformly exchanged between data consumers—why restrict that to only client-side use? C/C++ can be used to create server-side ISAPI applications, or even EXEs and DLLs that work directly with the Web server software.

When deciding between compiled languages (such as C/C++, Java, or Visual Basic) and interpreted languages (such as VBScript, JavaScript, and PERL) you need to evaluate several items. The first thing you should evaluate is the server platform. If your server is running UNIX, you may find it very difficult to get your Visual Basic routines to run. While third-party plug-ins to servers may allow you to stretch your server's usefulness, they are not always the best choice. Know what your Web server's capabilities are and where they can be compromised. Microsoft platforms run Internet Information Server (IIS).

Typically, this allows you to create custom ISAPI DLLs and ISAPI filters. It also allows you to create COM objects in Visual Basic or C/C++. Java servletts and Java-coded COM objects can also be made to run on Microsoft platforms without much difficulty. Microsoft's IIS allows the use of Active Server Pages using any scripting language for which you have a runtime module (JavaScript and VBScript come with IIS, and PerlScript is available at http://www.activestate.com). XML can be used on the server obviously since it is a platform-independent technology.

UNIX servers can usually run CGI applications more easily than Microsoft Windows servers do. They also have been running PERL for quite some time and, therefore, are a little less buggy than the PERL plug-ins for Microsoft platforms would be. UNIX servers do not run Visual Basic or Visual Basic script. They can, however, run JavaScript and Java servletts very well. They, too, allow development of EXEs and DLLs that work directly with the Web server. These can be coded in C/C++ or Java (or in many other languages not mentioned in this book, for that matter). XML is available for use on UNIX. While there is a plug-in for Active Server Pages to run on UNIX platforms, they still are not as well supported as their native home on a Microsoft Web server.

As you can see, most of the server-side technologies are available on both platforms, but have strengths in some areas in which the others may be weak. I might lose a merit badge or two by saying that both platforms are necessary to fill different needs. There is a not-so-quiet argument over which platform is the best. In general, both sides think they are the best solution for every problem.

The next thing to consider is what your current development team is comfortable with. If this "team" consists only of yourself, you might want to consider not only what you are familiar with, but also what is popular. Should your needs grow, and you need to hire new people, it will be easier to find someone skilled in the most popular languages than to find someone who knows the same things you do!

More important than your comfort level are the needs of the server. If your server is going to be under high demand, it will be better to use a compiled language. This uses fewer server resources (memory especially) but also makes responses quicker because the code is closer to what the processor understands.

So what about client-side applications? How do I know which is the best to choose here? This is where things get a little more specific. While the availability and usefulness of all the technologies are still present on the client side (with the exception of ISAPI and CGI), there are very specific circumstances under which each should be used.

Java is a particularly good tool for small applets and applications on Internet sites. With the advent of Dynamic HTML (DHTML), much of what Java applets were used for (for example scrolling text, hover buttons, and so on) on Web sites have been replaced by DHTML code. Java is a good tool when you need to have client-side code available, but hidden to the user. Source code can be a very useful tool when crackers attempt to breach security. If your company's logic needs to stay private, yet still remain on the client side, Java is excellent.

exam
ⓦatch

Understand which platforms run each scripting language, and know which language will provide better performance on each platform.

When Languages Are Executed

We have two main types of processes in Web applications: client-side and server-side. Client-side processes can be simple data manipulation or displaying of some type of dynamic content. On the server side we could have split processing occurring: some in our scripts, some in the objects, and then some inside the database itself. These processes are broken down into tiers. The Web by design is a multitiered application architecture. In this section we will go over the division of processes and a brief history of application development and how it leads into Web application development.

Multitiered Applications

A tier in an application is where a process of an application takes place. For an instance, an example of a single-tiered application would be a word processor. In a word processor application, all processes are taking place in that instance of the word processor and on that one single machine. For a more detailed explanation of an application's tiers, see Figure 7-1. On the first level we have a single-tier application, in our example, a word processor application. In the beginning, these single-tiered applications were fine; but with the advent of networking application, developers learned that we could centralize data and then use clients to access that data. At first, the clients were dumb terminals with very little processing power. Then PCs came around, with a fair amount of processing power available to the developer to leverage. This allowed a developer to split up applications into multiple tiers. One tier contains just the client services, which are what the user sees and interacts with. For example, the browser you use would be considered the client services. The next tier in the application contains the business services, which are any rules or special handling that needs to be done before a transaction takes place or data is entered into our database. For instance, if we need to do an inventory check or credit card validation before we complete the transaction and write the information to our database, these processes are completed in the business services tier. As you can see in Figure 7-1, in traditional client-server development or two-tiered applications, the business tier was sometimes split between the client and the database. On the database, this was accomplished using either database functions or stored procedures. Stored procedures or database functions allow you to run some logic against the data being sent to the database before the transaction is actually completed. Finally, we end up at our Web application model, where we have three tiers. Our client services are located in the Web browser; the business tier is located on our Web server or object server (this business tier could be an object served by MTS or a Javabean); then, finally, our data services are provided by some database server. In our Web model, we could further divide this into an n-tier application and store multiple objects on several servers.

So how does this n-tier model benefit you as a developer? In traditional one- and two-tier application development, a developer would have to update each individual client each time there was just a slight change in the business rules. You can imagine what would happen if you had thousands of clients and had to deploy a new application every other month or so due to some policy change. A deployment to a large amount of clients could get to be an administrative nightmare. With three- or n-tier development,

FIGURE 7-1   Division of processing in multiple tiers

Single-tiered applications

Word Processor

User & Business Services	Data & Business Services	**Two-tiered application**
Client Software	Database Server	**Ex: Client/Server**

User Services	Business Services	Data Services	**Three-tiered application**
Web Browser	Web Server	Database Server	**Ex: Web Application**

deployment is not such a big issue anymore. By separating your rules into objects on the middle tier, you just expose properties and methods to the clients accessing them; all the logic is contained in a centralized location provided by some object server. This allows updates to occur in one location, and all clients will be subsequently updated without any input from you. Web applications by nature are centralized; they are developed with all logic contained on a Web server.

Relational Database vs. Nonrelational Database

In this section we will be going over the various database types available to the Web developer. These include relational databases, server-based systems, and file-based systems. We will also cover nonrelational data stores such as flat files.

Relational Databases

We touched upon what a relational database is in the SQL section of this chapter. In our previous example, we used two tables in order to pull related data from both. We had a primary key and a foreign key that established the relation between the two tables. Essentially, this is what a relational database is—a database consisting of one or more related tables. The tables are then made up of rows and columns, with each individual row being a record.

Figure 7-2 shows the components of a table in a relational database, in this case, Microsoft Access. This table consists of a table of data that is made of records, which are then broken down into fields. In this example, we are using a contacts database. Our table is all our contacts, our record is the individual company, and then our company is broken down into fields like CompanyName and CompanyAddress. Even though we have this table in our database, this table has no relationship to anything else. We need to create another table that will become related to this primary company table.

In this example, we have a main table that consists of the primary company information, but for each company we may have more than one contact. In order to handle this data, we need to create a contacts table and then create a relationship with our company table. We do this by creating a

FIGURE 7-2   A typical table in a relational database

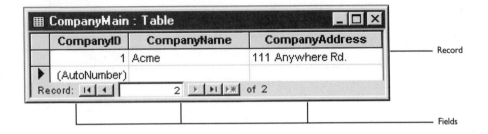

field in our contacts table that identifies the record in the company table to which this contact record is related. This field in the contacts table that contains the identifier of the company table is called the *foreign key*, because is designates data that is not local to the table. This foreign key contains the identifier of the company table. This identifier key of the company table is called its *primary key*. Primary keys contain a unique value in order to distinguish the record in the table from other records in the table. Figure 7-3 illustrates this relationship between the tables.

This relationship that is created in our example is called a one-to-many relationship, meaning that one company may have multiple contacts for that company.

You could also have a one-to-one relationship, in which you have one record in one table related to one record in another table.

Next we'll go over the two primary database systems: file based and server based.

FIGURE 7-3

Related tables

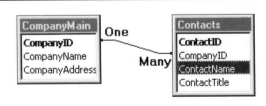

File-Based Databases

A file-based database is a database that has all of the resources needed to connect to the database located within the database itself. File-based databases do not require that you install some piece of software in order to access the data contained within them. Microsoft Access is an example of a file-based system. In order to access the contents of an Access database, the only thing required is an open database connectivity layer (ODBC). You don't need to install the Access application in order to be able to expose the underlying data to your Web application. Another file-based database is a set of simple ASCII text files. Many databases in use on the Web are simple flat-file systems. With a flat-file database you do not need to install any additional software in order to expose the underlying data to your application; you can open the file using what's available to you via the operating system.

Server-Based Databases

Server-based databases are databases that require a server to be running in order to obtain the data. Examples of these are Oracle or SQL Server. These applications provide more features than a typical file-based system; many of these database servers provide features that are not available in file-based systems:

- ■ **Backup scheduling**   Most of these systems contain utilities that allow you to back up your database tables. This can facilitate recovery in case of failure. Now most database systems can give you up-to-the-minute backup and recovery in case of failure. It is vital to have these backup systems in place, especially in an e-commerce application.

- ■ **Transactional systems**   Transactional systems allow you to do a full recovery in case of failure in the transaction. If a user comes in and, in the process of a transaction, something fails, then the transaction reverts back to the beginning as if nothing has occurred—no partial or orphaned data will exist in the database.

- ■ **E-mail notifications**   These allow you to set up notification in case of various events: database failures, backup completion, and so on.

- ■ **Security**   Usually you can set up security on the individual tables, and even define what a user can have access to. If you want to allow one user to be able to read a record in a table, but not be allowed to modify that record, databases have built-in security to allow you to do this.

- ■ **Logging**   Most events that occur in the server will be logged, allowing you as an administrator to spot problems as they occur.

If you were going to implement a large e-business application, then you would most likely need to use a database server instead of a file-based system. Of course, the additional features that a database server provides will cost more in resources and the price of the software will be higher, but you'll have a much more stable system.

Nonrelational Databases

Unlike the relational databases, nonrelational systems normally contain all the data in one large file. In the early days of Web development, most of the databases were nonrelational systems. PERL, one of the most widely used scripting languages used in Web development, was developed with working with flat-file databases in mind. Because of this focus, PERL is an exceptional language for working with text files. It can perform fast searches on text files by loading them into an array and performing string matches.

Flat-file databases normally contain fields of data in one file and a character or separator then designates these fields. The following is an example of our company database example as a flat-file database:

```
Acme&&111 Anywhere Rd.&&John Smith&&Sales Manager&&
Acme&&111 Anywhere Rd.&&Mary Doe&&EBusiness Manager&&
```

If you look at this flat-file database, you'll see the company information repeated for each contact that exists in the database. Each field in the database is then separated by "&&" as a delimiter. No relationship exists between two tables.

In order to deal with this data, a developer would run a routine to split each record into fields or an array and then perform some loop to go through the records and modify or pull data that met some specific criteria.

Nonrelational systems tend to be file-based systems. Although they tend to not require as many of the server's resources as do relational database and, particularly, server-based systems, there are some disadvantages to nonrelational systems:

- They tend to get very large due to repeated data. In our example, every contact contains the company information.

- Performance can be degraded on larger databases. This is mainly due to the fact that they can grow to be very large.

- There is very little transactional support, if any.

- They can require extensive coding to manipulate and display data.

CERTIFICATION OBJECTIVE 7.04

Integration of a Database with a Web Site

We described the various components of a Web application: the scripting and languages used by both client side and server, and the databases behind them. Together these technologies make up a Web application. In order for you to get a clear picture of where these technologies take place or reside in our Web application, we should go over the concept of multitiered applications.

Technologies Used to Connect the Two

Now that you understand what tiers make up an application, you need to know how to connect them all. We went over the various technologies used to develop applications and to store our data; we need a way to connect the two in order for it to do a Web application any good. Just because you write the code and create a database, this doesn't necessarily mean that the two know how to "talk" to each other; settings need to be done in order for it all to come together. In this section, we will be creating a database connection on the Web server and then accessing it via some code.

One of the main things to understand about these various database connectivity technologies is that you need to have the connector reside on the server that requires the connection, not on the database server itself. This means that you can create a Web site on an NT server and then use an ODBC driver to connect to an Oracle database on a UNIX box, as long as you have the appropriate driver on the NT box. You do not need to add additional software to the UNIX server in order to connect to it; this is the nature of database servers.

Open Database Connectivity (ODBC)

ODBC is an application programming interface or API used to connect to various databases. These datastores could be an Oracle database, SQL Server database, text database, or any other type of datastore for which an ODBC driver is available.

ODBC can be installed by obtaining the latest Microsoft Advanced Data Connector or MDAC from Microsoft's Web site at http://www.microsoft.com/mdac.

Java Database Connector (JDBC)

Similar to ODBC, JDBC provides an interface for a developer to access a database. The vendor will need to provide a driver in order to access the underlying database. In order to install JDBC on your machine, you will need to install the Java Development Kit; once you download and install the JDK, you will have installed the JDBC API as well. More information on installing the JDK can be obtained from the Sun Microsystems's Web site at http://java.sun.com.

Once you have installed the JDK with the JDBC API, you will also need to install the appropriate driver from your vendor. This information can be found from your vendor or its Web site.

Connecting to the Database in Your Code

Once you have your drivers configured on your Web server, you can then reference the connection via code. This basically entails specifying an object to hold the database connection and passing our ODBC or JDBC connection information to this object in order to let it know what setting on our system to use to connect to the database. This connection information could be set up on the server itself or passed right in the code. In most cases, you would need to specify the server on which the database is located and the login and password used to get access to the server.

If you were going to use ODBC you would need to create a database connection and pass the ODBC connection information to the active data object (ADO) that Microsoft provides for connecting to databases. ADO is an object that a developer can use to connect to a variety of data sources using SQL type query language. In Exercise 7-1, we will run through the code required in order to create a database connection in ASP code.

EXERCISE 7-1

Create an ODBC Database Connection

1. First, create the ADO Database connection object and assign it to a variable:

```
Set DBConn = Server.CreateObject("ADODB.Connection")
```

2. Next, pass our ODBC connection information in either of two ways:

```
DBConn.Open "DSN=MyODBCEntry;PWD=;UID=sa"
```

This method passes a data source name (DSN) that is set up via the Control Panel and entered into the system registry. This DSN contains information on the location of the database, the server type, and the drivers to use to connect to the database. We could also pass this information directly in our code in this way:

```
DBConn.Open
"DBQ=c:\Database\MyDB.mdb;DefaultDir=c:Temp;Driver={Microsoft
  Access Driver (*.mdb)};DriverId=25;FIL=MS
  Access;ImplicitCommitSync=Yes;
MaxBufferSize=512;MaxScanRows=8;PageTimeout=5;SafeTransactions=0;
Threads=3;UID=admin;UserCommitSync=Yes;"
```

The previous method passes all the information that ODBC will need in order to connect to an Access database, as in this example.

Exercise 7-2 shows you how to create a connection, but instead of using ODBC, we'll use JDBC to create the connection to our database. As in the previous example using ODBC, it takes two steps to do the same thing with JDBC.

EXERCISE 7-2

Create a JDBC Database Connection

1. First you need to load the appropriate driver for the database management system you're going to use:

```
Class.forName("jdbc.DBMSDriver");
```

Here you're specifying to load the JDBC driver to DBMS.

2. Next we need to make the connection using our specified driver to the database server, by passing the server's URL and security information to the database:

```
Connection DBConn DriverManager.getConnection(url, "LogonID",
  "LogonPassword");
```

The URL is usually a pointer to your data source name on the Web server.

After you establish the connection and instantiate your database objects, you can manipulate them directly via scripting. Then it's up to you to decide how to design your application and make it all work.

QUESTIONS AND ANSWERS

You are developing an e-commerce application, and customers need to have certain contract pricing applied to them. You must apply certain rules that the customer needs to meet in order to purchase an item. To which tier of the application—user services, business services, or data services—would these rules be applied?	Business rules are applied in the business services tier of an application.
You're developing an application for a company intranet. All users will be using Internet Explorer, and you have in-house developers experienced in developing with Visual Basic. What client-side technology would be the most efficient use of the resources you have available?	Use VBScript as your client-side technology since you know all users will be using Internet Explorer (which supports VBScript) and your in-house skills are Visual Basic. VBScript is a subset of Visual Basic, making the learning curve shorter than it would be with JScript or JavaScript.

CERTIFICATION SUMMARY

There are too many Web technologies available to cover them all in one chapter of a book; we have, however, covered the primary technologies that you will encounter as a Web professional.

In this chapter, we discussed the various scripting and language technologies available to you as a Web developer. We then compared these different technologies and evaluated the situations in which you should use each technology.

We then discussed the various tiers of an application. Tiers break down the application into a defined model, which is divided into the user services, business services, and data services tier.

Finally, we went over database development and learned how to connect databases to our Web application.

TWO-MINUTE DRILL

❑ API is an acronym for application program interface. These interfaces are the set of commands that an application uses to request and carry out lower-level services performed by a computer's operating system or access functionality of another program.

❏ Extending the functionality of your application is most certainly one of the biggest advantages of using API.

❏ Common Gateway Interface, or CGI, defines the communication link between the Web server and Web applications.

❏ SQL (often pronounced "sequel"), or Structured Query Language, is the common communication method between databases. The history of SQL began in the late 1970s, when IBM began developing it in a lab in San Jose, California. SQL is a nonprocedural language that will let you decide what data you want to select from a database.

❏ ISAPI (Internet Server Application Programming Interface) is a set of program calls that allows you to create a Windows Web-based application that will run faster than a CGI application.

❏ A special kind of ISAPI DLL is called an ISAPI filter. An ISAPI filter can be instructed to execute for every HTTP request. It can also be instructed to execute only for certain file types. You can create an ISAPI filter for logging, encryption or decryption, authentication, or many other purposes.

❏ Dynamic Link Library (DLL) is a collection of functions or a collection of programs that can be called upon by another program. The word "library" suggests that it can store a vast set of functions that can be "checked out" when they are needed. These functions are then stored in a file, usually with a .dll extension.

❏ Client- and server-side scripting are important elements in Internet development. They allow the interaction of customers with data of all types.

❏ Java was developed in 1995 specifically for use in distributed applications and, more specifically, for the Internet.

❏ JavaScript carries some of the syntax of Java and even carries some of the same functions. However, JavaScript is different in that it is interpreted rather than compiled.

❏ Practical Extraction and Reporting Language (PERL) is an interpreted scripting language. While PERL is generally used on

UNIX-platformed Web servers, it has been ported to many other operating systems as well. Since PERL is interpreted, it is compiled just before execution. It can be compiled into either C code or cross-platform byte-code.

❑   C is a very powerful and very flexible programming language. There are no limitations to what can be done with C. Any application can be written in it.

❑   C++ is more than just a very strange-looking grade. C++ is yet another language to choose from that also has its good points. So, logically, if C replaced B, wouldn't C++ be the next generation language to replace C? The reason the next version of C is named C++ is that in the C language, in order to increment a value by one, you use the operator ++, hence C++. C++ is the next step past C, but only in that it has added a few things for a new environment.

❑   Visual Basic is a programming language from Microsoft. The word "visual" comes from the idea that dragging and dropping objects and controls on the form can create the program's interface. BASIC is the name of the language from which VB was formed.

❑   VBScript is provided by Microsoft and is a smaller subset of its Visual Basic programming language.

❑   JScript is an interpreted script language from Microsoft that is designed for use within Web pages. It adheres to the ECMAScript standard developed by Microsoft and Netscape. It is basically Microsoft's equivalent to the earlier and more widely used JavaScript.

❑   Extensible Markup Language (XML) is a flexible way to define commonly used information formats. The format and the data itself may then be shared on the World Wide Web, in intranets, and even in desktop applications.

❑   Virtual Reality Modeling Language (VRML) is a language used for describing three-dimensional image sequences and user interactions with them. VRML allows you to build a sequence of visual images into Web pages.

❑   An ASP can be an ordinary HTML page that includes one or more scripts that are processed on the Web server before the page is sent to the user. An ASP is somewhat similar to CGI applications in that they both involve programs that run on the server.

❑ A relational database is a database consisting of one or more related tables.

❑ Unlike the relational databases, nonrelational systems normally contain all the data in one large file.

SELF TEST

1. The language used to perform updates and to pull data from a relational database is known as

   A. SQL

   B. VBScript

   C. ASP

   D. JavaScript

2. When a connection is established to a database using either ODBC or JDBC, the following information is not required:

   A. Driver information

   B. Database location

   C. Login username and password

   D. The language being used to display the data

3. You have developed a Web application for your company. This application has DHTML that is presented to the user via the Web browser. In what tier of the application does this activity occur?

   A. Business services

   B. Data services

   C. User services

   D. Internet services

4. A PERL script running out of process on a UNIX server would most likely be an example of

   A. A CGI application

   B. An ISAPI application

   C. A Visual Basic application

   D. A Java applet

5. The field in a table that directly relates to a primary key of a record in another table is known as a

   A. Domestic key

   B. International key

   C. Static key

   D. Foreign key

6. This type of database is totally self-contained and does not need to have supporting software installed in order to access the information. The only requirement needed is a driver or the operating system.

   A. Relational database

   B. File-based database

   C. Server database

   D. Normalized database

7. This server-side scripting technology runs as an ISAPI filter on the Web server.

   A. CGI

   B. PERL scripts

   C. Java applets

   D. ASP

8. Which technology is not normally run in the process of the Web browser?

   A. DHTML

   B. HTML

C. JavaScript

D. CGI

9. You are working on a project for a real estate agency that wants to be able to provide potential clients with a walk-through experience of homes via a Web browser. Which technology would be the best way to attempt to provide this experience?

A. VRML

B. SQL

C. Visual Basic

D. Java

10. You have a database from which you need to retrieve all records from a table called MyTable. Using SQL, how would you perform this task?

A. GET * ROWS FROM MyTable

B. SELECT * FROM MyTable

C. LOAD * RECORDS FROM MyTable

D. DROP * FROM MyTable

11. Your Web application contains logic that implements specific rules that need to be checked before you continue a transaction. In which application tier does this checking of rules occur?

A. Business services

B. Data services

C. User services

D. Internet services

12. This development language requires that a virtual machine be placed on the computer in order to execute applications. Select the best answer.

A. VBScript

B. ASP

C. Java

D. PERL

13. Which of these is a method of defining data using plain text markup consisting of tags?

A. ODBC

B. JDBC

C. SQL

D. XML

14. This is provided for developers as a low-level interface for accessing certain functions. It frees the developer from having to write extensive code in order to access common tasks.

A. PERL

B. API

C. SQL

D. VBScript

15. You are developing a company's Internet site. You do not know what browsers are going to be accessing this site. You need to implement a client-side scripting technology that will accommodate the largest percentage of browsers. Which

client-side scripting technology will be best suited for this task?

A. VBScript

B. PerlScript

C. CGI

D. JavaScript

16. This scripting language is one of the original scripting languages used in the early days of Web application development; it is most suited for searching and manipulating text file databases.

A. ASP

B. PERL

C. Java

D. ColdFusion

17. In a relational database system, you have one master table that contains records that are related to another table that has several associated records. For example, you have a table containing a list of manufacturers and then a related table that has several products for an individual manufacturer. What type of relationship is this?

A. One to one

B. Ten to one

C. One to many

D. Broken

18. You are developing a company database application that uses Web technologies. Where would the interaction with the database occur? Select the best answer from the following choices.

A. User services

B. Client-side scripting

C. Web browser

D. Web server

19. Which type of Database Management System usually provides some type of inherent security features and transactional support?

A. Flat-file database

B. File-based database

C. Relational database

D. Server-based database

20. You need to provide your Web application with simple functionality of scrolling text areas. You do not have any in-house scripting skills. You also need to be able to reach the broadest amount of Web sites possible because this is for an Internet site. Which technology would be best for this task?

A. DHTML

B. VBScript

C. Java applets

D. SQL

SELF TEST ANSWERS

1. **A** is correct. SQL stands for Structured Query Language and is used for accessing relational database systems.

   B and **D** are incorrect, because these are scripting technologies and not used for directly manipulating relational databases. **C** is incorrect, because ASP (Active Server Pages) is an architecture used for processing server-side scripts and not for directly connecting to databases.

2. **D** is correct. Connection information is independent of the scripting language being used; once a connection is established, practically any scripting language can be used using the same connection information for all languages.

   A, **B**, and **C** are incorrect, because they are required in order to access a database management system.

3. **C** is correct. DHTML is something the user sees or interacts with; anything the user interacts with is known as the user services tier of an application.

   A and **B** are incorrect, because these tiers do not interact with the user directly. **D** is incorrect, because there is no Internet services tier of a Web application.

4. **A** is correct. CGI applications are run separately from the server and typically are run as UNIX systems using the PERL scripting language.

   B is incorrect, because ISAPI applications usually run in process and on a Windows operating system. **C** and **D** are incorrect, because these are not server-based Web applications.

5. **D** is correct. The field is known as the foreign key; this foreign key contains the identifier of the related record of the master table.

   A, **B**, and **C** are incorrect, because no such keys exist in a relational database.

6. **B** is correct. Most file-based databases such as Microsoft Access or CSV files need only a driver or the OS in order to access and manipulate the data.

   A is incorrect, because a relational database could be either a file-based or server-based database. **C** is incorrect, because server-based databases need server software to be installed in order to access the underlying database. **D** is incorrect, because normalization of a database has nothing to do with to the way you connect to it.

7. **D** is correct. Active Server Pages (ASP) run in process on Internet Information Server as an ISAPI filter through the asp.dll.
   A and **B** are incorrect, because CGI scripts run like executables, as an out-of-process application. **C** is incorrect, because Java applets run on the client side in the process of the Web browser.

8. **D** is correct. CGI applications are run on the Web server and are totally separate from the Web browser accessing the application.
   A, **B**, and **C** are incorrect, because all of these technologies are supported and run in the same process of the Web browser.

9. **A** is correct. Virtual Reality Modeling Language is made for providing users with a virtual world that they can "walk" through.
   B, **C**, and **D** are incorrect, because none of these technologies is able to perform this task.

10. **B** is correct. In order to retrieve information from a database using SQL, you would need to use the SELECT statement.
    A, **C**, and **D** are incorrect, because none of these statements would retrieve information from a database table.

11. **A** is correct. Rules are logic that is unique to the business organization. This logic is processed in the business services tier of an application.
    B and **C** are incorrect, because these tiers usually don't contain business logic. **D** is incorrect, because there is no Internet services tier of a Web application.

12. **C** is correct. Operating systems need to provide a Java Virtual Machine on their platforms in order to run Java applications.
    A, **B**, and **D** are incorrect, because they don't require a virtual machine to be loaded on the OS; some scripting technologies require a scripting engine in order to interpret script commands.

13. **D** is correct. XML is a method of defining data using tags to surround values. It is an extension of SGML and is laid out much as standard HTML documents are laid out.
    A, **B**, and **C** are incorrect, because these are not used for defining data; rather they are used for pulling and presentating data.

14. **B** is correct. Only the API (Application Programming Interface) provides an interface for developers to access lower-level functions. APIs can greatly reduce the amount of

code that a developer will need to write, which in turn frees up the developer's time to focus on higher-level application functions.

A, C, and **D** are incorrect, because these technologies are languages and do not expose an interface.

15. **D** is correct. JavaScript would be the best choice in this case. JavaScript is supported by most of the browsers available on the market.

A and **B** are incorrect, because VBScript is supported only by Internet Explorer without the use of a special plug-in for other browsers, and PerlScript would need an engine to be installed on the client machine accessing your site before you could use it. **C** is incorrect, because CGI scripts run on the server and not on the client.

16. **B** is correct. PERL was developed in the early days of Web development with the initial intention of manipulating text files.

A, C, and **D** are incorrect, because all of these technologies have become available fairly recently and are optimal for connecting to relational databases or in the case of Java platform independence.

17. **C** is correct. This is a one-to-many relationship; one record from a table has several associated records in another table. In this example, one manufacturer has many products.

A is incorrect, because in a one-to-one relationship there are no multiple records; you have one record for one record. **B** and **D** are incorrect, because these are not valid relations in a relational database.

18. **D** is correct. Most interactions with a database management system occur on the Web server.

A, B, and **C** are incorrect, because these are all client-side technologies. Because HTTP is a static protocol, it is hard to maintain a connection to a back-end DBMS in a Web application without installing some type of helper application on the client.

19. **B** is correct. A server-based DBMS would be the best choice; although server-based systems can be relational databases, not all relational based databases provide the features that were described in this question.

A and **B** are incorrect, because these are file-based systems and do not provide all of the features described in the question. **C** is incorrect, because not all relational database systems are server based. A good example of this is Microsoft Access.

20. **C** is correct. Java applets will provide you with the broadest reach of browser support. Most applets are available to accomplish this task either as freeware or for a small price. Many HTML editors can assist you in easily adding Java applets to your page. **A, B,** and **D** are incorrect, because DHTML is fairly new and is supported only by 4.0 and later browsers. DHTML development also requires some extensive scripting abilities. VBScript is available natively by Internet Explorer browsers. SQL is not a client-side technology.

i-Net+ ™

COMPUTING TECHNOLOGY INDUSTRY ASSOCIATION®

8

Networking and Infrastructure

I n this chapter, you will learn about some of the systems and networks that help the Internet communicate efficiently. Although the Internet is a decentralized collection of networks, each network is nevertheless connected to another using special systems and tools that help route traffic efficiently from its source to the intended destination. By the end of this chapter, you will be able to identify exactly how these hosts and systems operate.

The Internet is nothing more than a collection of networks that (usually) work closely together. By the end of 1996—which was well before the Internet became popular—the Internet was comprised of over 100,000 networks. All networks on the Internet communicate via TCP/IP, which is a packet-switching protocol. A packet-switching protocol does not establish dedicated connections in order to communicate. A circuit-switching network, such as those run by telephone companies, uses dedicated connections; but a packet-switching protocol uses various programs, algorithms, and network lines to get information from the source to its destination any way it can. TCP/IP divides information into discrete bits and then delivers it through various pipelines, which are called *routers*.

A packet-switching protocol and/or network can use a different network path to communicate each time a transaction occurs. For example, when you send two e-mails to your friend at two different times, it is possible for the packets that comprise each e-mail message to travel a different path each time. A distributed network allows computers to communicate via several different paths. Because the Internet is a packet-switching network, it requires several key elements to make sure that this communication occurs efficiently.

These backbone elements that allow users to communicate on the Internet include Internet Service Providers (ISPs), routers, high-speed backbone networks, Network Access Points (NAPs), and the Domain Name Server (DNS) system. These elements are separate though closely related, because they comprise the backbone of the Internet. This chapter will focus on these elements so that you can further understand how the deceptively simple tasks of checking e-mail or browsing the Web involve a constantly evolving, rather complex network infrastructure.

Core Components of the Current Internet Infrastructure

The Internet has been evolving for some time. Its structure is somewhat different than when it was dominated by the U.S. government. The Internet was then governed by the National Science Foundation (NSF). Until 1995, the NSF network (known as NSFNet) was governed by the U.S. government, which made rules and limitations concerning who could use it and how it was run. Because of such limitations as lack of funds and slow connection speeds, the NSF imposed what was called an Acceptable Use Policy (AUP), which determined exactly how the Internet could be used by organizations and businesses. However, since 1995, the NSFNet has been privatized, and it is now run by companies such as MCI WorldCom, Sprint, PacBell, UUNET, and others. In addition, MCI cooperates with the NSF to maintain high-speed networks and other critical Internet connection points.

No longer governed solely by the NSF, the new Internet structure essentially consists of ISPs that communicate via a backbone comprised of Network Access Points (NAPs), high-speed networks Routing Arbiters (RAs), and Metropolitan Area Exchanges (MAEs). Before you learn about these elements, however, you should first understand the function of an ISP.

e x a m
ⓦatch

A router is nothing more than a dedicated computer that helps IP packets get from one destination to another. A router is necessary whenever an IP packet has to travel from one local network to another. A router composes lists of other routers using special tables of information that it stores in memory. These tables are called routing tables. Whenever one router talks to another, this communication helps networks figure out exactly where an IP packet goes. Routers often require updates to their routing tables so that they can send IP packets to the correct location. Although it is beyond the scope of this chapter to discuss exactly how routers communicate with each other, you should understand that routers are the things that connect different networks to each other. Many different types of routers exist. Some are suitable only for connecting small networks to each other, whereas others are responsible for connecting entire parts of the country so that they can communicate.

Internet Service Provider (ISP)

Whenever you use your modem, cable modem, DSL line, or T1 line , this connection is provided by an Internet Service Provider (ISP). An ISP is a vendor that sells Internet time to you. This particular Internet element is responsible for providing specific services, including Web, FTP, e-mail, e-commerce servers (such as IBM Net.Commerce), and so forth. An ISP is connected to the Internet via a router. Usually, an ISP is connected to the client via a telephone line. Sometimes the telephone line is a simple Plain Old Telephone System (POTS) connection. Increasingly, however, users are able to connect to their ISPs via higher-speed connections that include

- **Integrated Switched Digital Network (ISDN)**   This connection method allows users to connect at speeds of up to 128 Kbps.

- **Digital Subscriber Line (DSL)**   DSL connections vary, although it is possible to have a DSL line that connects at speeds of up to 1.544 Mbps and even higher (8.5 Mbps). Typical speeds, however, are slower (between 384 Kbps and 768 Kbps). Many different types of DSL are available. Asynchronous Digital Subscriber connections, for example, allow different upload and download speeds. For example, an ADSL line may have a 512 Kbps download speed, but only a 128 Kbps upload speed.

Traditional POTS service via modem can be no faster than 56 Kbps. However, most people are lucky if they can connect at speeds faster than around 50 Kbps. Actual speed is somewhat less due to problems in the line, as well as the natural limitations of POTS equipment.

You have now learned a bit about how a client connects to an ISP. Now it's time to learn a bit more about how ISPs connect to each other.

Network Access Points

An ISP always requires access to a Network Access Point (NAP). A NAP is nothing more than a central point that allows Internet Service Providers (ISPs) to exchange information with each other. The technical term for the activity of exchanging information between ISPs is "peering." Peering is the result of a special arrangement between ISPs. This activity allows any two ISPs to arrange to share traffic. This way, the two ISPs can give each other a direct connection to its networks without having to have this traffic go out to still other networks. Whenever one ISP exchanges information with another, it does so via a NAP. A NAP regulates how peering operates, but a NAP itself does not do the peering; this is the job of the ISP only. Furthermore, a NAP is not a router. A NAP is a self-contained network that operates at high speeds and acts as a mediator between ISPs. ISP routers connect to a NAP so that the ISP can communicate with all parties on the Internet (for example, government, commercial, and international networks).

Because a NAP is a central point of information exchange between ISPs, it is a key part of the Internet backbone. A NAP is also a common source of congestion on the Internet. A NAP uses routers that can get overburdened very quickly.

When the Internet first began, the National Science Foundation (NSF) invented the first NAP. However, the current structure is no longer dominated by the NSF. Commercial entities now pay for NAPs. Some companies, such as MCI, work closely with the NSF to create NAPs where they are needed.

How Does a NAP Work?

A NAP implements routing by implementing a routing policy. This policy helps coordinate ISP traffic. A service provider within a NAP is called an

Autonomous System (AS). In other words, this ISP is in a peering relationship. Most ISPs are regional, meaning that they establish a local network, and then communicate with the networks immediately around them. There are times, of course, when one ISP will have to communicate outside its own region, say when a user in London sends an e-mail message to Bombay, India. Not all messages, however, need to travel across long distances. Imagine what would happen if an e-mail you sent had to travel all the way across the world in order to get to an ISP that was physically quite near you. Imagine further what would happen if mail sent from 50 million users had to do the same thing. The network would get bogged down quite quickly.

Fortunately, however, NAPs solve this problem. This is because a NAP allows traffic that originates and terminates within a particular region to stay in that region. Peering allows one ISP to communicate to others whenever a long distance connection is necessary. A NAP also helps coordinate ISP traffic so that no one ISP gains an advantage; in some ways, a NAP can act like a good traffic cop; it helps ISPs coordinate their traffic. A NAP, however, is a high-speed connection point. For example, it is not uncommon for a NAP to communicate at between 155 Mbps and 1Gbps or more.

Figure 8-1 shows how a NAP allows ISPs to communicate with each other. It is possible for one regional ISP to communicate directly with another. A NAP is designed to allow an ISP to communicate outside its own region in a well-structured, coordinated way.

Inter- and Intra-NAP Communication

If one ISP wishes to update its routing table with its information, it uses special protocols. If an ISP wishes to have its router update its routing table with another within its autonomous system (AS), it uses the Interior Gateway Protocol (IGP). If one ISP router communicates outside its AS, it uses the Border Gateway Protocol (BGP). BGP is an improvement on another protocol called the Exterior Gateway Protocol (EGP). It is possible for an ISP to use either BGP or EGP, although the latter is becoming increasingly common.

FIGURE 8-1

Network Access Points

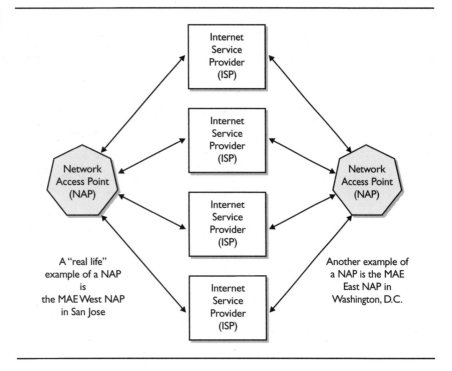

FIGURE 8-1

Network Access Points

Although it is not important for you to learn the details of IGP and EGP, you should nevertheless understand the following facts:

- Each of the protocols mentioned in this section is designed to update routing tables.

- Different protocols are necessary because the routers share different relationships with each other.

- Whenever one router updates the other, this process is called *polling*.

- These protocols are specific to Internet routers. Networks that wish to have routers update each other's router within LANs use protocols such as the Routing Information Protocol (RIP) and Open Shortest Path First (OSPF).

One of the benefits of BGP over EGP is that it will poll a router only when it notices a change. Also, instead of updating the entire routing table, BGP will send only that part of the routing table that needs an update. This saves bandwidth.

Connection Speeds

Bandwidth is a key factor in making sure that the Internet works well. Generally speaking, bandwidth is the measurement of how much information can fit on a network wire. Technically speaking, bandwidth is the measurement of how many bits per second can be sent over a particular connection. The technologies you have learned about all use connections of varying speeds. Internet backbone connections use extremely high speeds, or rates. The relevant rates include

- Optical carrier (OC)
- Digital Signal X
- T standards
- E standards

The following is a discussion of the typical connection speeds for NAPs and backbone networks.

The Digital Signal (DS) standards provide the base for other standards, including the T and E carrier standards. The DS0 rate is 64 Kbps. The DS0 speed is fundamental for many other standards. This is because these other standards, such as the T and E rates, are multiples of 64 Kbps. Table 8-1 gives the typical DS rates.

You should note that each of these network types can carry both voice and data.

Synchronous Optical Network (SONET) networks employ fiber-optic cable. As a result, they can use speeds that are faster than most other networks. The basic element for the OC standard is 51.84 Mbps. In other

TABLE 8-1

DS Rates

Specification	Rate
DS0	64 Kbps
DS1	1.544 Mbps
DS2	6.132 Mbps
DS3	44.736 Mbps
DS4	274.176 Mbps

words, an OC-1 line is 51.84 Mbps. An OC-2 line operates at twice that base amount, and so forth. Table 8-2 gives the signal rates this type of network uses.

The T and E carrier specifications are based on the DS0 model, given earlier. For example, a T1 line is nothing more than 24 DS0 (64 Kbps) signals combined into one channel. Whenever separate channels are combined into one, this is called *multiplexing*. Table 8-3 gives two common T1 rates.

exam
ⓦatch

You should note that it is possible to use a fractional T1 or E1. In other words, it is possible to "demultiplex" these channels. Many ISPs, for example, sell only certain channels of their T1 or E1 connections. Whenever an ISP sells part of an E1 line, it is said to sell a fractional T1. This same concept applies to E Carrier standards, as well.

TABLE 8-2

SONET Rates

Specification	Rate
OC-1	51.84 Mpbs
OC-2	103.68 Mpbs
OC-4	207.36 Mbps
OC-12	622.08 Mbps
OC-48	2.488 Gbps

Specification	Rate
TI	1.544 Mpbs
T3	44.736 Mbps

The E Carrier standards apply mostly in Europe. Although they are roughly equivalent to T Carrier standards, they are different enough to merit their own discussion (see Table 8-4).

Backbone

A NAP can connect high-speed backbone networks. A backbone network is generally

- **Fault tolerant** It uses several redundant connections to make sure that one failure (that is, fault) does not bring down the entire network.

- **High-speed** It connects at speeds that are state of the art for its time.

The National Science Foundation Network (NSFNet) originally provided the Internet backbone service. As of this writing, only about seven backbone networks exist in the United States. Although only seven backbone networks exist, many different sites exist on these networks. Companies that provide high-speed backbone services include Ameritech, MCI WorldCom, Pacific Bell, and Sprint. Backbone networks exist in Los Angeles, Houston, Atlanta, San Francisco, Denver, and other parts of the world.

One example of a backbone network is the Very High Speed Backbone Network Service (vBNS); the networks in this service operate at extremely high speeds. This is possible because they operate using Synchronous

Specification	Rate
EI	2.048 Mbps
E2	8.448 Mbps
E3	34.368 Mbps

Optical Network (SONET) technology. Table 8-5 shows some locations of vBNS sites, as well as their speeds.

Metropolitan Area Exchange (MAE)

A Metropolitan Area Exchange (MAE) is a specific example of a NAP. ISPs connect to MAEs in order to get access to the Internet. Two types of MAEs exist: tier 1 and tier 2. Tier 1 MAE connections employ high-speed Fiber Distributed Data Interface (FDDI) connections. FDDI networks operate at relatively high speeds and have redundant connections. This is because they are dual Token Ring networks. A Token Ring network of this nature can operate up to 100 Mbps. The beauty behind the dual Token Ring strategy is that if one ring network fails, the second can take over. If no problem exists, it is possible to enlist the backup connection, and the network can communicate at 200 Mbps. Presently, tier 1 MAEs include

- MAE West (San Jose, California)
- MAE East (Washington, D.C.)

Tier 2 MAEs include

- Los Angeles
- Houston
- Chicago
- Dallas
- New York

TABLE 8-5	City or Institution	Carrier Rate	Connection Speed
vBNS Sites and Speeds	Denver	OC-48	2.488 Gbps
	San Francisco	OC-48	2.488 Gbps
	Seattle	OC-48	2.488 Gbps
	UCLA	OC-3	155.52 Mbps
	Northwestern	OC-3	155.52 Mbps
	Boston University	DS-3	44.736 Mbps

Tier 2 MAEs can use either FDDI or Asynchronous Transfer Mode (ATM) networks. An ATM network is not a Token Ring network, as is FDDI. However, ATM networks are extremely fast, traveling at rates of either 155.520 Mbps or 622.080 Mbps. Whether they are FDDI or ATM, backbone networks are extremely high-speed in nature. They help create the commercial backbone of the Internet. Tier 2 MAEs are generally regional connection points, as opposed to the two coastal tier 1 MAEs. MCI and other companies are constantly adding more MAEs as the Internet becomes more truly worldwide. A MAE often has several different ISPs operating in its region. The primary reason for this is fault tolerance. Although the MAE connections are somewhat slower than their vBNS counterparts, they have been established longer, making them central to the Internet.

Routing Arbiter

You have already learned about how a NAP enforces routing policies. A Routing Arbiter (RA) is the backbone element that enacts those policies. The RA takes the place of the old NSFNet Acceptable Use Policy (AUP). Whenever one NAP connects to another, they use an RA. An RA is a collection of devices that provide routing maps, address resolution, and redundant connectivity. Therefore, the purpose of the RA is to make sure ISPs communicate efficiently and that packets don't get dropped (that is, lost) too often.

In its effort to control the routes that an ISP uses to communicate with another, an RA consults the following items to help coordinate routes:

- **The Internet Routing Registry (IRR)**   This registry is a central database of routes.

- **Route Servers (RS)**   These servers forward packets according to the routes in the IRR.

With the information derived from an IRR, a NAP can then help providers communicate more efficiently.

Viewing NAPs and vBNS Backbones

1. Open your browser. It does not matter which type you use (options include Netscape Navigator, Internet Explorer, or Lynx).

2. Go to the following URL: http://www.vbns.net/. As of this writing, this URL brings up the screen shown in Figure 8-2.

3. This Web site gives information about NAPs and high-speed backbone networks run by MCI. Select the Reports link. Your screen should resemble Figure 8-3.

FIGURE 8-2   vBNS Web site

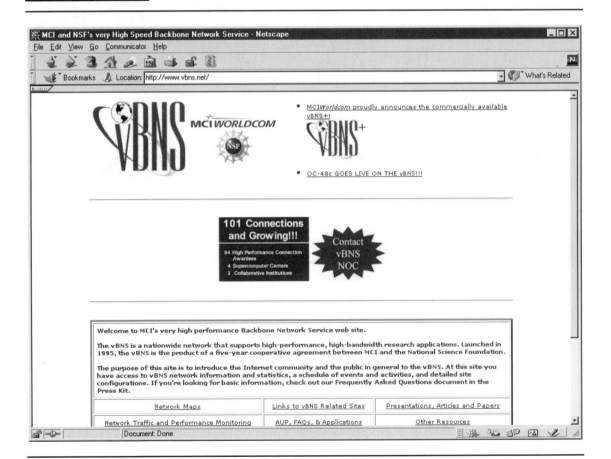

FIGURE 8-3 The vBNS Reports page

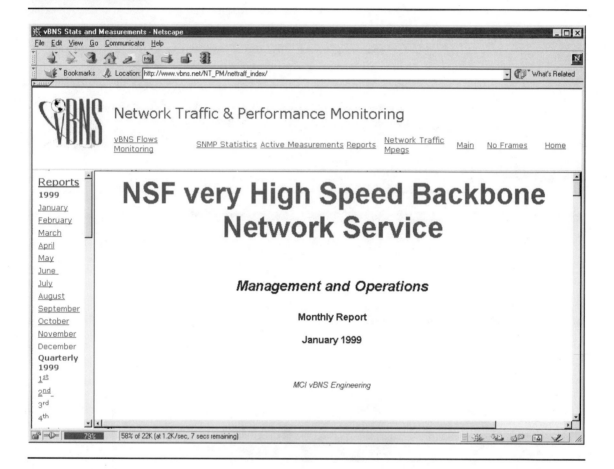

4. Note that you can view reports on a monthly basis. Choose the latest month. As of this writing, October 1999 was the latest report month.

5. Once you have chosen the latest month, note the total packet count for that month on this vBNS network. As of October 1999, the packet count was 350 billion.

6. Note that these reports tend to refer to a network protocol called SNMP (Simple Network Monitoring Protocol). This protocol is an application-layer protocol meant to monitor TCP/IP networks. It is ideal for collecting usage statistics about routers.

7. Scroll down to view a map of the ATM and NAP connections that comprise the MCI vBNS.

8. Scroll down past the map to view the latest networks that have connected to it.

9. Now, go back to the home page (http://www.vbns.net/). Click the Network Maps link (http://www.vbns.net/netmaps/logical.html).

10. You should see a screen significantly similar to that shown in Figure 8-4.

FIGURE 8-4   The MCI vBNS Logical Network Map

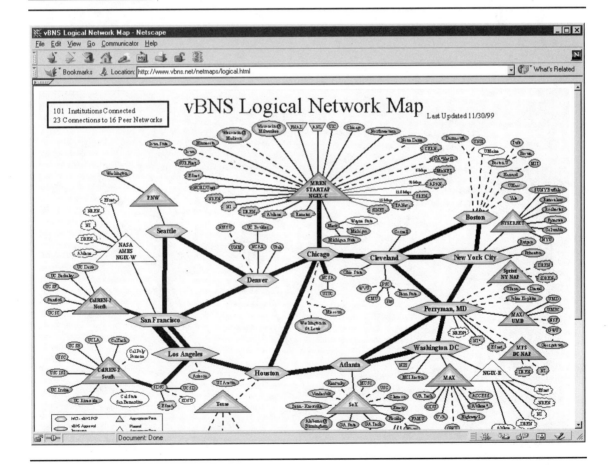

11. View the latest networks that have joined this particular vBNS.

12. Select the Backbone Map link at the bottom of this page.

13. You should see a map similar to that shown in Figure 8-5.

You now have a clearer idea of the high-speed networks that connect your NAPs, which then connect your ISPs.

FIGURE 8-5   The vBNS Backbone Network Map

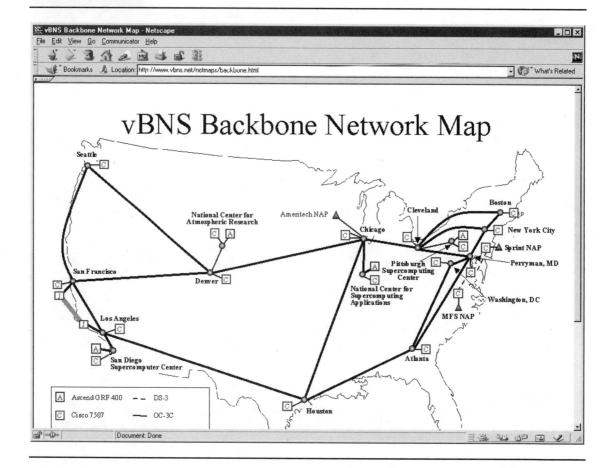

Internet Connectivity from Source to Destination for Various Types of Servers

Thus far, you have learned about the high-speed, redundant connection points that allow the Internet to function. You have also learned about how a NAP allows one ISP to communicate with another. In the next section, you will learn more about how common Internet servers communicate with each other. As you read through this section, consider that these servers communicate with each other largely unaware that they are traveling across a vBNS or via a NAP. An e-mail or Web server's job is to establish connections between itself and a client, or between itself and other servers. Much of an IT professional's job is to ensure that these connections occur as efficiently as possible.

E-mail

Whenever you send an e-mail message, you are using at least two different types of servers. First of all, you are using a Simple Mail Transport Protocol (SMTP) server. An SMTP server simply receives e-mail, and then forwards it to the proper location. Its job is to determine whether it can deliver the message locally or whether it has to send it off to another server, who then may know what to do with it. E-mail servers are closely integrated with DNS servers. Most of the problems experienced by all e-mail servers have to do with misconfigured—or misunderstood—DNS entries.

An SMTP server is known as a Mail Transfer Agent (MTA). SMTP servers use TCP port 25. SMTP servers can also

- Accept e-mail messages from a Mail User Agent (MUA), such as Microsoft Outlook, Eudora, or Pine.
- Rewrite the original e-mail message headers so that one SMTP server can send the message to another.
- Route messages to the proper destination.

Thus far, you have learned about mail transfer agents and mail user agents. These elements are essential for sending e-mail. However, you also need an element that can receive and store e-mail. For this, you need a mail delivery agent (MDA). On the Internet, POP3 servers act as MDAs. POP3 gets its name because it is the third iteration of the Post Office Protocol. Earlier versions of POP were proposed, but never widely implemented. POP3 uses TCP port 110. POP3 does not send e-mail. Rather, it is a protocol that receives a message, and then drops it off to an MUA. Essentially, a POP3 server receives an e-mail message, stores it, and then forwards it upon request.

The only e-mail servers that use standard authentication measures are POP3 servers. For example, whenever you check your e-mail, you generally have to give a username and a password. It is possible, also, for SMTP servers to require a form of authentication. However, SMTP servers do not ask for usernames and passwords. Rather, they use the Domain Name Server (DNS) system to help them verify that a message they have received is actually coming from where it says it is. Specifically, some SMTP servers conduct what are called reverse DNS lookups, which are essentially queries sent by the SMTP server to DNS that help it determine the name of the server sending the e-mail.

When you send and receive e-mail, you are actually beginning a chain of events. First, your e-mail client program sends the message to an SMTP server, which then forwards the message to another SMTP server, and so forth, until the message reaches its destination, a POP3 server. The message will remain at the POP3 server until a properly authenticated user downloads the message.

on the job

You should note that many end users have problems with their e-mail clients due to improperly configured SMTP and POP3 server entries. As a result, they may not be able to either send or receive e-mail messages. Use ping to determine whether the SMTP and/or POP3 servers are up, and then check the SMTP and POP3 entries in the client to identify the problem.

Web and E-commerce Sites

A Web site is simply a specialized server that listens on TCP port 80 of a particular IP address. A Web server can also listen on TCP port 443, which is the Secure Sockets Layer (SSL) port. Web servers use the Hypertext Transfer Protocol (HTTP) in order to communicate. However, you should note that a Web browser generally doesn't communicate directly with the Web server. The HTTP request first must travel through various routers before it ever reaches the Web server.

A Web server is usually only part of the equation. Although a Web server does serve up documents, it can also cooperate closely with additional elements, including

- Database servers
- Additional Web servers
- Application servers

An application server is often called a middleware server. Middleware includes Java servlets, which are small Java programs that help format and process information as it passes between a Web server and a database server. Additional examples of middleware servers include Allaire's Cold Fusion, Microsoft's Active Server Pages (ASP), and Netscape's Java Server Pages (JSP). The purpose behind middleware is to extend the abilities of a Web server. Middleware allows a Web server to conduct more complex transactions, such as transfer information to and from databases.

These servers are also the chief causes of latency in a Web site. You will want to make sure that all servers can connect to each other quickly.

Slow Servers and Latency

One slow server can cause problems for several others downstream. Whenever one network host experiences a delay because it has to wait for a slow server, it is said to experience latency. *Latency* is the delay experienced by a client or server that has requested information (or some sort of transaction) from a server. Here is a short list of elements that can contribute to latency:

- **Congested routers** *Congestion* is a term generally used to refer to routers. When a router gets too busy breaking up packets and sending them off to other routers, it is said to be congested.

- **Overburdened database servers** Web servers often refer to databases. This is especially the case for e-commerce sites. It is quite common for the database to get overworked. As a result, the Web servers are either forced to return "too busy" error messages, or they must wait for another database connection to open up.

- **Slow networks** Just as when traffic slows down due to overcrowding on a freeway, a network segment that is too slow for the connections it has to carry can cause problems for conjoining segments.

- **Downed networks** If one network fails, the traffic will often get dumped onto another, causing more pressure on the other network.

CERTIFICATION OBJECTIVE 8.03

Internet Domain Names and DNS

Put simply, the Domain Name Server (DNS) system allows you to map common names to IP addresses. DNS is a fundamental service, because it allows people to use names, which are generally more memorable than IP addresses. The Internet communicates via TCP/IP. Two forms of TCP/IP exist: IPv4 and IPv6. Currently, the most common form of IP is IPv4, which uses 32-bit addresses, such as 198.133.219.25 or 205.181.158.215. Each IP address is unique and refers to a specific host on the Internet. DNS was first defined by RFCs 1034 and 1035. The two parties involved in DNS are resolvers and servers. A *resolver* is simply a client that makes DNS queries. As you might suspect, a *server* fulfills requests made by resolvers.

However, you have probably noticed that you rarely, if ever, enter numeric information into your Web browser. When you browse the Web, you enter names such as http://www.cisco.com or http://www.syngress.com, not the actual IP addresses of 198.133.219.25 and 205.181.158.215, respectively. You are able to enter actual names because your Web browser is able to query a special server called a Domain Name Server (DNS). The primary function of a DNS is to resolve user-friendly names to IP addresses. Without a DNS, you would be forced into always using IP address numbers, which is not an attractive option to most people.

The Domain Name Server system, therefore, is a distributed network of computers that provides a fundamental naming service for the entire Internet. Before 1984, only one naming server existed at the University of California at Berkeley. This server contained one large text file that resolved names to IP addresses. However, as the Internet grew, this file got too large, and the DNS became too bogged down by traffic: the DNS system was created.

DNS Has a Hierarchical Structure

Hosts within the domain name system are said to reside within the domain namespace. The domain namespace is hierarchical. There are root-level, top-level, and secondary domains. For example, you are likely familiar with companies such as IBM and Compaq, as well as universities such as Oxford and CalTech. Each of these organizations has DNS entries and participates in the DNS namespace. Figure 8-6 shows the DNS hierarchy.

For now, don't get too concerned with any particular names. Just concentrate on how this image illustrates the hierarchy. First, there is the root-level domain. It is unnamed and is represented by a dot (.). Then come the top-level domains (.edu, .com, and .org), followed by the secondary domains. As shown in Figure 8-6, secondary domains can include the company and organizational names you may already be familiar with. For example, if you have ever gone to the http://www.yahoo.com Web site, the "yahoo" part of this particular DNS address is an example of a secondary domain name.

FIGURE 8-6 The DNS hierarchy

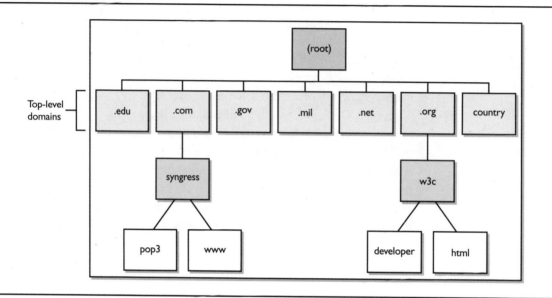

The Role of the Root Domain

The root-level domain, which is unnamed, consists of several hosts that work in tandem to form the very top of the DNS tree. As of this writing, the root domain servers include

- a.root-servers.net
- b.root-servers.net
- c.root-servers.net
- d.root-servers.net
- e.root-servers.net
- f.root-servers.net

The servers listed in the root domain are constantly updated (at least once a day). After it is updated, its hosts distribute their DNS information with all other root servers, then down to the top-level domains. This domain has no name.

Top-Level or Original Domain

Currently, seven top-level domains exist. These include the .edu., .com, and .org domains (see Figure 8-6). These seven domains are known as the original domains.

Country-Level Domains

The "int" domain is no longer common. In its place are the extremely common country codes. These country codes include

.uk	United Kingdom
.us	United States
.ca	Canada
.au	Australia
.ru	Russia

Second-Level Domains

Second-level domains generally include the names of organizations and companies. These include

- Microsoft.com
- Amazon.com
- Berkeley.edu

If you work for a company on the Internet, chances are that it has a Web presence. You can access that Web server as www.*yourcompany*.com. The name of the Web server, then, is www. The only reason that many Web servers are called "www" is that Webmasters simply chose this as a convention. The host named "www," then, is part of the "yourcompany" second-level domain, which is itself part of the .com domain.

Subdomains and Fully Qualified Domain Names (FQDN)

Another name for a fully qualified domain name (FQDN) is an absolute path name that identifies a particular hosts's relationship to the root domain. An FQDN is simply a domain name that is not relative to any other domain. Note that second-level domain names can then have subdomains. For example, imagine that Syngress has an e-mail server with a DNS entry of POP3. This server belongs to the syngress secondary domain. Finally, you know that syngress is part of the .com top-level domain, which is beneath root (.). Therefore, its fully qualified domain name would be POP3.syngress.com, because the proper definition of an FQDN is that it is relative to the root (.) domain.

Reading a FQDN

You already understand the theory behind domains and subdomains: once IBM gets its own domain, it can then create its own. However, you need to understand the practical way to read a subdomain. First of all, you read domain names from left to right. The information in the leftmost space before the dots is more specific. As you move on, the information is more general (see Figure 8-7).

Therefore, you should understand that you read the most specific information first. The research subdomain is more specific than the "bigtimecompany" secondary domain, which is more specific than the .com domain. As discussed previously, the root domain is not named.

Additional Information

Before you learn more about why IBM is in the .com domain and Oxford is in the .edu domain, it is important to understand a few things about DNS:

- It is common for an organization to be assigned a domain name, and then, in turn, create its own subdomains. As long as the organization is recognized by the rest of the DNS system, the subdomains are valid, as well.

- Many organizations run their own DNS servers. Each of these servers in turn must be recognized by DNS servers in its own domain.

FIGURE 8-7

Reading DNS names

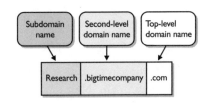

- The DNS system is decentralized in the sense that no one server has all of the information.

- You have to register domain names. The International Corporation for Assigned Names and Numbers (ICANN) manages the domain namespace. You can contact many different organizations and sites to register a domain name. Once you have registered a domain, you can populate that domain with any host names you wish; you do not have to register every DNS name that is part of your domain.

- It is possible to run DNS internally in a nonrouted network. If you plan to provide name resolution via DNS internally, then you really don't have to register your domain. Domain name registration is necessary only when you plan on having your network participate on the Internet.

- You can use the ping and nslookup programs to troubleshoot DNS connectivity. Using ping, you can use deductive logic to find out the source of a problem. For example, if you can ping a host by its IP address, but not by its DNS name, then you have a DNS-related problem. This problem may exist with the client (for example, it does not have the proper DNS server entered in the DNS entry), or with the server (for example, the server may be down, or the network connection to the server may be experiencing a problem). Using nslookup, you can query the databases of the DNS server in your domain. You can even switch to other domains to learn information about other companies.

Zones vs. Domains

Name servers have text files that define a part of the domain namespace. For example, a primary DNS domain usually has a forward zone file and a reverse zone file. These files contain information about hosts within each of these domains. A zone file that exists on a DNS server contains information about various hosts.

Recursion and Iteration

The idea behind DNS is that a client can issue a query, which is then sent up or down the DNS hierarchy. Generally, the client queries a root server. This root server can do one of two things:

- Answer to the query directly.
- Provide the name of an authoritative server for a subdomain that will be able to provide additional information.

Whenever a DNS gets a query to resolve a name into an IP address, these queries can be of two types: recursive and iterative. Recursive queries occur when a resolver creates a request that requires the DNS to follow the entire request path until it is fulfilled. As you might suspect, this form of query is much more taxing on servers. Recursive queries often occur when a resolver queries a name server that is not authoritative for that domain. When a DNS client makes a recursive query, the DNS that is being queried becomes responsible for obtaining the information. The DNS then must track all requests until it finds the authoritative server for that domain. One of the main problems with recursion is that multiple recursive queries can bog down a server.

Iteration, on the other hand, occurs when the DNS gives its best answer to the query sent by the client (that is, the resolver). The key difference between iteration and recursion is that in iteration, the server already knows the answer. In iteration, the client directly asks a local DNS about information. The DNS can then either

- Answer from its own cached information.
- Query another name server.

An iterative request can travel down many name servers until the request finds a server that is authoritative for that domain. Once this occurs, the name server will reply, satisfying the resolver's request. Iteration is also less taxing on DNSs.

Name Server Types

When you create a DNS, you have to choose exactly what type of server it will be. Depending upon your situation, you can choose the following DNS types:

- **Primary** This server contains the authoritative information for an entire zone.

- **Secondary** Also called a slave server, a secondary server receives its database (that is, zone file) from a primary through a zone transfer. In a zone transfer, the primary server gives its database (that is, its zone file) to the secondary server. It is possible to establish times and conditions under which a zone transfer will take place.

- **Forwarding** Also called a forwarder, this type of server allows systems that can't communicate with the root name servers on the Internet to still get information from a specific source. Pure forwarding servers do not keep their own zone databases, although it is common to have a server be both a primary and a forwarding server. This way, a DNS can still resolve a request. You can use forwarders to control exactly how a DNS will communicate with the Internet. As a result, forwarders are quite common in firewall settings, because you can direct a DNS to query only specific servers. A forwarding server can also help process recursive queries. Finally, a forwarding server can also reduce expenses because all queries sent that must travel outside of your network are first processed by the forwarding server, which may have already cached the entry a host has asked for. A caching server does not forward requests.

- **Caching** These servers do not have their own authoritative databases for their zone or for any other. Rather, they build up a database by satisfying the queries of other DNSs. Through the process of answering queries, they learn more about the DNS domain namespace and can then help to inform other servers. The primary benefit of caching servers is that they help speed up name resolution. The other thing to remember about caching servers is that they hold DNS information for only a certain period of time. This is because they do not use a static table, as does a secondary or primary server. Each entry has a Time To Live (TTL) field. When the TTL for an entry in a caching server expires, the entry is flushed from the system.

A forwarding server can help control access to the Internet. Whenever a host queries DNS, a forwarding server can process the request by taking it and then querying another DNS (see Figure 8-8).

The Start of Authority (SOA) File and DNS Entry Types

Thus far, you have learned about the various types of servers and their general hierarchy. Now you need to understand specifically how an actual

| FIGURE 8-8 | A forwarding server |

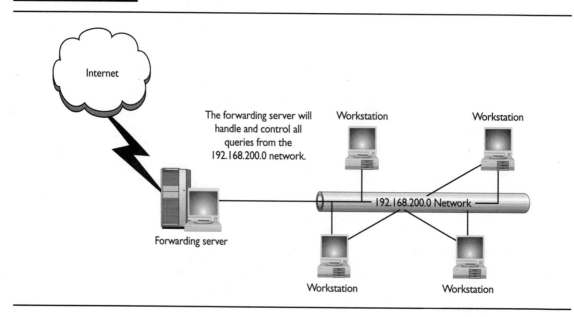

DNS operates. A DNS reads simple text files that contain information about the host with a particular IP address. Besides the actual configuration files the DNS reads, the primary file that contains the DNS information is called the Start of Authority (SOA) file. The SOA file contains information that establishes the following parameters:

- The name servers (primary and secondary) for the entire domain
- E-mail contact information
- The serial number, which identifies the name server
- Values that govern how often the primary server will update its files with the secondary server
- Name and address information for specific hosts

Figure 8-9 shows a sample SOA file. This particular file declares the DNS namespace for the fictional writers.com domain. This simple domain has several hosts, including coleridge, keats, blake, and levinas.

The most common entries simply provide a name for an IP address. However, there are additional entries that are equally important. Here is a list of the most common entries:

- **A**   Provides information that maps a name directly to an IP address. The most common entry.
- **CNAME**   Allows you to provide an alternative name to a host already named in the DNS file. In Figure 8-9, the computer named blake (IP address 10.100.100.8) also has the name heidegger. The only way to give two names to the same host is by using CNAME entries.
- **HINFO**   Short for "host information." This record gives information about the system on the resolved host. For example, all HINFO records contain information about the CPU type and operating system.
- **MX**   Short for "mail exchange." This type of record is essential for naming the e-mail server on your domain.

FIGURE 8-9   A sample SOA file

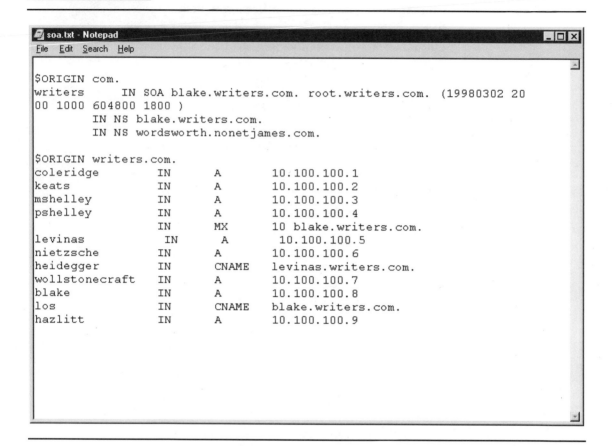

```
soa.txt - Notepad                                                    _ □ ✕
File  Edit  Search  Help

$ORIGIN com.
writers      IN SOA blake.writers.com. root.writers.com.  (19980302 20
00 1000 604800 1800 )
         IN NS blake.writers.com.
         IN NS wordsworth.nonetjames.com.

$ORIGIN writers.com.
coleridge       IN      A       10.100.100.1
keats           IN      A       10.100.100.2
mshelley        IN      A       10.100.100.3
pshelley        IN      A       10.100.100.4
                IN      MX      10 blake.writers.com.
levinas         IN      A        10.100.100.5
nietzsche       IN      A       10.100.100.6
heidegger       IN      CNAME   levinas.writers.com.
wollstonecraft  IN      A       10.100.100.7
blake           IN      A       10.100.100.8
los             IN      CNAME   blake.writers.com.
hazlitt         IN      A       10.100.100.9
```

■ PTR   Short for "pointer record." These entries help create reverse DNS lookup domains. PTR records go into a separate file from the entries named above.

Note that the IN entry is short for "Internet." It is possible to create a DNS system for protocols other than TCP/IP. Because the Internet standardized to TCP/IP in 1983, DNS uses IN to mean TCP/IP. Chances are that all DNS entries you will see will be preceded by an IN entry.

on the
job

*Creating DNS records is somewhat complex, and it is especially
daunting for the new user. Perhaps the most common cause for errors
are typos. The most common mistake occurs when the zone creator
user forgets to enter a trailing dot at the end of a fully qualified
domain name. In Figure 8-9, all of the names have dots. If you omit
the dot, you will confuse the DNS system into thinking that you have
a completely different domain name. As you run into problems, look
to check your typing first.*

IN-ADDR.ARPA and Reverse DNS Lookup

You now understand how the DNS system maps names to IP addresses.
You should note, however, that the DNS system does the reverse as well:
it allows you to map IP addresses to names. This is often called *reverse
mapping*, or *reverse DNS lookup*. Reverse DNS lookup is made possible
by a pseudo domain structure called IN-ADDR.ARPA. This domain name
is attached to the end of an IP address that has its normal order reversed.
For example, if you have an IP address of 205.181.158.215, and it
has a reverse DNS entry, it is possible to search its name. When DNS
resolves the 205.181.158.215 IP address to a name, it uses this
IN-ADDR.ARPA address:

158.181.205.IN-ADDR.ARPA

Note that this address is the exact opposite of the IP address, with the
IN-ADDR.ARPA address stuck on the end. This convention makes the
IN-ADDR.ARPA domain part of the network zone controlled by the
primary DNS for that zone.

You should also note that if you were to actually create an
IN-ADDR.ARPA entry, it would look like this:

PTR 158.181.205.IN-ADDR.ARPA

Remember, the PTR entry allows you to define an actual DNS entry in a
reverse lookup zone.

exam
Ⓦatch

Now that you have read this particular section, you should understand that resolving names to IP addresses is not the same thing as resolving IP addresses to names. When you enter a name, such as www.syngress.com, into a Web browser (or a program such as ping), you are using a DNS to resolve that name to its IP address. Of course, a DNS can also resolve IP addresses to names. This is called reverse DNS lookup. Servers interested in securing connections can use reverse DNS lookup to try and verify exactly where a connection is coming from. For example, some servers will not allow connections from computers unless they can verify its participation in a DNS domain.

on the
Ⓙob

When you create a primary DNS domain, you will generally have to create two zone files. One will be a forward zone file that contains A, CNAME, and MX records. The second file will be a reverse zone file that contains PTR records for each host that is in the forward zone file. Although it is not absolutely essential to create a reverse zone, your company may not be able to access all of the resources on the Internet if you omit this file. The reason for this is that many Internet servers conduct a reverse DNS lookup, which traces your IP address to a resolved name. By doing a reverse DNS lookup, the server can determine more information about you, including what country you are in. At one time, users foreign to the United States could not export certain types of encryption. Whenever Netscape or Microsoft wished to give away its browsers that used high encryption (over 40 bits), they were required to conduct a reverse DNS lookup. One of the companies I worked for was in the United States, but it was not equipped for reverse DNS. Subsequently, I could not download browsers that had high encryption.

Registering DNS Names

Although the International Corporation for Assigned Names and Numbers (ICANN) manages DNS names, you can go to many different sites to register a name, including Network Solutions, Incorporated (http://www.networksolutions.com/) (see Figure 8-10).

Using the Network Solutions Web site, you can register a domain name. You can first conduct searches to determine if your domain name has

FIGURE 8-10	The Network Solutions homepage

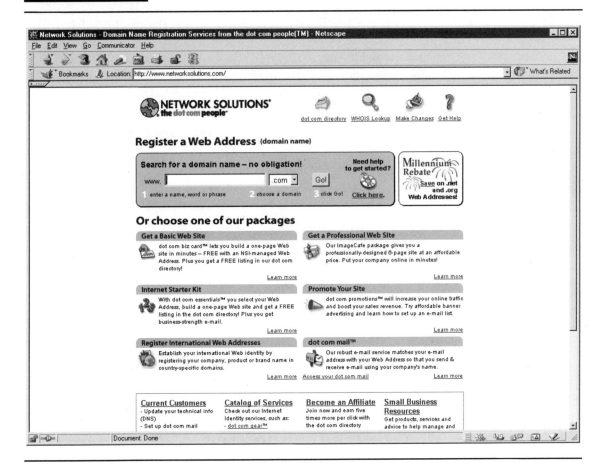

already been taken. As of this writing, it costs $70.00 to register a domain name for two years. It then costs $35.00 a year to renew your registration.

Once you get your own domain name, you can then decide to run your own DNS, which will allow you to take control of the DNS space you have received. For example, it is possible to manage the syngress.com namespace by creating forward and reverse lookup zones, as well as subdomains.

whois and nslookup

The whois service allows you to determine information about a DNS domain. Figure 8-11 shows a the results of a whois query of the syngress.com domain.

The results show that NetworkSolutions.com has registered the NS1.INFOBOARD.NET and NS2.INFOBOARD.NET servers as the DNSs for Syngress. It is likely that NS1.INFOBOARD.NET is a primary DNS and that NS2.INFOBOARD.NET is a secondary server.

FIGURE 8-11 Conducting a whois query on the syngress.com domain

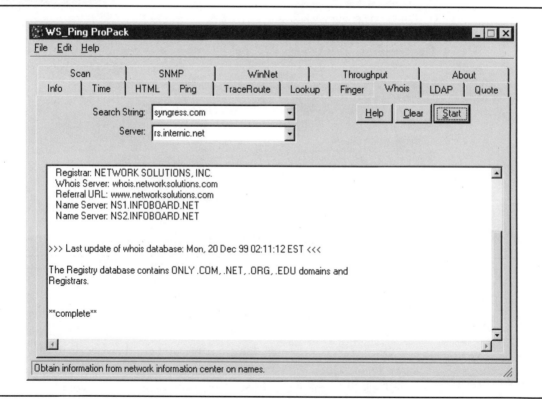

on the

Üob

You should note that the International Corporation for Assigned Names and Numbers (ICANN) is responsible for managing the DNS namespace for the entire Internet.

EXERCISE 8-2

Studying DNS Name Resolution

1. In Windows 95/98 or NT, find the hosts file. In Windows 98/98, the file exists in the C:/windows directory, assuming your system is installed on a C:\ drive. In Windows NT, it is in the \winnt\system32\drivers\etc file. If you wish, just type **hosts** in the Start | Find menu.

2. Make a copy of the hosts file in case you make a mistake or experience a problem. Place it on your desktop.

3. Open the hosts file that exists in the Windows directory using Notepad. One way to do this is to right-click the file while pressing the SHIFT key at the same time. You can then use the Open With… option to select Notepad.

4. Once you have opened the hosts file, it should appear significantly similar to Figure 8-12.

5. This file is designed to provide local resolution. It is present on any computer that uses TCP/IP. You can edit this file to provide name resolution to an IP address. Keep this file open.

6. Establish an Internet connection.

7. Open a command prompt (MS DOS prompt).

8. Use the ping utility to query the following address: www.ibm.com. This utility allows you to test your ability to connect to other hosts. Simply enter **ping www.ibm.com**.

9. Notice that in Windows, you receive four replies. Notice the IP address, as well.

10. Go to your hosts file. Create some space at the very bottom of the host file.

FIGURE 8-12   A sample hosts file

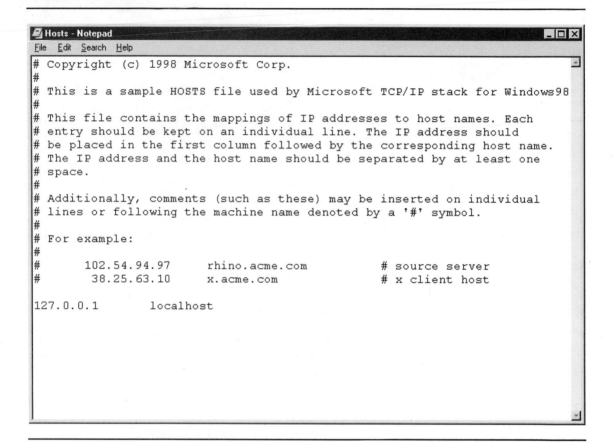

```
# Copyright (c) 1998 Microsoft Corp.
#
# This is a sample HOSTS file used by Microsoft TCP/IP stack for Windows98
#
# This file contains the mappings of IP addresses to host names. Each
# entry should be kept on an individual line. The IP address should
# be placed in the first column followed by the corresponding host name.
# The IP address and the host name should be separated by at least one
# space.
#
# Additionally, comments (such as these) may be inserted on individual
# lines or following the machine name denoted by a '#' symbol.
#
# For example:
#
#      102.54.94.97     rhino.acme.com          # source server
#      38.25.63.10      x.acme.com              # x client host

127.0.0.1        localhost
```

11. Enter the IP address you read at the very left-hand side of the hosts file. For example, I would enter it immediately beneath the loopback address (127.0.0.1) shown in Figure 8-13.

12. Press the space bar a few times and then enter your first name. Your hosts file should look similar to Figure 8-13.

13. Now, save the hosts file. Make sure this file is in the directory you found it in.

14. Using your command prompt, ping your name. For example, if I were to do this, I would type **ping james**.

FIGURE 8-13   An edited hosts file

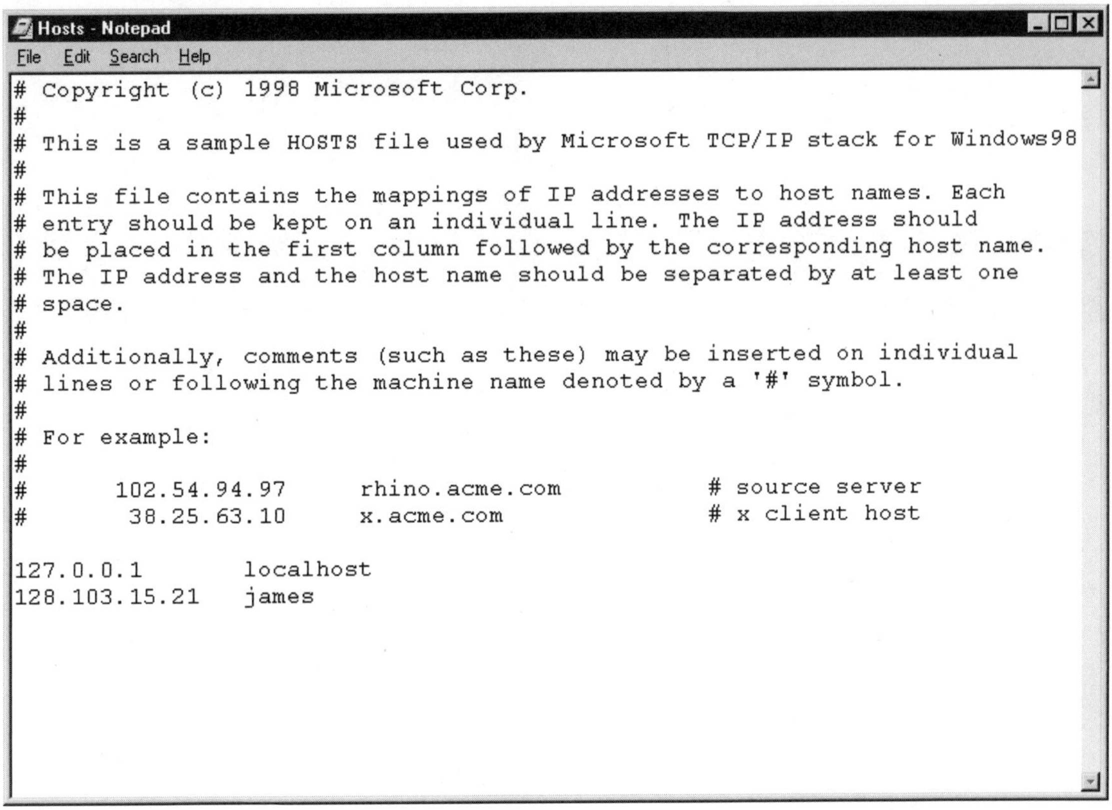

```
Hosts - Notepad                                                    _ □ ×
File  Edit  Search  Help
# Copyright (c) 1998 Microsoft Corp.
#
# This is a sample HOSTS file used by Microsoft TCP/IP stack for Windows98
#
# This file contains the mappings of IP addresses to host names. Each
# entry should be kept on an individual line. The IP address should
# be placed in the first column followed by the corresponding host name.
# The IP address and the host name should be separated by at least one
# space.
#
# Additionally, comments (such as these) may be inserted on individual
# lines or following the machine name denoted by a '#' symbol.
#
# For example:
#
#      102.54.94.97      rhino.acme.com          # source server
#       38.25.63.10      x.acme.com              # x client host

127.0.0.1       localhost
128.103.15.21   james
```

15. You should receive replies similar to the following:

```
C:\WINDOWS\Desktop>ping james
Pinging james [128.103.15.21] with 32 bytes of data:

Reply from 128.103.15.21: bytes=32 time=218ms TTL=235
Reply from 128.103.15.21: bytes=32 time=201ms TTL=235
Reply from 128.103.15.21: bytes=32 time=214ms TTL=235
Reply from 128.103.15.21: bytes=32 time=196ms TTL=235

Ping statistics for 128.103.15.21:
Packets: Sent = 4, Received = 4, Lost = 0 (0% loss),
Approximate round trip times in milli-seconds:
Minimum = 196ms, Maximum =  218ms, Average =  207ms

C:\WINDOWS\Desktop>
```

16. You have received a response from the IBM, not because it has a machine named james, or any other name. You have received a response because your system first read the local hosts file you just edited before it went out and queried a DNS server.

You have just studied some of the hosts, networks, and systems that help the Internet communicate efficiently. Now take a brief look at some scenarios and answers.

QUESTIONS AND ANSWERS

A small business has ten employees. Each requires a connection to the Internet to do the following:
    Read simple e-mail messages.
    Browse corporate Internet and extranet Web sites to upload information via simple HTML forms.
They will not be accessing the Internet often. What speed of connection will this business require?
	This business requires either a DSL connection or a fractional T1 line. First of all, this company does not have numerous employees, nor will it be accessing the Internet very often. Second, consider the fact that the documents these employees are uploading are not complex or large. HTML forms do not require large amounts of bandwidth. Therefore, they do not need the amount of bandwidth found in a full T1 line (1.544 Mbps).

A company has decided that it is going to create a new division. It already has a domain name (bigcompany.com). Due to consumer interest, the company has been able to create a dedicated sales division. It will include 50 new employees. In regard to DNS, what can you do as an IT administrator to help organize the 50 new machines you will have under your control?	Out of several possibilities, one of the most pressing is to create a subdomain of bigcompany.com. Arguably, the most logical name for this subdomain would be *sales*.bigcompany.com. Doing this will help organize your company's assets and make them easier to manage.

You have not been able to ping a host by its DNS name of blake.yourcompany.com. However, you can ping the machine by its IP address. What has gone wrong?	Although several explanations are possible, the three most plausible are
	    The DNS your client uses has gone down.
	    The DNS your client uses is unavailable due to a routing problem or a bad network connection.
	    The DNS information for your client is misconfigured or not entered.
	If you can ping the host by its IP address, that means that it is participating on the network. Because you can't get name resolution, you will have to first make sure your client is configured correctly, then begin to ask questions about what is going wrong with the server.

CERTIFICATION SUMMARY

In this chapter, you have learned about the hosts and systems the Internet uses to ensure efficient communication. You learned about high-speed network connections that connect the world's networks. You then learned about NAPs and how they help one ISP communicate with another. As you learned about the high-speed networks that create a NAP, you learned about connection speeds. Finally, you learned the basics of DNS.

TWO-MINUTE DRILL

❑ Because the Internet is a packet-switching network, it requires several key elements to make sure that this communication occurs efficiently.

❑ These backbone elements that allow users to communicate on the Internet include Internet Service Providers (ISPs), routers, high-speed backbone networks, Network Access Points (NAPs), and the Domain Name Server (DNS) system.

❑ No longer governed solely by the NSF, the new Internet structure essentially consists of ISPs that communicate via a backbone comprised of Network Access Points (NAPs), high-speed networks Routing Arbiters (RAs), and Metropolitan Area Exchanges (MAEs).

❑ A NAP is nothing more than a central point that allows Internet Service Providers (ISPs) to exchange information with each other. The technical term for the activity of exchanging information between ISPs is "peering." Whenever one ISP exchanges information with another, it does so via a NAP, which regulates how peering operates.

❑ If an ISP wishes to have its router update its routing table with another within its autonomous system (AS), it uses the Interior Gateway Protocol (IGP). If one ISP router communicates outside its AS, it uses the Border Gateway Protocol (BGP). BGP is an improvement on another protocol, the Exterior Gateway Protocol (EGP).

❑ A NAP implements routing by implementing a routing policy. This policy helps coordinate ISP traffic.

❑ A backbone network is generally

  ❑ **Fault tolerant** It uses several redundant connections to make sure that one failure (that is, fault) does not bring down the entire network.

  ❑ **High-speed** It connects at speeds that are state of the art for its time.

❑ A Metropolitan Area Exchange is a specific example of a NAP. Two types of MAEs exist: tier 1 and tier 2. Tier 1 MAE connections employ high-speed Fiber Distributed Data Interface (FDDI) connections.

❑ You have already learned about how a NAP enforces routing policies. A Routing Arbiter (RA) is the backbone element that enacts those policies. The RA takes the place of the old NSFNet Acceptable Use Policy (AUP). Whenever one NAP connects to another, they use an RA. An RA is a collection of devices that provide routing maps, address resolution, and redundant connectivity.

❑ Whenever you send an e-mail message, you are using at least two different types of servers.

❑ One slow server can cause problems for several others downstream. Whenever one network host experiences a delay because it has to wait for a slow server, it is said to experience latency.

❑ Put simply, the Domain Name Server (DNS) system allows you to map common names to IP addresses. The DNS system is a fundamental service, because it allows people to use names, which are generally more memorable than IP addresses.

❑ The Domain Name Server system is a distributed network of computers that provides a fundamental naming service for the entire Internet.

❑ Hosts within the domain name system are said to reside within the domain namespace. The domain namespace is hierarchical.

❑ The root-level domain, which is unnamed, consists of several hosts that work in tandem to form the very top of the DNS tree.

❑ Currently, seven top-level domains exist. Top-level domains include .edu, .org, and .com.

❑ Second-level domains generally include the names of organizations and companies, such as redhat.com and microsoft.com.

❑ A DNS reads simple text files that contain information about the host with a particular IP address. Besides the actual configuration files the DNS reads, the primary file that contains the DNS information is called the Start of Authority (SOA) file. Information in the SOA file can include entries, such as A, CNAME, and MX records. DNS uses these record entries to provide name resolution.

❑ You now understand how the DNS system maps names to IP addresses. You should note, however, that the DNS system does the reverse as well: it allows you to map IP addresses to names.

❑ The International Corporation for Assigned Names and Numbers (ICANN) manages DNS names.

SELF TEST

1. You are running a firewall to make sure that hackers cannot penetrate your network. You wish to use DNS to resolve host names. You wish to control how DNS queries are made to the Internet. You also wish to use a server that does not keep its own database, or zone. Which of these servers can help you do this?

   A. A primary server

   B. A secondary server

   C. A caching server

   D. A forwarding server

2. Sarah runs a small ISP. She wishes to cut down on traffic passing through her router. She also wishes to work closely with another ISP so that she can pass data more efficiently to it. Her goal is to bring faster connectivity to her customers. What should she do?

   A. Buy a new router.

   B. Initiate a peering relationship.

   C. Create a NAP.

   D. Install a secondary DNS.

3. Sarah has created a peering relationship with another ISP. The peering relationship is working well. As is common, her routers wish to update their information from routers outside her peering relationship. What protocol should she install on her routers so that they can update their tables with routers outside her peering relationships? (Choose all that apply.)

   A. Exterior Gateway Protocol

   B. Interior Gateway Protocol

   C. Extended Gateway Protocol

   D. Border Gateway Protocol

4. Ming is responsible for connecting his company to the Internet. His company is in Des Moines, Iowa, in the United States. He calculates how much bandwidth his company needs. He is able to estimate that between all of the e-mail checking, Web browsing, and DNS queries, this network will require about 1.3 Mbps of bandwidth. Which line should he choose?

   A. An OC3 line

   B. A DS0 line

   C. A T1 line

   D. An E-1 line

5. You have not been able to resolve queries all day. You cannot contact your ISP to discover the problem. You have tried to use the ping program to determine the problem yourself. You find that you are not able to ping by IP address, either. You can establish a dial-up connection to your ISP, and you can ping the e-mail and servers that belong to your ISP. Of the following choices, which can explain the problem? (Choose all that apply.)

A. A backbone network used by the ISP is down.

B. The ISP's secondary DNS is down.

C. The ISP's routers are down.

D. The ISP's primary DNS is down.

6. You have just installed a new e-mail client. After installing and configuring it, you find that you can send e-mail, but you can't receive it. You can ping the POP3 server by IP address as well as by its name. Which of the answers below gives the best solution for this problem?

A. Contact the ISP and inform it that its POP3 server is down.

B. Contact the ISP and inform it that its SMTP server is down.

C. Check and fix your SMTP server entry.

D. Check and fix your POP3 server entry.

7. You notice that your Web server is taking an unacceptable amount of time responding to requests. This server is part of your e-commerce site that allows users to add their names to a database of contacts before purchasing items. Which of the servers listed here is most likely causing this problem?

A. The DNS

B. The database server

C. The SMTP server

D. The POP3 server

8. You have just created a primary DNS. You have created both forward and reverse

zones. How would you describe this DNS? (Choose all that apply.)

A. The database is authoritative for the entire bigcompany.com domain.

B. This server is a resolver.

C. The server resolves IP addresses to domain names.

D. The server resolves domain names to IP addresses.

9. In the URL server.research.bigcompany.com, what is the top-level domain name?

A. research

B. bigcompany *second level domain name*

C. bigcompany.com

D. .com

10. You wish to create a DNS that backs up the primary DNS. You wish this server to receive its database from the primary DNS. What type of server will you create?

A. A caching server

B. A forwarding server

C. A secondary server

D. A second-level server

11. What are the two network types commonly implemented in a MAE?

A. ATM and FDDI

B. SONET and ADSL

C. Ethernet and Token Ring

D. ISDN and T1

12. You run a large ISP. You have just engaged in a peering relationship with several other ISPs to increase the routing efficiency between networks. What element of your NAP helps define the way routing information is transferred?

    A. The Acceptable Use Policy (AUP)

    B. A Router Server (RS)

    C. The Routing Arbiter (RA)

    D. An Internet Routing Registry (IRR)

13. You are establishing DNS for the sales subdomain. This subdomain is beneath the staff.syngress.com domain. You are populating this subdomain with several hosts, including a Web server named www. If you wished to access this server from outside the domain, how would you refer to it in a Web browser?

    A. http://www.sales.syngress.com

    B. http://www.syngress.com

    C. http://www.staff.syngress.com

    D. http://www.sales.staff.syngress.com

14. You wish to have your company participate on the Internet. You wish to use the following DNS name: yourcompanyname.com. You also wish to create your own DNS system that is authoritative for your entire domain. Which of these answers explains what you have to do next in order to use it?

    A. Register this DNS name with Network Solutions.

    B. Register this DNS name with Network Solutions, and then create a primary DNS domain.

    C. Register this DNS name with Network Associates, and then create a second-level DNS domain.

    D. Register this DNS name with Network Solutions, and then create a caching server.

15. You wish to enable systems to resolve IP addresses to names. What domain allows this?

    A. The IN-ADDR.ARPA domain

    B. A caching domain

    C. A top-level domain

    D. A second-level domain

16. You have a host with the following class A IP address: 10.90.80.70. You are using a standard subnet mask. You wish to enable reverse DNS lookup for it. What would the entry look like in the reverse DNS zone file?

    A. IN PTR IN-ADDR.ARPA.70.80.90

    B. IN PTR 70.80.90.IN-ADDR.ARPA

    C. IN PTR 80.90.10.IN-ADDR.ARPA

    D. IN PTR 70.80.90.IN-ADDR.ARPA

17. You have just installed a POP3 server. You have been asked to update the DNS database so that DNS knows where the POP3 server is. What type of record do you use?

    A. PTR
    B. MX *mail exchanger*
    C. A
    D. HINFO

18. You have a server named server1.bigcompany.com. You wish to give it an alternative name of www. What record would you use?

    A. PTR
    B. MX
    C. A
    √ D. CNAME

19. Mary has received complaints from end users that they can't connect to their systems. She suspects DNS resolution is the problem. What tools can she use to troubleshoot DNS connectivity?

    A. arp
    √ B. ping
    C. traceroute
    √ D. nslookup

20. Your company wishes you to be extremely thorough in documenting each host that is part of your DNS domain. What DNS record entries can allow you to identify the nature of each host, including its operating system type and version?

    A. CNAME
    B. A
    √ C. HINFO
    D. IN

SELF TEST ANSWERS

1. **D** is correct, because a forwarding server handles requests for a particular domain by accepting them and then forwarding them to another server. A forwarding server can also reduce expenses because all queries sent that must travel outside your network are first processed by the forwarding server, which may have already cached the entry a host has asked for.

   A, B, and **C** are incorrect, because a primary server keeps its own database, as does a secondary server. A caching server does not forward requests.

2. **B** is correct, because peering allows two ISPs to share information more efficiently. Specifically, peering allows two ISPs to share information without having to use outside networks.

   A is incorrect, because buying a new router will not necessarily allow Sarah to work closely with another ISP. **C** is incorrect, because even though a NAP allows peering relationships, small ISPs do not create their own NAPs.

3. **A** and **D** are correct, because both BGP and EGP allow a router to communicate with other routers in order to update their routing tables.

   B is incorrect, because the Interior Gateway Protocol (IGP) is suited only for routers within an autonomous system (AS).

4. **C** is correct, because a T-1 line runs at 1.544 Mbps. This figure is the closest to Ming's requirement for 1.3 Mbps.

   A is incorrect, because an OC3 line runs at 155.52 Mbps, which is far faster than what he needs. **B** is incorrect, because a DS0 line runs at only 64 Kbps. Finally, an E-1 line is closer to Ming's needs, but the E standards apply in Europe, while Ming lives in the United States. Besides, if Ming were in Europe, he would choose a fractional E-1 line as opposed to a full E-1 line.

5. **A** and **C** are correct, because they can explain why you can contact the ISP but can't get outside that ISP. By establishing a dial-up connection, you have pretty much proved that your connection is not the problem. The problem lies with your ISP. Of the answers given, **A** and **C** are the most plausible, because they would mean that your ISP has a problem connecting to the outside world.

   B and **D** are incorrect, because pinging IP addresses only fails, as well. If only the DNSs were down, you could still ping by IP address.

6. **D** is correct. Chances are the problem comes because you incorrectly entered the name of the POP3 server. Many ISPs use separate servers (or at least IP addresses) to handle SMTP and POP3. If you enter the name of either server incorrectly, your e-mail client will not be able to contact them.

    B and **C** are incorrect, because they would address server-side and client-side SMTP problems. SMTP is the protocol that sends mail, as opposed to receiving it. **A** is incorrect, because when you use ping you can prove that the site is still up.

7. **B** is correct, because it is the server most directly connected to the Web server. **A**, **B**, and **D** are incorrect, because even though each of these can cause too much network traffic, they still are not part of the series of connections that creates an e-commerce solution.

8. **A**, **C**, and **D** are the three answers that best describe a primary DNS server. First of all, a primary DNS is the authoritative server for that domain. It also is responsible for resolving domain names to IP addresses and resolving IP addresses to domain names.

    B is incorrect, because a resolver is another name for a DNS client, not a DNS.

9. **D** is the correct answer. Top-level Internet domain names include .com, .edu, .org, and country names.

    A is the name of a subdomain of a secondary domain. **B** is a second-level domain name. **C** is a combination of the top- and second-level domain names.

10. **C** is correct, because a secondary DNS server receives its database from a primary DNS server.

    A is incorrect, because a caching server does not have its own database. It simply builds up its own database of information by keeping (that is, caching) answers it receives by answering queries made to it. Also, a caching server does not have its own database. Similarly, **B** is incorrect, because a forwarding server does not receive its database from the primary server. **D** is incorrect, because a second-level server does not exist; do not confuse secondary servers with the idea of a second-level domain.

11. **A** is correct. At present, Metropolitan Area Exchanges use ATM or FDDI connections. **B** is incorrect, because SONET is used for vBNS backbone connections, whereas ADSL is used for small business and end user Internet connectivity. **C** is incorrect, because even though the Internet is comprised largely of Ethernet networks, the answer is far more general than the network types given in **A**. **D** is incorrect, because it gives connection speeds and types, as opposed to network types.

12. **C is correct.** A Routing Arbiter (RA) is responsible for enacting NAP policies. **B** is incorrect, because the Route Server is the actual device that transfers information. **A** is incorrect, because routing arbiters replaced acceptable use policies. **D** is incorrect, because the IRR is the central database of routes consulted by a router server.

13. **D is correct.** It represents the proper DNS name, because it represents the proper hierarchical relationship. You are adding a host named www to the sales domain, which is beneath the staff domain, which is beneath the syngress.com domain. **A** is incorrect, because the www entry here would make the machine part of the sales subdomain, but omits the staff subdomain. **B** is incorrect, because the www entry refers to a host that is part of the syngress.com domain, not the sales.staff subdomain. **C** is incorrect, because it places the www host in the staff subdomain, not sales.staff.

14. **B is correct.** The first step to take is to register your name with ICANN. One way to do this is to visit the Network Solutions Web page, or contact them via telephone. The Network Solutions company will then arrange to register your name with ICANN for a nominal fee. Second, you then have to create a primary DNS domain. This way, you can then create forward and reverse zones and create subdomains. **A** is incorrect, because it omits establishing your own DNS. **C** is incorrect, because Network Solutions, not Network Associates, is one place to go. In addition, you would not create your own second-level domain. Second-level domains are such names as .com and .edu; creating such domains is left up to ICANN. **D** is incorrect, because a caching server would not create an authoritative DNS zone.

15. **A is correct.** The IN-ADDR.ARPA domain allows you to create a system that allows hosts to resolve IP addresses to names. **B** is incorrect, because there is no such thing as a caching domain. **C** and **D** are incorrect, because each defines the DNS namespace hierarchy, and is not directly responsible for resolving IP addresses into host names.

16. **C is correct.** Note that the first thing you would do is use the PTR entry. Second, you would take the IP address and remove the host portion (70). You would then take the network address and reverse it. Therefore, you would begin with 80.90.10, so that the network address is the highest. You then append this address to the IN-ADDR.ARPA domain. **A, B,** and **D** are incorrect, because they do not properly reverse the network portion of the address, nor do they drop the host name.

17. **B** is correct. MX (mail exchanger) records allow DNS to define where e-mail will be sent.
A, C, and **D** are incorrect, because they define entries having to do with reverse lookup, forward lookup, and hardware information records.

18. **D** is correct. A CNAME (canonical name) record entry allows you to give an alternative DNS name to a host that has already been defined in your DNS namespace.
A is incorrect, because PTR records are for placing reverse DNS lookup entries in reverse zone files. **B** is incorrect, because MX records allow you to tell DNS where your mail server is, whereas an A record maps DNS names to IP addresses in a forward zone file. Therefore, **C** is incorrect.

19. **B** and **D** are correct. Although each of these tools can help troubleshoot TCP/IP, nslookup and ping are the ideal ones to use. You can use ping to determine whether problems exist in name resolution, whereas you can use nslookup to learn about the contents of the DNS database.

20. **C** is correct. The HINFO (host information) record allows you to specify additional information about your host. This can include type of operating system, as well as information about the hardware that the host uses. Such information can be quite helpful in documenting a LAN, although it can also present a security risk. If a hacker obtains HINFO records, he or she then has a great deal of information to help map out the network and then exploit it.
A, B, and **D** are incorrect, because none of these records allows you to specify additional information other than alternative names, forward address mapping, and the fact that the host is using TCP/IP as its networking protocol.

i-Net+ ™

COMPUTING TECHNOLOGY INDUSTRY ASSOCIATION®

9

Protocols

CERTIFICATION OBJECTIVES

H

ave you ever wondered how the Internet works? How office networks work? How AOL™ works? By now, everyone has seen that we can send an e-mail to someone in another country as easily as we send it to our neighbor next door. But exactly how did it get there? Why did it go to that person as opposed to someone else? Sure, there had to be cables (or antennas) connecting the two locations together, but how did it actually get from point A to point B? And why did it take the path that it did?

The answer is that in all of these situations, the networks are set up in accordance with certain rules. These rules govern things such as which computer talks when, what "language" they use, which pathway they will take, how they will communicate that the message has been received, and so on. These rules are called *protocols*.

In this chapter we are going to learn about the different protocols that are in use both on the Internet and in corporate networks. We will learn how TCP/IP (Transmission Control Protocol/Internet Protocol) came to be the dominant protocol in the computer industry, how it works, and what tools are available to troubleshoot it. We will also learn about the various remote access protocols and the diagnostic tools available for them.

CERTIFICATION OBJECTIVE 9.01

Nature, Purpose, and Operational Essentials of TCP/IP

TCP/IP came into existence in the late 1960s and early 1970s as a result of research conducted by the Department of Defense Advanced Research Project Agency (ARPA). The focus of the research was figuring out a way to reliably carry data over unreliable communications links. They had to come up with some method of transporting data whereby each individual piece of data (called a datagram) was independent of all the others, because they wanted a system that was robust enough to operate in case one of the communication links went down.

FIGURE 9-1

Communication between computers, based on TCP/IP

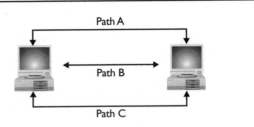

Path A

Path B

Path C

Take the example in Figure 9-1. These two computers need to communicate. Both of them are set up to use TCP/IP. When one machine sends information to the other, that information can travel down Path A, Path B, or Path C. To the computers, it doesn't matter which path is taken, because the rules of the TCP/IP suite will handle all of the details. If something happens to Path A, and it is no longer available, then the TCP/IP suite will detect that change and compensate accordingly.

Independent Communication

The main strength of the TCP/IP is that it allows the devices on a network to communicate with each other and lets them know whether they are up and functioning and whom they can talk to. In this way, if a device has gone down, or the pathway to that device has gone down, all of the other devices will learn about it, and they will stop trying to communicate with that device. Once the protocol has done that, it can then determine the best path to use to send datagrams from one host to another. (*Host* is a TCP/IP term for a computer or other peripheral device that can understand TCP/IP.)

Data Integrity and User Accessibility

Next, the protocol is concerned with the actual data: Is it all there? Is any of it corrupted? Does any of it need to be resent? And finally, the protocol is concerned with whether the data has made it to the user in a format that the user can understand.

TCP/IP: The Protocol of the Internet

The reason TCP/IP has become the dominant protocol is twofold: it's not proprietary, and it's very fault tolerant. Because it is nonproprietary, vendors can write their own implementation of TCP/IP and let the marketplace decide whether to use it. It is fault tolerant in that once it is configured correctly, TCP/IP can carry packets from place to place over numerous routes. Thus it is not susceptible to a single line failure's disrupting traffic.

Background and Reference Points on Protocol: The OSI Reference Model

Before we go any further in our discussion of TCP/IP, we need to spend a little time understanding some background information about protocols in general. To do that we need to define some terms that are widely used in the industry and explore the OSI reference model.

Definition and Examples

A *protocol* is the set of rules that governs how devices on a network communicate with each other. Different networks can have different protocols. In fact, the same physical network can have multiple protocols running on it. How exactly does a protocol work? Let's take an example from the beginning of the chapter.

Suppose that you have a friend in Europe to whom you need to send a message. You have a couple of different options in getting that message there. You can talk with your European friend on the phone. You can also mail your message. Or you can send it via e-mail. All three scenarios require you to follow certain rules or protocols. In dialing a number, or putting a stamp and address on an envelope, or typing in an e-mail address, you have to conform to the rules of the network that you are operating in. Let's look more closely at the last example, since that is what we are really interested in.

How E-mail Works

Figure 9-2 demonstrates how e-mail works. The e-mail client running on workstation A contacts mail server A and says, "Here is a message I need for

FIGURE 9-2

How e-mail works

you to deliver." Mail server A responds by saying, "Thanks for the message. Don't worry about it anymore. I will make sure that it gets to its destination." From there, the e-mail is sent out over a multitude of routers that connect the Internet until it finally makes its way to the destination e-mail server, mail server B, which it turn delivers it to workstation B.

The main point is that, in order to communicate on any network, you have to be using the protocols for that network. These protocols work in conjunction with each other to reliably deliver information from point A to point B. In the case of the Internet, that collection of protocols is known as the TCP/IP Protocol Suite. We will call it TCP/IP for short.

The Seven Layers of the OSI Reference Model

Throughout the history of networking, there have been (and continue to be) numerous protocols in use. In order for network professionals to be able to discuss these different protocols and understand how each one works, there has to be a common reference point to which networking professionals can map the different protocols. That reference point is called the OSI (Open Systems Interconnect) reference model.

The OSI reference model is exactly what it sounds like: a networking model that we can reference so that we can see how the different protocols work. You need to be aware of the OSI reference model because every IT professional can go back to this reference point when he or she discusses disparate protocols, in order to understand how each one works. For the purpose of our discussion, I will always identify the layer at which a specific protocol is operating.

The OSI reference model is divided into seven layers. They are shown in Figure 9-3.

FIGURE 9-3

The seven layers of the OSI reference model

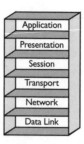

What does this mean to you right now? Not much. But as we learn about various protocols, we will see that they operate at different layers to accomplish different goals. Keep in mind that these layers are not actual protocols; rather, each layer is a logical grouping of the protocols that operate together to accomplish similar goals. Each of these protocols will have functions that, for the most part, are specific to the layer in question.

Layers Are Logical Points of Separation

A protocol that operates at the network layer is concerned with making sure that the data gets from one network to the next. It isn't concerned with what's in the data, or with how it looks to the user, just with getting it from one place to another. By the same token, protocols that operate at the application layer are concerned with making sure that the data that is being sent from one machine to another is in a format that the user can understand.

Why All the Complexity?

There are different layers so that no one entity has to be responsible for writing all of the code needed to make networking work. 3Com is, among other things, a network interface card (NIC) vendor. When 3Com makes a NIC, it also writes drivers for that NIC. Those drivers are pieces of software that operate at the data link layer. They control how the NIC communicates with other NICS.

The people at 3Com are not concerned with writing an application that allows users to transfer files, because that is not what they do best. Instead, they provide the NIC and corresponding protocols that allow two computers to talk to each other, and they leave it up to another vendor to write applications that make use of the networking connectivity that they provide.

Operational Essentials of TCP/IP

Now that we've defined what a protocol is, and we have the OSI reference model to use as a guide, let us turn our attention to how TCP/IP works.

In the same way that people have unique phone numbers, each TCP/IP host has a unique identification number. A unique 32-bit binary number identifies each TCP/IP host. Binary numbers are actually quite simple. In a binary system, you have only two choices in numbers: 0 or 1. That is why computers are referred to as binary machines, because at their base level all they do is count 1's and 0's. How does all that apply to TCP/IP? All TCP/IP address are really binary numbers. Here is an example of an IP address that I am sure a lot of you will recognize:

11001100100011111001000100101011

Even if you don't recognize it, I am sure that your computer would. That's one of the addresses that Yahoo.com uses. The reason you don't recognize it is that you do not have to know the binary addresses of all the sites you visit, because the TCP/IP stack takes care of it for you.

It's All Binary These Days

Let's examine that address in more detail. It is actually composed of four different sections, called octets, that help identify what type of address it is. In its octet binary form it appears as

11001100.01000111.11001000.01001011

Notice that each octet has 8 bits, and each bit is either a 0 or a 1. But wait, there's more. So that you and I don't go crazy trying to read binary all day long, we convert all of these numbers into decimal for easier reading.

Converting Binary to Decimal

11001100.01000111.11001000.01001011 is 204.71.200.74. How did I get to that answer? Actually, if you do a little math, it's very easy. Since each octet is comprised of 8 bits, each bit represents an exponential increase of 2, as in $2^0\,2^1,2^2,2^3,2^4,2^5,2^6,2^7$, and so on.

For example, 00000001 in binary is equal to 1 in decimal; 00000010 in binary is equal to 2 in decimal; and so on. Here it is for each bit:

```
00000001 = 1
00000010 = 2
00000100 = 4
00001000 = 8
00010000 = 16
00100000 = 32
01000000 = 64
10000000 = 128
```

With this in mind, let's go back to the first octet of Yahoo.com's number. 11001100 equals 204 because, taken together, the bits add up to 204:

```
10000000 = 128
01000000 = 64
00001000 = 8
00000100 = 4
128+64+8+4 = 204
```

Now that we know how to read binary numbers, let's turn our attention to how all TCP/IP addresses are divided.

Network vs. Host

All TCP/IP addresses are divided into two portions: a network portion and a host portion. The *network* portion identifies what network that particular device is on. The *host* portion identifies that host uniquely on that network. In other words, no two hosts on the same network can have the same host number, but two hosts on separate networks can have the same host number. How do you know who is on what network? That is where the network portion of the TCP/IP address comes in.

Networks, Networks, and More Networks

There are three primary types of networks (actually there are five types, but only three are available to identify single hosts): Class A, Class B, and Class C (shown in Figure 9-4).

CLASS A   Class A networks are identified by the fact that the first octet is used for network addressing, and the last three octets are used to identify the host. In decimal form, all IP addresses from 1 to 127.*x.x.x* are Class A networks. This means that a computer with an address of **100**.1.1.2 is different from a machine with and address of **101**.1.1.2. Both of them have the same host portion (in this case the last three octets of the address), but since they have a different network address, 100 to 101, they are on different networks.

There can be up to 126 Class A networks attached to the Internet, each having up to 16,777,216 hosts, because that is how many possible combinations there are with the first octet being used to identify the network and the final three used to uniquely identify hosts.

CLASS B   Class B networks are identified by the fact that the first two octets are used for network addressing, and the last two octets are used to identify the host. In decimal form, all IP addresses from 128 to 192.*x.x* are Class B networks. That means that a computer with an address of **170**.1.1.2

FIGURE 9-4

The three classes of networks

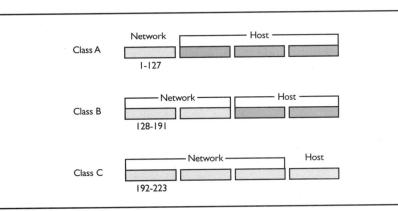

is different from a machine with an address of **170.2.1.2**. Both of them have the same host portion (in this case, the last two octets of the address), but since they have a different network address, 170.1 to 170.2, they are on different networks. There are 16,384 possible Class B networks on the Internet, with each network having up 65,534 hosts.

CLASS C Class C networks are identified by the fact that the first three octets are used for network addressing, and the last octet is used to identify the host. In decimal form, all IP addresses from 193 to 223.*x* are Class C networks. That means that a computer with an address of **207.158.63.1** is different from a machine with an address of **207.158.64.1**. Both of them have the same host portion (in this case, the last octet of the address), but since they have a different network address **207.158.63** to **207.158.64**, they are on different networks. There are 2,097,152 possible Class C networks on the Internet, with each network having up to 255 hosts.

Putting It in Action

Figure 9-5 shows a simple network setup. If I have a machine with an IP address of 200.0.0.2, no other machine can have that particular IP address on that network. If I want to connect that network with other networks, then I have to make sure that both networks are adhering to the same standards.

For example, if you want to connect to the Internet, you have to first make sure that the IP addresses that you are using are valid for use on the Internet. (The way that you do this is to register your IP address with the Internic at http://www.internic.net.)

If I have one machine with an IP address of 200.0.0.2 and another machine with the address 200.0.0.3, and they are both on the same

FIGURE 9-5

A simple network setup

200.0.0.2   200.0.0.3

segment, they can communicate back and forth to each other because of the protocols that are in operation at the network layer of the OSI reference model. In this case, the IP protocol will put the IP address of the machine to which it is sending the packet in the header of the packet it is sending.

The header portion of the packet is the portion where administrative information is stored. It is not the actual data that the user is sending, but rather it is the information that the computers need to know in order to determine where the data packet should go.

In this example, the computer with IP address of 200.0.03 will receive the packet and examine the address and say, "Oh this IP datagram is destined for me. I'm going to take it and I'm going to process the information contained in it." All other machines on that IP network would read the first portion of that IP address and say, "Oh this isn't for me. I'm going to drop the packet." That's how IP hosts communicate with each other if they are on the same segment.

What About Routing?

But what if they're not on the same segment? That's the next concept we need to learn about.

Routing Between Networks

If you want to communicate, to pass packets between an IP host on one network and an IP host on another network, you have to have a router between them. A router is a device that has two or more network interfaces in it; each network interface is connected to a different network. Its sole job is to take packets from one network and, if they meet certain criteria, to pass them on to the other network. Routers operate at the network layer of the OSI reference model.

In TCP/IP networks, routers have valid IP addresses for each segment that they connect to. Let's add a router to our example and see how things work now.

If I have a host on a network segment, and it wants to talk to another host on the same segment, no router has to get involved with that transaction because those two machines are communicating over the same segment. But if the two machines are not on the same segment, then they don't have way of knowing about each other. Enter the router. As already explained, a router's sole purpose is take all packets that it receives, to examine them, and to decide on the basis of the network address whether or not to forward them to the other network.

In the example in the previous section, if the machine with IP address of 200.0.0.2 sent
a packet addressed to 200.1.0.2, the router would do the following things:

1. It would look at the destination network IP address contained in the packet's header.

2. Based on the address—in this case, 200.1.0—it would copy it over to its other NIC to transmit to the appropriate network—again, in this case, 200.1.0.

All of this activity would be happening at the network layer of the OSI reference model. The TCP/IP involved would be IP.

exam
ⓦatch

Understand how TCP networks handle routing and be able to view network layouts and label the various components that make up the network.

Determining Address Validity (Subnet Masks)

There is one final piece of the puzzle that we haven't covered yet. That piece is subnet masks. In practice, subnet masks are used to subdivide networks so that administrators can utilize the addresses in a given network more efficiently. Let's see how this works.

Consider the IP address 10.5.0.1. Based on what we learned earlier, that is a Class A network. We know that because any addresses that begin with numbers from 1 to 127 are classified as Class A networks. Because it is a Class A network, I need to identify the first octet as the network portion of the address. To do that, I give it a default subnet mask.

What Is a Subnet Mask?

A *subnet mask* is a binary number that gets associated with the TCP/IP address. This is required with the TCP/IP. Essentially, a subnet mask tells the computer which portions of the IP address to use to identify the network, and which portions to use to identify the host. Based on our example above, the default subnet mask for that address would be

255.0.0.0

How Does It Work?

The TCP/IP compares the IP address with the network mask through an operation known as a logical AND. This mathematical operation compares the bits of both the IP address and the subnet mask with the portion of the subnet mask that has ones in it. If both are identified as 1's, then TCP/IP knows that it is part of the network address.

10.5.0.1 in binary equals 00001010.00000101.00000000.00000001
255.0.0.0 in binary equals 11111111.00000000.00000000.00000000

The first octet of the subnet mask is concerned with the network portion of the address, and the other three identify the host portion. We can see that, because the subnet mask has 1's in the first octet, thereby identifying it as network specific.

But what if you want to take one network address (10.*x.x.x*) and use it for multiple networks? Is that possible? Why would you want to do it? The answers to those questions are the focus of the next section.

Subnetting Networks

Subnetting networks is a practice that is widely used on TCP/IP networks. Consider our earlier example. If we have a network of 10.0.0.0 assigned to us, then that means that we have a possible 16,777,216 hosts, and only one network. More than likely you won't be needing all of those addresses. But what if you "borrowed" portions of the host id to create subnetworks inside your big network? You would lose some of your 16 million hosts, but you would gain the flexibility of having multiple networks. How does it work?

First, you will extend the default subnet mask. In this example, let's extend it by 8 bits or one octet. Our subnet mask now reads 255.255.0.0. Applied to our original IP address of 10.5.0.1, we now find the following:

10.5.0.1 in binary equals 00001010.00000101.00000000.00000001
255.255.0.0 in binary equals 11111111.11111111.00000000.00000000

This means that this host is on subnet 10.5 as opposed to being on network 10 with a host of 5.0.1. In this manner we could have all sorts of networks: 10.1, 10.2, 10.3 . . . 10.254.

We would do this to allow multiple networks to exist within one network address space.

Public vs. Private IP Addresses

If you want to connect to the Internet, you have to get a publicly registered IP address. This can be done by contacting the Internic at http://www.internic.net. When you register your IP address, you are telling the whole Internet, "Hey, if you want to contact me I am at IP address such

FROM THE CLASSROOM

Increase the Speed of Your Network

You can increase the speed of your network by dividing segments that communicate often into their own subnet. This can be most beneficial in an environment used for applications in which you have several processes split up among several machines. For example, say you have a Web application that is multitiered, in that you have one machine running a database, another that serves files for the Web server, an SMTP mail server, an application or logic server for the Web, and a Web farm. All these servers frequently pass information back and forth to each other and rarely communicate with the rest of your network.

For an environment like this you could place all of these servers into their own subnet. By minimizing the amount of machines on the subnet, this allows the machines to pass packets to each more efficiently by not having to pass information over the rest of the local area network or LAN, i.e., routers, gateways, bridges, and the like. For further optimization, hard code the individual machines' IP addresses and place an entry in each machine's *hosts* file for all the machines on this small subnet.

—*Patrick J. Santry,*
i-Net+, MCT, MCSD, MCP+SB

and so." If someone wants to send you something, all they need is your IP address. That is why you need a registered IP address; it guarantees to you that it will be unique on the Internet.

A private IP address is an address that is not legal out on the Internet. It is an address that you create and assign internally within your organization to allow computers to communicate with each other over IP without using registered addresses.

What's the difference between the two? From a purely technical standpoint there is no difference. That is, they use the same technologies to work. The difference is one of a more political nature. A publicly registered IP address is kept in the router tables of the routers that connect the Internet together. The question that then comes up is, if Internet connectivity is desired (which in most cases it is), then why would you ever want to use a private IP addressing scheme? The answer is threefold:

- It costs your company more money to register more IP addresses.

- It increases your security risks by exposing more hosts to the Internet.

- You can use technologies such as proxy services or NAT (Network Address Translation) or a protocol gateway to effectively use one IP address for your whole company.

You should now have a good understanding of how addressing works in a TCP/IP network. Addressing is the most important aspect of TCP/IP that a network engineer needs to know. Addressing in a TCP/IP network is handled by the IP (Internet Protocol) of the TCP/IP stack. Once the addressing has been taken care of, it then becomes the responsibility of the TCP (Transmission Control Protocol) to make sure that the proper process running on the destination machine gets the data. Now that we understand how TCP/IP gets from point A to point B, let's learn about some more protocols that allow us to connect networks together.

The Purpose of Remote Access Protocols

Remote Access Protocols allow you to access all of the resources on your network as if you were directly connected to it. For example, if you were traveling and needed to access your corporate data that was on a server back at your home office, you would use Remote Access Protocols to access that data. In this section, we are going to learn about the different Remote Access Protocols that we can use.

SLIP

SLIP (Serial Line Internet Protocol) is an older protocol that is not widely used anymore in networking. SLIP allows you to establish a dial-up connection with a host computer over the Plain Old Telephone System (POTS). SLIP operates at the data link layer of the OSI reference model. SLIP works by allowing you to use IP over a serial connection, in effect bringing the IP network to you. Its drawbacks are that you can only run IP and that it doesn't support compression. You can establish a SLIP connection between your host and the computer that you are dialing, and then you will get a valid IP address for that network.

PPP

PPP (Point-to-Point Protocol) is the primary protocol that most people use to connect to the Internet. PPP is the replacement for SLIP. PPP supports compression and encryption, and you can use it to connect to a variety of networks. If you connect to the Internet from home over a modem, chances are you are using PPP.

You use Point-to-Point Protocol when you establish a dial-up connection over your modem to connect to your ISP (Internet Service Provider). PPP operates at the data link layer of the OSI reference model. Once your modem has negotiated its connection with the host computer (the one that you are dialing), PPP takes over and establishes the IP connection with the server you dialed. In doing that, PPP will support data compression, which will allow faster access; it will support encryption (for security), and you can also use PPP as the foundation for establishing a VPN (Virtual Private Network) using the next protocol we will learn about: PPTP.

PPTP

PPTP is an enhancement of the PPP protocol. The T stands for Tunneling. PPTP allows you to send information over a public network (the Internet) securely. With this protocol, you establish a PPP connection over your phone line, and then you establish another PPP connection over that connection and create the VPN. The VPN is an encrypted conversation that only the computer that initiates the connection and the destination computer can participate in.

Point-to-Point/Multipoint

The term *point-to-point* refers to two computers that have a direct connection with each other. An example of this is your computer dialing into an ISP. You are setting up a point-to-point connection between those two devices.

Multipoint technology allows you to have multiple connections between two computers. This is used to ensure fault tolerant communications so that if one link goes down, you have another link ready to conduct the transaction.

These are examples of the Remote Access Protocols that are used in the TCP/IP suite. Next we will learn about the different services that are offered over all of the protocols that we have just discussed.

CERTIFICATION OBJECTIVE 9.03

Application of Various Protocols or Services

Now that we have a good understanding of how the TCP/IP suite gets information from one point to another, let's learn about the protocols that make use of that information. In this section, I am going to list several different types of protocols that are in the TCP/IP suite and define what they do.

Typically, these protocols work by monitoring a given port for a request from a client. A port is an opening that a protocol monitors for activity, which would be a request made from a client. For example, with HTTP, the client or browser makes a request using the HTTP command GET and directs this request to the default TCP port of 80. The Web server monitors this port and replies to the client in the appropriate manner in order to handle the request.

Table 9-1 lists the common protocols and the default ports used for each of these protocols.

POP3

POP3 (Post Office Protocol 3, or Point of Presence Protocol 3) is a remote access protocol that allows you to receive e-mail from any server on the Internet (with which you have an account) from any computer connected to the Internet. The only requirements that you have to meet is that your computer has a POP3-compatible e-mail reader (Outlook, Netscape, or Eudora, just to name a few) and that your e-mail server is configured to accept POP3 requests. POP3 is a protocol that operates at the application layer.

TABLE 9-1

Common Protocols and Their Default Ports

Protocol	Default Port Used
POP3	110
SMTP	25
Telnet	23
HTTP	80
HTTPS	443
FTP	21
LDAP	389
Gopher	70

SMTP

SMTP (Simple Mail Transfer Protocol) allows you to send mail from your e-mail client to your e-mail server. Your server then processes that message and sends it on its way to its destination e-mail server, where that server may deliver it to a client using the POP3 protocol. SMTP operates at the application layer of the OSI reference model.

As you can see, POP3 and SMTP work hand in hand in delivering and receiving mail. SMTP is the sending portion, and POP3 is the receiving portion.

LDAP

LDAP (Lightweight Directory Access Protocol) is a protocol for setting up a directory for networks. A directory is a listing of information, much like a telephone book that can be queried for information. Microsoft's Active Directory, Novell's NDS, and Netscape's Directory are all LDAP-compliant directories. LDAP operates at the application layer.

FTP

FTP (File Transfer Protocol) is a protocol that operates at the application layer, allowing you to send files from one machine to another over a TCP/IP network. Its typical usage today is from within a browser when you want to download a file from a Web site.

Telnet

Telnet is a utility that operates at the application layer of the OSI reference model. Telnet allows a remote user to access a server that is running the Telnet service as if that user were sitting at that computer. In Figure 9-6, I am Telnetted into a Cisco Router.

Gopher

Gopher is a protocol or an application that was formerly widely used on the Internet. It is not used that widely anymore due to the overwhelming

Establishing a Telnet
session with a Cisco router

```
Telnet - 207.158.84.60                                              _ □ ×
Connect  Edit  Terminal  Help
Cisco Internetwork Operating System Software
IOS (tm) 3000 Software (CPA25-CG-L), Version 11.0(4), RELEASE SOFTWARE (fc1)
Copyright (c) 1986-1995 by cisco Systems, Inc.
Compiled Mon 18-Dec-95 19:15 by alanyu
Image text-base: 0x0301F254, data-base: 0x00001000

ROM: System Bootstrap, Version 5.2(5), RELEASE SOFTWARE
ROM: 3000 Bootstrap Software (IGS-RXBOOT), Version 10.2(5), RELEASE SOFTWARE (fc
1)

Dallas uptime is 12 weeks, 4 days, 13 hours, 19 minutes
System restarted by power-on
System image file is "flash:cpa25-cg-1.110-4", booted via flash

cisco 2500 (68030) processor (revision L) with 2044K/2048K bytes of memory.
Processor board ID 01888628, with hardware revision 00000000
Bridging software.
SuperLAT software copyright 1990 by Meridian Technology Corp).
TN3270 Emulation software (copyright 1994 by TGU Inc).
X.25 software, Version 2.0, NET2, BFE and GOSIP compliant.
1 Ethernet/IEEE 802.3 interface.
2 Serial network interfaces.
32K bytes of non-volatile configuration memory.
4096K bytes of processor board System flash (Read ONLY)
 --More-- █
```

popularity of the World Wide Web. Gopher allows you to search databases
across the Internet. It is an application layer protocol.

DNS

The DNS (Domain Name Server) system is used so that we don't have to
keep track of all of the decimal numbers that represent computers. Think
back to our discussion on how we converted binary to decimal. Remember
how you marveled at how easy that made everything? Well, DNS makes it
even easier by setting up a system of servers that keeps track of all of those
IP addresses and maps them to names. So when you and I type
http:\\www.yahoo.com into our browser, our computer sends a request to
one of these DNSs and says, "Hey what IP address belongs to this name?"
The server replies with the correct IP address, and your computer then
sends the data to the destination. DNS is an application layer protocol.

DHCP

DHCP (Dynamic Host Configuration Protocol) is used to automate the assignment of TCP/IP addresses, as well as other crucial bits of information. DHCP is comprised of a server portion and a client portion. Here is how it works: The client sends out a request for any DHCP servers. One or more answer, saying that they are available. The client then sends out another request, but this time to only one of the DHCP servers that replied, asking for an IP address. The DHCP server looks in its records, chooses an IP address, as well as any other information the administrator wants it to send, and sends it to the DHCP client. In this manner, an administrator can pass out IP addresses automatically to the entire network. As you can see, it is a very efficient way of setting up a TCP/IP network. DHCP is an application layer protocol.

on the **Job**

In a large network environment, using DHCP is the right way to manage your IP address assignment. DHCP allows you to connect clients to the network and not have to worry about maintaining a list of IP addresses that are available for the new client to use. Using DHCP, the client will just make a request to your DHCP server for an IP address, and then the DHCP server will provide an IP address that is not currently in use. This avoids any IP conflicts that can occur when two machines have the same IP address. IP conflicts can cause clients not to be able to participate in the network and other problems on your network. DHCP is a great way to make your network easier to manage, and it lessens the likelihood of an IP conflict on your network.

HTTP and HTML

HTTP (HyperText Transfer Protocol) is an application layer protocol that allows client machines running browsers to retrieve HyperText Markup Language documents that reside on HTTP (Web) servers. HTTP handles the operation of the client making a request to the server and the server responding to the request.

Once the client browser receives a response from the Web server, the Web server usually responds by sending HTML (HyperText Markup Language). HTML is what the browser translates to generate the Web page that you finally see in the browser.

These are examples of utilities and services that you can use in TCP/IP networks. Next, we will turn our attention to tools that we can use to troubleshoot problems that can affect TCP/IP networks.

exam
ⓦatch

Understand the different protocols and the clients that support them.

CERTIFICATION OBJECTIVE 9.04

Using Diagnostic Tools to Troubleshoot TCP/IP and Remote Access Protocols

The next area that we need to focus our attention on is identifying and understanding the diagnostic tools that you have as a network professional for identifying and resolving TCP/IP-related problems.

Ping Your Problems Away

The first tool that we have at our disposal is a tool called PING (see Figure 9-7). PING is a utility that operates at the IP layer, sending ICMP (Internet Control Message Protocol) packets from one host to another to determine whether it is up. An ICMP packet is sent from one machine to another, and if the other machine is up, it will respond by sending the other packet back to the first sending machine and that way the machine that sent the original packet knows that the other machine is up.

For example, if I am sitting at a machine with an IP address of 192.168.1.1 and I want to know if another machine is up and running, I would do the following:

1. Go out to a DOS prompt.

2. Type **ping** and the IP address of the host I am interested in.

FIGURE 9-7

Running a ping to contact a
domain name

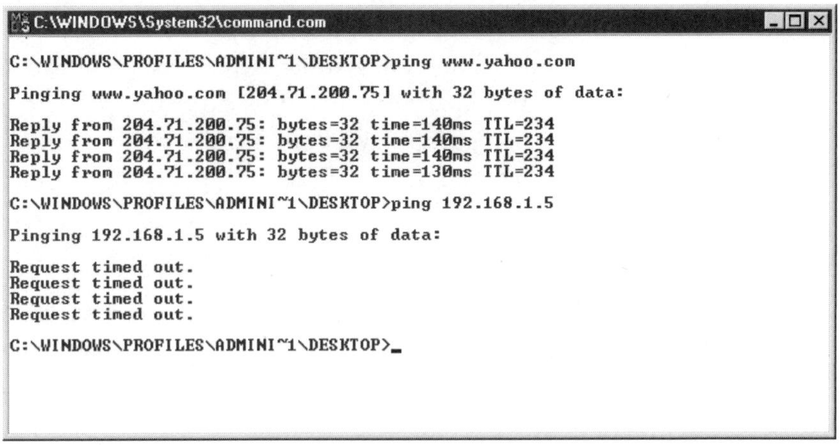

```
C:\WINDOWS\System32\command.com                                    _ □ ×

C:\WINDOWS\PROFILES\ADMINI~1\DESKTOP>ping www.yahoo.com

Pinging www.yahoo.com [204.71.200.75] with 32 bytes of data:

Reply from 204.71.200.75: bytes=32 time=140ms TTL=234
Reply from 204.71.200.75: bytes=32 time=140ms TTL=234
Reply from 204.71.200.75: bytes=32 time=140ms TTL=234
Reply from 204.71.200.75: bytes=32 time=130ms TTL=234

C:\WINDOWS\PROFILES\ADMINI~1\DESKTOP>ping 192.168.1.5

Pinging 192.168.1.5 with 32 bytes of data:

Request timed out.
Request timed out.
Request timed out.
Request timed out.

C:\WINDOWS\PROFILES\ADMINI~1\DESKTOP>_
```

Then, depending on whether or not that host was up and working, I
would either get the response "ping successful" or the response "destination
host not found."

If I get the response "destination host not found," that doesn't necessarily
mean that that machine is not up and active. It could also mean that one or
more routers between the two machines were not functional.

You can see an example of running a ping in Figure 9-7, in which we
ping www.yahoo.com to see whether it is reachable from our local machine.

Trace Route

Trace route is a utility that we can use to find a route that is being used by
the Internet protocol to pass packets between two machines. Here is how
you use it:

At the DOS prompt of our first machine, type **TRACERT**, press the
spacebar, and then type the IP address of the machine you want to know
about. When we do that and press ENTER, the Trace route packets will go
back and forth between machine A and machine B and let us know what
routers it had to cross.

The Trace route utility will go out and show us the routers that the
packets had to travel to get from one computer to another. If there were no

routers that they had to travel over, the Trace route will come back very quickly. If there are multiple routers that they had to go over, then it will show you in reverse order each router that it had to go through to get to the destination. It will do this for up to thirty routers.

In Figure 9-8, we run a Trace route to see the route our IP packets take to get from our client machine to the final destination of www.yahoo.com.

WinIPCFG/IPConfig

Another utility that we have at our disposal is called WinIPCFG. In the NT environment this utility is called IPConfig (Figure 9-9). WinIPCFG (pronounced Win IP Config) returns to you the IP configuration information for that workstation. The information that it will return is the workstation's IP address, subnet mask, DNS servers, and gateway. WinIPCFG is a very good troubleshooting tool that you can use to determine whether or not TCP/IP is loaded and working correctly on that particular machine.

ARP

ARP stands for Address Resolution Protocol. With the ARP utility, you can find out the MAC (Media Access Control) addresses of all of the machines

---

FIGURE 9-8

Running a trace route to trace the route of IP packets

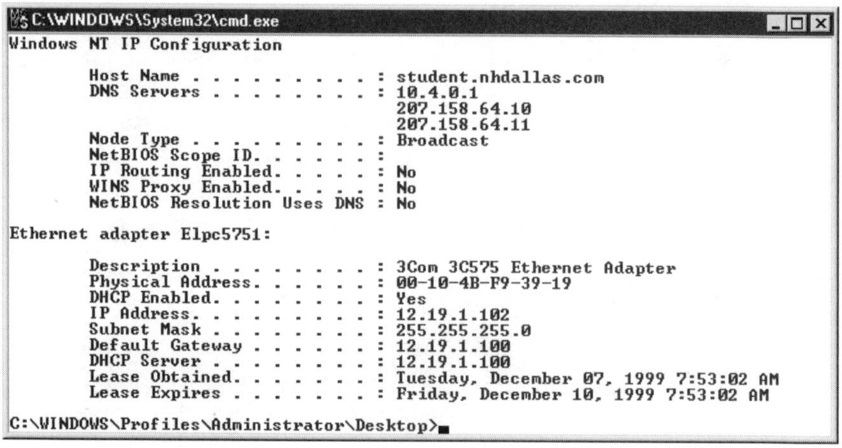

```
C:\WINDOWS\System32\cmd.exe                                          _ □ ×
Windows NT IP Configuration

        Host Name . . . . . . . . . : student.nhdallas.com
        DNS Servers . . . . . . . . : 10.4.0.1
                                      207.158.64.10
                                      207.158.64.11
        Node Type . . . . . . . . . : Broadcast
        NetBIOS Scope ID. . . . . . :
        IP Routing Enabled. . . . . : No
        WINS Proxy Enabled. . . . . : No
        NetBIOS Resolution Uses DNS : No

Ethernet adapter Elpc5751:

        Description . . . . . . . . : 3Com 3C575 Ethernet Adapter
        Physical Address. . . . . . : 00-10-4B-F9-39-19
        DHCP Enabled. . . . . . . . : Yes
        IP Address. . . . . . . . . : 12.19.1.102
        Subnet Mask . . . . . . . . : 255.255.255.0
        Default Gateway . . . . . . : 12.19.1.100
        DHCP Server . . . . . . . . : 12.19.1.100
        Lease Obtained. . . . . . . : Tuesday, December 07, 1999 7:53:02 AM
        Lease Expires . . . . . . . : Friday, December 10, 1999 7:53:02 AM

C:\WINDOWS\Profiles\Administrator\Desktop>_
```

IPConfig

```
C:\WINDOWS\System32\cmd.exe                                           _ □ X
Windows NT IP Configuration

        Host Name . . . . . . . . . : student.nhdallas.com
        DNS Servers . . . . . . . : 10.4.0.1
                                    207.158.64.10
                                    207.158.64.11
        Node Type . . . . . . . : Broadcast
        NetBIOS Scope ID. . . . . :
        IP Routing Enabled. . . . . : No
        WINS Proxy Enabled. . . . . : No
        NetBIOS Resolution Uses DNS : No

Ethernet adapter Elpc5751:

        Description . . . . . . . : 3Com 3C575 Ethernet Adapter
        Physical Address. . . . . : 00-10-4B-F9-39-19
        DHCP Enabled. . . . . . . : Yes
        IP Address. . . . . . . . : 12.19.1.102
        Subnet Mask . . . . . . . : 255.255.255.0
        Default Gateway . . . . . : 12.19.1.100
        DHCP Server . . . . . . . : 12.19.1.100
        Lease Obtained. . . . . . : Tuesday, December 07, 1999 7:53:02 AM
        Lease Expires . . . . . . : Friday, December 10, 1999 7:53:02 AM

C:\WINDOWS\Profiles\Administrator\Desktop>■
```

that your computer knows about. The MAC address is the address assigned to the NIC by its vendor. Using ARP, you can see what MAC addresses have what IP addresses. In other words, you would be able to isolate what machine is claiming what IP address.

In Figure 9-10, we are issuing the ARP command with the parameter of –a. Running this command will display all network adapters on the machine and

Results of running the ARP command on a Windows client

```
C:\WINDOWS\System32\command.com                                       _ □ X
C:\WINDOWS\PROFILES\ADMINI~1\DESKTOP>arp –a

Interface: 192.168.1.3 on Interface 2
  Internet Address      Physical Address      Type
  192.168.1.1           00-c0-f0-0d-fc-35     dynamic

C:\WINDOWS\PROFILES\ADMINI~1\DESKTOP>
```

their corresponding IP, MAC addresses, and the type of IP address assignment to the card—either dynamic using DHCP, or statically assigned.

Netstat

The final utility that we are going to discuss is called Netstat. Netstat stands for Network Status. You can use this utility to find out all sorts of information about TCP/IP on your machine. For example, let's say that you need to see how many TCP/IP packets your computer had processed. To do this, you go to a DOS prompt, and type **Netstat –e**. As in Figure 9-11, you'll see the results of running Netstat on a Windows client, the total bytes that were sent and received, and detailed information on the bytes.

All of the utilities that we have talked about have been command-line utilities. That is, you enter their names at the command line, and the utility runs and gives you the information. There is another type of diagnostic tool that is very beneficial in figuring out network problems. That tool is called a network analyzer, and it will be the last tool that we discuss in this chapter.

on the **Job**

Knowing how to use these network tools to diagnose IP connectivity problems is vital. These software tools will allow you to pinpoint where your connection problems originate, and using these tools should always be your first step in diagnosing a problem.

FIGURE 9-11

Results of running Netstat to find packet information

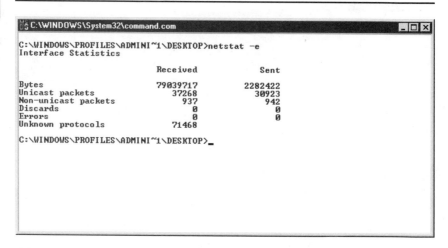

```
C:\WINDOWS\System32\command.com                                    _ □ X

C:\WINDOWS\PROFILES\ADMINI~1\DESKTOP>netstat -e
Interface Statistics

                            Received            Sent

Bytes                       79039717         2282422
Unicast packets                37268           30923
Non-unicast packets              937             942
Discards                           0               0
Errors                             0               0
Unknown protocols              71468

C:\WINDOWS\PROFILES\ADMINI~1\DESKTOP>_
```

Network Analyzers

Network analyzers, also called *sniffers*, are tools that look at all of the packets that are out on the network and show you all sorts of information about them. They can be TCP/IP packets, Apple Talk packets, or IPX/SPX packets, among others. By using this utility, you can capture packets that are out on the wire and see where they came from, where they are going, and what data they have in them. From a network troubleshooting perspective, having some type of network analyzer is essential to being able to properly diagnose problems when they occur on a network.

Now that you have a better idea of all of the troubleshooting utilities that you can use, here are some possible scenario questions and their answers:

QUESTIONS AND ANSWERS	
What utility should you use to see whether a another IP host is up?	PING
You need to configure a router remotely; what utility is best suited for this?	Telnet
Your network has slowed down to a crawl; how should you determine what happened?	Use a packet analyzer to see what is happening on the network.

CERTIFICATION SUMMARY

What we learned in this chapter was that in order for networks to work, we need an agreed-upon set of rules to follow. Those rules define how machines find out about each other, how they send information from one to another, how they determine how to "talk" to each other, and so on. These rules are called *protocols*.

The protocol suite that connects the Internet is called the TCP/IP suite. TCP/IP became the protocol of choice because it is nonproprietary and very fault tolerant. It is made up of hundreds of different protocols that work together to allow computers to communicate. Each protocol operates a different layer of the OSI reference model, doing a specific task. The OSI reference model is made up of seven layers. The layers are physical, data link, network, transport, session, presentation, and application.

The reason we have the OSI reference model is so that we have a common frame of reference for a discussion of networking. Some of those protocols control how the computer interfaces with the user, while other protocols control how the computer interfaces with the NIC.

We learned that in the TCP/IP suite machines are identified by their IP address combined with their subnet mask. Both of these items are 32-bit binary numbers that are used by computers to identify networks and computers. We learned how to convert those numbers into decimal notation.

There are three main types of addresses: Class A, Class B, and Class C. Class A networks are few in number, but large in size. There are more Class B networks than Class A, although each Class B network has fewer hosts than each Class A network. Class C networks are more numerous than Class A and Class B, but Class C networks have fewer hosts than the other two.

We explored some of the many different protocols that are in use on the Internet: LDAP, Telnet, PPP, and PPTP. We learned that each protocol is responsible for a specific task and that working together, they make networks work.

Finally, we also learned about some of the different diagnostic tools that we could use to troubleshoot the different protocols. They include PING, Trace route, WinIPCFG, and network analyzers.

With this information, you should have a good understanding of how TCP/IP works and what tools you can use to troubleshoot it.

 # TWO-MINUTE DRILL

❑ TCP/IP came into existence in the late 1960s and early 1970s as a result of research conducted by the Department of Defense Advanced Research Project Agency (ARPA).

❑ The main strength of the TCP/IP is that it allows the devices on a network to communicate with each other and lets them know whether they are up and functioning and whom they can talk to.

❑ The protocol is concerned with the actual data: Is it all there? Is any of it corrupted? Does any of it need to be resent ? And finally, the protocol is concerned with whether the data has made it to the user in a format that the user can understand.

❑ The reason TCP/IP has become the dominant protocol is twofold: It's not proprietary, and it's very fault tolerant.

❑ A protocol is the set of rules that governs how devices on a network communicate with each other.

❑ The OSI reference model is exactly what it sounds like: a networking model that we can reference so that we can see how the different protocols work. You need to be aware of the OSI reference model because every IT professional can go back to this reference point when he or she discusses disparate protocols, in order to understand how each one works.

❑ In the same way that people have unique phone numbers, each TCP/IP host has a unique identification number. A unique 32-bit binary number identifies each TCP/IP host.

❑ All TCP/IP addresses are divided into two portions: a network portion and a host portion. The network portion identifies what network that particular device is on. The host portion identifies that host uniquely on that network.

❑ There are three primary types of networks (actually there are five types, but only three are available to identify single hosts): Class A, Class B, and Class C.

❑ A subnet mask is a binary number that gets associated with the TCP/IP address.

❑ The TCP/IP compares the IP address with the network mask through an operation known as a logical AND. This mathematical operation compares the bits of both the IP address and the subnet mask with the portion of the subnet mask that has ones in it. If both are identified as 1's, TCP/IP then knows that it is part of the network address.

❑ If you want to connect to the Internet you have to get a publicly registered IP address. This can be done by contacting the Internic at http://www.internic.net. When you register your IP address, you are telling the whole Internet, "Hey, if you want to contact me I am at IP address such and so." If someone wants to send you something, all they need is your IP address. That is why you need a registered IP address: it guarantees to you that it will be unique on the Internet.

❑ Remote Access protocols allow you to access all of the resources on your network as if you were directly connected to it.

❑ There are some diagnostic tools that you have as a network professional for identifying and resolving TCP/IP-related problems: PING, Trace route, WinIPCFG/IPConfig, ARP, Netstat.

❑ Network analyzers, also called sniffers, are tools that look at all of the packets that are out on the network and show you all sorts of information about them.

SELF TEST

1. TCIP was developed

   A. As a response to Apple Talk

   B. To move datagrams across the network independent of each other

   C. In the 1980s

   D. By IBM

2. The OSI reference model is used to

   A. Deliver packets from one network to another.

   B. Compare MAC addresses.

   C. Create a point of comparison for discussion of different protocols.

   D. Troubleshoot WinIPCFG.

3. In order for a host to contact another host on the same segment, what information needs to be entered?

   A. IP address and subnet mask

   B. DNS name, IP address, and subnet mask

   C. IP address, subnet mask, and router

   D. IP address, Win address, and subnet mask

4. DNS was developed to

   A. Match MAC addresses with IP addresses.

   B. Maintain names of routers across the Internet.

   C. Provide IP address to host name resolution.

   D. All of the above.

5. If you have an IP address of 189.1.0.0 and a subnet mask of 255.0.0.0, which of the following is correct?

   A. You are subnetted for a Class C address.

   B. You are subnetted for a Class A address.

   C. You are subnetted for a Class B address.

   D. That is an invalid address assignment.

6. FTP stands for

   A. Filter Time out Protocol

   B. File Transfer Protocol

   C. Finite Transmission Protocol

   D. None of the above

7. Given an IP address of 207.158.4.200 and a subnet mask of 255.255.255.0, how many octets of the IP address are used to define the host?

   A. One

   B. Two

   C. Three

   D. Four

8. DHCP can be configured to

   A. Automatically assign IP addresses to workstations.

   B. Automatically assign subnet mask information to the workstations.

C. Automatically assign DNS server information to the workstations.

D. All of the above.

9. A workstation can ping its own IP address and IP addresses of other hosts on the same segment as itself, but it cannot ping addresses out on the Internet. No other workstations are affected. What is the most likely cause of the problem?

A. The subnet mask is incorrect.

B. Its IP address is incorrect.

C. Its router address is incorrect.

D. WINS has not been enabled.

10. You are troubleshooting a Windows 98 workstation over the phone. The user has called in and said that she has no Internet access. You have verified that others on that segment and throughout the enterprise have Internet access. What utility should you have the user execute to determine what the problem is?

A. Windows Explorer

B. IP Config/All

C. Netstat

D. WinIPCFG

11. You are at a Windows 98 machine and you go to a DOS prompt. You type in **arp –a** and press ENTER. What information does it tell you?

A. Your IP configuration

B. The IP addresses of all the routers that you have contacted

C. The IP addresses and MAC addresses of all hosts you have contacted on your segment

D. None of the above

12. What protocol is used to deliver Web pages from a Web server to a browser?

A. IP

B. DNS

C. HTML

D. HTTP

13. SMTP and POP are two protocols that work together to allow you to

A. Browse the World Wide Web.

B. Send files using FTP.

C. Communicate using e-mail.

D. Read newsgroups.

14. DNSs are needed

A. So that you don't have to keep track of all the routers that connect you to the Internet

B. To make e-commerce more secure

C. To allow you to have to remember only host names and not IP addresses

D. To allow you to send e-mail

15. You are trying to ping an IP address that you can't get to. You get no response. You want to see what route your packets are taking. What command do you issue to see that information?

A. WinIPCFG

B. IPConfig

C. Trace route

D. Netstat

16. What two protocols work together to deliver Web pages from servers to clients?

A. SMTP and POP3

B. Telnet and PING

C. Trace route and WinIPCFG

D. HTTP and HTML

17. You suspect that an employee is using the company network for illegal purposes. What type of tool can you use to monitor everything that this employee is doing on the network?

A. Network analyzer

B. Trace route

C. DHCP

D. HTTP

18. One of your users is complaining that she can't access a Web site that is on the Internet. You verify that this is true. You then ping an Internet IP address, and it is successful. What is the most likely cause of the problem?

A. The user deleted the system directory.

B. The network is down.

C. DNS isn't working on that machine.

D. The NIC is bad.

19. The device that connects two or more networks is called

A. Hub

B. Switch

C. Router

D. NIC

20. You are trying to connect to the Internet from home over a modem. You dial the ISP's (Internet Service Provider's) number, and your modem makes a connection to its modem. You wait a few seconds, and then you are disconnected. What protocol do you need to troubleshoot in this scenario?

A. HTTP

B. PPP

C. DNS

D. POP3

SELF TEST ANSWERS

1. **B** is correct. The whole purpose behind TCP/IP is to make each datagram independent of all others.
   A and **B** are incorrect, because TCP/IP was not a commercial development; it was originally developed as a U.S. government initiative. **C** is incorrect, because development on TCP/IP began in the 1960s.

2. **C** is correct. The OSI reference model is designed to be an abstract point of reference for network engineers.
   A, **B**, and **D** are incorrect, because these issues relate directly to the operation of the network protocols, whereas the OSI reference is just an abstraction and not a functioning application.

3. **A** is correct. Since there is no route being crossed, the only essential information is the IP address and subnet mask.
   B is incorrect, because DNS names eventually get resolved to an IP address; therefore, it would just add an additional layer. **C** is incorrect, since the two machines are on the same subnet and, therefore, do not need packets to cross into other subnets to communicate. **D** is incorrect, because WINS is not necessary in a TCP/IP network; WINS performs names resolution.

4. **C** is correct. DNS is a collection of IP addresses to host name mappings.
   A is incorrect, because MAC to IP addresses are performed at a lower level than name resolution. **B** is incorrect, because domain name resolution is for all IP addresses on the network. **D** is incorrect because **A** and **B** are incorrect.

5. **D** is correct. 190.1.0.0 is a Class B address. 255.0.0.0 is the default Class A subnet mask. The subnet mask is illegal.
   A, **B**, and **C** are incorrect, because the example given is an invalid address.

6. **B** is correct. FTP is used to transfer files from one computer to another, thus the acronym stands for File Transfer Protocol.
   A and **C** are incorrect, because they are not the correct long form of the acronym. **D** is incorrect, because there is a correct answer in the answers provided.

7. **C** is correct, because the first three octets are being used to define the network in this typical Class C subnet mask.
A, **B**, and **D** are incorrect.

8. **D** is correct. One of the great things about DHCP is that it allows the administrator to configure the TCP/IP information needed by workstations automatically. **A**, **B**, and **C** are correct, but they are not the best answers to this question, because DHCP can perform all the tasks supplied by the answers.

9. **C** is correct. If other workstations are getting out, then you know the problem is isolated to this one machine. Because the machine can reach other hosts in its network and not machines outside the network, the most likely cause is an incorrect routing address. Routers enable one machine to access resources on other network subnets; if the router address is incorrect on the client, it will not be able to reach other hosts on other subnets, but will still be able to reach hosts in its own subnet.
A and **B** could be correct, but since the client can reach others in its network, the most likely cause would be an incorrect router address entry in the machine's IP configuration. **D** is incorrect, because WINS is not needed to ping IP addresses on a network.

10. **D** is correct. WinIPCFG gives you information about TCP/IP on that particular workstation.
A is incorrect, because Windows Explorer has no relationship with IP configuration on a machine—it is used for browsing files on a machine. **B** is incorrect, because IPConfig is not available on a Windows 98 machine. **C** is incorrect, because it does not provide you with complete IP configuration on a machine.

11. **C** is correct. ARP is the utility that checks to see which machines on your segment your machine knows about.
A is incorrect, because the utility used to perform an IP configuration check is WinIPCFG. **B** is incorrect, because the utility used for this would be a Trace route. **D** is incorrect, because there is a correct answer available in the pool of answers.

12. **D** is correct. HTTP (Hypertext Transfer Protocol) is used to send Web pages written in HTML (Hypertext Markup Language).
A is incorrect, because IP is not a transport protocol. **B** is incorrect, because DNS is used for name-to-IP resolution and not for transport. **C** is incorrect, because HTML

is the markup language used to construct Web documents and not a transport protocol for Web documents.

13. **C** is correct. SMTP sends mail out, and POP3 retrieves mail.
A is incorrect, because the protocol used for browsing the World Wide Web is HTTP. **B** answers itself in specifying the FTP protocol. **D** is incorrect, because NNTP is used for newsgroups.

14. **C** is correct. Domain Name Server is the mechanism whereby IP addresses are mapped to host names.
A is incorrect, because routing tables do not usually need name resolution as they are specified in your network settings and assigned via DHCP. **B** is incorrect, because DNS has nothing to do with security—it is just for name resolution. **D** is incorrect: DNS does make setting up e-mail clients easier by using the mail server's friendly name, but e-mail clients can still work by entering in the IP address of the mail server.

15. **C** is correct. Trace route shows you in reverse order the routers that your packet had to travel over to get to its destination.
A is incorrect, because WinIPCFG is used for finding out the IP configuration of Windows 95/98 clients. **B** is incorrect, because IPConfig is used for finding IP configuration of Windows NT and Windows 2000 clients. **D** is incorrect, because Netstat is used for finding out IP connection information of the local machine.

16. **D** is correct. HTTP is the delivery protocol for HTML.
A is incorrect, because SMTP and POP3 are used for sending and receiving Internet e-mail. **B** is incorrect, because Telnet is an application for establishing remote sessions with a host and PING is used for testing IP connectivity. **C** is incorrect, because Trace route and WinIPCFG are used for checking IP configuration and connectivity.

17. **A** is correct. Network analyzer could be used to monitor all incoming and outgoing traffic to that employee's workstation.
B is incorrect, because Trace route is for checking the hops an IP packet uses to get to its destination and does not tell you anything about the content of the packets. **C** is incorrect, because DHCP is used for dynamically configuring a network client's IP address information. **D** is incorrect, because HTTP is used for transporting HTML documents over the Internet.

18. **C is correct.** DNS provides IP address–to–host name resolution. Since you were able to ping successfully, chances are that DNS was not working.
    A is incorrect, because a user who deleted the system directory would not even be able to boot her machine, let alone run her browser application. **B** is incorrect, since we were able to connect to the Web site using an IP address. **D** is incorrect, because we were able to connect via the IP address, and NIC cards have nothing to do with name resolution to IP address.

19. **C is correct.** Routers by definition connect networks.
    A, B, and **D** are incorrect; although all take a part in providing network connectivity, they do not connect different networks.

20. **B is correct.** Point-to-Point protocol is the protocol used to connect remote users to TCP/IP networks.
    A is incorrect, because HTTP is used for transporting HTML pages. **C** is incorrect, because DNS is used after a connection is established for name resolution. **D** is incorrect, because POP3 is used for receiving e-mail.

i-Net+™

COMPUTING TECHNOLOGY INDUSTRY ASSOCIATION®

10

Hardware and Software

CERTIFICATION OBJECTIVES

10.01   Hardware and Software Connection
         Devices and Their Uses

10.02   Registering an Internet Domain Name

Y ou should now be familiar with many Internet concepts, such as its infrastructure, protocols, languages, and security. In this chapter, we step away from these global concepts in order to take a closer look at the preliminary steps to getting and keeping a computer connected to the Internet, as well as to becoming a part of the Internet with your own domain.

CERTIFICATION OBJECTIVE 10.01

Hardware and Software Connection Devices and Their Uses

Connecting a computer to the Internet can be as simple as installing a modem and plugging it into a phone jack. It can also be as complicated as connecting a multisegment network to the Internet through a single high-speed, direct line, while maintaining network security. This section looks at some of the various methods of gaining Internet access, and the hardware and software tools they employ.

Modems

The key to connecting a computer or network to the Internet lies in the ability to access the phone and cable lines that the Internet uses. This is the job of the computer's modem. Modems are responsible for creating and maintaining the computer's connection to the Internet, as well as sending and receiving data. Some modems are also responsible for compression and error correction of incoming or outgoing data. The most commonly used modems are analog, ISDN, DSL, and cable (for more details, refer to Table 10-1, later in the chapter in "Cable").

Analog Modems

When modems were first introduced, phone communications were strictly analog. However, computers use digital (binary) signals, so analog modems

FROM THE CLASSROOM

The Modem Handshake

So, what is all that buzzing and pinging you hear when your modem tries to connect to the Internet over the phone lines? It's called a *handshake*, and it's a process that two communicating modems must perform in order to establish the rules of the connection.

- When you access the Internet, your modem first dials up the modem of another computer, usually your Internet Service Provider's server. The receiving modem picks up and answers with a *guard tone* to let the sending modem know that it has reached another modem, and not a person or fax machine, etc . . .

- The receiving modem then tries to establish the speed at which the two modems will communicate. It sends a *carrier* tone to indicate its fastest possible speed. If the sending modem

is able to communicate at that speed, it will respond with a tone of its own. If there is no response, the receiving modem drops that carrier and tries another. This continues until the receiving modem suggests a speed that the sending modem is capable of using.

- Once a speed has been established, both modems test the line quality and adjust for noise or interference. This is called *equalization*, and it sounds like static. The modem speakers are then turned off, so this is the last sound you hear from the modem.

The two modems then establish the protocols for error correction and compression. Once this is completed, regular communication can begin.

—Amy Thomson, B.Sc., A+, MOUS Master

were created with the ability to convert signals from digital to analog and back. The conversion of your computer's digital signals into analog is called *modulation*. The conversion of analog signals to digital is called *demodulation*. Modems got their names from this process of signal MOdulation/DEModulation.

The most common speeds of analog modems are 14.4 Kbps, 28.8 Kbps, 33.6 Kbps, and 56.6 Kbps. 56.6 Kbps is probably the fastest that analog modems will ever be able to achieve, due to the restrictions of analog lines themselves.

on the job

When you're downloading information from the Internet, you may notice that your 56.6K modem is not working at 56.6K. There may be several reasons for this, including heavy line traffic and phone-line noise (interference). Also, recall that during the handshake, a common transmission speed is established between the two modems. This means that communication can only occur at the speed of the slower modem. Finally, the time it takes data to be error-checked, uncompressed, and processed can also contribute to your modem downloading at a speed that is a fraction of its potential.

Analog modems may be internal or external. There is no performance difference between the two, but each has benefits and disadvantages. Internal modems are inside the computer, so they are out of the way, and therefore less likely to be damaged. However, external modems are easier to replace and troubleshoot.

Analog modems connect to phone lines through a regular phone jack, using an RJ-11 connector (the same one the phone uses). Analog modems use the same frequency band on the phone line (0–4 KHz) as voice communications, which prevents their concurrent use of the line. This means that you must have separate phone lines if you want to use the Internet and the phone or fax machine at the same time.

Phone lines using analog signals (analog lines) do not communicate well over long distances, have little fault tolerance, and are quite limited in their transmission speed. In the 1960s, an effort was made to overcome these limitations by replacing analog lines with faster, better-performing digital lines. Today, digital lines make up most of the phone system. However, analog lines are still found in older areas and are still used to connect buildings to main feeder lines located at the phone company's switching stations (see Figure 10-1). Because analog lines still exist, and because analog modems are less expensive than other modem types, they are still very popular with home computer users and small businesses that do not require frequent or speedy access to the Internet.

While most lines in the phone system are digital, analog lines are still used to connect buildings to the local switching station

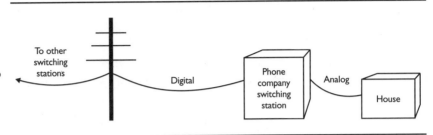

ISDN

The Integrated Services Digital Network (ISDN) standard was developed more than 10 years ago to take advantage of the benefits of the increasing number of digital phone lines. ISDN communications are purely digital, so they are faster than analog systems, and they work well over long distances.

Because analog lines are still used to connect buildings to switching stations, a digital ISDN line must be installed in its place to make your Internet connection purely digital. There are two types of ISDN lines—Basic Rate Interface (BRI) and Primary Rate Interface (PRI). BRI ISDN is much more common and is the focus of this discussion. ISDN lines are composed of three channels. Two of the channels, used for data transmission, are called B channels. Each B channel can transmit at 64 Kbps. Combined, this means 128 Kbps. The third channel is called a D channel, and it is used in setting up and terminating the dial-up connection.

on the **Job**

PRI ISDN is made up of 23 B channels!

Because there are two data channels in an ISDN line, two separate sets of data can be sent at once. This means you can use a phone or other attached device and still remain connected to the Internet. Of course, your connection rate to the Internet will be cut in half until the second B channel is freed up. Because ISDN lines are very intolerant to interference, only one can be installed at a single location.

The device that allows you to access digital lines is not really a modem, since it is not required to modulate and demodulate data. However, the term "modem" has come to mean any device that allows a computer to connect to a phone or cable line. The connection device is actually called a Network Termination 1 (NT1) device, but is more commonly referred to as an ISDN adapter.

ISDN communications are end-to-end digital. ISDN hardware does not really qualify as a modem, since the signal does not need to be modulated and demodulated.

ISDN adapters, like analog modems, can be external or internal, and they connect to a wall outlet using an RJ-11 or RJ-45 connector. Unlike analog modems, there are differences between the two. Internal ISDN adapters cost less and can take full advantage of the ISDN line's speed capabilities. External ISDN adapters usually connect to the computer via a serial or parallel port. These ports are limited to transmission speeds of about 115 Kbps, which is quite a bit slower than 128 Kbps the ISDN line is capable of. In order to take full advantage of an external ISDN adapter, it can be connected to the computer via a network cable and NIC. However, this option is more costly and involves more configuration of the computer.

ISDN technology is quite popular in small- and medium-sized businesses because of its improvements over analog lines and modems. ISDN has a wider bandwidth, which means that more networked users can access the Internet through the line at once. Also, the latency of ISDN (the period of time it takes to dial up and establish an Internet connection) is about half that of analog. The service and installation costs of ISDN technology are quite a bit more expensive than those of analog.

o n   t h e
Ⓙ o b

An Internet connection is only as fast as the slower component. In order to benefit from using ISDN, the computer you connect to must be using technology that matches or exceeds yours in speed and bandwidth.

DSL

DSL (Digital Subscriber Line) is a recent development in Internet communications (it was introduced in 1998). DSL is similar to ISDN in that the technology is used only for the connection between buildings and the phone company's switching stations (recall that this distance is typically comprised of analog lines). However, unlike ISDN lines, which replace analog lines, DSL actually makes use of existing analog lines.

Here's how it works: Analog lines are simply copper wire lines that transmit analog signals within the 0–4 KHz frequency band. This is just a very small portion of what the copper line is capable of using. DSL technology uses a splitter to divide the copper wire into two channels: 0–4 KHz for analog signals and 6 KHz–1.1 MHz for high-speed digital signals. Because the phone line is split into two separate channels, the DSL modem and phone do not interfere with each other; they can be used at the same time.

There are more than ten different types of DSL technology, but the two most common are asymmetric (ADSL) and symmetric (SDSL). ADSL gets its name from the fact that most of its bandwidth is used for incoming data. In ADSL, incoming data moves downstream. This arrangement is ideal for Internet users since most Internet communications, such as viewing Web pages and downloading files, travel in the downstream direction. Users spend very little Internet time sending requests and uploading files, so a small upstream bandwidth is sufficient. The transmission rate of ADSL depends on the modem speed and the service provided, but it can support speeds of 144 Kbps to 6 Mbps downstream, and between 64 Kbps and 640 Kbps upstream.

Symmetric DSL divides the channel's bandwidth equally for the upstream and downstream directions. This means that SDSL transmits at the same rate it can receive. The transmission rates of SDSL vary from 144 Kbps to 3 Mbps, but the most common speed is 1.5 Mbps.

All types of DSL require the same basic hardware:

- **Phone line**   DSL can use existing analog or digital phone lines running between your building and the phone company. You must activate a phone service account on the line in order to use it for DSL.

- **Line splitter**   Some types of DSL are called splitterless. This means that the signal splitter is located at the phone company office. However, ADSL and SDSL are splitter based, meaning that the signal splitter is located at the client's home or business. The DSL service provider is typically responsible for the installation and configuration of the splitter.

- **Modem**   This is the device that provides a connection between the computer and the phone line. The term "DSL modem" is a bit of a misnomer because the device is not required to modulate and demodulate signals, since the channel it uses is purely digital. In any case, it is an external device that plugs into the phone jack using the same type of cable and connectors as a regular phone. The modem also has a power connection for the wall outlet, and is designed to stay on, regardless of the on or off status of the computer.

■ **Network card**   The modem connects to the computer's internal Ethernet network card. With 10–100 Mbps transfer rates, it is the only port on the computer capable of keeping up with the speed of the modem. For this reason, DSL modems are sometimes called *Ethernet bridges*. Ethernet network cards are discussed in more detail later in this chapter.

Most DSL service providers will supply, install, and configure all of the required hardware. Once the splitter is installed on the phone line, the modem is connected to it. The phone line offers a direct connection to the DSL service provider, so there is no dial-up. There is always current on the line, so as soon as the modem is plugged in, the connection is established. This connection is never terminated unless the modem loses power or is disconnected from the phone line. The only leg of the connection that is ever terminated is between the network card and the modem when the computer is shut down.

on the **Job**

A common problem with DSL technology is that the modems can "go to sleep" (stop responding). This can be easily fixed by unplugging the modem from the wall, and then plugging it back in.

DSL provides many advantages for Internet communication, but has some disadvantages, too. The technology is so new that it's not available in many areas, and few standards have been set for the technology. Also, the speed and performance of the DSL connection suffers as the distance between the client and service provider increases. In fact, the DSL modem is not likely to work at all if it is located more than three miles from the service provider.

Cable

Fast on the heels of DSL is cable Internet access. Cable was first developed as an Internet access medium in 1996, and cable access began its appearance in homes and businesses in early 1999. Cable technology makes a break from conventional access methods by using TV cable lines, rather than phone lines.

TV cable lines are installed as a shared resource, forming a bus network that connects all users within a neighborhood to the cable company (called the head end of the cable network). Figure 10-2 illustrates the network layout of TV cables. TV cables contain hundreds of channels, each with a different frequency range. Downstream data from the Internet uses a 6 MHz wide band within the frequency range of 42–750 MHz, and upstream data uses frequencies between 5 and 40 MHz. Because there are so many channels available with cable, computer signals do not interfere with the reception of TV signals.

Like DSL, cable communications can be symmetric or asymmetric. Asymmetric cable can support downstream speeds up to 50 Mbps, but the actual experienced speed (depending on the type of modem and service) is usually around 3–10 Mbps. Asymmetric upstream speeds can be as high as 10 Mbps, but are more likely to fall between 200 Kbps and 2 Mbps. Symmetric cable speeds are around 500 Kbps–5 Mbps in either direction.

The hardware setup for cable is similar to that of DSL. First, a technician will install a splitter at the client's location to allow for more than one wall outlet (for example, one for the modem and one for a TV). The cable modem is external, and plugs into the wall outlet using coaxial cable with a BNC connector (the same one your TV uses). The modem usually communicates with the computer via an Ethernet network card, although a Universal Serial Bus (USB) connection can also be used. Figure 10-3 shows a typical cable modem setup.

Unlike the hardware used in ISDN or DSL, a cable modem really is a modem. Cable lines carry analog (radio) frequencies, so the modem is responsible for converting digital signals into analog, and vice versa. The first time a cable modem is plugged in, it scans the channels for the cable network's head-end modem. The channel being used by the head end will vary depending on your location and service provider.

The modem is connected to the Internet as soon as it finds the channel with the head end. Like TV channels and DSL connections, your cable Internet connection is always there, so there is no dial-up. The modem connection is never dropped and is available for you to use as soon as your

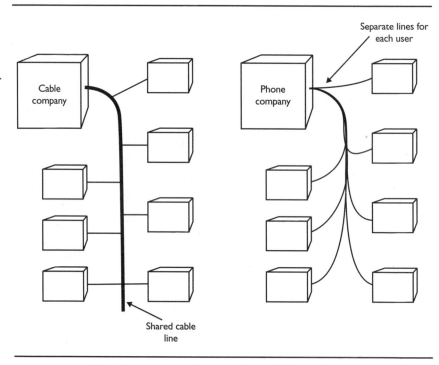

FIGURE 10-2

In the phone system, each customer has a separate line to the phone company. In the cable system, users in a neighborhood share one line to the cable company

computer starts up. Like DSL modems, cable modems can "go to sleep" and need to be disconnected, and then plugged back in. When this happens, the modem must begin scanning again for the head end. Fortunately, the

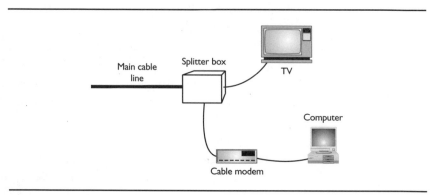

FIGURE 10-3

The cable goes through a splitter, then into the cable modem. The modem connects to the computer's internal Ethernet card

modem will "remember" which channel it last used, and will try there first before it scans the other cable channels.

Cable Internet access is becoming more and more popular with home users because it can support very high-speed connections, and is available at a price only slightly more expensive than regular analog. Also, recall that this technology uses a regular cable channel, so phone and TV service are unaffected when you go online. The modem is always connected to the Internet, and there is no dial-up.

However, there are a number of disadvantages of using cable, most of which stem from the network structure of the cable system. While cable is capable of even greater speeds than DSL (50 Mbps vs. 6 Mbps), it generally runs at speeds that are the same as, or slower than, DSL. Because cable lines are a shared resource, the speed of a cable connection will depend on the number of users online in the area. As more people access the Internet, the traffic on the line increases. This means an overall decrease in the speed of each connection.

The security of a cable connection can also be an issue. In phone-line communications, each user has a separate line to the service provider that cannot be accessed by other computers. However, data being sent to the head end in a cable network travels along the very same lines as data from other users. In fact, users on a cable network can "see" each other's computers in the Windows Network Neighborhood icon. Because it may be possible for another user to access your information before it reaches the head end, many cable modems are equipped with encryption capabilities. Data is encrypted by the modem, and then decrypted by the modem at the head end for upstream data, and vice versa for downstream data.

Finally, cable connections are susceptible to line noise and other types of interference. Recall that upstream data uses the frequency range 5–40 MHz. This range tends to get interference from CD radios and home appliances. Even worse, since the line is shared, noise from each connection can combine to create poor upstream communications for all users.

Table 10-1 summarizes the main characteristics of analog, ISDN, DSL, and cable modems.

TABLE 10-1			A Summary of Analog, ISDN, DSL, and Cable Modems	

	Analog	**ISDN**	**DSL**	**Cable**
Line type	Phone	Phone	Phone	Cable
Signal type	Analog	Digital	Digital	Analog
True modem?	Yes	No	No	Yes
Connection type	Dial-up	Dial-up	Direct	Direct
Year of implementation	Early 1980s	Late 1980s	1998	1999
Monthly service price	~$20.00	~$80.00	~$200.00	~$40.00
Availability	Widespread	Widespread	Limited	Limited
Types	N/A	BRI PRI	ADSL SDSL	Asymmetric Symmetric
Typical speed	14.4–56.6 Kbps	BRI: 64–128 Kbps	ADSL: 144 Kbps–6 Mbps downstream, 64–640 Kbps upstream SDSL: 144 Kbps–3 Mbps	Asymmetric: 3–10 Mbps Symmetric: 500 Kbps–5 Mbps
Experienced speed	Much slower	No change	No change	Slower, depending on amount of Internet traffic
Location of modem	Internal or external	Internal or external	External	External
Other hardware required	N/A	N/A	Signal splitter, internal Ethernet card	Signal splitter, internal Ethernet card

| TABLE 10-1 | A Summary of Analog, ISDN, DSL, and Cable Modems *(continued)* |

	Analog	**ISDN**	**DSL**	**Cable**
Advantages	Low cost Easy to set up Can be used on any phone line	Faster than analog Does not interfere with phone	Faster than ISDN Does not interfere with phone No dial-up	Theoretically faster than DSL Does not interfere with phone or TV No dial-up
Disadvantages	Slow Susceptible to interference	Dial-up Bottleneck between external modem and computer	Availability Must be within 3 miles of service provider	Availability Security Speed is affected by local traffic Susceptible to interference

exam
ⓦatch

You are bound to be asked questions that test your knowledge about the differences among modems. Make sure you are very familiar with Table 10-1.

Modem Setup and Commands

As you know, DSL and cable modems are installed and maintained by the service provider. There is no dial-up to configure, and the modems are hardwired to find and communicate with the service provider's modem. The only piece of the equipment that must be configured is the network card, so that it knows how to connect with the modem. However, analog and ISDN modems must be installed and set up by the user. The configuration of dial-up modems, and their language of communication, is the focus of this section.

Modem Setup

The first step in setting up a modem is to install it and configure it for use by the computer. To install an internal modem, plug it into an available ISA or PCI expansion slot inside the computer. If the modem is plug-and-play, the operating system will automatically detect and configure it, and then load the proper driver for it. If the modem is not plug-and-play, you need to assign it an IRQ and I/O address, typically IRQ 4 and I/O address 3E8-3EF. You can load the driver by running the setup program on the manufacturer-provided disk that came with the modem.

External modems attach to the computer through a serial port and use that port's IRQ and I/O address. However, if the modem is not plug-and-play, you will be required to install the modem's device driver.

Now the modem needs to be configured for dial-up access. This is a relatively simple process carried out by the setup program provided to you by your Internet service provider. When you launch the setup program, you will be asked to provide information about yourself and enter your Internet password. The program will then use the modem to dial up the service provider and establish a connection. The necessary setup information will be automatically downloaded into your computer, and the dial-up configuration is completed.

EXERCISE 10-1

Installing an Internal Analog Modem

1. Power down the computer and open the case, taking care to follow ESD safety procedures.

2. Insert the modem into an available expansion slot. Press straight down with both thumbs until the card is fully seated. If the card does not fit smoothly, gently rock the card from end to end (not back and forth) while you apply downward pressure.

3. Once the modem card is fully seated, insert and tighten the retaining screw that holds the card to the computer's chassis.

4. After booting the computer, run the driver software that came with the modem and the dial-up software supplied by your ISP.

Modem Commands

The language that your computer uses to direct the actions of the modem is known as the *modem command set*. The Hayes AT command set has emerged as a standard in the computer industry and is supported by most modems. The AT set includes commands to dial, answer incoming calls, and terminate a dial-up connection. Although some communications software requires you to manually input AT commands, most newer software takes care of it for you. Table 10-2 shows some commonly used AT commands.

Network Interface Card

Network interface cards are often used to connect a computer to a cable or DSL modem. The network interface card may be referred to as a *network*

TABLE 10-2	Command	Description	Usage
The AT Command Set for Hayes-Compatible Modems	D	Dial the given phone number	ATDT5551234 (T = tone dialing) ATDP5551234 (P = pulse dialing)
	9,	Used to get an outside line	ATDT9,5551234 (the , indicates a pause)
	*70	Disable call waiting	ATDT*70,5551234
	A	Answer the phone	ATA
	H	Hang up	ATH0 (Hang up) ATH1 (Hang up and enter command mode)
	M	Speaker control	ATM0 (speaker is always off) ATM1 (speaker turns off during carrier detect) ATM2 (speaker is always on)
	+++	Escape online mode and switch to command mode	+++
	O	Switch back to online mode	ATO0 return online ATO1 return online and redo handshake

adapter, or *NIC*. Network cards are also (and usually) used for connecting computers together in a network structure. The NIC allows a computer to see and transfer packets of information to and from other computers that are physically connected to the same network.

Computers on a network do not require individual Internet connections; rather, a single server can be set up to provide Internet access to all computers on the network. This is often a more cost-efficient and lower maintenance option than providing one Internet connection per computer on a network.

When you set up a network to access, or be accessed from, the Internet, there are several things to consider. You must select a NIC that supports the proper access method, topology, and cable type of the network. All of these factors are known collectively as the *network architecture*. When a network is configured to access the Internet, the most common choice is the Ethernet standard. Ethernet NICs offer a great deal of versatility and are easier to configure than most other types of networks. Also, they are capable of speeds of 10–100 Mbps, so they are the only standard capable of keeping up with high-speed Internet communications.

Ethernet Access Methods

Network access methods are standards that computers on the network use to send data to other computers, and to resolve and/or avoid transmission conflicts. If two computers try to send data over the network at the same time, a collision occurs, and the access method dictates what action each computer should then take.

CSMA / CD   Carrier Sense Multiple Access / Collision Detection. This is a type of first-come, first-served access method whereby computers on the network can send packets of information at any time, and if a collision between two or more computers occurs, each will resend its packet after a random amount of time.

CSMA / CA   Carrier Sense Multiple Access / Collision Avoidance. This type of access method is similar to CSMA/CD, except that after a collision has occurred on the network, one computer will first send out a "signal" to warn other computers that it is about to send a packet. This access method is more organized than CSMA/CD, so it may be more suitable for use on networks with a high number of Internet accesses or hits.

Ethernet Topology

The term *topology* refers to the physical layout of the network's devices and cables. These are the most commonly used topologies:

- **Bus**   This layout includes a main cable backbone, which runs the length of the network. Each computer on the network attaches to the backbone via its own cable. This topology is the simplest to set up, but has very low fault tolerance. A break or fault in the backbone results in a complete network failure.

- **Star**   In a star topology, each computer's network cable connects to a central network hub. If a cable breaks in a star network, the only computer affected is the one attached to that cable. However, a hub failure will result in a failure of the entire network. Hubs are described in more detail later in this chapter.

Ethernet Cabling

The term *network cabling* refers simply to the type of cable used to connect network computers and devices together. This section describes the most common types and their characteristics.

- **Twisted pair**   This is the most common (and least expensive) type of network cable. Twisted-pair cable attaches to a NIC with an RJ-45 connector, which resembles a large phone jack. Twisted pair can transmit at either 10 Mbps or 100 Mbps.

- **Coaxial**   This is a more popular choice when long distance or signal interference is an issue. Coax cable looks just like the cable used for cable TV, and uses the same BNC connector. Coax cable is able to transmit at 10 Mbps or 100 Mbps.

- **Fiber optic**   This cable type has no theoretical distance or speed limitations; and because it transmits light instead of an electrical signal, it is unaffected by electromagnetic interference. Fiber-optic cable is the most expensive type, and typically transmits at speeds of 100 Mbps–2 Gbps at distances up to two kilometers.

Most NICs come with at least two types of connectors, usually an RJ-45 for twisted pair and a BNC for coaxial.

Hub

Recall that each computer in a star network attaches to a device called a hub, which has many cable ports and provides a central connection point for computers on a network. When a passive hub receives information through one of its ports, the hub copies the information and sends it to every other port. This means that network information is broadcast to every computer on the network, but it is read only by the destination computer.

An active hub performs in much the same way, but will also repeat (boost the signal of) the information. This is beneficial for use with long network cables, which can experience a decrease in signal strength over distance (called *signal attenuation*). Figure 10-4 shows a typical star network with a hub.

Hubs are suitable for smaller local area networks (LANs), but their method of data transfer makes them unsuitable for larger networks. Because the hub copies and sends data to all computers on the network, it generates a lot of unnecessary network traffic. The amount of traffic on a network with a hub increases exponentially as more computers are added.

Bridge

When a network becomes too large to connect to one hub, or when transmission performance suffers from excessive network traffic, the

FIGURE 10-4

The hub acts as a central connection point for all computers on a star network

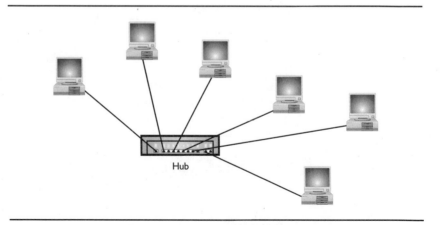

Hub

network is often divided into smaller segments, or LANs. When there are fewer computers on a network, there is less local traffic and increased speed. A bridge can then be used to maintain connectivity between the two (or more) network segments or LANs. Figure 10-5 shows a three-LAN network connected by a bridge.

The bridge provides a physical connection among LAN hubs, and it is also responsible for passing data packets back and forth among the network segments. The bridge is selective about the data it passes along;

FIGURE 10-5

A bridge is often used to connect small LANs or network segments

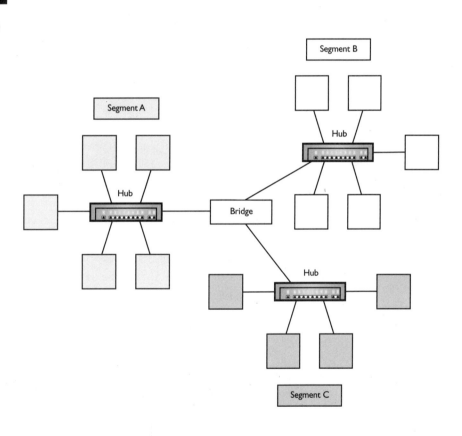

it is able to determine whether the sending and receiving computers reside in the same or different segments of the network.

Here's how it works: Each segment of the network connects to a separate port on the bridge. The bridge then creates routing tables, of which computers can be accessed through each port. When the bridge receives data, it will access the routing table of the sending port and look there for the destination address. If the sending and receiving computers are listed in the same routing table, the bridge assumes they are on the same segment, and will not send the data any further. If the bridge cannot find the destination address in the routing table, it assumes the receiving computer resides on a different segment. If this is the case, the bridge will broadcast the data to all other ports (segments).

When computer ABCDE1 addresses a packet to computer LMNOP3, the packet is received by the segment A hub, and then sent to the bridge. When the bridge receives the packet in port 1, it will access the port 1 (segment A) routing table. Since LMNOP3 is listed in that routing table, the bridge will filter out the data packet (see Figure 10-6).

Now consider that ABCDE1 sends a packet addressed to BMQRF3. When the bridge accesses the segment A routing table, it will not see a listing for BMQRF3. The bridge will assume that BMQRF3 resides in another segment, and the data will be broadcast to segments B and C.

As you can see, the bridge can determine when data must be passed from one segment to another, but cannot determine which segment to send the data to. The bridge must therefore broadcast the data to all possible segments. This can result in a lot of unnecessary traffic to computers and segments that will not even read the data packet. For this reason, bridges are not suitable for large or busy networks.

Router

A router, like a bridge, can be used to connect networks. However, routers are capable of much more sophisticated addressing. Routers are typically used on complex multi-LAN networks, like the one shown in Figure 10-7. Routers use IP, rather than MAC addresses, so they are suitable for use in Internet environments.

FIGURE 10-6

FIGURE 10-6   The bridge uses the routing table to determine whether to filter or broadcast data packets

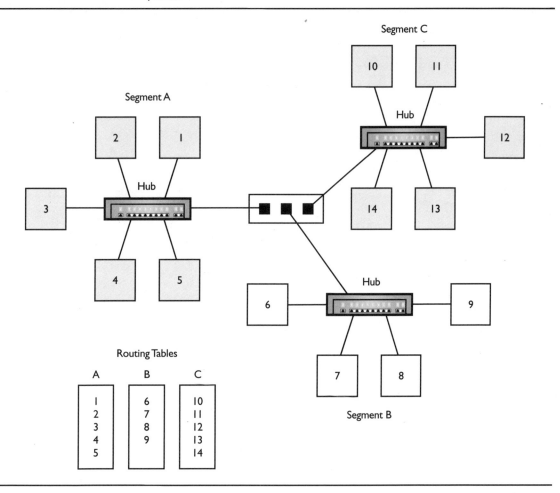

When a router receives a data packet, it examines the contents of it, then uses its knowledge of the layout and current condition of the network to send the packet on the best route toward its destination. In particularly large networks, data may be sent to many routers before it finally reaches its destination. Each router uses its own routing table to select the right direction for the next hop of the transmission.

Routers can be used on large, complex networks to send data packets on the best route toward the proper destination

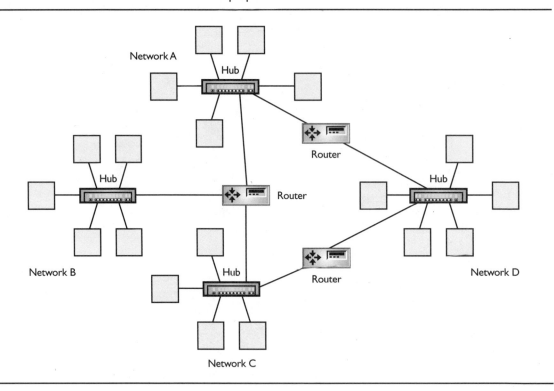

Routers can also provide fault tolerance on a large network. As you can see in Figure 10-7, there is more than one route between the networks. If one router is unable to transmit a data packet, another router may be used. Furthermore, routers keep track of the condition of the network, and may choose to send a packet on a route with less traffic or interference. Because the router will send data only to one specific address, it does not create broadcast storms to all computers on the network as bridges can.

Switch

A switch is another device that can be used to connect networks. The switch uses a specific addressing scheme for delivery of packets, much as a router does. That is, rather than broadcasting data all over the network (like a bridge), the switch is able to read the destination IP address of a packet and send it to the proper network segment.

However, switches are much simpler than routers and cannot determine the full route that the data must follow in order to reach its destination. The switch's routing table is limited to only devices that are physically connected to the switch, or very nearby. This means that the switch cannot be used to send data that is more than a few hops away. For this reason, switches tend to be placed very close to origin and destination devices in the network.

Figure 10-8 shows an example of the devices covered by a switch's routing table. The switch cannot be used to send data to the other LANs in the network because it simply does not know their locations, or which route is the best to use. In Figure 10-8, the switch passes data back and forth between segments. Any data that must pass beyond this area is sent to a router, which can then determine the proper route for the data.

on the
ⓙob

You may hear a switch referred to as a "switching hub" or "multiport bridge." To make matters even more complicated, some switches are now available with routing capabilities!

Gateway

The function of a gateway is to connect networks that use different protocols. For example, one network may use TCP/IP, while another is using IPX/SPX. The gateway translates data so that the networks can communicate with each other. Gateways are very important in Internet access, since so many protocols are in use today.

The gateway may be a dedicated hardware device whose sole purpose is to perform protocol conversions, or it may be software loaded on a network server. All data passing between dissimilar protocols must first pass through the gateway.

A gateway can exist anywhere on a network, as long as data can pass through it before it reaches its destination. In many networks that require Internet access, the network server performs gateway functions. Networks that access the Internet must have a gateway in order to connect. The gateway translates the protocol of the network into the protocol of the

FIGURE 10-8

A switch is usually located on the network where there is little distance between source and destination devices. The gray area shows the devices listed in this switch's routing table

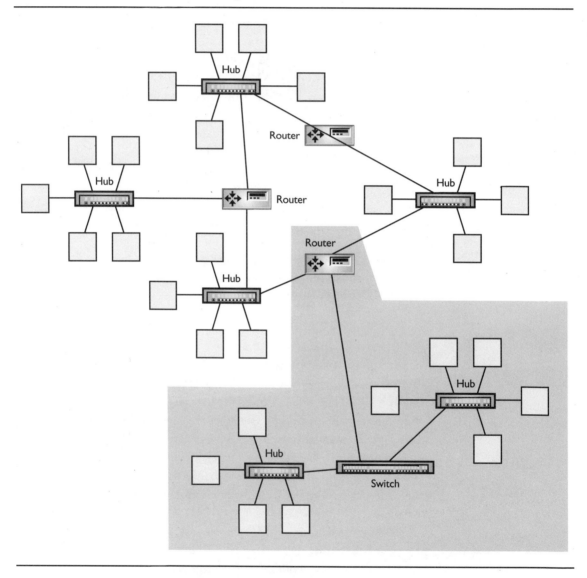

Internet, and translates between e-mail, messaging, and file transfer protocols.

Here are some questions that you should be able to answer, based on the information about hardware devices included in this chapter.

QUESTIONS AND ANSWERS

We are a small company with two networks that we would like to connect. What is the easiest and least expensive way to do this?	A *bridge* is ideal for small networks, especially when ease of use and cost are issues.
Our bridged network is growing, and users are complaining of slow network traffic. What should we do?	Use a *router*. They do not create broadcast storms, as bridges can.
We have a large network located in one building, and we want to connect other LANs from a different building. Which option is most cost efficient?	Use a *switch*. It acts like a router with a limited addressing capacity. However, it is well suited for attaching one or two LANs to an existing network structure, and is cheaper than a router.

NOS

A network operating system (NOS), like a regular operating system, is software that controls the functions of the computer, but also includes the features required to connect to and communicate with a network. Some popular network operating systems include Novell NetWare, Microsoft Windows NT, and UNIX.

Although these NOSs can be used to support peer-to-peer networks, in which all computers manage their own connection and configuration information, they are designed for client/server relationships. In a client/server network, all network requests go through and are managed by the server. This means less individual configuration and tighter security.

Most NOSs come in either client or server editions for just this reason. The client NOS is used by the workstations on the network, and the workstations have the ability to connect to the network and communicate with the server. The server software, on the other hand, is responsible for managing user accounts and profiles, allocating resources, tracking errors, and ensuring the security of the network.

Internet-in-a-Box

Internet-in-a-box (Ibox) is a relatively new technology that provides networks with one-step connections to the Internet. When the Ibox is installed and properly configured, it supplies the tools necessary to connect the network to the Internet by acting as a gateway, configuring the network for Internet access and providing Internet software tools, such as e-mail and Web browsers. Iboxes vary greatly in their features and capabilities, but generally include these features:

- **Dynamic host configuration protocol (DHCP) server**   The Ibox can dynamically allocate IP addresses to all computers on the network, typically the responsibility of the network server.

- **Web caching**   Many Internet users visit the same sites often. A Web cache retains those Web sites so that the next time they are accessed by a user, they are supplied by the Ibox, rather than being downloaded from the source. This saves time and frees up bandwidth for other tasks.

- **Firewall Security**   This is software that protects the network from being accessed by other Internet users. Firewalls are discussed in more detail later in the chapter.

- **Web browser**   The Ibox contains its own browser for hosting and viewing pages on the World Wide Web.

- **Search engines**   This is software that allows Internet users to search the Internet for Web sites based on the topic they enter.

- **File transfer protocols**   Many Iboxes support FTP (File Transfer Protocol) and HTTP (Hypertext Transfer Protocol). These protocols are necessary for downloading (copying) files and viewing Web pages.

- **E-mail and news programs**

The use of an Ibox can greatly decrease the amount of configuration and maintenance involved in connecting a network to the Internet. The device itself is considered firmware because it is a physical piece of equipment (hardware) that has programs and other software hardwired into it. The

Ibox can be plugged in at any point in the network, and more than one can be installed to allow for more users, or to enable load balancing or fault tolerance.

However, Iboxes are relatively new, so there are no standards among them. Also, most Iboxes will only support one type of network protocol (either IPX or TCP/IP). Finally, because the programs are hardwired into the device, they cannot be easily changed or updated.

exam
ⓦatch

You may hear the term "Internet-in-a-box" used to describe an ISP Internet package or a suite of Internet software. Many manufacturers use the term to describe their products as easy to use. However, the i-Net+ exam will be looking for your knowledge of the firmware device just described.

Firewall

A firewall is a security system that prevents outside users from accessing private network resources. Firewalls can be set up between segments on a large network, but are more commonly employed for security between a network and the Internet. Firewalls can also be used to restrict the Internet resources network to which users can have access.

Firewall Types

There are several types of firewalls, but the most common are packet-level and application-level firewalls. They differ in their screening methods, level of security, ease of configuration, and resulting network performance.

PACKET-LEVEL FIREWALL   A *packet-level firewall* is a basic type of security whereby packets are allowed or denied access to the network based on source and destination IP addresses. This type of firewall is usually managed by a router, which has been configured with IP address filtering rules. The router examines each packet and screens out all data from unidentified IP addresses.

This type of firewall is transparent to users, meaning that they probably won't know it's there, and Internet access will not suffer. Packet firewalls are fast, inexpensive, and can be simple to set up if you plan to use only a few security rules. However, the more screening rules you add, the greater the chance of creating conflicting rules that allow access from unwanted sources. Packet-level firewalls are also susceptible to IP spoofing, which occurs when an outside computer masks itself with a valid IP address.

APPLICATION-LEVEL FIREWALLS   *Application-level firewalls* (also called *application gateways*) use additional software, called a proxy, to filter incoming or outgoing data. A proxy is a software program that makes Internet connections and requests on behalf of the user. When the user makes a data request, it is actually sent to the proxy instead of the actual Internet location. The proxy examines the request, and then makes a decision about whether or not to forward it. Incoming data is intercepted by the proxy, examined, and then passed along or dropped according to the network's screening rules.

This is the most secure type of firewall because it screens data on the basis of content rather than IP address. It is not susceptible to IP spoofing, and it retransmits packets as its own, thereby masking the IP addresses of computers on the network. Also, in the event of an attack, application firewalls provide a more detailed account of which types of information outsiders tried to access. However, application-level firewalls are usually not fully transparent to users. They can slow down the network, resulting in performance degradation.

CIRCUIT-LEVEL FIREWALL   A *circuit-level firewall* (*circuit gateway*) is a type of application-based firewall that uses the same rules and principles as an application-level firewall. The circuit-level firewall's security features are applied at startup; and, once an Internet connection has been made, the connection stays open and data packets are not individually examined and screened.

This type of firewall is not nearly as secure as an application-level firewall, but it does provide some security and "masks" the IP addresses of computers on the internal network. It is more secure than packet-based firewalls and allows more flexibility than application-level firewalls.

Firewall Architecture

It is important to select carefully both the firewall type and the proper physical layout for your security system. Packet screening simply involves the configuration of an existing router. However, when you use application-level or circuit-level firewalls, the location and combination of security devices is very important. The most common firewall architectures are described here.

DUAL-HOMED HOST FIREWALLS   In this setup, the proxy computer (called the host) is placed between the Internet and internal network, so there is no possible direct connection between Internet users and network users; all data must pass through the proxy server. The proxy server also acts as a router, so the regular network routing method must be disabled to use this architecture. Figure 10-9 illustrates a typical dual-homed firewall setup.

SCREENED-HOST FIREWALLS   This type of configuration provides more protection than a dual-homed host firewall, because it combines the use of the proxy server with a packet-filtering router. In effect, it is a combination of application- and packet-level firewalls. The screening router is placed

---

FIGURE 10-9

In a dual-homed host firewall setup, the proxy server is located between the internal network and the Internet

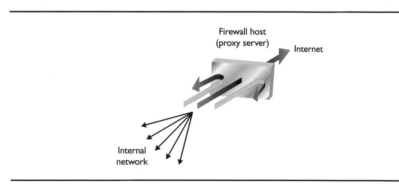

Firewall host
(proxy server)

Internet

Internal
network

FIGURE 10-10

A screened host firewall includes a router that first screened packets based on IP address information

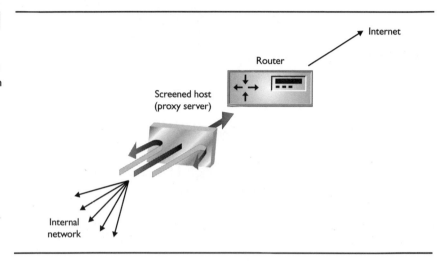

Internet

Router

Screened host
(proxy server)

Internal
network

between the Internet and the proxy server. The proxy server, then, is referred to as a *screened host*, because the router performs IP-based filtering before the packets reach the server. Figure 10-10 shows an example of a screened host firewall.

CERTIFICATION OBJECTIVE 10.02

Registering an Internet Domain Name

Every Web site on the Internet has an IP address so that it can be located and accessed by Internet users. Because IP addresses can be difficult to remember, the Internet relies on the Domain Name Server (DNS) service to translate addresses into more logical domain names. For example, a company's Web site address may be 124.122.108.92, and its domain name is www.company.com.

Without your own Internet domain name, your Web site and e-mail address are attached to your ISP's name—for example, you@ISP.com. Registering your own domain name makes it easier for people to find you because they will be looking for your business, not your ISP.

All Internet domain names must be registered with an organization called Internet Network Information Center (InterNIC), and your ISP can usually do this on your behalf. Your ISP will charge you a fee for hosting your own Web site through its service, and there is also a monthly fee to InterNIC for maintaining the domain name.

Ideally, a company's Internet domain name should be similar to the name of the company itself. This makes it easy for users to remember, and allows people to guess the name if they don't know it. For example, the domain name of Syngress is syngress.com. and the domain name of CompTIA is comptia.org.

However, Internet domain names must be unique; no two Web sites can exist with the same name. Domain names are assigned on a first-come, first-served basis, so you should be prepared with a backup name in case your first choice is already taken. You may also need to give some consideration to the root domain (extension) of your domain name. The most popular is .com, but nonprofit organizations may be found at .org and networking organizations may be found at .net. Furthermore, different countries can employ alternative extensions, such as .ca in Canada, .au in Australia and .us in the United States.

CERTIFICATION SUMMARY

This chapter examined the hardware and software devices necessary to maintain a network and allow that network access to the Internet. You learned about different types of modems and the hardware required to properly set up a network for Internet access. You also learned about software and firmware designed for Internet and network access, and, finally, how to register an Internet domain name.

There are four types of modems: analog, cable, ISDN, and DSL. Analog modems are the oldest type and are used mainly by home users and small businesses. They are the least expensive and slowest of the four types. ISDN modems use digital lines, and can achieve speeds up to 128 Kbps. A special ISDN line must be installed at your location to use an ISDN modem. DSL is a service that splits a regular phone line into two channels—one for the phone and one for digital communications. DSL can achieve speeds up to 6 Mbps. Cable modems are fairly recent and make use of existing cable lines. They use analog signals, and they can achieve speeds up to 10 Mbps.

To create a network, each computer must have a NIC. The most popular card for use in networks with Internet access is the Ethernet card, because of its speed and ease of use. Each computer in a star network attaches to the network hub. The hub is responsible for providing a physical connection between all computers and sending data from one port to all others. When connecting two segments of a network, you can use a bridge. The bridge filters out data that does not need to be sent to a different segment, but passes along all other information to all computers on the network. A router is more sophisticated, and can determine the best route to use when sending data on the network. It uses IP addressing and does not cause broadcast storms. A switch is similar to a router, but it is capable of less sophisticated addressing. A gateway is a device or program that translates between networks using different protocols.

There are many important software tools required for maintaining a network and accessing the Internet. A network operating system (NOS) is similar to a regular operating system, but also provides computers with file and resource sharing capabilities. NOSs usually come in client and server versions. Internet-in-a-box is firmware that plugs into a network and provides it with file transfer, e-mail, browser, and Internet search programs. When you connect a network to the Internet, security is a must. Firewalls are security systems used to prevent external Internet users from accessing internal network computer resources.

Finally, to get your business or organization on the Internet, you can register your own Internet domain name. Your name must be registered with InterNIC, and domain names are assigned on a first-come, first-served basis, so it's possible you may not be able to use the name you want. Most ISPs will do the legwork for you.

 # TWO-MINUTE DRILL

❑ Modems are responsible for creating and maintaining the computer's connection to the Internet, as well as sending and receiving data. Some modems are also responsible for compression and error correction of incoming or outgoing data.

❑ The most commonly used modems are analog, ISDN, DSL, and cable.

❑ The most common speeds of analog modems are 14.4 Kbps, 28.8 Kbps, 33.6 Kbps, and 56.6 Kbps. 56.6 Kbps is probably the fastest that analog modems will ever be able to achieve, due to the restrictions of analog lines themselves.

❑ The Integrated Services Digital Network (ISDN) standard was developed more than ten years ago to take advantage of the benefits of the increasing number of digital phone lines. ISDN communications are purely digital, so they are faster than analog systems, and they work well over long distances.

❑ An Internet connection is only as fast as the slower component. In order to benefit from using ISDN, the computer you connect to must be using technology that matches or exceeds yours in speed and bandwidth.

❑ DSL is similar to ISDN in that the technology is used only for the connection between buildings and the phone company's switching stations. However, unlike ISDN lines, which replace analog lines, DSL actually makes use of existing analog lines.

❑ Fast on the heels of DSL is cable Internet access. Cable was first developed as an Internet access medium in 1996, and cable access began its appearance in homes and businesses in early 1999. Cable technology makes a break from conventional access methods by using TV cable lines, rather than phone lines.

❑ DSL and cable modems are installed and maintained by the service provider. There is no dial-up to configure, and the modems are hardwired to find and communicate with the service provider's modem. The only piece of the equipment that must be configured is the network card, so that it knows how to connect with the modem.

❑ Network interface cards are often used to connect a computer to a cable or DSL modem. The network interface card may be referred to as a network adapter, or NIC. Network cards are also (and usually) used for connecting computers together in a network structure. The NIC allows a computer to see and transfer packets of information to and from other computers that are physically connected to the same network.

❑ Network access methods are standards that computers on the network use to send data to other computers, and to resolve and/or avoid transmission conflicts. If two computers try to send data over the network at the same time, a collision occurs, and the access method dictates what action each computer should then take.

❑ Each computer in a star network attaches to a device called a *hub*, which has many cable ports and provides a central connection point for computers on a network. When a passive hub receives information through one of its ports, the hub copies the information, and sends it to every other port. This means that network information is broadcast to every computer on the network, but is read only by the destination computer.

❑ Bridges, routers and switches are used to connect networks.

❑ The function of a gateway is to connect networks that use different protocols.

❑ A network operating system (NOS), like a regular operating system, is software that controls the functions of the computer, but also includes the features required to connect to and communicate with a network.

❑ Internet-in-a-box (Ibox) is a relatively new technology that provides networks with one-step connections to the Internet.

❑ A firewall is a security system that prevents outside users from accessing private network resources.

❑ Every Web site on the Internet has an IP address so that it can be located and accessed by Internet users. Because IP addresses can be difficult to remember, the Internet relies on the Domain Name Server (DNS) service to translate addresses into more logical domain names. For example, a company's Web site address may be 124.122.108.92, and its domain name is www.company.com.

SELF TEST

1. A home computer user has asked for your advice regarding the purchase of a modem. The user intends to access the Internet about two hours each week, mostly to send and receive e-mail. The user is concerned about cost and the ease of the equipment setup. What should you recommend?

   A. Analog modem

   B. ISDN

   C. DSL modem

   D. Cable

2. Analog modems are available in different speeds. Which data transfer speed is not supported by analog modems?

   A. 33.6 Kbps

   B. 14.4 Kbps

   C. 56.6 Kbps

   D. 64 Kbps

3. When an analog or ISDN modem goes through its dial-up procedure, you can hear some tones and static coming from it. What is the cause of these noises?

   A. The modem is establishing an encryption protocol with the computer.

   B. The two modems are establishing a communication speed and testing the line for noise.

   C. The two modems are establishing error correction and compression protocols.

   D. The sending modem is asking the receiving modem permission to send a large data packet.

4. Your business uses a fax machine, a phone, and the Internet. Typically, they share the phone line, but, lately, it has been inconvenient to have to use one device at a time. Which connection type will allow you to use these devices concurrently on the same line, and still allow you to stay within your budget of $60.00 a month?

   A. Analog modem

   B. BRI ISDN

   ✓ C. DSL

   D. Cable

5. A client with high-speed Internet requirements is interested in getting ISDN service. Which type of ISDN modem should you recommend?

   ✓ A. Internal, because they are not prone to computer-modem bottlenecks

   B. External, because they are easier to install and troubleshoot

   C. Internal, because they are less prone to interference

   D. External, because they are less prone to interference

6. There are several types of DSL service, the most common being ADSL and SDSL. Which is more suitable for most Internet users?

    A. ADSL, because it is much easier to configure than SDSL

    B. SDSL, because it is much cheaper and more fault tolerant than ADSL

    C. ADSL, because it divides the bandwidth unequally between upstream and downstream

    D. SDSL, because it is about four times faster than ADSL

7. Which of the following fits this description?

    This modem offers high-speed Internet access, direct connection (no dial-up), uses analog signals, and allows concurrent use of phone and Internet.

    A. ISDN

    B. DSL

    C. Cable

    D. None of the above

8. A client wants a high-speed, high-security Internet connection with no dial-up and doesn't want the Internet access to interfere with the use of the phone. The client is curious about a cable connection and is willing to pay any amount. Should you recommend cable?

    A. No, because the customer is willing to pay any amount, and DSL is much faster.

    B. No, because cable doesn't provide a direct connection.

    C. Yes, because cable meets all of the client's requirements.

    D. No, because cable does not offer high security.

9. You are trying to manually dial up another modem using tone dialing, and at the command line, you entered the following command: ATDT5551234. The modem will not dial properly. What is the problem?

    A. The command should read ADTD5551234.

    B. The command should read ATDT555-1234.

    C. The command should read ATDP5551234.

    D. None of the above.

10. A client is interesting in setting up a single LAN to access the Internet. He has not yet decided on a modem type, and wants to set up the network first. What critical piece of hardware do you recommend?

    A. Bridge

    B. Router

    C. Splitter

    D. Ethernet cards

11. Which type of device will broadcast all data from one port to all other ports, and will repeat signals to prevent signal attenuation?

A. Active hub

B. Passive hub

C. Switching hub

D. Bridge

12. Your business network is made up of three LANs connected by a bridge. The network has gradually gotten bigger, and users are beginning to complain about how slow the network is. What should you do?

  A. Use another bridge to divide the network into four, rather than three, segments.

  B. Replace the bridge with a router.

  C. Change the protocol of one of the segments, and install gateway software on the server to translate between them.

  D. Move the firewall outside the network so that local traffic doesn't have to go through it.

13. Your network has five segments, connected by four routers. You have just replaced the NIC of one of the computers. What should you do next to ensure that the routing tables can find that computer?

  A. Use the network server's administration tools to manually enter the new MAC address in any of the routing tables.

  B. Use the network server's administration tools to manually enter the new MAC address in all of the routing tables.

C. Turn the computer on and log in.

D. Do nothing. The routers will automatically detect the new MAC address and update their routing tables.

14. According to the following illustration, which networks will lose connectivity if the router at position 4 stops working?

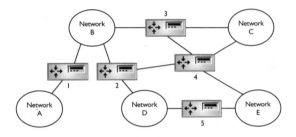

  A. A, B, and D

  B. C and E

  C. All of them

  D. None of them

15. Refer to the illustration in question 14—which number indicates the best place to put a switch?

  A. 1

  B. 2

  C. 3

  D. 4

16. The Internet uses many different e-mail, file transfer, and messaging protocols. What allows you to access these services, even when your computer uses a different protocol?

A. Router

B. Switch

C. Gateway

D. Web browser

17. Many network operating systems are available in peer-to-peer, client, and server versions. Which version is best for installing on computers that will log into a high-security network and access the resources of a central computer?

A. Peer-to-peer.

B. Client.

C. Server.

D. All of the above will perform this task equally.

18. Your company is considering the purchase of an Internet-in-a-box for the network's Internet access. The network is server-based with 20 IPX clients on one segment and 8 TCP/IP clients on another segment. The Internet connection itself is ISDN. Should you recommend an Ibox?

A. Yes. The Ibox will control dial-up procedures, and will double as either a router or switch.

B. No. An Ibox cannot be used on a client/server network.

C. Yes. The Ibox will provide the network with Internet tools such as e-mail, Telnet services, and Web browsers.

D. No. An Ibox cannot be used with ISDN.

19. A three-segment star network with two routers has a client/server configuration and ISDN Internet access. One segment uses TCP/IP, and the other two use IPX/SPX. Which of the following describes most accurately the likely role of a firewall on this network?

A. To establish and maintain user profiles to ensure that users do not access restricted information

B. To protect the network from external access by Internet users

C. To translate data between the TCP/IP segment and IPX/SPX segments

D. To ensure that all segments can communicate with each other

20. Your company is an American nonprofit organization looking to register its own domain name. The company's name is Blitz, so you have decided on the domain name www.blitz.com. However, you are informed that this domain name is already in use. Which of the following is a suitable alternative?

A. www.blitz.net

B. www.blitz.ca

C. www.blitz.am

D. www.blitz.org

SELF TEST ANSWERS

1. **A.** You should recommend an analog modem. These modems are very popular with home users because they do not require additional lines or configuration of existing lines. The analog modem simply plugs into an existing phone jack in the wall. Analog modems are also the least expensive, which satisfies the customer's desire to save money. Although analog modems deliver poor performance compared to other modem types, they offer sufficient quality to support a few hours of browsing and e-mail a week.

   B, C, and **D,** are all incorrect, because they do not satisfy the user's need for ease of setup or cost. ISDN requires a special digital line installation, and the service and equipment is far more expensive than that of an analog modem setup (analog cost is about a quarter that of ISDN). A DSL modem can take advantage of existing phone lines, but a splitter must be installed at the user's location, and an Ethernet network card must be installed in the computer. Although no special lines must be installed to use a cable modem, an Ethernet card must be installed in the computer. Although ISDN, DSL, and cable provide a better Internet connection, it is not worth the extra money for the two hours a week the user will spend using the Internet.

2. **D.** Analog modems do not support speeds of 64 Kbps. The fastest transfer rate for analog modems is 56.6 Kbps. This is not a limitation of modem technology; rather, it's a limitation of the analog phone lines that the modem must use.

   A, B, and **C** are all incorrect, because they are all valid modem speeds. As you might guess, older analog modems are slower. The fastest analog modems today are 56.6 Kbps, and this is also the most popular speed used today.

3. **B.** The noises you hear during dial-up are caused by the two modems establishing a communication speed and testing the line for noise. The receiving modem will send a carrier tone, which indicates its highest possible speed. It will continue sending different tones until the sending modem responds that it can use one of the suggested speeds. Once a communication speed has been established, both modems test the quality of the phone line and adjust their speed in the presence of line noise. This step is called *equalization*.

   A is incorrect, because it states that the noise is caused by the modem establishing an encryption protocol with the computer. Any encryption of data between the computer and modem is established when the modem is first installed and configured in the computer. This process does not create any noise from the modem. **C** is incorrect, because it suggests the noise is caused when the two communicating modems establish error correction and compression protocols. While this is an important step in the modem handshake, it occurs after the modem speakers have been turned off, so you will not hear any noise from the modem during this procedure. **D** is also incorrect. The sending modem does not ask to send a large packet; it simply sends the packet along. In fact, any further signals between the two modems will not cause noise that you can hear.

4. **B.** Basic Rate Interface (BRI) ISDN uses a special digital phone line that is actually made up of two channels, each capable of transferring 64 Kbps. Because the channels are separate, you can use any two phone-line devices at the same time (Internet, phone, fax machine, and so on). ISDN prices vary, but are typically below $60.00 a month.

   A is incorrect, because this is probably the type of modem already being used. Although analog modems are the least expensive, they support low data-transfer speeds, and they hog the phone line; when you are online, you cannot use the phone or fax machine. **C** is incorrect, because it does not conform to the budget guidelines. While DSL is an excellent solution for those wanting concurrent phone and Internet access on the same line, prices can be hundreds of dollars a month. Although **D** is within the price guideline, it will not allow the concurrent use of phone devices on the same line. Cable modems use TV cables, and the phone and fax machine must use phone lines.

5. **A.** You should recommend an internal modem, because they are not prone to computer-modem bottlenecks. The key to this situation is that the client requires a high-speed Internet connection. ISDN supports transfer speeds up to 128 Kbps, but an external ISDN modem connects to the computer through a serial port, which is limited to about 115 Kbps. An internal modem can transfer data along the computer's internal bus as fast as the data is received.

   B is incorrect, because it suggests recommending an external modem. Although they are easier to troubleshoot, they are not suitable for high-speed connections because of the bottleneck problem. **C** and **D** are incorrect, because there is no difference between internal and external ISDN modems in terms of their susceptibility to interference.

6. **C.** ADSL is more suitable than SDSL for most Internet users, because the bandwidth is divided unequally between upstream and downstream. In ADSL, only 1/4–1/10 of

the bandwidth is dedicated for upstream data, and the rest is used for downstream data. This is ideal for most Internet access, since users spend a great deal of time downloading information (getting files, viewing Web pages, and so on). Very little Internet time is spent sending data or requests upstream.

A is incorrect, because it states that ADSL is easier to configure than SDSL. The same configuration is required for each type. The bandwidth difference between ADSL and SDSL depends on the splitter used, not the configuration of the computer or modem. **B** is incorrect, because there is no difference between ADSL and SDSL in terms of fault tolerance. **D** is incorrect, because it states that SDSL is about four times faster than ADSL. While speeds vary according to the modem and line conditions, ADSL is usually faster than SDSL. SDSL speeds range from 144 Kbps to 3 Mbps. ADSL speeds range from 64 Kbps to 640 Kbps upstream and up to 6 Mbps downstream.

7. **C.** Cable modems offer high-speed Internet access (up to 10 Mbps downstream) and also offer a direct connection. The connection is never dropped, so there is no dial-up. Cable modems use TV cables, which transmit radio (analog) signals; and, because they do not make use of phone lines, they do not interfere with the use of the phone.

A is incorrect, because it offers speeds of only up to 128 Kbps, and must perform a dial-up every time you access the Internet. The D in ISDN stands for "digital," and ISDN connections are digital from end to end. The only characteristic of ISDN listed is that it allows for concurrent use of the phone and Internet. **B** is also incorrect. While DSL does provide high-speed access, a direct connection, and concurrent use of the phone, it uses digital signals. DSL uses a splitter that divides the phone line into two channels: an analog channel for phone and fax use and a digital channel for Internet communications. **D** is incorrect, because it suggests that none of the options listed are correct.

8. **D.** You shouldn't recommend cable because it does not offer high security. Because cable lines are shared between homes within a neighborhood, the data you send travels on the same public line as the data from other users. It is possible that others could intercept your data with their computers.

A is incorrect, because although DSL is more expensive than cable, it does not support maximum speeds as high as those of cable (6 Mbps vs. 10 Mbps). **B** is incorrect, because it states that cable doesn't provide a direct connection. Cable modems connect to regular TV cable lines, which always have a signal on them. There is no dial-up because the connection is never broken. **C** is incorrect, because it does not satisfy the client's need for high security.

9. **D.** The command entered, ATDT5551234, is a valid AT command. This particular command means "Using the AT command set, Dial using Tones," and the number is 5551234. If the modem will not carry out this command, there is another problem (perhaps a problem with the modem itself or the receiving modem).
   A is incorrect, because this is not the proper syntax for the AT dial command. Most commands must start with AT, not AD. **B** is also incorrect, because the phone number should be entered with no spaces or dashes. **C** is incorrect, because although this is a valid AT command, it is used to specify pulse dialing, not tone dialing.

10. **D.** Remember: The purpose of the LAN is to provide users with Internet access. Ethernet cards are the only NICs capable of supporting high-speed Internet communications, and they are necessary for creating a network, with or without Internet access.
    A and **B** are incorrect, because the client is connecting only a single LAN to the Internet. The function of a bridge or a router is to connect two or more separate LANs. **C** is incorrect, because splitters are only used in certain types of Internet access, such as DSL and cable. Since the client hasn't yet decided on an access type, you don't know whether a splitter will be required. Furthermore, most ISPs will provide and install a splitter if one is required for your Internet connection. Finally, a splitter cannot be used in the setup of a network, which is the primary focus of this scenario.

11. **A.** Hubs are used to connect computers in a star network. Each computer plugs into a hub port, and when one computer sends data, the hub resends it to all other hubs. The data is ignored by all computers except the receiving computer. While a passive hub simply sends data packets, an active hub will boost (repeat) the signal to ensure that it doesn't degrade before it reaches its destination.
    B is incorrect, because it simply resends data without boosting or repeating it. **C** is also incorrect, because it will not broadcast all data to all ports. Rather, a switching hub is able to determine which port is associated with the destination address, and it will send data to the proper port only. **D** is incorrect, because although a bridge performs broadcasting to all ports, it will not repeat signals.

12. **B.** You should replace the bridge with a router. Bridges are notorious for causing excessive network traffic, because they broadcast all data packets to all segments. Routers use a routing table to send data only to the destination computer, so each packet gets sent to only one computer.
    A is incorrect, because it suggests making another division in the network and adding

another bridge. This will probably make things worse, since now you will have three bridges broadcasting data to all other computers, instead of just two. **C** is also incorrect, because it states that you should change the protocol of one of the segments and install gateway software. The problem here is broadcast storms caused by the action of the bridge. If you change the protocol of one segment and make all traffic go through a gateway, you will slow down the network even more. **D** is incorrect, because firewalls are used to protect an internal network from an outside one (like the Internet). All local traffic can pass from one segment to another without having to go through the firewall, so this solution probably won't make any difference at all in the speed of the network.

13. **C.** Routers maintain the IP addresses of computers on the network, not their MAC addresses. Replacing the network card will have no effect as long as the IP address of the computer isn't changed.
    A, B, and **D** are all incorrect, because they suggest that the routing table keeps track of MAC addresses, which are based on the network card in each computer. Routing tables do not maintain MAC address lists, so they will be unaffected by the changing of a network card in a computer.

14. **D.** Routers are typically set up in a network to provide fault tolerance. This means that there are many routes that packets can take to get to their destination. In this particular scenario, all data from all networks can get to their destinations by alternate routes.
    A, B, and **C** are all incorrect. Although a failure of router 4 would mean longer trips for packets, all networks are still connected through other routes. Even networks C and E will still be connected (albeit in a roundabout way).

15. **A.** Position 1 is the best place to install a switch. Recall that a switch has a limited routing table, so it only knows the addresses of networks directly connected to it, or maybe two hops away. Because position 1 has only two direct connections, and is connected to networks instead of routers, it is an ideal place for a switch. Position 5 is a pretty good place for a switch, too.
    B and **C** are incorrect, because positions 2 and 3 are each connected to two networks and to a router that connects to more networks and routers. This is more address information than the switch can maintain, so it would be unable to correctly send packets to the proper destination. **D** is also incorrect. This is probably the worst place

on this network to put a switch, because it is the center of the network and must route more packets than any other position.

16. **C.** The purpose of a gateway is to translate between different protocols. Gateways may be used on a network in which different segments use different protocols. You must use a gateway to access e-mail and files of different protocols on the Internet. **A** and **B** are incorrect, because these are both network connectivity devices. They route and resend packages between networks, and can be used in maintaining an Internet connection, but they do nothing to translate protocols. **D** is also incorrect. A Web browser is a program that lets you view HTML Web pages on the Internet. It does not translate between e-mail, file, or messaging protocols.

17. **B.** Client network operating systems are designed to be installed on a workstation computer in a client/server network. The NOS allows the computer to log into the network, and then it works in conjunction with the server NOS to implement network rights and restrictions for the workstation.
A is incorrect, because in this type of network, all computers can access all resources on the network, provided each user knows the proper password. This makes for a low-security network. **C** is incorrect, because this version of the NOS is responsible for administering the network and maintaining its security and access rights. Although a server NOS can be used on a workstation, this is not what they were designed for, so it is not the best choice. **D** is incorrect, because it states that all of the above will perform the task equally. Although all the choices given could be made to work, they will not function in the client role as well as specially designed client software.

18. **C.** The Ibox may also act as a gateway and DHCP server. There is no reason for the company not to use an Ibox if it is already interested in getting one.
A is incorrect, because it states that you should recommend the Ibox because it will double as a router or switch and perform the Internet dial-up. Iboxes can provide software-based programs and configurations, but will not route data on the network, and do not have dial-up capabilities. In addition to the Ibox, the network must have dedicated routing and dial-up hardware. **B** is incorrect, because it states that an Ibox cannot be used on a client/server network. This is simply untrue; the Ibox works just as well on client/server networks as on peer-to-peer networks. **D** is also incorrect, because it states that the Ibox can't be used with an ISDN Internet connection. The

Ibox manages the internal network, regardless of the method by which data is retrieved from the Internet.

19. **B.** The firewall is a security mechanism that allows only authorized data requests to and from the Internet and can block requests to the network from unrecognized external IP addresses or communication programs.
    A is incorrect. This is the role of the network's server. **C** is incorrect, because this is the job of a gateway. **D** incorrect. This is the job of the network's two routers.

20. **D.** The .org extension is reserved for nonprofit organizations, like the one in this scenario.
    A is incorrect, because the .net extension is reserved for networking organizations. **B** is incorrect, because the .ca extension can only be used for domains located within Canada. **C** is incorrect, because the .am extension doesn't exist. The extension that defines a name as being American is .us.

11

Servers and Bandwidth Technologies

CERTIFICATION OBJECTIVES

11.01	Internet Bandwidth Technologies (Link Types)
11.02	Servers: Their Purpose, Functionality, and Features

This chapter introduces the topics of Internet bandwidth technologies and connectivity options. You will learn about the high-speed digital data link connections using T1/T3 connections, and their European E1/E3 counterparts. You will be introduced to various packet-delivery protocols and standards, including Frame Relay, X.25, ATM, and DSL.

You will also be given an overview of Internet server technologies, including their purpose, function, and features. While software vendors have their own specific server implementations, they generally share a set of core features and functions based on the Internet standards and protocols for their services. You will be given an overview of Internet Information servers including Proxy, Mail (SMTP), List, Web (HTTP), News (NNTP), Certificate, Directory (LDAP), Mirror servers and sites, and File Transfer (FTP) servers.

CERTIFICATION OBJECTIVE 11.01

Internet Bandwidth Technologies (Link Types)

Internet bandwidth technologies include various link types such as T1/E1 and T3/E3 standards for high-speed networking and data communications. The various signal formats and framing types used for packet-switching networks are discussed in the next sections.

T1 and E1 Standards

T1 is simply ITU-T's (International Telecommunication Union-Telecommunication Standardization Sector, formerly the CCITT) North American name for the 1.544 Mbps standard pipe that can be used to pass signal traffic. T1 stands for TDM (time-division multiplexing) signal number 1. These pipes, or circuits, consist of 24 56-Kbps or 64-Kbps channels, known as DS-0s.

The European standard, called E1, contains higher bandwidth (2.048 Mbps) because it is supported by 32 DS-0s. Telephone companies often refer to T1s as DS-1s, where DS stands for Digital Signal.

Physical Media

T1s/E1s can be transmitted over several types of media, such as copper wire and fiber-optic cabling. Depending on the medium used, signal attenuation issues need to be addressed, generally by the provider. As an example, copper wire is considered a common, shorter-haul medium, because it is susceptible to loss of signal strength. Therefore, signal repeaters are required at intervals of 5000–6000 feet minimally. Fiber-optic cabling is considered more of a long-haul medium, which supports signal strength. Therefore, this medium only needs repeaters to be at intervals of 25–30 miles.

Pulse Code Modulation

The most common technique used to digitize an analog signal into the DS-0 format is called PCM (pulse code modulation). This process involves two steps:

1. The incoming analog signal is "sampled" at a rate of 8000 times per second and converted into subsequent pulses known as PAMs (pulse amplitude modulation).

2. Each PAM is assigned an equivalent 8-bit binary value. This provides a digital output to the analog signal.

It may be interesting to note that the 8000 samples per second multiplied by the 8-bit output is equivalent to the 64 Kbps rate of the DS-0. These DS-0s are then multiplexed together into the T1 circuit via TDM (time-division multiplexing).

Time-Division Multiplexing

Time-division multiplexing is a technique used to transmit a number of small signals (in this case, the DS-0s) into one continuous, larger signal.

It is analogous to the way train cars make up a train. TDM interleaves a piece (8 bits) of each incoming signal, one after another, into each of the T1's 24 timeslots. The compilation of these timeslots comprises one frame. Subsequent frames are then used to continue transferring the data.

Framing

Framing is an error-control procedure used to multiplex a logical data stream. In order to provide better data organization (between the bytes, so to speak), the signal is formatted using the framing process. A frame is a compilation of 1 byte from each of the 24 DS-0 timeslots, plus a framing bit. This makes each frame 193 bits. T1s use one of two types of framing, D4 or ESF (Extended Superframe). D4 has been superceded by ESF. Caution should be taken when ordering T1s and PRI-T1s, since there are two framing types the provider can give you. According to standard, a PRI-T1 requires ESF, but there are times when the provider can only provide D4 framing because of legacy equipment.

T3/E3

Depending on the nature of the carrier, a T3 circuit may multiplex 24–28 T1s together via TDM to create a T3 (DS-3). These circuits carry up to 44.736 Mbps of bandwidth. DS-3 circuits are about four to six times the cost of DS-1 circuits; thus, they are much more cost effective for large bandwidth requirements. E3 circuits designed for the international market carry up to 34 Mbps of bandwidth. E3 circuits multiplex 16 E1 lines.

Frame Relay

Frame Relay is a variable packet size transport service. Frame Relay was originally designed to carry data and, therefore, uses a variable frame size. The specification allows frame sizes as large as 4096 octets. Frame Relay resides at Layer 2 in the OSI model. Frame Relay access (Layer 1 of the OSI model) may be provided over T1, E1, or ISDN digital carrier facilities.

Frame Relay is one of the most popular wide area networking services used. Due to its low bandwidth needs, prevalence in outlying areas, and popularity, it is very cost effective for businesses to implement. It is commonly implemented in branch offices. Frame Relay is a protocol stack that defines the wide area network (WAN) protocols used to move data from one local area network (LAN) to another.

The Frame Relay standards evolved from X.25 (discussed in the next section) and were designed to take advantage of newer digital and fiber-based networks, which were much less susceptible to the errors encountered in their analog counterparts at the time X.25 was developed. As such, the Frame Relay standards do not bother with ensuring packet delivery and correct sequencing of packets, like the earlier X.25 standard did. Instead, Frame Relay assumes that higher-level protocols such as TCP/IP will ensure correct sequencing and handle the retransmission of packets lost within the network due to errors. Because of these differences, Frame Relay can scale upward to T3 speed (44.736 Mbps), whereas X.25 topped off at speeds of 56 Kbps. Practically speaking, most Telco carriers offer Frame Relay up to T1 (1.544 Mbps) or internationally E1 (2.048 Mbps) speeds. The trade-off for higher speed is that if a packet does encounter errors, it takes longer for the retransmission to occur, as the higher-layer protocols must ensure that this happens.

DLCI

Frame Relay is an encapsulation method that operates at Layer 2 and runs on top of nearly any serial interface. Frame Relay is a packet-switching technology that multiplexes multiple logical data streams onto one physical link. These data streams are called *virtual circuits*, and each is identified by a *data-link connection identifier*. The acronym for this is DLCI, which is pronounced "dell-see."

Virtual Circuits

Frame Relay can create two types of virtual circuits. The first is a *permanent virtual circuit (PVC)* and the second is a *switched virtual circuit (SVC)*. A PVC is manually created by an administrator with a source and destination, and operates very much like a leased line. As its name implies, it is a permanent connection and remains until it is manually removed. An SVC, on the other hand, is dynamically created by software through a call setup procedure. This is similar to the process by which two people operate a telephone. When communication is required, a call is placed, and it is disconnected when the transmission has ended.

Error Correction

Frame Relay also has error correction built into it, but not nearly to the extent that X.25 has. Similar to the cyclic redundancy check (CRC) in an Ethernet network, Frame Relay uses a Frame Check Sequence (FCS) that is appended to the end of each frame passed. When a station receives a frame, it computes a new FCS on the data portion and compares it to the FCS that was in the frame. If they are different, it drops the packet without notifying the sending station. While this may sound bad, it is in fact a good thing. Because of this technique, Frame Relay is faster at transferring data than X.25, because no time is lost in the overhead of having to process error checking or having to resend information. Instead, Frame Relay relies on the next layer that is communicating over it to handle error recovery, which most level-3 protocols do. If the protocol that is running over Frame Relay is connection oriented, such as the TCP half of TCP/IP, there are no problems, since it will handle its own error recovery and flow control. However, if the protocol is connectionless, like that of UDP, the application that is implementing it must be specifically coded for self-recovery.

X.25

X.25 is similar to Frame Relay in that it is a packet-switched technology that typically operates as PVC. Since data on a packet-switched network is capable of following any available circuit path, it is usually depicted as clouds in graphical representations, as shown in Figure 11-1.

X.25 was introduced at a time when WAN links, traveling through the public switched network, were primarily analog lines producing errors and poor transmissions. X.25 sought to remedy this through built-in error correction and flow control. The trade-off for this reliability is performance. With all the acknowledgments, buffering, and retransmission that happens within X.25, latency becomes an issue. In the grander scheme of things, for protocols that provide their own error detection and correction, such as TCP, it is a poor performer.

FIGURE 11-1

Basic X.25 configuration

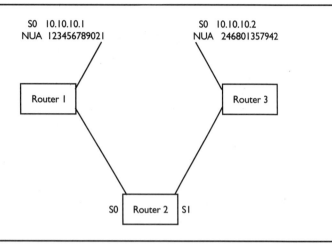

X.25 encompasses the first three layers of the OSI model. On each end of an X.25 connection, along the Physical layer of the OSI model, is a data terminal equipment (DTE) device and a data circuit–terminating equipment (DCE) device. Each DTE on an X.25 network is given a unique address, which can be used much like a telephone number.

Asynchronous Transfer Mode (ATM)

At first glance, ATM seems very close to Frame Relay. ATM's use of switching and multiplexing technologies, virtual circuits, and dynamic bandwidth allocation demonstrates that it was at least based on the foundations of Frame Relay. Where Frame Relay ends as an excellent WAN technology, ATM continues to the LAN. ATM blurs the lines between LAN and WAN technologies, creating for the first time a viable all-in-one solution.

One important difference between ATM and Frame Relay is the guarantee of delivery. Earlier we discussed how Frame Relay is a Layer-2 technology that relies on the encapsulated Layer-3 protocol for error recovery. ATM differs in that, depending on the transmission, it has the capability to provide a guaranteed delivery at a specific rate.

ATM's packet sizes are created at a fixed length, instead of varying like Frame Relay and X.25. The ATM cell is 53 bytes long and is referred to as a *cell*. A 5-byte header contains the address information and other fields of information used to route the cell through the network. Following the header is a 48-byte information field called a *payload*. Because of this fixed length, ATM can predict and control the number of packets, to control bandwidth utilization.

Having a cell of a fixed length also means that buffers can be designed at a set length, thereby allowing hardware switching. Using switching technology in hardware rather than in software tables helps minimize latency for time-critical data such as video and sound.

One of the reasons ATM is so fast is because of its use of virtual channels and virtual paths to route traffic through the network. By implementing virtual channel connections (VCC), the routes to be used by the ATM routing device are determined before data is even transferred. Using this method, the transfer of data does not require complex routing decisions to be made in real time through software-based routing tables. Routing decisions are made in the hardware, thereby minimizing latency in data transfer.

The VPI and VCI numbers in ATM are similar to the DLCI number found in Frame Relay in that they only have relevance locally. In this case, "locally" refers to a segment, which can be either between a host and a switch, or between two switches. Even though two switches might recognize the VCC by different numbers, it is still the same circuit.

Also, as in Frame Relay, virtual circuits can be categorized into two groups: PVCs and SVCs. A PVC is a connection between endpoints that is not dynamically established or removed. If you'll recall, PVC connections are manually implemented and manually released. Implementation in an ATM network is typically found at the WAN level. An SVC is a connection that is dynamically established and released. It is most often found at the LAN level, all the way to the desktop.

ATM is often referred to as a shared-media LAN. One obvious characteristic of shared-media LANs is that, with each new user, it becomes less available for everybody else. Hosts must contend for access to the transmission medium, since in a shared-media LAN, the network is available to only one user at a time.

ATM LANs can operate over several different types of media. Using a special piece of hardware, ATM can run at 155 Mbps over Category 5 twisted pair. While this is the most widely adapted configuration to the desktop, ATM also has the capability to run at 25 Mbps over two pairs of Category 3 or 4 cable. Finally, for higher ATM speeds and distances of more than 100 meters, fiber-optic cable is required. Over fiber, ATM can run up to 622 Mbps.

DSL

DSL is the acronym for Digital Subscriber Line technology, which is a relatively new technology that makes use of copper telephone lines sometimes referred to as POTS lines (Plain Old Telephone System). DSL significantly increases bandwidth between the telephone companies and their customers when compared to POTS service.

DSL offers users a choice of connection speeds ranging from 32 Kbps to more than 50 Mbps. It is useful for delivering bandwidth-intensive applications like video on demand and distance learning. DSL takes existing voice cables and turns them into a high-speed digital link; the maximum DSL speed is determined by the distance between the customer site and the Telco's Central Office (CO). Most Internet Service Providers (ISPs) offer a range of speeds so customers can choose the rate that meets their specific business needs. At the customer premises, a DSL modem connects the DSL line to a (LAN or an individual computer. Once installed, the DSL modem provides the customer site with continuous connection to the Internet. To use DSL, you will need a DSL modem and a network interface card (NIC).

Types of DSL

There are several forms of DSL, each designed around specific business goals. They are best categorized by the modulation methods used to encode data, as described next.

- ■ **ADSL** Asymmetric Digital Subscriber Line (ADSL) is the most popular form of DSL technology. The limitation of ADSL is that both the upstream and downstream transfer rates are asymmetric, or uneven. In practice, the bandwidth from the provider to the user (downstream) is higher than the upstream link. This is due in part to the limitation of the POTS system, and the desire to accommodate the typical Internet user needs where the majority of data is being sent to the user (programs, graphics, sounds, and video) with minimal upload capacity required. Downstream speeds typically range from 1.5 Mbps to 9 Mbps. Upstream speeds typically range from 64 Kbps to 1.5 Mbps.

■ **HDSL** High bit-rate Digital Subscriber Line (HDSL) is often deployed as a substitute for T1/E1 links. HDSL is becoming popular as a way to provide symmetric data communication (data transfer rates for upstream and downstream communications are equivalent) at rates up to 1.544 Mbps (2.048 Mbps in Europe) over moderate distances via POTS connections. Traditional T1 requires repeaters every 6000 feet to boost the signal strength. HDSL has a longer range than T1/E1 without the use of repeaters to allow transmission over distances up to 12,000 feet.

■ **SDSL** Symmetric Digital Subscriber Line (SDSL) is a two-wire implementation of HDSL and supports T1/E1 on a single wire pair to a distance of 11,000 feet. The name has become more generic over time to refer to symmetric service at a variety of rates over a single loop.

CERTIFICATION OBJECTIVE 11.02

Servers: Their Purpose, Functionality, and Features

Internet information servers are the technology used to provide access to data, resources, and information on the Internet and the World Wide Web. Specialized information servers have evolved to address specific Internet protocols and services. This section provides an overview of Internet servers used for content caching and security (Proxy), e-mail and list servers (SMTP), Web (HTTP), News (NNTP), digital certificates, directories (LDAP), Telnet, mirror servers, and file transfer (FTP).

Proxy Servers

One of the primary functions of a proxy server is to act as a gateway to and from the Internet. Proxy servers are also known as *extensible firewalls*. Being extensible means the functionality of the server can be extended, or made to perform other functions not originally designed as part of the server.

Proxy servers also can work as *content cache servers*. A content cache server stores the Web pages most frequently accessed by the network users. This speeds up the return of Web pages to clients' browsers because they come from a local server rather than the Internet. In most cases, the access speed of the local network is faster than the Internet.

Proxy servers also act as *gateways*. A gateway is a system, hardware, and software that acts as an interface allowing two different systems to communicate. Using a proxy server as a gateway, you can secure your network against unauthorized access. Your users can access other networks on the Internet while you prevent access to your network by unauthorized users.

Proxy servers allow users on the Internet to access the Web servers on your internal network. This feature is known as *reverse proxy*. In addition to reverse proxy, proxy servers have the ability to do *packet filtering*. Packet filtering can make your network more secure by providing you with greater control over how information is accessed.

In general terms, a proxy is the authority to act for another. In the context of a network, a proxy provides a path in and out of the network. Proxy servers have the authority to act on behalf of the local clients.

Clients connect to proxy servers when they make a request for resources located on the Internet. The proxy server gets the resource and returns it to the client. A proxy server can also allow selective computers or protocols to access the internal network. You only present one IP address to the Internet; the proxy server hides your network. Figure 11-2 illustrates how clients can hide from the Internet behind a proxy server.

Proxy Servers and the Internet

The Internet and its protocols comprise an *open system*. An open system in this case means that the protocols are published and equipment is interoperable. These open systems are all interconnected into what we call

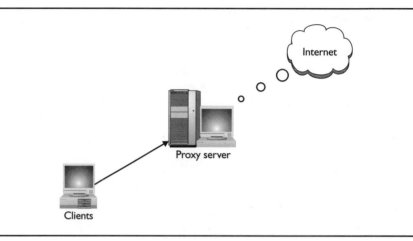

FIGURE 11-2

Hiding from the Internet
behind a proxy server

the Internet. There are numerous private LANs all tied into the public Internet. Although these organizations are interconnected, private networks still need to be isolated from the larger public network for reasons of security and safety. Proxy servers allow you to isolate your private network while still having some degree of manageable access to the Internet.

CERN Compliance

CERN stands for the Conseil Europeen pour la Recherche Nucleaire, or the European Laboratory for Particle Physics. The CERN organization is based in Switzerland. Much of the support for the HyperText Transfer Protocol (HTTP) and the Web libraries has its origins at CERN. As the products evolved, the CERN proxy protocol became the standard that was accepted by the Internet. Web browsers such as Internet Explorer and Netscape Navigator are examples of CERN-compliant applications.

Communications between CERN-compliant proxy servers and clients is done using HTTP. HTTP has commands that clients send to the server. Among these commands are Get and Post. The Get command is used to forward the Uniform Resource Locator (URL) to the server requesting the resource named in the URL. The Post command is used to send the request containing the URL and the data. The user provides this data, generally by using an HTML (HyperText Markup Language) form.

Proxy Server Caching

A Web Proxy service maintains a local copy of HTTP and FTP objects on the local hard disk. This is called *caching*. Not all objects are cached. Some objects change frequently, even each time they are accessed, so caching them is a waste of processing time. Some objects have a security context and are cached for the security reasons. There are two forms of caching: *passive* and *active*.

exam
Watch

Know what the cache types are and how they work.

Passive caching is the predominant cache method used. It is also known as *on-demand caching* because it is available on demand when the client makes the request. As mentioned earlier, a request is the URL of the desired resource.

In a normal (nonproxy server) situation, the client contacts the Web server on the Internet. The Web server responds to the request and sends the requested objects directly back to the client. The proxy server sits in the middle of this process. The client contacts the proxy server with the request. The proxy server goes to the Internet with the request, retrieves the requested object, and then caches that object. If you, or any other client, request the object again, the proxy server gets the object from the local cache rather than from the Web server on the Internet.

Several techniques are used to ensure that the cached information is still current. One technique is to set an expiration time on the object, known as the Time To Live (TTL). When a client requests an object that is cached, the proxy server checks the TTL to determine if the requested object is still valid. If the TTL has not expired, the object is returned to the client. If the TTL has expired, the proxy server goes out to the Internet and retrieves the object, and the TTL process begins again.

Active caching supplements passive caching. The intent of active caching is to maximize the probability that an object will be in local cache when the client requests the object from a proxy server. To accomplish this, the proxy server may automatically retrieve objects from the Internet. It chooses objects by considering such factors as

- **Frequency of request** Objects that are more frequently requested are kept in the cache. If the TTL on one of these objects expires, a new object is requested.

- **Time To Live** Objects having a greater TTL are better to cache than objects with shorter TTLs. In other words, if an object has a short TTL and is seldom requested, it is not advantageous to cache it because the TTL will have expired by the time the next request arrives.

- **Server activity** The proxy server seeks to cache more objects during times of low activity than it does during periods of high activity.

WinSock Proxy Service

Windows Sockets (WinSock) is a set of application programming interfaces (APIs) that applications can use to communicate with other applications in the network. Many applications may be running on the same computer, even though the processes are being conducted across the network. The APIs support the following functions:

- Initiating an outbound session as a client
- Accepting an inbound session as a server
- Transferring data on the established connection
- Terminating the session

WinSock is a port of the Berkeley Sockets API for UNIX. It has extensions for the Win16 and Win32 message-based application environments. It supports the Windows TCP/IP protocol stacks, and supports other protocols such as IPX/SPX.

WinSock supports a point-to-point connection-oriented session. It also supports a point-to-point or multipoint connectionless session.

The WinSock Proxy service offers the following features:

- Support for WinSock 1.1–based applications (for example, Telnet)
- Secure IP
- Control of inbound and outbound access
- Filtering of Internet sites by domain or IP address
- Data encryption through SSL

The WinSock Proxy service works with Windows-based client computers. It allows WinSock applications to run remotely. However, the WinSock Proxy service does not support Windows Sockets 2.0 API.

The WinSock Proxy service is a client/server process that runs only on Windows NT 4.0 Server running Proxy Server. It allows client applications to run as if they are directly connected to the Internet.

On the client computer, WinSock DLLs are replaced with the WinSock Proxy client DLLs. During installation, the original DLLs are renamed and the proxy DLLs are given the same name. This allows the WinSock applications to link to the proxy DLLs when the application is run.

The WinSock Proxy service sets up a control session between the client and the server to allow for messages. The session uses the UDP protocol with a simple acknowledgement protocol added for reliability. The control session uses UDP port number 1745 on both the WinSock Proxy server and client. This control session serves the following functions:

- **Routing information**   When the session is first established, the server sends the client the LAT (local address table). This table contains the list of internal IP addresses and subnets.

- **Establishing the TCP connection**   When the client makes the connection to the remote application, the server uses the control session to establish this virtual connection. After the connection is established, the control session is not used for data.

- **Message traffic**   The control session is used for nondata requests, such as a request for a host name resolution (DNS).

SOCKS Proxy Service

The SOCKS Proxy service is a cross-platform mechanism used to establish secure communications between the server and the client. This service allows for transparent access to the Internet using Proxy Server. This service does not support applications that use UDP, nor does it support the IPX/SPX protocol.

The SOCKS protocol acts as a proxy. It allows a host on one side of a SOCKS server to access a host on the other side of a SOCKS server. You do not need a direct IP connection to do this. SOCKS has two operations: *Connect* and *Bind.*

The Connect operation is used when the SOCKS client needs to connect to an application server. This connection request includes information such as the SOCKS protocol version number, command code, destination IP address and port number, and a user ID.

The SOCKS Proxy service receives the request. The server replies to the client with a status such as granted, rejected, or failed. If the client request was rejected or failed, the server may return an error code indicating why, and close the connection without further action.

If the request to connect is successful, the server executes the Bind operation. The Bind operation provides access control.

The Guardian Between You and the Internet

The computer that runs the proxy server has two NICs: one connected to your network, and one connected to the Internet. This physically isolates your LAN from the Internet.

Packet Filtering

Packet filtering is a scheme whereby certain packets are passed through to the network and others are discarded. You can block or enable reception of certain types of packets through certain ports. Ports are only opened as needed. Packets are allowed in for only the minimum duration required and only on specified ports.

SMTP Servers

The main standard for Internet mail, on which other standards are built, is the Simple Mail Transfer Protocol (SMTP). Before this standard was implemented and available, electronic mail was transferred between systems using the file transfer protocol, which was very inefficient. SMTP was developed to support the transfer of mail across the Internet.

The purpose of SMTP servers is to transfer mail reliably and efficiently. SMTP is independent of the particular transmission subsystem. The SMTP service uses the SMTP protocol to deliver e-mail messages. Remote mail servers transfer messages from themselves to the SMTP server designated as the domain. The SMTP service uses TCP port 25 to listen for a connection. The SMTP service receives e-mail from other SMTP servers or directly from applications themselves.

SMTP uses a style of asymmetric request-response protocol. If mail delivery fails, sendmail (one of the most popular SMTP implementations) will queue mail messages and retry delivery later.

Mail Transfer Agents (MTAs)

MTAs are permanently running programs on hosts with permanent connections to the Internet. Host computers running MTA software are commonly known as *mail servers*. An MTA "listens" for incoming e-mail from both local and remote MTAs, examines the e-mail, and either saves it locally (in a spool file) for retrieval by the destination user or identifies a remote MTA and transfers the e-mail to it.

Several MTAs may be involved in the transfer of e-mail from originator to destination across the Internet. The intermediate MTAs are known as *mail relays*. Typical MTAs are programs such as sendmail and exim. A different type of MTA will listen for requests from users for any e-mail saved for them and will transfer the e-mail to the user.

Mail User Agents (MUAs)

An MUA is a client application used to send and receive e-mail. It provides a user interface for composition and local storage of e-mail messages, and also has facilities to communicate with MTAs. There are numerous MUAs available under modern Windows-based environments; typical examples include Eudora and Microsoft Outlook. On UNIX-based systems, character-based (non-Windows) programs such as elm and Pine are popular.

Domains

On SMTP servers, domains are used to organize messages for delivery. Each SMTP site has at least one domain known as the *default domain.* Strictly speaking, having the one domain is sufficient to operate, but it may not always be desirable. You can create additional domains and configure them as remote domains or local domains. You can also delete domains, but you can never delete the default domain.

Local Domain

A *local domain* is a domain that is served by the local SMTP server. The local domain has an entry in the DNS table. When a message arrives at the SMTP server and is addressed to the local domain, the SMTP server puts the message in a local Drop folder. The local SMTP server cannot send the message to a remote SMTP server. If it cannot put the message in a local Drop folder, it must return a nondelivery report (NDR) to the sender.

NDRs go through the same delivery process as regular messages and are subject to the same restrictions. If an NDR cannot be delivered to the sender, the SMTP server places a copy of the message in the Badmail folder. You can also send NDR notification to another location. You should check the Badmail folder periodically. Deleting messages and NDRs from the Badmail folder helps system performance, especially if there are numerous messages.

Remote Domains

A *remote domain* is a domain that is not local. This means there is no Drop folder for that domain on the local SMTP server. Mail addressed to remote domains is forwarded to the SMTP server specified for that domain. The SMTP uses DNS entries to locate the remote domain SMTP server.

SMTP server uses the following process to deliver remote mail:

1. **Sort messages** SMTP sorts the messages by domains. This allows the service to send the messages to a group, optimizing the connection and the transfer.

2. **Queue the messages** SMTP puts them in a queue ready to send.

3. **Connect to the remote server** SMTP attempts to connect to the remote server. If the connection cannot be made, or if the server is not ready, the messages remain in the queue. The delivery is attempted again at a designated time, up to the maximum number of attempts specified.

4. **Verify recipients** Message recipients are verified. If the recipient is not at the remote server (not verified), an NDR is generated for that message.

5. **Send** Once the verification is complete and the recipient is verified, the message is sent and acknowledged.

List Servers

Mailing lists are commonly used to provide support for products and services and to allow people to discuss common interests. List servers work with standard e-mail (POP3) accounts and send messages through your ISP's SMTP server.

E-mail list management software solutions have been developed to make managing e-mail lists more efficient. The most popular commercial list server software is LISTSERV. LISTSERV performs several functions that would otherwise have to be managed manually as in the days before any e-mail list management software existed. LISTSERV was the first software introduced to automate the administration of e-mail lists, and currently offers a full set of features for the list member, list owner, and site maintainer to manipulate their list/site configurations. A public domain version of list server software, Majordomo, is also available.

In order to use LISTSERV, the server software must be installed on a server with a dedicated connection to the Internet. When a list is set up, an e-mail address is created for the list, which is then used to post messages to the list. Once a message is sent, it is delivered to the central server where the mailing list management software resides. The software then completes the operation by automatically distributing the message to every subscriber on the list.

Web (HTTP) Servers

One of the most popular applications today is publishing on the World Wide Web (WWW), sometimes referred to as W3, or just *the Web*. Organizations have discovered that the Web is a wonderful place to publish information internally and externally. The WWW service has an intuitive interface that works as well inside the corporate firewall as it does internationally on the Web. The Web is founded on standards developed by the Internet community. The advantage of using standards-based products is communication with others who might be using other software or hardware.

You do not actually "go" to the Web page as in a login, Telnet, or FTP session. Your Web browser requests an HTML page from the remote site specified by the URL. As your browser interprets this HTML document while downloading it from the remote site, it may encounter requests for other objects such as pictures, audio, and other multimedia format files corresponding to the MIME (Multipurpose Internet Mail Extensions) standard.

The Web can tie together many servers throughout the world or within your organization into what appears to users as unified information content. With this power, the Web is preferable to storing information in the form of files on different servers.

WWW Service

HTTP is the protocol of the World Wide Web. HTTP grew out of a need for a standards-based protocol to simplify the way in which users access information on the Internet. It is a generic, stateless, object-oriented protocol. HTTP is at the Application layer of the protocol model. HTTP categorizes data, allowing systems to be built independently of the data being transferred.

Virtual Servers

The WWW service supports a concept called *virtual servers*. A virtual server can be used to host multiple domain names on the same physical Web server. You need a unique IP address for each virtual server that you host. This is sometimes referred to as *multihoming*.

on the
job

Each virtual server requires a unique IP address that is assigned to the NIC.

Web Server Functionality

The HTTP protocol is based on a client/server model. There must be a server-side application and a client-side application. The client and the server interact to perform a specific task. When a client clicks a hyperlink, the HTTP protocol performs the following:

1. The client browser uses HTTP to communicate with the server.

2. A connection is established from the client to the server. The server monitors TCP port 80 by default.

3. Once the connection is made, the requested message is sent to the server. The requests are typically for a resource file.

4. The server sends a response message to the client, along with the data the client requested.

5. The server closes the connection unless the client's browser has configured a keep-alive option.

HTTP Requests

The client communicates with the server in the form of a *simple request method*, which consists of a URL and a protocol version. The following is an example of an HTTP request:

Get http://www.microsoft.com/cert_train/iis HTTP 1.0

The preceding request contains the following elements that are interpreted by the Web server:

- **get**   Specifies the request method.
- **URL**   //www.microsoft.com/cert_train/iis; specifies which object to get.
- **HTTP 1.0**   The version of the protocol to be used.

The following elements may be used in an HTTP request:

- **Request**   Such as "get."
- **Resource**   The URL path to the object.
- **Message**   The message makes a simple request into a full request and can include additional information such as a MIME, request modifiers, and client information.
- **Response**   The HTTP response message.

HTTP Server Response Messages

The client sends a request to the HTTP (Web) server. The server receives the request and responds with a status message. The message includes the protocol version, and a success or error code. A MIME message follows containing server information, entity information, and possibly body content. Table 11-1 contains examples of server status messages.

Message	Type	Description
2.xx	Success	The request was successfully received.
3.xx	Redirection	Further action must be taken to complete the request.
4.xx	Client error	The request contains bad syntax, or the request cannot be fulfilled.
5xx	Server error	The server has failed to fulfill a valid request.
1xx1	Informational	This series has been reserved for future use. It is not currently used.

exam
Ⓦatch

Know the syntax of a request and how to construct a URL.

MIME Types

If your server has files that use different file formats, your server must have a MIME mapping for each different file type or extension. If you don't have this, your client's browser may not be able to retrieve the file. These mapping associations are identified in the HTTP header.

HTTP Ports and Connections

The HTTP server monitors port 80 for Web client connections. Changing the port number on the server requires that the clients specify the same port number when they attempt to connect. This may act as a small security screen because the client needs to know which port is in use but, as in the case with FTP, this is not much of an obstacle to an experienced hacker.

EXERCISE II-I

Connecting to Your HTTP Server

This exercise will demonstrate the ability of your browser to connect to the Web server. You will also modify the TCP port and reconnect to the server specifying the new port number.

1. Log in to Windows NT as Administrator.

2. Start Internet Explorer.

3. In the Address box, type **Serverxx**, where **xx** is the number of your server.

4. Press ENTER. Your browser should connect to your server.

5. Close IE.

6. Open Internet Service Manager.

7. Expand your server so that you can see the Default Web Site.

8. Right-click the Default Web Site.

9. Click Properties.

10. Ensure that the Web Site is selected.

11. What is the default TCP port?

12. Modify the TCP port number to 3300.

13. Click APPLY.

14. Open Internet Explorer.

15. What message did you get?

16. Click OK to clear the error message.

17. In the Address box, type **http://serverxx:3300**.

18. Press ENTER.

19. What happened?

20. Close IE.

21. Switch to the Web property sheet.

22. Set the TCP port to 80.

23. Click APPLY.

24. Close the MMC.

News (NNTP) Servers

The Network News Transport Protocol (NNTP) provides a robust and scalable service for newsgroup servers. NNTP allows you to host and participate in newsgroup-style discussion, and allows users to read articles and to post articles for others to read.

NNTP service supports both client-to-server and server-to-server communication over the Internet. NNTP supports popular extensions and

FROM THE CLASSROOM

Developing an Internet Computing Environment for E-business

A successful e-business requires developing a computing environment integrating your e-business applications, networks, databases, servers, systems, databases, and other information technology assets. When deploying Web-based applications that your customers, suppliers, and employees depend on, you must build in *scalability* to accommodate growth. Scalability means your server environment and platform can scale to meet a dramatic surge in demand once you have deployed your e-business infrastructure. If an e-business fails to predict demand when deploying applications, it risks losing potential online sales, making customers and suppliers frustrated or dissatisfied when system response time increases and performance decreases. Network and server *security* is key. As you open your business to the world, you want to make sure that your systems and applications execute in a secure environment that allows for access control, and maintain privacy and confidentiality of your data. Certificate servers, proxy servers, and encryption using SSL and user authentication are key technology components. For your e-business strategy to be successful, you should plan, design, and implement applications and systems that are

reliable. Server downtime and sluggish performance are unacceptable in the e-business world. For example, when you deploy your systems, you should consider having backup systems and mirror servers and sites to prepare for system outages. To ease your transition into an e-business, you should deploy *server-centric* applications that are maintained in one central location. In a server-centric environment, Java applications and applets can be written once and run on any platform. This makes systems and network management much more cost and time efficient. Also consider centralizing information directories and resources using a directory server based on LDAP. Finally, you must *integrate* your Web-enabled applications with your core business systems and/or legacy-based applications and data. By deploying applications that are easily integrated, you are better able to leverage existing resources, including servers, databases, applications, and other information technology assets. Begin to think of your entire information infrastructure as a whole instead of a collection of individual components.

—Maxwell Miller, Ph.D., CIW, CWT, i-Net+

is fully compatible with other NNTP clients and servers. NNTP supports the following content formats:

- Multipurpose Internet Mail Extension (MIME)
- HyperText Markup Language (HTML)
- Graphics Interchange Format (GIF)
- Joint Photographic Experts Group (JPEG)

NNTP Service

The NNTP service is a client/server process. The news client uses the TCP/IP protocol and makes the connection to the NNTP server through port 119. When the inbound connection is made, the server authenticates the client. After authentication takes place, the user then gets a list of available newsgroups from the server. The user selects which newsgroups to view, but no articles from the newsgroup have been sent yet. The server verifies that the client is authorized to access this newsgroup and sends the client a list of articles available in the newsgroup. The client selects and requests certain news articles. The NNTP server then sends the client the contents of the selected articles.

NNTP servers allow the server administrator to limit the size of articles that may be posted. The size of newsgroup postings can also be limited. You can specify if other servers will be allowed to pull articles from this server, and what to do with control messages. You can post control messages or just log them in the log.

You can specify the SMTP server where postings for moderated groups are forwarded. This can be a host name or a path name. If you use the host name, the NNTP service needs to be able to find the host name in a DNS table. If you use the directory path, the path must either be on the local machine or a virtual directory.

Moderated Newsgroups

When you want to have articles read by someone who will be responsible for approving or rejecting the article, consider creating a *moderated newsgroup*. An article posted to a moderated newsgroup is not actually posted until the moderator posts it. In a moderated newsgroup, when the user posts a message, the NNTP server sends that message to the moderator. The NNTP service uses the SMTP server to send messages to the moderator.

The moderator receives a message. The moderator reviews the article and either rejects it or posts it. When the moderator posts the article, it becomes available to all readers of the newsgroup.

If the moderator rejects the article, the moderator can elect to return the article to the sender with an explanation about why the article is being rejected. Otherwise, the moderator simply discards the message.

Newsgroup Limits and Expirations

You can establish a limit for the length of time an article may be kept through a *news expiration policy*. You can set this expiration limit for one or more newsgroups, and these policies can vary from newsgroup to newsgroup.

Certificate Servers

It is highly desirable, especially in an environment on which security is a concern, to be able to determine or authenticate with whom you are communicating. You cannot see or hear the person on the other end when you communicate electronically. With electronic communication, it is difficult to ensure secure communication because it happens so fast and at such great volume.

Digital Certificates

Digital certificates are a form of authentication. They provide the mechanism necessary to conduct private communications in an open environment. They also provide a method to "prove" the origin of the communications. These requirements work both ways. As a user, you want to be sure that the host and processes you are accessing are, in fact, what you think they are. The same logic holds true for the host. The host processes also need to validate who is on the other end of the communication process.

In the physical world of documents, you have a certain interaction that assures you (at least at some level) of the authenticity of the documents and the process. For example, consider the use of a passport. The customs official who looks at your passport and then accepts it as proof of your identity, trusts that your government did an adequate job of identifying you before issuing you a passport. There has to be a level of trust in the certifying authority.

In order to guarantee authenticity of public keys, a certificate server is used to provide digital certificates as a secure method of exchanging public keys over a nonsecure network such as the Internet.

Certificate Servers

The purpose of a *certificate server* is to generate digital certificates in standard X.509 format. These certificates are used for public key applications, including

- Server and client authentication under the Secure Sockets Layer (SSL) protocol

- Secure e-mail using Secure/Multipurpose Internet Mail Extensions (S/MIME)

- Secure payment using Secure Electronic Transaction (SET)

Server Components

A typical certificate server consists of the following three elements:

- The *server engine* is the core component and acts as the data pump for the requests it receives from the users and other servers. It pushes information between the components during request processing and certificate generation. The engine monitors each request through the various processes to ensure data processing.

- A *Web server* often acts as *intermediary* component that receives the request for a new certificate from the requestor (Web client). The intermediary submits the request to the server engine on behalf of the requestor. Internet Information Server is an intermediary that handles requests from HTTP clients and forwards the requests to the server engine. Intermediaries can be written to be client specific, transport specific, or policy criteria specific.

■ The *server database* maintains status information and a record of all issued certificates. It also maintains server logs and queues. The database stores all certificates issued by the server so administrators can track, audit, and archive server activity. In addition, the server database is used by the server engine to store pending revocations prior to publishing them. The server queue maintains status information as the server is processing a certificate request.

Directory Servers (LDAP)

Information describing the various users, applications, files, and other resources available on a network is often collected in a special database referred to as a *directory* server. These objects may reside on the same LAN, on an intranet, or on the worldwide Internet. As the number of networks and information applications in use has increased dramatically, specialized directories of information have also grown, resulting in islands of data that cannot be easily shared across networks, and are difficult to maintain and administer. Directory servers were designed to ease the use of these objects across distributed networked computers.

The Lightweight Directory Access Protocol, or LDAP, is an open-industry standard that defines a method for accessing and updating information stored in directories. Since LDAP is a vender-neutral standard, it is being widely adopted by software vendors and application developers

QUESTIONS AND ANSWERS

Do I need to install a certificate server to operate a Web site?	No, you never need to install a certificate server. Certificates add to security, but their absence does not affect functionality.
If I only have an intranet, should I install a certificate server?	Maybe. The functionality that certificates offer can be useful on a large internal network. On smaller networks, the need to authenticate at this level may not be so critical.
If public keys are available to everyone, how can the system be secure?	It takes two keys to make the system work. If you don't have both keys, you can't decrypt.

for use with the Internet, intranets, and extranets. Many LDAP servers are available from different vendors, including IBM, Netscape, Novell, and Microsoft.

LDAP is based on a client/server computing model and has evolved from the X.500 standard. Originally developed to access X.500 directory access protocol (DAP), LDAP has since become independent, and servers are supporting the LDAP protocol. Some of the main advantages of LDAP over X.500 and DAP include

■ LDAP runs over TCP/IP rather than the OSI protocol stack, making LDAP much more widely available to Internet-based systems.

■ LDAP uses a simpler functional model, making LDAP easier to understand and implement.

■ LDAP uses strings to represent data rather than complicated structured syntaxes such as Abstract Syntax Notation.

Telnet

Telnet is a terminal emulation program for TCP/IP networks such as the Internet that is assigned to port 23. Telnet provides a remote terminal using a character-based interface over the Internet. It provides a user with remote access to a host using a standard terminal emulator such as a VT-100. It is described in RFC854 and was first published in 1983.

The Telnet client runs on your computer and connects your PC to a server on the network. You can then enter commands through the Telnet program and they are executed as if you were entering them directly on the server console. Telnet provides a common method to remotely control Web servers. The Telnet server daemon *telnetd* runs a login shell program that implements the Telnet service.

The Network Virtual Terminal

Communication is established using the TCP/IP protocols, and communication is based on a set of facilities known as a Network Virtual Terminal (NVT). At the client end, the Telnet client program is responsible for mapping incoming NVT codes to the actual codes needed to operate the user's display device, and is also responsible for mapping user-generated keyboard sequences into NVT sequences.

The NVT uses 7-bit codes for characters. The terminal is only required to display the "standard" printing ASCII characters represented by 7-bit codes, and to recognize and process certain control codes. The 7-bit characters are transmitted as 8-bit bytes with most significant bit set to zero. An end-of-line is transmitted as the character sequence CR (carriage return) followed by LF (line feed). If it is desired to transmit an actual carriage return, this is transmitted as a carriage return followed by a NULL (all bits zero) character.

Mirror Servers

A *mirror server* is a backup server that duplicates all the processes and transactions of the primary server. If, for any reason, the primary server fails, the backup server can immediately take its place without losing any downtime.

Server mirroring is an expensive but effective strategy for achieving fault tolerance. It's expensive because each server must be mirrored by an identical server whose only purpose is to be there in the event of a failure.

Mirror *sites* are Web sites that provide duplicate content at a different URL. Mirror sites are used to store mirror copies of applications and content that is colocated in nearby geographic regions close to the end user. This eliminates unnecessary network traffic across wide geographic boundaries.

File Transfer Protocol (FTP) Servers

FTP is a client/server process for transferring files between host computers. FTP uses two connections: the *control connection* and the *data connection.* These connections may have one of two states:

- **Passive open**   A state waiting for transmission
- **Active open**   A state initiating the transmission

The control connection starts the process between the client and the FTP server. The control connection uses port 21 on the server side and an open port on the client side that is greater than 1023. This connection is maintained for the duration of the session.

The data connection is managed by a set of programs known as the *data transfer* process. The server maintains a passive open state at port 21 listening for an FTP connection request from the client. When a request arrives, the server sets up the control session and receives FTP commands from the client. This session remains until the user types **Bye** or **Quit**.

The data transfer connection gets set up only when there is data to transfer between the server and the client. After the data transfer is complete, the connection is closed. The next time data is to be transferred, a new data connection is established. The control connection remains open through multiple data transfers. The server data port is always 20.

When you enter an FTP command, a return code and its associated message appears after the command. Figure 11-3 contains an example of command usage and the resulting return codes.

Sockets

An FTP port, or a *socket*, represents the endpoint of a network connection. Two numbers identify TCP sockets:

- **IP address**   The IP address identifies the computer on the network.

- **TCP port number**   The TCP port number identifies a process or application at the computer.

An example of such a number is 201.200.199.250(20).

FIGURE 11-3

FTP command and
return codes

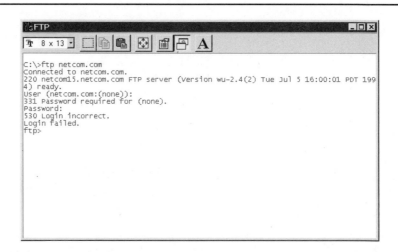

```
C:\>ftp netcom.com
Connected to netcom.com.
220 netcom15.netcom.com FTP server (Version wu-2.4(2) Tue Jul 5 16:00:01 PDT 199
4) ready.
User (netcom.com:(none)):
331 Password required for (none).
Password:
530 Login incorrect.
Login failed.
ftp>
```

A *TCP port* is the address of a server on an IP network. When an application uses TCP, it calls an assigned port for access. For example, the FTP service always monitors TCP port 21 for activity.

TCP ports are divided into two general categories: *well-known ports* and *dynamic ports*. A TCP port can be referred to by several different names, including

- TCP port number
- Port address
- TCP port
- Port number
- Port
- Data port

TCP ports can be numbered from 0 to 65,535. Port numbers 0 through 1023 are reserved for server-side use and never change. Port numbers 0 through 1023 are called *well-known ports* because they never change. These well-known ports are preassigned by the Internet Assigned Numbers Authority (IANA). You can always expect FTP to monitor port 21 in a standard configuration.

Ports 1024 through 65,535 are reserved for client-side applications. These port numbers are assigned dynamically by the operating system when an application makes a request for service. An application may be assigned a given port number on one occasion and another port number on a different occasion, even though the application may be performing the same function on both occasions.

A server-side application that uses TCP always has at least one preassigned, or well-known, port number. By way of example, FTP uses two port numbers for its service:

- Port 20 for data
- Port 21 for control

EXERCISE 11-2

Entering FTP Commands

1. Log on as Administrator.
2. Using Windows NT Explorer, select the \interpub\ftp root folder.
3. Right-click the right side pane.
4. Click New.
5. Click Text Document.
6. Type **From_Server01** in the dialog box. Press ENTER to create the file, and you are done.

EXERCISE 11-3

Observing Various Return Codes

1. Log in as Administrator.
2. Open a command prompt.
3. Type **ftp server01** and press ENTER.
4. Which return code was returned?
5. Enter **anonymous** for a username.
6. Press ENTER to supply a null password.
7. Which return codes were returned?
8. Open Internet Service Manager.
9. Expand the Server01 site.
10. Right-click the Default FTP Site.
11. Select Properties.
12. Click Current Sessions.
13. Which user is logged in?
14. Return to the command prompt.
15. Type **Bye**.

16. Press the up arrow key. The previous command, ftp server01, should be displayed. If it is not displayed, type **ftp server01**.

17. Press ENTER.

18. Enter **anonymous** for a username.

19. Type **Max@S4.com** and press ENTER.

20. Return to the MMC, Default FTP Site Properties.

21. Click Current Sessions.

22. Which user is logged in?

23. Return to the command prompt.

24. Change directories to the \inetpub\ftproot folder.

25. Type **dir** and press ENTER.

26. What do you see listed?

27. Type **get From_Server01.txt** and press ENTER.

28. Type **bye** to quit the FTP session. Close the command prompt.

29. Click CANCEL in the Default FTP Site Properties.

CERTIFICATION SUMMARY

This chapter reviewed the topics of Internet bandwidth technologies and connectivity options. You learned about the high-speed digital data link connections using T1/T3 connections and their European E1/E3 counterparts. You were introduced to various packet-delivery protocols and standards, including Frame Relay, X.25, ATM, and DSL.

You learned about Internet servers, including their purpose, function, and features. While software vendors have their own specific server implementations, they generally share a set of core features and functions based on the Internet standards and protocols for their services. You were given an overview of Internet Information servers, including Proxy, Mail (SMTP), List, Web (HTTP), News (NNTP), Certificate, Directory (LDAP), Mirror servers and sites, and File Transfer (FTP) servers.

TWO-MINUTE DRILL

❑ T1 is simply ITU-T's (International Telecommunication Union-Telecommunication Standardization Sector, formerly the CCITT) North American name for the 1.544 Mbps standard pipe that can be used to pass signal traffic.

❑ The European standard, called E1, contains more bandwidth (2.048 Mbps) because it is supported by 32 DS-0s.

❑ T1s/E1s can be transmitted over several types of media, such as copper wire and fiber-optic cabling.

❑ The most common technique used to digitize an analog signal into the DS-0 format is called PCM (pulse code modulation).

❑ Time-division multiplexing is a technique used to transmit a number of small signals (in this case, the DS-0s) into one continuous, larger signal.

❑ Framing is an error-control procedure used to multiplex a logical data stream.

❑ T1 signals are held to a standard that requires each byte (8 total bits) to contain at least one binary pulse. This standard is called *ones density*.

❑ X.25 is similar to Frame Relay in that it is a packet-switched technology that typically operates as permanent virtual circuit (PVC).

❑ SVCs (switched virtual circuits) are a lot like telephone calls: a connection is established, data is transferred, and then the connection is terminated.

❑ PVCs (permanent virtual circuits) are closer to a leased line idea in that their connection is always present.

❑ Frame Relay is not a certain type of interface; rather, it is an encapsulation method that operates at Layer 2 and runs on top of nearly any serial interface.

❑ One important difference between ATM and Frame Relay is the guarantee of delivery.

❑ One of the reasons ATM is so fast is because of its use of virtual channels and virtual paths to route traffic through the network.

❑ Asymmetric Digital Subscriber Line (ADSL) is the most popular form of DSL technology.

❑ The limitation of ADSL is that both the upstream and downstream transfer rate is asymmetric, or uneven. Downstream speeds typically range from 1.5 Mbps to 9 Mbps. Upstream speeds typically range from 64 Kbps to 1.5 Mbps.

❑ High Bit-Rate Digital Subscriber Line (HDSL) is often deployed as a substitute for T1/E1 links.

❑ Symmetric Digital Subscriber Line (SDSL) is a two-wire implementation of HDSL, and supports T1/E1 on a single wire pair to a distance of 11,000 ft. The name has become more generic over time to refer to symmetric service at a variety of rates over a single loop.

❑ Proxy servers act as a gateway to the Internet.

❑ Proxy servers can be extensible firewalls.

❑ Proxy servers also act as content servers.

❑ Reverse proxy is when users on the Internet access your Web server through Proxy Server.

❑ SOCKS Proxy service allows host-to-host communication to occur in a secure fashion.

❑ Expiration of content is controlled by the Time To Live (TTL).

❑ Passive cache is storing Internet objects on the local disk.

❑ Active caching attempts to predict which objects will be requested frequently, and stores those objects on the local disk before they are requested by a client.

❑ The main standard for Internet mail, on which others are built, is the Simple Mail Transfer Protocol (SMTP).

❑ The purpose of SMTP servers is to transfer mail reliably and efficiently.

❑ The SMTP service uses TCP port 25 to listen for a connection.

❑ MTAs are permanently running programs on hosts with permanent connections to the Internet. Host computers running MTA software are commonly known as mail servers.

❑ MUA is a client application used to send and receive e-mail.

❑ List servers work with standard e-mail (POP3) accounts and send messages through your ISP's SMTP server.

❑ The most popular commercial list server software is LISTSERV.

❑ A public domain version of list server software, Majordomo, is also available.

❑ HyperText Transfer Protocol (HTTP) is a generic, stateless, object-oriented protocol.

❑ A virtual server can be used to host multiple domain names on the same physical Web server.

❑ The HTTP protocol is based on a client/server model. There must be a server-side application and a client-side application.

❑ An HTTP server monitors port 80 for Web client connections.

❑ The Network News Transport Protocol (NNTP) provides a robust and scalable service for newsgroup servers.

❑ The news client uses the TCP/IP protocol and makes the connection to the NNTP server through port 119.

❑ NNTP servers allow the server administrator to limit the size of articles that may be posted. The size of newsgroup postings can also be limited.

❑ Digital certificates are a form of authentication.

❑ Information describing the various users, applications, files, and other resources available on a network is often collected in a special database referred to as a directory server.

❑ The Lightweight Directory Access Protocol, or LDAP, is an open-industry standard that defines a method for accessing and updating information stored in directories.

❑ LDAP is based on a client/server computing model and has evolved from the X.500 standard.

❑ LDAP was originally developed to access X.500 directory access protocol (DAP).

❑ Telnet is a terminal emulation program for TCP/IP networks such as the Internet.

❑ Telnet provides a remote terminal using a character-based interface over the Internet, using a standard terminal emulator such as a VT-100. It is described in RFC854 and was first published in 1983.

❑ The Telnet server daemon *telnetd* runs a login shell program that implements the Telnet service.

❑ A mirror server is a backup server that duplicates all the processes and transactions of the primary server.

❑ Server mirroring is an expensive but effective strategy for achieving fault tolerance.

❑ Mirror *sites* are Web sites that provide duplicate content at a different URL.

❑ FTP is a client/server process based on the TCP protocol.

❑ Use FTP to transfer files between the server and the client.

❑ With FTP, the client must initiate the connection.

SELF TEST

The following Self Test questions will help you measure your understanding of the material presented in this chapter. Read all the choices carefully, as there may be more than one correct answer. Choose all correct answers for each question.

1. What is the data speed of a T1 connection?

    A. 1.544 Mbps

    B. 45 Mbps

    C. 2.048 Mbps

    D. 1.480 Mbps

2. What is the data speed of an E3 connection?

    A. 1.544 Mbps

    B. 2.048 Mbps

    C. 34 Mbps

    D. 45 Mbps

3. Which process is widely used by local exchange carriers to convert analog signals into digital transmissions?

    A. TDM

    B. DS-0

    C. PCM

    D. PPP

4. Which of the following is an error-control procedure used to multiplex a logical data stream?

    A. Encoding

    B. Framing

    C. DS-1

    D. SMTP

5. Which statement(s) are true about Frame Relay?

    A. Frame Relay is a variable packet-size transport service.

    B. Frame Relay uses a variable frame size.

    C. Frame Relay resides at Layer 2 in the OSI model.

    D. All of the above.

6. Which of these is *not* a characteristic of PVCs?

    A. They must each be set up manually.

    B. They are similar to a leased line.

    C. The connections can be established very quickly when the bandwidth is needed.

    D. They require a DTE and a DCE to operate.

7. Which layer(s) of the OSI model does X.25 cover?

    A. 1 and 2

    B. 1, 2, and 3

    C. 2 and 3

    D. 2, 3, and 4

8. Which statement is true of X.25?

    A. It is a cell-based technology.

    B. It is a packet-based technology.

    C. It supports only PVC.

    D. All of the above.

9. Which statement about an ATM packet is *not* true?

   A. It is 56 bytes long.

   B. It contains a 5-byte header.

   C. The information field is 48 bytes long.

   D. Because of its fixed length, it can control bandwidth utilization.

10. ATM guarantees which of the following that Frame Relay does not?

    A. Direct broadcast

    B. Delivery

    C. Error checking

    D. Flow control

11. You are the Webmaster at a small business with an e-commerce site. Your bandwidth requirements are growing and your ISDN service cannot keep up, but you cannot afford a T1 or faster connection. You need a bidirectional high-speed connection for HTTP, NNTP, and FTP. What is the best possible solution?

    A. ADSL

    B. HDSL

    C. SDSL

    D. All of the above

12. Proxy servers can be used in which of the following ways?

    A. Gateway to the Internet

    B. Directory services

    C. Content cache server

    D. All of the above

13. Which of the following statements is true about SOCKS Proxy service?

    A. SOCKS Proxy service is a cross-platform service.

    B. SOCKS supports UDP, IPX/SPX.

    C. SOCKS supports TCP/IP.

    D. All of the above.

14. Which following statement is false about the Simple Mail Transfer Protocol?

    A. SMTP is POP3 compliant.

    B. The SMTP service uses TCP port 25 to listen for a connection.

    C. SMTP uses a style of asymmetric request-response protocol.

15. The Marketing department has decided to create an e-mail distribution list for its customers to advertise monthly product specials. You have been tasked with determining what advantages a list server has over using a standard e-mail client. Your research has determined which of the following? (Choose all that apply.)

    A. List servers are SMTP and POP3 compliant.

    B. The most popular commercial list server software is LISTSERV.

    C. List servers are NNTP compliant.

    D. All of the above.

16. Which of the following statements is true about Web servers?

    A. The default port for Web client connections is 80.

B.   HTTP is the protocol supported by Web servers.

C.   HTTP communications are secure.

D.   None of the above.

17.   Which statement about news servers is false?

A.   NNTP is the protocol supported by news servers.

B.   The NNTP service is a client/server process.

C.   The default NNTP server is port 120.

D.   NNTP service supports both client-to-server and server-to-server communications.

18.   You are the security expert on a Web site development team. The specification for an e-commerce system you are implementing requires secure user authentication. Which of the following solutions will meet those needs?

A.   Encrypted communications using SSL

B.   Digital certificates

C.   Username and password access control

D.   All of the above

19.   Which of the following statements are true about LDAP?

A.   LDAP is an open-industry standard.

B.   LDAP runs over the OSI protocol stack.

C.   LDAP has evolved from the X.500 standard.

20.   Which statement(s) are true about the Telnet service?

A.   Telnet is a terminal emulation program for TCP/IP networks.

B.   Telnet is assigned to port 23.

C.   The Telnet server daemon *telnetd* runs a login shell program.

D.   All of the above.

21.   Which statement(s) are true about the mirror servers?

A.   Serves as a backup server that duplicates all the processes of the primary server.

B.   Uses port number 121.

C.   Server mirroring is an expensive but effective strategy for achieving fault tolerance.

D.   All of the above.

22.   To transfer files using FTP, what must be in place?

A.   A default gateway

B.   An FTP server

C.   An HTTP server

D.   An FTP client

23.   Which port does the FTP service monitor for a connection request?

A.   20

B.   21

C.   1024

D.   Any available port

SELF TEST ANSWERS

1. **A.** 1.544 Mbps.
   B, C, and **D** are incorrect. A T1 is 1.544 Mbps; a T3 is approximately 45 Mbps; the European version of a T1 (referred to as an E1) is 2.048 Mbps.

2. **C.** 34 Mbps.
   A, B, and **D** are incorrect. A T1 is 1.544 Mbps; an E1 is 2.048 Mbps; a T3 connection is 45 Mbps.

3. **C.** The most common technique used to digitize an analog signal into the DS-0 format is PCM (Pulse Code Modulation).
   A is incorrect. TDM is time division multiplexing used to multiplex multiple signals on the same carrier. **B** is incorrect because a DS-0 is a type of digital signal. **D** is incorrect as PPP is the point-to-point protocol.

4. **B.** Framing is an error-control procedure used to multiplex a logical data stream. In order to provide better data organization, the signal is formatted using this process.
   A is incorrect because encoding using PCM is not an error control procedure. **C** is incorrect because a DS-1 is a type of digital signal. **D** is incorrect because SMTP is an e-mail protocol.

5. **D.** Frame Relay is a variable packet-size transport service originally designed to carry data, and it therefore uses a variable frame size. The specification allows frame sizes as large as 4096 octets. Frame Relay resides at Layer 2 in the OSI model. Frame Relay access (Layer 1 of the OSI model) may be provided over T1, E1, or ISDN digital carrier facilities.

6. **C** is correct.
   A, B, and **D** are incorrect. PVC connections are permanent and take time to set up. SVC, on the other hand, is automatically created by software through a call setup procedure. This is similar to the process by which two people operate a telephone. When communication is required, a call is placed, and it is disconnected when the transmission has ended.

7. **B** is correct.
   A, C, and **D** are incorrect. X.25 encompasses the first three layers of the OSI model. On each end of an X.25 connection, along the Physical layer of the OSI model, is a data terminal equipment (DTE) device and a data circuit-terminating equipment (DCE) device. Each DTE on an X.25 network is given a unique address, which can be used much like a telephone number.

8. **B.** X.25 is a packet-based technology. ATM is an example of a cell-based technology. **C** is incorrect because although X.25 typically operates as PVC, it can also support SVC. **A** is incorrect.

9. **A.** An ATM packet is 53 bytes in length, not 56 bytes. ATM's packet sizes are created at a fixed length, instead of varying like Frame Relay and X.25. The ATM cell is 53 bytes long and is referred to as a *cell.* A 5-byte header contains the address information and other fields of information used to route the cell through the network. Following the header is a 48-byte information field called a *payload.* Because of this fixed length, ATM can predict and control the number of packets, to control bandwidth utilization.

10. **B.** ATM guarantees delivery, which Frame Relay does not.
C and **D** are incorrect because both Frame Relay and ATM have error checking and flow control. **A** is incorrect because ATM does not directly do broadcast, but it can pseudo-broadcast by replicating each broadcast packet across each virtual circuit that is set up to receive them.

11. **B** and **C.** HDSL is often deployed as a substitute for T1/E1 links. HDSL is becoming popular as a way to provide symmetric data communication (data transfer rates for upstream and downstream communications are equivalent) at rates up to 1.544 Mbps. SDSL is a two-wire implementation of HDSL and supports T1/E1 on a single wire pair to a distance of 11,000 feet.
A is incorrect. ADSL is limited because the bandwidth from the provider to the user (downstream) is higher than the upstream link.

12. **A** and **C.** Proxy servers also act as *gateways.* A gateway is a system, hardware and software, that acts as an interface allowing two different systems to communicate. Proxy servers also can work as a *content cache server.* A content cache server stores the Web pages most frequently accessed by the network users.
B is incorrect. Directory servers are used to implement directories and LDAP.

13. **A** and **C.** SOCKS Proxy service is a cross-platform mechanism that supports secure communications. This service allows for transparent access to the Internet using Proxy Server.
B is incorrect. SOCKS does not support applications that use UDP, nor does it support the IPX/SPX protocol.

14. **B** and **C.** The main standard for Internet mail on which other standards are built is the Simple Mail Transfer Protocol (SMTP). The SMTP service uses TCP port 25 to

listen for a connection. SMTP uses a style of asymmetric request-response protocol. If mail delivery fails, sendmail (one of the most popular SMTP implementations) will queue mail messages and retry delivery later.

A is incorrect because POP3 is an e-mail protocol for transferring messages to e-mail clients, not between servers.

15. **A** and **B.** List servers work with standard e-mail (POP3) accounts and send messages through your ISP's SMTP server. E-mail list management software solutions have been developed to make managing e-mail lists more efficient, The most popular commercial list server software is LISTSERV.

C is incorrect because newsgroup servers are NNTP compliant, not list servers.

16. **A** and **B.** The HTTP server monitors port 80 for Web client connections. Changing the port number on the server requires that clients specify the same port number when they attempt to connect. HyperText Transfer Protocol (HTTP) is the protocol of the World Wide Web and is used for Web server transactions.

C is incorrect. HTTP is not a secure protocol. SSL is used for secure Web communications.

17. **C.** The news client makes the connection to the NNTP server through port 119, not port 120. NNTP provides a robust and scalable service for newsgroup servers. NNTP allows you to host and participate in newsgroup-style discussion, and allows users to read articles and to post articles for others to read. NNTP service supports both client-to-server and server-to-server communication over the Internet.

18. **B.** Digital certificates and certificate servers are a form of authentication and are used as a secure method of exchanging public keys over a nonsecure network such as the Internet.

A is incorrect because SSL is used for secure communications using encryption, and is not used for authentication. **C** is incorrect because usernames and passwords can be used for authentication, but are not secure unless this data is encrypted.

19. **A** and **C.** LDAP is an open-industry standard that defines a method for accessing and updating information stored in directories. LDAP is based on a client/server computing model and has evolved from the X.500 standard.

B is incorrect because LDAP runs over TCP/IP rather than the OSI protocol stack, making LDAP much more widely available to Internet-based systems.

20. **D.** Telnet is a terminal emulation program for TCP/IP networks such as the Internet that is assigned to port 23. Telnet provides a remote terminal using a character-based interface over the Internet. The Telnet server daemon *telnetd* runs a login shell program that implements the Telnet service.

21. **A and C.** A mirror server is a backup server that duplicates all the processes and transactions of the primary server. If, for any reason, the primary server fails, the backup server can immediately take its place without losing any downtime. Server mirroring is an expensive but effective strategy for achieving fault tolerance.
    B is incorrect because mirror servers are not assigned to a port.

22. **B and D.** FTP is a client/server process. You don't need a default gateway if you are on the same network segment.

23. **B.** Data connection is managed by a set of programs known as the Data Transfer Process. The server maintains a passive open state at port 21 listening for an FTP connection request from the client.
    A is incorrect because the server data port is always 20. The data transfer connection gets set up only when there is data to transfer between the server and the client. **C** and **D** are incorrect because these are not valid port numbers.

12

i-Net Security

Not too long ago, the concept of the Internet was largely unknown to anyone but a rather small, elite group. Just six years ago, Microsoft's Web server was stored away in a half-forgotten closet, and companies such as GM, Ford, and others had little Internet presence to speak of. E-mail was largely unknown to them. Now these corporations and many others boast enormous, complex Web sites and have adopted e-mail and other Internet services as mission-critical business tools. Many organizations and corporations have rapidly embraced technologies related to the Internet. One of the results of the almost mad rush to obtain a presence on the Internet and take advantage of its services has been that many organizations have fallen victim to intrusions. Some of these intrusions have led to the disclosure of proprietary information, loss of credibility through Web graffiti, and incidents in which the company's bottom line and reputation was actually hurt by its presence on the Internet.

Of course, rapid corporate adoption of the Internet is not the only reason for Internet-related security issues. TCP/IP v4, the most commonly used internetworking protocol, is an open standard. This means that anyone who wants to study how it works and discover its weaknesses can do so. One of the chief weaknesses of TCP/IP is that it was not built from the ground up with security in mind. It does not contain an effective means for authentication and does not natively support encryption. The only way to make TCP/IP more secure is to create add-ons that enhance its security without reducing its efficiency. You should also note that hackers have more sophisticated tools at their disposal than ever before. Almost anyone can attempt fairly sophisticated hacks by just making a few searches on the Internet. Also, due to marketing pressures, many companies are releasing operating systems and applications without properly testing them, which means that you and your end users inherit "buggy" systems and programs that can open up security holes.

This chapter will discuss some of the concepts, problems, and solutions related to security on the Internet. For example, you will learn about how a virtual private network (VPN) can help ensure enhanced security through encryption. You will also study access control, auditing, and other standard security procedures that you will have to understand before you are certified as a professional. Now, let's go over a few concepts that will help you become familiar with Internet security.

Internet Security Concepts

This chapter explores industry-standard concepts and best practices:

- **Authentication**   The ability to verify the identity of a user, host, or system process

- **Access control**   The determination of who and what is allowed into an operating system or network

- **Encryption**   The use of algorithms and protocols to scramble information so that users cannot engage in electronic eavesdropping or data tampering

- **Data confidentiality**   The use of encryption to make sure that information remains secret

- **Data integrity**   The use of encryption and other means to make sure that no one has tampered with (that is, altered) information in transit

- **Auditing**   The ability to determine who has accessed the system, and when

- **Nonrepudiation**   The ability to prove that a transaction has in fact occurred

These concepts will be discussed in detail. Pay close attention, because you will be implementing them as you go about your daily activities as an administrator. Many security applications, such as firewalls and intrusion detection systems, can get quite complex. Unless you have a clear understanding of these foundational concepts, you will feel that the applications run you rather than your running them. Furthermore, as you study for various Internet-related exams, you will find that these concepts give you a framework upon which you can base the rest of your knowledge.

exam

ⓦatch

The concepts you have just read about may seem rather dry and boring compared to reading about the latest exploits of hackers and phreakers such as Mudge, Captain Crunch, and the crew at L0pht Heavy Industries (http://www.l0pht.com). However, the exploits conducted by these people are based upon their detailed knowledge of how these services and mechanisms work in regard to specific operating systems. Note that the exam will focus on specific applications of these concepts. Learn them carefully. As you go about your computing, try to apply each of these principles to your activities so that you can think through test questions designed to see whether, for example, you know the difference between data confidentiality and data integrity.

Security Documents and Organizations

Many security organizations and standards exist. Some are sponsored by national governments, such as the National Institute of Standards and Technology (NIST), which was sponsored by the U.S. Department of Defense (DOD). This organization created the famous Trusted Computer System Evaluation Criteria (TCSEC), which is also known as the Orange Book, because it was originally published with an orange cover. Although it was written in 1983 and revised in 1985, many security professionals still refer to this book. This is mainly because operating system design has not changed significantly since the NIST created the Orange Book.

The Orange Book rates the security protection of various operating systems according to an alphabetical scale (D through A). Systems given a D rating are the least secure, whereas an A-grade system is specially designed to give granular control over system users and processes. The most common rating is C2, which certain Novell, UNIX, and NT systems can achieve with some work. However, the C2 rating is very specific: When rating a system, you must consider not only how you configure the operating system, but also how you configure the particular machine (that is, server) that operating system is installed in. In other words, C-2 compliance refers to the way in which an operating system works with a specific server. Even if a Windows NT installation on a Compaq server is C-2 compliant, installing that exact same operating system on a Dell server, may not warrant a C-2 rating. The primary goal of the Orange Book standard is to create trusted systems. The idea was that if you could create a secure system, a hacker could not spread from it to another and then to another.

The TCSEC standard is a common example of a proprietary standard adopted by the Internet community. However, additional, international standards exist, including

- The International Organization for Standardization (ISO) 7498-2
- BS 7799 (1995 and 1999 versions)

These standards documents have helped create our understanding of authentication, access control, and encryption. This document also provides the standard definitions for data confidentiality, data integrity, and nonrepudiation. Before you learn more about the ISO 7498-2 document, you should first learn more about ISO and its most famous standard, the OSI/RM, which comprises the foundation of the 7498 series of documents.

The International Organization for Standardization is responsible for the Open Systems Interconnection model. This model is shown along with the four-layer TCP/IP model. These two models provide an abstract description for each activity that occurs on your network. To understand how to implement security measures intelligently, you must first study these two models. Most security references assume that you understand each layer and its function (see Figure 12-1).

The OSI/RM

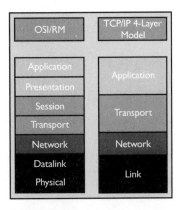

Figure 12-1 shows how the OSI/RM and the TCP/IP model map to each other. In general, the OSI/RM is more specific in its description of how TCP/IP works, and it is the model used in this chapter. Table 12-1 gives a short discussion of the responsibility of each layer.

You should remember that this model describes packet generation. In regard to security, this model also helps you understand just how specific security implementations, such as firewalls and intrusion detection systems, operate. The Application, Transport, and Network layers of this model are of special interest for security purposes.

Additional organizations include the Computer Emergency Response Team (CERT). CERT is dedicated to helping all computer users maintain security. It is not focused on any one platform. You can gain much information about past hacker attacks, including ways to protect yourself against them. You can learn more about CERT at http://www.cert.org.

Now that you have reviewed some of the common standards and issues in regard to security, let's delve a bit more deeply into each of them.

TABLE 12-1	Layer	Responsibility
OSI/RM Summary	Application	Renders information for use with specific applications, such as FTP, HTTP, and so forth.
	Presentation	Formats information from one language type to another.
	Session	Establishes and maintains connections.
	Transport	Provides reliable transport and error control mechanisms, including checksum, and ports. TCP and UDP run at this layer.
	Network	Provides for actual network addresses between two systems. IP runs at this layer.
	Datalink	Maps physical addresses to network addresses. Contains two sublayers: Media Access Control (MAC) and Logical Link Control (LLC). The MAC layer provides hardware addresses, whereas the LLC is responsible for how NIC drivers operate.
	Physical	Sends and receives bits of data.

Authentication

Authentication is the ability to verify the identity of a particular person, network host, or system process. In real life, you can authenticate a person in many different ways. In person, you can determine identity by means of sight, fingerprints, or by a signature on a document. If you are speaking to someone remotely over a telephone, you can authenticate via that person's voice, or by sharing some secret information. However, the advent of the Internet has made it somewhat difficult, if not impossible, to use these simple means. According to security standards such as ISO 7498-2 and the TSEC standard, you can authenticate in these ways:

- **What you know**   A password is the most common example of this form of identification.

- **What you have**   This form of authentication requires that you present a physical token of some sort. In the analog world, this can be a key or an actual piece of paper. On the Internet, digital signatures and certificates provide this service. Smart cards, which are small cards that have microprocessing and mass storage capacity, are the most advanced form of "what you have" authentication.

- **What you are**   Biometrics is the study of authentication via physical traits, including retinal scans, fingerprints, and voice identification.

- **Where you are**   Also called proof of origin. It is possible for systems to authenticate packets depending upon where they come from. Although this form of authentication is not very secure, it is still practiced by the UNIX rlogin programs. For example, a UNIX system (host A) using the rlogin series of programs will allow another host (host B) to log in without a password. This is because host A has a special file named rlogin.hosts that specifies a user from a specific host to bypass the authentication subsystem and enter the host. However, because it is possible for users to "spoof" IP addresses and other information in an IP packet, this practice is increasingly falling out of favor.

There are some specific ways that you can enhance authentication across networks and internetworks.

Again, these concepts are essential for understanding how authentication works. Before you can create a VPN or fully understand how a network login process, such as authenticating with a Windows NT domain, works, you should understand these concepts.

Authentication and Encryption

In order to authenticate users across the Internet, you generally have to use some kind of encryption. The main reason for this is that you can use encryption as a "what you have" form of authentication; if you can provide a digital certificate, you can at least begin to prove your identity. There are several ways to use encryption for the purposes of authentication and encryption.

You should note that you don't absolutely have to use encryption. In other words, Internetworking technology does not require you to use it. As you continue your networking and Internetworking career, you will notice that many sites allow clear-text communication. Nevertheless, you should use encryption for security purposes.

Certificates

Digital certificates are the primary means of authenticating users, hosts, and servers. They use public key encryption, as well as one-way encryption. Using the information in a certificate, unknown parties can build trust with each other. Digital certificates involve the use of a trusted third party, called a certificate authority (CA). Arguably, the most popular CA is VeriSign (http://www.verisign.com). A CA verifies that a public key is valid by checking information concerning a person or a particular vendor. A CA can create a key pair for a user, or it can verify a public key that has already been created. Many different types of certificates exist, including

- **Server**   A server certificate is designed to authenticate servers. For example, a Secure Sockets Layer (SSL) session requires a certificate to reside on a server.

- **Individual**   You can use a certificate to prove that you have written a particular e-mail message.

- **Certificate-level**   You can obtain a special type of certificate to become your own certificate authority.

Digital certificates provide enhanced authentication services, because they contain additional information about the system you are connecting to. Such information can include

- The public key of the person or host that has the digital certificate

- Creation and expiration dates

- A specially encrypted message, called a digital signature, from the CA

- The server's DNS name

- The name of the company

All digital certificates are in a special format mandated by the X.509 standard. Public key infrastructure (PKI) is a term reserved for organizations and bodies that create, store, and manage digital certificates. PKI is generally a distributed system, meaning that many different hosts and servers work together to create a single solution. PKI generally involves the following:

- Certificate authorities

- Registration authorities

- Certificate management systems

- Certificate directories (also called X.509 directories)

Whereas the CA creates certificates, it is possible for a different organization to register those certificates and make them valid. Such distribution can enhance security, because it distributes the information to more than one party; if a hacker compromises the CA, it is still possible for the registration authority to operate securely. It is also possible to distribute the responsibility for managing the keys to yet other parties. In other words, you can use another party to revoke or renew a certificate. PKI allows you to store keys in various locations. A certificate directory is nothing more than a clearinghouse that contains all of the digital certificates you have created. A certificate directory allows you to publish your certificate to a larger audience, such as anyone who accesses a particular site on the Internet. Finally, a PKI allows for the possibility to revoke certificates in case one gets compromised, or if the certificate is no longer needed.

Digital Signatures

A digital signature is the electronic equivalent of your own "real" signature that you use when signing a check. A digital signature has two major uses:

- It provides proof of origin. In the same way that a "normal" signature generally proves that you created and/or approved of a document, a digital signature allows you to show where it came from. Because the signature proves that a transmission came from you, it effectively authenticates that document or message.

- It provides data integrity. A digital signature enables you to prove within a reasonable doubt that a message was not altered as it traveled across a public network. A digital signature uses public key cryptography and one-way encryption to achieve this goal. Perhaps the best analogy for this particular use of a digital signature is the use of seals placed on envelopes sent via snail mail; if the seal on the letter is broken, this is a possible sign that someone has opened the envelope and (possibly) tampered with the message. As a result, you cannot trust that message, and should ask your friend to send it again.

Perhaps an applied example will help. Imagine that you wish to send a confidential e-mail to a friend. You then run this message through a one-way (that is, hash) algorithm to create a mathematical digest of the original message. You use your private key to encrypt that hash, and then send the e-mail accompanied by the encrypted digest. When your friend gets the message, he generates his own digest of your message, and then decrypts the original digest you made using your public key. His software then determines whether the two hashes match. If they do, then it is likely that no one has altered the message. If the hashes do not match, then there is a problem with the message, and you will have to take another course of action to communicate the original message.

You should note that digital signatures do not encrypt transmissions. They simply provide evidence that a message sent from point A has arrived at point B in unaltered form.

Nonrepudiation

As mentioned earlier, nonrepudiation is the practice of being able to verify that a transaction—or any occurrence, for that matter—has actually happened. You can achieve nonrepudiation through many means. For example, you can use digital signatures. Consider the purpose of a standard signature on a check you use to pay for something you have bought. This signature provides three services. First, it proves that the correct (that is, authorized) person has written this check. A bank can read the signature and authenticate the user. Second, the signature forbids anyone from adding to or taking away from what the check says. The signature finalizes the transaction. If you make any subsequent changes, you will have to authorize and finalize them with yet another signature (or at least an initial). Third, the signature proves that the transaction actually occurred.

Here is another example illustrating nonrepudiation. Let's say you go to the computer store to buy a new server. When you purchase it, you get a receipt. This receipt is a standard way to ensure nonrepudiation. When you leave the store, you use this receipt as proof that you did, in fact, purchase the item, and that you aren't trying to steal it. You can even use this receipt to prove that you purchased your server from this particular store in case you need to return it.

For nonrepudiation on the Internet, a digital signature helps you prove that a certain transaction has taken place, because you have the signature of the person with whom you had the transaction. You can produce this signature at any time, just as you would a standard receipt from a store. Therefore, when you purchase a server across the Internet, you use digital signatures to prove that the purchase has occurred. The site from which you bought the server can then take this information and generate standard receipts and e-mail messages, and then deliver them to you.

Strong Authentication

Strong authentication involves combining certificates, digital signatures, and the authentication measures mentioned earlier. In short, if you combine the first three forms of authentication, you can strongly authenticate users. Specific ways to enable strong authentication include

- **Kerberos** MIT professors originally developed the Kerberos system. It allows you to authenticate users via encryption. Once a user is authenticated, a Kerberos server then grants "tickets" to system resources, such as printers, additional networks, databases, and file servers. These tickets are viable for only a period of time. Kerberos has an added security feature in that it does not transport passwords over the network wire, which eliminates the threat of "sniffing" password information. It is an IETF standard, although Microsoft will implement an altered version of Kerberos for its Windows NT 2000 operating system.

- **Smart cards** Essentially a credit card on steroids, this type of card is considered smart because it has two capabilities beyond the standard credit card you probably have in your wallet: First, a smart card can store information in persistent memory. Depending on the card, it can store as little information as your government identification data, or as much information as your entire medical history. Second, a smart card can have an on-board microprocessor with volatile RAM that acts much like a minicomputer. Such cards are about three to five times as thick as a standard credit card. Some cards have their own power source, whereas others require a smart card reader. Using a smart card, you can use "what you have" authentication to begin an encrypted session that then begins a password exchange sequence.

- **One Time Passwords (OTP)** The concept of a one-time password involves "what you know" authentication, but enhances the practice by never using the same password twice. Generally, OTP protocols involve beginning a session—for instance, with an FTP server. After you initiate the session, the FTP server will send out a specific message as a challenge. You cannot answer this challenge unless you enter this challenge message into a specially designed OTP application. This application may be software running on your Windows 98 system, or it may reside on a dedicated device, which may be shaped like a calculator or like something that could fit on your key ring. You then enter the challenge phrase into the OTP application, where it returns a value. You send this value back to the FTP server, where you are then authenticated. The FTP server can then determine how much access it will grant.

Access Control

Access control is not the same principle as authentication. Access control involves the ability to grant or deny system resources to authenticated users. Perhaps an analogy will help explain the difference between authentication and access control: You may wish to allow someone you know into your house. To do so, all you need to do is verify who this person is, and then let her in. However, once this person is in the home, there may still be areas of the house to which you wish to restrict access. Although you have authenticated this person and allowed her access into your home, you can still indicate certain places that are off limits. In an operating system, you can base access control on specific criteria, including

- Usernames
- Group membership
- The location of a server
- Authentication parameters

Most operating systems, however, enforce access control through special lists.

Access Control List

An *access control list* is a special file or series of values that helps determine the level of access a user has to a specific resource. An operating system refers to these lists to control access to system resources. One of the more important concepts to understand in access control is the use of objects. An object can be any system resource, including

- System files
- Shares established on a system
- Files that exist in shares
- The ability to change the system itself
- Access to other machines

Access control lists regulate access to these objects. Specifically, an access control list regulates a user's ability to use either an operating system or the objects served by an operating system. An ACL does this by associating specific rights to a username and/or group. Whenever a user makes a request for an object, the operating system checks the ACL to determine whether it can grant the request. UNIX, on the other hand, does not have a centralized ACL for each of its systems. Each application or service contains its own ACL.

on the job

You should note that Windows 95/98 really have no access control measures to speak of. It is possible to use crude password protection for logins, as well as screen savers, and it is also possible to establish a password-protected share. However, Windows 95/98 systems do not have proper access control lists. Windows NT does not have extensive security measures unless you format the drive with the NT File System (NTFS). ACLs in NT are not based upon the user, but rather on the object upon which you are applying security. Objects can include files and folders, for example.

Firewall

Whereas an ACL governs access for a specific operating system, a firewall governs access in and out of an entire network. As shown in Figure 12-2, a firewall is a machine or series of machines that lies between your own, trusted network, and other networks over which you have no control. These machines contain special software that enables you to exert granular control over network traffic.

A firewall filters all traffic that passes between your network and the outside world. No other way should exist to enter your network. Although a firewall often does not check access from a modem bank (that is, a collection of modems that enables network access), it is still possible to use your firewall to check such access. You can also use a firewall to create virtual private networks.

A common perception is that a firewall prevents traffic only from coming into a network. However, this is not the case. You can use a firewall to prevent traffic from exiting a network, as well. For example, if your company security policy forbids the use of company e-mail across the Internet, you can use your firewall to enact that particular policy.

Firewalls contain their own access control lists, called rules. A firewall rule is a statement that helps it determine how to react to a particular situation. Before you learn more about firewall rules, you need to learn more about the different types of existing firewalls.

FIGURE 12-2   Firewall separating your network from others

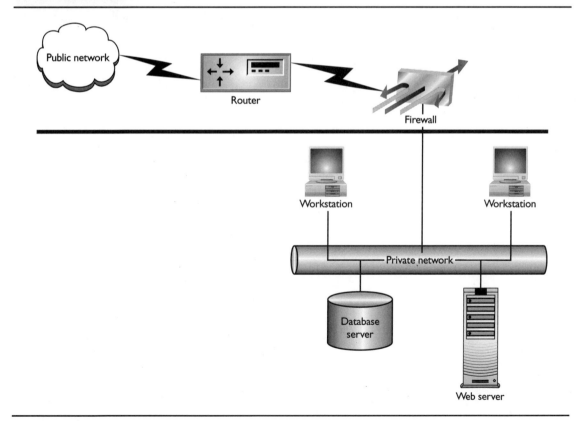

Most industry-standard firewalls are based on this principle: all traffic is denied unless it is explicitly allowed by a firewall rule. However, some firewalls work in the opposite way: they allow all traffic, which means that you must create rules to deny traffic you do not want to come in or out of the network.

A firewall offers enhanced logging. However, a firewall is a perimeter solution; its logs do not offer you the ability to check internal systems. You will have to check system logs and Intrusion Detection System (IDS) logs, for example, to learn about internal activity. You will learn more about Intrusion Detection Systems later in the chapter.

FIREWALL TYPES   Three types of firewalls exist: packet-filtering firewalls, application gateways, and circuit-level gateways. Table 12-2 contains a summary of each type.

TABLE 12-2 Firewall Type Summary	Firewall Type	Description
	Packet filter	A packet filter inspects source and destination IP addresses, as well as ports. This type of firewall operates at the network layer of the OSI/RM. Its chief benefit is that it inspects packets quickly, and it is quite difficult to overwhelm. However, a packet filter cannot delve as deeply into a packet as the other firewall types.
	Application-level gateway	As you might suspect, an application gateway operates at the application layer of the OSI/RM. This firewall is arguably the most thorough, because it not only can determine source and destination IP address, but also inspect actual data inside the packet. However, application-level gateways tend to be slower than packet filters.
	Circuit-level gateway	The chief benefit of this type of firewall is network address translation (NAT), which is the ability to use reserved IP addresses internally, and Internet-capable addresses externally. Circuit-level gateways operate at the transport layer of the OSI/RM. Circuit-level gateways are quicker than application-level gateways, although not as quick as packet-filtering firewalls. The drawback to a circuit-level gateway is that you must modify all software in order for it to communicate with the firewall. This can be prohibitively costly.

FIREWALLS AND THE DEMILITARIZED ZONE (DMZ)

It is possible to combine firewall types to create a coordinated solution. As shown in Figure 12-3, you can place a packet-filtering firewall (that is, a packet filter) on both sides of a network. This buffer network is called a *demilitarized zone (DMZ)*. You can then place an application-level gateway within it. This extra element further secures your network.

Packet Filters

Although all firewalls require you to establish rules, packet-filtering firewalls require extensive rules. Table 12-3 shows an example of a firewall rule specifically for SMTP in a firewall that denies all access unless explicitly granted.

This rule allows only SMTP activity. All other activity is restricted. In other words, if you had a firewall with only these rules, no one in your

FIGURE 12-3

A demilitarized zone

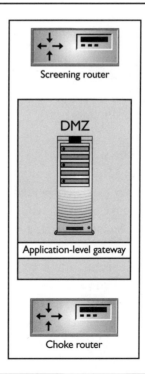

Screening router

DMZ

Application-level gateway

Choke router

TABLE 12-3		Firewall Rule				
Source IP Address	Destination IP Address	Protocol	Source Port	Destination Port	Explanation
All external	SMTP Server 10.100.100.2	TCP	> 1023	25	Allows external SMTP clients and servers to send messages to your internal SMTP server
SMTP server 10.100.100.2	All external	TCP	> 1023	25	Allows your internal SMTP server to send messages to external SMTP servers
All internal	All external	TCP	> 1023	25	Allows internal e-mail clients to communicate with external servers

company could receive e-mail from a POP3 server, nor could they browse the Web or use FTP. You would have to create rules for each of these services.

It bears repeating that the chief drawback of application-level and circuit-level gateways is that they are slower than packet filters. However, as you can see, creating packet-filter rules can be quite time consuming and complex.

Proxy Server

Application-level gateways and circuit-level gateways are proxy based. A proxy mediates between one party and another. In the case of the Internet, a proxy mediates between inside users and outside traffic. A proxy receives requests from external users, investigates the nature of the request, and then passes the request on to the appropriate location. A packet filter, on the other hand, simply checks for source and destination IP addresses, as well as ports, and a few other fields in a packet.

However, a proxy server can do more than process requests from outside. A proxy server also processes requests coming from inside the network with an external destination address. Part of this process is that a proxy server can save requests and keep them in a database for a certain period of time. Then, the proxy server can service subsequent requests from this database. This process of storing past requests in order to serve future requests is called *caching*. It saves a great deal of resources, because it allows a server to fulfill a request without having to establish a new connection every time. A proxy server can also engage in network address translation.

In the cases of application-level gateways and circuit-level gateways, a proxy server is particularly powerful because the proxy function helps lock down all traffic so that the firewall can control it better. Now that you understand firewalls, it is time to take a look at encryption, a technology that enables authentication, firewalls, and most transactions that occur over the Internet.

Configuring Proxy Servers

As you configure a proxy server, remember that you will have to configure both the clients and the server. In regard to the server, you generally will have to obtain a static IP address. At one time you had to use a rather advanced server, such as a UNIX server or Windows NT platform. Today, you can obtain any number of proxy servers that will run on Windows 98, Windows NT, or UNIX. They have become popular in homes that wish to share PPP connections, as well as Ethernet connections. If your proxy server is doing NAT, then you will have to configure internal and external IP addresses. In regard to the client, you will have to obtain this information:

- The port numbers of the services you wish to proxy.
- The IP address of the proxy server.
- Information specific to the service you are proxying. For example, if you are going to use FTP, you likely won't need to supply any information, although some proxies require that you enter a default username and password. However, if you are proxying SMTP or POP3, you will have to enter the SMTP and POP3 server names or IP addresses, as well as a username and password.

Some proxies are rather limited, and can support only a limited number of protocols. For example, many freeware proxy servers support only HTTP. Others support more application-layer protocols, including

- HTTP
- FTP
- SMTP
- POP3

More ambitious proxy servers provide support for

- Network News Transport Protocol (NNTP)
- Telnet
- Ping
- Traceroute
- ICQ
- Instant Messenger
- RealPlayer

Such proxy servers generally do not engage in true NAT, because they simply communicate via agents that reside on each host. These agents "talk" to the main proxy server and forward all of the protocols to the proxy server. Examples of this type of proxy server include WinGate (http://www.wingate.com) and pppshar (http:////www.pppindia.com/intl/pppshar/).

Enterprise-grade proxy servers, such as Microsoft Proxy server or Linux servers with the ability to conduct proxying (called IP chaining), allow support for any protocol supported by TCP/IP. They generally do not install agent software on the clients, but they do require software that is modified to support proxy servers. In some cases, however, the proxy server—for example, Microsoft—provides software to allow interoperability. Proxy server has a Winsock proxy that only needs to be installed from a network share. Once you conduct this installation, you then do not have to specially configure any of your Internet clients. This is because they will use the specially engineered proxied Winsock.

Encryption

Encryption is the science of turning plaintext into ciphertext. Encryption requires the use of algorithms, which are procedures and mathematical calculations written either by individuals or agencies. Encryption provides these services:

- **Data confidentiality**   The ability to hide information by means of encryption

- **Data integrity**   The ability to verify that information has not been tampered with

- **Authentication**   Encryption allows you to verify a person or server's identity because it has the ability to encrypt and decrypt messages

You have already seen how authentication uses encryption for data integrity. When you learn about SSL, you will learn about how encryption can hide information. Encryption works through the use of keys. You use a key, which is generally a simple text string, to encrypt information.

It is important that you understand that encryption provides these two services by employing three different types of encryption:

- **Symmetric encryption**   The use of one key that both encrypts and decrypts information. For example, if you choose the word "bill," this one word is the basis of encrypting and decrypting information.

- **Asymmetric encryption**   This form of encryption is more complex, and it involves the use of a key pair. This form of encryption is much more secure. Asymmetric algorithms include ElGamal and RSA. The most common is RSA, which is used by both Microsoft Internet Explorer and Netscape Navigator.

- **One-way encryption**   The use of hash algorithms to create information that is theoretically irretrievable. Once you have run text through a hash algorithm, you cannot get it back. You will see the use of this form of encryption, below. You can use one-way encryption to create hash code. Examples of one-way encryption include MD2 and MD5 and Secure Hash Algorithm (SHA).

You should note that key length is an important issue in encryption. As a general rule, the longer the key, the stronger the password. Key length is important both when a developer creates an algorithm, and when an end user chooses a password. Another important issue is the actual strength of the algorithm used. Strength is generally determined by how much it has been publicly tested. Another factor is how well documented the algorithm is. Symmetric key encryption algorithms include

- **Data Encryption Standard (DES)**   This is the most popularly used form of encryption, not necessarily because it is the most secure, but because it has been adopted by the U.S. government and several large companies. It uses a 56-bit key and allows the possibility of over 70,000,000,000,000,000 (that's over 70 quadrillion) possible keys.

- **Triple DES**   Somewhat more secure, this form of encryption is more powerful than DES.

- **The RC series of algorithms (RC2, RC4, and RC5)**   Invented by Ron Rivest of RSA, these algorithms are somewhat more secure than DES and triple DES. RC4 is considered to be the fastest, if not the most secure. The RC series is considered more secure because it uses longer keys.

- **The Advanced Encryption Standard (AES)**   Although no encryption algorithm has been chosen as of this writing, this standard is sponsored by the U.S. government as a replacement for DES. RC6, MARS, Rijndael, Serpent, and Twofish are all finalists for this standard.

Public and Private Keys

Asymmetric encryption uses a key pair. This key pair is uniquely and mathematically related, but it is just about impossible to take advantage of this relationship. In other words, it is very difficult for anyone to guess the meaning of one key because he or she has the other. As you learn more about SSL, S/MIME, and digital signatures, you will appreciate the power of the relationship between public and private keys. You must remember three things about public and private keys:

- You can freely distribute the public key.

- You must always keep the private key secret. It should stay hidden on your machine.

- What a private key encrypts, a public key can decrypt. Likewise, what a public key encrypts, a private key can decrypt. Take time to think about this relationship, because each of the three techniques discussed in the following is based upon it.

You can use public key encryption in these ways:

- **Data encryption**   You can encrypt a message or data stream to someone's public key. This means that only the person who has the private key can decrypt it. Because you are supposed to be the only one with this private key, anyone can decrypt it.

- **Data integrity**   You can use asymmetric encryption (along with one-way encryption) to "sign" a document. If you encrypt a document to your own private key, this means that anyone with your public key can decrypt the message to reveal the symmetric key and the hash code. You will learn more about digital signatures shortly.

- **Safe key transport**   Public key encryption allows you to transmit keys securely because you can embed a symmetric key within a message encrypted to someone's public key. The primary protocol for describing safe key transport is the Diffie/Hellman protocol.

It is important to note that you can use public key encryption for various purposes, depending upon whether you encrypt information to someone else's public key, or to your own private key. The former encrypts data so that it remains private. The latter merely signs data.

Digital Signatures

You have already been introduced to how digital signatures use public key cryptography to associate unique characteristics to a message. You can also use a hashing algorithm to create a message digest. A *message digest* (also known as *hash text*) is cryptographically generated text that is of a fixed length. Because hashing algorithms are faster than public keys, many applications, such as SSL and S/MIME, use hash algorithms as opposed to public key algorithms. You will learn about S/MIME later in this chapter.

The process is quite simple. If you wish to send an e-mail, for example, you create a message, run it through a hashing algorithm, and then encrypt this code to the recipient's public key. The recipient can then receive the message and decrypt it. The recipient then uses the original hash and puts it through another hashing algorithm to calculate a new hash code. The recipient compares this new hash code to the original. If the values are the same, the recipient can be reasonably sure that no one tampered with the message. This process is popular because it is fast, and because the hash codes are small and, therefore, easily transported across slow network connections, such as a modem.

Global vs Country-Specific Encryption Standards

Encryption has become a controversial topic, mainly because it is possible to use encryption to hide illicit activities, such as terrorism and child pornography. Until recently, it was illegal to export 128-bit encryption from the United States, for example. Many countries have their own encryption standards. As you have read, the official encryption standard is currently DES, although this will change with the adoption of the Advanced Encryption Standard (AES).

One of the country-specific encryption practices is the idea of key escrow, which involves the creation of powerful encryption algorithms by one body, which then reserves the right to hold all of the possible keys. In this system, a user would be able to encrypt a document that is unreadable by all but the intended recipients. However, in the case of a declared emergency, a certain body, such as the CIA or MI5, could decrypt the message immediately. An example of key escrow is the U.S. government's ill-fated clipper chip plan. The clipper chip allows all users to deploy very advanced encryption. However, the U.S. government reserves the right to hold all possible keys in case it needs to read messages and data encrypted by the plan. For example, if the government wished to foil a drug smuggling or terrorist plan, agents could crack anything encrypted by the clipper chip. Needless to say, this proposal is extremely controversial.

One example of a global encryption standard is the one published by the Organization for Economic Cooperation and Development (OECD). Additional standards have been put forth by these bodies:

- The Internet Engineering Task Force (IETF)
- The World Wide Web Consortium (W3C)
- The Standardizing Information and Communication System (also known as ECMA)

No global standard exists as yet. It is likely that organizations such as ISO, the Internet Engineering Task Force (IETF), and the World Wide Web Consortium (W3C) will help create a global standard in cooperation with various governments such as the United States, Great Britain, and Germany.

Secure Sockets Layer (SSL)

Secure Sockets Layer (SSL) is a method of encrypting a specific session between a client and a server. Specifically, it is a transport-layer protocol commonly used in Web-based, e-commerce transactions. It has three chief benefits:

- It allows for authentication using public key encryption and certificates. Although client-side authentication is rare, it is possible for a client to authenticate a server by checking its digital certificate.
- Data is made confidential.
- The encryption session begins quickly and transparently, if the server's certificate is valid.
- The integrity of information being transmitted is (reasonably) ensured.

Whenever a client begins an SSL session in a Web browser, two things will happen: First, the URL window will change from the normal http:// to https://. Second, you will see a lock icon that is closed. It is also highlighted.

SSL uses port 443. If you are running a packet filter, for example, you would have to open up port 443 to allow your users to take advantage of it. Therefore, whenever you place a Web server inside a firewall, you will likely have to open up two ports: port 80 (for standard HTTP access) and port 443. Netscape Communications, the same people who brought you the Navigator browser, presented the final version (3.0) of Secure Sockets Layer in 1996. SSL works in this way:

1. The client and the server engage in an initial handshake.

2. The client obtains a digital certificate from the server.

3. The client checks the validity of the certificate. It is also possible for the server to check the client's certificate.

4. If the certificate is valid, the server will issue a session key, which is symmetrically encrypted with a key generated by the server on the fly. This session key is a message that is symmetrically encrypted, and then embedded within a message that has been signed to the client's public key. This ensures that only the client can read this information. This is because anything encrypted to a client's public key can be decrypted by its private key.

5. Data transported is signed to the recipient's public key. The recipient decrypts this information with his or her private key, and then decrypts the symmetrically encrypted session key. The client then reads the hash code value to ensure that data has not been tampered with.

SSL requires certificates in order to begin an encrypted session. You can use SSL to encrypt sessions that request specific files, as well as directories. You can read more about SSL in RFC 1913. You can go to http://www.rfc-editor.org to read this RFC. If this site is down, go to AltaVista or Yahoo! to search for a good RFC site.

exam
Watch

When you take the test, make sure that you understand the purpose of the three types of encryption. Be especially aware that the session key is created through symmetric encryption, and that it is the item that allows you to finish authentication and log in.

S/MIME

S/MIME is the industry-standard method for encrypting e-mail. You should note that S/MIME is an example of encryption at the application layer of the OSI/RM, because it encrypts the actual message itself, rather than the transport stream. S/MIME uses public key and private key encryption. Like SSL, S/MIME is an instance of applied encryption, because it uses a combination of public key encryption, private key encryption, and one-way encryption.

Auditing

Hands-on application of concerns at the operating system and network level. You have to find ways to discover what is happening with specific operating systems, as well as what is happening to the network wire itself. For example, you will have to implement auditing in these operating systems:

- Windows NT
- UNIX (all flavors, including Solaris, Linux, HP-UX, AIX, SCO, and IRIX)
- Assorted router operating systems (CISCO's IOS, 3COM)
- Novell NetWare

Note that regardless of operating system type, auditing can consume system resources. This is because the auditing subsystem, just like any other series of processes and applications, requires memory. Also, on a busy system, audit logs can take up valuable hard drive space. You should consider choosing only critical systems for your audit, including

- **Successful local login**   Although this option can consume resources, it does provide a great deal of information about how the system is being used.
- **Successful remote login**   Some auditing subsystems allow you to determine exactly where a login comes from.
- **Failed logins**   Auditing failures can help you detect brute force attacks, or recognize when a hacker tries to guess user passwords through repeated, high-speed guessing.

- **Changes in user privileges** Once a hacker assumes control of a server, he or she will try to create a user account or elevate the permissions of an account to root, or administrative privileges.

- **System restart and shutdown** Some attacks involve conducting denial of service attacks against a machine. Because a denial of service attack involves somehow disabling a system, making it restart or simply shut down is a logical choice. You should enable this option because it helps you determine whether someone else has found a way to control or crash your machine's ability to boot at will.

- **System processes** Some operating systems assign a highly privileged process identification number (PID). If you are not able to control system processes, you will want to audit them to see how the system is using them. Doing so can help you establish an audit trail. There are a couple of ways you can audit UNIX systems.

The UNIX last command, shown in Figure 12-4, allows you to view any users who have logged in interactively. In an interactive login, the user sits in front of the machine. The command also logs any processes, such as the system boot process, that use the system.

Figure 12-5 shows the UNIX lastlog command, which shows all users that have logged in remotely. Both of these commands can help you audit your system and see who has been using it.

Now that you have learned about a few manual auditing options, let's take a look at a few ways to automate auditing in a network.

Web Server Logs

Because Web servers invite anonymous traffic, you should audit these servers often. Make sure that you search for ping and port scans, as well as access attempts to password-protected areas of the site. You should also search for requests made for nonexistent files, as well as requests for Common Gateway Interface (CGI) programs and other executable that sites use to extend your server's ability to communicate with end users and your back-end databases. CGI scripts have been known to open up security holes. If you can search your logs for any requests that seem out of place, you may be able to lock down a security issue.

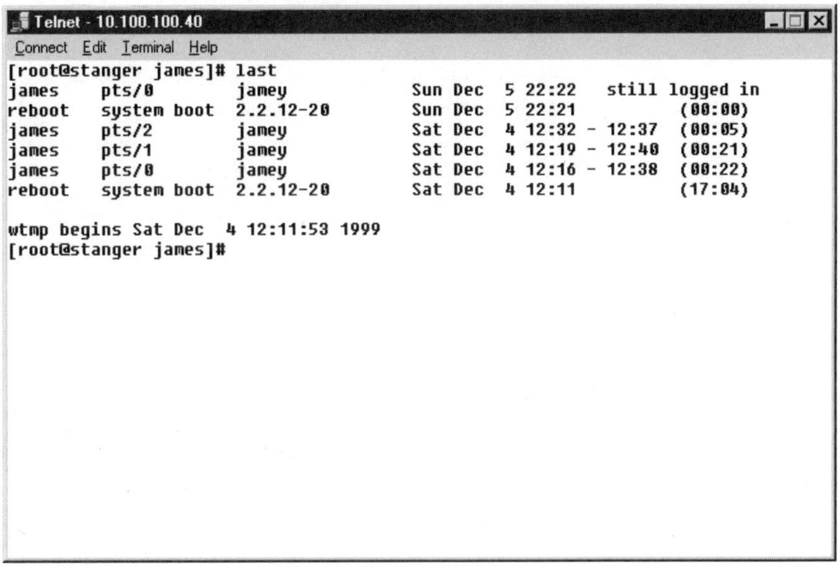

FIGURE 12-4

FIGURE 12-4

Using the UNIX
last command

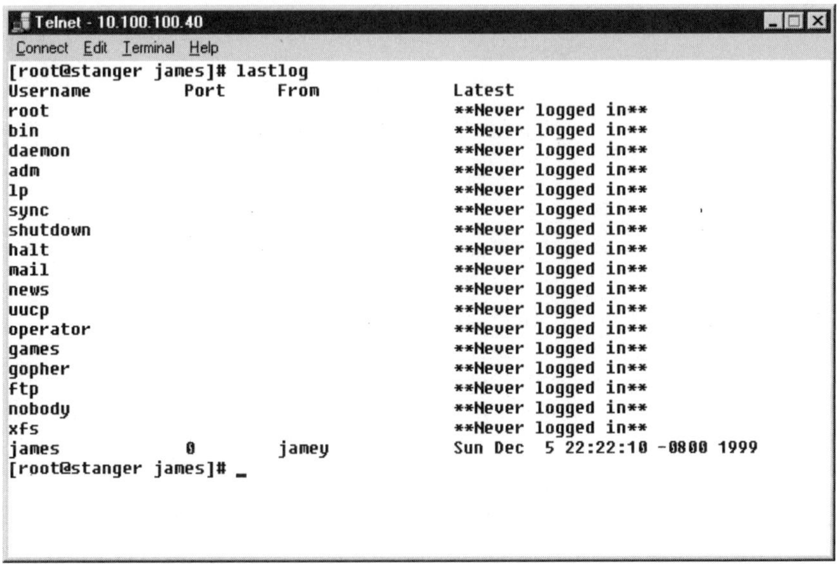

```
 Telnet - 10.100.100.40                                              _ □ ×
 Connect  Edit  Terminal  Help
[root@stanger james]# last
james      pts/0         jamey            Sun Dec  5 22:22    still logged in
reboot     system boot   2.2.12-20        Sun Dec  5 22:21             (00:00)
james      pts/2         jamey            Sat Dec  4 12:32 - 12:37     (00:05)
james      pts/1         jamey            Sat Dec  4 12:19 - 12:40     (00:21)
james      pts/0         jamey            Sat Dec  4 12:16 - 12:38     (00:22)
reboot     system boot   2.2.12-20        Sat Dec  4 12:11             (17:04)

wtmp begins Sat Dec  4 12:11:53 1999
[root@stanger james]#
```

FIGURE 12-5

Using the UNIX
lastlog command

```
 Telnet - 10.100.100.40                                              _ □ ×
 Connect  Edit  Terminal  Help
[root@stanger james]# lastlog
Username        Port     From            Latest
root                                     **Never logged in**
bin                                      **Never logged in**
daemon                                   **Never logged in**
adm                                      **Never logged in**
lp                                       **Never logged in**
sync                                     **Never logged in**
shutdown                                 **Never logged in**
halt                                     **Never logged in**
mail                                     **Never logged in**
news                                     **Never logged in**
uucp                                     **Never logged in**
operator                                 **Never logged in**
games                                    **Never logged in**
gopher                                   **Never logged in**
ftp                                      **Never logged in**
nobody                                   **Never logged in**
xfs                                      **Never logged in**
james           0        jamey           Sun Dec  5 22:22:10 -0800 1999
[root@stanger james]# _
```

Intrusion Detection Utilities

An Intrusion Detection System (IDS) is a series of applications and services designed to detect and, if so configured, to thwart illicit activity. Two types of IDS exist:

- **Host based** This form of IDS uses agents that reside on each host. In this system, centralized manager software reads the transmissions sent from agent software. The agents read the logs that reside on each system and search for suspicious activity. This form of IDS is ideal for switched networks. Once you have activated auditing for your operating system, you can install a third-party IDS to augment auditing.

- **Network based** The most simple type of host-based IDS uses an application that scans the network wire for all hosts on a particular subnet. This type of IDS is ideal for hub-based networks, because most network switches tend to open connections in a manner that isolates an IDS from the rest of the network. A host-based IDS searches for these activities:

  - A large number of files deleted in succession
  - A large number of users created or deleted in succession
  - Repeated login failures
  - Root logins
  - A service being started or stopped
  - A system restart
  - A system shutdown
  - The opening or closing of a specific port

A network-based IDS is ideal for identifying traffic as it comes across the network wire. This might include

- Activity to or from a specific IP address
- Activity to or from a specific port
- ICMP and/or UDP

- SYN floods
- "Half-open" TCP scans

An IDS can log such instances and then send alerts, launch applications, and/or reconfigure existing systems—such as firewalls and routers—to deal with the attack. You can coordinate your IDS with your firewall, as well as with additional programs to help thwart hackers.

Intrusion detection systems are fairly new to the scene, and are not foolproof. They only know about hacker attacks for which they have been programmed, for one thing. Although some IDS applications can, in a sense, "learn" network baseline activity by gathering statistics about usage, if a hacker devises a new attack, it is possible that an IDS will not catch it. On the other hand, an IDS can also "cry wolf" by generating what are called false positives. While an IDS is quite effective, this is not a perfect technology.

Log Files

Although an IDS is a popular item of discussion, few tools are more effective in checking security than a well-configured log daemon. Log file locations vary from system to system. In Windows NT, you can view system log files in Event Viewer. In UNIX systems, you can view log files in various locations. For example, the default location in Linux 5.0, 5.1, and 6.1 is /var/log. An example of a UNIX boot log file is shown in Figure 12-6.

You are not limited to just checking boot log files. You can also check messages sent from the UNIX kernel. These messages include notes about open and closed sessions, as well as failed logins. By default, they are in the /var/log/messages file, as shown in Figure 12-7.

Finally, operating systems have a log file devoted to security issues. In UNIX, the /var/log/secure file reports the most urgent security messages (see Figure 12-8).

The Windows NT counterpart to this file is the Security log file found in Event Viewer, shown in Figure 12-9.

Event Viewer shows more events than just those related to security. However, this is the most relevant area for this chapter.

FIGURE 12-6

The /var/log/boot file

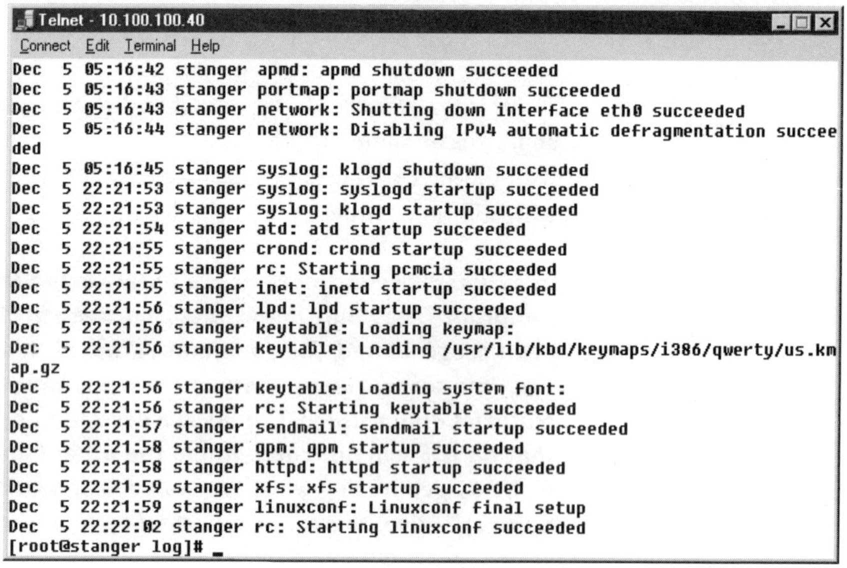

```
Telnet - 10.100.100.40                                              _ □ X
Connect  Edit  Terminal  Help
Dec  5 05:16:42 stanger apmd: apmd shutdown succeeded
Dec  5 05:16:43 stanger portmap: portmap shutdown succeeded
Dec  5 05:16:43 stanger network: Shutting down interface eth0 succeeded
Dec  5 05:16:44 stanger network: Disabling IPv4 automatic defragmentation succee
ded
Dec  5 05:16:45 stanger syslog: klogd shutdown succeeded
Dec  5 22:21:53 stanger syslog: syslogd startup succeeded
Dec  5 22:21:53 stanger syslog: klogd startup succeeded
Dec  5 22:21:54 stanger atd: atd startup succeeded
Dec  5 22:21:55 stanger crond: crond startup succeeded
Dec  5 22:21:55 stanger rc: Starting pcmcia succeeded
Dec  5 22:21:55 stanger inet: inetd startup succeeded
Dec  5 22:21:56 stanger lpd: lpd startup succeeded
Dec  5 22:21:56 stanger keytable: Loading keymap:
Dec  5 22:21:56 stanger keytable: Loading /usr/lib/kbd/keymaps/i386/qwerty/us.km
ap.gz
Dec  5 22:21:56 stanger keytable: Loading system font:
Dec  5 22:21:56 stanger rc: Starting keytable succeeded
Dec  5 22:21:57 stanger sendmail: sendmail startup succeeded
Dec  5 22:21:58 stanger gpm: gpm startup succeeded
Dec  5 22:21:58 stanger httpd: httpd startup succeeded
Dec  5 22:21:59 stanger xfs: xfs startup succeeded
Dec  5 22:21:59 stanger linuxconf: Linuxconf final setup
Dec  5 22:22:02 stanger rc: Starting linuxconf succeeded
[root@stanger log]# _
```

FIGURE 12-7

The var/log/messages file

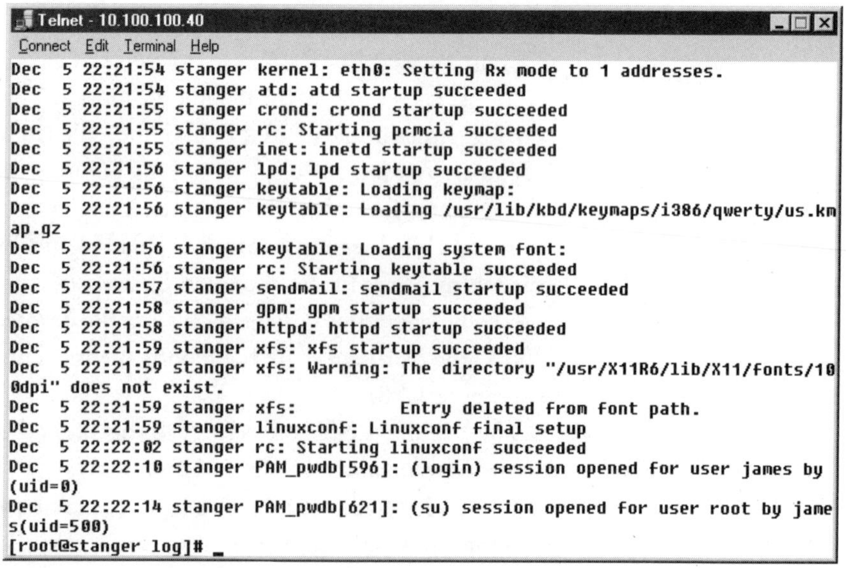

```
Telnet - 10.100.100.40                                              _ □ X
Connect  Edit  Terminal  Help
Dec  5 22:21:54 stanger kernel: eth0: Setting Rx mode to 1 addresses.
Dec  5 22:21:54 stanger atd: atd startup succeeded
Dec  5 22:21:55 stanger crond: crond startup succeeded
Dec  5 22:21:55 stanger rc: Starting pcmcia succeeded
Dec  5 22:21:55 stanger inet: inetd startup succeeded
Dec  5 22:21:56 stanger lpd: lpd startup succeeded
Dec  5 22:21:56 stanger keytable: Loading keymap:
Dec  5 22:21:56 stanger keytable: Loading /usr/lib/kbd/keymaps/i386/qwerty/us.km
ap.gz
Dec  5 22:21:56 stanger keytable: Loading system font:
Dec  5 22:21:56 stanger rc: Starting keytable succeeded
Dec  5 22:21:57 stanger sendmail: sendmail startup succeeded
Dec  5 22:21:58 stanger gpm: gpm startup succeeded
Dec  5 22:21:58 stanger httpd: httpd startup succeeded
Dec  5 22:21:59 stanger xfs: xfs startup succeeded
Dec  5 22:21:59 stanger xfs: Warning: The directory "/usr/X11R6/lib/X11/fonts/10
0dpi" does not exist.
Dec  5 22:21:59 stanger xfs:           Entry deleted from font path.
Dec  5 22:21:59 stanger linuxconf: Linuxconf final setup
Dec  5 22:22:02 stanger rc: Starting linuxconf succeeded
Dec  5 22:22:10 stanger PAM_pwdb[596]: (login) session opened for user james by
(uid=0)
Dec  5 22:22:14 stanger PAM_pwdb[621]: (su) session opened for user root by jame
s(uid=500)
[root@stanger log]# _
```

FIGURE 12-8

FIGURE 12-8

The /var/log/secure file

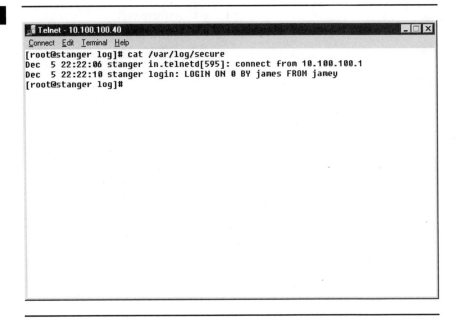

FIGURE 12-9

The Security log file in
Windows NT

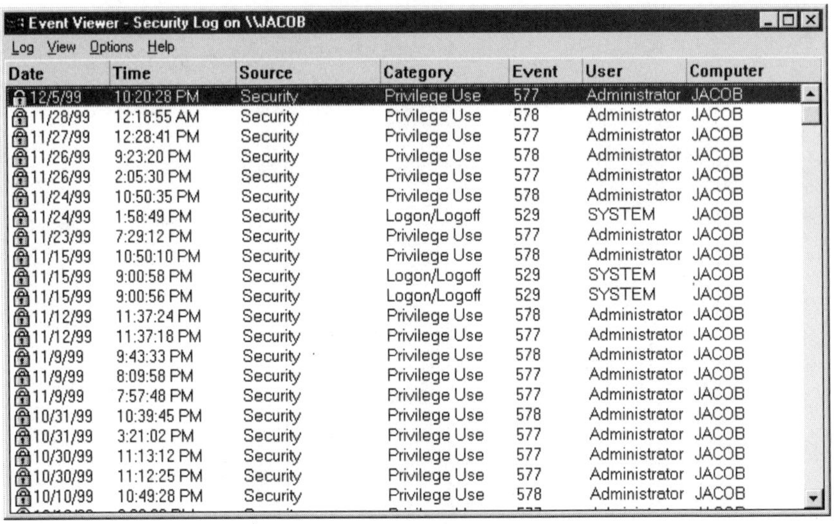

Auditing Log Configuration

The UNIX syslogd and the processes captured by the Windows NT Event Viewer are essential for determining what, if anything, has happened on a host. Similarly, log files generated by Web servers, routers, FTP servers, and other services and daemons are essential tools for discovering activity.

You can customize log files so that they deliver relevant information. In UNIX systems, you can edit the /etc/syslog.conf file to generate information according to parameters you set (see Figure 12-10). Be sure to audit all log files regularly. One of the most overlooked duties is log file checking. The most effective way to determine security at the perimeter is to check router and firewall logs.

Figure 12-11 shows the dialog box that allows you to enable auditing in Windows NT. You get there from User Manager. If you wish to audit Windows NT properly, you should format it with NTFS, rather than with FAT.

FIGURE 12-10

The UNIX syslog.conf file

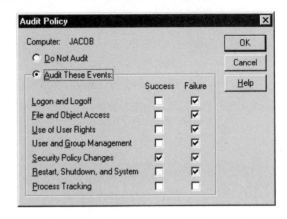

FIGURE 12-11

Auditing options in
Windows NT

SET (Secure Electronic Transactions)

SET is a series of procedures that enable e-commerce to conduct financial transactions sites a secure way to exchange information with banking institutions. Although SET is not currently popular in the United States, it has been adopted by most European countries. SET uses SSL, digital certificates, and additional technologies. This form of doing business over the Internet is effective because parties receive certain information only if it is relevant for their particular needs. For example, a merchant does not receive the actual credit card number. The merchant is simply informed that the bank approved the transaction.

Set Terminology

These are the parties and terminology involved in a SET transaction:

- **Card holder, or user**   The client who wishes to transact online. The user generally has a "wallet," which is an application specifically designed to represent standard currency in digital format.

- **Issuer**   A credit card company that gives a credit card to a user.

- **Merchant**   The firm or organization that has goods to sell.

- **Merchant bank**   The bank that the merchant uses to provide credit card and digital cash services to a user.

- **Acquirer** A party that processes merchant authorization and payment messages between the merchant and the merchant's bank. Sometimes, a merchant bank has its own acquirer function, but not always.

- **Payment gateway** A piece of software or a service run by the acquirer that processes transactions between the merchant and the merchant bank.

CERTIFICATION OBJECTIVE 12.02

The Internet, Intranets, and Extranets

The Internet is really nothing more than a vast collection of networks connected by routers. A public network, the Internet has no inherent security measures. It is your duty as a networking professional to ensure that your network is sufficiently separated from the rest of the Internet. You can do this through firewalls, proxy servers, IDS applications, and authentication through login environments, such as the Windows NT domain.

exam
⊕atch

An intranet is the same thing as the Internet, except on a much less ambitious scale. An intranet offers Web sites, e-mail, and access to information relevant for a specific company. Access to an intranet is allowed only to authenticated employees. In addition, an intranet has added authentication, because information shared on an intranet is often valuable and sensitive. The main thing that defines an intranet is that it is located on an internal network that is separate from the public Internet.

An extranet involves a secure network established between two private networks over public lines. Generally, an extranet has the same elements as an intranet: Each company is able to communicate via e-mail and has the option of using Web sites to conduct transactions. The chief difference is that the companies communicate via encryption, which is usually enabled by two firewalls working together. It is possible to use the Lightweight Directory Access Protocol (LDAP) in such situations. LDAP is a part of the X.500 standard that is designed to provide centralized directory services for a network. It stores information hierarchically. LDAP can provide access to small databases, such as a global e-mail contacts database. LDAP also provides the ability for users to log in to centralized login servers, such as Novell's Directory Services (NDS).

Nevertheless, you should note that an extranet is open only to certain users. For example, if two large companies wished to cooperate with each other, they could establish an extranet that allows only certain parties from each of these two companies to communicate.

Generally, an extranet is valuable to large corporations and banks that wish to communicate with each other for these reasons:

- **Facilitates research opportunities** An extranet provides ways for companies to standardize secure communications as they conduct research within their own company, or in cooperation with other companies.

- **Creates virtual enterprises** A virtual enterprise is where two or more companies combine for a specific period of time to cooperate on a project. An extranet allows a virtual enterprise to communicate securely.

- **Engages in transactions** Large corporations often use extranets to coordinate activities between company divisions that are not physically near each other.

- **Easier information exchange** Using an extranet, it is possible to conduct electronic data interchange (EDI) transactions between two different businesses or business divisions. EDI is a means for businesses to exchange complex data between different operating systems and still retain formatting and data relationships.

- **Banking services** Many e-commerce implementations rely upon extranets to securely exchange banking information.

Different Security Requirements for the Internet, Intranets, and Extranets

The Internet has virtually no security requirements. An intranet requires considerable security, because even though it is open to only authorized company employees, the majority—close to 80 percent—of hacking originates from employees themselves. You can employ auditing, as well as S/MIME and intrusion detection services to make sure your intranet is as secure as possible. An extranet, on the other hand, requires the most security, because you are connecting two private networks via a public, exposed network. As a result, you will not only require auditing and encryption methods, but will also require additional encryption and enhanced authentication. One of these additional means of encryption is the virtual private network.

CERTIFICATION OBJECTIVE 12.03

Virtual Private Networks

A virtual private network (VPN) is an example of a tunneling protocol. In fact, the specific protocol that allows virtual private networks is called the Point to Point Tunneling Protocol (PPTP). This protocol operates at the network layer and encrypts all transmissions, making it difficult for hackers to sniff information. PPTP also works closely with the datalink layer. A VPN is so named because it is a practice that allows users to communicate securely over public lines. Normally, a private network, such as one created over leased frame relay lines, is secure from outside "sniffing" attacks. However, when you send information over the Internet, it is possible for complete strangers to use a protocol analyzer (that is, a packet sniffer) to read it, even though they are not authorized. A virtual private network provides a relatively safe private tunnel through such public networks. A VPN tunnel is composed of these elements:

- **A tunnel initiator (TI)**   Technically, an initiator is software that handles the first part of a VPN connection. Accomplished through software, a TI resides either on a client or on another VPN server wishing to establish a connection.

- **A connection to a WAN, or the Internet**

- **One or more tunnel terminators (TT)**   A tunnel terminator is nothing more than software that ends the connection.

You should make sure you are familiar with the fact that most Internet dial-up connections use the Point to Point Protocol (PPP). This protocol is currently popular because it allows for higher connection speeds, data compression, error correction, and the use of PPTP. It is also useful because it is possible to automatically configure IP addresses, default gateways, and DNS services through it, as well. The older way to make dial-up connections is by using the Serial Line Interface Protocol (SLIP). It is still in limited use, although PPP is preferable.

VPN and Encrypted Communications

A VPN server encrypts information so that only an authorized client can decrypt it. To encrypt transmissions, a VPN conducts a key exchange, whereby the server encrypts information to the client's public key. This key exchange is "on the fly," meaning that the server and the client negotiate a connection, and then transfer public keys. Once the public keys have been transferred, the VPN server can grant a session key, which is encrypted to the client. The session key is a form of "what you have" information that the client can then use to begin the VPN session. The client can then decrypt all information sent by the server with its private key. The two networks, then, can communicate via any client they wish (for example, HTTP, FTP, SMTP, POP3, Telnet, and so forth) through the tunnel.

Connecting Two Company Sites via an Internet VPN (Extranet)

There are two types of VPN: those established between firewalls and those established between a VPN server and a client computer, such as a Windows 98 system. This discussion assumes a session between a server and a client, although the encryption principles remain the same. Generally, the secure connection that allows an extranet to exist involves establishing a VPN connection between two private networks over public lines. In other words, if two companies create a new VPN-based network over the Internet, they are creating an extranet. In fact, one way to implement an extranet is to allow specific companies and users access to a company intranet.

A VPN connection of this type is generally a long-term connection—meaning that once you establish it between one firewall and another, it will remain up, generally for months at a time. In other words, it is not something that terminates and restarts, as does a dialup connection. Although VPN connections are technically not dedicated (that is, absolutely permanent and hard-wired), the nature of these connections is generally long term.

Once established, an extranet can, of course, allow users to communicate via S/MIME and digital certificates. In other words, you can double up on encryption: you can begin a VPN connection, and then use S/MIME to encrypt e-mail messages within the tunnel. This can afford an extra layer of encryption; if a hacker were to compromise the VPN connection through a hijacking attack, then the hacker would not be able to read the e-mail messages, because they have been encrypted through a completely different means (through S/MIME, PGP, or some other means of encryption).

Connecting a Remote User to a Site

Remember that an extranet can often be an intranet that allows controlled access from the outside. If a user from one company wishes to log in to the extranet, it is possible to use a browser to begin the authentication process. That user first authenticates with a firewall, then is able to enter the extranet. Whenever a client connects to a VPN using a dial-up connection, this is done through the Point to Point Transfer Protocol (PPTP). This is a tunneling protocol that allows you to send encrypted transmissions via a point-to-point (PP) connection.

First, an end user establishes a standard network connection. This can be an Ethernet-based connection or a dial-up connection. This particular connnection is not encrypted. The end user then establishes a second connection, which involves public key encryption. After authentication, all data sent between the client and the server is encrypted. Generally, VPN connections use RSA public key encryption, as well as a symmetrically encrypted session key, which is encrypted to the public key of the client.

It is standard practice to connect to a VPN using only TCP/IP. However, users can tunnel additional protocols, including NetBEUI and IPX/SPX. Most VPN connections allow these additional settings:

- **Software compression** The ability to compress packets as they pass through the wire. Both the client and the server must support this option.

- **Password encryption** If supported by the client and the server, all elements of the transaction, including the initial passwords, are encrypted.

- **Creation of client-side log files** Such log files are ideal for troubleshooting connections.

- **Automatic assignment of IP addresses and name servers** DHCP settings are popular, especially in large networks.

- **Manual configuration, if desired** As with IP addresses, this option is popular in large networks.

EXERCISE 12-1

Creating a VPN Connection in Microsoft Windows 98

1. In Windows 98, click the My Computer icon.

2. Double-click the Dial-up Networking icon.

3. Double-click the Make a New Connection icon.

4. Enter **Test** in the "Type a name for the computer you are dialing" field. This does not have to be the name of the actual computer.

5. In the Select a Device section, select Microsoft VPN Adapter. Note: If you have not upgraded your TCP/IP stack, which happens when you upgrade Dial-up Networking (DUN), you may not be able to create a VPN connection. Contact Microsoft for the latest version of DUN (http://www.microsoft.com).

6. Click Next.

7. Enter the host name or IP address of the computer that has the VPN service running. For the purposes of this exercise, enter **vpn.testconnection.com**. This, of course, is not a real computer.

8. Click Next, and then click Finish.

9. You aren't through yet. Go back in to the Dialup Networking window from My Computer, and right-click on the Test connection you have just created. Click the Server Types tab.

10. Notice that the three protocols used in Microsoft VPN are selected by default. De-select all but TCP/IP. The only box that should have a check next to it is TCP/IP.

11. Click the TCP/IP Settings button. The TCP/IP Settings button should appear.

12. Notice that by default the IP address, DNS, and WINS settings assume a DHCP server. When you establish a VPN connection for real, you may have to specify an IP address and name server settings.

CERTIFICATION OBJECTIVE 12.04

Suspicious Activities

Suspicious activities include attacks waged from inside the network, as well as those that arise from outside the firewall. This section will list activities covered by the i-Net+ exam. However, suspicious activities are generally not as obvious as they are described to be. In other words, the reason they are called suspicious activities is that they are generally not easy to detect. The first thing that a hacker wants to do is to identify the resources out on the network. The second thing is to assume control over the systems, preferably by obtaining a root account. Third, the hacker wants to spread to other systems. Above all, the hacker wishes to avoid detection. Secrecy, stealth, and an overworked IT professional who doesn't have time to check system logs are a hacker's best friends.

One of the latest suspicious activities during the network mapping phase is for hackers to conduct scans from diverse locations. In the past, a hacker considered himself lucky if he was able to discover systems through simple port scans. In the past couple of years, hackers have been able to team up and send what seems to be innocuous data from various locations. This data, such as a stray ACK packet here, or maybe a ping message there, seems to be nonthreatening, because it takes place over a long period of time (say, a month), and comes from several locations. However, the hackers who are transmitting these packets are paying careful attention to information derived from these packets. This information can include the type of operating system, the version of various services (such as IIS, SQL Server, Oracle8*i*, and so forth), and additional information that allows a hacker to obtain control over a system.

Before you learn more about multiple login failures, packet sniffing, denial of service attacks, and buffer overflows, you should first understand that hackers come up with new activities all the time. Every month or so, what was once a new attack becomes obsolete, because most IT professionals have patched them. Nevertheless, the categories described here will remain relevant; it is only the particular attacks and procedures that will change regularly.

Multiple Login Failures

Not every login failure is evidence that an attack is under way. A new user or one who has forgotten his or her password may be trying to figure out how to legitimately enter the system. However, multiple login failures are also evidence of a hacker trying to use a dictionary program such as L0pthCrack or John the Ripper. A dictionary program is an example of a brute force program designed to find any way possible to crack passwords.

A dictionary program uses a large text file of words. It will throw each word in this file at the authenticating server in the hope that at least one of these words will be the same as the actual password. This is why a strong password, for example, is at the very least a variation on any word that you might normally find in a dictionary. This is why you would never want a password that is someone's name or any other name or thing found in a dictionary. Also, if you are a science fiction nut, it is generally a bad idea to name yourself after a character, because most dictionary files have thorough lists of such information.

Upon failing dictionary mode, most cracking programs will then resort to statistical calculations and other means to crack the password. For example, some programs will add numbers to the beginning and ending of words. This is why you would never want to have a password such as 1yourspouse'sname1, and so forth.

Sniffing and Cracking Attacks

It is possible for a hacker to place a network interface card (NIC) into promiscuous mode. In a hub-based network, this enables one machine to capture traffic on the entire subnet. In a switched network, a hacker may be able to sniff traffic only between himself and one other host. Nevertheless, it is possible for a hacker to obtain sensitive information, including encrypted packets. Of course, if the information is not encrypted, then the hacker can obtain usernames, passwords, and other information. If it is encrypted, the hacker can use cracking programs such as L0phtCrack to analyze and crack the encryption found on the wire.

It is also possible to use cracking programs such as CAIN to find and attack Windows-based shares (see Figure 12-12). Once CAIN finds these shares, it runs dictionary and brute force attacks against the shares. Given enough time and enough information, a program like CAIN will eventually defeat the password.

Denial of Service Attacks

A denial of service attack crashes a server, or specific processes and systems that reside on a server. Sometimes a hacker wishes to conduct a denial of service (DOS) attack against a server out of pure malice. Many beginning hackers enjoy the simple sense of achievement they get when they bring down their first host.

FIGURE 12-12   The CAIN Share Discovery and Cracking program

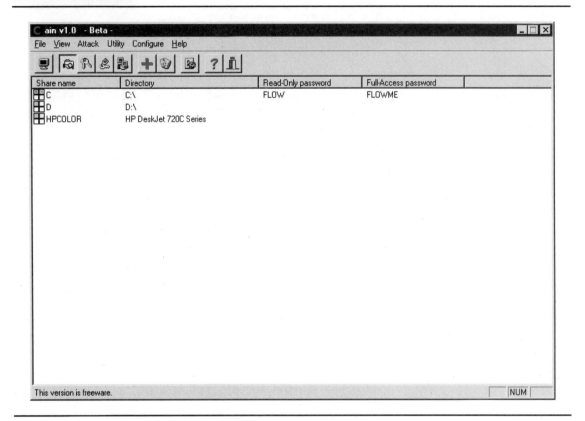

More sophisticated reasons exist for denial of service attacks, however. For example, TCP/IPv4, the most common version, is open to spoofing. In other words, it is possible to forge your own TCP/IP packets. This can allow talented hackers to assume the identity of a legitimate host on a network. However, if a hacker wishes to assume a host's identity, that hacker will first want to make sure that this legitimate host is not participating on the network. A denial of service attack can get rid of that host so that the hacker can begin his spoofing activities. In addition, many networks rely heavily upon trust relationships between one computer and another. A denial of service attack against a trusted host can allow a hacker to imitate a trusted host and then spread throughout the system. Many different denial of service attacks exist:

- **Scanning** Hackers generally map out a network before attacking it. A good way to map a network is to conduct ping scans to determine which hosts are up. They then conduct port scans of each host to see what types of services are up and (possibly) vulnerable.

- **E-mail bombing** An e-mail bombing program generates a large number of e-mail messages, all of which contain large attachments. The result of such attacks is that they overload an account. Especially in slow network connections (less than 128 Kbps), this can effectively wipe out a user's e-mail account.

- **Nuking attacks** Unpatched operating systems are vulnerable to attacks that send unexpected information to an open port. Doing so causes a denial of service attack called *nuking*.

- **Ping floods** With a program called SMURF, it is possible to forge IP packets that send ICMP request messages to another host. Let's call this host B. Your SMURF program causes host B to send ICMP reply packets not to you, but to another host, host C. The result is that you have sent only one ping to host B, and host B sends one ping to host C. Now, imagine what would happen if you and a bunch of your friends used your SMURF program to send thousands and even millions of ICMP packets to many different hosts, all of which then replied to host C. Host C would crash under the strain.

- **The Ping of Death** Some unpatched Windows NT systems are not able to accept ICMP packets over 65,535 bytes long. Using special programs, it is possible to create an ICMP packet exceeding this length, which crashes the system.

- **Syn floods** This form of attack takes advantage of the three-way TCP handshake process. Remember that TCP is a connection-oriented protocol. It first establishes a control connection before it transmits any information. What would happen if a hacker were to begin a

TCP connection on your host by sending a SYN request, but then never replied with an ACK packet? Your computer would devote resources to keeping that connection open until it timed out. This would be no big deal if only one connection stayed open for a little while. But what would happen if a hacker were to send thousands or millions of SYN requests? Your system would crash under the strain.

- **UDP attacks** A UDP attack could involve sending many UDP packets to one host, as in a ping flood attack. However, it is also possible to attack a system by sending UDP packets that then overlap once the receiving host puts them back together again. In nonpatched Windows NT and Linux systems, this overlapping of UDP packets crashes the system, resulting in the "blue screen of death" and a kernel panic, respectively.

Hijacking

In another form of attack, hijacking, a hacker successfully intercepts and controls a data stream originating from one computer and meant for another. For example, assume computer A, named jacob, wishes to establish an SSL session with computer B, named sandi. Normally, jacob would begin the SSL negotiation process with sandi. However, it is possible (though very difficult) for a hacker residing in the middle of this connection to intercept packets sent by jacob. After knocking the host named sandi out of the picture via a DOS attack, the hacker can then imitate sandi and send back packets. The result is that the session will be encrypted. However, jacob thinks that it is communicating to sandi, when in fact it is communicating with the hacker machine. This kind of attack is also called a "man in the middle" attack.

System Bugs and Back Doors

A system bug consists of a program, application, or service that contains code that results in unexpected or dangerous behavior. For example, many Internet browsers, including Microsoft Internet Explorer and Netscape Navigator, have bugs in them that allow for window spoofing. Using

JavaScript or VBScript, a malicious Web site can manipulate a user's browser so that the address window (that is, where you enter the URL) appears to be from one site, such as www.yahoo.com, but is in fact at another. Other browser-based bugs allow hackers to view the contents of your hard drive while you are visiting their Web site.

Bugs are not limited to Web browsers, however. The first iteration of Windows NT 4.0 had a system bug that allowed users to connect to port 139 and enter random code. The result of this attack was that the computer's CPU went up to 100 percent, resulting in a denial of service attack. Many known system bugs exist, with more being found all the time. One common source for Windows NT bugs is the NTBugTraq page (http://www.ntbugtraq.com/).

The best way to deal with system bugs is to research your particular operating system. Find your operating system vendor, and then see if they have developed any updates. These are sometimes called *system patches*. It is vital that you discover your system's patch level and that you further determine whether this patch level is the best one for your particular system.

A back door is a concern related to system bugs. The chief difference between a system bug and a system back door is that a system bug is generally considered to be a mistake or oversight on the part of the programmer. A back door, on the other hand, is the result of intent. The most common example of a back door is an unknown username and password that exists on the system.

Sometimes, a back door is not malicious; it is simply there to help technical support provide help and advice for system administrators. Older routers and operating systems often had back doors placed in them for such legitimate purposes. However, it is possible for other, illegitimate back doors to exist. Careful study of the username and password database, as well as of the baseline function of your operating system, can help you determine the existence of any back doors.

Perhaps the most often exploited system bug is a program, file, or service that has a buffer overflow.

Buffer Overflows

Whenever a programmer creates a program using C, C++, or one of many other languages, he or she has to create a buffer to hold information used by the program. Some of this information includes variables used by the programs. The programmer generally assigns a default size to this buffer, because he or she only expects variables of a certain size to go into the buffer. However, it is possible for a hacker to manipulate the program so that it sends information into the buffer that is too large. The result is that the buffer gets overcrowded and overflows its limits. A buffer overflow can lead to one or more of these problems:

- The service or application crashes, resulting in a denial of service attack.
- The entire operating system crashes, resulting in a denial of service attack.
- The operating system, service, or application crashes, leaving behind a crashed shell or space where a hacker can execute arbitrary code.

The third problem is the most serious, because a buffer overflow can allow a hacker to issue commands to a service or operating system.

Illicit Services

In the past couple of years, hackers have spent a great deal of time creating illicit services that reside on UNIX, NT, and Novell systems. One well-known illicit server is the BackOrifice 2000 program. This program is quite powerful, as it has the ability to log keystrokes and store them in a hidden file, map shares, and even start a hidden HTTP server that allows file upload and download, among many other services. This illicit service can even encrypt transmissions, making detection somewhat more difficult. The original BackOrifice program ran only on Windows 95 and 98. However, BO 2000 operates on any 32-bit platform, which includes Windows NT.

Another less ambitious server is NetBus. Although it does not have all of the features of BackOrifice, it nevertheless can compromise a host. It opens up a server on port 12345, which you can then use a client to manipulate. The client is shown in Figure 12-13.

Each of these programs is representative because it uses a fairly simple client to access a server that resides on a compromised host. Many additional illicit servers exist. Some open hidden FTP and HTTP servers; others are more complex and use their own servers.

Trojans

A *trojan* is an illicit program that appears to have a legitimate function. For example, it is possible to disguise an illicit program such as BackOrifice or NetBus so that it looks like a simple installation program. Generally, if a user installs a trojan, the user thinks that he or she is installing a game or application. However, unbeknownst to the user, the program gets installed on the system and then goes on to thwart the operating system's authentication functions.

FIGURE 12-13

The NetBus client interface

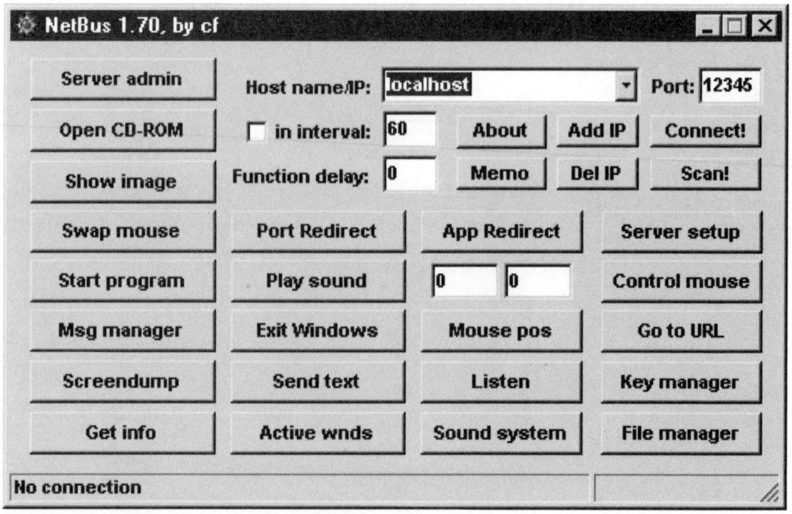

In UNIX systems, many trojan programs have been gathered together as a root kit, which consists of illicit programs that replace legitimate programs, such as ls (used to list files), su (used to become a super user, or root), and cd (used to change from one directory to another). Many trojan programs exist in Windows NT systems. For example, one hacker placed NetBus into a trojan called Whack-A-Mole and sent it out on the Web. Everyone who double-clicked on this file and played the game also loaded this illicit server on their computers.

Viruses and Worms

A virus is a small program that takes control of the operating system. A virus generally has a payload. Depending upon the virus, the payload can be something annoying, such as a sound playing at a particular time, or downright destructive: the old Michelangelo virus, for example, erased entire hard drives. There are three main types of viruses:

- **Boot sector** The most common type, this virus infects the master boot record of a floppy or hard disk. Once the disk is activated, the virus goes into memory. If a user places an infected floppy disk into an uninfected system, the virus will then infect the uninfected system.

- **Macro** Programs such as Microsoft Word, Corel WordPerfect, and Microsoft Excel use special languages to create macros. Usually, a macro is a valuable work-saving tool. However, it is possible to create malicious programs using these powerful macro languages. Some macro viruses are capable of erasing and modifying data.

- **File** This type of virus attaches to specific files and activates once the file is put into use.

All viruses rely upon some sort of human intervention in order to spread. For example, a user generally has to insert a floppy or double-click a file in order to activate the payload.

A worm, on the other hand, is somewhat more ambitious, because it can spread by itself, given certain conditions. For example, the so-called Melissa virus had many wormlike qualities, because even though it took advantage of Word and Excel macros, it used Microsoft Outlook to automatically spread to other systems. Although Melissa victims had to double-click an e-mail attachment to get infected, the rest of the process was automatic, given the condition that the users used Microsoft Outlook, and that they had their macro settings to their default, as most people do.

exam
ⓦatch

Take careful note of the different types of suspicious activities discussed in this chapter. Specific attacks and programs are always changing. However, the principles discussed in this section will remain the same for a long time. In other words, just because the WinNuke programs are now quite old, this doesn't mean that denial of service attacks are now unimportant.

Physical Attacks

It is possible for a hacker to obtain physical access to a computer. Once this is accomplished, he or she can insert disks into it. Programs on this disk might completely bypass the operating system's security measures and allow the hacker to control it. It is also possible for a hacker to simply shoulder surf passwords and then take control of it.

Other physical attacks include actually stealing the server itself, or grabbing a hard drive or some other element.

EXERCISE 12-2

Researching Suspicious Activities

1. Open your browser and enter this URL: http://www.antiocode.com.

2. Identify the types of attacks and programs available to you.

3. Go to this URL: http://www.insecure.org.

4. Finally, use a search engine such as Yahoo! (http://www.yahoo.com) or AltaVista (http://www.altavista.com) and conduct searches using some of the keywords found in this chapter. For example, use AltaVista and enter the following text string, including the quotes: **"denial of service attack"**.

5. Use a search engine and enter these words: **Trojans, NetBus, BackOrifice, cracking, hacking**.

6. Now that you have seen the darker, generally less productive side of hacking, go to this Web site: http://www.ntbugtraq.com/. Search this site's contents. If you wish, click the Subscribe link to subscribe to a very useful e-mail list that informs you about the latest Windows NT–related security issues.

7. Go to this site: http://www.cert.org/. Search this site's contents.

In this exercise, you have received a taste of the kind of attacks that exist on the Web, as well as the sites that exist to help protect you from hackers.

Access Security Features for an Internet Server

An Internet server, such as an HTTP server, has many security features associated with it. For example, it is possible to

- Log users
- Enforce authentication via passwords
- Encrypt transmissions
- Enforce strong authentication
- Encrypt files and folders

Usernames and Passwords

The basic means of authentication for a Web site, as well as most other Internet servers (Telnet, FTP, and so on) is a username and password. Figure 12-14 shows how it is possible to require a user to provide a username and password before he is allowed access into a particular directory.

FIGURE 12-14   Web server authenticating a user for access to a restricted directory

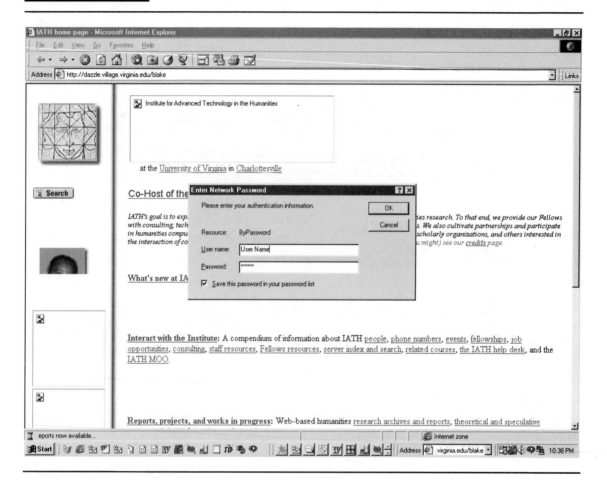

A user who enters the wrong information and fails authentication will receive a message similar to that shown in Figure 12-15.

It is possible to restrict access to an entire site, as well. You can do this by requiring password protection for all documents within a directory; as soon as a user tries to gain access to the documents inside this directory, the server will ask the user for authentication information. Some Web servers, such as IIS, allow you to restrict access for an entire virtual server. For example, if your Web site has two virtual servers, it is possible to allow the first to be completely open, and to require usernames and passwords for the second.

FIGURE 12-15   Results of failed authentication

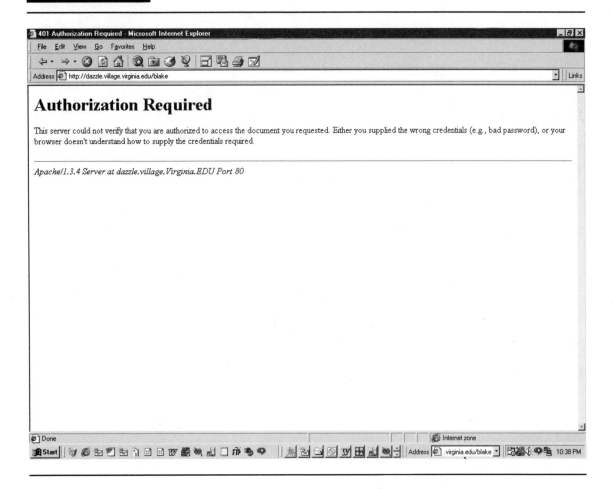

File-Level Protection

It is possible to encrypt specific files, as well. You can do this by using encryption programs to require a password before an application can open it. For example, Microsoft Word contains its own encryption program that applies a symmetric key to it. Pretty Good Privacy (PGP) uses strong algorithms to encrypt files, using public key encryption. As discussed earlier, it is also possible to sign documents with your private key, allowing anyone with a public key to verify the file's integrity.

If a client is using Netscape Navigator and the site is operating a Netscape server, it is possible to begin an SSL session if a user selects a specific file. A similar scheme exists between IIS and Microsoft Internet Explorer. As of this writing, however, this technology is not universal, although there are plans to make it so.

Certificates

Certificates allow for enhanced authentication as well as encryption. Once a Web server has a certificate, you can apply this certificate to certain directories. Once a user requests a specific object (that is, a file, directory, or site), the server will then begin an SSL session before it sends information. Once a client begins an SSL session, he or she can check a server's certificate. Most Web browsers automate this process, but it is possible to check these certificates. If a browser detects an expired certificate, or one that has been revoked, you will be given options, including the choice to move on with the transaction.

Because a certificate provides enhanced authentication, you should choose to continue such a transaction only after careful consideration.

File-Level Access

When you apply file-level access to a source, you generally have three choices. You can employ these permissions:

- **Read** Allows users to view a file. They can also copy it to their hard drive.

- **Write** Allows users to modify the file in any way. This means that they can add information, as well as taking information away from that particular file. They can also delete the file, if they wish. If a directory (as opposed to a file) has write access, then a user can create and delete files inside that directory.

- **Execute**   Execute permission allows users to execute binary files (such as an e-mail application or any other program).

- **No access**   The user cannot read or modify the file.

As you learn more about permissions, you will find that many more permission types exist. Windows NT using NTFS has many additional permissions, including list, which allows users to list files in a directory, but not actually read their contents. This permission type is a subset of the read permission, but is much more restrictive than read, because standard read permission allows you to view the contents of the file.

It is possible to combine permissions. When you do, the file has both permissions. For example, if a file is given read and execute permissions to everyone, then all users—even those not created on the system—will be able to read and execute that file. If a file is given read and write access, then users can both read and write to that file. The only exception to this is the no access permission. If a file is marked as no access, then this overrides all other permissions. No access, therefore, always means no access. Finally, it is possible to remove read permissions and still allow execute permissions. This means that a user can execute a program without being able to view its location. When creating CGI scripts, for example, on a Web page, everyone will have to execute it. However, just because everyone can execute it does not mean that everyone should be able to view its contents.

You should also note that you can control access to a Web server by denying access to certain IP addresses. You can enforce restrictions either through the operating system, or through the Web server. For example, UNIX systems provide ways to forbid access to certain services using the TCPWrappers daemon. Windows NT Servers 4.0 and 2000 allow you to prohibit IP traffic by address and subnet. Microsoft IIS has the same capability.

Anti-Virus Software and Its Use

Anti-virus software searches for specific viruses, worms, and trojans, as well as other suspect executables. This type of software identifies exactly how a program behaves; it then works to inform you about the problem and effect repairs if possible. Sometimes, an anti-virus program can only identify problems, rather than fixing them. This may be because the nature of the infection is so advanced, or because an actual fix was not yet known when the vendor released the anti-virus program.

Anti-virus programs search for virus signatures. A signature is simply the way the virus tries to take over the computer. Once a virus's signature is known, it is possible to detect and kill it. All anti-virus programs have a signature list, which is nothing more than a list of viruses that it can kill. Effective anti-virus programs update these lists often, usually once or twice a month. Additional updates come in the event of a virus, trojan, or worm that is particularly destructive. It is vital that you keep your servers and client computers updated as much as possible. If your users have gone longer than a month without an update, then they have gone too long.

Browser/Client Anti-Virus Programs

The most common type of anti-virus program is one that resides on an end user's computer. Common examples of this type of program include Norton AntiVirus (http://www.norton.com) shown in Figure 12-16, Mcafee VirusScan (http://www.mcafee.com), and Pccillin (http://www.pccillin.com).

Most of these anti-virus programs allow you to specify scans of items you download from Web sites. Others will scan e-mail attachments.

Protecting Servers

A server can use the same applications as a client. Therefore, you can simply install Norton AntiVirus on your system and make sure you keep it updated. However, it is possible to enable on-the-fly anti-virus scanning on your

FIGURE 12-16

The Norton AntiVirus
program

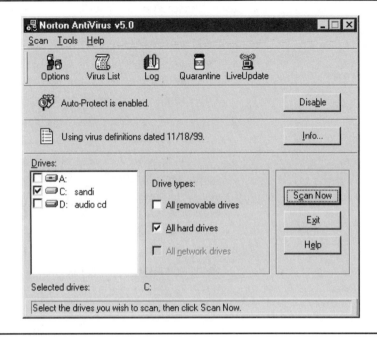

e-mail servers. The ability to scan e-mail attachments is quite different from the ability to use a standard anti-virus scan.

E-mail attachment scanning places e-mail attachments in a special directory whenever the e-mail receives messages with attachments. Because this can take some time, the e-mail server will provide user identification numbers for the attachments and the e-mail message. This means that some messages will be delayed, which may cause end users to complain. Also, it is possible for hackers to conduct denial of service attacks against an e-mail server equipped with this type of scanner. By simply sending multiple infected messages to the server, hackers can either crash the entire server or disable the scanning feature.

EXERCISE 12-3

Conducting an Anti-Virus Scan on Your Network Host

In this exercise, you deploy an anti-virus program on your Web site. You will register with the Trend Micro HouseCall anti-virus Web site, then download either a Java or ActiveX program, depending upon whether you are using Netscape or Internet Explorer. This program will then inspect your hard drive for viruses. Note: The process is somewhat more simple if you use Microsoft Internet Explorer.

1. Open your Web browser and enter this URL:
   http://housecall.antivirus.com/pc_housecall/
   You should see a picture similar to the one in Figure 12-17.

2. Enter your e-mail address. This is necessary to obtain the ActiveX control.

3. You will have to wait several minutes while the site investigates your computer. Depending upon the speed of your network connection and CPU, this could take a few minutes. Note: If you are using Netscape Navigator, you will have to download the HouseCall program, run it, and then close and reopen Netscape.

4. If you are using Microsoft Internet Explorer, you will receive a security warning, asking whether you wish to install and download the program. Click the More Info button to obtain more information.

FIGURE 12-17

The Trend Micro
HouseCall Web site

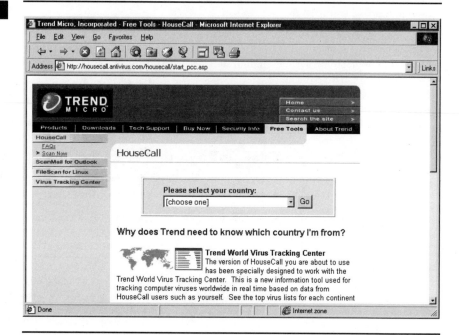

5. After the control is downloaded (and, if you are using Netscape Navigator, you have restarted your browser), your browser should provide you with a graphical representation of all drives on your computer, including your floppy drives, CD ROM, and hard drives.

6. Select one of these items, and then click the Scan button.

7. The anti-virus program will scan your system for viruses.

You have now conducted a virus scan of your computer. Note that if you find any problems, this service will not clean them up for you. It will only identify issues, and then give you directions on how to solve them.

Now that you have a better idea of how to identify hacker activity and protect yourself against it, here are some possible scenario questions and their answers.

QUESTIONS AND ANSWERS

Your Web server has been restarted several times in the last two days. Your server technician has verified that all physical elements (that is, power supplies and hard drives) are working well. What is a possible cause of the server shutdown?	A hacker has conducted a denial of service attack against it, forcing it to reboot. Another answer may be that a hacker has obtained control over the server, installed an illicit service, and then restarted it to make sure the service can take effect.
You notice that several key files ending in .doc and .xsl (Microsoft Word and Excel files) keep getting deleted. You have an anti-virus program, and you have scanned the hard drive repeatedly. You still suspect that a virus exists. What should you do now?	The likely problem is that your anti-virus program is using older signatures, and that you have been infected with a recent virus, trojan, or worm. You have several options. First, you should update the virus definitions (that is, the signature files) that your anti-virus program uses. Second, you may want to obtain a better anti-virus program. Finally, it is possible that someone has physically attacked your computer and deleted these files. You should consider locking down all physical access to the computer.
You have found that your server is vulnerable to a specific attack. What do you do?	The best way to recover from a problem is to find the operating system's vendor and see if they have issued an update file, which is sometimes called a systems patch or a hot fix. Microsoft, for example, issues Service Packs to ensure that its servers are the most secure. As of this writing, the latest service pack is Service Pack 6. Microsoft is developing postservice pack fixes.

CERTIFICATION SUMMARY

In this chapter, you have learned the basics of Internet security. You have learned about the security standards and organizations that help keep IT professionals alerted concerning security problems. Some of these include ISO and CERT. You have also learned about the types of services and mechanisms that exist in order to make systems secure. These include authentication, data integrity, data confidentiality, and nonrepudiation.

You then learned about authentication and encryption, including the three different types of encryption used in a network. You read about access control, including how firewalls and proxy servers enhanced network authentication. You also read about intrusion detection, as well as how to identify and classify specific attacks and threats, including denial of service, buffer overflow, and bug-based attacks. You then identified ways to secure Internet-based services, such as a Web server.

Auditing is a fundamental security tool, and you learned about some of the ways UNIX and NT systems audit their security. You have also learned about SSL, SET, and VPN connections. Finally, you have learned about viruses and how to protect yourself against them.

 # TWO-MINUTE DRILL

- ❑ The OSI/RM and the ISO 7498-2 document provide information about key services and mechanisms provided by an operating system.
- ❑ *Authentication* is the ability to verify the identity of a user, host, or system process.
- ❑ *Access control* is the determination of who and what is allowed in to an operating system or network.
- ❑ *Encryption* is the use of algorithms and protocols to scramble information so that users cannot engage in electronic eavesdropping or data tampering.

❑ *Data confidentiality* is the use of encryption to make sure that information remains secret.

❑ *Data integrity* is the use of encryption and other means to make sure that no one has tampered with (that is, altered) information in transit.

❑ *Auditing* is the ability to determine who has accessed the system, and when.

❑ *Nonrepudiation* is the ability to prove that a transaction has in fact occurred.

❑ *What you know*–the most common example of this form of identification is a password.

❑ *What you have*–this form of authentication requires that you present a physical token of some sort. In the analog world, this may be a key or an actual piece of paper. As far as the Internet is concerned, digital signatures and certificates provide this service. Smart cards are the most advanced form of "what you have" authentication.

❑ *What you are*–biometrics is the study of authentication via physical traits, including retinal scans, fingerprints, and voice identification.

❑ *Where you are*–also called proof of origin. It is possible for systems to authenticate packets, depending upon where they come from. Although this form of authentication is not very secure, it is still practiced by the UNIX rlogin programs. For example, a UNIX system (host A) using the rlogin series of programs will allow another host (host B) to log in without a password. This is because host A has a special file named rlogin.hosts that specifies a user from a specific host to bypass the authentication subsystem and enter the host. However, because it is possible for users to spoof IP addresses and other information in an IP packet, this practice is increasingly falling out of favor.

❑ *Digital certificates* provide enhanced authentication services, because they contain additional information about the system you are connecting to. Digital certificates are the primary means of authenticating users, hosts, and servers.

❑ The *X.509 standard* mandates a special format for all digital certificates.

❑ A *virtual private network* (VPN) is an example of a tunneling protocol. It operates at the network layer and encrypts all transmissions, making it difficult for hackers to sniff information.

❑ *Public key infrastructure* (PKI) is a term reserved for organizations and bodies that create, store, and manage digital certificates.

❑ A *digital signature* is the electronic equivalent of your own "real" signature that you use when signing a check.

❑ *Nonrepudiation* is the practice of being able to verify that a transaction—or any occurrence, for that matter—has actually happened.

❑ *Strong authentication* involves combining certificates, digital signatures, and the authentication measures mentioned (what you have, what you are, what you know, and where you are). In short, if you combine the first three forms of authentication, you are able to strongly authenticate users.

❑ *Kerberos* is a centralized server that uses OTP and encryption to grant access to network resources.

❑ *Smart cards* contain the ability to store and/or process information. They are often used to strongly authenticate users.

❑ *OTP*–one-time passwords are, as the name suggests, passwords used only once. You use them to identify.

❑ A *virus* is an illicit program designed to take over control of a host.

❑ A *trojan* is an illicit program that can take over a host, and then replicate itself to other hosts under certain conditions.

❑ *Auditing* is the ability to determine what has happened on a network host.

❑ *SET* is a series of procedures that enable e-commerce to conduct financial transactions sites in a secure way to exchange information with banking institutions.

SELF TEST

1. Your Web server has been attacked. No users can connect to it to view Web pages. You must restart it in order to use it again. Which of the following best describes this attack?

   A. A virus attack

   B. A bug-based attack

   ✓C. A denial of service attack

   D. A buffer overflow attack

2. Several new users have been hired. You need to create three new users. They are named james, jacob, and joel. You will do this in Windows NT User Manager. All users will need to read messages in the f:\reports directory. They will also need to run programs in the g:\programs directory, although they do not necessarily need to read the files, because the files will be run via a batch script. What are the minimum permissions that you need to assign in regard to these directories?

   A. Read and execute permissions to both directories.

   ✓B. Execute permissions to the programs directory, and read permissions to the reports directory.

   C. Read permissions to the programs directory, and write permissions to the reports directory.

   D. Read and execute permissions to the programs directory, and read permissions to the reports directory.

3. You have just updated your anti-virus program. After running it on your F:\ drive, you receive an alert telling you that your master boot record has been corrupted. Which type of virus infects the master boot record?

   A. File infector

   B. Boot signature

   C. Macro

   ✓D. Boot sector

4. You have just initiated an advanced authentication scheme using voice printing and smart cards. Which of the authentication principles listed here best describes the use of voice printing and smart cards? (Choose all that apply.)

   A. What the person does

   ✓B. What the person has

   ✓C. What the person is

   D. Password-based authentication

5. You have just gone to VeriSign and had them create a key pair for you. You receive an e-mail message back from VeriSign containing what you have asked for. Specifically, it contains the public and private keys VeriSign created. What must you do next with these keys?

   A. You will install both keys, then distribute both freely, depending upon how you wish to use public key encryption.

B. You will install the private key, store the public key, and then distribute the public key freely and keep the private key secret.

C. You will install and distribute both, and then distribute the private key and keep the public key secret.

D. You will encrypt messages to the recipient's public key.

6. You have just engaged in a transaction with Amazon.com. This company has sent you an e-mail confirming your transaction. It has also kept a confidential record of the transaction. Which of the concepts given here best describes this practice?

A. Data confidentiality

B. Data integrity

C. Authentication

D. Nonrepudiation

7. What is the purpose of a certificate authority (CA)? (Choose all that apply.)

A. To create public keys

B. To verify public keys

C. To create private keys

D. To verify users

8. You wish to encrypt a transmission so that no one but the recipient can read it. In other words, you wish to achieve data confidentiality. You wish to use public key encryption. What should you do?

A. Encrypt your message to your private key.

B. Encrypt your message symmetrically.

C. Encrypt your message asymmetrically.

D. Encrypt your message to your recipient's public key.

9. What is the purpose of PKI? (Choose all that apply.)

A. To manage certificates

B. To create SSL sessions

C. To create SET sessions

D. To revoke certificates

10. You have just been attacked by a hacker. The hacker program automatically activated itself, and then used the normal workings of your operating system, complete with some of its applications, to spread to other systems. Given this information, what type of hacker program attacked your system?

A. A buffer overflow

B. A virus

C. A trojan

D. A worm

11. You are conducting an audit of your network. You are concerned that your systems may be vulnerable to some new attacks originating from inside the network. You are especially interested in tracking scanning attacks. You wish to discover the details about what has happened to a particular internal subnet. What can you do? (Choose all that apply.)

A. Enable auditing, if it is not already on.
B. Check the security logs.
C. Check the firewall logs.
D. Check the IDS application logs.

12. You have just installed a service patch on your server. You run netstat and notice that port 12345 is open. You notice that this is the NetBus port. You run your anti-virus programs, which destroy the infection. You go to another server and run a virus checker and find that it is sound. You then update another server using the same service patch. You run netstat and notice that it, too, now has port 12345 open, which indicates a NetBus infection. What is happening, here?

A. You are the victim of a worm.
B. You are the victim of a trojan.
C. You are the victim of a virus.
D. You are the victim of a denial of service attack.

13. Your IDS alerts you that a network host has been brought down. It is a Linux server that you are using as a DNS server. You analyze the network connections to this Linux server using a packet sniffer and find that thousands of TCP connections have been begun on this host. What is the name for this type of attack?

A. A UDP flood
B. An ICMP flood

C. A SYN flood
D. A ping flood

14. Your affiliate in Germany requires SET in order to conduct e-commerce. Specifically, it requires you to contact a body that can process merchant authorization and payment messages in Bonn. In regard to SET, what is the official name for a body that can do these things?

A. An acquirer
B. A merchant
C. A merchant bank
D. A CA

15. You have just been attacked by a hacker. The attack focused on your Netscape Web server, which is running on your HP-UX UNIX system. You can tell from system logs that the Web server experienced a buffer overflow. You are not familiar with any known attacks against this server. Which of the sites given here will likely contain information about buffer overflow issues in regard to Netscape servers?

A. The FBI Web site
B. Search engines that discover information about the Netscape Web server
C. Newsgroups concerning security and Netscape servers
D. The CERT WEB site

16. An auditor has been able to gain access to the root account of your Web server. When

you ask about how this happened, the auditor replies that she was able to grab some packets off of the wire and then use L0phtCrack against them. After two days, she had the password. What is the name for this type of attack?

A. Denial of service

B. Buffer overflow

C. Hacking

√ D. Cracking

17. Todd works as a Webmaster for a startup company devoted to creating Web pages for its partners. He wishes to limit access to the development and partner areas of the company Web site, but keep other areas of the site open for all other visitors. Specifically, only Webmaster employees should be able to access the development site, whereas only partners should be able to access the partner site. What should he do?

A. Enable SSL, and then make sure that the authentication SSL field is filled in with the appropriate user information.

B. Enable password protection on the Web site so that only Webmasters and partners can enter the site.

C. Set your firewall to deny port 80 for all people but Webmasters and partners.

√ D. Enable password protection on the directories that house the files relevant for both Webmasters and partners.

18. You wish to encrypt transmissions between two companies to create an extranet over public lines. How will you encrypt the transmissions?

√ A. By using a VPN

B. By using SSL

C. By using S/MIME

D. By using SET

19. You wish to authenticate users using your Web server. You also wish to use your Web server to encrypt information using the most appropriate means available to a Web server. You are using Apache Web server on a Linux server. What can you do to ensure authentication and encryption?

A. Use a VPN and SSL.

B. Deploy a firewall and password protection.

√ C. Use SSL and password protection.

D. Use S/MIME and SSL.

20. You wish to ensure that e-mail attachments are virus free. You have already installed and updated client-side software. What else can you do?

A. Filter e-mail at the router.

B. Install the same anti-virus program that the clients have on the server.

C. Install two anti-virus programs on the clients.

√ D. Install anti-virus programs that scan e-mail attachments.

SELF TEST ANSWERS

1. **C.** A denial of service attack is one that crashes the server.
   A is incorrect, because a virus attack can be many things, including a denial of service attack. **B** is incorrect, because a system bug can lead to more serious security breaches. **D** is incorrect, because the scenario never mentions how the denial of service attack was waged.

2. **B** is correct. Users need to execute programs in the programs directory, and only need to read files in the reports directory. The programs directory need only execute permissions, because users will not need to see the programs they are executing, because they are using a batch file.
   A and **D** are incorrect, because they would allow too many permissions. Remember: The programs directory does not need read permissions. Likewise, the reports directory does not need execute permissions, because users will read only the files. **C** is incorrect, because it would not allow execution on the programs directory, and it would allow users to write to the reports directory; you want to allow them only to read this directory, not write to it.

3. **D.** A boot sector virus infects the master boot record.
   B is incorrect, because there is no such thing as a boot signature virus. A macro virus infects Microsoft Word files; but **A** is incorrect, because a file infector virus attacks specific files, not the master boot record.

4. **B** and **C** are correct. Authentication is based upon various principles discussed in the chapter. Two of them are what the person has and what the person is. If a person has a smart card, at least one of the principles being used here is what the person has. Also, if the user's voice is being used as a means for authentication, then the user is being authenticated by what the person is, because voice is unique to a person.
   A is not an authentication principle. **D** is incorrect, because it provides an example of "what you know" authentication, as opposed to an authentication principle itself.

5. **B** is correct. When you receive your key pair from a CA, you first place this private key on your hard drive and keep it secret. This key never goes anywhere, and is generally nontransferable. In other words, once it is on this system, you don't want to move it. As far as the public key is concerned, you can freely distribute it.

A and C are incorrect, because you would never distribute your private key. D is incorrect, because even though it does describe the proper process for using public key encryption for data confidentiality, it does not necessarily describe the next step you would take with these keys.

6. **D** is correct. "Nonrepudiation" is the generic term for the ability to verify that a transaction or occurrence has in fact happened. Because Amazon.com sent you a confirmation e-mail and also kept a record of the transaction, it will be able to prove that the transaction occurred. Similarly, you can prove that the transaction occurred, because you have a receipt in the form of the e-mail. Nonrepudiation also involves the ability to prove that a transaction or transmission has not, in fact, occurred; you can challenge this transaction by mustering information, such as credit card statements, to prove that you did not make the transaction.
   A, B, and **C** are incorrect, because they list other principles. Nonrepudiation can occur through the transfer of encrypted messages.

7. **A, B,** and **D** are correct. A certificate authority can generate a key pair (which includes the public key), or it can receive and validate an already existing public key. It can also verify specific users.
   C is incorrect, because a CA does not create a private key.

8. **D** is correct. You can use public key encryption in two ways. To achieve actual data confidentiality, you need to encrypt the message to your recipient's public key. This means that no one but the recipient will be able to decrypt the message.
   A is incorrect, because this describes the practice of signing a message; anyone with your public key could read this message. **B** is incorrect, because we are discussing asymmetric key encryption only.

9. **A** and **D** are correct. PKI (public key infrastructure) describes a series of bodies that manage certificates. Part of managing certificates can, in cases in which the certificate is compromised, include certificate revocation.
   B and **C** are incorrect, because although PKI can help generate and distribute the certificates that allow SSL and SET sessions, SSL and SET do not necessarily rely upon PKI to begin sessions.

10. **D** is correct. A worm can spread automatically (without user intervention) under certain circumstances. This includes the ability to take advantage of e-mail client and browser security settings. **B** is incorrect, because a virus is its own category, and does not spread to other systems automatically; a virus generally requires that a user activate it in some way. **C** is incorrect, because although a worm can be placed in a trojan, a trojan can contain many different types of threats, including illicit servers and viruses. **A** is incorrect, because it describes an activity that a worm can accomplish, rather than describing what a worm is.

11. **A, B,** and **D** are correct. You should first enable auditing on your systems, and then check the logs. Firewall and IDS logs are particularly rich sources of information. **C** is incorrect, because a firewall does not log activity internal to a subnet.

12. **B** is correct. The service patch you are using is in fact a trojan. You are not the victim of a virus, per se, because NetBus is an illicit server.
NetBus is not a worm, either, so **A** is incorrect. Finally, a NetBus infection is not necessarily a denial of service attack, so **D** is incorrect.

13. **C** is correct. A SYN flood causes a server to open up half-open SYN connections.
A, B, and **D** are incorrect, because they specify attacks that use the wrong protocol.

14. **A** is correct. An acquirer is a party that processes merchant authorization and payment messages between the merchant and the merchant's bank. Sometimes, but not always, a merchant bank has its own acquirer function.
B is incorrect, because even though it uses SSL, the acquirer is not responsible for SSL. **C** is incorrect, because the acquirer does not ever directly communicate with the end user. **D** is incorrect, because it does not manage certificates in any way.

15. **D** is correct. CERT (the Computer Emergency Response Team) is responsible for alerting users to the latest hacker exploits. It is the site most likely to contain alerts concerning problems with a particular Web server.
A, B, and **C** are incorrect, because even though these sites may contain information, they will not contain relevant information that is easy to search.

16. **D** is correct. Another name for cracking is cryptography. Although this attack also involves sniffing packets off of the wire, its focus was on grabbing packets, and then running a common cracking program against them.
    A and **B** are incorrect, because they describe other forms of attack. The word "hacking" is a generic term that describes various forms of activity.

17. **D** is correct. You can use your Web server to enable password protection on specific directories that house the site's files. You can limit access to various directories according to their contents. For example, you can create one directory that contains files for Webmaster developers, and another directory that contains files and information relevant to business partners.
    A is incorrect, because an SSL session provides data confidentiality and data integrity, not data access control. As of this writing, there is no way to manipulate the headers in the manner described. **B** is incorrect, because it would deny access to the entire site for all people, except Webmasters and partners. **C** is incorrect, because it would deny all users access to the site.

18. **A** is correct. You would use a VPN to encrypt these transmissions at the network layer. SSL is suitable for Web-based traffic. S/MIME is appropriate for e-mail, and SET describes the ability for banks and e-commerce sites to communicate securely.

19. **C** is correct. SSL is the most common, efficient solution for ensuring encryption via the Web. Password protection on a directory will ensure authentication. You should make sure you understand that both are necessary here. SSL does not yet ensure authentication; you require an additional step to make sure authenticated users can communicate via an encrypted data stream.
    A is incorrect, because a VPN is generally not necessary for ensuring encryption via a single Web server and a client. A VPN would be more appropriate in an extranet setting. **B** is incorrect, because it is, again, a solution that is not appropriate to a single Web server solution. **D** is incorrect, because even though SSL is correct, S/MIME is used for encrypting and authenticating e-mail messages, not Web transaction.

20. **D** is correct. It is possible to scan e-mail attachments at the e-mail server.
    A is incorrect, because it is not possible to use a router to scan attachments. **B** is incorrect, because installing a simple anti-virus program will not scan e-mail attachments. **C** is incorrect, because no number of simple anti-virus programs will solve this problem.

i-Net+

COMPUTING TECHNOLOGY INDUSTRY ASSOCIATION

13

Business Concepts

T he first part of this chapter deals with the issues of copyright and trademark, and the associated issues of licensing. These are all forms of intellectual property law that are equally important in the electronic world as they are in the physical world.

The second part of this chapter is concerned with the issues surrounding globalization and localization of Web sites and the issues of conducting business and e-commerce around the world.

CERTIFICATION OBJECTIVE 13.01

Copyright and Patent

The intellectual property laws in the United States protect the following types of property:

- **Copyright law**   Protects "original works of authorship"
- **Trademark law**   Protects words, names, and symbols used by manufacturers and businesses to identify their goods and services
- **Patent law**   Protects new, useful, and "nonobvious" inventions and processes

This lesson will focus on the U.S. copyright and trademark law for applications, including the Internet and e-business.

Copyright Law

Copyright is a form of legal protection provided by the laws of the United States (Title 17, U.S. Code) to the authors of "original works of authorship," including literary, dramatic, musical, artistic, and certain other intellectual works. This protection is available to both published and unpublished works. Since copyright law is part of federal law, it does not vary from state to state.

Circular 66, which is available from the U.S. Copyright Office, describes information on registering digital and electronic works such as Web, FTP, and Gopher sites that are made available over networks such as the Internet. Specific Internet considerations are discussed in a later section of this chapter. You can download Circular 66 from http://lcweb.loc.gov/copyright/circs/circ66.pdf.

What Are Protected Works?

Copyright protection is as old as the nation. The framers of the Constitution delegated to the national government the authority to enact laws for the protection of copyrights. Specifically, Article I, Section 8, Clause 8 of the U.S. Constitution empowers Congress to promote the progress of science and useful arts, by securing for limited times to authors and inventors the exclusive right to their respective writings and discoveries.

The philosophy behind copyright protection was to encourage individuals to create literary works and works of art by ensuring economic gain. In 1996, Congress enacted the Copyright Act, which protects "original works of ownership," including literary and other original works:

- Literary works, including fiction, nonfiction, poetry, newspapers, magazines, computer software and software manuals, training manuals, catalogs, brochures, ads (text), compilations such as business directories, Web pages

- Architectural works, including drawings, drafts, models, CAD

- Musical works, including advertising jingles, songs, instrumentals, sound files

- Sound recordings, including music, sounds, or words

- Pictorial, graphic, and sculptural works, including photographs, posters, maps, paintings, drawings, graphic art, display ads, cartoon strips, cartoon characters, stuffed animals, statues, paintings, works of fine art

- Dramatic works, including plays, operas, and skits

- Pantomimes and choreographic works, including dance and mime works

- Motion pictures and other audiovisual works, including documentaries, travelogs, training films and videos, animation, television shows, television ads, and interactive multimedia works

Work for Hire

Generally a copyright is owned by the person (or persons) who create the work. However, when a work is created by an employee within the scope of his or her employment contract, the employer owns the copyright to the works since it's a "work for hire."

The copyright law also applies to independent contractors creating commissioned works. In order to qualify as a creator working on a specially commissioned work for hire, the creator must sign a written agreement stating that the work is for hire prior to commencing development of the product.

How to License Copyrighted Materials

With computer technology it is extremely easy to copy and publish works created by others without their permission. Just because the technology exists to copy these works, that does not mean you have the legal right to do so. If you use copyrighted material owned by others without getting permission through a license or assignment, you can incur liability for hundreds of thousands or even millions of dollars in damages.

These rights, however, are not unlimited in scope. Limitation takes the form of a "compulsory license" under which certain limited uses of copyrighted works are permitted upon payment of specified royalties and compliance with statutory conditions. Using copyrighted material without getting permission can have disastrous consequences. An assignment is generally understood to transfer all of the intellectual property rights in a particular work. A license provides the right to use a work and is generally quite limited.

Copyright Infringement

A violation of the exclusive rights of a copyright owner is known as a copyright infringement. Copyright owners can recover actual or, in some cases, statutory damages for a copyright infringement. Furthermore, courts have the power to issue injunctions to prevent or restrain copyright infringement and to order the impoundment and destruction of infringing copies.

Avoiding Copyright Infringement

If you use copyrighted material without getting permission, the owner of the copyright can prevent the distribution of your product and obtain damages from you for infringement, even if you did not intentionally include copyrighted material. Any of the copyright owners whose copyrights are infringed may be able to get a court order preventing further distribution of their works.

When You Don't Need a Copyright

Not every work is eligible for copyright protection. You don't need a license to use a copyrighted work in four circumstances:

- If the material you use is factual or an idea
- If the work is in the public domain
- If your use is fair use
- If the material you use consists of government documents

Factual Data

These materials, by their very nature, are ineligible for copyright protection:

- Works that have not been fixed in a tangible form of expression—for example, choreographic works that have not been notated or recorded, or improvisational speeches or performances that have not been written or recorded

- Titles, names, short phrases, and slogans; familiar symbols or designs; mere variations of typographic ornamentation, lettering, or coloring; mere listings of ingredients or contents

- Ideas, procedures, methods, systems, processes, concepts, principles, discoveries, or devices, as distinguished from a description, explanation, or illustration

- Works consisting entirely of information that is common property and containing no original authorship (for example, standard calendars, height and weight charts, tape measures and rulers, and lists or tables taken from public documents or other common sources)

Works in the Public Domain

A license is not required to use a work in the public domain. Such a work, one that is not protected by copyright, can be used by anyone. Because it is not protected by copyright, no one can claim the exclusive rights of copyright for such a work.

An example of works in the public domain are plays of Shakespeare. Works enter the public domain in several ways: because the term of the copyright expired, because the copyright owner failed to "renew" his copyright under the old Copyright Act of 1909, or because the copyright owner failed to properly use copyright notice (of importance only for works created before March 1, 1989, at which time copyright notice became optional).

The public domain also contains works that previously had copyright protection and lost that protection due to mistakes made by the creators in protecting their works. While it's next to impossible to lose copyright protection under today's laws, previous statutes were not as forgiving. As a result, *all works published before 1978 that did not contain a valid copyright notice are considered to be in the public domain.*

Owners of works published between January 1, 1978 and March 1, 1989, that did not contain a valid copyright notice were given a five-year grace period to correct the problem of publication without notice before their work was placed in the public domain.

Copyrighted works may enter the public domain if the copyright owner specifically grants the work to the public domain.

Expired Copyright

The public domain contains all works for which the statutory copyright period has expired. As a result, anyone is free to copy any work that was first published in the United States more than 75 years ago. In addition, you are free to copy any work published before 1964 for which the copyright owner failed to renew his copyright.

What Is the Fair Use Doctrine?

As previously discussed, the U.S. Constitution and Title 17 Section 106 and 106A of the U.S. Code provide certain protections to the owner of a copyright. However, Section 107 of the Copyright Act carves out a safe zone in which individuals can engage in the fair use of a copyrighted work and not violate the law. Specifically, Section 107 states that the fair use of a copyrighted work, including such use by reproduction in copies or by any other means specified by that section, for purposes such as criticism, comment, news reporting, teaching, scholarship, or research, is not an infringement of copyright.

In determining whether the use of a work is a "fair use," consider the following factors:

- The purpose and character of the use, including whether such use is of a commercial nature or is for nonprofit educational purposes.

- The nature of the copyrighted work (for example, the worthiness of the expression and creativity of the work seeking copyright protection).

- The amount and substantiality of the portion used in relation to the copyrighted work as a whole (for example, the quantity as well as the quality and importance of the copied material must be considered).

- The effect of the use upon the potential market for or value of the copyrighted work.

Government Documents

Documents and publications authored by the federal government are not copyrighted and, therefore, are considered to be in the public domain. Consequently, if you obtain a government document from the Internet, such as a law, statute, agency circular, federal report, or any other document published or generated by the federal government, you are free to copy or distribute the document.

Scope of Copyright

Copyright protects against copying the "expression" in a work, not against copying the work's ideas. The difference between "idea" and "expression" is one of the most difficult concepts in copyright law. The most important point to understand is that one can copy the protected expression in a work without copying the literal words. When a new work is created by copying an existing copyrighted work, copyright infringement exists if the new work is "substantially similar" to the work that was copied. The new work need not be identical to the copied work.

Section 106 of the Copyright Act generally gives the owner of a copyright the exclusive right to do and authorize others to do the following:

- **Reproduction**   The right to copy, duplicate, transcribe, or imitate the work in fixed form

- **Modification**   Preparation of derivative works based upon the copyrighted work

- **Distribution**   Distribution of copies of the copyrighted work to the public by sale or other transfer of ownership, or by rental, lease, or lending

- **Public performance**   Public performance of the copyrighted work, in the case of literary, musical, dramatic, and choreographic works, pantomimes, and motion pictures and other audiovisual works

- **Public display**   Public display of the copyrighted work, in the case of literary, musical, dramatic, and choreographic works, pantomimes, and pictorial, graphics, or sculptural works, including the individual images of a motion picture or other audiovisual work

Term of Copyright Protection

The length of time a copyright is valid depends on three factors:

- Who created the work
- When the work was created
- When it was first distributed commercially

For copyrighted works created on and after January 1, 1978, the copyright term for those created by individuals is the life of the author plus 50 years. The copyright term in the case of "work for hire" is 75 years from the date of first publication (distribution of copies to the general public) or 100 years from the date of creation, whichever expires first.

How to Copyright Your Material Anywhere

Copyright protection is granted automatically when an "original" work of authorship is created or "fixed" in a tangible medium of expression. The legal definition of these terms is defined in copyright law. Neither the originality nor the fixation requirement is strict.

- *Original* means that the work is original in the copyright sense if it owes its origin to the author(s) and was not copied from a preexisting work. Only minimal creativity is required to meet the originality requirement. No artistic merit or aesthetic quality is required. Works can incorporate preexisting material and still be original. However, when preexisting material is incorporated into a new work, the copyright on the new work covers only the original material contributed by the author. The preexisting material is still protected by the original copyright.

- *Fixed* refers to a work that is created to be "sufficiently permanent or stable to permit it to be perceived, reproduced, or otherwise communicated for a period of more than transitory duration." An author can "fix" words by writing them on a piece of paper, dictating them into a tape recorder, typing them on a typewriter, or entering them into a computer. Finally, a work can be original without being novel or unique.

- *Copies* are material objects from which a work can be read or visually perceived either directly or with the aid of a machine or device, such as books, manuscripts, sheet music, film, videotape, or microfilm. *Phonorecords* are material objects embodying fixations of sounds (excluding, by statutory definition, motion picture soundtracks), such as cassette tapes, CDs, or LPs.

on the Job

The official registration with the Copyright Office is optional. However, if you ever file an infringement suit, you must register the works before hand. Registering your works early is a good idea since it will make you eligible to receive reimbursement for attorneys' fees and statutory damages in the event of a lawsuit.

Notice of Copyright

The use of a copyright notice is no longer required under U.S. law, although it can be beneficial. (Because prior law did contain such a requirement, the use of notice is still relevant to the copyright status of older works.) The use of the copyright notice is the responsibility of the copyright owner and does not require advance permission from, or registration with, the Copyright Office.

Use of the notice may be important because it informs the public that the work is protected by copyright, identifies the copyright owner, and shows the year of first publication. Furthermore, in the event that a work is infringed, if a proper notice of copyright appears on the published copy to which a defendant in a copyright infringement suit had access, then no weight is given to such a defendant's interposition of a defense based on innocent infringement in mitigation of actual or statutory damages. Innocent infringement occurs when the infringer did not realize that the work was protected. The notice for visually perceptible copies should contain all these elements:

- **The symbol** © (the letter c in a circle), or the word "Copyright," or the abbreviation "Copr."

■ **The year of first publication of the work.** In the case of compilations or derivative works incorporating previously published material, the year date of first publication of the compilation or derivative work is sufficient. The year date may be omitted when a pictorial, graphic, or sculptural work, with accompanying textual matter, if any, is reproduced in or on greeting cards, postcards, stationery, jewelry, dolls, toys, or any useful article.

■ **The name of the owner of copyright in the work,** or an abbreviation by which the name can be recognized, or a generally known alternative designation of the owner—for example, © 1999 Mary Doe.

Registering Your Copyright

To register a work you must perform the steps listed in Exercise 13-1.

EXERCISE 13-1

Registering Your Electronic Copyright Works

1. Complete the copyright application form, available at http://www.loc.gov/copyright/forms/.

2. Enclose a check for $30.00 for each application, made payable to the Copyright Office. This is a nonrefundable filing fee (effective through June 30, 2002).

3. Enclose a nonreturnable deposit of the work being registered. The deposit requirements vary in particular situations. For digital and/or electronic information you should submit in these two formats:

   ■ Print out the entire Web site on hard copy to submit.

   ■ For sound, interactive multimedia elements, burn these digital files into a compact disk and submit.

   ■ As a supplement to the hard copy of a Web site, you can submit the Web pages in a CD format as well.

   Note: See the section "Special Deposit Requirements," later in the chapter.

4. Mail all of these documents in the same envelope or package to

Library of Congress
Copyright Office
Register of Copyrights
101 Independence Avenue, S.E.
Washington, D.C. 20559-6000

Special Deposit Requirements

Special deposit requirements exist for many types of works. The following are prominent examples of exceptions to the general deposit requirements:

- If the work is a *Web site*, print out the entire site (as viewed from a browser) and press a digital copy of the site, including all files, onto a CD. The underlying computer code (HTML, JavaScript, and so on) for the site does not need to be printed out.

- If the work is an unpublished or published binary *computer program,* the deposit requirement is one visually perceptible copy in source code of the *first 25 and last 25 pages* of the program, the operating software, and any manual(s) accompanying it. For a program of fewer than 50 pages, the deposit is a copy of the entire program.

- If the work is *multimedia*, including sound files, images, movies, animation, and so on, the deposit requirement is one complete copy of the digital files in CD format *and* a separate written description of its contents, such as a continuity, press book, or synopsis.

If you are unsure of the deposit requirement for your work, write or call the Copyright Office and describe the work you wish to register. Applications and fees received without appropriate copies or identifying material will not be processed and ordinarily will be returned. Unpublished deposits without applications or fees are also usually returned. In most cases, published deposits received without applications and fees can be immediately transferred to the collections of the Library of Congress.

on the **job** *Complete the application form using black ink pen or type information into the electronic form available from the Copyright Office. You may photocopy blank application forms. However, photocopied forms submitted to the Copyright Office must be clear, legible, and on a good grade of 8 and 1/2-inch by 11-inch white paper suitable for automatic feeding through a photocopier. The forms should be printed, preferably in black ink, head-to-head so that when you turn the sheet over, the top of page 2 is directly behind the top of page 1. Forms not meeting these requirements may be returned, resulting in delayed registration.*

Further Information

For further information, contact the U.S. Copyright Office, which is part of the Library of Congress, at http://lcweb.loc.gov/copyright, or call (202) 707-3000.

Copyright Issues and Restrictions

The registration process is fairly straightforward, and the fees are not high. Since copyright protection attaches immediately and automatically upon fixation (reduction to a tangible form) of the work in question, why should you go to the trouble of filing a federal copyright registration? There are two fundamental reasons: the ability to sue and the ability to collect statutory damages.

Although copyright attaches upon fixation, you cannot actually sue someone for infringing your copyright until you have registered your work with the Copyright Office. And if you register your work within three months from the date of first publication, or at least prior to the date of infringement, you can collect statutory damages from the infringer. Otherwise, you are stuck with actual damages, which, depending upon the situation, may be nominal.

FROM THE CLASSROOM

Assume you develop a Web site and do not register the content for copyright protection. As we know, Web pages are considered a tangible form and are, therefore, protected by copyright laws. If one of your competitors copies your site and places the content on its Web site, then your copyright has been infringed.

In order to sue for copyright infringement, you must have registered your Web site with the Copyright Office. If you are in a hurry to file the lawsuit, be prepared to pay an additional $200 fee to expedite the application. Assuming your competitor doesn't have any valid defense such as fair use, then you can collect for your losses, plus any

profits that your competitor accrued by virtue of the infringement.

If you register your Web site within three months of its first publication, then you are able to recover statutory damages in lieu of any virtually nonexistent actual damages. Statutory damages can be awarded up to $100,000, plus attorneys fees and court costs, depending upon the nature and malevolence of the infringement. This would certainly affect your decision-making process if you were deciding whether to sue someone for copyright infringement.

—*Maxwell Miller, Ph.D., CIW, CWT, i-Net+*

Copyright and the Internet

Copyright law protects expression independent of the medium, therefore almost any original expression that is fixed in a tangible form is protected as soon as it is expressed. For example, a graphic created in a graphics program is protected as soon as the file is saved to disk. Similarly, a Web page is protected as soon as the HTML file is saved to disk.

Most of the digital works on the Internet are eligible for copyright protection, including the text of Web pages, ASCII text documents, contents of e-mail and Usenet messages, sound, graphics, executable computer programs, source code, and other multimedia objects. The Internet has yielded at least two significant technological advances. First is the replacement of tangible objects for the transfer of information with electronic transmission as made possible by a new form of embodiment (digital works). Second is the capacity to create exact copies at little to no cost.

Web sites and their content are copyrightable works of authorship. Recent technological developments offer new possibilities for using, exploiting, and infringing on those copyrights. Although lawsuits have been filed, regulatory guidelines do not exist for resolving these newly raised issues due to the lack of a consensus on the legal implications of basic and widespread activities on the Internet.

Hypertext Linking

In order for a Web page to be linked, the unique URL of the Web page must be copied and incorporated into the HTML of the linking page. Since a URL is simply an address, and addresses cannot be copyrighted, no one may claim originality. A domain name is only a means to better remember the underlying numeric address, which is, in fact, an arbitrary designation for an IP address.

Copyrighting Electronic/Digital Works

A basic requirement for any claim of copyright infringement is that the allegedly infringed work qualify as a protected work of authorship. Just as these laws apply to printed works, recordings, graphics, and so on, they apply equally to digital works, so Web pages and all of their content are copyrightable works.

Web pages developed in HTML, XML, JavaScript, and other languages can be considered "computer programs" as defined by statute: "A set of statements or instructions to be used directly or indirectly in a computer in order to bring about a certain result." Indeed, Web authoring and scripting languages are instructions used indirectly (via the Web browser) in a computer to build the page as it is viewed by the user. Web pages are applications written for other applications, namely, Web browsers. Unlike the source code of most other computer programs, the source code of Web pages is not secret and can be viewed in any Web browser or text editor.

Web Page Elements

Web pages usually contain text, images, audio, video, and other multimedia elements. These elements may independently qualify for copyright protection as literary or audiovisual works or sound recordings. Even though Web pages are computer programs and are protected as such, they are mostly used as platforms or carriers for copyrighted works that happen to be stored in digital format. Therefore, when a Web site is being copyrighted, several forms may have to be filed with the Copyright Office, depending on the type of media embedded in a particular Web page.

Browsing Web Pages

Browsing the World Wide Web is considered viewing and not copying. Viewing Web pages is not any different from viewing a page in a magazine, newspaper, or printed book that is publicly accessible. In fact, viewing does not involve copyright laws at all, since there is no form of copying going on.

On the Web, it is the person who uploads a copy of the works who is liable for copyright infringement, not the person who views it. Applied to the Internet, this means that viewing Web pages does not involve copyright laws at all.

on the **Job**

Web pages are considered copyrightable works, so digital reproduction (for example, "screen captures") of Web pages is protected by copyright law. Before embedding images of Web pages, you need to gain the explicit permission from the copyright owner. Embedding hypertext links (URLs) to other Web sites is not considered a copyright infringement.

QUESTIONS AND ANSWERS

Is it okay to copy and use information I find on the Net without getting permission?	You are free to copy public domain material that you find on the Internet, but you should not copy copyrighted material without getting permission from the copyright owner.
Is it true that any information posted on a Web server is in the public domain, and that I can do anything I want with material that I get from a Web server?	Individuals and organizations put material on a Web server to make it accessible by others. However, the fact that it is on an Internet or a public Web server does not mean that the creators give up their copyright. You still need permission to be able to copy that information.
Is it okay to post copyrighted material on my Web site if I don't charge users for access to it?	Unless your use of the copyrighted work is fair use, you need a license to copy and use the work in your Web site even if you won't be charging people to view it. You also need a public display license.

CERTIFICATION OBJECTIVE 13.02

Trademark Law

A *trademark* is a word, phrase, symbol or design, or combination of words, phrases, symbols or designs, that identifies and distinguishes the source of the goods or services of one party from those of others. A *service mark* is the same as a trademark except that it identifies and distinguishes the source of a service rather than a product. Normally, a mark for goods appears on the product or on its packaging, while a service mark appears in advertising for the services.

Trademarks and service marks are used by manufacturers of goods and providers of services to distinguish their goods and services from goods manufactured and sold by others. For example, Netscape and Netscape Navigator are registered trademarks of Netscape Communications Corporation used to identify that company's Web browser and distinguish that software from other vendors' Web browsers.

Establishing Trademark Rights

Trademark rights arise from either actual use of the mark, or the filing of a proper application to register a mark in the Patent and Trademark Office (PTO), stating that the applicant has a bona fide intention to use the mark in commerce regulated by the U.S. Congress.

As with a copyright, federal registration is not required to establish rights in a mark, nor is it required to begin use of a mark. However, federal registration can secure benefits beyond the rights acquired by merely using a mark. For example, the owner of a federal registration is presumed to be the owner of the mark for the goods and services specified in the registration, and to be entitled to use the mark nationwide.

Two Types of Rights

There are two related but distinct types of rights in a mark: the right to register and the right to use. Generally, the first party who either uses a mark in commerce or files an application in the PTO has the ultimate right to register that mark. The PTO's authority is limited to determining the right to register.

The right to use a mark can be more complicated to determine. This is particularly true when two parties have begun use of the same or similar marks without knowledge of one another and neither has a federal registration. Only a court can render a decision about the right to use, such as issuing an injunction or awarding damages for infringement. A federal registration can provide significant advantages to a party involved in a court proceeding.

Unlike copyrights or patents, trademark rights can last indefinitely if the owner continues to use the mark to identify its goods or services. The term of a federal trademark registration is 10 years, with 10-year renewal terms. However, between the fifth and sixth year after the date of initial registration, the registrant must file an affidavit setting forth certain information to keep the registration alive. If no affidavit is filed, the registration is canceled.

Searching for Trademarks

An applicant is not required to conduct a search for conflicting marks prior to applying with the PTO. However, some find it useful. In evaluating an application, an examining attorney conducts a search and notifies the applicant if a conflicting mark is found. The application fee, which covers processing and search costs, will not be refunded even if a conflict is found and the mark cannot be registered.

Use of the TM, SM, and ® Symbols

Anyone who claims rights in a mark may use the TM (trademark) or SM (service mark) designation with the mark to alert the public to the claim. It is not necessary to have a registration, or even a pending application, to use these designations. The claim may or may not be valid.

The registration symbol, ®, may only be used when the mark is registered in the PTO. It is improper to use this symbol at any point before the registration issues. You should omit all symbols from the mark in the drawing you submit with your application; the symbols are not considered part of the mark.

Obtaining a Trademark

The most effective trademark protection is obtained by filing a federal trademark registration application in the U.S. PTO. Federal law protects unregistered trademarks, but such protection is limited to the geographic area in which the mark is actually being used.

State trademark protection under common law is obtained simply by adopting a trademark and using it in connection with goods or services. This protection is limited to the geographic area in which the trademark is actually being used. State statutory protection is obtained by filing an application with the state trademark office.

Registering Domain Names as Marks

Lately, the PTO has received an increasing number of applications to register Internet domain names. One of the most commonly asked questions is whether a domain name can be registered as a trademark. Domain names are not protected by copyright laws, since each is a simple name, but they are protected as trademarks. If an Internet domain name is used to identify and distinguish the goods and/or services, it may be registered as a trademark. (Trademark applications for Internet domain names usually seek registration of service marks.)

In order to register an Internet domain name, an applicant must show that it offers services via the Internet. Specimens submitted in support of the application to show use of the mark must show use of the Internet domain name as a source identifier.

The PTO has recently clarified how it classifies services associated with the World Wide Web. To obtain further information on the *Identification and Classification of Certain Computer Related Goods and Services*, download the document available at http://www.uspto.gov/web/offices/tac/domain/domcl.html.

on the **!** **()** o b

The use of an Internet domain name as a mere address (similar to use of a telephone number or business address on stationery, business cards, or advertisements) is not an example of using the name as a source identifier and, therefore, does not qualify for trademark protection.

on the **!** **()** o b

Cybersquatting—the practice of registering names of companies, famous people, or trademarks as Internet domain names with intent to sell them for profit—has been a growing problem. Congress is passing legislation to protect copyrights and trademarks from registration by cybersquatters.

Classifying Web Services

The PTO uses the phrases "connection" provider, "access" provider, and "content" provider to differentiate and classify services rendered via the Internet. An entity providing the technical connection needed for communication is called a connection provider. The closely related service rendered by online content providers such as America Online® or Prodigy® is an access provider. An access provider, according to the PTO, furnishes "multiple-user access to a global computer information network."

Most applicants will be content providers who furnish information via the Internet. However, all content providers do not offer registerable services that can be used by an Internet domain name. For example, Internet domain name locations that simply contain advertisements or other information normally expected or routine in promoting an entity's goods or services are not registerable services. Therefore, Internet domain names must meet the same requirements for registration as all trademarks and service marks. If a domain name does meet these requirements, it will be registered.

Further Information

For further information on registering a mark, contact the U.S. Patent and Trademark Office at http://ftp.uspto.gov/web/menu/tm.html, or call (800) 786-9199.

Trademark Scope

Trademark law in general, whether federal or state, protects a trademark owner's commercial identity (goodwill, reputation, and investment in advertising) by giving the trademark owner the exclusive right to use the trademark on the type of goods or services for which the owner is using the trademark. Any person who uses a trademark in connection with selling goods or services in a way that is likely to cause confusion is infringing on that trademark.

Trademark owners can obtain injunctions against the confusing use of their trademarks by others, and they can collect damages for infringement, just as with copyright violations.

CERTIFICATION OBJECTIVE 13.03

Issues Related to Working in a Global Environment

As more of the world becomes connected to the Internet, analysts are predicting that international or global e-commerce will become a huge opportunity for U.S. companies. While this creates opportunities for expanding to new markets, it also creates a number of challenges for working in a global environment. These challenges include language and cultural barriers, legal and regulatory issues surrounding international trademarks, and copyright protection of brands and marks.

Additional technological challenges include working in a multivendor e-business environment with multiple vendors in the supply chain, accepting different forms of currency, and developing an e-commerce strategy.

Selecting the Appropriate Business Model

As geographical boundaries shrink and digital currency becomes more dominant, the globalization of e-businesses is becoming a reality. Localization and translation of content become a necessity. Dealing with governmental regulations and a global commercial economy raises new challenges in terms of trading partners and international trade issues. Many of these issues carry over from processes developed for conducting business internationally. Others are being defined as new challenges are encountered.

Globalization of business—taking business conducted in the U.S. overseas—can take on a number of forms, including

- **Global business**   Treats the world market as an integrated whole and focuses on seamless integration of processes independent of geography.

- **Multinational**   Similar to a holding company; a multinational treats its holdings as a portfolio of separate business entities, each with its own profit-and-loss statement, and reporting back to corporate headquarters.

- **International firms**   Somewhat of a hybrid of the other two; applies the core competencies and business process of the parent company on a local or regional basis. In turn, the experience gathered at the local level may be fed back to the parent company.

The first step is to decide which type of global business you want to establish. Then you can design the infrastructure to support your business activities.

Working in a Multivendor Environment

Underlying the globalization trend is the rapid deployment of Internet-based (also referred to as e-business) technologies. These technologies have fostered the implementation of global interconnected networks that connect suppliers, distributors, resellers, business partners, and customers throughout the world. This interconnected chain is referred to as the supply chain.

Building a Global E-business Computing Framework

E-business applications are built using open standards, meaning that they are not bound to one specific platform, vendor, or technology. This open-architecture approach ensures that Web-enabled applications will integrate with existing applications running on any platform and with any data in your network, and will scale as demand dictates. These applications need to span multiple platforms and vendor applications—not just today, but in the future, as your computing environment evolves and changes.

E-business solutions by their very nature support distributed computing solutions and multiple hardware/software vendors, cross-platform applications, and open scalable solutions that are standards based. A Web-enabled e-business infrastructure builds on the traditional client/server model, integrating Internet-based technologies with legacy data and applications. This enables organizations to connect their corporate enterprise systems within the organization using intranets and global networks, and to connect to partners, vendors, and suppliers using extranets. The critical success factors in developing a global e-business computing framework include

- **Standards based** Using open standards technologies, cross-platform applications can run and interoperate on platforms and operating systems from multiple vendors (for example, IBM, Microsoft, Netscape, Oracle, Sun, Apple) by using standard protocols such as TCP/IP, HTTP, and HTML, Java, SSL and Java.

- **Cross-platform applications** The Internet is a heterogeneous network composed of multiple hardware and software platforms, operating systems, languages, browsers, and systems. There's no doubt that e-business applications must also be able to run universally multiple operating systems, platforms, and networks.

- **Scalable** Scalability allows your environment and platform to adjust, or scale, to meet a dramatic surge in demand once you have deployed your e-business infrastructure. If an e-business fails to predict demand when deploying applications, it risks losing potential online sales, making customers and suppliers frustrated or dissatisfied when system response time increases and performance decreases. If the explosion of e-business in the last few years is any indication, you should plan for growth. Scalable architecture plans for this growth. When you are deploying applications that you want your customers, suppliers, and employees to depend on, your applications and systems must be run in a *scalable* environment, in order to accommodate growth.

- **Network and system security**   As you open your business to the world, you need to ensure that your systems and applications execute in a secure environment that allows for access control and maintains the privacy and confidentiality of your data. Security is often a challenge. Traditionally business transactions were handled person-to-person; you could ask for physical identification, accept the payment, and close the transaction. With the rise of e-business, it is more difficult to identify those who are transacting with your company, because now transactions and transfers of data are handled electronically.

- **Server-centric**   Keep your applications centralized so you don't spend all your time upgrading and deploying. To ease your transition into an e-business, you should deploy server-centric applications, which are maintained in one central location. In a server-centric environment, Java servlets and applets can be written once and run on any platform. Similarly, any server-based solutions, including CGI and Active Server Pages, make systems and network management much more cost and time efficient.

- **Reliability**   For your e-business strategy to be successful, you should plan, design, and implement applications and systems that are reliable. System overload and sluggish performance are unacceptable in the e-business world! When you deploy your systems, you should consider having backup systems to prepare for system outages.

- **Quick integration**   Integration is the process of combining your Web-enabled applications with your core business systems and legacy resources. By deploying applications that are easily integrated across core business systems, companies are better able to leverage existing resources, including databases, applications, and other information technology assets.

■ **Usability** Companies have the opportunity to shield their users from the complexity of their systems by deploying Web-enabled applications that are intuitive and easy to use, thereby improving customer satisfaction and decreasing the overall training investment. In the world of e-business, easy-to-use applications are critical, because the client can be anywhere: a desktop, a laptop running a Web browser, or perhaps even a handheld digital device.

Application Reuse and Modularity

As your demand increases and your applications begin to scale, you don't want to develop new applications or rewrite code. Solutions include developing applications in cross-platform languages such as Java that can be written once and run anywhere, regardless of the platform or operating system, and can reuse existing software modules. This reduces development costs and time to market.

Component reuse and modular design is at the core of e-business application development. Reusing and re-purposing components and software (instead of having multiple teams develop software modules that solve the same problems) also reduces development costs and time to market.

Developing a Global E-business Strategy

There's more to developing a global e-business strategy than deploying a company intranet and Internet site. You need a plan to craft your business into a global e-business that crosses barriers of currency, language, time, and geography.

Developing an implementation path toward a global networked business model should start small and build on success. A company should begin by selecting one application or business process to transform that will have the greatest impact on its business. Critical business processes that provide the highest return on investment (ROI) include customer relationship management, supply chain management, e-commerce, knowledge management, and e-learning.

Movement toward a global e-commerce model usually requires a change in attitudes about the role of information, tools, and systems, as well as reengineering of some internal processes. The implementation team must be multidisciplinary with representatives not only from IT, but from all stakeholders. Once implemented, the application should be constantly monitored, modified, and improved. Then it's on to the next e-business target application.

The Internet does not change the principles of your business strategy. For an organization to be successful, it must understand markets, segmentation, targeted messages, and offerings. Using the conventional marketing model, market segments must be large to be manageable. Products and stores cannot be easily or cost effectively customized for individuals. Information-based products cannot be personalized. Supply chains contain weeks of slack, forcing consumers to take what is in stock. The tools used in the past to capture and analyze segmentation information were cumbersome, time consuming, and expensive.

The Internet changes the size of a manageable segment and the kinds of tools used to measure, evaluate, and manage those segments. Other major differences include

- **E-commerce** Web sites and business-to-business e-commerce interconnect e-tailors and suppliers worldwide, resulting in a larger market and greater profits due to the increased efficiencies in conducting business.

- **The supply chain** When drop ship arrangements and airfreight companies are used as distribution intermediaries, this allows orders to be turned without the retailer's taking physical ownership of inventory. These arrangements reduce slack in the supply chain and allow near real-time fulfillment of orders.

- **Customer relationship management** Personalization and customization of customer profiles becomes a reality. Since more is known about a customer as an individual, products could be built to order.

Shared IT Infrastructure

As you transform your business to an e-business and take advantage of the internet to gain access to the global marketplace, establishing common business practices across your enterprise becomes increasingly important. Moving from geographically dispersed infrastructure management and local practices to shared service centers and global rules can increase efficiency, lower costs, and reduce complexity.

With a shared IT infrastructure, you can consolidate business processing, eliminating the need to synchronize and reconcile data. Your organization can share common business rules and remove redundancies in order to increase efficiency. And with shared service centers, you can unify information, making it readily available, in a consistent format, to all members of the extended enterprise.

Web-Enabling Existing Applications

With Internet technology evolving as rapidly as it is, an organization must be prepared to adapt to these changes quickly without causing inconvenience to its customers or interruption to its internal operations. The fastest and most risk-free solution is to extend and modernize existing applications by Web-enabling them. A natural starting point for many companies is to put their existing legacy applications and data online to allow business partners to share information and data. This can result in immediate cost savings, increased operational efficiencies, and greater profits.

Dealing with Multiple Currencies

Processing international currency transactions becomes a key issue for working in a global e-business environment. E-commerce transactions often involve multiple currencies from countries all around the world. Systems must be built to deal with currency conversion between the consumer and the banking and merchant organizations. Online transaction payment software must be able to translate the client's currency into the merchant's (your organization's) preferred currency.

This is already a reality for businesses conducting e-commerce in the European Economic and Monetary Union (EMU). The EMU eliminates borders by offering a common currency model—the euro—for conducting business among member countries in Europe. Together, the Internet and the euro are changing the way companies do business around the world.

Understanding the EMU and the Euro

The EMU is responsible for establishing and managing a multiple currency system to facilitate trading among European trading partners. Right now the European economies are in a transition stage. A transitional phase of three years has been established in which the euro currency is represented in each EMU nation by two units: the National Currency Unit (NCU) and the euro unit.

This transitional period exposes businesses to a multicurrency environment. During the transition phase, from January 1, 1999, until January 1, 2002, it will be beneficial to have insight into the operations of your business in both the euro and the NCU. Sooner or later the euro will be the only legal tender, and there will be no other choice for accounting records.

Companies such as DataCash (http://www.datacash.com) and Oracle Corporation (http://www.oracle.com) have developed currency management systems that incorporate the concept of the euro and other monetary units into transaction-based e-commerce systems.

The Global Supply Chain

The latter half of the 1990s saw an explosion in the use of the global Internet and its accessibility to individuals, corporations, and organizations. This revolution has dramatically changed the way organizations conduct business with their consumers and with each other. The geographic boundaries that once offered limited access to goods and services are crumbling, and companies of all sizes are busy building commerce solutions and adapting to new ways of doing business.

Supply Chain Management (SCM) uses the low cost of the Internet to leverage tighter integration across suppliers, manufacturers, and distributors.

SCM is about optimizing business processes and business value in every corner of the extended enterprise, from your supplier's supplier to your customer's customer.

SCM uses e-business concepts and Web technologies to manage beyond the organization, both upstream and downstream. Manufacturers and vendors can share sales forecasts, manage inventories, schedule labor, optimize deliveries, and improve productivity. Suppliers need to be able to provide their business partners with secure access to their existing Web site and maintain these product catalogs when they are making pricing and/or inventory changes.

Traditional vs. Global E-business Supply Chain

Table 13-1 illustrates the differences between a traditional supply chain and a global e-business supply chain.

TABLE 13-1 Traditional vs. Global E-business Supply Chain

Resource	Traditional Supply Chain	Global E-business Supply Chain
Infrastructure	Based on dedicated private networks.	Based on a shared global interconnected network.
Information	Data and information are shared when feasible within the company and with great cost and complexity outside the company.	Data and information are shared whenever demand requires and with worldwide access.
People/Teams	Involve intracompany teams to build and manage processes with additional members added with difficulty.	Involve intercompany teams, with global members joining and leaving quickly.
Access Control and Security	Physically controlled by connection to internal corporate network or simple user ID and password.	Permission controlled when data is accessible from anywhere on the globe, with sophisticated security for authentication and authorization.

Some of the advantages of an e-business supply chain include

- *Lowers operating costs through reduced inventory requirements and helps to eliminate costly stockpiling.*

- *Improves customer satisfaction by maintaining adequate stock. Improves productivity and information flow process through better data integrity, fewer order entry errors, and less rework, leading to lower costs, improved efficiencies, and an increase in the accuracy and timeliness of data shared across the extended enterprise.*

- *Links together all players in the global supply chain, from raw material providers to final point of distribution.*

- *Distributes real-time market and process information to all players, allowing them to anticipate and adjust their operations in response to market conditions.*

Globalization Issues Relating to Language and Localization

International Data Corporation (IDC) predicts that by 2002, 60 percent of Internet users and 40 percent of e-commerce shoppers will originate from outside the United States. Users who visit Web sites constructed in their own language are three times more likely to make an online purchase than are those visiting Web sites in languages other than their own. With this trend in the globalization of e-commerce, it is clear that to remain competitive and be a leader in your marketplace worldwide, you must deploy language-specific Web sites targeted to each of your global markets.

Cultural and Localization Issues

Creating e-commerce sites as part of a global strategy involves more than delivering content that has been translated and localized for the native audience. It also requires an understanding of the cultural issues relating to a specific continent, country, or region.

Before you enter a new market, you must do your homework. Find a consultant with experience in your target market. Use best area practices and lessons learned from other U.S. companies that have expanded into those markets. Do competitive intelligence research to determine which strategies are successful and which are not. And be aware that content suited for an American audience in many cases will have to be not only translated but rewritten for different worldwide audiences.

For example, consider a U.S. company that wants to expand its marketplace to Asia by establishing a beachhead in Japan. There are many other issues to consider besides translating the Web site to Japanese. Localization issues require an understanding of the culture, the norms, and context of doing business in Japan. The marketing and advertising needs to be localized toward the Japanese market. The Japanese people are turned off by negative advertising, they prefer money transfers instead of credit cards, and they don't use personal checks as Americans do.

Assembling a Globalization Team

Part of the process of creating a global e-commerce strategy is putting together a team at the implementation level that understands your target market. Transforming your corporate message to a local audience requires a cross-functional team that includes members of your U.S. corporate operations, as well as local authors, language editors, translators, marketing team, and legal experts to authenticate the legitimacy and appropriateness of the message broadcast by an organization across its global Web sites.

Furthermore, Web site developers, designers, technical editors, and graphic artists are needed to ensure that each language implementation of your e-commerce site is suitably designed and functions correctly for each country-specific market.

Managing a Globalization Team

Managing multiple Web sites around the globe creates a whole new set of challenges that include managing human and technical resources, dealing with variability in technological infrastructure, and legal/regulatory issues in the markets in which you are conducting business. Managing updates to multiple Web sites around the world is now a much more complex problem. There is a whole host of other business-related problems that must be tackled, including a brand identity strategy, trademark/copyright issues, and other business-related issues such as channel strategies of using distributors vs. a direct sales model, and the like. These issues are outside the scope of the i-Net+ certification, but must be part of your overall global e-business strategy.

Unicode

The Unicode Worldwide Character Standard is a character coding system developed for computers to support the interchange, processing, and display of written texts of the languages of the modern world. Unicode provides the foundation for internationalization and localization of content for e-commerce and Web sites and computer software.

The Unicode Standard contains a large number of characters in order to capture the written languages of the world. It also contains characters with computer-control–like functions.

Unicode was developed to standardize on a system for document and data interchange. The Internet and the World Wide Web rely on the use of marked-up text, which is essentially similar to the features provided by formatting characters in the Unicode Standard for use with plain text.

Further information on the development of this standard can be obtained from the Unicode Consortium at http://www.unicode.org.

Advantages of Unicode

The traditional method of internationalizing a software application or a Web site is to translate the literal strings. This is problematic, because not all literal strings are translated correctly. The context is important in language and is lost in literal translation, so human judgment is required to interpret the translation, which is expensive and time consuming. This also introduces possibilities for creating bugs and inaccuracies in the translated works.

Unicode is a general technique used to internationalize content, to prepare it so that the code never needs modification. The actual content is separated from the rules of translation. The formatting then becomes language independent, meaning that dates, times, numbers, and currencies all call up logic that provides the formatting based on local language and country-code requirements.

Other functions such as sorting and searching become language independent. Once this process is concluded, you have an internationalized program. Changes to the source code containing the business logic are not required to localize that program. Instead, just the content files are typically handed off to contractors or translation agencies to be modified.

While the initial cost of producing internationalized code is higher than that of localizing to a single market, the cost of scaling to multiple country-code versions is much lower in the long run.

Newly developed standards for HTML, XML, and other scripting and authoring languages support Unicode. Versions 4.5+ of Netscape Navigator and 5.0+ of Internet Explorer both support Unicode.

Legal and Regulatory Issues

With the explosion in e-commerce, U.S.-based companies are expanding to over 200 countries around the globe. One of the costs of doing business internationally is the necessity to abide by foreign laws, rules, and regulations.

Since many of the progressive nations around the world are modeling their trade and commerce laws after U.S. laws and regulations that may become part of an international standard, the natural starting point for any company is to make sure that it is in total compliance with domestic laws. The legal profession is developing legal protections to ensure that U.S. products and services can be advertised, marketed, and sold online domestically and internationally without unnecessary governmental interference, taxation, limitations, and risk.

U.S. copyright and trademark laws are also being adopted by other nations. Web-based commerce issues are closely linked to copyright and trademark laws, and compliance with U.S. laws is a great start for a global e-commerce strategy.

Abiding by Foreign Laws

In order to conduct e-commerce internationally, your organization must be familiar with the laws, regulations, and trade policies of the country in which you are conducting business. By carefully choosing the global markets you enter, you can minimize your risks and maximize your gains.

Forrester Research issues reports, on a regular basis, that rank the best countries for conducting e-commerce and e-business. Currently, the Internet market is led by these countries:

- United States
- Canada
- United Kingdom
- Germany
- Japan
- Finland, New Zealand, and Sweden: where the next wave will hit
- Switzerland, Austria, Ireland, Israel, and South Africa: the up-and-comers

Seeking Professional Guidance

There are many ways to build a global e-business in order to enter foreign markets. To get started, seek counsel from consultants, accounting firms, and lawyers that specialize in international business. They can assist your company in evaluating and preparing for the legal and regulatory issues you will encounter abroad, to avoid costly mistakes. You may also want to consider going into partnership with a foreign company. A foreign government is less likely to harass a U.S. firm working with a respectable local company.

CERTIFICATION SUMMARY

This chapter summarized the legal and regulatory laws dealing with copyright, trademark, and licensing. These are all forms of intellectual property law that are equally important in the electronic world as they are in the physical world. Many of the legal issues surrounding Internet copyright and trademark law are still in their infancy, and clear answers don't always exist. Your organization should gain expert legal opinion for the specific issues relating to copyrights and trademark use on the Internet.

The second part of this chapter was concerned with the issues surrounding globalization and localization of Web sites and the issues of conducting business and e-commerce around the globe. The critical success factors for developing a global e-business technology framework were discussed. Issues involved in developing a global e-business strategy and global supply chain were also addressed. Finally, country-specific localization issues were discussed, including translation, Unicode, and legal and regulatory requirements useful for operating in a global economy.

 TWO-MINUTE DRILL

- ❑ The intellectual property laws in the United States protect the following types of property:
  - ❑ **Copyright law**   Protects "original works of authorship"
  - ❑ **Trademark law**   Protects words, names, and symbols used by manufacturers and businesses to identify their goods and services
  - ❑ **Patent law**   Protects new, useful, and "nonobvious" inventions and processes
- ❑ Copyright is a form of legal protection provided by the laws of the United States (Title 17, U.S. Code) to the authors of "original works of authorship," including literary, dramatic, musical, artistic, and certain other intellectual works. This protection is available to both published and unpublished works. Since copyright law is part of federal law, it does not vary from state to state.
- ❑ Generally a copyright is owned by the person (or persons) who create the work. However, when a work is created by an employee within the scope of his or her employment contract, the employer owns the copyright to the works since it's a "work for hire."
- ❑ Copyright is not unlimited in scope. Limitation takes the form of a "compulsory license" under which certain limited uses of copyrighted works are permitted upon payment of specified royalties and compliance with statutory conditions.

❑ An assignment is generally understood to transfer all of the intellectual property rights in a particular work. A license provides the right to use a work and is generally quite limited.

❑ A violation of the exclusive rights of a copyright owner is known as a copyright infringement.

❑ If you use copyrighted material without getting permission, the owner of the copyright can prevent the distribution of your product and obtain damages from you for infringement, even if you did not intentionally include copyrighted material. Any of the copyright owners whose copyrights are infringed may be able to get a court order preventing further distribution of their works.

❑ A license is not required to use a work in the public domain. Such a work, one that is not protected by copyright, can be used by anyone. Because it is not protected by copyright, no one can claim the exclusive rights of copyright for such a work.

❑ Web sites and their content are copyrightable works of authorship.

❑ A *trademark* is a word, phrase, symbol, or design, or combination of words, phrases, symbols, or designs, which identifies and distinguishes the source of the goods or services of one party from those of others. A *service mark* is the same as a trademark except that it identifies and distinguishes the source of a service rather than a product.

❑ There are two related but distinct types of rights in a mark: the right to register and the right to use.

❑ Anyone who claims rights in a mark may use the TM (trademark) or SM (service mark) designation with the mark to alert the public to the claim. It is not necessary to have a registration, or even a pending application, to use these designations.

❑ The registration symbol, ®, may only be used when the mark is registered in the PTO.

❑ Underlying the globalization trend is the rapid deployment of Internet-based (also referred to as e-business) technologies. These technologies have fostered the implementation of global interconnected networks that connect suppliers, distributors, resellers, business partners, and customers throughout the world. This interconnected chain is referred to as the supply chain.

❑ E-business applications are built using open standards, meaning that they are not bound to one specific platform, vendor, or technology. This open-architecture approach ensures that Web-enabled applications will integrate with existing applications running on any platform and with any data in your network, and will scale as demand dictates.

❑ E-business solutions by their very nature support distributed computing solutions and multiple hardware/software vendors, cross-platform applications, and open scalable solutions that are standards based. A Web-enabled e-business infrastructure builds on the traditional client/server model, integrating Internet-based technologies with legacy data and applications.

❑ Processing international currency transactions becomes a key issue for working in a global e-business environment. E-commerce transactions often involve multiple currencies from countries all around the world. Systems must be built to deal with currency conversion between the consumer and the banking and merchant organizations

SELF TEST

1. You are a Webmaster, and your company has just launched its first e-commerce site on the Internet. You are responsible for publishing a series of white papers and case studies given to you by the marketing department. The marketing team has asked you whether the site should be registered for copyright, patent, and/or trademarks. You advise them

   A. The site can be trademarked because it contains original works of authorship.

   B. The site can be copyrighted because it contains schematics of new inventions.

   C. The site can be copyrighted because it contains original works of authorship.

   D. The site can be patented because it offers goods and services.

2. You have contracted out sections of your Web site development to independent contractors. Your boss tells you to make sure that your company retains all rights to the content so you can create derivative works and/or translate the content for individual Web sites. You decide

   A. Since you are paying the contractors under a work-for-hire agreement, your company is automatically protected.

   B. Since you are paying the contractors to produce a commissioned work, the creator must sign a written agreement stating that the work is for hire, prior to commencing development of the product.

   C. Since the contractor is creating the works, he owns all rights to them, and you must license the content.

   D. The original works created by the contractor can be trademarked.

3. Your Web development team has included a Zip archive file in the distribution of your software code. You are in charge of making sure that all software that you use for distribution has been properly licensed. What do you need to do?

   A. Contact the vendor and inform the vendor that you are distributing your software in Zip archive format.

   B. You need do nothing, since you are not modifying the Zip source code.

   C. Seek permission from the vendor through a license.

   D. Seek permission from the vendor through an assignment.

4. You are incorporating documents from every department to post on your e-commerce site. You inform your content suppliers that works do not need to be copyrighted when

   A. The material you use is factual or an idea.

   B. The works are in the public domain.

   C. The use is "fair use."

   D. All of the above.

5. You are creating a not-for-profit Web site that highlights literary works of Shakespeare. You are not sure whether you need to license or seek approval before publishing these works. A call to the Copyright Office informs you

   A. Since the material is being published is not for profit, you can publish it.

   B. You are free to publish his works, since the copyright protection has expired and the works are in the public domain.

   C. Since the works were never copyrighted in the United States, you can publish them.

   D. You may not publish Shakespeare's works, since his heirs still own the copyright.

6. You are asked by the sales department to make the product catalog on your e-commerce site available to your suppliers and distributors and allow them to reproduce and/or print the catalogs as they see fit but not to change anything. The best course of action is

   A. You put the information in the public domain.

   B. You authorize your business partners to copy, duplicate, and print the product catalog.

   C. You register the works for copyright protection to ensure that no changes are made.

   D. All of the above.

7. The legal department has asked the marketing department to register the domain name for your new e-commerce Web site. Since you are the Webmaster, and the people in marketing don't understand the use of digital trademarks and copyrights, they have come to you for advice. You advise them

   A. Domain names cannot be copyrighted, since they are a simple name.

   B. Domain names can be trademarked if they are used to distinguish your companies' goods and services.

   C. Domain names can be copyrighted since they are original.

   D. Domain names cannot be trademarked if their use is equivalent to a telephone number.

8. To obtain both a trademark and a service mark, you must go through the following process:

   A. Submit an application to the Copyright Office with your registration fee and materials.

   B. Submit an application to the Copyright Office and the PTO with your registration fee and materials.

   C. Submit an application to the PTO with your registration fee and materials.

   D. Trademarks and service marks cannot be registered.

9. Your departmental users are posting sensitive internal information to your public Web site. You send out a memo reinforcing the policies for posting information, which says

   A. It is illegal to publish copyrighted material to the company Web site.

   B. Material should not be posted to the Web site if it is proprietary information without approval from an appropriate company officer or manager.

   C. It is a copyright infringement to post confidential information.

   D. All of the above.

10. Examples of Global e-commerce business models include

    A. Treating both domestic and international business as an integrated whole

    B. Treating holdings in foreign business entities as a separate profit center reporting back to corporate

    C. Using a hybrid approach of running separate business units independently while applying core competencies of the parent company to assist the local or foreign entities

    D. All of the above

11. E-business technologies have the following attributes:

    A. Built on open standards in a multivendor environment

    B. Designed to leverage proprietary solutions

    C. Designed to deploy cross-platform applications

    D. All of the above

12. You are replacing your legacy and mainframe systems with a Web-based architecture. Some of the advantages to customers, users, and partners you plan to include are

    A. Applications will be built to run within any standards-based Web browser.

    B. Usability will be greatly improved by creating graphical based Web interfaces.

    C. Information sharing will be greatly enhanced by connecting systems and platforms that were formally an island to themselves.

    D. All of the above.

13. Your company is planning to launch its first global e-commerce site in Italy. Some of the issues relating to international currency transactions include

    A. Systems must be built to deal with currency conversion between the consumer and the banking and merchant organizations.

    B. You must determine whether or not to take credit card transactions.

    C. Online transaction payment software must be able to translate the clients' currency into the merchant's (your organization's) preferred currency.

    D. You must make sure that taxes are collected when you convert currencies.

14. One of the goals of transforming your company into an e-business is to optimize your supply chain. Some of the benefits will include

    A. Operating costs will be lowered through reduced inventory requirements, which will help to eliminate costly stockpiling.

    B. All players in the global supply chain, from raw material providers to final point of distribution, will be linked.

    C. Real-time market and process information will be distributed to all players, allowing them to anticipate and adjust their operations in response to market conditions.

    D. All of the above.

15. You are the project manager tasked with localizing the corporate e-commerce site for Japan. Besides translating the content into Japanese, you must also consider

    A. Gaining an understanding of the cultural issues relating to Japan

    B. Determining which e-commerce strategies work in the Japanese market

    C. Using XML to code your Web site

    D. All of the above

16. You have successfully deployed localized versions of e-commerce sites in Japan and Germany. Now you are finding that maintaining these sites is extremely labor intensive. Select the possible reason(s) for this.

    A. Managing human and technical resources around the globe

    B. Managing updates to multiple Web sites around the world

    C. Dealing with differences in technology infrastructures in different countries

    D. All of the above

17. You have heard that Unicode is a new standard that provides a foundation for internationalization and localization of content, and you're eager to try this out on your own sites. Some of the benefits of Unicode include

    A. You no longer need to use HTML and XML to code Web pages.

    B. You have a standard format for document and data interchange that is language independent.

    C. You no longer have to manage multiple language versions of your Web sites.

    D. You can replace JavaScript with Unicode.

18. Understanding legal and regulatory issues is one of the costs of doing business in a global marketplace. The company attorney has just briefed the Web design team on some of the key issues, which are

    A. Understanding and complying with U.S. laws on copyright, trademarks, and service marks serves as a natural starting point.

    B. Since foreign governments create their own laws, U.S. laws are irrelevant.

    C. In many countries, bribes are the only acceptable way of conducting business, and laws do not matter.

    D. Strategically select the countries in which you want to conduct business, and avoid countries that are considered too risky.

19. Developing a global presence does not change the principles of your overall business strategy, but it does require a change in your thinking toward

    A. Your business processes and procedures

    B. The relationships in the supply chain between your company, suppliers, distributors, and business partners

    C. The relationship with your customers

    D. All of the above

20. When you enter new global markets, it is a good idea to seek counseling from

    A. International attorneys, and accountants experienced in global e-business

    B. Your competitors

    C. Foreign governments

    D. All of the above

SELF TEST ANSWERS

1. **C** is correct.

   A is wrong, because trademarks protect words, names and symbols. Copyrights protect original works of authorship. **B** is wrong, because new inventions must be patented. **D** is wrong, because goods and services are not protected by patents but by trademarks.

2. **B** is correct.

   A is incorrect, because work-for-hire arrangements do not automatically afford protection. **C** is wrong, because you can have the contractor sign a work-for-hire agreement, so your company retains all rights. **D** is wrong, because original works are protected by copyrights, not trademarks.

3. **C** and **D** are correct.

   A is wrong, because you must gain permission to distribute copyrighted software. **B** is wrong, because you must obtain a license to modify or change the source code.

4. **D** is correct. None of the above need to be copyrighted.

5. **B** and **C** are correct.

   A is incorrect, because even if you don't plan to resell the works, you must still abide by copyright law. **D** is incorrect, since the copyright protection expires after 75 years.

6. **B** is correct.

   A is incorrect, because if the information is in the public domain your partners can modify the works. **C** is incorrect, because you do not need to register a copyright in order to be granted copyrighted privileges.

7. **A**, **B**, and **D** are correct.

   C is incorrect. Domain names cannot be copyrighted in any way, shape, or form. If a domain name is used to distinguish a specific product or service, it may be trademarked or given a service mark.

8. **C** is correct.

   A and **B** are incorrect, because the Copyright Office deals with copyrights, not trade and service marks. **D** is incorrect, because trademarks and service marks can be registered with the PTO.

9. **B** is correct.

   A, **C**, and **D** are wrong. While it is not illegal or a copyright infringement to post internal company information, it is inappropriate and may violate company policy.

10. **D** is correct.

11. **A** and **C** are correct.

    B and **D** are wrong. E-business applications are designed to run on multiple hardware platforms, operating systems, and vendor tools and applications.

12. **D** is correct.

13. **A** and **C** are correct.

    B is incorrect, because determining the form of payment is not the same as converting between foreign and domestic currency. **D** is incorrect, because tax collection is an issue independent of currency conversion.

14. **D** is correct.

15. **A** and **B** are correct.

    C is wrong, because whether the site is coded in XML or HTML does not matter to the end user.

16. **D** is correct.

17. **B** is correct.

    A and **D** are incorrect, because Unicode does not replace scripting languages. Rather, it is a standard that is used for coding characters used in modern spoken languages. **C** is incorrect, because you still need to maintain the content in your Web sites with the language of the target audience.

18. **A** and **D** are correct.

    B is incorrect, because many countries are using U.S. laws as a standard for modeling their own laws. **C** is incorrect, because laws are always important in any country.

19. **D** is correct.

20. **A** and **C** are correct.

    B and **D** are wrong. Your competitors will not share confidential trade secrets with you unless you decide to partner with them.

i-Net+ ™

COMPUTING TECHNOLOGY INDUSTRY ASSOCIATION®

14

E-commerce and Your Internet Audience

CERTIFICATION OBJECTIVES

W ith the widespread commercialization of the Internet, Web advertising and marketing is an important priority for companies conducting business and commerce on the Web. A variety of approaches have emerged for attracting customers and, more important, retaining those customers for repeat business after the first sale.

The first part of this lesson will discuss some of the tried-and-true approaches of Web advertising, including the use of cookies for personalizing and customizing a user's experience. The push and pull models of information access and retrieval are discussed and compared. In addition, the various forms of Web advertising, including banner ads and click-through advertising, are discussed.

In the second part of this lesson, both the business and technology elements of e-business and e-commerce are described. These include business-to-consumer and business-to-business e-commerce, online catalogs, electronic data interchange, customer relationship management, and e-commerce trends.

CERTIFICATION OBJECTIVE 14.01

Web Technologies to Attract and Retain Customers

A variety of approaches have emerged for attracting customers and retaining customers purchasing goods and services over the Internet. One of the first technologies for personalizing a customer's online experience was cookies, first introduced by Netscape Communications and widely adopted by the industry at large.

Cookies

One of the first technologies for customizing and personalizing the user experience of Web surfers involved the use of cookies. A cookie is an HTTP header, consisting of a text string that stores information about the user and the browser. This data is saved to file on the user's local hard disk.

Applications of Cookies

Cookies are used in e-commerce and Web applications in these ways:

- *Personalization* of Web sites is one of the most common uses of cookies. Cookies help to save information about a customer, such as the username and password. Each time a user logs in to a site, the user does not need to renter that information. Cookies also provide Web developers with a means of keeping site content updated and relevant to a customer's interests, and provide information about the type of Web browser used to access a site. Cookies can store database information, custom page settings, or just about anything that would make a site individualized and customizable. One of the most popular applications of cookies is by information portals such as Yahoo! and Excite. They use cookies to store personalization settings for each user. When a user logs in to one of these portals, the user's unique user interface and content profile is retrieved and displayed in the browser.

- *E-catalogs* often rely on cookies to remember what a person orders while shopping online. This is done with a "shopping cart" metaphor by maintaining state information. Since HTTP is a "stateless" protocol, it is impossible to differentiate between separate user visits to a Web site. To make differentiation possible, Web servers mark a visitor by storing a piece of information about the visitor in a cookie. This allows customers to shop on your site, save their order, and return later to modify or place their order.

- *Targeted Web advertising* is one of the main e-commerce applications of cookies. A customer profile can be built and used to target the specific banner ads to specific customers, and to ensure that they are never presented the same ad twice during a session.

on the job

Newer Web server technologies, such as Web application servers, are able to store state information (as cookies do), as well as session information, such as user navigation though a site. This further enhances the online shopping experience for the user while simultaneously collecting valuable feedback about user shopping behaviors.

Server-Push and Internet Advertising

Two predominant technologies have been used to access information and content on the Web. The initial model of Web access was based on the idea that users must pull in content by visiting a Web site. This was the traditional approach of entering a URL in a Web browser and downloading a Web page. As the Web grew and new technologies emerged, push technologies appeared that automatically delivered information, such as news headlines or product updates, directly to a user's computer in a customized format at designated times, and without the user having to request the information updates manually.

In the push-based model, information providers do not wait for visitors. The objective is to reach out to an audience by pushing content to them. This technology has had a significant impact in the field of Internet marketing and advertising.

Push is not a specific technology solution or product, but rather a general concept used to describe a way to deliver information automatically over a network. Push is actually a diverse group of companies and technologies that deliver content—either data or applications—over computer networks such as the Internet or internal corporate intranets. Broadly defined, push technology is a form of Internet protocol multicasting (also known as Webcasting). IP multicasting routes data to specific computers on a network that are identified by an IP address or class.

The objective of many commercial Web sites is to bring eyes to advertising sponsors in order to support charging advertising fees. Merely creating a Web site and then hoping people will visit is a passive and ineffective strategy. It is critical for advertisers and e-commerce sites to ensure that customers come back to a site so these repeat customers can generate revenue.

News and Information Delivery

Push technology has been around for quite some time. The most common use of push publishing is to send users and customers information about services, products, or news. Mailing lists and e-mail newsletters are effective marketing and advertising tools; e-mail messages can target a specific audience to advertise a product and/or service. For example, ChannelWeb delivers an

Executive Briefing Newsletter that sends out industry news and information, and embeds links to advertisers and sponsors. Since the content is highly directed to the interests of the subscriber, the advertising is similarly targeted.

List Servers

Electronic mailing lists provide forums for Internet users to participate in discussions or to receive e-mail messages sent in bulk. The software responsible for the management and distribution of these mailing lists to thousands of subscribers is commonly called a *list server*. A list server automatically distributes an e-mail message from one member of a list to all other members on that list, as shown in Figure 14-1.

One of the most common list servers is called LISTSERV. Other popular mailing list software includes majordomo and listproc. Users subscribe to a list by submitting their names and e-mail addresses. List servers are very popular for sending electronic newsletters to customers, employees, analysts, investors, and business partners. This will help you build a strong relationship with your customers and partners and strengthen customer loyalty.

Push and the World Wide Web

Ultimately, the purpose of push is to help users find information on the Internet. Web portals have evolved from the days of push to allow users to personalize their content and information delivered to their browsers,

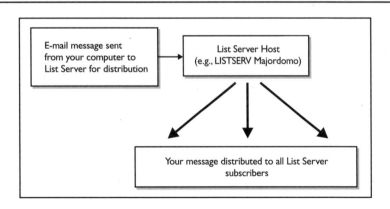

FIGURE 14-1

Process for list server distribution of e-mail

including customized news feeds, stock quotes, and other information. Portals have developed their own server-push solutions that work with any Web browser client to allow users to set up customized information channels that periodically update content in a user's browser.

on the Job

Push is taking on new forms on the Web, especially in the area of customized information and content delivery for e-commerce. One of the most important ways to add value to your service is to create ongoing customer relationships. Use cookies to create a customer profile for each of your users and provide them with relevant and fresh information based on past visits to your site, buying patterns, and so on. You can use this information gathered on the Web to keep customers up to date on specials and new products with newsletters and targeted e-mails.

Client-Pull Technology

The purpose of using client-pull technology is the same as that of using server-push technology: to refresh the HTML document content being viewed in a Web browser. For example, let's say you want to create a site that downloads stock price information every five minutes, but the server only downloads content at 20-minute intervals. You can use a client-pull solution as an alternative or in combination with a server-side push approach. The advantage of a client-pull solution is that you are not dependent on the server to refresh content viewed in a browser.

<META> Tag

By using client-pull you can update pages in both Netscape and Microsoft browsers using the <META> tag in the header of an HTML document. There is a special HTTP header field called Refresh that reloads the document at a preset interval. The content being updated can be the same HTML document, or another HTML document as defined in the URL parameter.

When an HTTP server sends a document to a client browser, a header field appears at the top of the document. The HTTP Refresh field implements the client-pull dynamic HTML document. The syntax for the <META> tag is as follows:

```
<META http-equiv="Refresh" content="field value">
```

The http-equiv attribute notifies the HTTP server to include a Refresh field with a value specified in the content attribute field. This value is passed (in quotes) in the string of headers that is sent to the client browser. Next, the rest of the document content is transmitted.

The field value of the content parameter in the Refresh field determines the update interval used to refresh the document content. If the value of this parameter is set to zero, there is zero delay, and the document is reloaded immediately after it is displayed. This value can be set to any integer value (x), and the browser will delay x seconds before reloading the document.

on the job

You can create crude animation effects by using the Refresh field with a 0 update parameter and pointing to a different document URL as you step through the animation. All the files being pointed to are various stages in the animation sequence.

EXERCISE 14-1

Creating a Client-Pull HTML Document

In this exercise, you will create a client-pull document that will reload the same Web page at a user-specified interval.

1. Create a new document in a text editor or an HTML editor.

2. Enter the following HTML text in your document:

```
<!DOCTYPE HTML PUBLIC "-//W3C//DTD HTML 4.0
Transitional//EN">
<HTML>
<HEAD>
<TITLE>Refresh Document</TITLE>
<META http-equiv="Refresh" content="3">
</HEAD>
<BODY>
This content will be refreshed at a preset interval...
<P>
Place an image file in the document to see screen
repaint itself.
</BODY>
</HTML>
```

3. Save the file as Refresh.htm and load it into your Web browser.

To better see the screen repainting after a refresh, embed a large image on the page; play with the content value integer to change the refresh rate.

Notice that the Refresh field's content value is the number of seconds the content is displayed in the browser before being reloaded repeatedly. Unless it is interrupted, this process will not stop until the browser is shut down.

EXERCISE 14-2

Refreshing a Different HTML Document

In this exercise, you will create a client-pull document that will reload a different document or site by adding that document's absolute URL. The URL is included after the delay time by adding a semicolon after the content parameter.

1. Create a new document in a text editor or an HTML editor.

2. Enter the following HTML text in your document:

```
<!DOCTYPE HTML PUBLIC "-//W3C//DTD HTML 4.0
Transitional//EN">
<HTML>
<HEAD>
<TITLE>Refresh Document</TITLE>
<META http-equiv="Refresh" content="3;
URL=http://www.comptia.org">
</HEAD>
<BODY>
This content will be refreshed at a preset interval...
<P>
</BODY>
</HTML>
```

3. Save the file as Refresh2.htm and load it into your Web browser.

Play with the content value integer to change the refresh rate.

Deciding Between Push and Pull Approaches

Client-pull documents can place a heavy burden on the server and the network, especially when the update frequency is short. Each time an automatic client-pull request is made, it consumes resources. Further, it may take several seconds between the time a browser makes a request to the server and the time when it begins to retrieve the document. If your situation requires a real-time solution, you will have to look at server-push technologies or other solutions such as Java applets and servlets for maintaining real-time connections. A good rule of thumb is to use client-pull technology for low-frequency updates.

FROM THE CLASSROOM

Web-Driven Kiosks as Customer Attractors

There are several ways client pull is useful for creating attractors to capture the attention of your audience. You can create a Web-driven kiosk effect by cycling through Web documents to capture the attention of your audience.

For example, let us say you create three client-pull HTML documents that loop through to one another. Each of the three documents presents information on your company's products and/or services. The code for each document will look like this: The document One.html contains

```
<META http-equiv="Refresh"
content="25;
URL=http://test.com/two.html">
```

The document Two.html contains

```
<META http-equiv="Refresh"
 content="25;
URL=http://test.com/three.html">
```

The document Three.html contains

```
<META http-equiv="Refresh"
content="25;
URL=http://test.com/one.html">
```

Uninterrupted, the browser will infinitely loop among the three documents at 30-second intervals. Users can click hyperlinks at any time to advance to one of the three pages without having to wait for the automatic client-pull action to be invoked. When they move on from your kiosk, new customers walking by will be attracted by the dynamic display.

—*Maxwell Miller, Ph.D., CIW, CWT, i-Net+*

CERTIFICATION OBJECTIVE 14.02

Internet, Intranet, and Extranet Technologies and Concepts

The Internet, corporate intranets, and extranets are all examples of modern-day networking and internetworking technologies. The protocols, standards, and computer languages that provide the foundation of the Internet are the same technologies used for building intranets and extranets. The differences between these various types of computing and telecommunications networks are found in their business applications.

The Internet

As you have learned previously, the Internet is perhaps best described as the world's largest interconnected network of networks. Many services are available on the Internet, including FTP, e-mail, the World Wide Web, newsgroups, and so on. What allows the global communication between varying computers, operating systems, network hardware, and software is a common set of open standards and communications protocols such as TCP/IP, HTTP, NNTP, SMTP, as discussed in Chapter 9.

The Internet is not only network and communications technology. It's a global community of people including corporations, nonprofit organizations, educational institutions, and individuals. As the Internet has been exploited for use in the business world, it has exploded with the widespread application of business-to-consumer e-commerce. Using a public Internet site, customers can purchase goods and services from merchants over the Internet using secure protocols and user-friendly Web browser access. The Internet also supports transaction-based, business-to-business e-commerce.

Corporate Intranets

Intranets (intraconnected networks) are based on the same open standards and technologies used for the Internet. Intranets are best defined as collections of Web sites belonging to an organization that are usually accessible only to members of that organization.

Often an intranet is located behind a firewall to prevent unauthorized access from outside the intranet. Intranets can also be thought of as extensions of local area networks (LANs) that are Web enabled. Intranets typically offer the following features:

- Online publishing and sharing of documents and files (for example, HTML, XML, and Word)
- Online search capability
- Application distribution (for example, ASP and Java applets)
- E-mail and messaging
- Groupware applications such as calendars and online directories
- Access to corporate databases and legacy systems

Extranets

Extranets (external networks), like intranets, are derived from Internet-based technologies and standards. Extranets connect an intranet site to the Internet (or intranet using the Internet). In a sense, extranets are extensions of an Internet/intranet site to another site on the Internet where information, data, applications, and resources are shared.

Common examples of extranets are links between business partners that need to share information between organizations in the supply chain. Extranets are the underlying technology infrastructure supporting business-to-business e-commerce.

exam
Ⓦatch

Make sure you understand the fundamental differences and tradeoffs between the Internet, intranets, and extranets from a business perspective as well as from a technical perspective. Be familiar with the business applications that each network type is suited for.

E-commerce Terms and Concepts

E-commerce may be described as the complete set of processes and systems that support conducting business electronically using the Internet or other private networks. E-commerce comprises the business activities between consumers, vendors, distributors, suppliers, and intermediaries using the Internet. The overall goals of e-commerce are very much business driven and include

- Increased market share
- Increased efficiency and accuracy through automation of business processes
- Reduced time to market when new products and services are introduced
- Reduced operating costs
- Improved profit margins through automated supply-chain management
- Improved customer service and support
- Instant communication with consumers and trading partners
- Better forecasting of customer needs and demand

The e-commerce field is multidisciplinary in nature. On the technical side, it includes the disciplines of computing, telecommunications, networking, security, multimedia, database design and management, EDI/EFT, and software development. On the business side, e-commerce includes core business processes including marketing, sales, advertising, procurement, purchasing, billing and payment, supply-chain management, and the like. As you learned in a previous lesson, the legal side of e-commerce involves intellectual property, privacy rights to information, taxation, and other governmental regulations.

exam
ⓦatch

Make sure you understand the overall goals of e-commerce from a business perspective as well as from a technical perspective.

Internet Commerce

Internet commerce has exploded in the past couple of years. As with any rapidly growing phenomenon, gauging the extent of e-commerce growth is not an exact science. The following statistics help provide guidance in estimating the scope of business opportunities.

- Consumers in the United States will spend $18.6 billion over the Web in 1999, more than doubling the $8 billion total in 1998, and effecting a 615 percent increase from the $2.6 billion they spent in 1997. (eMarketer)

- In 1999, the average annual online expenditure per buyer is $479. By 2002, this number is expected to double to $976 per buyer. (eMarketer)

- By 2000, nearly 56 percent of U.S. companies will sell their products online, up from 24 percent in 1998. (NUA)

- The United States has the fastest growing number of Internet users and largest proportion of e-commerce consumers. (Roper Starch Worldwide)

- Almost 42 percent of the total U.S. adult population (over 18) are regular Internet users. This is an increase of almost 20 percent from the previous year. (Internet Advertising Bureau)

- Small businesses that use the Internet have grown 46 percent faster than those that do not. (American City Business Journals)

- The number of online buyers will grow at an average annual rate of 20 percent, rising from 38.8 million at year-end 1999 to 67.2 million in 2002. (CyberAtlas)

- Nearly 470,000 U.S. homes already buy new cars via the Internet. (Forrester Research)

- One year ago, just over half of the people on the Internet were making purchases. Now, three-quarters are buying, and 82 percent of these are filling their online shopping carts with multiple purchases. (Greenfield Online)

- About 28 percent of the U.S. population was online in 1998; by 2003, that percentage will jump to 62 percent. (IDC)

■ By 2003, nearly 80 percent of businesses will be online, compared with just 36 percent in 1998. (IDC)

■ In 1999, U.S. online retail sales should reach $20.2 billion as 7 million Internet shoppers make their first electronic commerce purchases. (Forrester Research).

The Internet Economy: Determining Your Niche

In June 1999, Cisco Systems commissioned a study carried out at the University of Texas in Austin. *The Internet Economy*, which was the report published as a result of this study, is updated every three months at http://www.internetindicators.com. According to this study, the Internet economy can best be understood when it is divided into four layers.

By deciding where your company falls in each of these layers, you can determine the competitive landscape, better define your unique business niche, and gain more insight on how to grow your e-business.

■ Layer 1: The Internet *Infrastructure* Layer ($115B in revenues in 1998). This layer includes companies that provide products and services to networks to support the Internet infrastructure. These are the "pipes" that data and content flow through. Examples in this category include

■ Internet backbone providers (AT&T and MCI Worldcom)

■ Internet service providers (Mindspring and AOL)

■ Networking hardware and software companies (Cisco, Lucent, and 3Com)

■ Fiber-optics vendors (Corning)

■ Line acceleration hardware manufacturers (Ciena and Tellabs)

■ Layer 2: The Internet *Applications* Layer ($56B in revenues in 1998). Products and services in this layer add value to the IP network infrastructure and make it possible to perform business activities online. The categories in this layer include

■ Internet consultants (USWeb/CKS and Proxicom)

■ Multimedia applications (RealNetworks and Macromedia)

- Web development software (NetObjects, Microsoft, and Vignette)
- Search engine software (Inktomi and Verity)
- Online training (DigitalThink and HungryMinds.com)
- Web-enabled databases (Oracle)

- Layer 3: The Internet *Intermediary* Layer ($58B in revenues in 1998). Internet intermediaries facilitate the meeting and interaction of buyers and sellers over the Internet to create an e-business marketplace. They leverage the investments made at the infrastructure and applications layers. Categories with examples are

  - Market makers in vertical industries (VerticalNet and PCOrder)
  - Online travel agents (TravelWeb.com and 1Travel.com)
  - Online brokerages (E*Trade and Schwab.com)
  - Content aggregators (Cnet and ZDnet)
  - Portals/Content providers (Yahoo!, Excite and Netcenter)
  - Internet ad brokers (24/7 Media)
  - Online advertising (ABCNews)

- Layer 4: The Internet *Commerce* Layer ($101B in revenues in 1998). Internet commerce involves the sales of products and services to consumers or businesses over the Internet. The categories in this Internet commerce layer include

  - E-tailers (Amazon.com and cozone.com)
  - Manufacturers selling online (Cisco, Dell and Gateway)
  - Fee/Subscription-based companies (theStreet.com and WSJ.com)
  - Airlines selling online tickets (United Airlines)

Many of these companies are players at several layers. For example, Microsoft and IBM are important players at the applications and Internet commerce layers. Cisco is a key player at the infrastructure and commerce layers. And AOL/Netscape are key players in the infrastructure, intermediary, and commerce layers.

Types of Internet Commerce

There are two forms of Internet commerce: business-to-consumer (B2C) and business-to-business (B2B) electronic commerce. Both are based on open industry standards. There is no dominant Internet commerce solution. Each implementation is likely to include both vendor-neutral standards in addition to proprietary technologies offered by the leading vendors.

Business to Consumer (B2C)

B2C e-commerce is based on transactions conducted between a consumer and a business. B2C commerce is characterized by low-volume, low-dollar transactions (for example, ordering a book or CD over the Internet). This is quickly changing as more expensive items, such as automobiles, are being sold directly from the manufacturer to the consumer.

A B2C e-commerce transaction is shown in Figure 14-2. The arrows marked B2C display a transaction in which a consumer places an order for a product over the Internet with a distributor or retailer, or directly from the manufacturer (corporation), which then fills the order. B2C transactions are conducted over the Internet using electronic storefronts and e-catalogs.

Business to Business (B2B)

Figure 14-3 extends the B2C solution to a B2B scenario as indicated by the arrows marked B2B. Transaction information (in this case, the partners

---

FIGURE 14-2

Schematic showing
business-to-consumer
e-commerce model

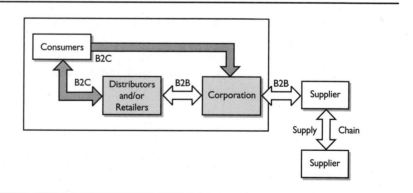

FIGURE 14-3

Schematic showing
business-to-business
e-commerce

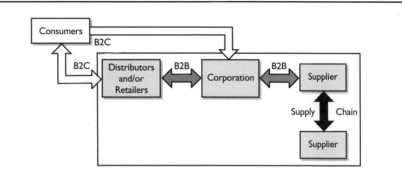

being distributors and/or retailers, some corporation, and the supply chain)
is being exchanged electronically between partners.

B2B e-commerce tends to be characterized by high-volume transactions
between trading partners in the supply chain or between the manufacturer
and distributors (reseller purchasing large quantity of units for resale). B2B
commerce tends to be conducted using extranets between businesses.

QUESTIONS AND ANSWERS

I want to create a B2C e-commerce site to market my products on the World Wide Web. What is the network model that I should use?	Build a B2C e-commerce Web site that is accessible via the Internet using standard Web browsers.
How can I create links in my supply chain between my company and our resellers and distributors?	Build a B2B extranet solution that links your internal database and Web systems with your reseller's and distributor's internal information systems.
How can I allow my employees greater access to their employment records, including benefit plans, performance reviews, and expense reimbursement software?	Create an intranet inside your organization that links to your LAN network and resources. Set up access control lists to protect user confidentiality and put your intranet behind a firewall to prevent unauthorized access from the Internet.

EDI

Electronic data interchange technology has been used for conducting electronic transactions for more than 20 years. EDI is a process and standard for the electronic exchange of data across computer networks. It is the process that allows electronic funds transfers (EFTs) between accounts, and it was first widely used in telephone banking and automatic teller machine applications.

EDI never caught on to the extent that e-commerce has with the widespread use of the Internet. Due to its high development and maintenance costs, primarily the banking industry and very large corporations have used EDI. That is changing, as e-business becomes ubiquitous.

EDI is becoming a fundamental component of B2B electronic commerce between trading partners. A great advantage of EDI is that data must be entered only once into an electronic format. This saves time and money by reducing redundancy in data-entry process and reducing the chances for data-entry error. Once in EDI, data is in an electronic format that is easily transferred across the supply chain.

Online Catalog and Merchant Systems

Electronic catalogs (e-catalogs) are online analogs of mail-order or printed catalogs. As an integral part of any e-commerce site or merchant system, e-catalogs support online shopping, ordering, and payment. Typically, e-catalogs offer more than their paper-based counterparts—such as more competitive online prices, interactive site and product exploration tools, and more detailed information on products and services.

Online merchant systems typically use the following elements:

- *Content* refers to the products, services, pricing information, and detailed product specifications listed in a catalog.

- *Presentation* deals with the look and feel of the catalog itself and the way it is presented to the user. Advanced e-catalogs often include multimedia capabilities, such as audio, video, and animation.

- *Back-end processing* refers to the integration between the e-catalog Web-based interface and the back-end systems to which it is connected, including databases, payment systems, and legacy information systems.

■ *Business logic* refers to the functionality of the front-end systems, including online search capability; online secure payment infrastructure; and online customer service, such as help-desk and customer relationship management.

■ *Usage tracking* refers to, the ability of an e-catalog system to track the number of hits to a site, customer demographics, and interface with a knowledge-based system to customize the presentation to its users.

There are several types of e-catalog systems. Some are stand-alone Web sites built for the explicit purpose of B2C e-commerce (for example, Amazon.com). Electronic malls are collections of online catalogs from various merchants integrated into a central B2C e-commerce site. The Internet Shopping Network is a good example of an electronic mall. With the increase in B2B e-commerce, e-catalogs are being used to facilitate transactions between strategic trading partners using OBI.

Open Buying on the Internet

Open Buying on the Internet (OBI) is a vendor-neutral standard that has emerged for electronic catalog systems. OBI defines the rules for conducting B2B commerce over the Internet. Most Internet-based procurement software relies on a proprietary system for exchanging transactions between companies. Some require both ends of a transaction to have the same software. Others take old EDI formats directly to the Web. As a result, many B2B systems are built using customized links between trading partners. This approach is expensive and labor intensive. As OBI becomes more widely adopted, B2B e-commerce will become an easier and more affordable option. Further information on OBI can be obtained at: http://www.openbuy.org/obi/.

Electronic Payment Systems on the Internet

Electronic payment systems in the e-commerce world are analogous to payment systems in the real world. They must be quick, reliable, and cost effective for the merchant and consumer. There are several payment systems in use, including smart cards, electronic money, credit card payments, and electronic checks.

- *Smart cards* are also referred to as stored-value cards. Smart cards started as debit cards such as prepaid phone cards or copy machine cards. Today's generation of smart cards have embedded integrated circuits (for example, American Express Blue Card) that might include a microprocessor, RAM, ROM, or EPROM. Applications of smart cards include digital currency, digital certificates for hardware-assisted encryption systems, or storage of important information such as health records. Usually used for in-person transactions.

- *Electronic money* is also referred to as digital cash. This is a PC-based electronic payment method that is integrated into Web browser software. Its purpose is to facilitate impulse buying for Internet shoppers. At some point, digital cash may replace credit cards for low-price transactions such as a newspaper issue or game play. CyberCash (http://www.cybercash.com) is a major player in this space.

- *Credit cards* are used in transactions over the Internet that involve the transmission of encrypted data containing credit card information, such as the number and expiration date, as well as privacy information, about the purchaser. One of the major problems with this system is the potential for fraud, since the owner of the card does not have to be physically present to use the card over the Internet. This is the dominant form of payment used for e-commerce transactions.

- *Electronic checks* are also referred to as e-checks. They are another payment system for making payments over computer networks. A digital version of a check is presented to a merchant over the Web. The merchant verifies the check through a financial institution, which in turn verifies the availability of funds in the customer's financial institution. Many electronic bill payment systems are based on electronic checks. One of the leading vendors is CheckFree (http://www.checkfree.com). The advantage of electronic checks for the customer is reduced monthly postage costs, increased accuracy in bill remittance, and greater convenience. For the merchant, the greatest advantage is the reduction of paper check processing costs.

Customer Relationship Management

Customer relationship management (CRM) is the business process of identifying, selecting, acquiring, developing, and retaining your most profitable customers. One of the cornerstones of business is that "the customer is always right," and keeping the customer as satisfied after the purchase and delivery of the product or service is just as important as effectively targeting the right customer in the first place. CRM helps companies cultivate a one-to-one customer service relationship with the customer over time.

When CRM solutions are used, customer information becomes accessible and consistent across the entire enterprise, and it is a strategic tool that organizations can use to create opportunities for cross-selling other types of products and services to an existing customer base.

CRM enables customers to engage with a business using the most effective service delivery channel, whether it is self-service over the Web or a traditional customer service call center or field service. Increased customer satisfaction means long-term customer retention.

Customer Self-Service

In an e-business world, self-service is critical. Customers expect interaction with the Web to be much more immediate and direct than real-world interaction. For example, a customer who purchased a power tool from a retail outlet searches the online help files of the manufacturer's Web site looking for troubleshooting information, and discovers that his machine has all the symptoms of a defective motor. The customer immediately contacts the 24-hour customer service hot line even during nonbusiness hours.

The customer service representative is already aware of the customer's need for help, since the product support sections of the Web site are integrated with the customer service application. In just a few minutes, the customer service representative can arrange for the warranty repair or replacement of the defective unit.

The benefits of self-service applications extend beyond your customers to your own organization. Many functions, such as expense report reimbursement, purchasing, human resources, and travel, can be moved to a self-service model in which those directly involved in the transaction initiate the processing activity through a Web browser on your corporate intranet. Other functions can be further automated by your linking self-service components to your supply chain using the Internet or an extranet.

For example, your salespeople can enter their own expenses; plan business travel; order their own supplies, and manage their retirement, education, and medical benefits using Web-based applications they access via a browser. Expense reports are routed automatically through the approval process, eliminating manual steps and paperwork. Your business partners can view schedules, orders, and requests for quotes, and perform many other activities at their convenience, while customers can review the status of their invoices and payments.

In business terms, by automating functions to a self-service model you can improve customer service and response time; reduce operating expenses; open new sales channels; and free up staff to focus on value-added activities, such as cross-selling and custom solutions.

Technical Support and Help Desk

CRM can help you move your company and e-business toward a customer-focused organization. One of the most effective uses of self-service is in technical support and help desk functions. Providing quality customer self-service involves Web-enabling existing back-end systems and building in secure access policies. Providing online information to frequently asked questions (FAQs), troubleshooting information, software distribution for update patches and upgrades, and moderated newsgroups are all tools used to enable customers to do more for themselves.

Web Call Back

Web call back is a relatively new technology that further enhances CRM. Web call back works by allowing customers to click a link on your e-commerce site and enter their phone numbers. The link immediately triggers a call to a specific phone number at your company. Your sales or customer service representatives answer, and the service informs them that they are being connected to a Web site visitor. Your company representative and your customer are immediately conferenced together, and your staff can effectively close a sale or answer the visitor's question. The phone calls are placed within seconds of the visitor's clicking the hot link.

Some of the other advantages of integrating a Web call-back feature into your e-commerce solution include

- Helps to increase impulse buying and close sales deals
- Gives real-time feedback to customers
- Reduces concern about credit card use
- Gives customers the personal touch with a live human being
- Helps customers navigate Web sites easily
- Directs customer calls to specific people and/or departments

Internet Marketing

Because of the Internet, the days of the mass marketing campaign aimed at anonymous customers are coming to an end. Internet marketing allows companies to personalize their marketing messages based on the various needs of distinct customers. Through the use of personalized targeted advertising, the most appropriate messages can be targeted toward the right customer at the right time. In turn, companies can quickly evaluate the effectiveness of marketing campaigns and modify them appropriately on the basis of customer feedback collected over the Web or through e-mail.

By integrating Internet marketing into a comprehensive marketing campaign, a merchant can target retail outlets, wholesale distributors, and direct sales channels differently through a variety of media, including television, direct mail, telemarketing calls, in-store promotions, and a globally available Web storefront. No matter how a customer buys the product, the information is captured and shared across all systems, including marketing and financial management systems.

When the customer visits the Web storefront for the first time and enters his name, he is welcomed to the site, asked how he likes the new table saw he recently purchased, and offered a 10 percent discount on a companion peripheral device of the same make. The pricing and offer are part of a campaign that is scheduled to run for six months, but the campaign will be modified dynamically depending on the results. A customer profile can then be created based on purchases, cancellations, returns, and customer service calls.

Online Marketing and Sales Tools

Internet marketing takes advantage of Web-based tools to enhance or broaden traditional marketing channels. Some of the functions that are easily handled include lead generation and lead qualification to consolidate and store leads and opportunities. Marketing campaigns can be designed to drive sales leads to the company Web site, where they are prioritized, qualified, and distributed, according to user-defined rule sets, and routed to individual salespeople. This can all be done in real time over the Internet.

Sales automation tools also leverage Web-based solutions. Examples of sales automation applications include automatic quote generators and tools for efficiently collecting prospect information. Many of these tools also have integrated contact management built in.

We have discussed many of the strategic reasons for marketing and advertising. This section focuses on the tactical side of the coin, and the specific techniques you can use to market your company's Web site and create brand awareness using the Internet and the Web.

- **Search engines**   Getting your Web site listed on a search engine or directory is a very cost-effective way of reaching prospects who might otherwise have been aware that you exist. A traditional search engine gives you a text box in which you enter keywords or phrases. The engine then submits this query to a database, which contains the URLs and descriptions of Web sites that are returned to the user. Some of the most common search engines are AltaVista, Inktomi, and HotBot.

- **Directories**   These organize information about sites into hierarchical lists, beginning with a topic, and descending through the layers of subtopics. Some directories, such as Excite, have self-service submission policies. Other directories, such as About.com and Magellan, rely on experts to report and review new sites. You must convince the experts in the pertinent directory category that your site is worth listing on their site. Yahoo!, the most popular of directories, has substantially different submission requirements available from its Web site.

- **E-mail newsletters and list servers**   These are some of the least expensive means for Internet marketing. E-mail newsletters and list servers are being used to lure customers to Web sites, introduce new products, offer special promotions targeted at specific audiences, and collect customer feedback.

- **Web advertising and banner ads**   These are a popular way to advertise and attract business to your Web site. Banner ads are placed on popular Web sites. They allow customers to click through the banner ad and be connected directly to your e-commerce site.

FROM THE CLASSROOM

Having Your Site Rank High in Search Engines and Directories

In order to attract customers to your site using a search engine, it is important to rank high on the hit list so that the customer sees your company listed near the top of the rankings. Here are some techniques you can use to ensure that you will get high rankings:

- **License use of keywords**   Many search engines, such as Yahoo!, charge a fee to allow merchants to license keywords that directly link to their Web site URLs. For example, suppose your business sells lighting systems. You may want to license keywords such as "lightbulb" and "lamps." Whenever a user submits these keywords in a query, your Web site URL will be returned at the top of the hit list or in a banner display ad.

- **Use descriptive, precise keywords in the TITLE statement**   Search engines index words that appear in the <TITLE> tag in your HTML document. This is a very important tool. To get your site at the top of the list of sites that a search engine supplies in response to a query, select a <TITLE> that is descriptive and precise.

- **Web site analysis tools**   Server log file analysis programs such as WebTrends (http://www.webtrends.com) can help you determine which search engines your visitors use most often and which keywords they used to reach your site. Your ISP may provide this or a similar tool as part of your service package.

—Maxwell Miller, Ph.D., CIW, CWT, i-Net+

Trends in E-commerce

WebTomorrow.com believes that the future of e-commerce will be characterized by five emerging trends:

- **Personalization**   As has been discussed throughout this lesson, all successful e-commerce merchants will be required to know their customers, not just by name, but also by their buying habits. By understanding consumer behavior and preferences, merchants can provide each customer with a personalized, interactive experience. Furthermore, company Web sites will be able to record where and on what a customer clicks and use that data to dynamically create pages that are custom designed according to that customer's preferences. Essentially, each customer's experience will be unique.

- **Instant fulfillment**   E-commerce customers will be able to get their product the same day that they order it. Consumers now must wait days for their merchandise to be delivered. Today's consumers are used to being able to take the product home with them. They see, they buy, and they carry it home. With the exception of downloadable products like software, e-commerce does not provide instant gratification. Future e-commerce companies will solve this problem by using local affiliate stores. After selecting a product, the shopper will be directed to stores closest to home or office, where the shopper can pick up the product, or from where the product can be delivered. This arrangement will also save the customer from having to pay shipping charges. This hybrid approach of combining brick-and-mortar sites with online e-business systems is already in place with such businesses as Amazon.com and Gateway.com, and it will continue to increase in popularity.

- **Custom pricing**   Eventually, e-commerce pricing will be highly flexible. Each customer will pay a different price on the basis of many factors, including how much product the customer has previously bought, how many ads the customer has read on the site, where the customer has just clicked from, how many friends the customer can refer, how much of the customer's profile he/she is willing to share, and so on. Companies like Priceline.com and eBay are paving the way for this dynamic pricing trend.

■ **Anywhere, anytime** In the future, customers will be able to buy from anywhere, at any time. They will use wireless devices, such as cellular phones, that are capable of live Web connections, or personal digital assistants, such as the Palm Pilot or Windows CE devices.

■ **Intelligent agents** Intelligent software agents will find the best products and best prices for customers. These autonomous intelligent agents will be able to be personalized and run 24 hours a day. Consumers will use agents to find the best prices for products and services. Companies will use agents in place of human purchasing agents. For example, a company that needs to order printer supplies will use an intelligent agent to monitor the quantity and usage patterns of printers within the company, launching the agents when supplies are becoming low. Then, the company's intelligent agent will automatically collect information on vendors and products that fit the needs of the company, evaluate the different offering options, decide which suppliers and products to pursue, negotiate the terms of transactions with these suppliers, and finally place orders and make automated payments.

CERTIFICATION SUMMARY

This lesson provided an overview of marketing and advertising approaches for attracting customers on the Web, and retaining those customers for repeat business in the future.

The first part of this lesson discussed some of the tried-and-true approaches of Web advertising, including the use of cookies for personalizing and customizing a user's experience. The push vs. pull model of information access and retrieval were discussed. In addition, forms of Web advertising, including banner ads, were explained.

In the second part of the lesson, the business and technological elements of e-commerce were described, including business-to-consumer and business-to-business e-commerce, online catalogs and merchant systems, EDI, customer relationship management, and e-commerce trends.

✓ TWO-MINUTE DRILL

- ❏ A *cookie* is an HTTP header that consists of a text string and that stores information about the user and the browser.

- ❏ Cookies save information about a customer, such as username, password, and any user-entered information.

- ❏ Cookies save information about the type of Web browser used to access a site.

- ❏ Web application servers are able to store state information, as well as session information such as user navigation through a site.

- ❏ Client pull is based on the idea that users must pull in content by visiting a Web site. This is the traditional approach of entering a URL in a Web browser and downloading a Web page.

- ❏ Server-push technologies automatically deliver information, such as news headlines and product updates, directly to a user's computer in a customized format.

- ❏ Push technology is a form of Internet protocol multicasting (also known as Webcasting).

- ❏ Web portals such as Yahoo! use Web-based push technology.

- ❏ Client pull updates Web pages using the <META> tag in the header of an HTML document.

- ❏ The protocols, standards, and computer languages that provide the foundation of the Internet are the same as the technologies used for building intranets and extranets.

- ❏ The Internet is best described as the world's largest interconnected network of networks.

- ❏ Intranets (intraconnected networks) are based on the same open standards and technologies used for the Internet and are usually accessible only to members of a particular organization.

- ❏ Extranets (external networks), like intranets, are derived from Internet-based technologies and standards.

- ❏ Common examples of extranets are links between business partners that need to share information between organizations in the supply chain.

❑ Extranets are made up of the underlying technology infrastructure supporting business-to-business e-commerce.

❑ E-commerce is the complete set of processes and systems that support conducting business electronically using the Internet or other private networks.

❑ The goals of e-commerce are business driven and include

   ❑ Increased market share

   ❑ Increased efficiency and accuracy through automation of business processes

   ❑ Reduced time to market when new products and services are introduced

   ❑ Reduced operating costs

   ❑ Improved profit margins through automated supply chain management

   ❑ Improved customer service and support

   ❑ Instant communication with consumers and trading partners

   ❑ Better forecasting of customer needs and demands

❑ The e-commerce field includes the disciplines of computing, telecommunications, networking, security, multimedia, database management, EDI/EFT, and software development.

❑ On the business side, e-commerce includes core business processes: marketing, sales, advertising, procurement, purchasing, billing and payment, supply chain management, and the like.

❑ The legal side of e-commerce involves intellectual property, privacy rights to information, taxation, and other governmental regulations.

❑ There are two forms of Internet commerce: business-to-consumer (B2C) and business-to-business (B2B) electronic commerce.

❑ B2C and B2B are based on open standards and are likely to include both vendor-neutral and proprietary technologies.

❑ B2C e-commerce is based on transactions conducted between a consumer and a business.

❑ B2C transactions are conducted over the Internet using electronic storefronts and e-catalogs.

❑ B2B is based on transactions exchanged between business and trading partners.

❑ Electronic Data Interchange (EDI) is a process and standard for the electronic exchange of data across computer networks.

❑ EDI is the process that allows electronic funds transfers (EFT) between accounts. It was first widely used in telephone banking and automatic teller machine applications.

❑ EDI is becoming a fundamental component of B2B electronic commerce between trading partners.

❑ A great advantage of EDI is that once the data is in an electronic format, it is easily transferred across the supply chain.

❑ Open Buying on the Internet (OBI) is a vendor-neutral standard that has emerged for electronic catalog systems.

❑ Applications of smart cards include digital currency, digital certificates for hardware-assisted encryption systems, or storage of important information such as health records.

❑ Electronic money is also referred to as digital cash and is a PC-based electronic payment method that is integrated into Web browser software.

❑ At some point, digital cash may replace credit cards for low-price transactions such as a newspaper issue or game play. CyberCash is a major player in this space.

❑ Credit card transactions over the Internet involve the transmission of encrypted data containing credit card information, such as the number and expiration date, as well as privacy information about the purchaser.

❑ Electronic checks (e-checks) are a payment system for making payments over computer networks. A digital version of a check is presented to a merchant over the Web. One of the leading vendors is CheckFree.

❑ Customer relationship management enables customers to engage with a business using the most effective service delivery channel, whether it is self-service over the Web or a traditional customer service call center.

❑ In an e-business world, self-service is critical.

❑ Many functions—such as expense report reimbursement, purchasing, human resources, and travel—can be moved to a self-service model in which those directly involved in the transaction initiate the processing activity through a Web browser on a corporate intranet.

❑ Web call back is a relatively new technology that further enhances CRM by allowing your customers to click a link on your e-commerce site and, within seconds, speak with a customer service representative.

❑ Internet marketing allows companies to personalize their marketing messages on the basis of various needs of specific customers.

❑ A customer profile can be created for each user based on purchases, cancellations and returns, and customer service calls.

❑ Web tools for marketing and sales include search engines, directories, list servers to send targeted e-mail and newsletters, and Web banner advertising.

SELF TEST

1. You are designing an e-commerce site. Two of your goals are to personalize the experience for end users, and to make it easy for them to make return visits to your Web site without having to log in each time they visit. Which technique(s) should you use?

   A. Use a client-pull model to automate the login process.

   B. Use cookies to store user information.

   C. Use the <META> tag to create a password field.

   D. All of the above.

2. A cookies is best described as

   A. An HTTP header that consists of a text-string

   B. An encrypted file saved to your local hard disk

   C. A tool for maintaining state information about a user visit to your site

   D. All of the above

3. As part of your e-commerce site security policy, you want to provide prompts every 15 minutes to your customers informing them they will be logged off if there isn't any online activity. What is the correct method(s) for accomplishing this goal?

   A. Use client-pull statements in Web pages.

   B. Use server-pull statements in Web pages.

   C. Use server-push technologies.

   D. A and C.

4. Which of the following statement(s) is true about list servers?

   A. List servers parse e-mail messages looking for text patterns.

   B. List servers are responsible for the management and distribution of mailing lists.

   C. List servers are used to send Web banner ads.

   D. All of the above.

5. Examples of popular list server(s) include

   A. LISTING SERVICE

   B. Minor Demo

   C. LISTSERVE

   D. Mailerdomo

6. Some of the applications of push technology include

   A. Relational database technology

   B. Web site portals that update news and information at preset intervals

   C. A B2B solution tool for encrypting data

   D. All of the above

7. Your company has decided to enter the Internet Age by developing a secure

intranet site for use by employees. What are the key features an intranet will provide your organization?

A. B2B commerce between your organization and its trading partners

B. Online publishing and sharing of documents and files

C. Groupware applications such as calendars and online directories

D. Access to the World Wide Web

8. You have successfully launched a B2C e-commerce site. The management team decides next to build a B2B extranet with your suppliers and trading partners. Which of the following statement(s) is true?

A. Extranets are derived from Internet-based technologies and standards.

B. Extranets enable secure communications to link your supply chain.

C. Extranets enable customers to create their own HTML pages.

D. All of the above.

9. Building an e-commerce storefront requires technical expertise and business expertise. Which of the following describe(s) the business goals for Internet-based commerce?

A. Increased market share, reduced costs, increased profit margins

B. Reduced time to market when new products and services are introduced

C. Increased market share at the cost of decreased efficiency and accuracy of transactions

D. Instant communications with customers and clients

10. You have been asked by the CEO to brief the sales department on the differences between B2C and B2B e-commerce. Which of the following statement(s) is true?

A. E-commerce and e-business systems are based on closed proprietary standards.

B. E-business emphasizes trading between partners in the supply chain.

C. E-commerce is based on transactions between a consumer and a business.

D. Both B2C and B2B Internet commerce are based on the same Internet standards.

11. You are implementing a B2B link between your company and its distributors. You have decided to use an EDI solution to match your business partner systems. Which statement(s) is true about EDI?

A. EDI has been widely used for Electronic Funds Transfers between banks.

B. EDI can be costly and complex to implement.

C. EDI is a process and a standard for the electronic exchange of data across networks.

D. All of the above.

12. Your company is designing its second-generation e-commerce platform. The CEO has suggested moving toward an online catalog system (e-catalogs) and asks you to explain the main benefits.

    A. E-catalogs are online versions of printed catalogs that are much easier to update.

    B. E-catalogs are useful only for B2C e-commerce situations.

    C. Electronic malls can be created to support multiple e-catalog merchants.

    D. E-catalog systems support online shopping, ordering, and payment.

13. Merchant systems include which of the following types of storefronts?

    A. Secure EDI

    B. Electronic malls, which are collections of online catalogs from different merchants

    C. OBI with embedded encryption

    D. Stand-alone Web sites built for the explicit purpose of B2C e-commerce

14. Prioritizing CRM is vital to being a successful e-business. What are some of the benefits of Web-based CRM solutions?

    A. CRM identifies, develops, and retains your best and most profitable customers.

    B. With CRM, customer data becomes accessible and consistent across the entire enterprise.

    C. CRM solutions are ideal for creating cross-selling products to your customers.

    D. All of the above.

15. Part of a comprehensive CRM solution includes building in customer self-service features. Which of the following applications lend themselves to self-service?

    A. Technical support and help desk functions

    B. Planning business travel, ordering supplies, and managing medical benefits

    C. Creating secure e-business applications

    D. All of the above.

16. You are a software manufacturer and you have just implemented an off-the-shelf CRM solution for your e-commerce site. You have heard about Web call back (WCB) and would like to integrate this into your CRM solution, and you need to justify it from a business perspective. Which of the following statement(s) is true?

    A. WCB is a client-side CGI technology.

    B. WCB is a programming function used to invoke subroutines.

    C. WCB lets your customers click a link to immediately speak with a customer agent.

    D. WCB is a middleware client/server technology.

17. You are the Webmaster in your company. The marketing department has come to you asking for suggestions on how your company can market its products on the Internet, and you give them some suggestions. Which of the following statements are accurate?

    A. Targeted e-mail advertising is effective for alerting customers to upcoming sales.

    B. Banner ads on high-profile Web sites are an excellent way to attract new customers.

    C. Personalize the user experience to increase repeat business to your e-commerce site.

    D. Your company should list itself in search engines and online directories.

18. Your marketing department has decided to take up your suggestion and list your e-commerce site in popular search engines and directories, such as Yahoo! and Excite. What techniques can you use to rank high when a user queries on keywords that are related to your products?

    A. License use of keywords that are close matches to your products or services.

    B. Use cookies to increase hit counts.

    C. Use descriptive and precise keywords in your <TITLE> and <META> statements.

    D. All of the above.

19. A recent report by a well-respected Internet marketing group has identified five trends that are critical to an e-commerce site. Which of the following apply?

    A. Personalization, instant order fulfillment, custom pricing

    B. Personalization, instant order fulfillment, proprietary technology

    C. Personal intelligent shopping agents and wireless e-commerce connectivity

    D. Wireless e-commerce connectivity and supply-chain management

SELF TEST ANSWERS

1. **B** is correct.

   A, **C**, and **D** are incorrect. Client pull does not allow you to create an automatic login process. The <META> tag is used to create a pull statement.

2. **D** is correct.

3. **D** is correct.

   B is incorrect, because server pull is not a valid technology.

4. **B** is correct.

   A is incorrect, because search engines are used to parse e-mail messages and look for keywords. **C** is wrong, because banner ads are written in HTML for Web sites.

5. **C** is correct and is the most popular list server product.

   A, **B**, and **D** are fictitious products.

6. **B** is correct.

   A is incorrect, because push is not a database technology. **C** is incorrect, because push technology is not used for data encryption. Data-encryption technologies include secure socket layer, public and private key encryption, and HTTPS.

7. **B** and **C** are correct.

   A is incorrect, because intranets are for internal use. Extranets are used to link your organization with trading partners. **D** is incorrect, because intranets do not provide Web access without a gateway or Internet connection from a service provider.

8. **A** and **B** are correct.

   C is incorrect, because the purpose of extranets is to provide supply-chain management, not to provide Web space for HTML pages.

9. **A**, **B**, and **D** are correct.

   C is incorrect, because the goals of e-commerce are to increase market share while at the same time improve the efficiency and accuracy of transactions.

10. **B**, **C**, and **D** are correct.

    A is incorrect, because both e-commerce and e-business systems are built using open industry standards.

11. **D** is correct.

12. **A, C,** and **D** are correct.
    B is incorrect; e-catalogs are being used to facilitate transactions between trading partners using OBI.

13. **B** and **D** are correct.
    A and **C** are incorrect, because EDI and OBI are B2B technologies, not merchant systems.

14. **D** is correct.

15. **A** and **B** are correct.
    C is incorrect, because application development is not a self-service function performed by your customers.

16. **C** is correct.
    A and **B** are incorrect, because WCB is not a client-side CGI technology or a programming function. **D** is incorrect, because WCB is not a middleware client/server technology.

17. **A, B, C,** and **D** are all correct.

18. **A** and **C** are correct.
    B is incorrect, because cookies do not increase hit counts with search engines.

19. **A** and **C** are correct.
    B is incorrect, because proprietary technology will prevent many users and customers from accessing your Web site. **D** is incorrect, because supply-chain management is aimed at B2B, not a B2C market.

A

About the CD

Thís CD-ROM contains a browser-based testing product, the *Personal Testing Center*. the *Personal Testing Center* is easy to install on any Windows 95/98/NT computer.

Installing the Personal Testing Center

Double-clicking on the setup.html file on the CD will cycle you through an introductory page on the *Test Yourself* software. On the second page, you will have to read and accept the license agreement. Once you have read the agreement, click the Agree icon and you will be brought to the *Personal Testing Center's* main page.

On the main page, you will find links to the *Personal Testing Center*, to the electronic version of the book, and to other resources you may find helpful. Click the first link to the *Personal Testing Center* and you will be brought to the Quick Start page. Here you can choose to run the Personal Testing Center from the CD or install it to your hard drive.

Installing the *Personal Testing Center* to your hard drive is an easy process. Click the Install to Hard Drive icon and the procedure will start for you. An instructional box will appear and walk you through the remainder of the installation. If installed to the hard drive, the Personal Testing Center program group will be created in the Start Programs folder.

Should you wish to run the software from the CD-ROM, the steps are the same as above until you reach the point at which you would select the Install to Hard Drive icon. Here, select Run from CD icon and the exam will automatically begin.

To uninstall the program from your hard disk, use the add/remove programs feature in your Windows Control Panel. InstallShield will run Uninstall.

Test Type Choices

With the *Personal Testing Center*, you have three options in which to run the program: Live, Practice, and Review. Each test type will draw from a pool of over 280 potential questions. Your choice of test type will depend on whether you would like to simulate an actual i-Net+ certification exam, receive instant feedback on your answer choices, or review concepts using the testing simulator. Note that selecting the Full Screen icon on Internet Explorer's standard toolbar gives you the best display of the *Personal Testing Center.*

Live

The Live timed test type is meant to reflect the actual exam as closely as possible. You will have 120 minutes in which to complete the exam. You will have the option to skip questions and return to them later, move to the previous question, or end the exam. Once the timer has expired, you will automatically go to the scoring page to review your test results.

Managing Windows

The testing application runs inside an Internet Explorer 4.0 or 5.0 browser window. We recommend that you use the full-screen view to minimize the amount of text scrolling you need to do. However, the application will initiate a second iteration of the browser when you link to an Answer in Depth or a Review Graphic. If you are running in full-screen view, the second iteration of the browser will be covered by the first. You can toggle between the two windows with ALT-TAB, you can click your taskbar to maximize the second window, or you can get out of full-screen mode and arrange the two windows so they are both visible on the screen at the same time. The application will not initiate more than two browser windows, so you aren't left with hundreds of open windows for each Answer in Depth or Review Graphic that you view.

Saving Scores as Cookies

Your exam score is stored as a browser cookie. If you've configured your browser to accept cookies, your score will be stored in a cookie named History. If you don't accept cookies, you cannot permanently save your scores. If you delete the History cookie, the scores will be deleted permanently.

Using the Browser Buttons

The test application runs inside the Internet Explorer 4.0 browser. You should navigate from screen to screen by using the application's buttons, not the browser's buttons.

JavaScript Errors

If you encounter a JavaScript error, you should be able to proceed within the application. If you cannot, shut down your Internet Explorer 4.0 browser session and relaunch the testing application.

Practice

When choosing the Practice exam type, you have the option of receiving instant feedback as to whether your selected answer is correct. The questions will be presented to you in numerical order, and you will see every question in the available question pool for each section you chose to be tested on.

As with the Live exam type, you have the option of continuing through the entire exam without seeing the correct answer for each question. The number of questions you answered correctly, along with the percentage of correct answers, will be displayed during the postexam summary report. Once you have answered a question, click the Answer icon to display the correct answer.

You have the option of ending the Practice exam at any time, but your postexam summary screen may reflect an incorrect percentage based on the number of questions you failed to answer. Questions that are skipped are counted as incorrect answers on the postexam summary screen.

Review

During the Review exam type, you will be presented with questions similar to both the Live and Practice exam types. However, the Answer icon is not present, as every question will have the correct answer posted near the bottom of the screen. You have the option of answering the question without looking at the correct answer. In the Review exam type, you can also return to previous questions and skip to the next question, as well as end the exam by clicking the Stop icon.

The Review exam type is recommended when you have already completed the Live exam type once or twice, and would now like to determine which questions you answered correctly.

Questions with Answers

For the Practice and Review exam types, you will have the option of clicking a hyperlink titled Answers in Depth, which will present relevant study material aimed at exposing the logic behind the answer in a separate browser window. By having two browsers open (one for the test engine and one for the review information), you can quickly alternate between the two windows while keeping your place in the exam. You will find that additional windows are not generated as you follow hyperlinks throughout the test engine.

Scoring

The *Personal Testing Center* postexam summary screen, called Benchmark Yourself, displays the results for each section you chose to be tested on, including a bar graph similar to the real exam, which displays the percentage of correct answers. You can compare your percentage to the actual passing percentage for each section. The percentage displayed on the postexam summary screen is not the actual percentage required to pass the exam. You'll see the number of questions you answered correctly compared to the total number of questions you were tested on. If you chose to skip a question, it will be marked as incorrect. Ending the exam by clicking the End button with questions still unanswered lowers your percentage, as these questions will be marked as incorrect.

Clicking the End button and then the Home button allows you to choose another exam type, or test yourself on another section.

i-Net+ ™

COMPUTING TECHNOLOGY INDUSTRY ASSOCIATION®

B

About the Web Site

At Access.Globalknowledge, the premier online information source for IT professionals (http://access.globalknowledge.com), you'll enter a Global Knowledge information portal designed to inform, educate, and update visitors on issues regarding IT and IT education.

Get *What* You Want *When* You Want It

At the Access.Globalknowledge site, you can

- Choose personalized technology articles related to your interests. Access a new article, review, or tutorial regularly throughout the week, customized to what you want to see.

- Continue your education, in between Global courses, by taking advantage of chat sessions with other users or instructors. Get the tips, tricks, and advice that you need today!

- Make your point in the Access.Globalknowledge community with threaded discussion groups related to technologies and certification.

- Get instant course information at your fingertips. Customized course calendars show you the courses you want, when and where you want them.

- Obtain the resources you need with online tools, trivia, skills assessment and more!

All this and more is available now on the Web at
http://access.globalknowledge.com
Visit today!

Glossary

Acceptable Use Policy (AUP)   AUP (as designed by the NSF) determined exactly how the Internet could be used by organizations and businesses.

Access control   Determination of who and what is allowed into an operating system or network. Access control involves the ability to grant or deny system resources to authenticated users.

Access Control List (ACL)   An ACL is a special file or series of values that help determine the level of access a user has to a specific resource. An operating system refers to these lists to control access to system resources. An ACL regulates a user's ability to use either an operating system, or the objects served by an operating system.

ACL   *See* Access Control List.

Active caching   Active caching takes passive caching as a foundation and builds upon it with increased performance and enhanced configuration options. Active caching helps maintain higher levels of client performance: when clients can access pages that are stored in a caching server, the transfer speed is increased, and overall session latency is reduced.

Active hub   An active hub performs in much the same way as a passive hub, but active hubs will also repeat (boost the signal of) the information. This is beneficial for use with long network cables, which can experience a decrease in signal strength over distance (called *signal attenuation*).

Active Server Page (ASP)   An ASP can be an ordinary HTML page that includes one or more scripts that are processed on the Web server before the page is sent to the user. An ASP is somewhat similar to CGI applications in that they both involve programs that run on the server.

Active Server Page (ASP) filter   This file-mapped filter executes script code stored in any file with an .asp extension.

Address Resolution Protocol (ARP) ARP is used to obtain the hardware addresses of hosts located on the same physical network. With the ARP utility, you can find out the MAC (Media Access Channel) address of all of the machines that your computer knows about. Using ARP you can see what MAC addresses have what IP addresses.

ADSL *See* Asymmetric DSL.

Advanced Encryption Standard (AES) Although no encryption algorithm has been chosen as of this writing, this standard is sponsored by the U. S. government as a replacement for DES. RC6, MARS, Rijndael, Serpent, and Twofish are all finalists for this standard.

Advanced Research Projects Agency (ARPA) ARPA is a U.S. government agency formed by the Eisenhower administration in 1957 with the purpose of conducting scientific research and developing advanced technologies for the U.S. military. One of ARPA's research areas was developing a large-scale computer network that could survive a serious nuclear attack. This network, ARPAnet, was to ensure reliable communications between individual computers (nodes), even in the event of massive failure. The architecture of ARPAnet provided the foundation for the Internet as we know it today.

AES *See* Advanced Encryption Standard.

All-in-one (universal) clients This type of client software enables users to access Web pages, FTP sites, Telnet sites, e-mail, and more through a single application. Rather than having several applications running at once, you can access diverse Internet services through a single program or suite of programs.

Analog modems Analog modems connect to phone lines through a regular phone jack, using an RJ-11 connector (the same one the phone uses). Analog modems use the same frequency band on the phone line (0–4 kHz) as voice communications, which prevents their concurrent use of the line.

AND operator   The AND operator between two words or other values means you are searching for documents that match both the search items, not just one of them.

Anti-virus software   Anti-virus software searches for specific viruses, worms, and trojans, as well as other suspect executables. This type of software identifies exactly how a program behaves, and then works to inform you about the problem and effect repairs, if possible. Sometimes, an anti-virus program can only identify problems, rather than fix them. This may be because the nature of the infection is so advanced, or because an actual fix was not yet known when the vendor released the anti-virus program.

API   *See* Application Program Interface.

Application gateways   *See* Application-level firewall.

Application layer   Renders information for use with specific applications, such as FTP, HTTP, and so forth.

Application Program Interface (API)   API is the code that instructs applications to interact with the operating system by working with programming code that enables the application request services and access functionality provided by the system. This interface is the set of commands that an application uses to request and carry out lower-level services performed by a computer's operating system, or access functionality of another program.

Application-level firewall   Application-level firewalls (also called *application gateways*) use additional software, called a *proxy*, to filter incoming or outgoing data.

Application-level gateway   An application-level gateway operates at the application layer of the OSI/RM. This firewall is arguably the most thorough, because it not only can determine source and destination IP address, but it also can inspect actual data inside the packet. However, application-level gateways tend to be slower than packet filters.

ARP *See* Address Resolution Protocol.

ARPA *See* Advanced Research Projects Agency.

ARPAnet *See* Advanced Research Projects Agency.

AS *See* Autonomous System.

ASP *See* Active Server Page.

Asymmetric DSL An emerging technology developed by the telephone companies that transmit data at 1.5 Mbps to 9 Mbps over standard copper telephone wires and twisted-pair cabling.

Asymmetric encryption This form of encryption is more complex and involves the use of a key pair. This form of encryption is much more secure. Asymmetric algorithms include ElGamal and RSA. Asymmetric encryption uses a key pair. This key pair is uniquely and mathematically related, but it is just about impossible to take advantage of this relationship.

Asynchronous Transfer Mode (ATM) A transmission protocol that segments user traffic into small, fixed size cells. Cells are transmitted to their destination, where the original traffic is re-assembled. During transmission, cells from different users are intermixed asynchronously to maximize utilization of network resources.

ATM *See* Asynchronous Transfer Mode.

Attributes Attributes allow you to control features or characteristics of a table and caption. Attributes give you the ability to control such things as spacing, the appearance of your table, and the positioning of caption text.

Audio Video Interleave files (AVIs) These movie files may contain both audio and video, and must be fully downloaded before they can be played. They are unlike RealMedia files, which provide a link to the actual file on the Web server. The benefit of having to download the entire file is that you can then play them at any time, and do not need to connect to the Internet while doing so. The quality of AVI files is similar to MPEG-1.

Auditing   Auditing is the ability to determine who has accessed a system and when.

AUP   *See* Acceptable Use Policy.

Authentication   Authentication is the ability to verify the identity of a particular person, network host, or system process. When authenticating users across the Internet, you generally have to use encryption in one way or another. *See also* Strong authentication.

Autonomous System (AS)   A service provider within a NAP.

AVIs   *See* Audio Video Interleave files.

B2C   *See* Business to Consumer.

Back door   A back door is a related concern to system bugs. The chief difference between a system bug and a system back door is that a system bug is generally considered to be a mistake or oversight on the part of the programmer. A back door, on the other hand, is the result of intent. The most common example of a back door is an unknown username and password that exists on the system.

Backbone   The high-speed infrastructure that connects the individual networks on the Internet. A backbone is a high-speed conduit for data to which hundreds and even thousands of other smaller networks are connected. Each backbone is operated and maintained by the organization that owns it.

Back-end processing   Refers to the integration between the e-catalog Web-based interface and the back-end systems that it is connected to, including databases, payment systems, and legacy information systems.

BackWeb   BackWeb provides software for e-business solutions that solve the problem of accessing timely, accurate, critical information delivery across corporate networks and the Internet.

Basic Rate Interface (BRI)   One-level service that is designed for home and small business users. BRI consists of two 64-Kbps bearer channels (or B channels) and one 16 Kbps delta channel (or D channel). The B channel is used for transmitting and receiving data and voice, and the D channel is used to send and receive information used for control and signaling. In North America, PRI is made up of 23 B channels and one 64 Kbps D channel.

BinHex   BinHex is a popular encoding method that is used to convert data from binary to ASCII. Binary is a common format for representing data, especially in executable programs, or files that use numeric data. ASCII uses numbers to represent characters. In ASCII, each letter, number, and character on a keyboard is represented as a number between 0 and 127. Because different platforms use ASCII, most computers and applications on the market can understand this format.

Biometrics   Biometrics is the study of authentication via physical traits, including retinal scans, fingerprints, and voice identification.

Bitmaps (BMPs)   *See* Raster graphics.

Body tags   The <BODY> ... </BODY> tags are used to define the bulk of your Web page's content. Like the body of a paragraph, it contains most of the information you want to relay to your page's reader. Text written between the <BODY> and </BODY> tags will display in the main window of a Web browser.

Boolean operators   Boolean statements are composed of Boolean operators such as AND, OR, and NOT. With these operators you can articulate your search to whatever degree is necessary by including and excluding relative subjects.

Boolean queries   Boolean queries tend to be used in simple queries to eliminate a certain property or information from a result set.

Boolean searches   Boolean searches are simply based upon evaluating a statement or expression for true or false. Boolean-based searches reflect logic that is typically used in programming languages, which is great for programmers, but can be too complicated for normal users.

Boot sector virus   The most common type, this virus infects the master boot record of a floppy or hard disk. Once the disk is activated, the virus goes into memory. If a user places an infected floppy disk into an uninfected system, the virus will then infect the uninfected system.

BRI   *See* Basic Rate Interface.

Bridge   A bridge can be used to maintain connectivity between the two (or more) network segments or Local Area Networks (LANs).

Buffer overflow   Whenever a programmer creates a program using C, C++, or many other languages, he or she has to create a buffer to hold information used by the program. Some of this information includes variables used by the programs. The programmer generally assigns a default size to this buffer, because he or she only expects variables of a certain size to go into the buffer. However, it is possible for a hacker to manipulate the program so that it sends information into the buffer that is too large. The result is that the buffer gets overcrowded and overflows its limits.

Bulleted lists   *See* Unordered lists.

Business logic   Refers to the functionality of the front-end systems including online search capability; online secure payment infrastructure; and online customer service, such as help-desk and customer relationship management.

Business to Consumer (B2C) e-commerce   B2C e-commerce is based on transactions conducted between a consumer and a business. B2C commerce is characterized by low-volume transactions (e.g., ordering a book or computer). This is quickly changing as more expensive items, such as automobiles, are being sold directly from the manufacturer to the consumer.

Button   A button is one of the most common elements you'll add to a form. When a button element is added to a form, it appears in the Web page as a 3-D Windows push button. The only attributes a button has are VALUE and NAME.

Byte-code   Byte-code is an abstraction of compiled code that serves as an instruction set.

C++   C++ is an object-oriented language that allows programmers to code in the style of everyday life, with interaction of one object to another. Each object has its own characteristics, properties, events, and methods of operation.

Caching   Caching is the process of storing requested objects at a network point closer to the client, at a location that will provide these objects for reuse as they are requested by additional clients. By doing so, we can reduce network utilization and client access times. *See also* Active caching; Distributed caching; File caching; Hierarchical caching; Parent sibling caching; Passive caching; Proxy caching; Single-server caching.

Caching Array Protocol (CARP)   The Caching Array Protocol (CARP) provides an alternative method to ICP to coordinate multiple caching servers. Instead of querying neighbor caches, participating CARP servers use an algorithm to label each server. This algorithm or hash provides for a deterministic way to determine the location of a requested object.

Call Back   *See* World Wide Web Call Back.

Caption tags   The <CAPTION>...</CAPTION> tags can be used to create a caption for your table. Captions are lines of text that often appear below the table, and tell the reader what information the table contains. This allows a person viewing the table to immediately recognize what data the table holds, without having to read surrounding paragraphs.

CARP   *See* Caching Array Protocol.

Carrier Sense Multiple Access/Collision Avoidance (CSMA/CA)   This type of access method is similar to CSMA/CD, except that after a collision has occurred on the network, one computer will first send out a "signal" to warn other computers that it is about to send a packet. This access method is more organized than CSMA/CD, so it may be more suitable for use on networks with a high number of Internet accesses or hits.

Carrier Sense Multiple Access/Collision Detection (CSMA/CD)   CSMA/CD is a type of first-come, first-served access method by which computers on the network can send packets of information at any time. If a collision between two or more computers occurs, each will resend its packet after a random amount of time.

Cascading style sheet   A cascading style sheet sets the style of a Web page by using multiple style sheets and/or files, and displaying them in a specific order.

Castanet   Castanet was a push technology used to distribute applications, including software code, content, and services, to any endpoint over a network, and to manage and maintain these applications remotely.

CERN   *See* Conseil European pour la Recherche Nucleaire.

CERT   *See* Computer Emergency Response Team.

Certificate   Certificates allow for enhanced authentication, as well as encryption. Once a Web server has a certificate, you can apply this certificate to certain directories. Once a user requests a specific object (i.e., a file, directory, or site), the server will then begin an SSL session before it sends information. Once a client begins an SSL session, he or she can check a server's certificate.

CGI   *See* Common Gateway Interface.

Channels   Channels are links to content that can be accessed through RealPlayer.

Check boxes   Check boxes are another common element in forms. When viewed through a Browser, the check box element appears as a square. When you click it, the check box will appear checked. The text appearing beside a check box is used to indicate choices for the user. When multiple check boxes appear on a form, the user can choose one or more of the check boxes.

CICS   *See* Customer Information Control System.

Circuit-level firewall   A circuit-level firewall (circuit gateway) is a type of application-based firewall that uses the same rules and principles as an application-level firewall described previously. The circuit-level firewall's security features are applied at startup; and, once an Internet connection has been made, the connection stays open and data packets are not individually examined and screened.

Circuit-level gateway   The chief benefit of this type of firewall is network address translation (NAT), which is the ability to use reserved IP addresses internally, and Internet-capable addresses externally. Circuit-level gateways operate at the transport layer of the OSI/RM. Circuit-level gateways are quicker than application-level gateways, although not as quick as packet-filtering firewalls. The drawback to a circuit-level gateway is that you must modify all software in order for it to communicate with the firewall. This can be very costly and prohibitive.

Circuit-switching network   A circuit-switching network, such as those run by telephone companies, uses dedicated connections; but a packet-switching protocol uses various programs, algorithms, and network lines to get information from the source to its destination any way it can.

Class A networks   Class A networks are identified by the fact that the first octet is used for network addressing, and the last three octets are used to identify the host. In decimal form, all IP addresses from 1–127.*x.x.x* are Class A networks.

Class B networks   Class B networks are identified by the fact that the first two octets are used for network addressing, and the last two octets are used to identify the host. In decimal form, all IP addresses from 128–192.*x.x* are Class B networks.

Class C networks   Class C networks are identified by the fact that the first three octets are used for network addressing, and the last octet is used to identify the host. In decimal form, all IP addresses from 193–223.*x* are Class C networks.

Client cache   The client cache stores these objects locally on the client computer, within memory and in an allocated section of hard disk space. The client cache is designed to reduce the load times for objects that are static in nature, or dynamic objects that have not changed since the client's last visit.

Clusters   Clusters are groups of systems linked or chained together that are used in the caching of information for a company or ISP. By having a cluster of cache servers you can reduce bandwidth while increasing production time of the user because the user does not have to wait for the page to be retrieved from the Internet.

CNAME   Allows you to provide an alternative name to a host already named in the DNS file.

Coaxial (coax) cable   This is a more popular choice (than twisted-pair cabling) when long distance or signal interference is an issue. Coax cable looks just like the cable used for cable TV, and uses the same BNC connector. Coax cable is able to transmit at 10 Mbps or 100 Mbps.

Common Gateway Interface (CGI)   Common Gateway Interface, or CGI, defines the communication link between the Web server and Web applications. CGI gives network or Internet access to specific programs of your choice.

Compiled program   A compiled program is converted into language that the computer can understand.

Compound queries   Individual queries can be combined to form a compound query. This allows for separate operators to be combined, retrieving the most accurate result set.

Computer Emergency Response Team (CERT)   CERT is dedicated to helping all computer users maintain security. It is not focused on any one platform. You can gain much information about past hacker attacks, including ways to protect yourself against them. You can learn more about CERT at http://www.cert.org.

Congestion   Congestion is a term generally used to refer to routers. When a router gets too busy breaking up packets and sending them off to other routers, it is said to be congested.

Conseil European pour la Recherche Nucleaire (CERN)
CERN (or, the European Laboratory for Particle Physics) is the organization based in Switzerland where the World Wide Web was started. Much of the support for the HyperText Transfer Protocol (HTTP) and the Web libraries has its origins at CERN.

Content cache server   A content cache server stores the Web pages most frequently accessed by the network users. This speeds up the return of Web pages to clients' browsers because they come from a local server rather than the Internet.

Cookie   A cookie (also known as a *Web cookie*) is a simple piece of information sent in the HTTP header during a Web transaction between a Web server and a browser. You can transmit (i.e., set) cookies using a scripting language, such as JavaScript or VBScript. The primary use of cookies is to maintain state. HTTP sessions generally "time out" quickly. In other words, the Web server normally drops the TCP connection shortly after a Web page has finished loading. Without cookies, any information entered by a user would be lost as soon as he goes to another site. If the server sets a cookie, however, this cookie store has information created during the session. The activity of using cookies to track user activity has prompted some to argue that cookie use can constitute an invasion of privacy. Although this notion is a bit extreme, you should note that Web sites do, in fact, track users all of the time. Tracking helps them tailor their site to customer interests, plan advertising campaigns, and even generate revenue through selling user profiles.

Copyright infringement   A violation of the exclusive rights of a copyright owner. Copyright owners can recover actual or, in some cases, statutory damages for a copyright infringement. Furthermore, courts have the power to issue injunctions to prevent or restrain copyright infringement and to order the impoundment and destruction of infringing copies.

Copyright law   Copyright law protects original works of authorship. Copyright is a form of legal protection provided by the laws of the United States (Title 17, U.S. Code) to the authors of "original works of authorship," including literary, dramatic, musical, artistic, and certain other intellectual works. This protection is available to both published and unpublished works. Since copyright law is federal it does not vary from state to state.

Country-level domain   The "int" domain is no longer common. In its place are the extremely common country codes.

Crawling   The process of crawling is the spider visiting your site, going through every page that is accessible via a hyperlink, and recording that information back to a database.

CRC   *See* Cyclic Redundancy Check.

Cross-browser coding   Cross-browser coding can be used to create HTML documents or parts of HTML documents that will run only in specific browsers. In other words, if users are viewing your Web page with

Netscape Navigator, they will see one version of your page. Users viewing with Internet Explorer will see another version, while users with other browsers will see yet another version of your Web page. Such cross-browser coding can be added to your HTML document using any one of a number of scripting languages, such as JavaScript or VBScript.

CSMA/CA   *See* Carrier Sense Multiple Access/Collision Avoidance.

CSMA/CD   *See* Carrier Sense Multiple Access/Collision Detection.

Customer Information Control System (CICS)   A monitor that controls interactions between users and applications; it also provides terminal routing, transaction logging, and password security.

Cyclic Redundancy Check (CRC)   An automatic error-checking method used by Microsoft's Disk Operating System (MS-DOS) when writing data to a hard or floppy disk in its drive mechanism. Later, upon reading, the same error check is conducted and the results of the two checks are compared to ensure the data has not been altered.

Daemon   A UNIX process designed to handle a specialized function (such as handling Internet server requests) and requiring a limited user interface.

Data confidentiality   The use of encryption to make sure that information remains secret.

Data Encryption Standard (DES)   A private key encryption scheme developed by IBM in the 1970s that has been adopted by NIST as the U.S. government standard.

Datalink layer   This layer maps physical addresses to network addresses. Contains two sublayers: Media Access Control (MAC) and Logical Link Control (LLC). The MAC layer provides hardware addresses, whereas the LLC is responsible for how NIC drivers operate.

Default gateway   A default gateway is a computer or other hardware that will forward messages and data to another network. If data is meant for a computer on a remote network, it is sent to the default gateway and forwarded from there. The way that your computer knows what computer is the gateway is by configuring it with the IP address of the default gateway.

DeMilitarized Zone (DMZ)   It is possible to combine firewall types to create a coordinated solution. You can place a packet-filtering firewall (e.g., a packet filter) on both sides of a network. This "buffer" network is called a DMZ.

Denial Of Service (DOS)   A DOS attack crashes a server, or specific processes and systems that reside on a server. Sometimes, a hacker wishes to conduct a DOS attack against a server out of pure malice. Many beginning hackers enjoy the simple sense of achievement they get when they bring down their first host.

DES   *See* Data Encryption Standard. *See also* Triple DES.

Desktop computers   *See* Personal computers.

DHCP   *See* Dynamic Host Configuration Protocol.

DHTML   *See* Dynamic HyperText Markup Language.

Dial-Up Networking (DUN)   Where you configure settings used to connect to an ISP or a remote TCP/IP network.

Digital certificates   Digital certificates are the primary means of authenticating users, hosts, and servers. They use public key encryption, as well as one-way encryption. Using the information in a certificate, unknown parties can build trust with each other. Digital certificates involve the use of a trusted third party, called a Certificate Authority (CA). Arguably, the most popular CA is VeriSign.

Digital Signal (DS)   The Digital Signal (DS) standards provide the base for other standards, including the T and E carrier standards. The DS0 rate is 64 Kbps. The DS0 speed is fundamental for many other standards. This is because these other standards, such as the T and E rates, are multiples of 64 Kbps.

Digital signature   A digital signature is the electronic equivalent of your own, "real" signature that you use when signing a check. It provides proof of origin and data integrity.

Digital Subscriber Line (DSL)   DSL allows users to connect at speeds ranging from 512 Kbps to 8 Mbps. Theoretically, the technology provides speeds up to 8.448 Mbps (megabits per second), but typical connections are considerably lower than this. While POTS uses analog signals to transmit data, DSL uses high-bandwidth digital copper telephone lines for the transmission of data and voice. *See also* Asymmetric DSL, Symmetric DSL.

Directories   Directories organize information about sites into hierarchical lists, beginning with a topic, and descending through the layers of subtopics.

Directory path   The directory path is the name and directory path of the file on the server being requested by the browser (optional). The directory path is sometimes called the *path statement.*

Distributed caching   Distributed caching is much like proxy clusters. The idea is that you have several proxy servers working together to reduce the load of retrieving the information from the Internet. This also acts as a fault tolerance so that if one of the proxy servers goes offline, the others will automatically be able to respond to the requests.

DLL   *See* Dynamic Link Library.

DMZ   *See* Demilitarized Zone.

DNS   *See* Domain Name System.

Domain name The domain name specifies the address of a specific Web server to which the browser is connecting. Similar to a telephone number, it must be unique. The first part of the domain name is usually the name of the company, person, or organization. The second part, called the *extension*, comes largely from a set of conventions adopted by the Internet community. The control and management of domain names was passed from NSF to Network Solutions, Inc. Network Solutions has had a monopoly on the distribution of domain names until 1999 when the process was opened up to other companies.

Domain name server The domain name server is a dedicated computer at your ISP. This sometimes uses the acronym DNS.

Domain Name System (DNS) The system designed to assign and organize addresses is called the Domain Name System (DNS). The DNS, devised in the early 1970s, is still in use today. The DNS was designed to be more user friendly than IP numbers. Because every IP address has an equivalent domain name, any server on the Internet can be specified using its IP number or domain name.

Domains *See* Local domain; Remote domain.

DOS *See* Denial Of Service.

DS *See* Digital Signal.

DSL *See* Digital Subscriber Line.

Dual-home host firewalls In this setup, the proxy computer (called the *host*) is placed between the Internet and internal network, so there is no possible direct connection between Internet users and network users—all data must pass through the proxy server. The proxy server also acts as a router, so the regular network routing method must be disabled to use this architecture.

DUN *See* Dial-Up Networking.

Dynamic Host Configuration Protocol (DHCP) DHCP allows you to assign and configure a user's network settings dynamically as he or she logs in to your network. DHCP manages the allocation of IP addresses and eliminates many of the problems associated with manually configuring a client computer.

Dynamic HyperText Markup Language (DHTML) As its name suggests, it allows a Web page to be dynamically altered once it has been loaded. While HTML allows you to format and display elements of a Web page in a static or unchanging manner, DHTML allows you to change dynamically, display, and move various elements.

Dynamic Link Library (DLL) A collection of functions or a collection of programs that can be called upon by another program. The word "library" suggests that it can store a vast set of functions that can be "checked out" when they are needed. These functions are then stored in a file, usually with a .dll extension.

Dynamic linking Used for program functions that are not used often in your program or are not accessed constantly.

E1 The European standard of T1, called E1, contains higher bandwidth (2.048 Mbps) because it is supported by 32 DS-0's. Telephone companies often refer to T1's as DS-1's, where DS stands for Digital Signal.

E-business *See* Electronic business.

E-commerce *See* Electronic commerce.

Electronic business (e-business) E-business is about using Internet technologies to transform key business processes to capitalize on new business opportunities; strengthen relationships in the supply chain with customers, suppliers, business partners, and distributors; and become more efficient and, in the process, more profitable.

Electronic commerce (e-commerce)   The complete set of processes and systems that support conducting business electronically using the Internet or other private networks. E-commerce describes the business activities among consumers, vendors, distributors, suppliers, and intermediaries using computer networks such as the Internet.

Electronic Data Interchange (EDI)   EDI is a type of e-commerce technology that has been around for over 20 years. EDI is a process and standard for the electronic exchange of data across computer networks. EDI is the process that allows Electronic Funds Transfers (EFT) between accounts, and was first widely used in telephone banking and Automatic Teller Machine (ATM) applications.

Electronic mail (e-mail)   These are messages that can be sent and stored from one computer to another. Using a mail client, you can create messages, attach files to them, and transmit them over the Net. The message first goes to a mail server, and is then sent to the mail server where the receiving user's e-mail account is located. When the user connects to the mail server with his or her mail client, these messages are downloaded and can then be displayed through the mail client.

Electronic mail (e-mail) bombing   An e-mail bombing program generates a large number of e-mail messages, all of which contain large attachments. The result of such attacks is that they overload an account. Especially in slow network connections (less than 128 Kbps), this can effectively wipe out a user's e-mail account.

Electronic mail (e-mail) clients   E-mail clients are applications that enable you to send electronic messages to other users on your intranet or Internet. A number of e-mail clients are available on the market, including Eudora Pro, Outlook Express, and many others.

Electronic mail (e-mail) reflector   E-mail can be sent to individuals or groups of people. This is done through distribution lists and software called an e-mail reflector. This software contains a listing of users who are to receive e-mail. An e-mail message that is to be sent to those on the list is then sent to the e-mail reflector. By sending a message to an e-mail address that is assigned to the software itself, the e-mail reflector forwards a copy of the message to each person on the distribution list.

Electronic marketing (e-marketing)   E-marketing takes advantage of Web-based tools to enhance or broaden traditional marketing channels. Some of the functions that are easily handled include lead generation and lead qualification to consolidate and store leads and opportunities.

E-mail   *See* Electronic mail.

E-marketing   *See* Electronic marketing.

Encapsulated PostScript (EPS)   EPS is the file format used by PostScript to allow users to preview a PostScript font or image. PostScript files contain only the commands used to print a graphic or font. To display this font or image, an EPS file is used. Such an EPS file would contain the PostScript commands needed to print the image, and can contain a bitmapped representation, allowing the user to see what the font or image will look like. The EPS file may contain text, graphics, or both to display this representation.

Encryption   The use of algorithms (procedures and mathematical calculations written either by individuals or agencies) and protocols to scramble information so that users cannot engage in electronic eavesdropping or data tampering. Four levels exist: None, trivial, moderate, and strong. Some of the types are Rot13, DES, Triple DES, RSA, MD5, and SHA. *See also* Asymmetric encryption; Symmetric encryption.

Enterprise-grade proxy server   Enterprise-grade proxy servers, such as Linux servers with the ability to conduct proxying (called IP chaining), allow support for any protocol supported by TCP/IP. They generally do not install agent software on the clients. However, they do require software that is modified to support proxy servers.

EPS   *See* Encapsulated PostScript.

Ethernet bridges   When the modem connects to the computer's internal Ethernet network card, with 10–100 Mbps transfer rates, it is the only port on the computer capable of keeping up with the speed of the modem. For this reason, DSL modems are sometimes called Ethernet bridges.

eXtensible Markup Language (XML)   XML is a flexible way to define commonly used information formats. The format and the data itself may then be shared on the World Wide Web, in intranets, and even in desktop applications.

Extensions   *See* Plug-ins.

External Networks (Extranets)   An extranet involves establishing a secure network between two private networks over public lines. Generally, an extranet has the same elements as an intranet: each company is able to communicate via e-mail, and has the option of using Web sites to conduct transactions. The chief difference is that the companies communicate via encryption, which is usually enabled by two firewalls working together. An extranet provides LDAP services so that companies can exchange information quickly.

Extranets   *See* External Networks.

Fair Use Doctrine   Section 107 of the Copyright Act carves out a safe zone in which individuals can engage in the fair use of a copyrighted work and not violate the law. Specifically, Section 107 states that the fair use of a copyrighted work, including such use by reproduction in copies or by any other means specified by that section, for purposes such as criticism, comment, news reporting, teaching, scholarship, or research, is not an infringement of copyright.

FCS   *See* Frame Check Sequence.

Fiber-optic cable   This type of cable has no theoretical distance or speed limitations; and, because it transmits light instead of electrical signal, it is unaffected by electromagnetic interference. Fiber-optic cable is the most expensive type, and typically transmits at speeds of 100 Mbps to 2 Gbps.

File caching   Because FTP sessions tend to involve larger amounts of data than a typical HTTP session, benefits from caching FTP objects can be substantial. Using file caching for an FTP request in a large company can reduce request time and bandwidth dramatically.

Filename   The filename is the name of the document being requested by the Web browser. The filename is part of the directory path. The default filename when entering only the server name is usually index.htm or index.html.

File Transfer Protocol (FTP)   An Internet protocol allowing the exchange of files. FTP was developed to transfer files between computers on a TCP/IP network. A program enables the user to contact another computer on the Internet and exchange files.

File Transfer Protocol (FTP) clients   FTP clients are applications that make the FTP easy to use.

File virus   This type of virus attaches itself to specific files and activates once the file is put into use.

File-based database A file-based database is a database that has all of the resources needed to connect to the database located within the database itself. File-based databases do not require that you install some piece of software in order to access the data contained within them.

Firewall security Firewall security is software that protects the network from being accessed by other Internet users.

Firewalls A firewall is a security system that prevents outside users from accessing private network resources. Firewalls can be set up between segments on a large network, but are more commonly employed for security between a network and the Internet. Firewalls can also be used to restrict which Internet resources network users can access. A firewall filters all traffic that passes between your network and the outside world. No other way should exist to enter your network. Although a firewall often does not check access from a modem bank (i.e., a collection of modems that enables network access), it is still possible to use your firewall to check such access. *See also* Application-level firewall; Circuit-level firewall; Dual-home host firewalls; Packet-level firewall; Screened-host firewalls.

Fishwrap Fishwrap, under development at MIT since 1993, was one of the first experimental personalized newspaper projects.

Fixed work Fixed means a work is created to be "sufficiently permanent or stable to permit it to be perceived, reproduced, or otherwise communicated for a period of more than transitory duration."

Flash Flash, developed by Macromedia, Inc., is a method of creating graphic-intensive Web pages that are high performance at lower speeds. Flash files can be added to Web pages as a way of displaying animation, providing audio, and allowing interaction. They are extremely compact and stream from any Web server. It is a multimedia technology that exploits vector graphics.

Forwarder   *See* Forwarding server.

Forwarding server   Also called a *forwarder*, this type of server allows systems that cannot communicate with the root name servers on the Internet to still get information from a specific source. Pure forwarding servers do not keep their own zone databases, although it is common to have a server be both a primary and a forwarding server.

FQDN   *See* Fully Qualified Domain Name.

Frame Check Sequence (FCS)   A term corresponding to CRC; an error-checking protocol for linking modems.

Frame Relay   Frame Relay is a variable packet-size transport service. Frame Relay was originally designed to carry data and, therefore, uses a variable frame size. The specification allows frame sizes as large as 4096 octets. Frame Relay resides at Layer 2 in the OSI model. Frame Relay access (Layer 1 of the OSI model) may be provided over T1, E1, or ISDN digital carrier facilities.

Framing   Framing is an error-control procedure used to multiplex a logical data stream. In order to provide better data organization (between the bytes, so to speak), the signal is formatted using the framing process. A frame is a compilation of one byte from each of the 24 DS-0 timeslots, plus a framing bit. This makes each frame 193 bits.

FTP   *See* File Transfer Protocol.

Full-text index   A full-text index stores all the full-text words and their locations for a given table. A full-text catalog stores the full-text index of a database. The full-text service performs the full-text querying.

Fully Qualified Domain Name (FQDN)   An FQDN is simply a domain name that is not relative to any other domain.

Gateway   A gateway is a method or an on-ramp for connecting to the Internet. A gateway is often a server node with a high-speed connection to the Internet. Most individuals and smaller organizations use an ISP as their gateway to the Internet. Using a proxy server as a gateway, you can secure your network against unauthorized access. *See also* Application-level gateway; Circuit-level gateway; Default gateway.

GIF   *See* Graphic Interchange Format.

Gopher   Gopher, introduced by the University of Minnesota in 1991, is a menu-based program used as an adjunct for finding files, definitions, and resources. Gopher is a client/server software and a simple protocol that enables users to search and retrieve files from Gopher servers on the Internet. Using the Gopher service, Internet providers can create links to other servers, annotate files and directories, and create custom menus for use by Gopher clients.

Graphic Interchange Format (GIF)   GIF is a bitmapped graphics file format employed for graphics exchange on a BBS and networks. GIF uses a high-resolution graphics compression technique.

Graphic Interchange Format (GIF) version 89a (GIF89a)   The GIF89a format allows you to save images as "interlaced." When the interlaced image is viewed through a browser or graphic viewer, the picture slowly fades into view. The image first appears fuzzy. As more of the image is loaded into the browser or viewer, waves of data fill missing lines of the image. This continues until the image appears at full resolution.

Graphical User Interface (GUI)   An overall and consistent interface for the interactive and visual program that interacts (or interfaces) with the user. GUI can involve pull-down menus, dialog boxes, onscreen graphics, and a variety of icons.

Hacker   This term originally meant a technologically adept individual who explored and expanded computers to their limits. Now, the term means a person with an illegal and potentially harmful intention to slip past a computer security system or firewall in order to change data, destroy data, insert viruses, or execute other unauthorized functions.

Handheld devices   Handheld devices are computers and other pieces of equipment that are small enough to fit and operate in your hand.

Hardware   Hardware is a vital part of the infrastructure supporting an Internet client. Hardware is a blanket term for physical components on which applications run, and that they use to connect to software available on servers or to perform some specific purpose.

HDSL   *See* High bit-rate Digital Subscriber Line.

Head tags   The <HEAD> ... </HEAD> tags contain such elements as the title of your Web page and other elements that are not directly shown to the person viewing the page.

Helper programs   Plug-ins are different from so-called "helper programs," which are separate applications that launch in their own Window. Helper programs were common among earlier versions of Web browsers. When the browser encountered a specific file type that it wasn't able to display, it would attempt launching a separate program.

Hierarchical caching   Hierarchical caching is when you place a cache server at each layer of your network in a hierarchical fashion, just as you do routers. Your highest cache server would be just inside your firewall, which would be the only server responsible for retrieving information from the Internet.

High bit-rate Digital Subscriber Line (HDSL) HDSL is often deployed as a substitute for T1/E1 links. HDSL is becoming popular as a way to provide symmetric data communication (data transfer rates for upstream and downstream communications are equivalent) at rates up to 1.544 Mbps (2.048 Mbps in Europe) over moderate distances via POTS connections.

Hijacking Another form of attack, called "hijacking," is when a hacker successfully intercepts and controls a data stream originating from one computer and meant for another.

HINFO *See* Host INFO.

Hops Increased distance between client computers and the origin servers add latency and increase the risk of bottlenecks. Most connections will pass over 10 to 20 routers before end to connectivity is established. These routers along the network path are referred to as *hops*.

Host *See* Server.

Host INFO (HINFO) This record gives information about the system on the resolved host.

Host on Demand Host on Demand keeps the session alive even if you use your browser to go to additional Web pages.

Host-based IDS This form of IDS uses agents that reside on each host. In this system, centralized manager software reads the transmissions sent from agent software. The agents read the logs that reside on each system and search for suspicious activity. This form of IDS is ideal for switched networks. Once you have activated auditing for your operating system, you can install a third-party IDS to augment auditing.

HOSTS files   HOSTS files are static files that map host names to IP addresses. In other words, when new hosts are added to a network, the HOSTS file is not automatically updated. You need to open the HOSTS file manually, and then add the new host or domain name to the file.

HTML   *See* HyperText Markup Language.

HTTP   *See* HyperText Transfer Protocol.

Hub   A device with many cable ports that provides a central connection point for computers on a network. *See also* Active hub; Passive hub.

Hyperlinks   Hyperlinks are associated with images or text (which usually appears underlined) in a Web page. They are entered in the <BODY>...</BODY> section of your Web page. When the user clicks the hyperlinked image or text, the browser takes them to a Web page or performs an action associated with the hyperlink. To create a hyperlink, you use the anchor tags <A>...</A> combined with the hyperlink reference (HREF=) that refers to the URL or action to be performed.

HyperText Markup Language (HTML).   HTML is a Web-based standard that describes how HTML documents are displayed in a Web browser or thin client. HTML has three commonly used elements for textual input: text, textarea, and password.

HyperText Transfer Protocol (HTTP)   HTTP is the client/server protocol used by the World Wide Web. It is used by Internet browsers to retrieve HTML (HyperText Markup Language) documents from Web servers, and by Web servers to send Web pages. HTTP operates together with the TCP/IP protocol to facilitate the transfer of data in the form of text, images, audio, video, and animation. HTTP allows Web authors the ability to embed hyperlinks and also allows for transparent access to an Internet site.

IANA   *See* Internet Assigned Numbers Authority.

Ibox   *See* Internet-in-a-box.

ICANN   *See* Internet Corporation for Assigned Names & Numbers.

ICMP   *See* Internet Control Message Protocol.

IDS   *See* Intrusion Detection System.

IETF   *See* Internet Engineering Task Force.

IGMP   *See* Internet Group Management Protocol.

IIS   *See* Internet Information Server.

Index   *See* Full-text index; Keyword index; Static index.

Infrastructure   An infrastructure is the underlying features or framework of a system. In the case of a city, these features would include telephone lines for communication, roadways for transportation, and other elements that allow the city to function. For the Internet and intranets, the infrastructure consists of such things as protocols for transport of data, network connections to enable proper communication, and so on. The infrastructure is the basic systems that allow it to function. *See also* Public Key Infrastructure.

Integrated Services Digital Network (ISDN)   ISDN is a set of standards for transmitting data over copper wires and other media. This media allows you to transmit and receive data at speeds up to 128 Kbps. Instead of a modem, you use an ISDN adapter. The ISP also uses an ISDN adapter at their end to allow ISDN connectivity. In addition to data, ISDN allows you to communicate by voice, as you would with POTS.

Intelligent agents   Intelligent software agents will find the best products and best prices for customers. These autonomous intelligent agents will be able to be personalized and run 24 hours a day. Consumers will use agents to find the best prices for products and services.

Interconnected Network (Internet)   Perhaps best described as the world's largest *Inter*connected *Net*work of networks. Instead of a centralized control of the Internet, many millions of individual networks and individual computers interconnect throughout the world to communicate with each other. The Internet is based on Internet clients, Internet servers, and communication protocols.

Internet   *See* Interconnected Network.

Internet Assigned Numbers Authority (IANA)   The IANA is a voluntary organization that has suggested some new qualifiers (beyond the ones from the ICANN) that further differentiate hosts on the Internet.

Internet bandwidth technologies   Internet bandwidth technologies include various link types such as T1/E1 and T3/E3 standards for high-speed networking and data communications.

Internet Caching Protocol (ICP)   ICP allows several joined cache servers to communicate and share information that is cached locally among the servers. ICP is based upon the transport layer of the TCP/IP stack, utilizing a UDP or connectionless-based communication between the configured servers.

Internet Control Message Protocol (ICMP)   ICMP is used to send messages and report errors on the delivery of packets. These control messages and error reports are sent between the server and the gateway to the Internet or another section of a large network.

Internet Corporation for Assigned Names & Numbers   The group in charge of managing the Domain Name System is the Internet Corporation for Assigned Names & Numbers (ICANN). ICANN is a nonprofit organization whose purpose is to verify that no duplicate domain names are assigned. As of June 1999, ICANN accredited 42 companies from 10 countries to offer domain name assignment services. Also sometimes called International Corporation for Assigned Names and Numbers.

Internet Engineering Task Force (IETF)   The organization providing standard coordination and specification development for TCP/IP networking.

Internet Group Management Protocol (IGMP)   IGMP is used to report the memberships of computers (hosts) in a particular multicast group. The IGMP protocol is used to inform the local router that it wants to receive memberships addressed to a multicast group.

Internet Information Server (IIS)   Internet Information Servers are the technology used to provide access to data, resources, and information on the Internet and the World Wide Web.

Internet Infrastructure layer   This layer includes companies that provide products and services to network to support the Internet infrastructure. These are the "pipes" that data and content flows through. Products and services in this layer add value to the IP network infrastructure and make it possible to perform business activities online.

Internet intermediaries   Internet intermediaries increase the efficiency of electronic markets by facilitating the meeting and interaction of buyers and sellers over the Internet to create an e-business marketplace. They leverage investments in the infrastructure and applications layers.

Internet Network Information Center (InterNIC)   All Internet domain names must be registered with an organization called Internet Network Information Center (InterNIC), and your ISP can usually do this on your behalf. Your ISP will charge you a fee for hosting your own Web site through their service, and there is also a monthly fee to InterNIC for maintaining the domain name.

Internet phone   Internet phone is a recent innovation to the Internet, allowing users to talk verbally with one another as if they were using a normal telephone. Communication takes place over the Internet, allowing one user with an Internet phone to talk with other users with Internet phones without having to pay for long distance charges.

Internet port number   An Internet port number, also referred to as a *socket number* to distinguish between running applications. In some cases, a port number may be required and is appended to the server name, such as http://www.location.com:4 (80 is the port number for the Web server). The port number can usually be omitted and the server's default port will be used. The most commonly used port numbers are FTP (port 21), Telnet (port 23), SMTP (port 25), and HTTP (port 80).

Internet Protocol (IP)   IP has the primary responsibility for routing packets between networks and hosts on a TCP/IP network. It also specifies the format that the packet will take.

Internet Protocol (IP) multicasting   IP Multicasting routes data to specific computers on a network that is identified by an IP address or class.

Internet Routing Registry (IRR)   This registry is a central database of routes.

Internet server   *See* Server.

Internet Server Application Programming Interface (ISAPI)
A set of program calls that allows you to create a Windows Web-based application that will run faster than a CGI application.

Internet Service Provider (ISP)   An ISP is your gateway to the Internet. An ISP maintains a dedicated high-speed connection to the Internet 24 hours a day. In order to connect to the Internet, you must first be connected to your ISP. You can obtain a dedicated line that provides a continuous connection to your ISP (for an additional fee), or connect to the Internet only when necessary using a modem.

Internet Society (ISOC)   The international organization (founded 1992) supporting, enhancing, and extending the Internet via government, organizational, and public research, education, and standards development.

Internet-in-a-box (Ibox)   Ibox is a relatively new technology that provides networks with one-step connections to the Internet. When the Ibox is installed and properly configured, it supplies the tools necessary to connect the network to the Internet by acting as a gateway; configuring the network for Internet access; and providing Internet software tools, such as e-mail and Web browsers. Iboxes vary greatly in their features and capabilities.

InterNIC   *See* Internet Network Information Center.

Interpreted program   An interpreted program must be fed one command at a time into an interpreter.

Intraconnected networks (Intranets)   Intranets (internal private networks) are usually restricted to internal access only by a company's employees and workers. Often, an intranet is located behind a firewall to prevent unauthorized access from a public network. An intranet is the same thing as the Internet, except on a much less ambitious scale. An intranet offers Web sites, e-mail, and access to information relevant for a specific company. Access to an intranet is allowed only to authenticated employees. Additionally, an intranet has added authentication because information shared on an intranet is often valuable and sensitive.

Intranets   *See* Intraconnected networks.

Intrusion Detection System (IDS)   An IDS is a series of applications and services designed to detect and, if so configured, thwart illicit activity. *See also* Host-based IDS or Network-based IDS.

IP   *See* Internet Protocol.

IRR   *See* Internet Routing Registry.

ISAPI   *See* Internet Server Application Programming Interface.

ISDN   *See* Integrated Services Digital Network.

ISOC   *See* Internet Society.

ISP   *See* Internet Service Provider.

Java   Java is a programming language developed by Sun Microsystems (http://www.sun.com) in 1995. Java was developed specifically for use in distributed applications and, more specifically, for the Internet. Java was based on the popular C++ language. Much of the syntax and libraries created for Java was modeled after those items popular with C++.

Java DataBase Connectivity (JDBC)   Similar to ODBC, JDBC provides an interface for a developer to access a database. The vendor will need to provide a driver in order to access the underlying database.

JavaScript   JavaScript is different from the compiled language Java. JavaScript carries some of the syntax of Java and even carries some of the same functions. However, JavaScript is different in that it is interpreted rather than compiled.

JDBC   *See* Java DataBase Connectivity.

Joint Photographic Experts Group (JPEG)   The committee, under the auspices of the ISO and the CCITT, that developed the JPEG graphics standard defining how to compress still pictures. JPEG can achieve compression ratios of up to 20:1, superior to GIF ratios, without noticeable picture-quality degradation. JPEG is another popular type of graphic. Along with GIF, JPEG is one of the most common image formats you'll use and come across on the World Wide Web. Files that use this format usually have the extension .jpg, but you may also see graphic files with the extension .jpeg. One of the benefits of JPEG is its use of compression. *See also* Progressive JPEG.

JPEG   *See* Joint Photographic Experts Group.

JScript   JScript is an interpreted script language from Microsoft that is designed for use within Web pages. It adheres to the ECMAScript standard developed by Microsoft and Netscape.

Kerberos   Kerberos is a client/server method for controlling access to specific network resources. MIT professors originally developed the Kerberos system. It allows you to authenticate users via encryption. Once authenticated, a Kerberos server then grants "tickets" to system resources, such as printers, additional networks, databases, and file servers. These tickets exist temporarily. Kerberos has an added security feature in that it does not transport passwords over the network wire, which eliminates the threat of "sniffing" password information.

Key escrow   Key escrow involves the creation of powerful encryption algorithms by one body, who then reserves the right to hold all of the possible keys. The result is that, normally, a user would be able to encrypt a document that is unreadable by all but the intended recipients. However, in the case of a declared emergency, a certain body, such as the CIA or MI5 could decrypt the message immediately.

Keyword index   The amount of information contained on a Web site can be overwhelming. The user wishes to locate what he or she is looking for quickly. The idea of "keywords" has become a very important part of searching a Web page for content.

Keywords   Keywords are the basic terms that make up the functionality of the language. These terms range from instructions to initiate and end a loop to those used for simply declaring the existence of a variable.

LAN *See* Local Area Network.

Latency Latency is the delay experienced by a client or server that has requested information (or some sort of transaction) from a server.

Layering Layering builds on the use of style sheets, enabling your page to layer one style on top of another. The content of one style sheet will replace or superimpose on sections of content that are currently visible to the user. This allows you to create dynamic presentations that change their content based on a user's interaction, or by the amount of time you've programmed to pass before the next layer appears. This can be done through the style sheets themselves, or by using the <LAYER> ... </LAYER> HTML tag set.

LDAP *See* Lightweight Directory Access Protocol.

Legacy client One type of legacy client is an application that was widely used before the Internet became popular. A second type of legacy client is an older application, such as the original version of Navigator or an older e-mail program. Although such applications are clearly Internet oriented, they nevertheless represent older technology. Legacy clients often impede the ability for a company to share information consistently between all workers in a company.

Lempel-Ziv Welch (LZW) compression This is an older form of compression, but it continues to be used in GIFs because it works so well. The compression makes the graphic smaller, so it takes up less hard drive space, and takes less time to download.

Lightweight Directory Access Protocol (LDAP) Allows e-mail clients to view remote centralized lists of employees and contacts. The LDAP is an open-industry standard that defines a method for accessing and updating information stored in directories. Since LDAP is a vendor-neutral standard, it is being widely adopted by software vendors and application developers.

LISTSERV   The most popular commercial list server software is LISTSERV. LISTSERV performs several functions that would otherwise have to be managed manually, as in the days before any e-mail list management software existed. LISTSERV was the first software introduced to automate the administration of e-mail lists, and currently offers a full set of features for the list member, list owner, and site maintainer to manipulate their list/site configurations.

Load testing   To perform load testing, you will often need to purchase software that tests your Web site. This will provide information as to probable problems encountered by users, and how fast the Web pages load. Your Web server software may also provide utilities that track the number of users, the days and times they commonly use certain Web pages, or other data.

Local Area Network (LAN)   A system using high-speed connections over high-performance cables to communicate among computers within a few miles of each other, allowing users to share peripherals and a massive secondary storage unit, the file server.

Local domain   A domain that is served by the local SMTP server. The local domain has an entry in the DNS table. When a message arrives at the SMTP server and is addressed to the local domain, the SMTP server puts the message in a local Drop folder.

Loopback function   A function that loops packets back to your computer.

Lossy compression   Lossy compression technique is one in which detail is compromised for size.

Lynx   The most popular text-only browser on the market is Lynx, developed at the University of Kansas for students to access UNIX servers. It has become a popular browser for accessing the Internet when only text needs to be viewed or when graphics are not required.

LZW compression   *See* Lempel-Ziv Welch compression.

Macro virus   Usually, a macro is a valuable work-saving tool. However, it is possible to create malicious programs using these powerful macro languages. Some macro viruses are capable of erasing and modifying data.

MAE   *See* Metropolitan Area Exchange.

Mail eXchange (MX)   This type of record is essential for naming the e-mail server on your domain.

Mail Transfer Agent (MTA)   MTAs are permanently running programs on hosts with permanent connections to the Internet. Host computers running MTA software are commonly known as mail servers. An MTA "listens" for incoming e-mail from both local and remote MTAs, examines the e-mail, and either saves it locally (in a spool file) for retrieval by the destination user, or identifies a remote MTA and transfers the e-mail to it.

Mail User Agent (MUA)   An MUA is a client application used to send and receive e-mail. It provides a user interface for composition and local storage of e-mail messages, and also has facilities to communicate with MTAs. There are numerous MUAs available under modern Windows-based environments; typical examples include Eudora and Microsoft Outlook.

Markup languages   Markup languages use symbols, characters, and statements to format a document. These are placed in the document to indicate how that area of the document should appear when viewed or printed. In HTML, the indicators that the author uses are called *tags*.

Media Player   Media Player allows you to view and/or listen to streaming video and audio. This allows you to watch broadcasts, listen to the radio, view video files, or listen to audio files on the Web. Like RealPlayer, Media Player also has a Web page where you can browse through different audio and video files to watch and hear.

Meta tags   These tags allow the developers to emphasize specific content within their page. Meta tags are added to the HTML code of your Web pages.

Metadata   Metadata can be added to the <HEAD> ... </HEAD> section to help define visual elements and how accessible your HTML document will be on the Web. Metadata is not a tag in itself, but is used to describe a group of tags.

Metropolitan Area Exchange (MAE)   An MAE is a specific example of a NAP. ISPs connect to MAEs in order to get access to the Internet. Two types of MAEs exist: tier 1 and tier 2.

Middleware   Software that functions as a translation or conversion layer.

MIDI   *See* Musical Instrumental Digital Interface.

MIME   *See* Multipurpose Internet Mail Extensions.

Minus operator   When the minus operator is present before a search item, the results will exclude all items containing that search term.

Mirror server   A mirror server is a backup server that duplicates all the processes and transactions of the primary server. If, for any reason, the primary server fails, the backup server can immediately take its place without losing any downtime.

Modem   *See* MOdulator/DEModulator.

Moderated newsgroup   In a moderated newsgroup, when the user posts a message, the NNTP server sends that message to the moderator. The NNTP service uses the SMTP server to send messages to the moderator.

MOdulator/DEModulator (modem)   The key to connecting a computer or network to the Internet lies in the ability to access the phone and cable lines that the Internet uses. This is the job of the computer's modem. Modems are responsible for creating and maintaining the computer's connection to the Internet, as well as sending and receiving data. The most common speeds of analog modems are 14.4 Kbps, 28.8 Kbps, 33.6 Kbps, and 56.6 Kbps. 56.6 Kbps is probably the fastest that analog modems will ever be able to achieve. *See also* Analog modems.

Mosaic   The Mosaic World Wide Web browser was developed by the National Center for Supercomputing Applications (NCSA). Mosaic was the first Web browser with a graphical user interface. It was released initially for the UNIX computer platform and later in 1993 for Macintosh and Windows computers.

Motion Picture Experts Group (MPEG)   MPEGs use compression to make the files smaller. They do this through a type of lossy compression, in which some redundant data is removed from the imaging. The lost data is generally unnoticeable. The way that MPEGs compress their data is interesting, since entire images are not stored. Rather than storing a movie as a series of frames, with one image following the other, MPEGs store their files by storing only the changes from one frame to the next. MPEG-1 provides a video quality that is slightly inferior to the video you'd see in a VCR. It provides a resolution of 352 by 240, and 30 frames per second (fps). MPEG-2 is the standard used by DVD-ROMs. *See also* MP3.

MOV files   *See* Quick Time Movie files.

MP3   MP3 stands for MPEG 1, Audio Layer 3. It is a standard and format that allows sound files to be compressed into a smaller size, while preserving the original sound quality.

MPEG   *See* Motion Picture Experts Group.

MTA   *See* Mail Transfer Agent.

MUA   *See* Mail User Agent.

Multicasting   Multicasting is the ability to send messages to a select group of computers. *See also* Internet Protocol multicasting.

Multipoint technology   Multipoint technology allows you to have multiple connections between two computers. This is used to ensure fault tolerance communications so that if one link goes down, you have another link ready to conduct the transaction.

Multipurpose Internet Mail Extensions (MIME)   MIME established standard ways a Web server can deliver files to a client for easy, automatic reading. The original purpose of MIME was to extend the ability for e-mail clients and servers. Most applications, however, use MIME to ensure compatibility. *See also* Secure MIME.

Musical Instrument Digital Interface (MIDI)   A protocol standardizing the interchange and communication between musical instruments, computers, synthesizers, and other MIDI equipment.

MX   *See* Mail eXchange.

Name tag   The NAME tag is used to provide the element with a name that can be referred to in scripts.

NAP   *See* Network Access Point.

National Science Foundation (NSF)   The NSF created NSFnet in 1986, which eventually replaces ARPAnet (1990), and substantially increases the speed of communication over the Internet.

Natural language queries   Natural language queries represent increased technology that allows users to search based upon naturally formed phrases, sentences, or questions. The effectiveness of searches based upon natural language becomes more reliant on the search engine technology rather that depending on the wording of the query.

Netscape Navigator   Netscape Navigator Web browser was introduced is 1994. Marc Andreesson left NCSA and co-founded Netscape Communications Corporation in Mountain View, California. In 1995, the Netscape Navigator Web browser quickly became the most widely used cross-platform Web browser on the market. Netscape integrated all of the features of Mosaic, and added many new features and capabilities as well.

Network Access Point (NAP)   A NAP is nothing more than a central point that allows Internet Service Providers (ISPs) to exchange information with each other.

Network analyzers (also called sniffers)   Network analyzers look at all of the packets out on the network and show you all sorts of information about them. They can be TCP/IP packets, Apple Talk packets, or IPX/SPX packets, among others. By using this utility, you can capture packets that are out on the wire and see where they came from, where they are going, and what data they have in them.

Network connection   A network connection consists of hardware and software working together, so that you can access network resources. In terms of hardware, your computer will need a modem or network interface card (NIC), which is used to pass data onto and pull data off of the transmission wire.

Network Interface Card (NIC)   NICs are often used to connect a computer to a cable or DSL modem. The network interface card may be referred to as a network adapter, or NIC. Network cards are also (and usually) used for connecting computers together in a network structure. The NIC allows a computer to see and transfer packets of information to and from other computers that are physically connected to the same network.

Network layer   This layer provides for actual network addresses between two systems. The Internet Protocol (IP) runs at this layer.

Network News Transfer Protocol (NNTP)   NNTP provides a robust and scalable service for newsgroup servers. NNTP allows you to host and participate in newsgroup-style discussion, and allows users to read articles and to post articles for others to read. NNTP service supports both client-to-server and server-to-server communication over the Internet. NNTP supports popular extensions and is fully compatible with other NNTP clients and servers.

Network Operating System (NOS)   An NOS, like a regular operating system, is software that controls the functions of the computer, but also includes the features required to connect to and communicate with a network. Some popular Network Operating Systems include Novell NetWare, Microsoft Windows NT, and UNIX.

Network Virtual Terminal (NVT)   Communication established using the TCP/IP protocols and based on a set of facilities known as an NVT. At the client end, the Telnet client program is responsible for mapping incoming NVT codes to the actual codes needed to operate the user's display device, and it is also responsible for mapping user-generated keyboard sequences into NVT sequences.

Network-based IDS   The simplest type of host-based IDS uses an application that scans the network wire for all hosts on a particular subnet. This type of IDS is ideal for hub-based networks, because most network switches tend to open connections in a manner that isolates an IDS from the rest of the network.

News expiration policy   Establishes a limit for the length of time an article may be kept. You can set this expiration limit for one or more newsgroups, and these policies can vary from newsgroup to newsgroup.

Newsgroups   Newsgroups are directories of messages and files available on a news server. They are similar to message groups that appear on dial-in Bulletin Board Services, where messages are posted publicly and can be viewed by everyone.

Newshound   Newshound service was one of the first newspapers to provide a subscription-based, e-mail–delivered, personalized news filter.

NIC   *See* Network Interface Card.

NNTP   *See* Network News Transfer Protocol.

Nonrelational databases   Unlike the relational databases, nonrelational systems normally contain all the data in one large file. In the early days of Web development, most of the databases were nonrelational systems.

Nonrepudiation   The ability to prove that a transaction has, in fact, occurred.

Nonstreaming media   Nonstreaming media is the opposite of streaming media. This type of multimedia covers most file formats. With nonstreaming media, you need to download a file—which may be extremely large in size—before you can play it through a browser or separate application. The benefit of this type of media is that you do not need to be connected to the Internet to view the file. All of the data is stored on your hard drive, allowing you to view it when you're not online. With streaming media, you need to be connected to the Internet, so that you can receive the streaming data from a Web server.

NOS   *See* Network Operating System.

NOT operator   The NOT operator between two words or other values means you are searching for documents that contain the first word before the NOT operator, but not the second word that follows it.

Notebook computer   A notebook computer is a larger handheld device that can be used to access the Internet, but is still small enough to carry around easily. It is roughly the size of a hardcover book, and has computing power comparable to desktop PCs. It can run the same applications, including operating systems and Internet client programs.

NSFnet   *See* National Science Foundation.

Nuking   Unpatched operating systems are vulnerable to attacks that send unexpected information to an open port. Doing so causes a denial of service attack called nuking.

NVT   *See* Network Virtual Terminal.

OBI   *See* Open Buying on the Internet.

ODBC   *See* Open Database Connectivity.

On-demand caching   *See* Passive caching.

One-Time Password (OTP)   The concept of a one-time password involves "what you know" authentication, but enhances the practice by never using the same password twice.

Open Buying on the Internet (OBI)   OBI is a vendor-neutral standard that has emerged for electronic catalog systems. OBI defines the rules for conducting B2B commerce over the Internet.

Open DataBase Connectivity (ODBC)   ODBC is an API used to connect to various databases. These datastores could be an Oracle database, SQL Server database, text database, or any other type of datastore for which an ODBC driver is available.

Open Systems Interconnection (OSI)   The OSI reference model is exactly what it sounds like—a networking model that we can reference so that we can see how the different protocols work. The reason you need to be aware of the OSI reference model is it is the reference point that every IT professional can go back to when discussing disparate protocols to help understand how each one works.

Operating system   Operating systems provide a platform on which other software can run, and provide a layer between applications and the underlying hardware. This layer is important to software developers, as it frees them from having to provide proprietary drivers for each piece of hardware.

Operator   *See* AND operator; Minus operator; NOT operator; OR operator; Plus operator.

OR operator   The OR operator between two words or other values means you are searching for items that contain one of the words.

Orange Book   *See* Trusted Computer System Evaluation Criteria.

Original work   Original means that the work is original in the copyright sense if it owes its origin to the author(s) and was not copied from a preexisting work. Only minimal creativity is required to meet the originality requirement.

OSI   *See* Open Systems Interconnection.

OTP   *See* One-Time Password.

PAC   *See* Proxy Auto Configuration.

Packet filter   A packet filter inspects source and destination IP addresses, as well as ports. This type of firewall operates at the network layer of the OSI/RM. Its chief benefit is that it inspects packets quickly, and it is quite difficult to overwhelm. However, a packet filter cannot delve as deeply into a packet as the other firewall types.

Packet filtering   Packet filtering is a scheme whereby certain packets are passed through to the network and others are discarded. You can block or enable reception of certain types of packets through certain ports. Ports are only opened as needed. Packets are allowed in for only the minimum duration required and only on specified ports.

Packet INternet Groper (PING)   A common utility program used to determine whether a computer is connected to the Internet properly. PING is a utility that operates at the IP layer sending ICMP packets from one host to another to determine if it is up.

Packet INternet Groper (PING) floods   Using a program called "SMURF," you can forge IP packets that send ICMP request messages to another host. Let's call this host "host B." Your SMURF program causes host B to send ICMP reply packets not to you, but to another host that we will call host C. The result is that you have sent only one ping to host B, and host B sends one ping to host C. Now, imagine what would happen if you and a bunch of your friends used your SMURF program to send thousands and even millions of ICMP packets to many different hosts, all of which then replied to host C. Host C would crash under the strain.

Packet switching   Packet switching provided the ability to break data into smaller chunks that are, at most, a few kilobytes in size. Each packet is transmitted separately, providing a more efficient use of the media (i.e., telephone lines or network cable). If one of these packets becomes corrupted, the entire file does not need to be resent, just that particular packet.

Packet-level firewall   This is a very basic type of security in which packets are allowed or denied access to the network based on source and destination IP addresses. This type of firewall is usually managed by a router, which has been configured with IP address filtering rules.

Packet-switching protocol   A packet-switching protocol and/or network can use a different network path to communicate each time a transaction occurs.

Page Description Language (PDL)   A high-level language that commands the printer's functions. Examples are PostScript and PCL.

Palmtop   A palmtop is an example of a handheld device that fits into the palm of your hand.

Parent sibling caching   The parent-sibling caching works much like the hierarchies caching except that the sibling caches are all working together. Each sibling cache is aware of what the other caches are storing and can quickly request from the correct cache server. If a new request comes in, the siblings will send the request to the "Parent" cache server, which will either return the requested information or retrieve it.

Passive caching   Also called *on-demand caching*. Passive caching represents the most basic form of object caching. Passive caching servers require less configuration and maintenance, but at the price of reduced performance. Passive caching, as the name implies, makes no attempt to "prefetch" Internet objects.

Passive hub   A passive hub receives information through one of its ports; the hub copies the information and sends it to every other port. This means that network information is broadcast to every computer on the network, but is only read by the destination computer.

Password   This form of authentication requires that you present a physical token of some sort. In the analog world, a key or an actual piece of paper serves as an example. As far as the Internet is concerned, digital signatures and certificates provide this service. Smart cards are the most advanced form of this kind of authentication.

Password element   The password element is similar to the text element, except that it hides whatever the user types by displaying asterisks instead of text. The password element appears as a box on a Web page, just like a normal text element.

Patches   Patches are used because (1) The product originally shipped with a flaw that could not be fixed in time; (2) A previously overlooked problem was discovered; (3) The vendor invented or adopted a new, popular technology, and wishes to update the operating system, service, or application; and (4) New hacker techniques that make existing practices untenable.

Patent law Patent law protects new, useful, and "nonobvious" inventions and processes.

Path statement *See* Directory path.

PDF *See* Portable Document Format.

PDL *See* Page Description Language.

Peering The technical term for the activity of exchanging information between ISPs. Peering is the result of a special arrangement between ISPs. This activity allows any two ISPs to arrange to share traffic.

PERL *See* Practical Extraction and Reporting Language.

Permanent Virtual Circuit (PVC) A PVC is a connection between endpoints that is not dynamically established or removed.

Personal computers Personal computers (or *desktop computers*) are designed for individual users. These computers can be placed on a desktop, and are made up of components that gather input from a user (such as through a keyboard or mouse), process data, store data on a hard disk, and output information (such as through a monitor). Other components, such as a modem or network card, enable the user to connect to other computers, like over the Internet.

PGP *See* Pretty Good Privacy.

Physical layer This layer sends and receives bits of data.

PING *See* Packet INternet Groper.

Ping of Death Some unpatched Windows NT systems are not able to accept ICMP packets over 65,535 bytes long. Using special programs, it is possible to create an ICMP packet exceeding this length, which crashes the system.

PKI   *See* Public Key Infrastructure.

Plain Old Telephone Service (POTS)   Dial-up connections that use telephone lines are a conventional method of accessing the Internet. This is often referred to as POTS, in which the media used for data transmission is also used for voice communication.

Plug-ins (extensions)   Plug-ins are programs that can be installed on your computer, and add their functionality to the Web browser. Another term for plug-ins is extensions, as these applications extend the capabilities of the browser. These are modules that become a part of the browser, adding new features or enabling the display of different types of multimedia.

Plus operator   The plus operator works in inverse manner to the minus operator. When the plus symbol is located preceding a word or search phrase, that indicates that term has to be present to match the search request.

Point of Presence Protocol   *See* Post Office Protocol version 3.

PointCast   PointCast offered a client application that any Internet user could download to gain free access news, sports results, entertainment and business information, and stock quotes. Using the PointCast application, an end user could define a profile that acted as an information filter allowing them to view only the specific type of content that they wanted to view.

Pointer Record (PTR)   This entry helps create reverse DNS lookup domains. PTR records go into a separate file.

Point-to-Point Protocol (PPP)   PPP is the primary protocol for connecting to the Internet. PPP is the replacement for SLIP. PPP supports compression and encryption. If you connect to the Internet from home over a modem, chances are you are using PPP. One of two standards for dial-up telephone connection of computers to the Internet, with better data negotiation, compression, and error corrections than the other SLIP, but costing more to transmit data and unnecessary when both sending and receiving modems can handle some of the procedures.

Point-to-Point Tunneling Protocol (PPTP)   PPTP allows you to send information over a public network (the Internet) securely. With this protocol, you establish a PPP connection over your phone line, and then you establish another PPP connection over that connection and create the VPN.

POP   *See* Post Office Protocol.

POP3   *See* Post Office Protocol version 3.

Port   Any client software that uses TCP/IP uses an identifier called a port. When FTP, Telnet, SMTP, or other software and protocols are running, they monitor this port constantly. In other words, the server listens to this port for requests for service, and the client application uses this port number to request services like Web pages, mail, and so forth.

Port number   *See* Well-known port number.

Portable Document Format (PDF)   PDF is an acronym for the Portable Document Format, and can usually be identified by the file extension of .pdf. This format is used to capture a document as an image, so that it can be viewed and printed exactly as intended. In other words, anyone viewing a PDF on any document will see it exactly the same way on any computer.

Portable Network Graphics (PNG)   PNG (pronounced "ping") is expected to be the license-free answer to GIFs. If you're creating graphic software that exploits the PNG format however, there is no fee. For this reason, the World Wide Web Consortium (W3C) has approved the PNG format as a standard to replace GIFs. A disadvantage to PNG graphics is that they cannot be animated, since you cannot store multiple images in a single PNG file. However, PNG does support interlacing. With PNG files, the image is displayed faster than GIF files, which is an added benefit for those downloading and viewing the interlaced PNG file at a slower baud rate.

Post Office Protocol (POP)   A standard that specifies how an Internet-connected computer handles electronic mail. Electronic mail programs for personal computers detect whether new mail has arrived in a user's mailbox on the service provider's computer and allows the user to read, download, reply to, print, or store it.

Post Office Protocol version 3 (POP3)   POP3 (also called *Point of Presence Protocol*) is a remote access protocol that allows you to receive e-mail from any server on the Internet (that you have an account on) from any computer connected to the Internet. The only requirements that you have to meet are that your computer has a POP3-compatible e-mail reader (Outlook, Netscape, and Eudora just to name a few) and that your e-mail server is configured to accept POP3 requests. POP3 is a protocol that operates at the Application layer.

PostScript   It is used to define the look of a page, when it is sent to an output device like a printer or plotter. PostScript fonts are also commonly referred to as outline fonts and scalable fonts.

POTS   *See* Plain Old Telephone Service.

PPP   *See* Point-to-Point Protocol.

PPTP   *See* Point-to-Point Tunneling Protocol.

Practical Extraction and Reporting Language (PERL)   Perl is an interpreted scripting language. While PERL is generally used on UNIX-platformed Web servers, it has been ported to many other operating systems as well. Since PERL is interpreted, it is compiled just before execution. It can be compiled into either C code or cross-platform byte-code.

Pre-fetching   Active caching servers use a proactive approach referred to as "pre-fetching" to maximize the performance of the server's cache by increasing the amount of objects that are available locally based upon several configurations and statistical analysis.

Presentation layer   Formats information from one language type to another.

Pretty Good Privacy (PGP)   Developed by Phil Zimmerman. Uses RSA methods and is available to the public for, e.g., encrypting messages.

Primary Rate Interface (PRI)   PRI is one level of service designed for larger user bases such as large enterprises. In Europe, PRI consists of 30 B channels and one D channel.

Primary server   This server contains the authoritative information for an entire zone.

Private IP address   A private IP address is an address that is not legal out on the Internet. It is an address that you create and assign internally within your organization to allow computers to communicate with each other over IP without using registered addresses.

Progressive JPEG   A progressive JPEG is similar to an interlaced GIF, in that the image slowly fades into view, as a series of lines that appear on your screen. As each wave of lines appear in the image, the graphic begins to get clearer. This allows the person viewing a JPEG on your Web page to identify what the image is as it's being downloaded, which is especially good for users accessing your site with slower modems.

Proof of origin   It is possible for systems to authenticate packets depending upon where they come from. Although this form of authentication is not very secure, it is still practiced by the UNIX rlogin programs.

Protocol   A protocol is a set of rules as to how data is packaged, transmitted, and received. It controls how data is sent over a network.

Proxy   A proxy mediates between one party and another. In the case of the Internet, a proxy mediates between inside users and outside traffic. A proxy receives requests from external users, investigates the nature of the request, and then passes the request on to the appropriate location.

Proxy Auto Configuration (PAC) files   PAC files allow the browser to reconfigure its proxy settings based on information stored within this file. During the initial client installation, a URL is supplied to direct the browser to check for updates on a periodic basis. The code is usually written in JavaScript and stored at a location within the local area network, or at the remote access point.

Proxy caching   Proxy caching works through a cooperative connection between the browser and the caching server, instead of the remote origin server. When a client is configured to use a particular caching proxy server (or, any proxy server for that matter), it directs all of its requests for a particular protocol (HTTP, FTP, Gopher, etc) to the port on the proxy server specified in the browser configuration. Because several different protocols can be proxied and cached, most browsers allow for different configurations for each protocol.

Proxy server   A proxy server is a computer that stands between the LAN and the Internet. The proxy server software on this network server allows computers on the LAN to access the Internet through the proxy server's IP address. The address consists of four sets of numbers that are three digits or less, which identify the computer on the TCP/IP network. *See also* Enterprise-grade proxy server.

PTR   *See* Pointer Record.

Public Key Infrastructure (PKI)   PKI is a term reserved for organizations and bodies that create, store, and manage digital certificates. PKI is generally a distributed system, meaning that many different hosts and servers work together to create a single solution.

Pulse Code Modulation (PCM)   The most common technique used to digitize an analog signal into the DS-0 format. The incoming analog signal is "sampled" at a rate of 8000 times per second and converted into subsequent pulses known as a PAM (Pulse Amplitude Modulation). Each PAM is assigned an equivalent 8-bit binary value. This provides a digital output to the analog signal.

Push technology   Push technology is not a specific technology solution or product, but rather a general concept to describe a way to deliver information automatically over a network. Push is actually a diverse group of companies and technologies that deliver content—either data or applications—over computer networks such as the Internet or internal corporate intranets.

PVC   *See* Permanent Virtual Circuit.

QTVR   *See* Quick Time Virtual Reality.

Queries   *See* Boolean queries; Compound queries; Natural language queries; Recursive queries.

Quick Time Movie (MOV) files   The MOV files enable you to view video and audio over the Internet, or from your hard disk. By using a browser with the QuickTime plug-in, or the QuickTime Player application, you can view a cartoon, a clip of a live-action movie, or other footage. Because MOV files have been around for a number of years, you can also view them through numerous other applications. Many image products support this file format, allowing you to play them.

Quick Time Virtual Reality (QTVR)   QTVR is an enhanced version of QuickTime. QuickTime is used to display different forms of multimedia on computers, including animation, audio, and video. QTVR goes beyond this, enabling browsers to display and rotate images as three-dimensional objects.

RA   *See* Routing Arbiter.

Radio buttons   Radio buttons are similar to check boxes in that they are used to gather input, by having a user click it to choose an option. Radio buttons are round, and look like an "o" in a browser. When selected, a small dot will appear in it to indicate the selection. Another difference between check boxes and radio buttons is that, while check boxes can be used to accept multiple choices, you can only click a single radio button.

RAP   *See* Remote Access Protocol.

Raster graphics (bitmaps or BMPs)   Raster graphics are sometimes referred to as *bitmaps*, as they map data directly to a grid of x and y coordinates. The display is mapped into a grid of x (horizontal) and y (vertical) coordinates. A drawback to BMP files is the lack of compression, which makes images in this format larger than many of the other types of graphics.

Raster Image Processor (RIP)   A hardware/software processor that prepares an image for raster display or for raster printing.

RealPlayer   RealPlayer is an application and plug-in that enables you to view and listen to streaming audio and streaming video over the Internet. Streaming means that you hear and/or listen to the media in real time. You can listen to a radio or TV broadcast live, or view video or audio files of previous broadcasts.

Recursive queries   Recursive queries occur when a resolver creates a request that requires the DNS to follow the entire request path until it is fulfilled. As you might suspect, this form of query is much more taxing on servers. Recursive queries often occur when a resolver queries a name server that is not authoritative for that domain.

Relational database   A database consisting of one or more related tables.

Remote Access Protocol (RAP)   An RAP allows you to access all of the resources on your network as if you were directly connected to it.

Remote domain   A remote domain is a domain that is not local. This means there is no Drop folder for that domain on the local SMTP server. Mail addressed to remote domains is forwarded to the SMTP server specified for that domain.

Request For Comment 822 (RFC822)   Back in 1982, RFC822 defined the standard format for text-based e-mail sent via SMTP.

Request For Comment 1521 and 1522 (RFC1521 and RFC1522)   These extensions allowed more freedom concerning what you can transfer via e-mail. RFC 1521 showed how users could create e-mail messages that used more sophisticated ASCII text, but were still compatible with older systems. RFC 1521 extended e-mail, yet made sure these e-mail extensions were backward compatible. RFC 1522 brought even more flexibility to e-mail by allowing users to send non-ASCII text.

RFC   *See* Request For Comment.

Rich Text Format (RTF)   A text formatting standard that enables a word processing program to create a file containing all the document's formatting instructions without using any special codes. It allows the exchange of text files between different applications and operating systems and is an almost universal file format for text files. Using this format, you can exchange text between different operating systems, word processors, and other software. For example, you could create a document using Microsoft Word on a Macintosh machine, save it as an RTF file, and then import it into an HTML editor like Microsoft FrontPage running on a Windows 98 machine. Because it is such a popular format, many of the word processors or textual readers or writers on the market support this format.

RIP   *See* Raster Image Processor.

Rivest Shamir Adleman (RSA)   A secure cryptographic system using a two-part key in which the public key is known and the private key is held by the owner.

Root kit   Many trojan programs have been gathered together as a root kit, which is nothing more than illicit programs that replace legitimate programs, such as ls (used to list files) su (used to become "super user," or root), and cd (used to change from one directory to another).

Root-level domain   The root-level domain, which is unnamed, consists of several hosts that work in tandem to form the very top of the DNS tree.

Route Server (RS)   These servers forward packets according to the routes in the IRR.

Routers   Routers (specialized hardware) intercept the packets and view the information contained in the header code. These routers use tables that provide a listing of other routers and computers on the network. Based on the destination contained in the packet's header, the router will either retransmit the packet to the destination computer or—if that computer is not part of the router's local network—retransmit the packet to another router. The router determines the best possible path for the packet to take on its way to the destination of the receiving computer.

Routing Arbiter (RA)   An RA is the backbone element that enacts those routing policies. The RA takes the place of the old NSFNet Acceptable Use Policy (AUP). Whenever one NAP connects to another, they use an RA. An RA is a collection of devices that provide routing maps, address resolution, and redundant connectivity. Therefore, the purpose of the RA is to make sure ISPs communicate efficiently and that packets do not get dropped (that is, lost) too often.

RS   *See* Route Server.

RSA   *See* Rivest Shamir Adleman.

RTF   *See* Rich Text Format.

Safe key protocol   Public key encryption allows you to transmit keys securely because you can embed a symmetric key within a message encrypted to someone's public key. The primary protocol for describing safe key transport is the Diffie/Hellman protocol.

Screened-host firewalls   This type of configuration provides more protection than a dual-homed host firewall, because it combines the use of the proxy server with a packet-filtering router. In effect, it is a combination of application and packet-level firewalls. The screening router is placed between the Internet and the proxy server. The proxy server, then, is referred to as a screened host because the router performs IP-based filtering before the packets reach the server.

Script tags   The <SCRIPT>...</SCRIPT> tags are used to indicate that the code appearing between these tags is a scripting language that is to execute as a program. For example, you might enter JavaScript or VBScript code that performs some action when a user clicks a button on a form.

SDSL   *See* Symmetric DSL.

Searches   *See* Boolean searches; Wildcard searches.

Secondary server   Also called a *slave server*, a secondary server receives its database (that is, zone file) from a primary through a zone transfer.

Second-level domain   Second-level domains generally include the names of organizations and companies.

Secure Electronic Transaction (SET)   SET is a series of procedures that enable e-commerce to conduct financial transactions sites with a secure way to exchange information with banking institutions. Although SET is not currently popular in the United States, it has been adopted by most European countries. SET uses SSL, digital certificates, and additional technologies.

Secure Hash Algorithm (SHA)   SHA takes a 264-bit message (maximum size) and produces a 160-bit message (maximum size). SHA is shielded against inversion attacks and brute-force collision.

Secure MIME (S/MIME)   S/MIME is the industry-standard method for encrypting e-mail. You should note that S/MIME is an example of encryption at the application layer of the OSI/RM, because it encrypts the actual message itself, rather than the transport stream itself. S/MIME uses public key and private key encryption. Like SSL, S/MIME is an instance of applied encryption, because it uses a combination of public key encryption, private key encryption, and one-way encryption.

Secure Socket Layer (SSL)   An Internet Security standard incorporated into Netscape Navigator and Netscape Commerce Server software; unlike Secure HTTP, SSL works with all the Internet tools, not just the WWW. It is a transport-layer protocol commonly used in Web-based e-commerce transactions.

Serial Line Interface Protocol (SLIP)   An SLIP allows you to establish a dial-up connection with a host computer over the Plain old Telephone System (POTS). SLIP operates at the Data Link layer of the OSI reference model. SLIP works by allowing you to use IP over a serial connection, in effect bringing the IP network to you.

Server   A server (also called a *host*) is a computer or software application that makes available (or serves the client) data and files. An Internet server works identically to a server except it does so on the Internet and makes mail, news, the Web, and other services available.

Server-based databases   Server-based databases are databases that require a server to be running in order to obtain the data.

Server database   The server database maintains status information and a record of all issued certificates. It also maintains server logs and queues. The database stores all certificates issued by the server so administrators can track, audit, and archive server activity. In addition, the server database is used by the server engine to store pending revocations prior to publishing the revocations.

Server engine   The server engine is the core component and acts as the data pump for the requests it receives from the users and other servers. It pushes information between the components during request processing and certificate generation. The engine monitors each request through the various processes to ensure data processing.

Server-side scripting   Server-side scripting allows the programmer to access server resources such as SQL Server databases, custom COM objects, MTS components, and more. Server-side scripting allows the programmer to place the business logic on the server.

Service mark   A service mark is the same as a trademark except that it identifies and distinguishes the source of a service rather than a product. Normally, a mark for goods appears on the product or on its packaging, while a service mark appears in advertising for the services.

Session layer   Establishes and maintains connections.

SET   *See* Secure Electronic Transaction.

SHA   *See* Secure Hash Algorithm.

Shockwave   Shockwave is another technology that was developed by Macromedia, Inc., that takes multimedia on the Web one step beyond. Using Shockwave, you can add multimedia to your Web page as objects. Not only can you view animation and video, and listen to audio, but you can actually interact with a Shockwave object. A Shockwave object that is added to a Web page has the ability to respond to mouse clicks. This means that you could create games that can be played over the Internet.

Simple Mail Transfer Protocol (SMTP)   A U.S. Department of Defense standard for electronic mail systems that have both host and user selections. User software is often included in TCP/IP PC packages; host software is available for exchanging SMTP mail with mail from proprietary systems. SMTP is installed on machines as part of the TCP/IP protocol suite. Because SMTP has a limited ability to queue messages on the receiving end, Post Office Protocol 3, or POP3, is the protocol often used on the receiving end of e-mail messages.

Single-line Digital Subscriber Line (SDSL)   This line uses a single wire pair with a maximum operating range of approximately 10,000 feet. SDSL is suitable for videoconferencing, etc.

Single-server caching   Single-server caching is the idea that you have one server acting as the caching server. This is generally seen primarily on a small LAN; more then 10 or 12 users will easily overrun a single cache server.

Slave server   *See* Secondary server.

SLIP   *See* Serial Line Interface Protocol.

Smart card   This type of card is "smart" because it has two capabilities beyond the standard credit card you probably have in your wallet: First, a smart card can store information in persistent memory. Second, a smart card can have an on-board microprocessor with volatile RAM that acts much like a mini-computer.

S/MIME   *See* Secure MIME.

SMTP   *See* Simple Mail Transfer Protocol.

SNA   *See* Systems Network Architecture.

Sniffers   *See* Network analyzers.

SOA   *See* Start Of Authority.

Sockets   An FTP port, or a socket, represents the endpoint of a network connection. Two numbers identify TCP sockets: IP address and TCP port number.

SOCKS Proxy Service   The SOCKS Proxy Service is a cross-platform mechanism used to establish secure communications between the server and the client. This service allows for transparent access to the Internet using Proxy Server. This service does not support applications that use UDP, nor does it support the IPX/SPX protocol.

Spider   A spider is simply an application running on a remote server that views raw HTML information and Meta tags and records information within the search engines database.

SQL   *See* Structured Query Language.

SSL   *See* Secure Socket Layer.

Start of Authority (SOA)   This identifies who/what has authoritative responsibility for a domain and also identifies the database's current version.

Static index   A static index allows visitors to your Web site to choose from a list of hyperlinks that will direct a visitor to the appropriate content. This is very similar to a book's table of contents. Static indexes allow us to define where content is located and assist visitors by placing these links in a readily accessible area such as the homepage.

Static IP addresses   Static IP addresses are IP addresses that are assigned to one—and only one—user. The IP address is manually entered into the TCP/IP configuration, and no other computer on the network is able to use that address. Static IP addresses are commonly used on networks and corporate intranets, allowing administrators to track what users are doing, control their access, and access the user's computer by connecting to the IP address of that user's computer.

Static linking   Static linking is used for functions that are used consistently and constantly throughout your program. Static linking is loaded at runtime and, therefore, uses more system memory (RAM).

Streaming media   Streaming media is a relatively new and popular method of transferring data to browsers. With this, data is sent in a continuous stream from the Web server to the browser on your computer. As the data is received, it is buffered and displayed. Streaming video involves a sequence of pictures that is compressed over the Internet, and then displayed through a plug-in or application when it arrived. Streaming audio sends sound files in a continuous stream, and then plays the sound through a plug-in or application.

Strong authentication   Strong authentication involves combining certificates, digital signatures, and the authentication measures of what you have, what you are, what you know, and where you are. In short, if you combine these three forms of authentication, you are able to strongly authenticate users.

Structured Query Language (SQL)   The common communication method between databases. The history of SQL began in the late 1970s, when IBM began developing it in a lab in San Jose, California. SQL is a nonprocedural language that will let you decide what data you want to select from a database. The term "nonprocedural" describes what data is returned as opposed to how the database performs the action.

Style sheets   Style sheets are embedded in HTML documents, or linked to an external file, which defines the default styles and characteristics of the Web pages used in a document or Web site. It can define how a page is laid out through the use of the <STYLE> ... </STYLE> tag set. By using style sheets, you are ensuring that each page used in your Web site has a consistent look or style. Using style sheets, you can address such issues as what the default background color or graphic will be for your pages, the size and color of text and hypertext links, fonts used, and so on.

Subnet mask A subnet mask is a binary number that gets associated with the TCP/IP address. The subnet mask allows the computer to distinguish what parts of the IP address are the network ID and host ID. A subnet mask is used to block parts of the IP address to distinguish the network ID from the host ID. Like an IP address, the subnet mask is made up of four sets of 1–3 digit numbers. If a set of numbers is 255, the corresponding set in the IP address is identified as part of the network ID. If the set of numbers in the subnet mask is a zero, the corresponding set in the IP address is part of the host ID.

Suspicious activities Suspicious activities include attacks waged from inside the network, as well as those that arise from outside the firewall. One of the latest suspicious activities during the network-mapping phase is for hackers to conduct scans from diverse locations.

SVC *See* Switched Virtual Circuit.

Switch A switch is another device that can be used to connect networks. The switch uses a specific addressing scheme for delivery of packets, much like a router does. That is, rather than broadcasting data all over the network (like a bridge), the switch is able to read the destination IP address of a packet and send it to the proper network segment.

Switched Virtual Circuit (SVC) A connection set up by signaling, with the user defining the endpoints when the connection is made.

Symmetric encryption The use of one key that both encrypts and decrypts information.

Syn flood This form of attack takes advantage of the three-way TCP handshake process. TCP is a connection-oriented protocol. It first establishes a control connection before it transmits any information. What would happen if a hacker were to begin a TCP connection on your host by sending a SYN request, but then never replied with an ACK packet? Your computer would devote resources to keeping that connection open until it times out. This is no big deal if only one connection stays open for a little while. But what would happen if a hacker were to send thousands or millions of SYN requests? Your system will crash under the strain.

System bug   A system bug is when a program, application, or service contains code that results in unexpected or dangerous behavior.

Systems Network Architecture (SNA)   A seven-layer communications architecture developed by IBM.

T1   *See* Time Division Multiplexing signal number 1.

T3 connection   A T3 connection can range in throughput from 3 Mbps to 45 Mbps. T3 connections are used by ISPs and Telcos.

Tagged Image File Format (TIFF)   A bitmapped graphics format for scanned images simulating gray-scale shading with resolutions up to 300 dpi. TIFF can usually be identified by the file extension .tif or .tiff. This file format was developed in 1986 by a committee of the Aldus Corporation (which is now owned by Adobe Software), Microsoft, and Hewlett-Packard as a common format for page-layout applications. Such applications would include desktop publishing, faxing, and image-editing applications. As was the intention of this committee, TIFFs are one of the most commonly used graphic formats, and supported by most imaging applications.

Tags   Tags are elements that tell a Web browser that the document uses HTML, and how information is to be formatted and displayed. A tag is a letter or statement between the < and > symbols.

TCP   *See* Transmission Control Protocol.

TCP/IP   *See* Transmission Control Protocol/Internet Protocol.

TCSEC   *See* Trusted Computer System Evaluation Criteria.

Telco   *See* Telecommunication Company.

Telecommunication Company (Telco)   One of the types of organizations that leases access to the Internet.

Teletype tag   The teletype tag, which is sometimes referred to as typewriter text, makes whatever text appears between the <TT>...</TT> tags appear as if they were typed on a typewriter. This allows you to make elements of your Web page take on a typewriter-style face.

Telnet   A virtual terminal protocol from the U.S. Department of Defense that interfaces terminal devices and terminal-oriented processes. Telnet is a client/server software and a simple protocol that enables users to log in to remote computers to run programs and access files. Like Gopher, Telnet goes back to the early days of the Internet and is less frequently used. It provides a user with remote access to a host using a standard terminal emulator such as a VT-100. It is described in RFC854 and was first published in 1983.

Telnet clients   Telnet clients are terminal emulation programs that run on TCP/IP networks. Telnet clients allow you to access information in a text-based manner.

Terminal emulation   Terminal emulation means that the software allows your computer to run like an older dumb terminal, and connect to mainframes, Bulletin Board Systems (BBSs), and other servers.

Text element   The TEXT element is used for situations when the user needs to enter a single line of text, such as name, username, age, and so forth.

Textarea element   The TEXTAREA element is also similar to the TEXT element, except that it can accept multiple lines of text. You often see the TEXTAREA element being used for accepting comments or feedback.

Thin client   A thin client may be a Web browser, network computer, personal digital assistant, or any device capable of displaying HTML. A thin client is a client that you can install and use on multiple platforms to access complex applications, services, and servers that reside on the back end (i.e., on the server side).

Tier   A tier in an application is where a process of an application takes place.

TIFF   *See* Tagged Image File Format.

Time Division Multiplexing (TDM)   TDM is used to transmit a number of small signals (in this case, the DS-0's) into one continuous, larger signal. TDM interleaves a piece (eight bits) of each incoming signal, one after another, into each of the T1's 24 timeslots. The compilation of these timeslots comprises one frame. Subsequent frames are then used to continue transferring the data.

Time Division Multiplexing (TDM) signal number I (TI)   T1 is simply ITU-T's (International Telecommunication Union-Telecommunication Standardization Sector, formerly the CCITT) North American name for the 1.544 Mbps standard pipe that can be used to pass signal traffic. These pipes, or circuits, consist of 24 56 Kbps or 64 Kbps channels, known as DS-0's.

Time To Live (TTL)   Set times a packet can travel through a network before being deleted.

Trace route   The trace route utility can find a route that is being used by the Internet protocol to pass packets between two machines. The trace route utility will show us the routers that the packets had to travel over to get from one computer to another. If there are no routers that they have to travel over, the trace route will come back very quickly. If there are multiple routers that the packets have to go over, then it will show you, in reverse order, each router that the packets have to go through to get to the destination. It will do this for up to 30 routers.

Trademark   A trademark is a word, phrase, symbol, or design, or combination of words, phrases, symbols, or designs, which identifies and distinguishes the source of the goods or services of one party from those of others.

Trademark law   Trademark law protects words, names, and symbols used by manufacturers and businesses to identify their goods and services. Trademark law in general, whether federal or state, protects a trademark owner's commercial identity (goodwill, reputation, and investment in advertising) by giving the trademark owner the exclusive right to use the trademark on the type of goods or services for which the owner is using the trademark. Any person who uses a trademark in connection with selling goods or services in a way that is likely to cause confusion is infringing on that trademark.

Transactional systems   Transactional systems allow you to do a full recovery in case of failure in the transaction. If a user comes in and in the process of transaction something fails, then the transaction reverts back to the beginning as if nothing has occurred—no partial or orphaned data will exist in the database.

Transfer protocol   The transfer protocol is the method of transferring or downloading information into a browser such as HTTP (for Web pages), FTP (for files), or NNTP (for USENET news). The transfer protocol determines the type of server being connected to, be it a Web, FTP, Gopher, mail, or news server.

Transmission Control Protocol (TCP)   TCP is used to provide connection-oriented, reliable sessions between computers. TCP is commonly used when large amounts of data are being sent, or acknowledgment of data being received is required.

Transmission Control Protocol (TCP) port   A TCP port is the address of a server on an IP network. When an application uses TCP, it calls an assigned port for access.

Transmission Control Protocol/Internet Protocol (TCP/IP)

The TCP/IP protocol suite is a set of protocols incorporated into software. Once installed on a computer, it can be used to communicate with other computers that also use TCP/IP. TCP/IP was established in 1982 as the data transfer protocol for ARPAnet. The Internet is based on scores of protocols that support each of the types of services and technologies deployed on the Internet. The basic suite of protocols that allow this mix of hardware and software devices to work together is called TCP/IP, which is a packet-switching system that encapsulates data transferred over the Internet into digital packets.

Transport layer   Provides reliable transport and error control mechanisms, including checksum and ports. TCP and UDP run at this layer.

Triple DES   This form of encryption is more secure and powerful than DES.

Trojan   A trojan is an illicit program that appears to have a legitimate function. *See also* Root kit.

Trusted Computer System Evaluation Criteria (TCSEC)

TCSEC, also called the Orange Book, was originally published with an orange cover. Although quite old (it was written in 1983 and revised in 1985), many security professionals still refer to this book. The Orange Book rates the security protection of various operating systems according to an alphabetical scale (D through A). Systems given a D rating are the least secure, whereas an A-grade system is specially designed to give granular control over system users and processes. The most common rating is C2, which certain Novell, UNIX, and NT systems can achieve with some work.

TTL   *See* Time To Live.

Twisted-pair cable   This is the most common (and least expensive) type of network cable. Twisted-pair cable attaches to a NIC with an RJ-45 connector, which resembles a large phone jack. Twisted pair can transmit at either 10 Mbps or 100 Mbps.

UDP   *See* User Datagram Protocol.

Unicode   The Unicode Worldwide Character Standard is a character coding system developed for computers to support the interchange, processing, and display of written texts of the languages of the modern world. Unicode provides the foundation for internationalization and localization of content for e-commerce and Web sites, and computer software.

Uniform Resource Locator (URL)   A unique address on the Internet, similar to an e-mail address. A URL specifies the address of a server, or a specific Web page residing on a server.

Universal clients   *See* All-in-one clients.

Unordered lists (bulleted lists)   Unordered lists are used when items in the list do not need to be listed in a set order. For this reason, in HTML, bulleted lists are more commonly referred to as unordered lists. They are created using the <UL> and </UL> tags.

URL   *See* Uniform Resource Locator.

Usage tracking   Refers to the ability of an e-catalog system to track the number of hits to a site, customer demographics, and interface with a knowledge-based system to customize the presentation to its users.

User Datagram Protocol (UDP)   UDP provides connectionless communication between computers. It does not guarantee that packets will be delivered, and is generally used to send small amounts of data or data that is not crucial for delivery. Any reliability of data being sent is the responsibility of the application, not this protocol.

User Datagram Protocol (UDP) attack   A UDP attack could involve sending many UDP packets to one host, as in a ping flood attack. However, it is also possible to attack a system by sending UDP packets that then overlap once the receiving host puts them back together again. In nonpatched Windows NT and Linux systems, this overlapping of UDP packets crashes the system, resulting in the "blue screen of death" and a kernel panic, respectively.

VBScript   VBScript is yet another interpreted scripting language. VBScript is provided by Microsoft and is a smaller subset of its Visual Basic programming language. VBScript is similar to other Web-based script languages like JavaScript, Tcl, PERL, and REXX.

Vector graphics   Vector graphics use geometrical formulas to represent images, and are the alternative method to creating images through bitmaps. While bitmaps are also called raster graphics, and represent images as a series of dots, vector graphics are distinguished as a series of lines.

Virtual Private Network (VPN)   A VPN allows you to encrypt all network communications. A VPN is an example of a tunneling protocol. It operates at the network layer and encrypts all transmissions, making it difficult for hackers to sniff information. A VPN is so named, because it is a protocol that allows users to communicate securely over public lines. Normally, a private network, such as one created over leased frame relay lines, is secure from outside "sniffing" attacks.

Virtual Reality Modeling Language (VRML)   VRML is a language used for describing three-dimensional image sequences and user interactions with them. VRML allows you to build a sequence of visual images into Web pages.

Virtual server   The WWW service supports the concept of virtual servers. A virtual server can be used to host multiple domain names on the same physical Web server. You need a unique IP address for each virtual server that you host. This is sometimes referred to as *multihoming*.

Viruses   A virus is a miniprogram specially designed to interrupt the normal workings of your computer. A virus generally has a payload.

Depending upon the virus, the payload can be something annoying, such as a sound playing at a particular time, or downright destructive. The old Michelangelo virus, for example, erased entire hard drives. *See also* Boot sector virus; File virus; Macro virus.

Visual Basic   Visual Basic is a programming language from Microsoft. The word "visual" comes from the idea that dragging and dropping objects and controls on the form can create the program's interface.

VPN   *See* Virtual Private Network.

VRML   *See* Virtual Reality Modeling Language.

Web   *See* World Wide Web.

Web Cache Communication Protocol   The Web Cache Communication Protocol was developed by Cisco in order to provide routers with the ability to redirect specified traffic to caching servers. With WCCP version 2, the previous limitations of single routers have been replaced with support for multiple routers. This is important in environments in which the router introduced a single point of failure.

Web caching   Caching is the process of storing requested objects at a network point closer to the client, at a location that will provide these objects for reuse as they are requested by additional clients. Web caching allows us as Network Administrators and System Engineers to reduce bandwidth peaks during periods of high network traffic.

Web cookie   *See* Cookie.

Web Proxy Automatic Discovery (WPAD) protocol   This protocol allows a browser to automatically detect proxy settings. Web Proxy Automatic Discovery (WPAD), is supported through the use of Dynamic Host Configuration Protocol (DHCP) and Domain Name System (DNS).

Once the proper settings are configured, DHCP and DNS servers can automatically find the appropriate proxy server and configure the browser's settings accordingly.

WebTV   WebTV is a Microsoft product that allows those without computers to access the Web through a television and a box that is similar in appearance to those used for cable TV. With these two requirements, you then sign up with a WebTV access service.

Well-known port number   Server applications or processes using TCP/IP have, at least, one assigned port number, which is called a well-known port number.

Well-known ports   Port numbers 0 through 1023 are called well-known ports because they never change. These well-known ports are preassigned by the Internet Assigned Numbers Authority (IANA). TCP ports can be numbered from 0 to 65,535. Port numbers 0 through 1023 are reserved for server-side use and never change.

Whitespace   Whitespace is the space between characters, where nothing has been entered. For example, when using a text editor, you may press the ENTER key several times, so that there are several spaces between lines.

Whois   The whois service allows you to determine information about a DNS domain.

Wildcard character   The asterisk wildcard will allow you to search for all items or phrases that match a particular pattern.

Wildcard searches   Wildcard searches allow for searches to match a certain pattern instead of a fixed word or phrase. The accepted character for wildcard searches is the asterisk. The asterisk can be placed at the beginning or the end of a search word or phrase.

Windows Internet Name Service (WINS)   WINS gives Windows NT Servers the ability to resolve NetBIOS computer names on a TCP/IP network. WINS keeps a database that is dynamically updated on the NT network, adding NetBIOS and IP addresses to it as new computers are found. When WINS is used on a network, client computers register their names with the WINS server as they connect to the network. The WINS server then maps the names of these computers to their IP addresses. When a WINS client requests a resource from one of these clients, the WINS server resolves the name and returns the IP address to the requesting computer.

Windows Sockets (WinSock)   WinSock is a set of APIs that applications can use to communicate with other applications in the network. Many applications may be running on the same computer, even though the processes are being conducted across the network.

Work for Hire   When a work is created by an employee within the scope of his or her employment contract, the employer owns the copyright to the works since it's a "work for hire."

World Wide Web (WWW / Web)   Tim Berners-Lee at CERN drafted a proposal for the Web in 1989. He conceived the architecture for the Web as a multimedia hypertext information system based on a client/server architecture. The Web was born at CERN in Geneva, Switzerland, in 1992.

World Wide Web (WWW / Web) browser   A Web browser is a client application that displays multimedia hypertext documents. The first-generation Web browser developed at CERN was character based. It was very primitive by today's standards and only capable of displaying text. It wasn't until the Mosaic browser became available in 1993 that the potential of the Web began to be realized. Web browsers provide the ability to interpret and display HyperText Markup Language (HTML) documents, which are documents that are written in HTML and contain indicators (called tags) that dictate how text and graphics are to be formatted. *See also* Mosaic.

World Wide Web (WWW / Web) Call Back   Web Call Back is a relatively new technology that further enhances CRM. Web Call Back works by allowing your customers to click a link on your e-commerce site and enter their phone number. The link immediately triggers a call to a specific phone number at your company.

World Wide Web Consortium (W3C)   This organization sets the standards that are to be followed in developing Web pages and the browsers that view them. Despite this, many browsers also include proprietary features. This means that in order to view a Web page that exploits these features, you must use that particular browser. These innovations occasionally become accepted standards by W3C, and are then implemented in other browser types.

Worm   A worm, on the other hand, is somewhat more ambitious, because it can spread by itself, given certain conditions. For example, the Melissa "virus" had many worm-like qualities, because it took advantage of Word and Excel macros.

WPAD   *See* Web Proxy Automatic Discovery.

WWW   *See* World Wide Web.

X.25   X.25 is similar to Frame Relay in that it is a packet-switched technology that typically operates as PVC. Since data on a packet-switched network is capable of following any available circuit path, it is usually depicted as clouds in graphical representations. X.25 was introduced at a time when WAN links, traveling through the public switched network, were primarily analog lines producing errors and poor transmissions. X.25 sought to remedy this through built-in error correction and flow control.

XML *See* eXtensible Markup Language.

Zone transfer In a zone transfer, the primary server gives its database (that is, its zone file) to the secondary server. It is possible to establish times and conditions under which a zone transfer will take place.

INDEX

NOTE: Page numbers in *italics* refer to illustrations or charts.

Numbers

8-second rule, Web site interest time, 285

A

A entry, SOA (Start of Authority) file and DNS entry types, 349

<A> tags, HTML anchor tags, 210

Access, relational databases, 302-304

access control, 513-527

    See also authentication; security

    encryption, 521-527

    firewalls, 435-438, 514-518

    lists (ACLs), 513-514

    overview, 513

    proxy servers, 518-522

accessing Web sites, testing multimedia, 256-258

ACLs (Access Control Lists), 513-514

ACTION attribute, forms in Web pages, 201

active caching

    proxy server caching, 468

    Web caching, 39-40

ActiveX controls, client-side security threats, 145

address bars, Internet client, 97

addresses. *See* IP addresses; URLs (Uniform Resource Locators)

ADSL (Asymmetric Digital Subscriber Line), 463-464

    See also DSL (Digital Subscriber Line)

advertising. *See* marketing

AES (Advanced Encryption Standard), 522

    See also encryption

agents, intelligent, 643

algorithms, encryption levels and, 147

ALIGN attribute, HTML table attributes, *196*

<ALIGN> tags, formatting HTML tags, 192

all-in-one (universal) clients, 92-94

analog modems, 410-412

    See also modems

    installing, 422

analysis tools for Web sites, 641

anchor tags, HTML <A> tags, 210

ANSI reserved words, C programming language, 290, *291*

Answers in Depth option, *Personal Testing Center,* 659

anti-virus software, 558-561

    See also security; viruses

    browser/client, 558

    e-mail attachment scanning, 559

    overview, 558

    patches and updates for clients, 144-145

    scanning network hosts, 559-561

    server protection, 558-561

"anywhere, anytime," trends in e-commerce, 643

APIs (application program interfaces), 278-279

    See also programming languages

    ISAPI (Internet Server), 281-283

Application layer, TCP/IP, 74-76

application reuse and modularity, multi-vendor environments, 597

application-level gateways, firewall types, 436, *516*

applications

    See also programming languages; software

    multitiered, 299-302

arbiters, routing (RAs), 332

ARP (Address Resolution Protocol)

    TCP/IP diagnostic tools, 394-396

    TCP/IP Internet layer, 77

ARPAnet, history of Internet, 2-3

ASP (Active Server Pages), 296

    See also programming languages

ASs (Autonomous Systems), NAPs (Network Access Points), 326

Asymmetric Digital Subscriber Line. *See* ADSL

asymmetric encryption, 521

ATM (Asynchronous Transfer Mode), 461-463

    See also bandwidth technologies

    cells, 461-462

    media, 462-463

    payloads, 462

    PVCs (permanent virtual circuits), 462

C

D

I

J

S

Custom Corporate Network Training

Train on Cutting Edge Technology   We can bring the best in skill-based training to your facility to create a real-world hands-on training experience. Global Knowledge has invested millions of dollars in network hardware and software to train our students on the same equipment they will work with on the job. Our relationships with vendors allow us to incorporate the latest equipment and platforms into your on-site labs.

Maximize Your Training Budget   Global Knowledge provides experienced instructors, comprehensive course materials, and all the networking equipment needed to deliver high quality training. You provide the students; we provide the knowledge.

Avoid Travel Expenses   On-site courses allow you to schedule technical training at your convenience, saving time, expense, and the opportunity cost of travel away from the workplace.

Discuss Confidential Topics   Private on-site training permits the open discussion of sensitive issues such as security, access, and network design. We can work with your existing network's proprietary files while demonstrating the latest technologies.

Customize Course Content   Global Knowledge can tailor your courses to include the technologies and the topics which have the greatest impact on your business. We can complement your internal training efforts or provide a total solution to your training needs.

Corporate Pass   The Corporate Pass Discount Program rewards our best network training customers with preferred pricing on public courses, discounts on multimedia training packages, and an array of career planning services.

Global Knowledge Training Lifecycle   Supporting the Dynamic and Specialized Training Requirements of Information Technology Professionals

- Define Profile
- Assess Skills
- Design Training
- Deliver Training
- Test Knowledge
- Update Profile
- Use New Skills

College Credit Recommendation Program   The American Council on Education's CREDIT program recommends 53 Global Knowledge courses for college credit. Now our network training can help you earn your college degree while you learn the technical skills needed for your job. When you attend an ACE-certified Global Knowledge course and pass the associated exam, you earn college credit recommendations for that course. Global Knowledge can establish a transcript record for you with ACE, which you can use to gain credit at a college or as a written record of your professional training that you can attach to your resume.

Registration Information

COURSE FEE: The fee covers course tuition, refreshments, and all course materials. Any parking expenses that may be incurred are not included. Payment or government training form must be received six business days prior to the course date. We will also accept Visa/MasterCard and American Express. For non-U.S. credit card users, charges will be in U.S. funds and will be converted by your credit card company. Checks drawn on Canadian banks in Canadian funds are acceptable.

COURSE SCHEDULE: Registration is at 8:00 a.m. on the first day. The program begins at 8:30 a.m. and concludes at 4:30 p.m. each day.

CANCELLATION POLICY: Cancellation and full refund will be allowed if written cancellation is received in our office at least six business days prior to the course start date. Registrants who do not attend the course or do not cancel more than six business days in advance are responsible for the full registration fee; you may transfer to a later date provided the course fee has been paid in full. Substitutions may be made at any time. If Global Knowledge must cancel a course for any reason, liability is limited to the registration fee only.

GLOBAL KNOWLEDGE: Global Knowledge programs are developed and presented by industry professionals with "real-world" experience. Designed to help professionals meet today's interconnectivity and interoperability challenges, most of our programs feature hands-on labs that incorporate state-of-the-art communication components and equipment.

ON-SITE TEAM TRAINING: Bring Global Knowledge's powerful training programs to your company. At Global Knowledge, we will custom design courses to meet your specific network requirements. Call 1 (919) 461-8686 for more information.

YOUR GUARANTEE: Global Knowledge believes its courses offer the best possible training in this field. If during the first day you are not satisfied and wish to withdraw from the course, simply notify the instructor, return all course materials, and receive a 100% refund.

REGISTRATION INFORMATION:

Course title _____

Course location _____ Course date _____

Name/title _____ Company _____

Name/title _____ Company _____

Name/title _____ Company _____

Address _____ Telephone _____ Fax _____

City _____ State/Province _____ Zip/Postal Code _____

Credit card _____ Card # _____ Expiration date _____

Signature _____